T0233816

Lecture Notes in Computer Science 9416

Commenced Publication in 1973
Founding and Former Series Editors:
Gerhard Goos, Juris Hartmanis, and Jan van Leeuwen

More information about this series at http://www.springer.com/series/7409

Ioana Ciuciu · Hervé Panetto
Christophe Debruyne · Alexis Aubry
Peter Bollen · Rafael Valencia-García
Alok Mishra · Anna Fensel
Fernando Ferri (Eds.)

On the Move to Meaningful Internet Systems: OTM 2015 Workshops

Confederated International Workshops:
OTM Academy, OTM Industry Case Studies Program,
EI2N, FBM, INBAST, ISDE, META4eS, and MSC 2015
Rhodes, Greece, October 26–30, 2015
Proceedings

 Springer

Editors

Ioana Ciuciu
University Babes-Bolyai
Cluj-Napoca
Romania

Hervé Panetto
University of Lorraine
Vandoeuvre-les-Nancy
France

Christophe Debruyne
Trinity College Dublin
Dublin 2
Ireland

Alexis Aubry
University of Lorraine
Vandoevre-les-Nancy
France

Peter Bollen
Maastricht University
MD Maastricht
The Netherlands

Rafael Valencia-García
Universidad de Murcia
Murcia
Spain

Alok Mishra
Atilim University
Ankara
Turkey

Anna Fensel
University of Innsbruck
Innsbruck
Austria

Fernando Ferri
National Research Council
Rome
Italy

ISSN 0302-9743   ISSN 1611-3349   (electronic)
Lecture Notes in Computer Science
ISBN 978-3-319-26137-9   ISBN 978-3-319-26138-6   (eBook)
DOI 10.1007/978-3-319-26138-6

Library of Congress Control Number: 2015953246

LNCS Sublibrary: SL3 – Information Systems and Applications, incl. Internet/Web, and HCI

Springer Cham Heidelberg New York Dordrecht London

Printed on acid-free paper

Springer International Publishing AG Switzerland is part of Springer Science+Business Media
(www.springer.com)

General Co-Chairs' Message for OnTheMove 2015, Rhodes, Greece

The OnTheMove 2015 event held during October 26–30, in Rhodes, Greece, further consolidated the importance of the series of annual conferences that was started in 2002 in Irvine, California. It then moved to Catania, Sicily, in 2003, to Cyprus in 2004 and 2005, Montpellier in 2006, Vilamoura in 2007 and 2009, in 2008 to Monterrey, Mexico, to Heraklion, Crete, in 2010 and 2011, Rome in 2012, Graz in 2013, and Amantea, Italy, in 2014. This prime event continues to attract a diverse and relevant selection of today's research worldwide on the scientific concepts underlying new computing paradigms, which of necessity must be distributed, heterogeneous, and supporting an environment of resources that are autonomous yet must meaningfully cooperate. Indeed, as such large, complex, and networked intelligent information systems become the focus and norm for computing, there continues to be an acute and even increasing need to address the implied software, system, and enterprise issues and discuss them face to face in an integrated forum that covers methodological, semantic, theoretical, and application issues as well. As we all realize, e-mail, the Internet, and even video conferences on their own are not optimal or even sufficient for effective and efficient scientific exchange.

The OnTheMove (OTM) Federated Conference series was created precisely to cover the scientific exchange needs of the communities that work in the broad yet closely connected fundamental technological spectrum of Web-based distributed computing. The OTM program every year covers data and Web semantics, distributed objects, Web services, databases, information systems, enterprise workflow and collaboration, ubiquity, interoperability, mobility, as well as grid and high-performance computing.

OTM does *not* consider itself a so-called multi-conference event but instead is proud to give meaning to the "federated" aspect in its full title[1]: It aspires to be a primary scientific meeting place where all aspects of research and development of Internet- and intranet-based systems in organizations and for e-business are discussed in a scientifically motivated way, in a forum of loosely interconnected workshops and conferences. This year's 14th edition of the OTM Federated Conferences event therefore once more provided an opportunity for researchers and practitioners to understand, discuss, and publish these developments within the broader context of distributed, ubiquitous computing. To further promote synergy and coherence, the main conferences of OTM 2015 were conceived against a background of three interlocking global themes:

- Trusted Cloud Computing Infrastructures Emphasizing Security and Privacy
- Technology and Methodology for Data and Knowledge Resources on the (Semantic) Web

---

[1] On The Move Towards Meaningful Internet Systems and Ubiquitous Computing – Federated Conferences and Workshops.

– Deployment of Collaborative and Social Computing for and in an Enterprise Context

Originally the federative structure of OTM was formed by the co-location of three related, complementary, and successful main conference series: DOA (Distributed Objects and Applications, held since 1999), covering the relevant infrastructure-enabling technologies, ODBASE (Ontologies, DataBases and Applications of SEmantics, since 2002), covering Web semantics, XML databases, and ontologies, and of course CoopIS (Cooperative Information Systems, held since 1993), which studies the application of these technologies in an enterprise context through, e.g., workflow systems and knowledge management. In the 2011 edition, security issues, originally started as topics of the IS workshop in OTM 2006, became the focus of DOA as secure virtual infrastructures, further broadened to cover aspects of trust and privacy in so-called cloud-based systems. As this latter aspect came to dominate agendas in this and overlapping research communities, we decided in 2014 to rename the event as the Cloud and Trusted Computing (C&TC) conference, and to organize and launch it in a workshop format to define future editions.

Both main conferences specifically seek high-quality contributions of a more mature nature and encourage researchers to treat their respective topics within a framework that simultaneously incorporates (a) theory, (b) conceptual design and development, (c) methodology and pragmatics, and (d) application in particular case studies and industrial solutions.

As in previous years we again solicited and selected additional quality workshop proposals to complement the more mature and "archival" nature of the main conferences. Our workshops are intended to serve as "incubators" for emergent research results in selected areas related, or becoming related, to the general domain of Web-based distributed computing. This year the difficult and time-consuming job of selecting and coordinating the workshops was brought to a successful end by Ioana Ciuciu, and we were very glad to see that some of our earlier successful workshops (EI2N, META4eS, ISDE, INBAST, MSC) re-appeared in 2015, in some cases in alliance with other older or newly emerging workshops. The new Fact-Based Modeling (FBM) workshop succeeded and expanded the scope of the successful ORM workshop. The Industry Case Studies Program, started in 2011 under the leadership of Hervé Panetto and OMG's Richard Mark Soley, further gained momentum and visibility in its fifth edition this year.

The OTM registration format ("one workshop or conference buys all workshops or conferences") actively intends to promote synergy between related areas in the field of distributed computing and to stimulate workshop audiences to productively mingle with each other and, optionally, with those of the main conferences. In particular EI2N continues to create and exploit a visible cross-pollination with CoopIS.

We were happy to see that also in 2015 the number of quality submissions for the OnTheMove Academy (OTMA) stabilized for the fourth consecutive year. OTMA implements our unique, actively coached and therefore very time- and effort-intensive formula to bring PhD students together, and aims to carry our "vision for the future" in research in the areas covered by OTM. Its 2015 edition was organized and managed by a dedicated team of collaborators and faculty, Peter Spyns, Maria-Esther Vidal, Anja Metzner, and Alfred Holl, inspired as always by the OTMA Dean, Erich Neuhold.

In the OTM Academy, PhD research proposals are submitted by students for peer review; selected submissions and their approaches are to be presented by the students in front of a wider audience at the conference, and are independently and extensively analyzed and discussed in front of this audience by a panel of senior professors. One will readily appreciate the resources invested in this by OnTheMove and especially the OTMA faculty!

As the three main conferences and the associated workshops all share the distributed aspects of modern computing systems, they experience the application pull created by the Internet and by the so-called Semantic Web, in particular developments of big data, increased importance of security issues, and the globalization of mobile-based technologies. For ODBASE 2015, the focus continued to be the knowledge bases and methods required for enabling the use of formal semantics in Web-based databases and information systems. For CoopIS 2015, the focus as before was on the interaction of such technologies and methods with business process issues, such as occur in networked organizations and enterprises. These subject areas overlap in a scientifically natural and fascinating fashion and many submissions in fact also covered and exploited the mutual impact among them. For our C&TC 2015 event, its primary emphasis was again squarely put on the virtual and security aspects of Web-based computing in the broadest sense. As with the earlier OTM editions, the organizers wanted to stimulate this cross-pollination by a program of famous keynote speakers from academia and industry around the chosen themes and shared by all OTM component events. We are quite proud to list for this year:

– Michele Bezzi
– Eva Kühn
– John Mylopoulos
– Sjir Nijssen

The general downturn in submissions observed in recent years for almost all conferences in computer science and IT is also affecting OTM, but we were still fortunate to receive a total of 130 submissions for the three main conferences and 86 submissions in total for the workshops. Not only may we indeed again claim success in attracting a representative volume of scientific papers, many from the USA and Asia, but these numbers of course allowed the respective Program Committees to again compose a high-quality cross-section of current research in the areas covered by OTM. Acceptance rates vary but the aim was to stay consistently at about one accepted full paper for two to three submitted (nearly one in four for CoopIS), yet as always these rates are subordinated to professional peer assessment of proper scientific quality. As usual we have separated the proceedings into two volumes with their own titles, one for the main conferences and one for the workshops and posters, and we are again most grateful to the Springer LNCS team in Heidelberg for their professional support, suggestions, and meticulous collaboration in producing the files and indexes ready for downloading on the USB sticks.

The reviewing process by the respective OTM Program Committees was performed to professional quality standards: Each paper review in the main conferences was assigned to at least three referees, with arbitrated e-mail discussions in the case of strongly diverging evaluations. It may be worthwhile to emphasize once more that it is an explicit OTM policy that all conference Program Committees and Chairs make their selections in a completely sovereign manner, autonomous and independent from any OTM organizational considerations. As in recent years, proceedings in paper form are now only available to be ordered separately.

The General Chairs are once more especially grateful to the many people directly or indirectly involved in the set-up of these federated conferences. Not everyone realizes the large number of persons that need to be involved, and the huge amount of work, commitment, and in the uncertain economic and funding climate of 2015 certainly also financial risk that is entailed by the organization of an event like OTM. Apart from the persons in their aforementioned roles we therefore wish to thank in particular explicitly our main conference Program Committee Chairs:

- CoopIS 2015: Georg Weichhart, with Heiko Ludwig and Michael Rosemann
- ODBASE 2015: Yuan An, with Min Song and Markus Strohmaier
- C&TC 2015: Claudio Ardagna, with Meiko Jensen

And similarly we thank the Program Committee (Co-)Chairs of the 2015 ICSP, OTMA, and Workshops (in their order of appearance on the website): Peter Spyns, Maria-Esther Vidal, Arne J. Berre, Gregoris Mentzas, Nadia Abchiche-Mimouni, Alexis Aubry, Fenareti Lampathaki, Eduardo Rocha Loures, Milan Zdravkovic, Peter Bollen, Hans Mulder, Maurice Nijssen, Miguel Ángel Rodríguez-García, Rafael Valencia García, Thomas Moser, Ricardo Colomo Palacios, Alok Mishra, Deepti Mishra, Jürgen Münch, Ioana Ciuciu, Christophe Debruyne, Anna Fensel, Maria Chiara Caschera, Fernando Ferri, Patrizia Grifoni, Arianna D'Ulizia, Mustafa Jarrar, António Lucas Soares, Cristovão Sousa.

Together with their many Program Committee members, they performed a superb and professional job in managing the difficult yet existential process of peer review and selection of the best papers from the harvest of submissions. We all also owe a significant debt of gratitude to our supremely competent and experienced Conference Secretariat and technical support staff in Guadalajara, Brussels, and Dublin, respectively, Daniel Meersman, Jan Demey, and Christophe Debruyne.

The General Conference and Workshop Co-Chairs also thankfully acknowledge the academic freedom, logistic support, and facilities they enjoy from their respective institutions — Technical University of Graz, Austria; Université de Lorraine, Nancy, France; Latrobe University, Melbourne, Australia; and Babes-Bolyai University, Cluj, Romania — without which such a project quite simply would not be feasible. We do hope that the results of this federated scientific enterprise contribute to your research and your place in the scientific network. We look forward to seeing you at next year's event!

September 2015   Robert Meersman
                                                                 Hervé Panetto
                                                                 Tharam Dillon
                                                                 Ernesto Damiani
                                                                 Ioana Ciuciu

Organization

OTM (On The Move) is a federated event involving a series of major international conferences and workshops. These proceedings contain the papers presented at the OTM Academy 2015, the OTM Industry Case Studies Program 2015, the OTM 2015 federated workshops, and the OTM 2015 federated conferences poster papers.

Executive Committee

General Co-Chairs

Robert Meersman   TU Graz, Austria
Hervé Panetto   University of Lorraine, France
Ioana Ciuciu   University Babes-Bolyai Cluj, Romania

OnTheMove Academy Dean

Erich Neuhold   University of Vienna, Austria

OnTheMove Academy Organizing Chairs

Peter Spyns   Vrije Universiteit Brussel, Belgium
Maria Esther Vidal   Universidad Simón Bolívar, Caracas, Venezuela

Industry Case Studies Program Chair

Hervé Panetto   University of Lorraine, France

EI2N 2015 PC Co-Chairs

Alexis Aubry   University of Lorraine, France
Eduardo Rocha Loures   PUC Parana, Brazil
Fenareti Lampathaki   National Technical University of Athens, Greece
Milan Zdravkovic   University of Niš, Serbia

FBM 2015 PC Co-Chairs

Robert Meersman   T.U. Graz, Austria
Peter Bollen   University of Maastricht, The Netherlands
Maurice Nijssen   PNA, The Netherlands
Hans Mulder   VIAgroep, The Netherlands

INBAST 2015 PC Co-Chairs

Rafael Valencia-García   Universidad de Murcia, Spain
Miguel Ángel   Universidad de Murcia, Spain
    Rodríguez-García

| Ricardo Colomo Palacios | Østfold University College, Norway |
| Thomas Moser | St. Pölten University of Applied Sciences, Austria |

ISDE 2015 PC Co-Chairs

Alok Mishra	Atilim University, Turkey
Jürgen Münch	University of Helsinki, Finland
Deepti Mishra	Atilim University, Turkey

META4eS 2015 PC Co-Chairs

Anna Fensel	STI Innsbruck, University of Innsbruck, Austria
Christophe Debruyne	Trinity College Dublin, Ireland
Ioana Ciuciu	University Babes-Bolyai Cluj, Romania

MSC 2015 PC Co-Chairs

Fernando Ferri	National Research Council, Italy
Patrizia Grifoni	National Research Council, Italy
Arianna D'Ulizia	National Research Council, Italy
Maria Chiara Caschera	National Research Council, Italy

Logistics Team

Daniel Meersman

OTM Academy 2015 Program Committee

Galia Angelova	Avigdor Gal
Marcelo Arenas	Claudia Jiménez
Christoph Bussler	Frédéric Le Mouël
Paolo Ceravolo	Anja Metzner
Philippe Cudré-Mauroux	Erich Neuhold
Manu De Backer	Hervé Panetto
Dejing Dou	Erik Proper

Industry Case Studies 2015 Program Committee

Michael Alexander	Ben Calloni
Sinuhe Arroyo	Luis Camarinha-Matos
˙Ian Bayley	Vincent Chapurlat
Peter Benson	Yannis Charalabidis
Gash Bhullar	David Cohen
Emmanuel Blanvillain	Eva Coscia
Serge Boverie	Tuan Dang
Dennis Brandl	Francesco Danza
Christoph Bussler	Michele Dassisti

Piero De Sabbata
Marc Delbaere
Jacques Durand
Dominique Ernadote
Donald Ferguson
Kurt Fessl
Sanford Friedenthal
Andres Garcia Higuera
Jean-Luc Garnier
Pascal Gendre
Ricardo Goncalves
Ted Goranson
Mattew Hause
Mathias Kohler
Sheron Koshy
Harald Kuehn
Antoine Lonjon
Peter Loos
Eduardo Loures
Gottfried Luef
Juan-Carlos Mendez
Arturo Molina

Jishnu Mukerji
Silvana Muscella
Yannick Naudet
Yasuyuki Nishioka
Ed Parsons
Andrea Persidis
Sobah Abbas Petersen
Daniel Sáez Domingo
Joe Salvo
Ayelet Sapir
Stan Schneider
Mark Schulte
Jean Simao
Dirk Slama
Richard Soley
Janos Sztipanovits
François Vernadat
Georg Weichhart
Lawrence Whitman
Detlef Zühlke
Milan Zdravkovic
Martin Zelm

EI2N 2015 Program Committee

Hamideh Afsarmanesh
Spiros Alesakis
João P.A. Almeida
Dimitris Apostolou
Dimitris Askounis
Rafael Batres
Frederick Benaben
Giuseppe Berio
Peter Bernus
Nacer Boudjlida
Prasad Calyam
Luis Camarinha-Matos
Osiris Canciglieri
J. Cecil
Vincent Chapurlat
Yannis Charalabidis
David Chen
Michele Dassisti
Claudia Diamantini

Antonio Dourado Correia
Cesare Fantuzzi
Andres Garcia Higuera
Ted Goranson
Ricardo Jardim Goncalves
Roland Jochem
Ulrich Jumar
Udo Kannengiesser
Thomas Knothe
John Krogstie
Sotiris Koussouris
Oscar Lazaro
Mario Lezoche
Qing Li
Ivan Lukovic
Duta Luminita
Babis Magoutas
Andreia Malucelli
Zoran Marjanovic

Juan-Carlos Mendez
Istvan Mezgár
Michele Missikoff
Néjib Moalla
Yannick Naudet
Shimon Nof
Ovidiu Noran
Angel Ortiz Bas
Hervé Panetto
Raul Poler
Erik Proper
David Romero Diaz
Luca Settineri
Richard Soley

Lawrence Stapleton
Kamelia Stefanova
Nenad Stefanovic
Janusz Szpytko
Miroslav Trajanovic
Yannis Verginadis
François Vernadat
Gianluigi Viscusi
Birgit Vogel-Heuser
Xiaofang Wang
Marek Wegrzyn
Georg Weichhart
Esma Yahia
Martin Zelm

FBM 2015 Program Committee

Roel Baardman
Herman Balsters
Ed Barkmeyer
Marco Brattinga
Cory Casanava
Matthew Curland
David Cuyler
Diederik Dulfer
Harald Eisenmann
Gordon Everest
William Frank
Pat Hallock
Terry Halpin
Clifford Heath
Stijn Hoppenbrouwers
Paul Iske
Mike Jackson
Mustafa Jarrar
Inge Lemmens
Mariette Lokin
Tony Morgan
Ellen Munthe-Kaas
David Newman
Sjir Nijssen

Leo Oberst
Baba Piprani
Erik Proper
Jos Rozendaal
Pierre Schlag
Robert Schmaal
Hayo Schreijer
John Sowa
Peter Spyns
Peter Straatsma
Yan Tang
Serge Valera
Hans van Bommel
Dirk van der Linden
Robert van Doesburg
Tom van Engers
Jan Vanthienen
Jos Vos
Adrian Walker
Miriam Wesselink
Matthew West
Jan Pieter Wijbenga
Martijn Zoet
Michael zur Muehlen

INBAST 2015 Program Committee

Giner Alor-Hernández
Ghassan Beydoun
Robert Brown
Luis Omar Colombo-Mendoza
Sergio de Cesare
Christophe Debruyne
Fajar Juang Ekaputra
Jesualdo Tomás Fernández-Breis
Frederik Gailly
Francisco J. García-Peñalvo
Francisco García-Sánchez
Przemyslaw Kazienko
Antonio A. Lopez-Lorca
Catalina Martínez-Costa

Jose Antonio Miñarro-Giménez
Miroslav Minovic
Ana Muñoz
Petr Novák
José Luis Ochoa
Mario Andrés Paredes-Valerde
Oscar Pastor Lopez
Alejandro Rodríguez-González
Marta Sabou
Maria Pilar Salas-Zárate
Estefania Serral Asensio
Vladimir Stantchev
Wikan Danar Sunindyo
Reza Zamani

ISDE 2015 Program Committee

Silvia Abrahao
M. Ali Babar
Nick Bessis
Barbara Carminati
Cagatay Catal
Ricardo Colomo-Palacios
Juan Garbajosa
Amar Gupta
Luis Iribarne
Orit Hazzan
Jukka Kääriäinen
Marco Kuhrmann
Casper Lassenius

Mahmood Niazi
Alexander Norta
Allen E. Milewski
Srini Ramaswamy
Ita Richardson
Daniel Rodriguez
Kassem Saleh
Adel Taweel
June Verner
Deo Praksah Vidyarthi
Adam Wojciechowski
Liguo Yu

META4eS 2015 Program Committee

Vladimir Alexiev
Adrian M.P. Brasoveanu
Stamatia Dasiopoulou
Alina Dia Miron
Marin Dimitrov
Efstratios Kontopoulos
Vikash Kumar
Andrea Kő

Cosmin Lazar
Erik Mannens
Jorge Martinez-Gil
Georgios Meditskos
Camelia-M. Pintea
Maria Poveda Villalón
Christophe Roche
Dumitru Roman

Ana Roxin
Magali Séguran
Peter Spyns
Thanos Stavropoulos

Doina Tatar
Dia Trambitas
Maria Esther Vidal
Fouad Zablith

MSC 2015 Program Committee

Frederic Andres
Richard Chbeir
Alessia D'Andrea
Deborah Dahl
Anna Formica
Tiziana Guzzo
Spyros Kokolakis
Nikos Komninos

Claudia Linnhoff-Popien
Stephen Marsh
Nitendra Rajput
Nicola Santoro
Riccardo Torlone
Fei-Yue Wang
Adam Wojciechowski

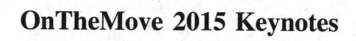
OnTheMove 2015 Keynotes

Data Semantics in the Days of Big Data

John Mylopoulos

University of Trento, Italy

Short Bio

John Mylopoulos holds a professor emeritus position at the Universities of Trento and Toronto. He earned a PhD degree from Princeton University in 1970 and joined the Department of Computer Science at the University of Toronto that year. His research interests include conceptual modelling, requirements engineering, data semantics, and knowledge management. Mylopoulos is a fellow of the Association for the Advancement of Artificial Intelligence (AAAI) and the Royal Society of Canada (Academy of Sciences). He has served as program/general chair of international conferences in artificial intelligence, databases and software engineering, including IJCAI (1991), Requirements Engineering (1997), and VLDB (2004). Mylopoulos is the recipient of an advanced grant from the European Research Council for a project titled "Lucretius: Foundations for Software Evolution."

Talk

"Data Semantics in the Days of Big Data"

In the good old days, the semantics of data was defined in terms of entities and relationships. For example, a tuple (widget:w#123, price: €10, date: 1970.07.30) in the SALES relation meant something like "widget w#123 was sold for €10 on July 30, 1970." This simple view of semantics no longer applies in the days of big data, where gigabytes of data are pouring in every day and the intended meaning is defined in terms of strategic objectives such as, "We want to grow our sales by 2% over three years," or tactical ones such as, "We want to grow sales for our clothing products by 2.5% over the next quarter in Lombardia." We review some of the elements of this new perspective on data and present some of the analysis techniques that are emerging along with big data technologies.

Reusable Coordination Components: A Silver Bullet for Reliable Development of Cooperative Information Systems?

Eva Kühn

TU Wien, Austria

Short Bio

Eva Kühn graduated as an engineer of computer sciences, with a PhD, habilitation, and professor position at TU Wien. Heinz-Zemanek Research Award for PhD work on "Multi Database Systems". She received a Kurt-Gödel Research Grant from the Austrian Government for a sabbatical at the Indiana Center for Databases at Purdue University, USA. She has several international publications and teaching experience in the areas of methods and tools for software development, software engineering, coordination languages, software integration, parallel and distributed programming, heterogeneous transaction processing, and space-based computing. Eva has been project coordinator of nationally (FWF, FFG, AT) and internationally (EU Commission) funded research projects as well as projects with industry. She has international software patents for research work on a new "Coordination System," and seven years of experience as Chief Technological Officer (CTO) of an Austrian spin-off company for software development. Sue has served as conference chair, program committee member, organizer, and coordinator of international conferences. She is a member of the Governing Board of the Austrian and European UNIX systems user group, of the ISO Working Group for the standardization of Prolog, of the Senate of the Christian Doppler Forschungsgesellschaft (CDG), and of the Science and Research Council of the Federal State of Salzburg.

Talk

"Reusable Coordination Components: A Silver Bullet for Reliable Development of Cooperative Information Systems?"

Today's emerging trends such as factory of the future, big data, Internet of Things, intelligent traffic solutions, cyber-physical systems, wireless sensor networks, and smart home/city/grid raise major new challenges on software development. They are characterized by high concurrency, distribution, and dynamics as well as huge numbers of heterogeneous devices, resources, and users that must collaborate in a reliable way. The management of all interactions and dependencies between the participants is a complex task posing massive coordination and integration problems. Must these be solved for each new application from scratch?

An alternative approach would be to identify similarities in their communication and synchronization behavior, to design corresponding "reusable patterns" with the help of a suitable and flexible coordination model, and finally to realize the patterns in the form of software components that run on a suitable middleware platform. In this keynote we discuss state-of-the-art coordination models and middleware systems to achieve this goal. The sharing of coordination components among different use cases on different platforms, reaching from energy-aware micro-controller platforms to enterprise server systems, is demonstrated by means of real-life scenarios from different domains. The vision is to compose advanced cooperative information systems from proven, configurable, reusable "coordination components," thus reducing software development risks and costs.

Durable Modeling and Ever-Changing Implementation Technologies

Sjir Nijssen

PNA Group, Netherlands

Short Bio

Dr. Sjir Nijssen is an emeritus professor and has been CTO at PNA in The Netherlands (www.pna-group.com) for the last 25 years. Dr. Nijssen first experienced the essential steps of working with facts in 1959 and 1960 while serving as a draft officer in the Royal Dutch Air Force, where at that time there was careful observation of planes of friends and enemies by boys on towers in the field, and girls plotting the information by the boys in one of the seven areas of The Netherlands, over telephone lines on a large table in atomic-free bunkers. The contents of the tables of the seven areas was verbalized by girls sitting at the next higher level and were then plotted by girls in the central command on a table covering the entire Netherlands. That information was used by the officers to direct interceptor planes. This was a world with very clear protocols on how to observe, how to formulate the facts, how to convert the facts into another representation of the facts on a land map table, verbalizing the information of the local tables into facts and transmitting these facts to the girls plotting the information read on the central table. Dr. Nijssen started with fact-based business communication modeling in the early 1970s, at Control Data's European headquarters in Brussels. Since then it has been more than his full-time occupation. It was there that NIAM (Natural language Information Analysis Method), a fact-based protocol to develop a conceptual schema and notation, was conceived. Prof. Robert Meersman was one of the pillars of the 22-person research lab at Control Data, from 1970 to 1982. From 1983, Dr. Nijssen held a position as professor of Computer Science for seven years at the University of Queensland in Australia. In 1989 he founded the company PNA, exclusively dedicated to delivering durable and tested business requirements, conceptual modeling, consulting, and educational services fully based on fact orientation. PNA currently employs about 30 people. Dr. Nijssen can be reached directly at `sjir.nijssen@pna-group.com`.

Talk

"Durable Modeling and Ever-Changing Implementation Technologies"

In the relative short history of information technology we have seen substantial improvements. However, between the wishes of the users and the implemented services there is still in many cases an enormous gap. And the problem of very substantial cost overruns in the development of these services is still a serious challenge in too many cases. Today we aim to fill this gap between the requirements and the running services with what is called a durable model. The road toward a durable model has been a long one and an overview will be given since the 1960s. During the 1970s and 1980s the term conceptual model was used to refer to a durable model, with many contributions from the IFIP WG 2.6 conferences and the landmark publication of the ISO Technical Report TR9007 in 1987, "Concepts and Terminology for the Conceptual Schema and the Information Base." Thereafter we discuss how durable modeling has evolved and been misused by various factions in the research and business world.

Since 2012 a co-creation has been established in The Netherlands consisting of government service organizations, universities, and innovative companies with the aim of developing an engineering protocol on how to "transform" laws, regulations, and policies into a durable model. The aim is to develop a national protocol that will be offered to all government departments and all other organizations in The Netherlands. Of course it will be offered to the world. We discuss the scientific foundation of this protocol, called CogniLex, as well as its practical version and report on experiences obtained so far. To the best of our knowledge, this is the most extensive protocol currently available. The skills of protocolled observation and transformation into facts, transforming the facts into another representation mode adequate for a specific purpose, and transforming the other representation mode back into verbalized facts are vital parts of any testing protocol, called ex-ante in Terra Legis. We demonstrate how certain legal domain protocol essentials like Hohfeld can be modeled in fact-based modeling, a durable modeling approach. We also demonstrate how fact-based modeling has been used to detect the needed extensions to the famous work of Hohfeld. If time permits, the transformation of such a durable model into UML, ER, OWL, SBVR, and DMN will be discussed.

From (Security) Research to Innovation

Michele Bezzi

Sap Labs, France

Short Bio

Michele Bezzi is Research Manager at SAP Product Security Research. He heads a group of researchers investigating applied research and innovative security solutions, addressing topics such as security tools for development, intrusion detection systems, and software security analysis.

He received his Master of Physics degree from the University of Florence in 1994 and his PhD in Physics from the University of Bologna in 1998. He has over 15 years' experience in industrial research in SONY, Accenture, and SAP. He has supervised several European projects, and has published more than 50 scientific papers in various research areas: security, privacy, pervasive computing, neural networks, evolutionary models, and complex systems.

Talk

"From (Security) Research to Innovation"

I present some concrete examples of research projects, and show how these research results have been used in SAP products and processes.

The security research team addresses different topics such as security tools for development, intrusion detection systems, and software security analysis. For example, in recent years, we prototyped an application level intrusion detection software, now released as a product — SAP Enterprise Threat Detection (ETD) — able to detect attacks, in real time, on complex software landscape. We also devise tools to support developers in secure development, allowing, for example, security testing during the code writing phase, as well as innovative tools for security governance. In this talk, starting from these examples, I also discuss challenges and opportunities in transferring research results to industrial products or processes.

Contents

IoT and CPS Applications

International Workshop on Enterprise Integration, Interoperability and Networking (EI2N) 2015

EI2N'2015 Co-Chairs' Message

International Workshop on Fact Based Modeling (FBM) 2015

FBM PC Co-Chairs' Message

**Workshop on Industrial and Business Applications of Semantic Web
Technologies (INBAST) 2015**

INBAST 2015 PC Co-Chairs' Message

Mobile and Social Computing for Collaborative Interactions (MSC) 2015

MSC 2015 PC Co-Chairs' Message

Ontologies, DataBases, and Applications of Semantics (ODBASE) 2015 Posters

ODBASE 2015 PC Co-Chairs' Message

On The Move Academy (OTMA) 2015

The 12th OnTheMove Academy PC Chairs' Message

In the past editions, the OTM Academy has yearly innovated its way of working to uphold its mark of quality and excellence. This year's innovation is the addition of a collaborative paper clinic session integrating the idea of "Ph.D. student buddies" who review and help to improve one another's submission under the guidance of an OTMA faculty member. The OTMA faculty members, who are well-respected researchers and practitioners, critically reflect on the students' work in a positive and inspiring atmosphere, so that the students learn to improve not only their research capacities but also their presentation and writing skills. OTMA participants learn how to review scientific papers. They also enjoy ample possibilities to build and expand their professional network thanks to access to all OTM conferences and workshops. OTM Ph.D. students publish their work in a highly reputed publication channel, namely the Springer LNCS OTM workshops proceedings. And last but not least, an ECTS credit certificate rewards their hard work.

Crucial for the success of OTM Academy is the commitment of our other OTMA faculty members whom we sincerely thank:

- Alfred Holl (University of Applied Sciences, Nuremberg, Germany)
- Josefa Kumpfmüller (Vienna, Austria), Student Communication Seminar
- Erich J. Neuhold (University of Vienna, Austria), OTMA Dean

The OTMA submissions were reviewed by an international programme committee of well-respected experts. We thank them for their effort and time:

- Galia Angelova (Bulgarian Academy of Science, Sofia, Bulgary)
- Marcelo Arenas (Pontificia Universidad Católica de Chile, Chile)
- Christoph Bussler (Tropo Inc., USA)
- Paolo Ceravolo (Università degli Studi di Milano, Italy)
- Philippe Cudré-Mauroux (Massachusetts Institute of Technology, USA)
- Manu De Backer (University of Ghent, Belgium)
- Dejing Dou (University of Oregon, Oregon, USA)
- Claudia Jiménez (Universidad de los Andes, Chile)
- Avigdor Gal (Technion – Israel Institute of Technology, Haifa, Israell)
- Frédéric Le Mouël (University of Lyon, Lyon, France)
- Hervé Panetto (Nancy University, Nancy, France)
- Erik Proper (Public Research Centre - Henri Tudor, Luxembourg)

We also express our thanks to Christophe Debruyne (Vrije Universiteit Brussel) who again volunteered to be the OTMA 2015 "social media master".

This year, five papers were submitted by Ph.D. students. One submission is published as regular papers, two as short papers and one as a poster paper. We hope that you find the ideas of these upcoming researchers promising and inspiring for your own research.

September 2015

Peter Spyns
Maria Esther Vidal

Adaptation Mechanisms for Role-Based Software Systems

Martin Weißbach[✉]

Chair of Computer Networks, Institute for Systems Architecture,
Technische Universität Dresden, Dresden, Germany
martin.weissbach1@tu-dresden.de

1 Introduction and Related Work

Software Systems have become incredibly large and complex, hence, difficult
to develop, maintain and evolve. Furthermore, those software systems do not
operate in a stable environment. Certain properties of the environment, e.g.
available bandwidth, through-put or workload of the hosting machine of the
software system, vary over time and might influence the system's performance
adversely under certain conditions. This issue is addressed by self-adaptive software systems, which are systems that can change their own behavior in response
to changes in its operational environment [2].

Moreover, in a distributed application, local changes might require changes of
remote parts of the application as well. Consequently, the adaptation runtime has
to provide mechanisms to ensure that such related operations can be executed
synchronously, i.e. either all operations are executed successfully or changes are
reverted to prevent the application from being in an inconsistent state.

Recently, role-oriented programming has come into focus to allow behavioral
adaptations on the level of programming languages. Roles are used on the design
and implementation level to cover context-dependent behavior of software entities to increase the expressivity of static and dynamic parts of an application.
In [1,3] approaches were presented to incorporate self-adaptive software systems
and role-oriented programming, but the execution of the planned changes was
not closer investigated.

This thesis further investigates the execution of adaptations of role-bases
software systems, especially of distributed role-based applications.

2 Discussion

The general concept of roles as adaptable entities can be applied at multiple
layers of a software system. Coarse-grained structural adaptations, e.g. exchanging components, would be possible as well as fine-grained modifications of the
component's behavior, if implemented using roles.

Our research will mainly cover two parts: First and foremost, we are concerned with the behavioral modification of software systems at runtime that
roles allow. We develop a set of adaptation operations that operate on roles

© Springer International Publishing Switzerland 2015
I. Ciuciu et al. (Eds.): OTM 2015 Workshops, LNCS 9416, pp. 3–4, 2015.
DOI: 10.1007/978-3-319-26138-6_1

rather than on components or runtime objects directly and will therefore be applicable to both layers what makes the adaptation more transparent to the system controlling the adaptation. The controlling system must further determine a safe point in time in the programs execution to alter the system without any loss of data. Hence, we will discuss a lifecycle for roles at runtime that supports the adaptation operations and helps to prevent unwanted behavior during the adaptation as well as data loss. Roles are usually bound to players, simply passivating a role when a player's behavior is supposed to be modified is not sufficient, e.g. when roles are exchanged it must be ensured that state information are preserved ant the new role is activated after it has been bound to the player. Second, when the application's context changes, multiple roles might have to be exchanged in a coordinated and synchronized manner, e.g. if two roles on remote nodes collaborate, it might be necessary to exchange both roles if one of them has to be exchanged due to context changes. Therefore, we are investigating mechanisms how the controlling system can ensure the safe transition of the application from an outdated source state to the desired target state. Crucial at this point is especially the decentralized execution of such operations in a distributed software system.

As possible evaluation criteria, the performance and reliability of the adaptation execution at runtime can be considered, especially in distributed and concurrent applications where invalid role configurations are supposed to be prevented during adaptation. Closely coupled to this issue is the interrupt time that is required to exchange roles at runtime. Naturally, that time frame is supposed to be minimal. Moreover, a formal proof that the algorithms and protocols that drive the execution of adaptation operations do not run into deadlocks and behave as specified would be also desirable.

Acknowledgments. This work is funded by the German Research Foundation (DFG) within the Research Training Group "Role-based Software Infrastructures for continuous-context-sensitive Systems" (GRK 1907).

References

1. Monpratarnchai, S., Tetsuo, T.: Applying adaptive role-based model to self-adaptive system constructing problems: a case study. In: 2011 8th IEEE International Conference and Workshops on Engineering of Autonomic and Autonomous Systems (EASe), pp. 69–78. IEEE (2011)
2. Oreizy, P., Gorlick, M.M., Taylor, R.N., Heimhigner, D., Johnson, G., Medvidovic, N., Quilici, A., Rosenblum, D.S., Wolf, A.L.: An architecture-based approach to self-adaptive software. IEEE Intelligent Systems **14**(3), 54–62 (1999)
3. Tamai, T., Monpratarnchai, S.: A Context-Role Based Modeling Framework for Engineering Adaptive Software Systems. APSEC **1**, 103–110 (2014)

Time Management in Workflows with Loops

Margareta Ciglic[✉]

Department of Informatics Systems,
Alpen-Adria-Universität Klagenfurt, Klagenfurt, Austria
margareta.ciglic@aau.at
http://www.aau.at/tewi/inf/isys/ics/

Abstract. The goal of this research is to enable proactive time management for workflows with loops. We want to offer time constraint patterns that allow the formulation of time constraints on activities that are contained in loops.

Furthermore we design an algorithm for timed workflow graph computation considering loops and given time constraints. We use the time constraints to bind unbounded loops such that we iteratively expand the workflow, compute the timed workflow graph and check the satisfiability of the time constraints.

We also deal with a fast recomputation of a timed workflow graph at the runtime, which is needed to care for slack distribution, situation assessment and enactment of escalation strategies.

1 Introduction

Time management plays an important role in business processes, since violation of deadlines and other time constraints may lead to serious consequences. To represent temporal aspects, the workflow definition is extended by activity durations and other time constraints. Beneath overall deadlines, durations and implicit time constraints, we focus on two types of time constraints: the upper-bound (UBC) and the lower-bound constraint (LBC). They define the longest (respectively, shortest) time interval between the starting or ending points of two activities [4].

The aim of proactive time management is to predict and avoid violations of time constraints. A viable way to do that, as described in Eder et al. [4], is the computation of a timed workflow graph (TWfG) for a given workflow where each activity is annotated with execution intervals (earliest and latest finishing times) that are used to check the satisfiability of given time constraints.

An execution of a workflow and its time constraints is constantly monitored at the runtime and may be modified proactively if time constraints violations are predicted.

Time management becomes challenging if a workflow contains loops, especially if the loops are not bounded. Take a look at the simple photography workflow shown in figure 1. It contains 3 loops, denoted with *LS* (loop split) and *LJ*

Supervisor: Johann Eder, Alpen-Adria-Universität Klagenfurt, johann.eder@aau.at

I. Ciuciu et al. (Eds.): OTM 2015 Workshops, LNCS 9416, pp. 5–9, 2015.
DOI: 10.1007/978-3-319-26138-6_2

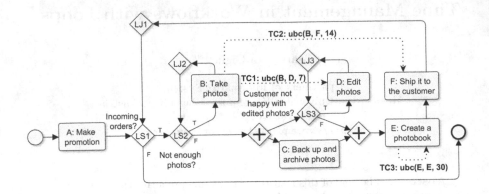

Fig. 1. Simple workflow example of a photography business

(loop join), that may iterate arbitrarily often. There are 3 time constraints for this workflow, defined by the customer and/or photographer:

TC1: ubc(B, D, 7) The customer wants to see the first edited photos at least 1 week after the shooting.

TC2: ubc(B, F, 14) According to the contract a photographer has to ship the photobook within 14 days.

TC3: ubc(E, E, 30) For each photobook a photographer gets a special price from the printing company if he/she orders it max. 30 days after the last order.

Each activity that is placed in a loop, might appear many times at runtime. Currently, there are no representations of constraints, which allow to specify which of these appearances of an activity are constrained. This limitation must be resolved with an extended definition of time constraints. One further problem is the satisfiability check of the time constraints, since the loops are not bounded and would have to be unfolded infinitely, which makes the calculation of the TWfG (and therefore also the satisfiability check of time constraints) impossible.

Loops, and problems related to them, do appear in workflows, therefore we tackle this challenge and search for a viable way to extend proactive time management to workflows with loops.

2   Related Work

The investigation of the research field workflow time management started back in the 90s. A short overview of the development of this field is given in [5]. An overview of time constraint types deliver Lanz et al. in [8] where they identify 10 classes of workflow time patterns. One of the categories of time patterns are recurrent process elements that also gives recommendations for specifying cyclic elements. First, Lanz et al. propose a general design choice for the number of cycles that a) can be determined by a fixed or dynamic number of iterations, b) depends on time lag and end date or c) depends on exit condition. A fixed number of iterations is often assumed in the literature, e.g. [3]. Lanz et al. further define that time lags between cycles can be fixed or may vary etc. The pattern solution for iteratively performed processes introduces a special time constraint between two process elements where the second one lies in the succeeding iteration.

Combi et al. [2] propose TNest, a new workflow modeling language for time constraints definition (among others), that can be used to express time constraints between two activities in different cycles of a loop, however the notation has a limited scope.

In the literature, loops are sometimes a) not handled at all [9], b) handled as a complex activity [10], c) rolled out into a sequence [12] or rolled out into conditional blocks (XORs) [7]. So far, most advanced loop handling was introduced by Pichler in [11]. He assigns branching probabilities to workflow graphs and uses this information to transform a cyclic workflow graph into an acyclic graph, called probabilistic unfolded workflow graph. To prevent an infinite growth of the graph, graph expansion stops when the probability of missing cases is below a certain threshold.

For the satisfiability check of time constraints, activities must be annotated with time information. There are several ways how to do that, e.g. Timed Petri Nets [6], Simple Temporal Network (STN) and its extended versions, Timed Game Automata (TGA) [1] or a timed workflow graph (TWfG) [4]. We use the TWfG to check the satisfiability of time constraints, because we believe that it is well suited for iterative graph expansion, computation of the time information and satisfiability check. TWfG computation works well for workflows without loops, however, it is not defined for workflows with loops.

As stated above, loops are frequently mentioned in the literature as a part of the workflow that is not the focus of the work and therefore they are not handled adequately [7,9,10,12]. Our contribution is to close this gap and to propose a time management solution for workflows with loops. We formulate time constraints definitions for workflows with loops and extend TWfG computation for adequate loop handling.

3   Research Goals

The challenge in proactive time management for workflows with loops can be divided into three main research goals:

1. Formulation of Time Constraints

The first problem is the definition of time constraints between two events where one or both of them appear in a loop. There is a need for an extended time constraint definition that can express the exact instance of an activity placed within a loop.

2. TWfG Computation and Time Constraints Satisfiability Check
Next problem is the TWfG computation in workflows with unbounded loops. A new algorithm that checks loop termination due to temporal constraints and the satisfiability of time constraints is needed.

3. Runtime Support
In order to keep the time information of the nodes in a TWfG accurate, a TWfG must be recomputed during the run time [4]. Since a recomputed TWfG must be quickly available at run time, an efficient recomputation algorithm that can cope with loops and status assessment are required and will be developed in scope of the thesis.

4   Work Plan and Research Methodology

According to the research goals, following work plan and solution ideas will be approached:

1. Formulation of Time Constraints
The first part of the solution copes with the definition of time constraints for workflows with loops. We extend the definition of the source and destination activity in an UBC/LBC such that we are able to address the exact appearance of an activity that is placed in a loop:

$source$:= [FIRST | LAST | EACH] activity_label [WITHIN loop_label]

$destination$:= [FIRST | LAST | EACH] [FOLLOWING | PRECEDING] activity_label
[WITHIN loop_label [SAME_ITERATION | NEXT_ITERATION | PRECEDING_ITERATION]]

With the extended definition of UBC/LBC, we would express the 3 time constraints from the example in figure 1 as follows:

TC1: ubc(LAST B WITHIN $LS2$, FIRST FOLLOWING D WITHIN $LS1$ SAME_ITERATION, 7)

TC2: ubc(LAST B WITHIN $LS2$, FIRST FOLLOWING F WITHIN $LS1$ SAME_ITERATION, 14)

TC3: ubc(EACH E WITHIN $LS1$, FIRST PRECEDING E WITHIN $LS1$ PRECEDING_ITERATION, 30)

2. TWfG Computation and Time Constraints Satisfiability Check
We design an algorithm that is capable to iteratively expand a workflow, compute a TWfG and check the satisfiability of time constraints (inclusive the overall deadline). This approach allows the use of time constraints to bind unbounded loops and consequently enables proactive time management in workflows with loops.

3. Runtime Support
We design runtime support that enables fast TWfG recomputation, slack distribution and support for dispatchment, status assessment and enactment of escalation strategies.

In our work we generate two artifacts: the language for the representation of time constraints and the algorithm for TWfG computation and time constraints satisfiability checking. The evaluation is performed with formal proofs and a prototypical implementation of the algorithm.

References

1. Cimatti, A., Hunsberger, L., Micheli, A., Posenato, R., Roveri, M.: Sound and complete algorithms for checking the dynamic controllability of temporal networks with uncertainty, disjunction and observation. In: 21st International Symposium on Temporal Representation and Reasoning (TIME 2014), pp. 27–36. IEEE (2014)
2. Combi, C., Gambini, M., Migliorini, S., Posenato, R.: Representing business processes through a temporal data-centric workflow modeling language: An application to the management of clinical pathways. IEEE Transactions on Systems, Man, and Cybernetics: Systems 44(9), 1182–1203 (2014)
3. Combi, C., Gozzi, M., Posenato, R., Pozzi, G.: Conceptual modeling of flexible temporal workflows. ACM Transactions on Autonomous and Adaptive Systems (TAAS) 7(2), 19 (2012)
4. Eder, J., Panagos, E., Rabinovich, M.I.: Time constraints in workflow systems. In: Jarke, M., Oberweis, A. (eds.) CAiSE 1999. LNCS, vol. 1626, pp. 286–300. Springer, Heidelberg (1999)
5. Eder, J., Panagos, E., Rabinovich, M.: Workflow time management revisited. In: Bubonko, J., et al. (eds.) Seminal Contributions to Information Systems Engineering, pp. 207–213. Springer, Heidelberg (2013)
6. Foyo, P.M.G.D., Silva, J.R.: Using time petri nets for modeling and verification of timed constrained workflow systems. ABCM Symposium Series in Mechatronics 3, 471–478 (2008)
7. Lanz, A., Posenato, R., Combi, C., Reichert, M.: Controllability of time-aware processes at run time. In: Meersman, R., Panetto, H., Dillon, T., Eder, J., Bellahsene, Z., Ritter, N., De Leenheer, P., Dou, D. (eds.) ODBASE 2013. LNCS, vol. 8185, pp. 39–56. Springer, Heidelberg (2013)
8. Lanz, A., Weber, B., Reichert, M.: Time patterns for process-aware information systems. Requirements Engineering 19(2), 113–141 (2014)
9. Lu, R., Sadiq, S.W., Padmanabhan, V., Governatori, G.: Using a temporal constraint network for business process execution. In: Dobbie, G., Bailey, J. (eds.) ADC 2006 Proceedings of the 17th Australasian Database Conference. CRPIT, vol. 49, pp. 157–166. Australian Computer Society (2006)
10. Marjanovic, O.: Dynamic verification of temporal constraints in production workflows. In: 11th Australasian Database Conference (ADC 2000), pp. 74–81. IEEE (2000)
11. Pichler, H.: Time management for workflow systems. A probabilistic approach for basic and advanced control flow structures. Ph.D. thesis, Alpen-Adria-Universitaet Klagenfurt (2006)
12. Son, J.H., Kim, J.S., Kim, M.H.: Extracting the workflow critical path from the extended well-formed workflow schema. Journal of Computer and System Sciences 70(1), 86–106 (2005)

Intercloud Communication for Value-Added Smart Home and Smart Grid Services

Philipp Grubitzsch[✉]

Computer Networks Group, Technische Universität Dresden,
01062 Dresden, Germany
philipp.grubitzsch@tu-dresden.de

Abstract. The increasingly decentralized generation of renewable energy enables value-added smart home and smart grid (SHSG) services. The device data on which those services rely are often stored in clouds of different vendors. Usually, the vendors' clouds all offer their own service interfaces. It is increasingly challenging for service providers to access the data from all these clouds. Hence, each cloud forms a data silo, where users' device data are captured. Intercloud computing is one suggested approach to solve this uprising vendor silo problem. Introducing a standardized service interface and simply interconnecting the clouds can easily result in an unnecessary communication overhead. Compared to other domains applying Intercloud computing, the device data in the SHSG domain has special characteristics. These characteristics should be considered for the design of an appropriate communication architecture. Thus, the focus of this research is on an efficient communication for discovering and delivering device data in an SHSG Intercloud scenario. Therefore, we present an architecture introducing an Intercloud Service (ICS) on top of the vendor clouds. An evaluation methodology is proposed to investigate the efficiency of the chosen solution for the ICS.

Keywords: Smart home · Smart grid · Intercloud computing

1 Introduction

Smart homes enable users a new quality of living by automation. In contrast, the smart grid is primarily an emerging technology to enable the shift from centralized energy production, based on fossil and nuclear sources, towards distributed production of renewable energy. Nevertheless, the smartness in both domains relies on *value-added services*. From several influence factors, they calculate new information and then present it to the users or make decisions to automatically control devices. In smart home, benefit of this services is a gain in comfort or to save money. In smart grid, they support the transmission and distribution side operators to keep the grid stable. One important influence factor for generating added value is the households real time *device data* like sensor measurements and device states.

© Springer International Publishing Switzerland 2015
I. Ciuciu et al. (Eds.): OTM 2015 Workshops, LNCS 9416, pp. 10–19, 2015.
DOI: 10.1007/978-3-319-26138-6_3

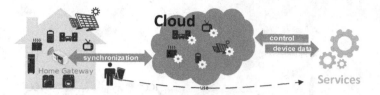

Fig. 1. SHSG cloud architecture

General Architecture: It is a trend in progress to move both, the value-added services [15] and the stored devices data [17] from the home into the cloud. Fig. 1 shows the common way how this is achieved for the device data. We call this approach the Smart Home/ Smart Grid (SHSG) cloud architecture. All devices in a household are connected to a *home gateway* [3,11,20]. Commonly, the home gateway uses an existing internet access (e.g. ADSL or Cable) to establish a bidirectional connection to a cloud. Every local device has a virtual counterpart in the cloud which fully represents its state. Synchronization is automatically triggered when devices send their live data to the home gateway, which then immediately pushes the data to the cloud. This changes the state of the corresponding virtual devices in the cloud. Vice versa, devices can also be remote-controlled by the cloud or a service. In that case, the virtual device representation changes and the cloud sends commands to the home gateway. To control devices and access their data, the cloud offers interfaces to users and services. Home gateways are bound to users, who can grant or revoke access rights to their devices and device data. Services or other users need access rights to request device data of a certain user's virtual devices.

The Data Silo Challenge: Today, many companies are trying to establish their own cloud solution. This increases the gap of service interface and data model interoperability between these solutions [19]. As a result, customers' data get captured in individual data silos (Fig. 2a). Nevertheless, the services generate more additional value with more available device data of more users. Hence, it has to be possible to access data from other silos to fully leverage the SHSG technology. In consequence, service providers are forced to support many different interfaces with their service implementation. Furthermore, they need to request device data separately from each cloud provider. Therefore, services have to know about each cloud. A centralized Google-like search index to work around this issue is not possible due data control concerns of the cloud providers. Dependency of a centralized index contradicts their business interests.

One suggested way to solve this issue is to utilize Intercloud computing [17]. As shown in Fig. 2b, our own approach follows this suggestion by extending the data silos with an *Intercloud Service* (ICS). It enables the silos to establish an *Intercloud-communication* (ICC) to access user-shared device data from other silos. Services use an *Intercloud API* (IC API) to transparently access the entire Intercloud by querying just a single arbitrary cloud, acting as *gateway cloud*. Thereby, services do not need to discover and collect the entire distributed data

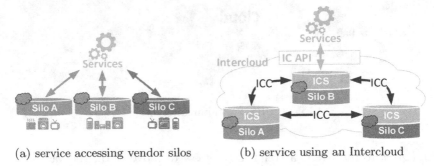

(a) service accessing vendor silos   (b) service using an Intercloud

Fig. 2. From silo challenge to Intercloud approach

from all clouds in the Intercloud, being *peer clouds*. The chosen gateway cloud has to process the query in two main steps: the ***discovery*** of the device data associated with the query, and the ***distribution*** of these data to the requesting services by collecting it from the peers and aggregating it for delivery.

The goal of this work is an efficient communication for discovery and distribution of device data in an SHSG Intercloud.

2 Related Work

SHSG clouds might be deployed on an Infrastructure as a Service (IaaS) solution like Amazon EC2[1] or MS Azure[2]. Beyond that, they themselves are usually provided as Platform as a Service (PaaS), which enables 3rd-party developers to create and run own value-added services on top of them. These services are then offered as Software as a Service (SaaS) to customers [16].

Numerous research has been conducted to clarify and classify SHSG services (SaaS) [5,12,16] and SHSG clouds (PaaS) [9,11,16,17]. Mostly, they have following requirements in common: a *data model* which supports many different devices encapsulated in a provided *service interface*, an *information management system* for virtual device and data management including appropriate privacy and access control, *bidirectional real time communication* with support of *data-centric* and *topic-based group* communication models and the ability to ensure *Quality of Service* (QoS) by a *Service Level Agreement* (SLA) model.

In [8] the authors suggest and evaluate a model for information management based on a classification of devices, user activities and communication. [2] investigates how Message-oriented-Middlewares (MOM) like XMPP, AMQP or DDS can be utilized to fulfill the requirements of the bidirectional real time communication for SHSG, while [3] examined these protocols for their suitability of *QoS*. QoS is important to ensure that a service can work as intended. In [4] the authors investigated QoS stovepipes and emphasizes the importance of the MOM

---

[1] http://aws.amazon.com/de/ec2/
[2] http://azure.microsoft.com

to achieve interoperability. [14] propose an SLA framework for monitoring QoS of smart grid services. Results of other research investigated show whole architectures or frameworks trying to address several of the mentioned requirements for smart grid [9] and smart home [20,21] clouds. All of them just show how to establish a single SHSG cloud, which will lead to vendor silos as mentioned in Sec. 1.

With the increasing number of cloud platforms in any domain, interoperability among several clouds moved into focus of research. Intercloud computing is the suggested way to achieve this [6,7,17,19]. Primarily, this relies on an interoperable *data model* and *service interface* and a communication management model between clouds, often called *broker*. The broker is responsible for provisioning of resources (discovery and distribution of services/ data) among all cloud entities in a QoS manner, determined by an SLA. Access control is supposed to be handled across several clouds. Trust between clouds is also an important concern. According to patterns of Intercloud communication, the MOM (and utilized protocols), should support a federated communication model.

An orchestration service (broker) to achieve C2C service interoperability with focus on QoS, access control and privacy across multiple cloud instances is described in [10]. [13] proposes a broker-based approach to interconnect arbitrary dynamic service plattforms (similar to PaaS-like clouds) with a simple trust model. An implementation utilizes XMPPs rostergroups for the trust model, presence function and further XMPP extension protocols (XEP) for discovering and availability tracking of the distributed services. [18] built a federated sensor network between three involved universities on top of XMPP Multi-User chat (MUC) rooms. An architecture for a Media Intercloud which takes almost all mentioned Intercloud requirements into account is proposed in [1]. They also utilize XMPP as MOM for the signaling and RDF/SPARQL for the data model/requesting in their API.

Research has rarely been conducted to extend the SHSG requirements to an Intercloud approach, yet. [17] proposed a decentralized model as cloud of clouds for the smart grid domain. Moreover, they demand a uniform and transparent (agnostic to C2C infrastructure) device data access for all stakeholders called GET API.

After thorough review of related work, there is no – to the best of our knowledge – complete architecture for an SHSG Intercloud, yet. None of the related Intercloud work has taken into account the special characteristics of the device data in order to obtain an efficient Intercloud communication within the SHSG domain. Only if this aspect is considered for the design of the *discovery* and *distribution* model, we expect a much more efficient communication.

3   Research Hypotheses

Our proposed architecture for an efficient Intercloud communication relies on the following hypotheses:

Hypothesis 1 - *A Semi-Distributed Directory Service with Partially Replicated Meta-Data Enables Efficient Resource Discovery in SHSG Scenarios, Yielding Data Control Concerns.*

As already mentioned, a centralized discovery solution is not desirable due to data control concerns. A dedicated solution is desired by each cloud provider. A semi-distributed directory service could avoid centralized storing of searchable SHSG device meta-data. Such meta-data could be key-value pairs of devices, location, or access permissions. These may be either replicated to all instances, trusted subsets, or not replicated. Having no directory services, queries would have to be sent broadcast-like to all peer clouds. However, with a rising number of clouds this approach appears to become inefficient. Thus, we want to elaborate possibilities for a partially replicated placement of meta-data. Semi-distributed directory services could be a reasonable possibility. Within that, part of the meta-data is shared among the directory services in an Intercloud compound while part of it remains at the individual clouds. Feasible replication strategies for exchanging and organizing the meta-data are required for an efficient query processing in the Intercloud. This leads to the following research questions:

Q1: What are the important device meta-data to be shared between the directory services of the clouds in order to achieve an efficient discovery communication between the clouds?
Q2: In order for our approach to surpass the efficiency of broadcasting queries, what are the thresholds for numbers of clouds and devices as well as device type distributions in the participating clouds?

Hypothesis 2 - *Dynamic topic grouping for data-centric communication avoids redundant data delivery for continuous device data*

As mentioned before, the requested device data might be distributed among many clouds. It can be delivered in two ways specified by the request itself: one time (PULL) or as subscription for a continuous delivery (PUSH). After successful retrieval of peer clouds from its directory service, the gateway cloud is also responsible for delivering the requested data to the querying service. Therefore, it must aggregate the result streams from the peer clouds and deliver them to the querying service. To address use cases in which two or more services request data sets for PUSH delivery, forming an intersection, we propose a data-centric communication applying topic grouping to avoid redundant transmission of the same data between clouds. We expect that this will significantly increase efficiency of network resource usage. This leads to the following research questions:

Q3: What are the circumstances for (re-)grouping (aggregate/split) the topics and what is the strategy for that?
Q4: When considering the resource costs of the platform infrastructure (processing, network), does the gain in network efficiency justify the additional required processing power for topic grouping?

Fig. 3. Directory Services - A) single centralized B) single distributed C) semi-distributed

4   Research Methods and Material

The Intercloud Service (ref. Fig. 2b) is the core component of our research prototype. The IC API will support both queries mentioned before, namely PULL and PUSH. They work with filter mechanisms on top of a device model. The interoperability of the IC API shall be deemed out of research scope; instead, we wish to focus on:

Discovery: Under hypothesis 1, we expect a directory service (DS) to perform better than an approach which broadcasts queries. We have taken several DS architectures into our considerations (Fig. 3); A) a single centralized DS was already excluded in Sec. 1 due to data control concerns; B) a single distributed DS (e.g. based on a distributed hash table or full replication) is also infeasible, because every cloud would also have the full data set; and finally C) an approach of multiple semi-distributed directory services with partially replicated meta-data meets our requirements best. Directory information is partially shared by trusted peering between clouds. This is similar to friends in a contact list of an instant messenger as we have prior described in [13]. Hence, every cloud has its own directory service, storing just the information provided by their trusted peers. In attempts to answer *Q1*, we identified three possible device meta-data for replication: the device model, the location and the access permissions. The information structure within the DS can effect the efficiency of searches on the meta-data. This affects the information which has to be stored in the directory services and therefore also their sizes and required processing time. Further issues to be discussed are privacy aspects of users' device data. This can lead from just sharing coarse grain data (e.g. instead of exact location just the city or region) up to not exchanging certain data. Further details of the strategy and also the structuring of the data in the DS are still being investigated. We plan to experiment with different existing solutions for storing and querying the device meta data. Possible candidates are LDAP-based DS, or index implementations of Apache Lucene[3] like Elasticsearch[4] or SolR[5].

Distribution: To address hypothesis 2, we outlined a data-centric delivery which uses dynamic topic grouping (Fig. 4). To deliver information topic based from the

---

[3] https://lucene.apache.org/
[4] https://www.elastic.co/products/elasticsearch
[5] http://lucene.apache.org/solr/

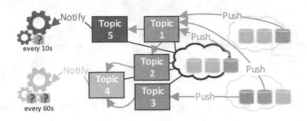

Fig. 4. Dynamic Topic Grouping - two services querying partially the same data

source side, the smallest information are key-value pairs described by the device model. From the service point of view, a topic is an aggregation of all information to serve a specific request. The topic grouping can be found between data source and service. Multiple requests can partially query for the same data but still differ in some details. For instance, the SLA/QoS may influence the outcome: SERVICE A requests DATA to delivered every 10 seconds, while SERVICE B requests DATA every 60 seconds for delivery. Therefore, just one stream per cloud is required to send DATA to TOPIC 1 every 10 seconds. The gateway cloud then also creates a new TOPIC 2 for SERVICE B and copies the value from TOPIC 1 every 60 seconds. Several other cases still have to be investigated.

The Intercloud Service is planned to build on top of *XMPP* as communication middleware. We have been evaluating several other middlewares; one of the outcomes is described in [18]. A major advantage for XMPP is the possibility of federated communication between servers and the extensive support of different communication patterns by extensions called *XEP*.

To prove our hypotheses, we want to compare our approach to a state-of-the-art architecture which serves as *baseline*. The baseline is using a broadcast mechanism for the discovery of device data. Thereby, a query for arbitrary device data results in a forward of the request to all known clouds. For the data distribution it uses a common request-oriented delivery. This means, data is transmitted separately for each individual request to the cloud, which initially has forwarded it. If two or more requests are sent for the same device data, it will result in redundant transmission.

For the suggested research method we are developing a hybrid testbed. It consist of an *emulator*, a *commercial cloud solution* and is controlled by a *testbed Manager*. The emulator is able to emulate thousands of clients on a single computer. A client is either a home gateway with several simulated devices producing real device data, or a generic value-added service requesting device data according to a predetermined pattern. Clients have a real network connection to several clouds. For the clouds we are using a solution from our industry partner KIWIGRID[6], extended by our proposed Intercloud Service. The testbed Manager comes with editors to setup and link devices, home gateways, value-added services and clouds, and a distributed execution environment.

---

[6] http://www.kiwigrid.com

With the proposed testbed we are able to produce and monitor real world network traffic for certain scenarios for device distribution (number in the clouds, device type heterogeneity), cloud configuration (linking between clouds, overall cloud number in Intercloud) and cloud architectures (baseline vs. our approach).

5 Discussion and Future Work

Each aspects of our conceptual progress, namely communication concept, testbed, and evaluation, needs to be individually reviewed.

Details of the **communication concept** for discovery and distribution remain to be conceived, followed by a determination of qualified data and their structure for the directory service. Further, the numerous special cases of PUSH data distribution need to be identified and investigated. For each of these cases, (re-)grouping strategies need to be designed.

Currently, the **testbed** is the most advanced part of our work. We are able to emulate all the clients and setup several clouds with the Intercloud communication of the baseline architecture. Therefore, we are currently developing a description language and an editor which allows us to create different scenarios of device type distribution, cloud constellation in the Intercloud, and to create query patterns for the emulated services. Next step for the testbed will be the implementation of the distributed execution environment. This will enable deployment of clients and clouds on available computers in our testbed network environment automatically.

For the **evaluation**, we plan to perform experiments in form of several scenarios. Table 1 shows the variables for each scenario and the measurands which serve as comparators to evaluate the performance of each architecture. With the chosen set of parameters we aim to show several possible constellations of clouds, distributed device data and network traffic and how each architecture will perform. Regarding research questions $Q2$ and $Q4$ we expect our approach to perform best in scenarios with many clouds, each managing a huge number of heterogeneous device types and services often requesting same subsets of data from their gateway clouds to the Intercloud. We assume, the choice for the right

Table 1. Parameters for evaluation experiments

Variables	Measurands
• architecture: own approach, baseline, others • # of clouds: 1,2,5,10,...,50 • # of homegateways per cloud: up to thousands • # of overall devices per cloud: up to thousands • heterogeneity of device type distribution • # of similar service requests	− network • average latency in ms • average bandwidth used in MBit/s • overall message count − processing • CPU load in % • memory used in MB

architecture depends on the kind of scenario in the future. With our evaluation method it shall also be possible to show which architecture performs better in a certain scenario. For the experiments we still need to design convincing scenarios, including reasonable combinations and values for the variables.

6   Conclusion

In this paper we propose an Intercloud approach for smart home and smart grid clouds to solve the uprising vendor silo problem of user's device data. Our approach focuses on an efficient communication to discover and distribute SHSG device data between participating clouds. For the proposed discovery approach, we address data control concerns of the cloud providers. Our suggested distribution mechanism supports QoS to fulfill certain SLAs while avoiding redundant data transmission for similar service requests. To prove our concept, a testbed currently in development is described. It will enable us to perform experiments for several possible future Intercloud scenarios and thus to answer our research questions.

Acknowledgments. This research is being conducted for my PhD efforts in context of the ZEEBus[7] project (fund number 16KIS0091) and is funded by the Federal Ministry of Education and Research (BMBF) in Germany. Gratitude shall be attributed to my supervisor Daniel Schuster, as well as my colleagues for proofreading. Additional thanks for the free pictographs of household appliances, used in Fig. 1 which where designed by Freepik[8].

References

1. Aazam, M., Huh, E.N.: Inter-cloud media storage and media cloud architecture for inter-cloud communication. In: 2014 IEEE 7th International Conference on Cloud Computing, pp. 982–985 (2014)
2. Albano, M., Ferreira, L.L., Pinho, L.M., Alkhawaja, A.R.: Message-oriented middleware for smart grids. Computer Standards & Interfaces **38**, 133–143 (2015)
3. Alkhawaja, A.R., Ferreira, L.L., Albano, M.: Message Oriented Middleware with QoS Support for Smart Grids, pp. 7–17 (2012)
4. Bakken, D.E., Schantz, R.E., Tucker, R.D.: Smart Grid Communications: QoS Stovepipes or QoS Interoperability? Tech. rep. (2009)
5. Bera, S., Misra, S., Rodrigues, J.J.: Cloud Computing Applications for Smart Grid: A Survey. IEEE Transactions on Parallel and Distributed Systems **PP**(99), 1 (2014)
6. Bernstein, D., Ludvigson, E., Sankar, K., Diamond, S., Morrow, M.: Blueprint for the intercloud - protocols and formats for cloud computing interoperability. In: Proceedings of the 2009 4th International Conference on Internet and Web Applications and Services, ICIW 2009, pp. 328–336 (2009)

---

[7] http://www.vdivde-it.de/KIS/kmu-innovativ/zeebus-1
[8] http://de.freepik.com

7. Bernstein, D., Vij, D.: Intercloud directory and exchange protocol detail using XMPP and RDF. In: Proceedings - 2010 6th World Congress on Services, Services-1, pp. 431–438, July 2010
8. Capitanelli, A., Papetti, A., Peruzzini, M., Germani, M.: A Smart Home Information Management Model for Device Interoperability Simulation. Procedia CIRP **21**, 64–69 (2014)
9. de Diego, R., Martnez, J.F., Rodrguez-Molina, J., Cuerva, A.: A Semantic Middleware Architecture Focused on Data and Heterogeneity Management within the Smart Grid. Energies **7**(9), 5953–5994 (2014)
10. Dowell, S., Barreto, A., Michael, J.B., Shing, M.T.: Cloud to cloud interoperability. In: Proceedings of 2011 6th International Conference on System of Systems Engineering: SoSE in Cloud Computing, Smart Grid, and Cyber Security, SoSE 2011, pp. 258–263 (2011)
11. Fan, Z., Kulkarni, P., Gormus, S., Efthymiou, C., Kalogridis, G., Sooriyabandara, M., Zhu, Z., Lambotharan, S., Chin, W.H.: Smart grid communications: Overview of research challenges, solutions, and standardization activities. IEEE Communications Surveys and Tutorials **15**(1), 21–38 (2013)
12. Fang, X., Misra, S., Xue, G., Yang, D.: Smart grid - The new and improved power grid: A survey. IEEE Communications Surveys and Tutorials **14**(4), 944–980 (2012)
13. Grubitzsch, P., Schuster, D.: Hosting and discovery of distributed mobile services in an XMPP cloud. In: 2014 IEEE International Conference on Mobile Services, pp. 47–54 (2014)
14. Hussain, S., Gustavsson, R., Saleem, A., Nordstrom, L.: SLA conceptual framework for coordinating and monitoring information flow in Smart Grid. In: 2014 IEEE PES Innovative Smart Grid Technologies Conference, ISGT 2014, pp. 1–5, February 2014
15. Kovatsch, M., Mayer, S., Ostermaier, B.: Moving application logic from the firmware to the cloud: towards the thin server architecture for the internet of things. In: Proceedings - 6th International Conference on Innovative Mobile and Internet Services in Ubiquitous Computing, IMIS 2012, pp. 751–756 (2012)
16. Markovic, D.S., Zivkovic, D., Branovic, I., Popovic, R., Cvetkovic, D.: Smart power grid and cloud computing. Renewable and Sustainable Energy Reviews **24**, 566–577 (2013)
17. Rusitschka, S., Eger, K., Gerdes, C.: Smart grid data cloud: a model for utilizing cloud computing in the smart grid domain. In: 2010 First IEEE International Conference on Smart Grid Communications (SmartGridComm), pp. 483–488 (2010)
18. Schuster, D., Grubitzsch, P., Renzel, D., Koren, I., Klauck, R., Kirsche, M.: Global-scale federated access to smart objects using XMPP. In: 2014 IEEE International Conference on Internet of Things(iThings), and IEEE Green Computing and Communications (GreenCom) and IEEE Cyber, Physical and Social Computing (CPSCom) (iThings), pp. 185–192 (2014)
19. Toosi, A.N., Calheiros, R.N., Buyya, R.: Interconnected Cloud Computing Environments. ACM Computing Surveys **47**(1), 1–47 (2014)
20. Yang, Y., Wei, Z., Jia, D., Cong, Y., Shan, R.: A cloud architecture based on smart home. In: 2010 Second International Workshop on Education Technology and Computer Science (ETCS), vol. 2, no. 60970130, pp. 440–443 (2010)
21. Ye, X., Huang, J.: A framework for cloud-based smart home. In: Proceedings of 2011 International Conference on Computer Science and Network Technology, ICCSNT 2011, vol. 2, pp. 894–897 (2011)

Dynamics in Linked Data Environments

Tobias Käfer(✉)

Institute AIFB, Karlsruhe Institute of Technology,
Kaiserstr. 12, 76131 Karlsruhe, Germany
tobias.kaefer@kit.edu

Abstract. Linked Data resources represent things in the world, which
change over time, i.e. the resources are dynamic. We want to address
open questions in building complex applications that consume and interact with Linked Data resources. Applications that consume Linked Data
need to know about the dynamics of Linked Data to efficiently obtain
fresh data to build their logic on. To address this problem of freshness, we
set up a study to observe the dynamics of Linked Data on the Web and
provide insights into the dynamics of Linked Data on the Web. Increasingly, the Web not only provides read-only Linked Data resources, but
also writeable Linked Data resources. We develop a model for dynamics
in the context of writeable Linked Data such that complex applications
can be built on this model. We last present an observer that tracks
the execution of applications that interact with multiple Linked Data
resources.

1 Introduction

The Linked Data principles[1] are a set of practices for data publishing on the Web.
Since their postulation, people and institutions have published a considerable
amount of data on the Web as Linked Data[2]. When building applications that
make use of this data, we are facing two problems:

P1 How to consume data considering that changes may occur to data on the
   Linked Data Web without notification?

The Web has a possibly infinite number of contributors, which may create,
retrieve, update, or delete (CRUD) data in parallel. Downloaded data thus can
get stale.

P2 How to program application logic on the Linked Data Web?

The Linked Data Web is built on Representational State Transfer (REST) [5] as
unified interface for interaction with Web resources.

On the interface, clients and servers exchange information about the current state of resources. To inform clients about resources they might want to

---

[1] http://www.w3.org/DesignIssues/LinkedData.html
[2] http://lod-cloud.net/

© Springer International Publishing Switzerland 2015
I. Ciuciu et al. (Eds.): OTM 2015 Workshops, LNCS 9416, pp. 20–25, 2015.
DOI: 10.1007/978-3-319-26138-6_4

interact with next in the application logic, servers can add links to those (next) resources in the state representation of the (current) resource. By adding links to other resources, hypermedia is formed, and because those links are the means to encode the application state, this practice is called Hypermedia-As-The-Engine-Of-Application-State (HATEOAS) in REST [5]. In the absence of HATEOAS descriptions, or if the application logic involves resources from multiple providers, clients need assistance regarding what their next steps should be.

In the following, we explicate the problems presented and derive research questions.

In their early days, the Linked Data principles were used to publish datasets in the form of self-descriptive resources for the entities in the data set. Linked Data resources represent things in the world, which change over time. To reflect those changes, datasets get updated, resulting in dynamic data. Linked Data-consuming systems often rely on local replications of the resource representations from the Web. If the original resource is updated, processing the local replications leads to outdated results. An efficient update strategy would anticipate changing resources and only update their representation's local replications, thus avoiding outdated results. Reflecting P1, we therefore address the question of *How do Linked Data datasets change?*, from which we derive the following research question:

RQ1 How to characterise the dynamics of Linked Data on the Web?

One challenge here is to derive a sample of Linked Data resources that is interesting to study and feasible to observe deriving snapshots with high consistency (a consistent snapshot is one that contains representations of resources that all are from the same point in time).

So far, we have only considered the retrieval of state. To achieve writeable Linked Data resources (e. g. for their use in application logic, cf. P2), the create, update, and delete operations from REST are used, which has led to the specification of the Linked Data Platform[3]. Therefore, we are next interested in *How are Linked Data datasets changed?*. To facilitate this considerably more complex analysis, we add more complexity to our approach in a stepwise fashion: We first have to clarify the notion of dynamics in REST:

RQ2 How to model change in Linked Data and REST?

The challenge is to find a model that allows for the expression of state transitions and that is coherent with REST. Moreover, the model needs to handle a possibly unlimited number of agents performing state manipulation in parallel.

With a model for change of Linked Data, we can reason over the application logic and the corresponding resource state changes in a formal model. To show

---

[3] http://www.w3.org/TR/ldp/

the applicability of processes in the context of this semantics, our next step is the observation of the execution of known processes:

RQ3 How to track agents performing processes in Linked Data?

The challenge in the context of the Web is that in REST, we cannot observe events (i. e. explicit state manipulation), but have to resort to the observation of resource state changes. With such a tracking framework, we can observe agents executing processes in Linked Data environments. The observation can be used e. g. for situative assistance or to check whether exhibited behaviour complies with instructions/specifications. We use this tracking in a project setting to track pilots in a virtual cockpit.

So far, we have not mentioned the importance of Linked Data and semantic technologies for our approach. For RQ1, semantics allows us for analysing the relations between entities. In the case of RQ2, we can regard the semantic links as semantically defined pointers to future actions according to the HATEOAS constraint of REST. For the techniques developed in the context of RQ3, semantic technologies allow for scalability by lowering the integration effort encountered when adding additional resources from different sources. The state of different resources may be described according to different data schemas, which semantic technologies help bridging easily.

2 Related Work

Related work exists in Data Bases. Rekatsinas et al. develop a model for source freshness based on historical observations [10]. Cho et al. derive an estimator for the frequency of change of resources on the HTML web [3]. In contrast to both analyses of data sources, our approach also allows for the analysis of links between entities and semantic information.

In Semantic Web, Umbrich et al. set up an observation of Linked Data [13], but they monitored a crawl starting in one seed resource. This has two drawbacks: first, incomplete change histories for resources, and second, a considerable bias in the data towards the domain of the seed resource. Our approach observes a bigger and constant sample with greater coverage of Linked Data.

For the investigation of the trade-off between consistency and size of a downloaded data set, there exists work in deriving consistent snapshots in distributed systems such as the work of Chandy and Lamport [2]. In REST, we cannot assume to run code on the components of the distributed system to compose consistent snapshots.

For the observation of applications in distributed systems, there is work in software engineering by Fidge [4] and distributed debugging by Bates [1]. Similarly to Complex Event Processing, their work assumes explicit monitoring information or access to events fired by the components in the distributed system. Such events are not available in REST.

3   Research Hypotheses

We derived two hypotheses from our research questions so far:

H1 We can observe Linked Data dynamics using our measurement devices.
H2 We can derive time-consistent views on the world using HTTP lookups.

4   Material

In this section, we describe using what resources we intend to test our hypotheses.

H1 In connection with RQ1, we build a system to monitor Linked Data on the
Web. We detect the changes by comparing snapshots.
In connection with RQ3, we are building a system to repeatedly download
relevant sources that the agent under consideration interacts with.
H2 We explore the consistency of Linked Data snapshots by building a model
for consistency with varying host-distribution of resources and network delay.
We empirically validate the model using Linked Data download software,
reflecting different use-cases of Linked Data technologies. We then evaluate
the trade-off between size of the snapshot and consistency.

5   Methods/Work Plan

For the building of systems such as the observation of Linked Data on the Web
and the observer to track agents, we apply the design science methodology.

For the investigation of the consistency of snapshots, we follow the methodology of reviewing literature, and building and empirically validating a mathematical model.

The analysis of Linked Data on the Web has been done in the first step using
descriptive statistics.

For the investigation of temporal dynamics in REST, we review literature,
and qualitatively evaluate the solutions for their applicability in REST.

6   Preliminary Results

We have proposed and set up the observation system for Linked Data on the
Web [7], and reported on the dynamics during the first half year of observation [6].

We are currently building the observer for agent behaviour to observe pilots
perform processes in a Virtual Reality cockpit. As a basis for this observation,
we have built a prototype in Linked Data-Fu [12] that consumes Linked Data
at the update rate of a Virtual Reality system [8,9], such that we know that we
can update our observer at a reasonable rate.

7   Future/Planned Work

The work outlined in this proposal can serve as a basis for process mining in Linked Data systems. Processes materialise in state change on resources. Then, on a history of state changes on resources, process mining techniques can be applied.

Moreover, process execution in Linked Data systems can be based on the results of the work proposed in this paper.

8   Conclusion

In this paper, I have presented the solution sketches to open research questions in creating Linked Data application, particularly in the presence of dynamic data.

During my PhD studies, I learnt that dynamic system behaviour is something that many disciplines have addressed, from distributed systems to software engineering to process modelling to logics and physics, to name a few. Without explicitly stating, they share intuitions and methods, from which I want to distil the relevant aspects for Linked Data dynamics.

Acknowledgments. I acknowledge supervision, mentoring, inspiration and advice from: Dr. Andreas Harth, Prof. Dr. Aidan Hogan, Dr. Martin Junghans, and Prof. Dr. Rudi Studer.

This project has received funding from the European Union's FP7 for research, technological development and demonstration under GA #605550 (i-VISION).

References

1. Bates, P.: Debugging heterogeneous distributed systems using event-based models of behavior. In: ACM SIGPlan Notices, pp. 11–22 (1988)
2. Chandy, K.M., Lamport, L.: Distributed Snapshots: Determining Global States of Distributed Systems. ACM TOCS **3**(1), 63–75 (1985)
3. Cho, J., Garcia-Molina, H.: Estimating frequency of change. ACM TOIT **3**(3), 256–290 (2003)
4. Fidge, C.J.: Fundamentals of distributed system observation. IEEE Software **13**(6), 77–83 (1996)
5. Fielding, R.T., Taylor, R.N.: Principled design of the modern Web architecture. ACM TOIT **2**(2), 115–150 (2002)
6. Käfer, T., Abdelrahman, A., Umbrich, J., O'Byrne, P., Hogan, A.: Observing linked data dynamics. In: Cimiano, P., Corcho, O., Presutti, V., Hollink, L., Rudolph, S. (eds.) ESWC 2013. LNCS, vol. 7882, pp. 213–227. Springer, Heidelberg (2013)
7. Käfer, T., Umbrich, J., Hogan, A., Polleres, A.: Towards a dynamic linked data observatory. In: Proc. of the 5th LDOW Workshop at the 21st WWW (2012)
8. Keppmann, F.L., Käfer, T., Stadtmüller, S., Schubotz, R., Harth, A.: High performance linked data processing for virtual reality environments. In: Poster & Demo Proc. of the 13th ISWC, Riva del Garda, Italy (2014)

9. Keppmann, F.L., Käfer, T., Stadtmüller, S., Schubotz, R., Harth, A.: Integrating highly dynamic RESTful linked data APIs in a virtual reality environment. In: Poster & Demo Proc. of the 13th ISMAR, Munich, Germany (2014)
10. Rekatsinas, T., Dong, X.L., Srivastava, D.: Characterizing and selecting fresh data sources. In: Proc. of SIGMOD, pp. 919–930 (2014)
11. Shannon, C.E.: Communication in the Presence of Noise. Proc. of the Institute of Radio Engineers **37**(1), 10–21 (1949)
12. Stadtmüller, S., Speiser, S., Harth, A., Studer, R.: Data-Fu: a language and an interpreter for interaction with read/write linked data. In: Proc. of the 22nd WWW, Rio de Janeiro, Brazil, pp. 1225–1236 (2013)
13. Umbrich, J., Hausenblas, M., Hogan, A., Polleres, A., Decker, S.: Towards dataset dynamics: change frequency of linked open data sources. In: Proc. of the 3rd LDOW Workshop at the 19th WWW (2010)

Industry Case Studies Program
(ICSP) 2015

ICSP 2015 PC Chair's Message

Cloud computing, service-oriented architecture, business process modelling, enterprise architecture, enterprise integration, semantic interoperability—what is an enterprise systems administrator to do with the constant stream of industry hype surrounding him, constantly bathing him with (apparently) new ideas and new "technologies"? It is nearly impossible, and the academic literature does not help solving the problem, with hyped "technologies" catching on in the academic world just as easily as the industrial world. The most unfortunate thing is that these technologies are actually useful, and the press hype only hides that value. What the enterprise information manager really cares about is integrated, interoperable infrastructures, industrial IoT, that support interoperable information systems, so he can deliver valuable information to management in time to make correct decisions about the use and delivery of enterprise resources, whether those are raw materials for manufacturing, people to carry out key business processes, or the management of shipping choices for correct delivery to customers.

The OTM conference series have established itself as a major international forum for exchanging ideas and results on scientific research for practitioners in fields such as computer supported cooperative work, middleware, Internet/Web data management, electronic commerce, workflow management, knowledge flow, agent technologies and software architectures, Cyber Physical Systems and IoT, to name a few. The recent popularity and interest in service-oriented architectures & domains require capabilities for on-demand composition of services. These emerging technologies represent a significant need for highly interoperable systems.

As a part of OnTheMove 2015, the Industry Case Studies Program on "Industry Applications and Standard initiatives for Cooperative Information Systems - The future for the Cyber Physical Systems", supported by OMG, IIC (Industrial Internet Consortium), IFAC TC 5.3 "Enterprise Integration and Networking", the SIG INTEROP Grande-Région, and the Greek Interoperability Centre on "Interoperability emphasized Research/Industry cooperation on these future trends. The focus of the program is on a discussion of ideas where research areas address interoperable information systems and infrastructure. 6 short papers have been presented, focusing on industry leaders, standardization initiatives, European and international projects consortiums and discussing how projects within their organizations addressed software, systems and architecture interoperability. Each paper has been reviewed by an international Programme Committee composed of representatives of Academia, Industry and Standardisation initiatives. We thank them for their dedication and interest.

We hope that you find this industry-focused part of the program valuable as feedback from industry practitioners, and we thank the authors for the time and effort taken to contribute to the program.

September 2015   Hervé Panetto

Continuous Data Collection Framework for Manufacturing Industries

Sudeep Ghimire[1,2(✉)], Raquel Melo[1,2], Jose Ferreira[1,2], Carlos Agostinho[1,2], and Ricardo Goncalves[1,2]

[1] Departamento de Engenharia Electrotécnica, Faculdade de Ciências e Tecnologia, FCT, Universidade Nova de Lisboa, 2829-516 Caparica, Portugal
{sud,ram,japf,ca,rg}@uninova.pt
[2] Centre of Technology and Systems, CTS, UNINOVA, 2829-516 Caparica, Portugal

Abstract. The combination of high-performance and quality with cost-effective productivity, realizing reconfigurable, adaptive and evolving factories leading to sustainable manufacturing industries is one of the emerging research challenges in the domain of Internet of Things. So, it is important to define strategies and technical solutions to allow manufacturing process to autonomously react to the changing factors. Continuous data collection from heterogeneous sources and infusion of such data into suitable processes to enable almost real-time reactive systems is emerging research domain. This research work provides a technical framework for continuous data collection in support of the supply network and manufacturing assets optimization based on collaborative production planning. This research work explores its connection to legacy systems, software components and hardware devices to provide information to the different data consumers. The most relevant achievement of this work is the framework to bridge differences among computing systems, devices and networks allowing uniformity for data access by application decoupling data consumers from data sources.

Keywords: Factories of future · Real-time systems · Collaborative networks

1 Introduction

SMEs manufacturing value chains are distributed and dependent on complex information and material flows. This requires new approaches to reduce the complexity of manufacturing management systems. But most of the SMEs currently do not have access to advanced management systems and collaborative tools due to their restricted in house resources and technical knowledge in developing enterprise system integration. It has been highlighted in 'Factories of the Future 2020 - Research Roadmap' [1] that it is an important research challenge to combine high-performance and quality with cost-effective productivity, realizing reconfigurable, adaptive and evolving solutions for factories to lead towards sustainable manufacturing industries. This required ubiquitous tools supporting collaboration among value chain partners and providing

© Springer International Publishing Switzerland 2015
I. Ciuciu et al. (Eds.): OTM 2015 Workshops, LNCS 9416, pp. 29–40, 2015.
DOI: 10.1007/978-3-319-26138-6_5

advanced algorithms to achieve holistic global and local optimization of manufacturing assets and to respond faster and more efficiently to unforeseen changes.

Cyber Physical Systems (refer [2] for details) have important requirement to achieve seamless integration between different types of systems and devices. Thus, Interoperable Architecture (refer [3] for more details) is an important research aspect within the scope of this research work. This led to new ubiquitous computing paradigm that facilitates computing and communication services anytime, everywhere, providing added values over real-time data. In fact, this emerging paradigm is changing every aspect of industrialization with potential impact in manufacturing domain. Global and localized networks, users, sensors, devices, systems and applications can seamlessly interact with each other and even the physical world in unprecedented ways. This clearly depicts the development of "systems-of-systems" that interact with real-world environment or of "systems" that have equally close connection with both the physical and the computational components.

2   Background

In most of the traditional enterprise applications, users are the producers of information. But in the context of today's manufacturing plans, automated data collection is common, although often complex and difficult to synchronize and maintain [4]. It has also been identified in 'Industry 4.0 -The new industrial revolution' [5] that new IT systems will be built around machines, storage systems and supplies. In this, data is gathered from suppliers, customers and the company itself and evaluated before being linked up with real production. The latter is increasingly using new technologies so that production processes are fine-tuned, adjusted or set up differently in real time [5].

The way in which manufacturing and service industries manage their businesses is changing due to emerging new competitive environments. One successful trend is collaborative production or collaborative networks by handling interoperability across organizational data and processes which have been studied by different researchers as in [6], [7] and [8]. Indeed, collaborative networks can take a large variety of forms, such as virtual organizations, virtual enterprises, dynamic supply chains, professional virtual communities, collaborative virtual laboratories [9] and collaborative non-hierarchical networks [10]. But to achieve collaborative environment enterprises face many challenges related to the lack and duration of interoperability and system integration [11] Also, with the increase in stakeholders in business processes, the amount and nature of data that has to be incorporated into decision-making steadily increases.

The rapid advances in computational power, coupled with the benefits of the Cloud and its services, has the potential to give rise to a new generation of service-based industrial systems whose functionalities reside in-Cloud (Cyber) and on-devices and systems (Physical). As we move towards an infrastructure that is increasingly dependent on monitoring of the real world, timely evaluation of data acquired and timely applicability of management (control), several new challenges arise. Future factories are expected to be complex System of Systems (SoS) that will empower a new generation of applications and services that, as yet, are impossible to realize owing to technical and financial limitations [12].

This research work addresses the issues of seamless data collection from real-world and existing computational resources decouple data sources from application logics. In the following sections background studies on continuous data collection, system integration, Internet of Things (IoT) and collaborative platforms are discussed and followed by the data collection framework developed in the scope of this research work. This research work addresses an important aspect of Cyber Physical Systems (CPS), which is seamless connectivity between physical world and cyber world. It is supported by application scenario involving SMEs collaborating for optimized production planning.

2.1   Motivation

Communication and connectivity enables cross-company innovation activities. Information flowing in and out of the company broadly support innovation and value co-creation. New impulses can come from a multitude of sources outside the own organization, and they have to be proactively integrated into an innovation process.

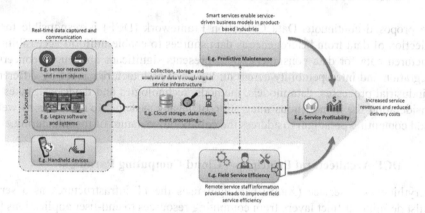

Fig. 1. Value creation through Smart Services and Cyber Physical Systems

Most of the companies enclosed in the borders of the European Union are considered Small and Medium Enterprises [13]. In 2012 the sectors that contributed most to the European SMEs were related to services and manufacturing. Both sectors combined employed 74 million people and produced €2.9 trillion of value added, with 85% of all European SMEs working in these two sectors [14]. In SMEs collaborative innovation is an important aspect for growth and sustainability.

In an interconnected Industry 4.0, ideas are much more valuable if they are embedded in an equally innovative periphery of devices or related solutions. These 'outside-in' and 'inside-out' processes are enabled by digital technologies as discussed in chapter "The Digital Basis of Industry 4.0 – Technology Enablers" of [15], such as community platforms or collaborative Product Lifecycle Management (PLM) tools, connecting knowledge resources. Fig. 1 adopted from [15] shows the value creation through smart services, the driving forces of both Factories of Future (FoF) and

Industry 4.0. It can be clearly noted that collection, storage and analysis of data through digital service infrastructure is an important aspect. Emergence and rising usage of CPS and IoT technologies is enabling data generated by sensor networks to be used by business intelligence software to identify trends and patterns, and help enterprises to make better decisions, and become more reactive to the surrounding environment [16][17]. Machine2Machine (M2M) technologies have the potential to be put to highly innovative and practical purposes [18]. Indeed, current research domain involves the process of connecting machines, equipment, software, and things in our surroundings. Things will use a unique internet protocol address, which permits the communication with each other without human intervention [19]. The European IMC-AESOP project [20] is an example of a state-of-art visionary undertaking by key industrial players such as Schneider Electric and Honeywell, investigating the applicability of cloud-based CPS [21] and Service Oriented Architectures (SOA) [22] in industrial systems.

3   Continuous Data Collection Framework

The proposed continuous Data Collection Framework (DCF) is responsible for the collection of data from heterogeneous data sources to enable uniform accessibility of structured data for data consumers. DCF presents significant challenges concerning integration and interoperability across all layers of architecture caused by differences in industrial processes, data models, methods, technologies and devices. It takes into consideration the homogenous integration of legacy systems, IoT devices as well as cloud computing paradigm to address the collaborative nature of manufacturing.

3.1   DCF Architectural Principles – Cloud Computing Paradigm

Everything as a service (XaaS) paradigm uses the IT infrastructures as a service whilst defining distinct layers from computing resources to end-user applications [23]. A general cloud architecture based on XaaS paradigm consists of three main layers, as depicted in Fig. 2.

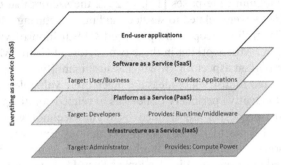

Fig. 2. A generic layered architecture based on XaaS paradigm [23]

The lowest layer, infrastructure as service (IaaS), provides processing, storage and other fundamental computing services over the network. The middle layer, platform as a service (PaaS), provides a runtime environment and middleware to deploy applications using programming languages and tools that the cloud provider supports. The higher layer features a complete application offered as software as a service (SaaS).

The DCF fits into the XaaS approach to provide a scalable real-time architecture, platform and software that support the business processes for manufacturing and logistic based on collaborative demand, production and delivery plans. In this sense, specifically DCF architecture focuses on SaaS layer but is designed to considering all the layers of XaaS for cloud based deployment.

3.2   DCF Architecture

The major components of DCF architecture presented in Fig. 3 are DCF client Node and DCF Cloud Edge, which will be explained in more detail in the following sub-sections. This generic architecture targets to streamline data collection from different data sources considering different standards, data models and communication protocols.

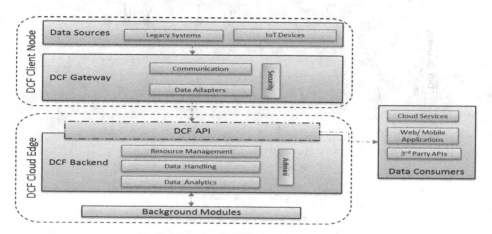

Fig. 3. DCF High Level Architecture

DCF architecture presents a clear demarcation between deployments at local and cloud infrastructure. The Client node is deployed at the local infrastructures of the enterprise and acts as the hub for connecting with the cloud services provided by DCF. Cloud edge is a multi-tenant cloud deployment of DCF backend components. These communicate amongst themselves through well-defined interfaces (DCF API). Different applications can access data on demand through the API. The following sections describe the components in details.

DCF Client Node.
DCF Client Node acts as the hub between the data source infrastructure of manufacturing enterprise and data processing services of DCF. Client node must address two major pools of data sources i.e. Legacy systems and IoT devices.

Legacy systems are traditional software systems currently used in the enterprises. There are multiple legacy systems at different levels viz. Enterprise Resource Planning systems (ERP), Manufacturing Execution Systems (MES), Production Monitoring and Control Systems (PMCS), Application Object Libraries (AOLS), Business Intelligence (BIs) etc. While IoT devices are sets of devices, sensors and actuators deployed at the manufacturing sites are used to perform sensing, monitoring and operative actions for a relatively wide manufacturing lifecycle and periodically transmitting information.

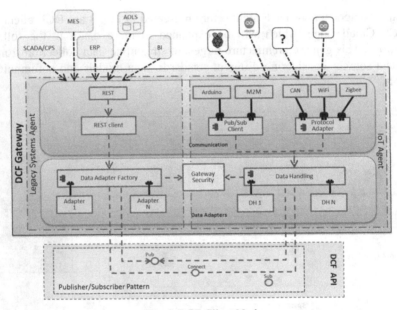

Fig. 4. DCF Client Node

DCF gateway component thus provides two independent components *Legacy Systems Agent* and *IoT Agent,* both of which follows the same architectural principles as described in previous section but instantiated to address specific needs of data sources. Fig. 4 provides the details of the DCF client node with instated cases of some data sources and components of the layers of DCF gateway.

Communication layer provides the components that facilities communication of data sources across various protocols. In the case of legacy systems the communication is bridged by well adopted REST pattern this enabling integration through HTTP protocol. For IoT paradigm supported standards like M2M are directly integrated through pub/sub client for device registration and continuous data collection. Other standards are supported by implementing protocol adapters.

Data Adapters layer provides components to enable data level integration and basic data handling functionalities so that the data follow a uniform reference data model. Legacy system agent implements data adaptor factory to enable seamless addition and instantiation of adapter implementations to handle data models from various data sources. IoT agent provides Data handling components to which different data handling logics can be added to deal with IoT devices deployed for various purposes. This layer also provides security to avoid unauthorized and anonymous access to the legacy systems and IoT devices.

DCF Cloud Edge.
DCF Cloud Edge provides the components that address the functional requirements for data processing and analytics; device and resources management and other higher level functionalities for event traceability, management of rules and constrains, complex event processing etc. DCF cloud Edge is composed of DCF Backend and Background modules as depicted in Fig. 5.

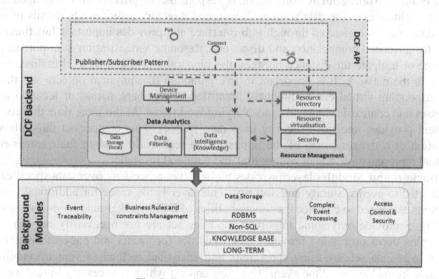

Fig. 5. Details of DCF Cloud Edge

DCF API provides communication interfaces for DCF client node. It provides interfaces for data producers to publish data/context by using Pub interface while data consumers can register to subscribe to data/context related using Sub interface. This publish/subscribe pattern is useful for providing data/context making use of PUSH approach that enable almost real-time access to data. This API also provides an interface for seamless connection between data source and sink to handle data synchronization, uniform connectivity and offline persistence.

Device Management is mainly responsible of connecting IoT devices to backend components. Devices and/or client nodes may use different standards or proprietary communication protocols so this component acts as the common point for management of all devices. These can be enabled/disabled, discarded or put on hold (in case of malfunctioning execution). It also can provide the visualization of all the available technical properties, show integration status (for e.g. "hardware not recognized", "hardware not working properly", etc), and especially accept remote commands (to perform managerial actions). This component enables configuration, operation and monitoring of DCF client nodes.

Data Analytics module provides data intensive functionalities like storage, filtering and business intelligence. Local data storage is necessary to handle the scenarios that might arise due to disruptive connections and also to forward immediate data to subscribers by keep track of access traceability. Data Filtering and Intelligence Knowledge module's main goal is to create knowledge bases from raw data. These are at the core of Data mining, which is mainly driven by machine learning, but also by data structure and purge, data visualization, and the use of human expertise to assess learning mechanisms. The two objectives of this section are the description of data (finding human readable patterns that describe data), and data pre-processing, in order to detect events or to prepare data for further analysis.

Resource Management component is responsible to provide core management functionalities over the data sources. Resourced directory provides the details of all the data sources registered through Pub interface and provides important functionalities for advanced composition and discovery. Resource virtualization is important to reduce or mitigate the distance between the physical world and their virtualized objects in the network. It is important in IoT paradigm that physical objects and their corresponding virtual can be uniquely identified by numbers, names or location addresses and context in time and space varying workspace. At the same time this component provides integrated security over data sources. This component thus allows creation of a dynamic map of the things in the real world through their consistent virtual representation, a map with spatial and temporal resolutions.

Background Modules layer provides higher level processing over data specifically related to events, storage and security. This layer is the space for additional components as needed to enhance the functionalities of DCF. Background modules shown in Fig. 5 provide only some important modules but are not necessarily only those. Complex event processing provides functionalities for events and patterns detection over large data sets by using constraints and analytical methods. Event traceability module keeps logs of all the events and their context which is necessary in real world scenarios not only to address creditability but also to perform events based analytics.

4   Application Scenario in Manufacturing Industry

Companies that work in the manufacturing sector face struggles in the effort to keep up with the technological development [24]. Most of the factories are still very dependent on human interventions for managing and supporting production. Due to the lack of suitable technical solution for proper planning and demand forecast the companies do not have full replenishment plan and timely management of stock levels. So the companies are totally dependent on the quick acquisition of raw materials at suppliers to start their production, and deliveries delays have a significant impact in the production. In this case, companies have to wait for arrival of raw materials for production or re-setup the machines for other production lines. In both cases this is translated directly in more down time for machines thus impacting profitability.

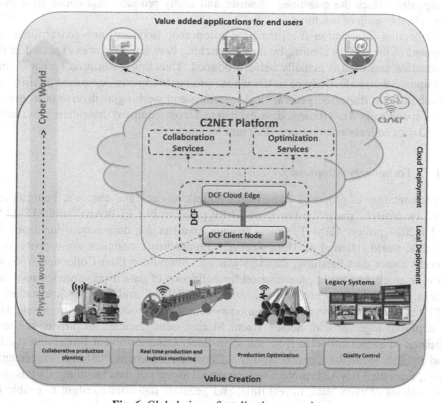

Fig. 6. Global view of application scenario

This scenario is addressed within the scope of H2020 C2NET[1] project. A number of manufacturing companies from the north of Portugal, operating in the Metal and Steel transforming industries are participating for development and validation of technical solution. C2NET is developing cloud based platform supported by IoT devices to help them solve issues related with production planning. In detail, C2NET platform will optimize machinery scheduling plans for production lines, will help understanding the status of their productions and also detect non-conformities during production. Fig. 6 shows the global view of the scenario with clear marking on the role of DCF proposed by the authors as discussed in section 3.

The proposed solution, embedded in the C2NET platform, will enable to track and trace their orders when acquiring raw materials with support provided by logistics companies. This is achieved by deploying IoT systems at the suppliers' logistic premises and also in trucks used for transportation. With that information companies can

---

[1] http://www.c2net-project.eu/

make real time decisions in case of probable delays, as well as understand the current status of their productions. The platform also manages the real time detection of non-conformity in products during the production process. This mechanism can help the companies reduce the quantities of waste and faulty products that could arise from errors in the setup of machines.

Collecting information from the production shop-floor and non-conformities are detected in the quality control, by direct matching between what was expected in the production and what is actually being produced. Thus this application scenario aims to improve the productivity of SMEs whose production line is dependent on different stakeholders at dispersed geographical locations and working as diverse independent units specifically via efficient data exchange across company boundaries and auto-mated data collection at the shop floor and logistics.

4.1   Technology Adoption

Implementation of proposed frameworks adopts services and enablers, being devel-oped by projects, under the European FI-PP program like FI-WARE[2] and FITMAN[3] and H2020 project C2NET, which provide enablers for data acquisition from the physical world (Internet of Things Service Enablement), complex event processing, context aware data handling, data analysis etc. Shop-floor Data Collection [4](SFDC) specific enabler, is the implementation for collection of data from various sensor net-works in a technology/protocol agnostic methodology, and also for integration of RFID tagged objects into the information system. In the production environment, SFD is deployed together with Secure Event Management[5] enabler, to provide a secure dispatch of events collected from the shop-floor. Complex Event Processing (CEP)[6] and Publish/Subscribe Context Broker - Context Awareness Platform[7] implementa-tions, from the FI-WARE project, are important aspects of data handling. CEP is used for analysis of event data, in real-time, and generate immediate insight to enable in-stant response to changing conditions. This implementation is thus used to react to situations rather than to single events. The situation is generated based on a series of events, which have occurred within a dynamic time window, called processing con-text. Context Broker enabler implements publication of context information by enti-ties, referred as Context Producers, so that published context information becomes available to other entities, referred as Context Consumers Those are interested in processing the published context information. Both of these enablers are the important components that are used for integration with the legacy system by use-case specific implementations.

---

[2] http://www.fi-ware.org/
[3] http://www.fitman-fi.eu/
[4] http://catalogue.fitman.atosresearch.eu/enablers/shopfloor-data-collection
[5] http://catalogue.fitman.atosresearch.eu/enablers/secure-event-management
[6] http://catalogue.fi-ware.org/enablers/complex-event-processing-cep-ibm-proactive-technology-online
[7] http://catalogue.fi-ware.org/enablers/publishsubscribe-context-broker-context-awareness-platform

5 Conclusion

In this paper, the challenges and issues in collaborative networking of manufacturing industries are discussed to justify the needs for unique and extensible data collection framework. Then the continuous data collection framework in diverse data sources environment is proposed and specified by detailing each of the components. The reference framework is currently being implemented by taking into consideration the scenario for SMEs in manufacturing industries. This research work clearly takes into consideration the complexity of a heterogeneous data generating systems across multiple domains and provides a scalable cloud enabled solution.

This research is an important part for realization of complete C2NET (Cloud Collaborative Manufacturing Network) and paves path towards efficient decision making and optimized production planning in real production scenarios. Moreover detection of various faults, plan deviations and on-time response to the events, are the added value that this work provides on top of the traditional information systems. However, in order to determine the extent to which this framework, and service delivery model, can be utilized in industrial scenarios, the instantiation of the framework has to be tested in an on-going project. This is the focus of the next phase of the current research work. At the same time, this work will open up new research paradigms on dynamic system integration; IoT devices interconnectivity; efficiencies and issues in cloud computing and improvisation of manufacturing processes.

Acknowledgement. The research leading to these results has received funding from the EC HORIZON2020 Program under grant agreement n° C2NET 636909 (http://www.c2net-project.eu/) and EC 7th Framework Programme under grant agreement n° FITMAN 604674 (http://www.fitman-fi.eu)

References

1. Commission, E.: Factories of the Future: Multi-Annual Roadmap for the Contractual PPP Under HORIZON 2020 (2013)
2. Lee, E.: The Past, Present and Future of Cyber-Physical Systems: A Focus on Models. Sensors **15**, 4837–4869 (2015)
3. Siong, H.Y., Keong, P.K., Yuan, A.J.: Interoperable Open Architecture For Land Platforms (2013). https://www.dsta.gov.sg/docs/dsta-horizons-2013/interoperable_open_architecture_for_land_platforms.pdf?sfvrsn=2
4. Microsoft: Manufacturing 2.0 – It's Time to Rethink Your Manufacturing IT Strategy (2009)
5. Dujin, A., Geissler, C., Horstkötter, D.: Industry 4.0 The new industrial revolution (2014)
6. Szejka, A.L., Aubry, A., Panetto, H., Júnior, O.C., Loures, E.: Towards a Conceptual Framework for Requirements Interoperability in Complex Systems Engineering. In: Meersman, R., et al. (eds.) OTM 2014 Workshops. LNCS, vol. 8842, pp. 229–240. Springer, Heidelberg (2014)

7. Lezoche, M., Yahia, E., Aubry, A., Panetto, H., Zdravkovic, M.: Conceptualising and structuring semantics in cooperative enterprise information systems models. Comput. Ind. **63**, 775–787 (2012)
8. Jardim-Goncalves, R., Grilo, A., Agostinho, C., Lampathaki, F., Charalabidis, Y.: Systematisation of Interoperability Body of Knowledge: the foundation for Enterprise Interoperability as a science. Enterp. Inf. Syst. **7**, 7–32 (2013)
9. Camarinha-Matos, L., Afsarmanesh, H.: Collaborative networks: a new scientific discipline. J. Intell. Manuf. **16**, 439–452 (2005)
10. Poler, R., Carneiro, L.M., Jasinski, T., Zolghadri, M., Pedrazzoli, P.: Intelligent Non-hierarchical Manufacturing Networks. Presented at the (2013)
11. Agostinho, C., Jardim-Gonçalves, R.: Sustaining interoperability of networked liquid-sensing enterprises: A complex systems perspective. Annu. Rev. Control **39**, 128–143 (2015)
12. Colombo, A., Karnouskos, S.: Towards the factory of the future: a service-oriented cross-layer infrastructure. In: ICT Shaping the World: A Scientific view, European Telecommunications Standards Institute (ETSI), pp. 65–81. European Telecommunications Standards Institute (ETSI), John Wiley and Sons (2009)
13. Publications, I.: The new SME definition. Off. J. Eur. Union **C**, 1–52 (2005)
14. European Commission: A Recovery on the horizon? - Annual Report on European SMEs 2012/2013 (2013)
15. Bechtold, J., Kern, A., Lauenstein, C., Bernhofer, L.: Industry 4.0 - The Capgemini Consulting View (2014)
16. Santucci, G., Martinez, C., Vlad-câlcic, D.: The sensing enterprise. In: FInES Workshop at FIA 2012, pp. 1–14 (2012)
17. Agostinho, C., Ducq, Y., Zacharewicz, G., Sarraipa, J., Lampathaki, F., Jardim-Goncalves, R., Poler, R.: Towards a Sustainable Interoperability in Networked Enterprise Information Systems: Trends of Knowledge and Model-Driven Technology. Accept. Publ. Comput. Ind. (2015)
18. With, S.A.: Powering Situational Awareness with M2M Technology (2013). http://www.surfnation.net/files/Powering_Situational_Awareness.pdf
19. Huang, Y., Li, G.: Descriptive models for Internet of Things. In: 2010 International Conference on Intelligent Control and Information Processing (ICICIP), pp. 483–486 (2010)
20. Automation, S.E., Bangemann, T.: IMC-AESOP outcomes: paving the way to collaborative manufacturing systems. In: IEEE 12th International Conference on Industrial Informatics (INDIN), pp. 255–260 (2014)
21. der Technikwissenschaften, D.A.: Cyber-Physical Systems: driving force for innovation in mobility, health, energy and production (2011)
22. Papazoglou, M.P., Heuvel, W.-J.: Service oriented architectures: approaches, technologies and research issues. VLDB J. **16**, 389–415 (2007)
23. Wink, D.M.: Pallis G: Cloud Computing: The New Frontier of Internet Computing. Internet Comput. **14**, 70–73 (2010)
24. Stöllinger, R., Foster-mcgregor, N., Holzner, M., Landesmann, M., Pöschl, J., Stehrer, R.: A Manufacturing Imperative in the EU – Europe's Position in Global Manufacturing and the Role of Industrial Policy (2013)

Determination of Manufacturing Unit Root-Cause Analysis Based on Conditional Monitoring Parameters Using In-Memory Paradigm and Data-Hub Rule Based Optimization Platform

Prabal Mahanta and Saurabh Jain[✉]

SAP Labs India Pvt. Ltd., EPIP Zone, Brookefield, Bangalore 560066, KA, India
{p.mahanta,saurabhjain03}@sap.com

Abstract. Different manufacturing plants have their disparate process of conditional monitoring for their processing units with diverse set of sensors which amounts to petabytes of data. This leads to conglomeration of problems limited not only to data management but also lack in ability to present the overall point of view of the critical observations at a real time scenario. Some of these observations impact the business revenue/cost process and due to lack of aggregation efforts, the overview is not available to the decision makers. With the intention of highlighting the critical performance factors and applied techniques we present the overall view point of a platform which will address such issues and assist decision makers with certain data points to make choices leading to profitability and sustainability of their business outlook. The platform will serve as a single point of aggregation for diversified but correlated data points and various custom data logic applied as per the business rules providing a correlation between data. This correlation will help reach an outcome where the user can trace the source of data point of the concerned manufacturing units where technical parameters can be optimized. This data flow and processing will result in root cause identification using the data hub platform and real time analytics can be made available using in-memory column store database approach.

Keywords: Big data · Manufacturing · In-memory · Data-Hub

1 Introduction

The introduction of smart devices and wireless sensors has given a way for diverse datasets for all units covering a manufacturing plant. This has led to proliferation of varied nature of unstructured/structured, noisy/incomplete datasets which keep multiplying over time at a considerable rate. The size of such data volumes prevents researchers from mining real-time insights into the data due to the disparate data sources and computing and data retrieval complexities [1].

© Springer International Publishing Switzerland 2015
I. Ciuciu et al. (Eds.): OTM 2015 Workshops, LNCS 9416, pp. 41–48, 2015.
DOI: 10.1007/978-3-319-26138-6_6

Adding to the present issues related to the research on such data, there have been research studies concentrating on the application of new paradigms for enhancing the manufacturing floor operations to optimize critical parameters concerning productivity and reducing downtimes. Various researches also try to correlate the supply chain, business performance and globalization surrounding the management practices which reveals that there has been considerable amount of computing practices and architecture enhancement required [2].

There are various evidences from a lot of case studies that suggest that manufacturing plants invests a lot of finance to prevent downtimes of certain units but very often they have to manually adhere to practices to prevent uncertain maintenance times for certain scenarios which could have prevented using mathematical modeling on the various parameter data that is available from different sensors [3].

The researches concentrates on the requirement of enabling centralized and secure capture of sensor and machine data from disparate sources and unify the structure to perform analysis with the use of new computing strategies. The strategy to implement pipeline workflow processing and cloud based standard services to perform preventive maintenance and downtimes [4].

Business value of insights into various functioning parameters in a manufacturing unit can lead to lesser cost to maintenance and increase profitability. In this paper we try to propose a platform where the problem of unified data structure enabled for modeling and analytic can be resolved using in-memory computing techniques.

If we study closely the case of a cement industry, there is some machinery issues which causes frequent coatings and blockages in the cyclone preheaters of rotary kiln plant for burning cement clinker. This causes plant workers to shut-down the production line for maintenance and this consumes about 8 hours for dissolving blockages using fans with considerable amount of power requirement. This leads to cost and also reduction in profit due to non-functioning of production line. The paper tries to concentrate on this particular incident and then integrate the cloud data hub concept to provide opportunities to investigate on other plant insights which currently have been overlooked until now.

2   Data Hub and Information Infrastructure

The main idea behind constructing the data hub is to unify and create an abstraction layer for data arriving from disparate sources like field devices and machinery sensors. The sensor data and product chemical measurement data may change every hour based on user/daily KPI/ overall production target which leads to the need of introducing encoding storage graph for preserving historical data and later using the same we can analyze and provide historical reports and using these reports we can provide future pattern for the performance of any machine and related productivity.

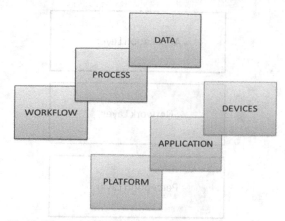

Fig. 1. Hierarchy Mapping of Technology Paradigm

Data hub will integrate the data sources from various sources using a centralized in-memory cloud platform services [5]. The platform will also provide reporting access via web to the concerned users. The historical data will be archived to achieve a compression ratio of 72. This platform will create a centralized access for high alert situations. The paper aims at defining an abstraction layer common to existing IoT environment in terms of architecture and also to ensure backward compatibility which will lead to early adoption. The platform will try to model various section using in-memory modeling concept [6] where the domain-technical, domain-functional, security and information models will be created using secured communication stack based on ISO-OSI network layer.

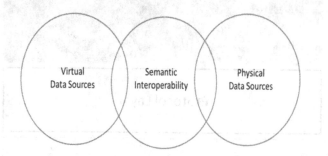

Fig. 2. Interoperability of connected data sources –physical and virtual.

Now when we consider conditional monitoring then our focus is on the three layers as shown in Figure 3.

If we can blow up the layers we can see that there are several components that tie up each layer and this can be visualized using the following figure.

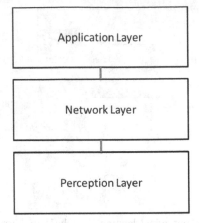

Fig. 3. Layers in a typical manufacturing unit

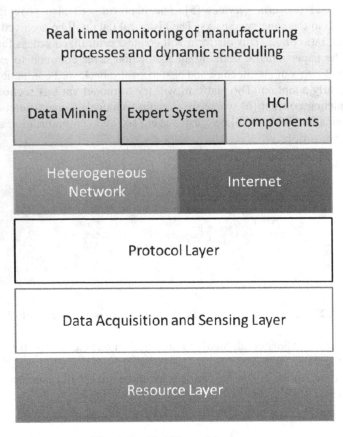

Fig. 4. Detailed View of the Layer

From our research, we realized that the cost to information ratio fairly on a higher side for the plants we studied and realized that this study will allow them to introduce a combination of environmental optimization for performance evaluation for production systems and generating an effective monitoring system for reporting usage.

3   Root Cause Analysis use Case

In any manufacturing plant daily operations, the management is concerned with the rate for increase in productivity which revolves around certain aspects of the production unit:

    a.   Key parameters for failure and increase in productivity.
    b.   Effect of changes in parameter value to productivity.
    c.   Cost to increase high yield rate.

To address the key points mentioned above we need to perform data mining on present data and past. We also realized from our study on cement manufacturing plants that any automated production process generates data in large volumes which contains sensor data, control operations data, worker data which may contain false positives too therefore it becomes important for any reporting operations that we pre-process and compress the data and store it in a cloud environment to avoid any on premise cost of manufacturing unit. The next step will be to prepare a production workflow to explore the data, analyze and present the outcomes and effective support processes [7] [8].

The idea is to present a design and implementation technique which is based on industry specific manufacturing rules for a distributed cloud based environment and preprocess data with compression ability for further data analytic for language integrated data mining and algorithm with real time monitoring and workload adjustment ability for various nodes involved adhering to domain-specific data characteristics [9]. There is a serious need to correlate the overall manufacturing process also which also involves:

    a.   Parameters in a process
    b.   Product quality and input material ratio
    c.   Yield rate and worker shift and worker recipe

We now look at one aspect of the problem in a typical cement manufacturing industry. There exists a problem of blockages with the cyclone preheaters of rotary kiln plants for burning cement clinker. This is due to combined effect of alkalis, chlorides and sulfates alongside components from the decomposition of raw material under the influence of extreme high temperature gases involved in the process. The process of blockage creation is caused by gradual deposition of composition in the narrow cross sections of top outlet ducts of any cyclone preheater and when this deposition thickens and dries out then it falls down and blocks the outlet preventing any further process. This blockage creates a downtime of several hours and this leads to loss in productivity for several tons of manufacturing material and also loss in wastage of raw material. The frequency of cyclone blockages depends on the onsite situation and its occurrence varies can happen daily or few times per year depending on technology installed in plant and the composition of the raw materials. The cause of these blockages differs from plant to plant and preventive measure is not uniform across the plants and there is no defined procedure for removing the blockages. It becomes of high importance to generate a pattern for the same to enable plant management to prevent blockages from hindering their production downtimes.

Now to understand the overall complexity we masked the industrial data and applied score to the production units using the composition X, Y, Z as input parameters across the plant unit and keeping into considerations the following assumptions:

- Diameters of the kiln were constant
- Raw materials were worker determined and hence randomness included.
- Temperature at recommended levels

A simple mathematical model which we used to model to determine the root cause analysis of this problem:

S1 = k1* C1~C1' + k2* C2~C2'
S2 = k3*C3~C3' + k4*C4~C4'
P = a*S1 + b*S2 + W'

Where,

S1 = Score determination for Chemical input X and Y represented as C1 and C2 with ranges C1 to C1' and C2 to C2' respectively

S2 = Score determination for Gas and water inputs for the overall process represented as C3 and C4 with ranges C3 to C3' and C4 to C4' respectively

P is the final product output score with error of wastage determined as W'

Here k1,k2,k3,k4 are weights determined based on the percentage composition specific to any industry standard and W' is the waste determined from the sensor data.

The Figure 5 shows that the daily production level pattern generated using the rule based engine and the outcomes were something we need to focus on.

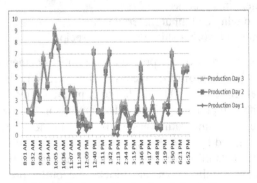

Fig. 5. Daily production level simulation

The outcomes suggested that

- Chemical composition determines the overall production

- Chemical composition is determined by worker and shift based worker output becomes very important to focus as lower output suggests proper training.

- Process and constraint required to be assessed.

- Machine parameters and value constraints are also part of the investigation.

Overall we realized that the protection thickness coating of a rotary cement kiln is important from the view point of productivity. We also realized that by the use of methods based on embedded vector nearest neighbor approach for historical process data we can identify more insights into the plant operations but detailed discussion here is beyond the scope of this paper [10][11].

4   Conclusion

There are various challenges that we came to realize while studying problems associated with a manufacturing industry issues. The concept of root cause analysis is not new but there previous research is not feasible to be adapted by the industry due to lack of knowledge about the data flow.

In this case we also realized that the use of IoT technology compliments such use cases and as a part of our future work we are currently working on the overall architecture and detailed computation requirements and trying to fit the model to various other industry where similar but different specific problems arise which actually accounts to the overall product quality and production rate in turn having an impact on profitability.

Acknowledgment. The Authors would like to thank their colleagues and friends for their immense support. They would also like to thank Ekta Arora, Vice President, Co-Innovation, Sap Labs, India for her support in the research.

References

1. Moreno-Cano, M.V., et al.: Future human-centric smart environments. In: Modeling and Processing for Next-Generation Big-Data Technologies, pp. 341–365. Springer International Publishing (2015)

2. Wong, C.W.Y., Lai, K., Bernroider, E.W.N.: The performance of contingencies of supply chain information integration: The roles of product and market complexity. International Journal of Production Economics **165**, 1–11 (2015)

3. Mohapatra, S., Lokhande, L.: Case Study: Developing Cloud Computing Strategy for Dabur. In: Cloud Computing and ROI, pp. 149–174. Springer International Publishing (2014)
4. Shah, M.: Big Data and the Internet of Things (2015). arXiv preprint arXiv:1503.07092
5. Färber, F., et al.: The SAP HANA Database–An Architecture Overview. IEEE Data Eng. Bull. **35**(1), 28–33 (2012)
6. Mahanta, P., Shah, D.: In-Memory Modeling and Analytics as-a Service in Cloud. Journal of Industrial and Intelligent Information **1**(4) (2013)
7. Hao, Q., et al.: Design of Chemical Industrial Park Integrated Information Management Platform Based on Cloud Computing and IOT (The Internet of Things) Technologies. International Journal of Smart Home **9**(4) (2015)
8. Gubbi, J., et al.: Internet of Things (IoT): A vision, architectural elements, and future directions. Future Generation Computer Systems **29**(7), 1645–1660 (2013)
9. Jayasinghe, D., et al.: An infrastructure for automating large-scale performance studies and data processing. In: 2013 IEEE International Conference on Big Data. IEEE (2013)
10. Bauer, M., et al.: Nearest neighbors methods for root cause analysis of plantwide disturbances. Industrial & Engineering Chemistry Research **46**(18), 5977–5984 (2007)
11. Bauer, M., Cox, J.W., Thornhill, N.F.: Measuring cause and effect of process variables. In: IEEE Advanced Process Control Applications for Industry Workshop 2005, Vancouver, Canada

"Wear" Is the Manufacturing Future: The Latest Fashion Hitting the Workplace

Gurbaksh Bhullar[✉]

Technology Application Network Limited (TANet), Waterton Technology Centre,
Bridgend, South Wales CF31 3WT, UK
gbhullar@control2k.co.uk

Abstract. The evolution of technology continues to bring socially accepted gadgets such as the smartwatch and other wearable devices into the world of work. The manufacturing sector along with most other sectors is bracing itself for all the functions that are readily acceptable in our daily lives to become part of the armoury of the shop floor personnel. Some of the simple forms of safety clothing such as gloves and safety glasses are mandatory when working in many manufacturing environments so it's an easy step to add the technology layers to these wearables to create the new Cyber links between people and their machines. In order to deploy these technologies however, we need to understand the barriers that hold back the implementation of these Cyber Physical Systems and the steps necessary for the full implementation Human-Machine linkages from Cloud systems to shop floor environments.

Keywords: Wearable · Smart · HoloLens · Oculus · Middleware · CPS

1 Introduction

As with life in general, things move on and evolve into something new and different from what came before. This is also true for the growth and evolution of the manufacturing sector along with most other sectors. Many of the past issues are constantly revisited in an attempt to reach utopia. Everything can always be made quicker, cheaper and with better quality, so as new technologies come and go, the old problems are revisited in order to apply these new developments. On the face of it, the new technology should resolve age old issues of error proofing, right first time, bottleneck analysis etc. along with other lean methodologies[1] but generally they bring their own dilemmas into the work place.

The obvious hurdles that comes with new technology is that in most cases, it is written in a completely new format, language or media. Ideally the migration path from old to new should be seamless and painless. However this is rarely the case as with new generations of developers, programmers and engineers that have not experienced the historical march that lead us to where we are now do not seem to be aware of the need for this bridge. How many times does new technology bring new answers

---

[1]   http://www.leanproduction.com/top-25-lean-tools.html

© Springer International Publishing Switzerland 2015
I. Ciuciu et al. (Eds.): OTM 2015 Workshops, LNCS 9416, pp. 49–56, 2015.
DOI: 10.1007/978-3-319-26138-6_7

for old problems? How many times can you re-invent total productive maintenance or introduce quality improvement programs to the sceptical and cynical work force?

2   Data Expansion and Miniaturisation of Devices

The mantra of flexible, scalable solutions and intelligent services in large-scale networking environments has echoed through the ages with each generation setting boundaries they believed would never be reached for decades. It wasn't that long ago (1980's) when 100Mb Disk drives seemed to be providing a capacity that would never be utilised but today we are populating drives with terabits of data on a daily basis. New technology continues to provide new solutions to keep increasing this data with technologies providing densities up to at least 10 Tbpsi by 2017[2]   (current shipping products have 735 Gbpsi areal[3]   density) as Hard Drives move to the solid state world and look likely to be around for higher capacity storage for many years to come.

Of course the size of devices continues to decrease, allowing the same footprint to host at least 10 times the capacity of its predecessors. With all this capacity and the ever increasing miniaturisation, it opens the way to having mass access to data and indeed with Wi-Fi connectivity, computerised devices can literally be made to fit in the palm of the hand. This opens the door to these smaller devices being "ready to wear" or even "ready to embed" and clearly the revolution of wearable devices is well underway as we step out of the world of science fiction and into reality.

3   Flexible Cyber Physical Systems

The human body is naturally adapted for hard work and high flexibility yet the world of technology keeps offering the opportunity to go beyond the normal constraints and allows the human to function safely and with less effort by attaching additional "hardware" in the form of skeletal support or more likely implants that help provide additional functionality to the human. Whilst we normally encounter these ideas in science fiction (Star Trek fans will no doubt relate to Seven of Nine[4], who portrays the common vision of how Cybernetic implants would look like), it is clear that this evolutionary cycle is the likely path for the continued development of the human race.

Of course embedded implants are still some years away but clearly we have already started down this path with the development of wearable devices.

---

[2]   http://www.forbes.com/sites/tomcoughlin/2013/09/07/when-will-we-see-higher-capacity-hard-disk-drives

[3]   The areal density is the average amount of data that can be stored in a unit of surface area on the disk

[4]   http://www.startrek.com/database_article/seven-of-nine

3.1   Google Glass / Alphabet

One of the early wearables was Google Glass (which will most likely be continued to be developed under Googles new company ALPHABET[5]), was a type of wearable technology with an optical head-mounted display (OHMD). It was developed by Google with the mission of producing a mass-market ubiquitous computer which displayed information on a smartphone-like hands-free format. The Google glass project was looking more towards new types of "pointer" devices where wearers communicated with the Internet via natural language voice commands. The touchpad located on the side of Google Glass, allowed users to control the device by swiping through a timeline-like interface displayed on the screen, sliding backward shows current events, such as weather, and sliding forward shows past events, such as phone calls, photos, circle updates, etc. This didn't serve the wearables market in the sense that the user ended up "interacting" with the glasses rather than just using them as a different form of medium presentation tool. On January 15, 2015, Google announced that it would stop producing the Google Glass prototype but remained committed to the development of the product. According to Google, Project Glass was ready to "graduate" from Google Labs[6]. It is likely with the emergence of other similar products hitting the market, Google will no doubt re-emerge from its hiding with a new strategy.

3.2   Facebook and Oculus Rift in the Automotive Industry

When Facebook announced its $2 billion acquisition of Oculus VR in March 2014, founder Mark Zuckerberg talked of applying virtual reality in different industries. A heated debated was sparked as to whether businesses could really use the technology to good effect. Car manufacturer Ford had a clear answer to that question: yes, it can revolutionize development[7].

Across many industries, experts have commented that virtual reality technology has great potential but many businesses are not maximizing it. Ford Motor Company, based in Dearborn, Michigan, has been using virtual reality technology to various degrees to develop its designs since the year 2000. But in the last seven years, the 111-year old business has made virtual reality central to its automotive development, using the Oculus Rift headset technology.

In an interview with Elizabeth Baron, virtual reality and advanced visualization technical specialist at the company, she reflected the use of technology at the design stage of production. "We want to be able to see the cars and our designs, and experience them before we have actually produced them." Ford uses the technology to examine the entire exterior and interior of a car design, as well as to drill right down to how a particular element looks, such as a dashboard or upholstery. This of course

---

[5]   http://www.theguardian.com/technology/2015/aug/10/google-alphabet-parent-company
[6]   https://en.wikipedia.org/wiki/Google_Glass
[7]   http://www.forbes.com/sites/leoking/2014/05/03/ford-where-virtual-reality-is-already-manufacturing-reality/

would require connectivity to several data sources including CAD[8] drawings, ERP[9] and MES[10] systems to be truly accurate.

Virtual reality technology continues to be improved with new interests being shown outside of the gaming world to provide better links between the virtual and physical world and as the technology becomes more widespread, clearly the opportunities to drive improvement are immense.

3.3   Microsoft's Venture into the World of Wearables

Clearly Microsoft have watched the development of Google Glass and developments in Oculus Rift and are finally entering the market with their HoloLens[11].

The standard use of the HoloLens, in familiarly computer aided design environments but the future applications will be much wider than the drawing office. The HoloLens headset offers what is being called mixed or augmented reality, but it is not clear how far HoloLens has travelled along the road to becoming a consumer product.

Director Mark Bolas, a VR veteran having worked in the field since the late 1980s, when asked "Why is virtual reality suddenly so hot" says "I find that question difficult to answer because I can't think of an area which it is not going to affect"[12].

Scientists, games developers, and some of the biggest forces in technology now seem convinced that virtual reality is an idea whose time has come. Now all they need to do is convince millions of us that we really want to strap on a headset and enter another world.

Much of the early developments are of course in the gaming world where restrictions such as secure connectivity, health and safely, demarcation issues, skills gaps and compliance to strict auditing standards are not as much of a challenge as they are in the manufacturing world. So clearly a much wider understanding of how wearable technology can be deployed in manufacturing environments is needed.

4   The Wearable Future

Coming back to the technology of today, and specifically to the manufacturing sector, it is clear that the most likely wearable devices will be in the form of visual headsets for present live data and glove technology since so many manufacturing processes

---

[8] Computer-aided drafting (CAD) is the use of computer systems to assist in the creation, modification, analysis, or optimization of a design (Wikipedia).

[9] Enterprise resource planning (ERP) is business management software—typically a suite of integrated applications that a company can use to collect, store, manage and interpret data from many business activities (Wikipedia).

[10] Manufacturing execution systems (MES) are computerized systems used in manufacturing. MES track and document the transformation of raw materials through finished goods (Wikipedia).

[11] https://www.microsoft.com/microsoft-hololens/en-us

[12] http://www.bbc.co.uk/news/technology-33149583

still require human hands for handling parts and equipment. Apple's smart watch[13] is open to development in the manufacturing sector but there doesn't seem to be a coherent strategy towards this at this stage.

Fig. 1. Wearable Technology with feedback

Figure 1 shows the typical way that glove technology can be deployed with workers on assembly lines given data straight to them instead of engaging with Human Machine Interface panels (HMI) or carrying additional diagnostic equipment. Figure 2 shows another application of glove technology where operators are required to handle several tools to perform normal tasks of tightening bolts, inserting correct components into the correct tool positions and of course tasks such as replacing tools back in the correct holders.

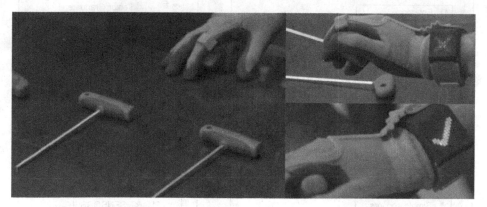

Fig. 2. Poka-Yoke (Error Proofing) Applications

Simple feedback can be provided where a simple "cross" or "tick" can be sufficient to provide sensible feedback to the operator on the selection of incorrect and correct selection of tools.

---

[13] http://www.apple.com/uk/watch

The examples shown are demonstrations of Proglove[14] which is a smart glove that enhances the most important tool of professionals: their hands. Whilst these initial CPS implementations might not sound exciting, the increase in efficiency and reducing errors, enabling workers in production, manufacturing and logistics to work faster, safer and easier are all welcomed in the manufacturing world and the increase in profit margins are the clear indicators to their success. ProGlove was developed as part of Cisco, Deutsche Telekom and Intel's accelerator program "challengeUp!" as indicated in footnote.

5   Interoperability for Cyber Physical Systems

So considering all the technological developments that are occurring and the visions that are forecast for the future of manufacturing, why aren't more manufacturing companies taking advantage of these breakthroughs?

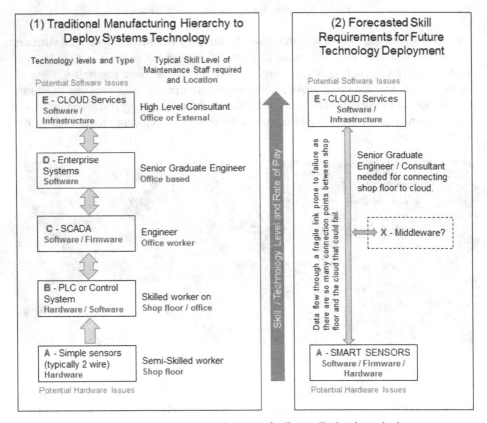

Fig. 3. Skills and Technology requirements for Future Technology deployment

---

[14] http://www.proglove.de – Third prize winners in Intel's "Make it wearable" competition https://makeit.intel.com

There is clearly a gap in the perception of what cyber physical systems can offer in the short term and ultimately what they will offer in the future. The challenge is managing the transition from the present manufacturing techniques and mind-sets found in most manufacturing companies, especially in the supply chains. In the automotive sector for example, Tier 1 suppliers[15] still struggle to interconnect basic machine cell systems to pull basic data from the production machines so the notion of trying to get them to interact with operators with intelligent systems seems a world away.

Figure 3 (1) Shows the current state of data connectivity found in many Tier 1 type companies regardless of sector where there are almost clear breakpoints (A, B, C, D and E) in technology and skill levels. At level A, where many of the hardware issues are normally encountered, the skill level required to test and replace simple two/three wire sensors such as thermocouples, proximity switches or solenoids can be kept to a minimum and breakdowns can easily be managed and resolved. From a Data transformation point of view, the transition of data between levels (between A and B, or B and C etc.) can be relatively simple and easily managed by dedicated staff.

To those not directly in the manufacturing field but who interact with the domain with almost an outsiders view, it seems crazy that manufacturers are not embracing the technology that is being presented to them. They see the advent of Smart sensors as devices that should directly connect to the cloud as shown in Figure 3 (2) somehow bypassing layers B, C and D. this means that smart objects / sensors on the shop floor (A) somehow link directly to cloud services (E). The dilemma is that interoperable cyber systems require a high level of knowledge and understanding to make this "almost" direct connection. This direct connectivity means if the system fails, the level of technical knowledge would need to be extremely high in order to repair any breakdowns in this connection. Of course if the system is working then it is not constantly required. This means highly paid staff basically hang around until a breakdown occurs and it is unlikely these staff members would be persuaded to perform manual labour jobs while they wait for such breakdowns. If this approach (Figure 3 (2)) was to be adopted and indeed worked, it would mean the jobs of the workers at level B, C and D would ultimately be redundant. This can pose ethical issues that are not discussed here but a solution to this transition needs to be found in the short term which involves inserting layer "X" which essentially be a form of Middleware[16].

Much of the development of wearable technology which can incorporate smart sensors as described earlier needs to have this link to this "X" layer in order to bridge the gap between hardware sensing systems and software presentation systems. Only then will we be able to use the full power of what smart technologies offers in the manufacturing sector bearing in mind that the systems need to have a full diagnostics capability to report faults and even automatically take corrective action as we know that stopping a manufacturing line can prove to be a very costly business. This is also

---

[15] http://www.tier1parts.com/what-is-tier-1-supplier

[16] Middleware is a computer software that provides services to software applications beyond those available from the operating system. It can be described as "software glue". Middleware makes it easier for software developers to perform communication and input/output, so they can focus on the specific purpose of their application (Wikipedia).

the subject of several Horizon 2020 funded projects such as CREMA[17], which is looking to provide a framework in Fig 3 (2). Of course many other companies such as Siemens know that the demise of the B C and D layers is coming and they are looking to provide the solutions to provide the middle layer of connectivity but just as the battle between smart cameras that could offer additional functionalities has been lost to the mobile phone market, the controls engineering field needs to embrace itself for the changes that are needed to fully implement the technologies that will be available to the manufacturing sector.

6   Next Steps

It is clear that wearable technology will be part of our daily lives, certainly in our social and domestic domains. The speed at which it gets deployed in the manufacturing sector and particularly on the shop floor is subject to many factors. Like all technologies, there has to be a critical mass which causes the technology to be adopted. The current rate of change of the technology causes alarm for most manufacturer, who are looking for stable, tested and proven systems. Of course peer pressure from competitors always speeds up adaption of new practices but the age old argument of Lower running costs, faster delivery times, increased customer satisfaction levels and higher profits are the surest way to win the deployment argument. The race to connect the shop floor to Cloud services has begun and winners have a huge opportunity to change the whole landscape of manufacturing systems integration. Indeed systems integrators through the deployment of Middleware services will open up the shop floor to newer connectivity layers, enabling smart watches, headsets and other wearable technologies to be easily implemented into this previously closed domain. With further refinement by integrating a range of sensor technologies and combining them with barcode and RFID scanning and wireless connectivity, new levels of data and information for manufacturing line and logistics management can be provided without any additional changes to working practices. This of course requires the usual change in direction for schools and colleges to focus the teaching to deal with this transition as well as governments understanding the new requirements in the workplace and the potential mass displacement of skilled and semi-skilled workers.

---

[17] http://www.crema-project.eu - H2020 CREMA - Cloud-based Rapid Elastic MAnufacturing. CREMA is an Research and Innovation project funded by the Horizon 2020 Framework Programme of the European Commission under Grant Agreement No. 637066

Evaluating the Utilization of the ProcessGene Repository for Generating Enterprise-Specific Business Processes Models

Maya Lincoln[1](✉) and Avi Wasser[2]

[1] University of Haifa, Haifa, Israel
mlincoln@haifa.ac.il
[2] ProcessGene Ltd, Haifa, Israel
avi.wasser@processgene.com

Abstract. Generic reference models are based on the assumption of similarity between enterprises - either cross industrial or within a given sector. They are formed mainly in order to assist enterprises in constructing their own, specific process models. The research presents an empirical evaluation of the quality of the ProcessGene process repository in generating individualized models.

Keywords: Industry blueprints · Reference models · Enterprise-specific

1 Introduction

Process modeling is considered a manual, labor intensive task, whose outcome depends on personal domain expertise, where errors or inconsistencies may result in bad process performance and high process costs [3]. Hence, generating enterprise-specific process models based on a process repository that contains predefined processes does not only save design time but also prevent errors when creating new business process models [1].

Nevertheless, the main thrust of business process management research has put little emphasis on the *content layer* that is supposed to populate structural process frameworks. "Real life" business process repositories, which contain practical content objects, have been somewhat disregarded except in illustrative examples. The lack of suggestions for standard structure, terminology and tools for the process content layer has restricted the development of "reference/best-practice models," leaving it mostly to vendors and commercial organizations.

Currently, most of the generic business process repositories are provided by industrial organizations, developed on the basis of experience accumulated through analyzing business activity and implementing IT systems in a variety of industries [2].

The objective of this paper is to assess the quality of the ProcessGene process repository[1] as an enabler and basis for the generation of enterprise-specific business process models.

---

[1] ProcessGene process repository, http://processgene.com/business-process-repository/

© Springer International Publishing Switzerland 2015
I. Ciuciu et al. (Eds.): OTM 2015 Workshops, LNCS 9416, pp. 57–60, 2015.
DOI: 10.1007/978-3-319-26138-6_8

After a review of the ProcessGene process repository (Section 2), we present an empirical evaluation of the repository effectiveness as a basis for the generation of enterprise-specific process models (Section 3). Section 4 includes conclusions and directions for future work.

2   The ProcessGene Process Repository

The ProcessGene process repository is an "all-inclusive" process database, aiming to include a large set of processes from different industries and organization types. Processes in the repository are organized in five hierarchal levels, grouped by operational functionalities. The highest process level (the most general grouping) includes categories such as: "Human Resource Management," "Procurement," "Financial Management," and "Inventory Management."

Each lower level includes process names that further detail their "parent" process. For example, "Human Resource Management" is further elaborated into "Recruitment," "Compensation," and "Worker Training." At the fourth level, the repository consists of 4,531 processes comprising 17,608 activities (fifth and most granular level). Processes are interconnected to each other and therefore the repository can be represented as a general graph.

3   Experiments

We now present an empirical evaluation of the ProcessGene repository effectiveness as a basis for the generation of enterprise-specific process models. First, we present the experimental setup and describe the data sets that were used. Based on this setup we present the implemented methodology. Finally, we present the experiment results and provide an empirical analysis of these results.

3.1   Data

We chose a set of 46 enterprise-specific process models that were created based on the ProcessGene repository as part of a BPM project each organization carried out. Therefore, each specific model represented a subset, or a sub-graph of the generic repository. The selected enterprises operate in different industries, are of various company sizes (considering workforce and financial aspects) and different geographical locations.

3.2   Evaluation Methodology

To evaluate the suggested method we conducted 46 experiments. At each experiment, the enterprise-specific model was compared to the ProcessGene repository. Based on this comparison, processes at the enterprise-specific model were marked as "equal" or "modified." Modified processes were further categorized into the following categories:

1. "Additional" - processes that were added to the enterprise-specific model and were not part of the ProcessGene repository.
2. "Modified Name" - processes that are represented in the ProcessGene repository using a different name (e.g. in one case the process "Evaluate Suppliers" was from an enterprise-specific model was matched to "Supplier Assessment" in the ProcessGene repository - since both were represented by the same activity set.
3. "Relocation" - processes that are represented in the ProcessGene repository and appear at a different sequential order in the enterprise-specific model.

In addition, we used the classification suggested in [4] and categorized each modified process as being part of one of the following functional areas: (1) Manufacturing; (2) Service; or (3) Business. This classification assisted us to further analyze the modified parts of the model.

3.3   Results and Analysis

Fig. 1 presents a summary of the experiment results. On average, 2.8% processes from the enterprise-specific model are "additional," and were added by the enterprise not based on the ProcessGene repository (see column #1). This was the case despite the diversity of the examined enterprises, highlighting the level of completeness and inclusiveness in the ProcessGene repository. This percentage was lower for the manufacturing and business parts of the model (1.6% and 2.8%, correspondingly) than for the service part of the model (3.9%). This can be explained due to the fact that manufacturing and business execution may be more standardized that service operations.

In addition, on average, 4.7% of the processes in the enterprise-specific model had a "modified name" (see column #2), again, highlighting the level of accuracy and compatibility of the ProcessGene repository. This percentage was significantly lower for the manufacturing part (0.7%) than for the service and business parts (8.3% and 5.2%, correspondingly), indicating the high level of conformity in manufacturing process terminology.

Finally, on average, 8.6% of the processes that were taken from the ProcessGene repository were relocated in the enterprise-specific model, reflecting a different execution sequence (see column #3). This percentage was significantly

Column #	1	2	3
Column name	% of "additional" processes	% of processes with a "modified name"	% "relocated" processes
Avg.-all	2.8%	4.7%	8.6%
Avg.-Manufacturing	1.6%	0.7%	4.7%
Avg.-Service	3.9%	8.3%	10.0%
Avg.-Business	2.8%	5.2%	11.2%

Fig. 1. Experiment results.

lower for the manufacturing processes (4.7%) than for the service and business parts (10% and 11.2%, correspondingly), indicating the high level of conformity in the order of manufacturing execution vs. service and business process execution.

To summarize, the experiments have demonstrated the effectiveness of the ProcessGene process repository in constructing enterprise-specific process models.

4   Conclusions

We presented an empirical evaluation of the effectiveness of the ProcessGene process repository in generating individualized models. This repository was found effective for the targeted task and therefore can save design time and also support non-expert designers in creating new business process models. The empirical evaluation and experiments provide a starting point that can already be applied in real-life scenarios, yet several research issues remain open, including: (1) extending the framework to include the activity level as well; and (2) applying the framework on additional process repositories.

References

1. Lincoln, M., Golani, M., Gal, A.: Machine-assisted design of business process models using descriptor space analysis. In: Hull, R., Mendling, J., Tai, S. (eds.) BPM 2010. LNCS, vol. 6336, pp. 128–144. Springer, Heidelberg (2010)
2. Lincoln, M., Wasser, A.: Applications for business process repositories based on semantic standardization. In: Herrero, P., Panetto, H., Meersman, R., Dillon, T. (eds.) OTM-WS 2012. LNCS, vol. 7567, pp. 173–182. Springer, Heidelberg (2012)
3. Müller, D., Reichert, M., Herbst, J.: Data-driven modeling and coordination of large process structures. In: Meersman, R., Tari, Z. (eds.) OTM 2007, Part I. LNCS, vol. 4803, pp. 131–149. Springer, Heidelberg (2007)
4. Wasser, A., Lincoln, M., Karni, R.: Accelerated enterprise process modeling through a formalized functional typology. In: van der Aalst, W.M.P., Benatallah, B., Casati, F., Curbera, F. (eds.) BPM 2005. LNCS, vol. 3649, pp. 446–451. Springer, Heidelberg (2005)

Impact of Internet of Things in the Retail Industry

Pradeep Shankara[1(✉)], Prabal Mahanta[1], Ekta Arora[1],
and Guruprasad Srinivasamurthy[2]

[1] SAP Labs India Pvt. Ltd., Bangalore, India
pradeep.s@sap.com
[2] SAP Labs LLC, Palo Alto, USA

Abstract. The rise of Internet of Things has led to many game changing efforts to create new business models and opportunities in various domains of industry. In this paper, we look into the impact that the concept of IoT will bring in Retail Industry in coming years with the point of view of new business outlook based upon parameters of security, reliability, integration, discoverability, and interoperability. The paper also presents new concepts that can be implemented for business profitability using various IoT Technologies with prime focus on the areas of embedded systems, cyber physical systems, generic sensors and security. In relation to the Retail Industry, the focus areas of development and support of IoT technology will shift from a mere data collection to knowledge creation which can enable value chain development using a framework concentrating more from a legal point of view. Not only has the technology paradigm shifted from a certain POV but businesses also changes in terms of scalability, dynamicity, heterogeneity and interconnectivity. The paper discusses about newer ideas and their business and social impact on the industry in terms of profitability and adaptability.

Keywords: IoT · Retail · Use cases · POV

1 Introduction

The current era of interconnected physical objects which are often referred to as "Things" are the building block of future trend of everything accessible anywhere realizing the concept of ubiquitous computing [1][2]. The innovation potential of IoT extending to new products, services and domains is endless and the range of domains it will affect will not only limited to smart cars, e-health, retail and smart logistics [3][4]. The innovation in this field is the results of the value add support and collaborative efforts from industry experts, academia and informatics.

This has also triggered software advancements in terms of storage and analytic aspects which can adhere to the data hierarchy related to the IoT. The retail industry has been evolving over time due to the impact of the Information Technology and this has led to adoption of various new business value propositions in terms of processes involved. The technology impact in Retail industry started with the introduction of E-Business proposition and this moved the overall model to look beyond adoption

© Springer International Publishing Switzerland 2015
I. Ciuciu et al. (Eds.): OTM 2015 Workshops, LNCS 9416, pp. 61–65, 2015.
DOI: 10.1007/978-3-319-26138-6_9

parameter to the deeper insights of actual discrepancies in scenarios involving business loss. Then the notion of the radio frequency identification (RFID) technology and the electronic product code (EPC) network arrived to the scene of mobile B2B e-Commerce and its integration into supply chain [5].

Evidence of impact of IT involving information quality, new organization processes, organizational scalability and flexibility have been positive with the performance optimization that it has brought to the domain leading to competition with new players and more choices for the consumer. The field of IoT has been developing rapidly and has consumed the concept of Ubiquitous computing leading to a new vision in terms of architecture and development layer model for IoT [6][7].

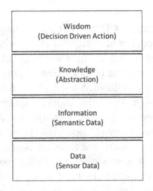

Fig. 1. IoT Knowledge Hierarchy

2   IoT and Retail Industry

There are various new innovations that were introduced in the area of embedded systems leading to a new paradigm adoption in the vast array of the heterogeneous devices leading to computing and networking optimizations. This led to the formation of the concept of smart grid and the feature of integration became the most important focus in the area of new technology innovation.

The innovations has bred web based service economy as the present focus of Internet of Things and platform enabling the service as a part of "Software As A Service" model enabling to bridge the gap between the representation of physical world in information systems and the physical world itself [6][8]. The overall challenge in any IoT project will be the following: a) Real-time information retrieval, b) Process Optimization, c) Responsiveness, d) Scalability, e) Network dependency.

3   Architecture

The innovation from the architecture surrounding any manufacturing domain in respect to the IoT has been very intensive and from the inclusion of various parameters like security and real time tracking the research outcomes in the areas of hybrid computation, network conditioning and heterogeneous interfacing has been quite formidable. The notion of a three dimensional aspect of communication, service and computation has to merge with the parameters like adoption, environment and field integration. The key parameters for success of IoT lie in the intelligent integration of Application Service, Information Integration, Data Exchange, and Field Sensing with control over the following key ROI [9][10][11]: a) Non-uniformity, b) Inconsistency, c) Inaccuracy, d) Verification.

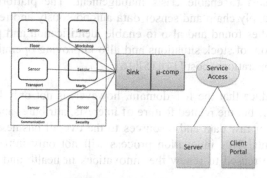

Fig. 2. General Architecture

The issue of content management in terms of sensitive information and secure sharing of such information will form the basis of design for architecture in case of Retail industry as it directly impacts the consumer.

4   Value Proposition for Business Process in IoT – Case Study

a)   **Beacon Assisted Shopping Experience.**

With the innovation in Bluetooth technology, the introduction of beacons to enable interaction with mobile devices in a shop floor based on proximity detection will define a unique experience for consumers who will be provided with information related to the particular section of items like offers, gifts and value added services. The cost-effectiveness and reliability of the overall architecture makes it more feasible and adaptable for retail stores and shopping malls. The methodology can also be applied to not only improve shopper experience and but also the detection of shoplifting [12].

b)   **Kinect Enabled Shopping Apparel Trials.**

Shopping experience and real time information regarding a particular garment is critical from sales point of view. We have seen the introduction of Virtual Fitting Rooms (VFRs) which have made it possible to be able to try out apparel without being physically present in the showroom or in case of physical presence simply stand in front of the garment and a 3D model of you with the garment will be displayed creating a physical interaction which is possible using full body maps and gesture recognition using Kinect and similar technology [13].

c) **Fresh Meat and Fruit Tracking and Smart Delivery**

The complex network of farm product delivery to the consumer table is one of the major research areas where IoT will impact with the advanced RFID technology enabling fresh farm products to reach consumers in time and in a hygienic manner with the use of smart data exchange platform and dynamic reporting, alert mechanisms to enable crisis management. The platform should enable exchange of supply chain and sensor data autonomously and report evidences in case of anomalies found and also to enable identification and prediction of precise trend for out of stock situations and also improving operational efficiencies, and reducing operational cost [14][15][16].

Finally we can deduce that the IoT domain, however, is not only limited to sensors and sensor networks but the related feature of interests, attributes and the autonomous integration of sensor raw data and resources to the overall business process and execution requirements. This innovation process will not only impact the domain of retail but it can be reused to renew the innovations in health and other critical domains.

Acknowledgement. The Authors would like to thank their colleagues and friends for their immense support. They would also like to thank their university connects and professors for supporting them in this theoretical research work.

References

1. Gubbi, J., et al.: Internet of Things (IoT): A vision, architectural elements, and future directions. Future Generation Computer Systems **29**(7), 1645–1660 (2013)
2. Atzori, L., Iera, A., Morabito, G.: Siot: Giving a social structure to the internet of things. Communications Letters, IEEE **15**(11), 1193–1195 (2011)
3. Vermesan, O., Peter, F. (eds.): Internet of things: converging technologies for smart environments and integrated ecosystems. River Publishers (2013)
4. Suciu, G., et al.: Smart cities built on resilient cloud computing and secure internet of things. In: 2013 19th International Conference on Control Systems and Computer Science (CSCS). IEEE (2013)
5. Wamba, S.F., et al.: Exploring the impact of RFID technology and the EPC network on mobile B2B eCommerce: A case study in the retail industry. International Journal of Production Economics **112**(2), 614–629 (2008)
6. Barnaghi, P., et al.: Semantics for the Internet of Things: early progress and back to the future. International Journal on Semantic Web and Information Systems (IJSWIS) **8**(1), 1–21 (2012)
7. Gyrard, A., et al.: Standardizing generic cross-domain applications in Internet of Things. In: Globecom Workshops (GC Wkshps). IEEE (2014)
8. De, S., et al.: An internet of things platform for real-world and digital objects. Scalable Computing: Practice and Experience **13**(1) (2012)
9. Ma, H.-D.: Internet of things: Objectives and scientific challenges. Journal of Computer science and Technology **26**(6), 919–924 (2011)

10. Zhou, L., Chao, H.-C.: Multimedia traffic security architecture for the internet of things. Network, IEEE **25**(3), 35–40 (2011)
11. Zhang, B., Ma, X.-X., Qin, Z.-G.: Security architecture on the trusting internet of things. Journal of Electronic Science and Technology **9**(4), 364–367 (2011)
12. Bohnenberger, T., Jameson, A., Krüger, A., Butz, A.: Location-aware shopping assistance: evaluation of a decision-theoretic approach. In: Paternó, F. (ed.) Mobile HCI 2002. LNCS, vol. 2411, pp. 155–169. Springer, Heidelberg (2002)
13. Vargheese, R., Dahir, H.: An IoT/IoE enabled architecture framework for precision on shelf availability: enhancing proactive shopper experience. 2014 IEEE International Conference on Big Data (Big Data). IEEE (2014)
14. Cuinas, I., Catarinucci, L., Trebar, M.: RFID from farm to fork: traceability along the complete food chain. In: Progress in Electromagnetics Research Symposium (PIERS 2011), Marrakesh, Morocco (2011)
15. Folinas, D., Manikas, I., Manos, B.: Traceability data management for food chains. British Food Journal **108**(8), 622–633 (2006)
16. Gu, Y., Jing, T.: The IOT research in supply chain management of fresh agricultural products. In: 2011 2nd International Conference on Artificial Intelligence, Management Science and Electronic Commerce (AIMSEC). IEEE (2011)

An Internet of Things (IoT) Based Cyber Physical Framework for Advanced Manufacturing

Yajun Lu and J. Cecil[✉]

Center for Information Centric Engineering, Oklahoma State University, Stillwater, USA
j.cecil@okstate.edu

Abstract. This paper outlines an IoT based collaborative framework which provides a foundation for cyber physical interactions and collaborations for advanced manufacturing domains; the domain of interest is the assembly of micro devices. The design of this collaborative framework is discussed in the context of IoT networks, cloud computing as well as the emerging Next Internet which is the focus of recent initiatives in the US, EU and other countries. A discussion of some of the key cyber physical resources and modules is outlined followed by a discussion of the implementation and validation of this framework.

Keywords: IoT · Cyber physical framework · Advanced manufacturing

1   Introduction

The term **Internet of Things (IoT)** is becoming popular in the context of the ongoing IT revolution which has created a greater awareness of emerging and smart technologies as well as phenomenal interest in IT based products in the world community. IoT can be described as the network of physical objects or "things" embedded with electronics, software, sensors and connectivity to enable it to achieve greater value and service by exchanging data with the manufacturer, operator and/or other connected devices [1]. In a nutshell, IoT refers to the *complex network of software and physical entities* which are embedded or implemented within sensors, smart phones, tables, computers, electronic products as well as other devices which have software elements to perform computing or non-computing activities. These *entities* are the '*things*' referred to in the term 'Internet of Things' which are expected to be capable of collaborating with other similar entities as part of the Internet and other cyber infrastructure at various levels of abstraction and network connectivity. The underlying assumption is that by interacting with each other, a large range of services can be provided using this network of collaborations. This subsequently enables these entities to provide greater value to customers and collaborating organizations.

Example of *things* are weather monitoring sensors, heart monitors, monitoring cameras in a manufacturing work cell in a factory, safety devices in a chemical processing plant, advanced home cooking equipment, etc. There are many risks and benefits to embracing such a vision. The benefits lie in being able to form collaborative partnerships to respond in a more agile manner to changing customer preferences

© Springer International Publishing Switzerland 2015
I. Ciuciu et al. (Eds.): OTM 2015 Workshops, LNCS 9416, pp. 66–74, 2015.
DOI: 10.1007/978-3-319-26138-6_10

while being able to seamless exchange data, information and knowledge at various levels of abstraction. Such an emphasis on adoption of IoT principles can also set in motion the realization of advanced next generation Cyber Physical relationships and frameworks which can enable software tools to control and accomplish various mundane as well as advanced physical activities.

In our IoT framework, we have explored the use of cloud principles to support information and data exchange among IoT devices and software modules. Cloud based technologies are becoming the focus of many industrial implementations [2-6]. In [7], a computing and service oriented model for cloud based manufacturing is outlined. Three categories of users are described including providers, the operators and consumers. Some of the benefits for cloud based manufacturing identified in [6] include reducing up-front investments, reduced infrastructure costs, and reduced maintenance and upgrade costs. In [5], the potential of cloud computing is underscored in transforming the traditional manufacturing business model and creating intelligent factory networks that support collaboration. A service oriented system based on cloud computing principles is also outlined for manufacturing contexts [5, 6, 8, 17].

2 Benefits of IoT Based Frameworks and Emergence of the Next Internet

In an IoT context, one of the core benefits is from the cyber physical interactions which help facilitate changes in the physical world. The plethora of smart devices emerging in the market serves as a catalyst for this next revolution which will greatly impact manufacturing and manufacturing practices globally. Imagine being able to design, simulate and build a customized product from a location hundreds or thousands of kilometers away from engineering and software resources, manufacturing facilities or an engineering organization. Today, using cloud technologies and thin clients such as smart phones and smart watches, the potential of using such IoT principles and technologies for advanced manufacturing is very high. Such cyber physical approaches also support an agile strategy which can enable organizations functioning as Virtual Enterprise partners to respond to changing customer requirements and produce a range of manufactured goods. With the help of advanced computer networks, such cyber (or software) resources and tools can be integrated with physical resources including manufacturing equipment. Thin clients, sensors, cameras, tablets and cell phones can be linked to computers, networks and a much larger set of resources which can collaborate in an integrated manner to accomplish engineering and manufacturing activities. When customer requirements change, such an approach can also help interfacing and integrating with a variety of distributed physical equipment whose capabilities can meet the engineering requirements based on the changing product design. Against this backdrop, it is important to also underscore recent efforts to develop the next generation of Internets.

In the US, the Global Environment for Network Innovations (GENI) is a National Science Foundation led initiative focuses on the design of the next generation of Internets including the deployment of software designed networks (SDN) and cloud based technologies. GENI can also be viewed as a virtual laboratory at the frontiers of network science and engineering for exploring Future Internet architectures and applications at-scale. In the context of advanced manufacturing (such as micro assembly [16]), such networks will enable distributed VE partners to exchange high bandwidth graphic rich data (such as the simulation of assembly alternatives, design of process layouts, analysis of potential assembly problems as well as monitoring the physical accomplishment of target assembly plans). In the European Union (EU) and Japan (as well as other countries), similar initiatives have also been initiated; in the EU, the Future Internet Research and Experimentation Initiative (FIRE) is investigating and experimentally validating highly innovative ideas for new networking and service paradigms (http://www.ict-fire.eu/home.html). Another important initiative is the US Ignite (http://us-ignite.org/) which seeks to foster the creation of next-generation Internet applications that provide transformative public benefit using ultra-fast high gigabit networks. Manufacturing is among the six US national priority areas (others include transportation and education).Both these initiatives herald the emergence of the next generation computing frameworks which in turn have set in motion the next Information Centric revolution in a wide range of industrial domains from engineering to public transport. These applications along with the cyber technologies are expected to impact global practices in a phenomenal manner.

GENI and FIRE Next Generation technologies adopt software defined networking (SDN) principles, which not only reduces the complexity seen in today's networks, but also helps Cloud service providers host millions of virtual networks without the need for common separation isolation methods such as VLAN [13]. SDN also enables the management of network services from a central management tool by virtualizing physical network connectivity into logical network connectivity [13]. As research in the design of the next generation Internets evolves, such cyber physical frameworks will become more commonplace. Initiatives such as GENI and US Ignite are beginning to focus on such next generation computer networking technologies which hold the potential to radically change the face of advanced manufacturing and engineering (among other domains).

3   Overview of IoT Based Cyber Physical Framework

IoT entities and devices will greatly benefit from the evolution of Cyber Physical approaches, systems and technologies. The term 'cyber' can refers to a software entity embedded in a thin client or smart device. A cyber physical system can be viewed as an advanced collaborative collection of both software and physical entities which share data, information and knowledge to achieve a function (which can be technical, service or social in nature). In a process engineering context, such cyber physical systems can be viewed as an emerging trend where software tools can interface or interact with physical devices to accomplish a variety of activities ranging from sensing, monitoring to advanced assembly and manufacturing. In today's network oriented technology context, such software tools and resources can interact with physical components through local area networks or through the ubiquitous Word Wide

Web (or the Internet). With the advent of the Next Generation Internet(s), the potential of adopting cyber physical technologies and frameworks for a range of process has increased phenomenally.

In the context of manufacturing, collaborations within an IoT context can be realized using various networking technologies including cloud based computing. According to the National Institute of Science and Technology (NIST), Cloud computing can be viewed as a model for enabling ubiquitous, convenient, on-demand network access to a shared pool of configurable computing resources (including networks, storage, services and servers) [9]; the computing resources can be rapidly provisioned with reduced or minimal management effort or interaction with service providers. Some of the benefits for cloud based manufacturing include reducing up-front investments and lower entry cost (for small businesses), reduced infrastructure costs, and reduced maintenance and upgrade costs [10]. In [11], Tao et al discussed the context of Internet of Things (IoT) and Cloud Computing (CC) which hold the potential to providing new methods for intelligent connections and efficient sharing of resources. They proposed a service system which consists of CC and IOT based Cloud Manufacturing.

The IoT based framework outlined in this paper was part of one US Ignite project dealing with advanced manufacturing and cyber physical frameworks [12]. The manufacturing domain of interest is the assembly of extremely tiny micron sized devices. This is one of the first projects involving Digital Manufacturing, cyber physical frameworks and the emerging Next Generation Internet (being built as part of the GENI initiatives).

The preliminary implementation of this IoT framework has been completed in the form of a collaborative Cyber Physical Test Bed whose long term goal is to enable globally distributed software and manufacturing resources to be accessed from different locations and used to accomplish a complex set of life cycle activities including design analysis, assembly planning, simulation and finally assembly of micro devices. The presence of ultra-fast high gigabit networks enables the exchange of high definition graphics (in the Virtual Reality based simulation environments) and the camera monitoring data (of the various complex micro manipulation and assembly tasks by advanced robots and controllers). Engineers from different locations interact more effectively when using such Virtual Assembly Analysis environments and comparing assembly and gripping alternatives prior to physical assembly.

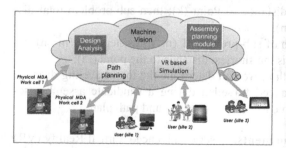 

Fig. 1. The IoT based cyber physical test bed   **Fig. 2.** The Virtual Assembly Environment

The resources of the cyber physical system (CPS) using cloud technologies are illustrated in figure 1. The users in different locations can access the CPS modules/resources through thin clients and IoT devices including tablets, cell phones, work cells, computers, and other thin clients. Thin clients refer to devices with less processing power that relies on the server to perform the data processing [14]. In this IoT based cyber physical frameworks, engineers can collaborate from geographically distributed locations and share resources as part of an agile collaboration process; they can interact with CPS resources using computers and/or thin client such as smart phones and tablets.The main cyber physical tasks were modeled using Extended Enterprise Modeling Language (eEML) shown Figure 3. The overall 'mini' life cycle activities in this cyber physical collaboration includes obtaining target micro design, generating assembly plan, developing path plan for assembly,performing assembly simulation and analyze using VR, assembling micro device and updating WIP/ assembly outcomes. The resources in this Cyber Physical implementation include the following (figure 1): assembly / path planning modules, VR based simulation environments (to analyze assembly/path plans, etc.), assembly command generators, machine vision based sensors/cameras (for guiding, monitoring physical assembly) and physical micro assembly equipment (to assemble the target micro designs). An overview of some of these resources is provided in the following sections.

Assembly Planning: The assembly planning module aims at determining the optimal assembly sequence to be completed by the micro gripper using various cyber physical resources for the assembly of micro devices. The outcome of the assembly plan generated is input to the Virtual Reality based assembly simulation environment. The Greedy Algorithm (GRA) is used to generate near optimal assembly sequences for the assembly planning module. Typically, a GRA seeks to make a locally optimal choice that looks best (at that current state) which help identify a nearly optimal global solution; this is the origin of the term 'greedy' in the context of a GRA. The key steps of such an algorithm are summarized below for the assembly of micro:

1. Initialize the distance d (i, j) between any point (i) and point (j) where i, j $\in$ {0, 1, 2...n}.
2. Find the point (k) which is the shortest distance to Home Point (0); then the total distance T (0, n) = d (0, k) + T (k, n).
3. Next, we need to find the solution of sub-problem total distance T (k, n). Find the point (m) which is the shortest distance to Point (k); then sub-problem total distance T (k, n) = d (k, m) + T (m, n).
4. Likewise, we can get the solution of sub-problem T (m, n) as step 3; T (m , n) = d (m, p) + T (p, n) where point (p) is the shortest distance to the point (m);
5. Using the above recursive algorithm, we can determine the total traveling distance (which is also the shortest distanced travelled during a candidate assembly sequence) corresponding to a feasible assembly sequence and path plan.

Virtual Assembly Analysis Environments: A set of advanced Virtual Reality (VR) based simulation environments was built using Unity3D platform to assist the analysis of the assembly/path plans interactively by engineers from different locations. The distributed engineers used the Next Internet (being developed under GENI) to propose, compare and modify assembly /path plans rapidly. The high gigabit data relating to these VR images were transmitted using this Next Generation Internet technology. Figure 2 is an example showing a view of the virtual environment with an avatar to help engineers and users interact with it; the VR assembly analysis environments were built using Unity 3D engine, C# and Java. Through these interactions, the most feasible assembly plan was identified. Subsequently, a different module in the cloud generated the various physical robot assembly commands based on the outcomes of the simulation analysis and assembly; these were then communicated to the work cell (in Stillwater, Oklahoma) selected to assemble the target micro designs.

Physical Resources: Two physical work cells are available in Stillwater for physical assembly which were part of this Cyber Physical Test Bed (CPTB). Work cell 1 has an assembly plate, cameras, and an advanced micro gripper. The base support of the assembly area has two linear degrees of freedom in the X axis and Y axis and one rotational degree of freedom. The gripper of the work cell can move in the Z axis. This work cell is capable of assembling micron-sized parts rapidly automatically using machine vision cameras. A second work cell was also part of this cyber physical- with a shape memory alloy based gripper and an assembly plate with 3 linear degrees of freedom along with cameras is also available. Figure 4 shows a view of one of the physical micro assembly cells used in this CPTB.

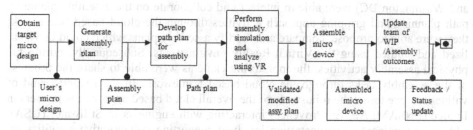

Fig. 3. Overview of the main cyber physical tasks in the collaborative framework

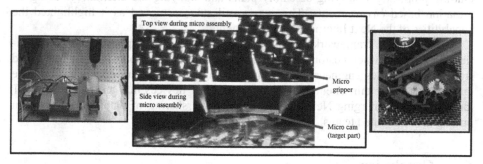

Fig. 4. (left): a physical micro assembly cell in progress   **Fig. 5.** a, b (middle/right): micro assembly tasks

4   Discussion and Test Cases

In our implementation, the cyber physical resources collaborated using the IoT cloud framework discussed in previous sections; user inputs were given through the web; subsequently, assembly plans were generated which were then compared and modified using the VR based simulation environments; finally, the validated plan was assembled using physical work cells. Several target micro and meso assembly designs (figure 5 a, b) were assembled using the implemented cyber physical framework; meso/micro composite part designs were built to study the capabilities of the two work cells; While there is no universally accepted definition of Meso assembly, we use the term meso scale to include part sizes greater than 1 mm, with accuracies greater than 25 microns.

The IoT based framework outlined in this paper is a step towards ubiquitous computing where engineers and users will not be required to have computing resources to accomplish engineering tasks; instead, they will be able to access and use resources in a 'cloud' through thin clients to conduct engineering activities. The approach developed uses a cloud based approach which seeks to make it easier for engineers who may be geographically distributed (and collaborating from different parts of the world) be able to conduct simulation and physical engineering activities using next generation Internet technologies.

Two rounds of validation was conducted. In the first set of collaborative activities (within the US), users at multiple locations (3 locations including Stillwater, Tulsa and Washington DC) were able to interact and collaborate on the assembly planning, path planning and gripping approach activities through the cloud based framework; they were able to propose, compare and modify assembly plans which could be visualized and studied using the Virtual Reality environments. Subsequently, during the physical assembly activities, the monitoring cameras were able to share the progress of the assembly tasks through the cloud based framework. In the second round of validations, we tested the robustness of the overall cloud based approach with users in France (ENSAM, Aix En Provence) interacting with engineers in Stillwater (USA). This inter-continental demonstration involved supporting collaborative activities including proposing/modifying assembly plans and studying the alternatives using simulation based environments. This was a milestone achieved as it highlighted the capabilities of the Next Internet across continents.

Cyber physical frameworks hold significant potential in support agile collaborations in industry; when customer requirements changes, adoption of such cloud based frameworks enables engineers and manufacturing partner organizations to exchange and interact using thin clients, computers and other devices that are part of the IoT landscape. The emerging Next Internet enabled the sharing of data and information among the distributed teams.

5   Conclusion

This paper outlined an IoT based framework to support collaborations among distributed partners in engineering and manufacturing contexts. This is being used as basis to develop a more comprehensive Cyber Physical Test Bed for the emerging domain of micro assembly. In most situations, micro devices assembly (MDA) resources are not located at a single organization; resources will be distributed among different organizations across different locations. For this reason, an IoT based framework is needed to support the collaborative and rapid assembly of micro devices. A cloud based approach was used to facilitate the collaboration of the various cyber physical components using advanced cyber infrastructure (related to the Next Internet as part of the GENI initiative).

Our cyber physical framework enabled the sharing of engineering resources using next generation Internet technologies. Such ICE frameworks facilitate the realization of global virtual enterprises where collaboration between distributed partners is possible especially when responding quickly to changing customer requirements. As IoT devices become ubiquitous, such interfaces and thin clients are expected to play an important role in facilitating collaborations in advanced manufacturing. The use of cloud technologies also helped in the design of this IoT based framework; with the popularity of such technologies in industry today, the next wave of manufacturing collaboration is underway which will further enable national and global collaborations.

Acknowledgement. Funding for the research activities outlined in this paper was obtained through grants from the National Science Foundation (NSF Grant 0423907, 0965153, 1256431, 1257803, 1447237), Sandia National Laboratories, Los Alamos National Laboratory, and the Mozilla Foundation.

References

1. http://en.wikipedia.org/wiki/Internet_of_Things
2. Cecil, J., Ramanathan, P., et al.: Collaborative virtual environments for orthopedic surgery. In: Proceedings of the 9th Annual IEEE International Conference on Automation Science and Engineering (IEEE CASE 2013), Madison, WI, August 17–21, 2013
3. Berryman, A., Calyam, P., Cecil, J., Adams, G., Comer, D.: Advanced manufacturing use cases and early results in GENI infrastructure. In: Proceedings of the Second GENI Research and Educational Experiment Workshop (GREE), 16th Global Environment for Network Innovations (GENI) Engineering Conference, Salt Lake City, March 19–21, 2013
4. Wu, D., Thames, L., Rosen, D., Schaefer, D.: Towards a cloud-based design and manufacturing paradigm: looking backward, looking forward. In: 32nd Computers and Information in Engineering Conference, Parts A and B Chicago, Illinois, USA, vol. 3, August 12–15, 2012
5. Tao, F., Zhang, L., Venkatesh, V.C., Luo, Y., Cheng, Y.: Cloud manufacturing: a computing and service-oriented manufacturing model. Proceedings of the Institution of Mechanical Engineers, Part B: Journal of Engineering Manufacture **225**(10), 1969–1976 (2011)
6. Xu, X.: From cloud computing to cloud manufacturing. Robotics and Computer-Integrated Manufacturing **28**(1), 75–86 (2012)
7. Cecil, J.: Information centric engineering (ICE) frameworks for advanced manufacturing enterprises. In: Demey, Y.T., Panetto, H. (eds.) OTM 2013 Workshops 2013. LNCS, vol. 8186, pp. 47–56. Springer, Heidelberg (2013)
8. Wang, X., Xu, X., Li, W., Mehnen, J. (eds.): ICMS: a cloud-based manufacturing system. Cloud Manufacturing, Springer Series in Advanced Manufacturing 2013, pp. 1–22. Springer Verlag, London (2013)

9. http://csrc.nist.gov/publications/nistpubs/800-145/SP800-145.pdf
10. Benefits of cloud computing. http://www.mbtmag.com/articles/2013/05/how-manufac turers-can-benefit-cloud-computing
11. Tao, F., Cheng, Y., Da Xu, L., Zhang, L., Li, B.H.: CCIoT-CMfg: cloud computing and Internet of Things based cloud manufacturing service system, 1 (2014)
12. Cecil, J.: https://vrice.okstate.edu/content/gigabit-network-and-cyber-physical-framework
13. http://www.serverwatch.com/server-tutorials/eight-big-benefits-of-software-defined-net working.html
14. http://www.devonit.com/thin-client-education
15. https://www.us-ignite.org/about/what-is-us-ignite/
16. Cecil, J., Kumar, M.B.R., Lu, Y., Basallali, V.: A review of micro-devices assembly techniques and technology. The International Journal of Advanced Manufacturing Technology, 1–13 (2015)
17. Panetto, H., Zdravković, M., Jardim-Goncalves, R., Romero, D., Cecil, J., Metzgar, I.: New Perspectives for the Future Interoperable Enterprise Systems. Computers in Industry (2015) (accepted-paper)

International Workshop on Enterprise Integration, Interoperability and Networking (EI2N) 2015

EI2N'2015 Co-Chairs' Message

After the successful ninth edition in 2014, the tenth edition of the Enterprise Integration, Interoperability and Networking workshop (EI2N'2015) has been organised as part of the On The Move Federated Conferences (OTM'2015) in Rhodes, Greece. The workshop is co-sponsored by the International Federation of Automatic Control (IFAC), and several IFAC Technical Committees 3.1, 3.3, 5.2, 5.3, 5.4. The workshop is moreover supported by the SIG INTEROP Grande-Région on "Enterprise Systems Interoperability", the French CNRS National Research Group GDR MACS, the Greek Centre on Interoperability and the Industrial Internet Consortium.

Today's rapidly evolving global economy has reiterated the urgent industrial need to achieve dynamic, efficient and effective cooperation of partner organizations within networks of larger enterprises. Enterprises must collaborate in order to prosper in the dynamic and heterogeneous business environment meeting sustainability constraints of present times. This in turn requires a substantial improvement of existing frameworks and technologies along with the exploration of innovative theories and the development of breakthrough technologies. Such innovations will serve as the foundation for more productive and effective collaborative global partnerships, and is a driver for sustainable businesses.

Enterprise integration, interoperability and networking are major disciplines studying collaborative, communicative enterprise systems. Enterprise Modelling Techniques, Next Generation Computing Architectures and Socio-technical Platforms along with Semantic Interoperability approaches are essential pillars supporting the achievement of sustainable enterprise systems.

The International Program Committee has reviewed 20 papers. After a rigorous review process, 9 papers have been accepted (45%). Every submitted paper was evaluated by at least two members of the program committee. It has been a great pleasure to work with these experts, who played a valuable role in providing feedback to the authors that allows the overall scientific field to evolve. We thank them for their precious voluntary contribution and continued interest.

We have divided this year's workshop in four sessions. The first three sessions consist of presentations of accepted papers, the last session is an interactive discussion called "Workshop Café". This special session is an integral part of the workshop since several years. The outcomes of these discussions will be reported during a plenary session jointly organized with the CoopIS'2015 and the OTM Industry Case Studies Program 2015, in order to share topics and issues for future research with a larger group of experts and scientists.

We would like to thank the authors, reviewers, sponsors and other colleagues who have together contributed to the continuing success of this workshop. We welcome all attendees and participants and look forward to an enthusiastic exchange of ideas and thoughts for the progress of science at the workshop.

September 2015

Alexis Aubry
Eduardo Rocha Loures
Fenareti Lampathaki
Milan Zdravkovic

Subject-Oriented BPM as the Glue for Integrating Enterprise Processes in Smart Factories

Udo Kannengiesser[1], Matthias Neubauer[2], and Richard Heininger[1(✉)]

[1] Metasonic GmbH, Münchner Str. 29 - Hettenshausen 85276, Pfaffenhofen, Germany
{udo.kannengiesser,richard.heininger}@metasonic.de
[2] Johannes Kepler Universität Linz, Institut für Wirtschaftsinformatik –
Communications Engineering, Altenbergerstaße 69 4040, Linz, Austria
matthias.neubauer@jku.at

Abstract. This paper presents how an existing approach to business process management, Subject-oriented BPM (S-BPM), provides a foundation for seamlessly integrating processes in production enterprises, from business processes to real-time production processes. The applicability of S-BPM is based on its simplicity and encapsulation of separate process domains. This supports agility as all stakeholders can be engaged and the effects of changes can be limited to individual modules of the process. An application and tool support developed in an ongoing European research project are presented to illustrate the approach.

Keywords: Seamless process integration · Smart factories · S-BPM · OPC UA

1 Introduction

As industry moves towards cyber-physical production systems (CPPS) and internet of things (IoT) manufacturing, the ways in which enterprise processes are conceptualised and executed are changing. Decentralising production using large numbers of inter-linked cyber-physical production resources breaks up the traditional boundaries drawn between different process abstraction layers. Smart devices and processes at all levels in the industrial control hierarchy need to interact if the vision of vertically and horizontally integrated production systems is to be realised [1, 2]. A number of integration approaches have been defined for this purpose, including IEC 62541 [3] and IEC 62264 [4].

Despite the availability and wide acceptance of such standards, designing integrated enterprise processes involving cyber-physical systems remains a challenge [5]. One issue is the lack of a process modelling language that is both understandable by all stakeholders and formally defined to allow model-driven execution. Most work on process modelling for production enterprises draws on existing approaches from the domains of software engineering and business process management (BPM). Examples include UML [6], BPMN [7, 8] and Petri Nets [9]. Yet, most of the current BPM approaches are not sufficiently formal to be immediately executed [10] and are difficult to be learned and applied by untrained modellers [11] such as business people and

© Springer International Publishing Switzerland 2015
I. Ciuciu et al. (Eds.): OTM 2015 Workshops, LNCS 9416, pp. 77–86, 2015.
DOI: 10.1007/978-3-319-26138-6_11

shopfloor workers. In addition, the centralised control-flow paradigm underpinning these modelling approaches is at odds with the decentralised control advocated for smart factories [5, 12]. Small changes in the production process (e.g. when a new product variant needs to be manufactured) can be quite difficult to implement and verify in a monolithic (centralised) process model. As agility is a principal motivation for smart factories [12, 13], there is a need for alternative approaches to integrated process modelling.

This paper shows that subject-oriented BPM (S-BPM) [14] provides such an approach. S-BPM has two distinguishing features that support agile processes:

1. Simple yet formal notation: S-BPM provides a common (and executable) language for all stakeholders including process participants not trained in a specialised modelling notation.
2. Encapsulation: S-BPM supports modular process architectures as it separates the concerns of different process domains and encapsulates them in "subjects" that are loosely coupled via messages.

Section 2 introduces S-BPM and highlights these features using examples from the business process domain. Section 3 explains how S-BPM can be applied for integrating business and production processes. Section 4 illustrates this approach based on prototypes developed within the Factories of the Future project SO-PC-Pro. Section 5 concludes the paper.

2   Subject-Oriented Business Process Management

Subject-oriented Business Process Management (S-BPM) [14] was first proposed by Albert Fleischmann in 1994 [15]. Formally, the S-BPM approach is based on the parallel activity specification scheme (PASS) which extends elements of the Calculus of Communicating Systems by Milner and Communicating Sequential Processes by Hoare [14, p.289f], This approach differs from traditional process modelling methods in that it is based on a decentralised view: Processes are understood as interactions between process-centric roles (called "subjects"), where every subject encapsulates its own behaviour specification [11]. Subjects coordinate their individual behaviours by exchanging messages. Such a communication-based approach differs from traditional BPM paradigms that require the orchestration of activities via tokens being passed along a central control flow. Messages in S-BPM may include information at any level of granularity, from simple notifications or requests to complex data structures (referred to as business objects).

2.1   Notation

S-BPM models include two types of diagrams: A Subject Interaction Diagram (SID) specifying a set of subjects and the messages exchanged between them, and a Subject Behaviour Diagram (SBD) for every subject specifying the details of its behaviour. SBDs describe subject behaviour using state machines, in which every state represents an action. There are three types of states in S-BPM: "receive" states for receiving messages, "send" states for sending messages, and "function" states for performing actions operating on business objects (i.e., actions performed without involving other subjects). Examples of a SID and a SBD are shown in Fig. 1 and Fig. 2, respectively. Details of the notational elements used can be found in [14].

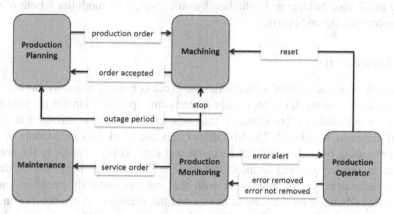

Fig. 1. Subject Interaction Diagram (SID) showing the communication between subjects in a production context

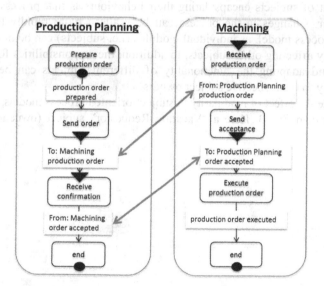

Fig. 2. Subject Behaviour Diagrams (SBD) showing the individual behaviours of the "Production Planning" subject and the "Machining" subject. Their interconnections through pairs of "send" and "receive" actions are represented using double-headed arrows (not part of the S-BPM notation).

Subjects may be executed by human or computational actors [11, 13], including cyber-physical systems or machines as indicated in Fig. 1 and Fig. 2. Their well-defined semantics (based on Abstract State Machines [16]) allow for automatic translation into executable code, including PLC code represented using IEC 61131-3 [17].

The simple notation using only few building blocks allows domain experts without formal training in process modelling to readily create valid S-BPM models. This is a departure from traditional approaches such as BPMN that require either extensive training of all stakeholders or facilitation by an experienced modeller – both of which are time-consuming and costly.

2.2   Encapsulation

Another key characteristic of subject-oriented process models is encapsulation: Every subject in a process model encapsulates a behaviour specification for performing the particular functionality represented by that subject. This idea is reflected in the two types of diagrams in S-BPM. The SID shows only the black-box behaviours of a subject, representing only the messages received and sent. This is similar to the notion of a service in service-oriented architectures (SOA). The detailed behaviour of the subject is usually opaque; for interacting with that subject one only needs to know its functionality (denoted by the subject name) and the messages it can receive and send [18]. The internal behaviour of a subject as described in its SBD is usually visible and modifiable only by the owner of that subject.

The benefit of subjects encapsulating their behaviours is that process models become modular. Changes in the process can be realised more rapidly than using a monolithic process model, as individual modules (i.e. subjects) can be modified without necessarily affecting other subjects. In addition, the responsibilities for providing, monitoring and adapting the functionality of different subjects can be clearly assigned, usually to the respective subject owners.

To illustrate the effect of modularity in subject-oriented process models, consider the example shown in Fig. 3. Here a "Vacation Requestor" subject (owned/executed by

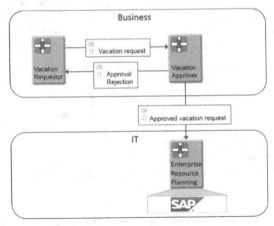

Fig. 3. A vacation process in which business and IT domains are integrated via encapsulation of subject behaviours

a company employee) sends a vacation request to a "Vacation Approver" subject (owned/executed by the employee's manager) who sends back either an approval or a rejection message. In case of approval, the "Vacation Approver" subject additionally notifies the "Enterprise Resource Planning" subject. That subject is owned by an IT expert, and its behaviour is executed by an SAP system.

If there are changes in the way the approved vacation request needs to be managed by the "Enterprise Resource Planning" subject, the IT expert can modify the internal behaviour of that subject without the other subjects (and their subject owners) having to know or care about – at least as long as the type of message (or the specific business object) conveyed to the subject is not affected by the change.

3   Vertical Process Integration Based on S-BPM

The concept of encapsulation can be applied to the vertical integration of enterprise processes across the different levels of the automation pyramid. The IEC 62264 control hierarchy [4] is shown on the left-hand side of Fig. 4. This hierarchy represents the processes in production companies at four levels: field instrumentation control (Level 1), process control (Level 2), manufacturing operations management (Level 3), and business planning & logistics (Level 4). As these levels impose distinct requirements on processes with respect to real-time processing, data storage, safety and security, the development of models and systems at each level has been undertaken rather independently. This has resulted in poorly integrated applications especially between the Low Level Control domain (LLC, i.e. Levels 1 and 2) operating in real time and the High Level Control domain (HLC, i.e. Levels 3 and 4) operating in non-real time. Systems developed for LLC include Programmable Logic Controllers (PLCs), and systems for HLC include ERP, MES and BPM systems.

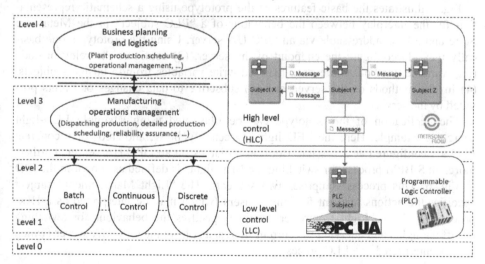

Fig. 4. Seamless process integration across the IEC 62262 control hierarchy (image adapted from [1]), based on subjects encapsulating domain-specific behaviours

A generic S-BPM process model is shown on the right-hand side of Fig. 4, encapsulating a LLC behaviour in a "PLC" subject. That subject is owned by an automation engineer, and its behaviour is executed by a workflow engine that communicates with a PLC via the OPC UA (IEC 62541) [3] standard.

When changes in LLC processes become necessary (e.g. when the control software of a production machine needs to be reconfigured), they can be easily managed by modifying the internal behaviour of the PLC subject and checking whether messages with other subjects need to be adapted. If messages need to be changed, the respective subject owners (e.g. a business person and an automation engineer) must come to an agreement on the specific message adaptations. However, they do not need to know about the detailed internal behaviour of each other's subjects.

4   Prototype

An interface to the OPC UA standard has been developed for the S-BPM tool Metasonic Suite (www.metasonic.de/en) within the EU FP7 funded project SO-PC-Pro (www.so-pc-pro.eu). The basic features of the interface have been derived from the structure of the OPC UA standard [3]. OPC UA applies the fundamental client-server concept to implement the interaction between different communication partners, e.g. a workflow engine and a plant floor PLC. To allow requesting services provided by an OPC UA server or within a network of OPC UA servers, OPC UA defines an AddressSpace model. In such an AddressSpace an OPC UA server defines which contents (i.e. nodes representing objects, variables, methods etc. for real objects) are visible/editable for clients. Servers also allow clients to monitor attributes and events at the server. Every client can subscribe to the attributes and events it is interested in and will then be notified accordingly.

Fig. 5 illustrates the basic features of the prototype using a schematic representation for the interplay between the behaviour of a "PLC subject" in the Metasonic Suite and a PLC addressable via an OPC UA server. Using the prototype, one basically may (1) configure the endpoint of the server, (2) configure the relevant node (e.g. variable, method, and event), (3) read/write variables from/to business objects, (4) invoke methods on the server, and (5) subscribe to data changes or events provided by the server.

The application of the prototype can be illustrated using a simple LED-light switching example. Here the LED lights 'green', 'yellow', and 'red' of a concrete PLC are configured as accessible Boolean variables on an OPC UA server. Furthermore, an S-BPM process for switching the LED lights is defined as shown in the SID in Fig. 6. This process comprises two subjects: The "Light Management" subject specifies the actions relevant for human users (which may be interpreted as a HLC process), and the "Light Controller" subject specifies the behaviour for switching on/off the lights and querying the current light status from the OPC UA server (which may be interpreted as a LLC process).

Business Process (Metasonic Suite)

Production Process (Programmable Logic Controller (PLC))

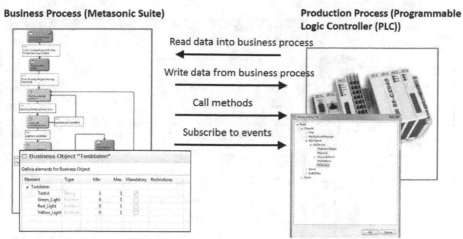

Read data into business process

Write data from business process

Call methods

Subscribe to events

Fig. 5. Schematic feature representation of the OPC UA interface

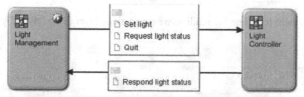

Fig. 6. Subject Interaction Diagram (SID) of a light switching process

The configuration for accessing the OPC UA services is done by using a so-called "refinement template" in Metasonic Suite: a GUI for configuring data interfaces to external systems. The concrete OPC UA refinement template shown in Fig. 7 allows (i) reading values from a PLC and store them in a business object and (ii) writing concrete values of a business object to variables of a PLC. The template thus facilitates configuring the concrete OPC UA server endpoint that provides the desired variables. Furthermore, one needs to choose the action and the relevant business object before mapping variables to each other. The user interface shown in Fig. 7 allows mapping multiple PLC variables to different fields of business objects.

After modelling and configuring all subject behaviours, the process can be executed in Metasonic's workflow engine. A screenshot of the generic user interface for executing the LED light switching process is shown in Fig. 8. In the example a user may choose one of three options: (1) set lights, (2) request light status, and (3) quit. When clicking "Set lights" the user will proceed to the step "Turn lights on/off" in which the status of the LED lights can be set as desired (i.e., on or off). The desired status will then be sent to the "Light Control" subject that writes this status as a value to the configured OPC UA server at runtime.

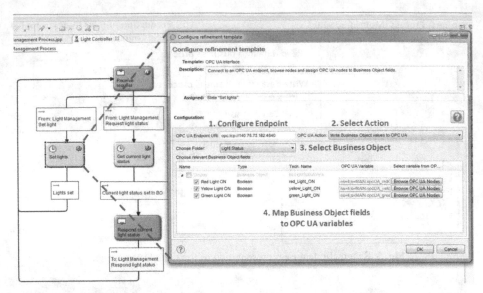

Fig. 7. Refinement template for reading/writing values from/to an OPC UA server variable

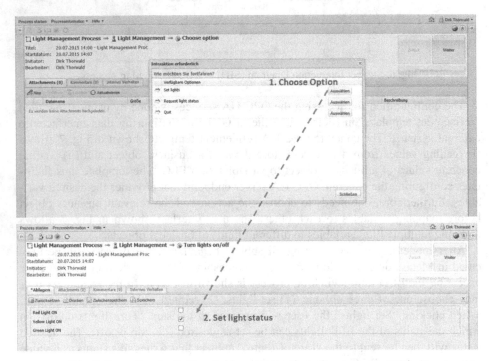

Fig. 8. Executing the light switching process (from the user's perspective)

The presented OPC UA interface is at the prototype stage. It has been tested within four different application scenarios. In the first application scenario a process for managing sun-blinds in a smart home has been modelled and executed. In the second scenario the prototype has been used to manage room lights in offices at different locations. In the third scenario, the power consumption of production machines in a medium-sized manufacturing company has been measured and analysed for process control and improvement. In the fourth scenario, an assembly process has been modelled in which the stress level of a worker (measured using a wearable sensor) is indicated by LED lights (green | yellow | red). Ongoing work comprises the conduction of user tests to improve the user interface and get feedback from process modellers in the field business information systems.

5   Conclusion

In his seminal paper on smart factories Zuehlke [12] concludes with a list of recommendations for future research and development:

- "reduce complexity by strict modularization and lean technologies,
- avoid centralized hierarchies in favour of loosely linked decentralized structures consisting of self-adapting modules,
- allow for self-organization on the system level wherever possible, [...]
- create and apply standards to all levels of the automation pyramid in order to reduce planning effort and allow re-use of components,
- and in the end: develop technologies for the human. A deserted factory is an aberration!"

The approach described in this paper follows these recommendations as it uses the modular, decentralised and simple modelling concepts provided by S-BPM, and interfaces with the OPC UA standard. Applying the approach across the entire enterprise can thus lead to process integration that is consistent with the foundational ideas of smart factories. This is a major condition for supporting agile processes in these factories and realising associated business models.

Acknowledgements. The research leading to these results has received funding from the EU Seventh Framework Programme FP7-2013-NMP-ICT-FOF(RTD) under grant agreement n° 609190 (www.so-pc-pro.eu).

References

1. Gerber, T., Theorin, A., Johnsson, C.: Towards a seamless integration between process modeling descriptions at business and production levels: work in progress. Journal of Intelligent Manufacturing 25(5), 1089–1099 (2014)
2. Colombo, A.W., Karnouskos, S., Bangemann, T.: A system of systems view on collaborative industrial automation. In: 2013 IEEE International Conference on Industrial Technology (ICIT), Cape Town, South Africa, pp. 1968–1975 (2013)

3. IEC 62541-1:2008 OPC Unified Architecture – Part 1: Overview and Concepts. International Electrotechnical Commission, Geneva
4. IEC 62264-1:2013 Enterprise-control system integration – Part 1: Models and terminology. International Electrotechnical Commission, Geneva
5. Horváth, I., Gerritsen, B.H.M.: Outlining nine major design challenges of open, decentralized, adaptive cyber-physical systems. In: Proceedings of the ASME 2013 International Design Engineering Technical Conferences and Computers and Information in Engineering Conference, Portland, OR (2013)
6. Kohler, H.J., Nickel, U., Niere, J., Zundorf, A.: Integrating UML Diagrams for production control systems. In: International Conference on Software Engineering, pp. 241–251. ACM, New York (2000)
7. Garcia-Dominguez, A., Marcos, M., Medina, I.: A comparison of BPMN 2.0 with other notations for manufacturing processes. Key Engineering Materials 502, 1–6 (2012)
8. Witsch, M., Vogel-Heuser, B.: Towards a formal specification framework for manufacturing execution systems. IEEE Transactions on Industrial Informatics 8, 311–320 (2012)
9. Gradisar, D., Music, G.: Production-process modelling based on production-management data: A Petri-Net approach. International Journal of Computer Integrated Manufacturing 20, 794–810 (2007)
10. Börger, E.: Approaches to modeling business processes: a critical analysis of BPMN, workflow patterns and YAWL. Software & Systems Modeling 11(3), 305–318 (2012)
11. Fleischmann, A., Kannengiesser, U., Schmidt, W., Stary, C.: Subject-oriented modeling and execution of multi-agent business processes. In: 2013 IEEE/WIC/ACM International Conferences on Web Intelligence (WI) and Intelligent Agent Technology (IAT), Atlanta, GA, pp. 138–145 (2013)
12. Zuehlke, D.: SmartFactory—Towards a factory-of-things. Annual Reviews in Control 34(1), 129–138 (2010)
13. Kannengiesser, U., Müller, H.: Towards agent-based smart factories. In: 2013 IEEE/WIC/ACM International Conferences on Web Intelligence (WI) and Intelligent Agent Technology (IAT), Atlanta, GA, pp. 83–86 (2013)
14. Fleischmann, A., Schmidt, W., Stary, C., Obermeier, S., Börger, E.: Subject-Oriented Business Process Management. Springer, Berlin (2012)
15. Fleischmann, A.: Distributed Systems – Software Design & Implementation. Springer, Berlin (1994)
16. Börger, E., Stärk, R.: Abstract State Machines: A Method for High-Level System Design and Analysis. Springer, Berlin (2003)
17. Müller, H.: Using S-BPM for PLC code generation and extension of subject-oriented methodology to all layers of modern control systems. In: Stary, C. (ed.) S-BPM ONE 2012. LNBIP, vol. 104, pp. 182–204. Springer, Heidelberg (2012)
18. Kannengiesser, U., Radmayr, M., Heininger, R., Meyer, N.: Generating subject-oriented process models from ad-hoc interactions of cognitive agents. In: 2014 IEEE/WIC/ACM International Joint Conferences on Web Intelligence (WI) and Intelligent Agent Technology (IAT), Warsaw, Poland, pp. 440–446 (2014)

Extended Service Modelling Language for Enterprise Network Integration

Qing Li[✉], Peixuan Xie, Xiaoqian Feng, Hongzhen Jiang, and Qianlin Tang

Department of Automation, Tsinghua University, Beijing 100084, People's Republic of China
liqing@tsinghua.edu.cn

Abstract. With the development of globalization and information technology, service oriented technologies and enterprise networks are arising quickly. Supply chain management, virtual enterprise, dynamic alliance, e-business and so forth are leading intra enterprise management and networked enterprise management to the enterprise networks management and integration. At the same time, Service Oriented Architecture (SOA) triggers series of servicization progresses in enterprise management, inter enterprise cooperation, manufacturing process, as well as IT related infrastructures. CEN/TC 310/WG 1 is developing the Service Modelling Language (SML) for Virtual Manufacturing Enterprises (VMEs). Based on Model Driven Architecture, SML tries to specify the Business Service Modelling (BSM) level of the Model Driven Service Engineering Architecture (MDSEA). In the paper, MDSEA and SML are extended for enterprise networks integration. A three levels modelling framework including business process modelling, service process modelling and operation process modelling are introduced. The Collaboration Point (CP) concept is developed to describe cooperation mechanism between enterprises so as to overcome the process and data fragmentation caused by enterprise organizational boundaries. The model mapping method among the three levels are also presented in the paper.

Keywords: Service · Modelling · Enterprise network · Integration

1   Introduction

With the development of globalization and information technology, service oriented technologies and enterprise networks are arising quickly. With the development of big data, internet of things and cloud computing, the two trends are changing the features of manufacturing:

- Supply chain management, virtual enterprise, dynamic alliance, e-business and so forth are leading intra enterprise management and networked enterprise management to the enterprise networks management and integration;
- At the same time, Service Oriented Architecture (SOA) triggers series of servicization progresses in enterprise management, inter enterprise cooperation, manufacturing process, as well as IT related infrastructures.

© Springer International Publishing Switzerland 2015
I. Ciuciu et al. (Eds.): OTM 2015 Workshops, LNCS 9416, pp. 87–96, 2015.
DOI: 10.1007/978-3-319-26138-6_12

In order to overcome the complexity of enterprise network integration, CEN/TC 310/WG 1 is developing the Service Modelling Language (SML) for Virtual Manufacturing Enterprises (VMEs). Based on Model Driven Architecture, SML tries to specify the Business Service Modelling (BSM) level of the Model Driven Service Engineering Architecture (MDSEA) [1].

In order to answer all requirements of enterprise network integration from business modelling, analysis and design to integrated distributed manufacturing system deployment and implementation, the original SML shall be extended.

In the paper, MDSEA and SML are extended for enterprise networks integration. A three levels modelling framework including business process modelling, service process modelling and operation process modelling are introduced. The Collaboration Point (CP) concept is developed to describe cooperation mechanism between enterprises so as to overcome the process and data fragmentation caused by enterprise organizational boundaries. The model mapping method between the three levels are also presented in the paper.

2   State of Art

Enterprise modelling methods have been developed for a long time. There are several modelling methods that have been applied widely in system integration projects. KBSI developed IDEF0 and IDEF3 methods to describe the relations among functional activities and business processes [2,3]. IDS-Scheer developed ARIS™ and Event Process Chain (EPC) to describe business processes with the related enterprise information, resources, organization and products [4]. UML is widely used as computer aided software engineering tools [5]. DFD is a traditional method to program operation processes [6].

In order to use models in system operation stage and reduce the complexity of system implementation and system adjustment, some enabling methods are developed: Workflow and related technology, BPMN/BPML (Business Process Modelling Notation / Business Process Modelling Language) for business process management [7], PSL (Process Specification Language) for process model information transformation [8], BPEL (Business Process Execution Language) for Web service application [9]. BPEL is developed to orchestrate services and deploy the solution as a Web service.

In order to present a systematic framework to support enterprise modelling based systems engineering, series of system architectures are developed. Zachman Framework, ARIS, CIMOSA, PERA and GERAM are the widely accepted some. Model Driven Architecture (MDA) describes a methodology to design and develop a software system step by step based on modelling and model mapping. Based on MDA, MDSEA presents a three levels modelling framework: business service modelling, technology independent modelling and technology dependent modelling [1].

In the "Service Modelling Language Technical Specification" developed by CEN/TC 310/WG 1, business service modelling (BSM) level modelling constructs and relationships are defined, some templates are also developed in the specification. However, the specification does not define the bottom two levels modelling methods, and it does not discuss how to map models from one level to another one. Therefore it is necessary to extend relative methods to present a total solution to model based enterprise network integration.

3   Service Oriented Modelling Framework for Enterprise Networks Integration

In the authors' research, the MDSEA is extended as the process modelling architecture depicted in Fig.1. The levels depict business process modelling across partner companies, service process modelling in every collaboration point, and operation process modelling (orchestration modelling) for service implementation [10,11].

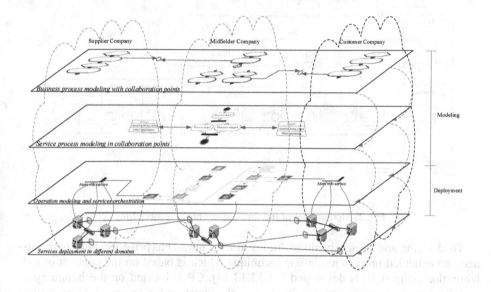

Fig. 1. Process model-driven mechanism of extended MDESA

(1) Business process modelling presents a model for operating businesses. Based on the model, analysts can identify collaboration points (CPs) that are shared by a company and its partner companies, so as to reduce modification of original business processes and information systems (ISs).

(2) Service process modelling depicts detailed operations in a CP. It distinguishes web services located in outside ISs and intra-ISs and designs a flow to integrate these web services together.

(3) Service orchestration transfers service process models to a BPEL-based operation model so that codes can be generated.

UML (unified modelling language) is the core modelling language of MDA. It presents a set of modelling languages for object-oriented programming. It is a computer aided software engineering tool. However, there is still a gap between the business model and software model in the MDA. UML is not suitable for business modelling, and it cannot be run directly. Currently, no modelling language can satisfy the requirements from business logic to computing logic. Therefore the extended MDSEA includes three-layer models: an extended event-driven process chain, UML and BPEL.

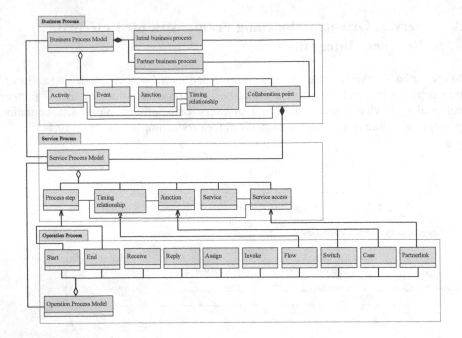

Fig. 2. Meta model of the three levels process modelling

To describe and design business logics among intra-enterprise ISs and their partners, an extended process modelling technique which is based on the concept of collaboration point (CP) is developed [11,12,13,14]. CP is located on the boundary of various computing environments. It presents the interface for process interoperations to cross over different computing environments as shown in Fig.1. The interface can support data exchange, command transferring, and monitoring.

Inside a CP, there is a complex operating logic that needs to be modelled and analyzed. CPs are realized as a set of web services, their operation/service modelling method is based on several common graphic symbols in UML. Detailed texts can be supplements besides the graphic language [11].

BPEL is a web service orchestration language. It presents sophisticated concepts and methods to link web services together and offer a complex function. Based on the concepts of BPEL, a service process can be transferred to a service orchestration model.

The meta-model of extended MDSEA process modelling is shown in Fig.2, in which constructs and their relationships are depicted. To simplify the meta-model, notations' relationships of operation process modelling are not shown in Fig.2. Their syntax and semantic rules can be found in BPEL technical documents [8,9].

4   Business Process Modelling Language for Enterprise Networks Integration

In enterprise network environments, an enterprise has business processes within its boundary. Some of these processes may interoperate with business processes of its partners in enterprise networks. Therefore, it is necessary to develop a mechanism to define the associations between different scenarios.

Collaboration Point is located on the boundary of scenarios that presents the interface for processes interoperation cross over different scenarios as shown in Fig. 3. The interface can support data exchange, command transferring, monitoring and so forth. It can be realized as a web service invoking interface, an agent or a broker.

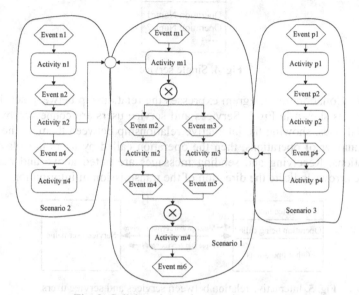

Fig. 3. Collaboration points between scenarios

In enterprise network environments, it is hard to design intra business processes with partner enterprises processes jointly. Few of partner enterprises will customize their service logic to satisfy a single enterprise's requirement. It is also very difficult to adjust the enterprise's business processes and ISs. Therefore, CPs will combine processes in different scenarios and minimize modifications of these processes.

While integrating cross scenarios processes, in order to keep integrity of business logics, the CP is not a simple API access or web services invoking. CPs include complex operating logics to complete a series of operations. These operations, including cross scenarios accesses, could be encapsulated as web services. Based on the APIs library of cross scenarios, through services encapsulation of APIs, services development and orchestration, the orchestrated process service will realize the function of a CP.

5   Service Process Modelling in Collaboration Point

Inside a CP, there is a complex operating logic which needs to be modelled and analyzed. Because CPs are realized as web services, its operation/service modelling method is based on several common graphical symbols in UML. Detailed texts can be supplements besides graphical language. The major model elements and model expressions list as follows [11]:

(1) Use UML Class Diagram to express services, as shown in Fig.4. Service names and operations are marked respectively in the Class Diagram. Service names need to be nouns or gerunds, such as "order service", "order information enquiry service". General names for operations are verb phrases, such as "enquire order information".

Fig. 4. Single service

(2) UML Collaboration Diagram expresses the relationship between services and service users, as shown in Fig.5. Services and service users are connected by double arrowed solid lines, showing the interactive relationship between them. If the service includes a number of operations, then the operation called by users is isolated from other operations. Receiving and sending messages are noted above and below the lines and the arrows indicate the direction of the transmission of information.

Fig. 5. Interactive relation between services and service users

(3) Combining the ideas of UML Activity Diagram and Collaboration Diagram, we express the interactive relationship between process services and their member services, as shown in Fig.6. The relationship diagram of services and service users is a basic form. The process service acts as the public service user of all the member services, and it calls the operation in a certain member service in a specific process step,

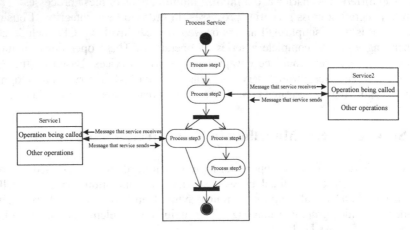

Fig. 6. Interactive relationship between process services and their member services

in other words, the operation in a member service achieves a specific process step. To express the relationship clearly, we draw the business process model by using UML Active Diagram and connect services and corresponding process steps with arrowed solid lines, showing that the process steps are achieved by this service operation.

6   Operation Process Modelling and Model Mapping Method

Operation/service model describe the operating logic in a CP. In order to implement the model, based on principles of MDA, the service process model shall be mapped to a run-time model and then transferred to run-time codes.

BPEL is a web service orchestration language. It presents a serious concepts and methods to link web services together and offers a complex function. Based on the concepts of BPEL, we developed a new service orchestration notations and language. Deferent from BPEL, the graphic description of services orchestration is mapped directly to Java codes and then deployed as standard web service. The notations of the orchestration language and related illustration are shown in Tab. 1.

Table 1. Notations of service orchestration method

Activity	Icon	Function
Start		Represent the beginning of a orchestration service process
End		Represent the end of a orchestration service process
Receive		Do a blocking wait for a matching message to arrive
Reply		Send a message in reply to a message that was received through a <receive>.
Assign		Update the values of variables with new data.
Invoke		Invoke a web service.
ParnterLink		Represent a called web service
Flow		Specify one or more activities to be performed concurrently.
Switch		Select exactly one branch of activity from a set of choices.
Case		Condition that one branch could run

Based on above concepts, a service process shown in Fig. 6 can be transferred to a service orchestration model, as shown in Tab. 2.

Table 2. Transformation from service processes cross over scenarios to services orchestration model

Semantic Transformation	Notation Replacement	Note
Process step		Process step is mapped to Assign
Service access		Collaboration point means there is an interface between two business processes. It can be replaced by an Invoke action with a Partner-Link which represents service access.
AND Junction		The couple of AND junctions can be transferred to a program sequence started with Flow.
XOR Junction		The couple of AND junctions can be transferred to a program sequence started with Switch and Cases.

Similar to the service orchestration, the business logic/flow editor can link services encapsulated from different applications in different ISs to form a complete automatic flow for a business process.

7   Cases Studying

The authors' research team implemented the modelling architecture and methodology in several projects. Detailed technologic discussion can be found in the authors' published papers.

In the reference [10], the modelling architecture with relative integrating platform is implemented in a grain trade e-marketplace construction project. In the same paper, a call centre information/service convergence project is also discussed.

The methodology is also used to solve problems of multi public cloud services integration [13,14].

8   Summary and Conclusion

In order to model inter processes collaborations among intra ISs and partner enterprises' ISs, the extended MDSEA for enterprise network integration has three modelling levels: business process modelling cross multiple scenarios with CPs, service process modelling within a CP, and services orchestration / operation process modelling to implement the CP.

Business process modelling presents a view to understand how the business system operated. Based on the model, analysts can find out CPs between the enterprise and its cloud vendors, so as to reduce modification of these business processes.

Operating/service logic modelling presents a view to understand how the CP can realize processes integration across public clouds and intra ISs, with which web services are distinguished and identified, and the flow logic among web services is also decided.

Based on the three levels modelling architecture, cross scenarios process integration principle is linked with its software realization.

Acknowledgements. This work is sponsored by the China High-Tech 863 Program, No. 2001AA415340 and No. 2007AA04Z1A6, the China Natural Science Foundation, No. 61174168, the Aviation Science Foundation of China, No. 20100758002 and 20128058006.

References

1. CEN/TC 310/WG 1: Service Modelling Language Technical Specification V1.1, February 13, 2015
2. KBSI: IEEE Standard for Functional Modeling Language – Syntax and Semantics for IDEF0. IEEE Std 1320.1-1998. IEEE (1998)
3. Mayer, R.J., Menzel, C.P.: Concurrent Engineering (IICE) IDEF3 Process Description Capture Method Report. KBSI Co. (1995)
4. Scheer, W.A.: Architecture for Integrated Information System. Springer-Verlag (1992)
5. Rumbaugh, J., Jacobson, I., Booch, G.: The Unified Modeling Language Reference Manual, 2nd edn. Addison-Wesley (2004)

6. Yourdon, E.: Just Enough Structured Analysis (2006). http://www.yourdon.com/
7. BPMI.ORG: Business Process Modeling Notation (BPMN), Version 1.0. Business Process Management Initiative (2004)
8. Schlenoff, C., Gruninger, M., Tissot, F., Valois, J., Lubell, J., Lee, J.: The Process Specification Language (PSL) Overview and Version 1.0 Specification. National Institute of Standards and Technology. http://www.mel.nist.gov/msidlibrary/doc/nistir6459.pdf
9. Andrews, T., Curbera, F., Dholakia, H., Goland, Y., et al.: Business Process Execution Language for Web Services, Version 1.1. http://www.oasis-open.org/
10. Li, Q., Zhou, J., Peng, Q.R., Li, C.Q., Wang, C., Wu, J., Shao, B.E.: Business processes oriented heterogeneous systems integration platform for networked enterprises. Computers in Industry 61(2), 127–144 (2010)
11. Li, Q., Wang, C., Wu, J., Li, J., Wang, Z.Y.: Towards the business–information technology alignment in cloud computing environment: anapproach based on collaboration points and agents. International Journal of Computer Integrated Manufacturing 24(11), 1038–1057 (2011)
12. Li, Q., Wang, Z., Li, W., Cao, Z., Du, R., Luo, H.: Model-based services convergence and multi-clouds integration. Computers in Industry 64(7), 813–832 (2013)
13. Li, Q., Wang, Z.Y., Cao, Z.C., Du, R.Y., Luo, H.: Process and data fragmentation-oriented enterprise network integration with collaboration modelling and collaboration agents. Enterprise Information Systems, (ahead-of-print), 1–31 (2014)
14. Li, Q., Wang, Z.Y., Li, W.H., Li, J., Wang, C., Du, R.Y.: Applications integration in a hybrid cloud computing environment: modelling and platform. Enterprise Information Systems 7(3), 237–271 (2013)

SAIL: A Domain-Specific Language for Semantic-Aided Automation of Interface Mapping in Enterprise Integration

Željko Vuković[1]([✉]), Nikola Milanović[2], Renata Vaderna[1],
Igor Dejanović[1], and Gordana Milosavljević[1]

[1] Faculty of Technical Sciences, Novi Sad, Serbia
{zeljkov,vrenata,igord,grist}@uns.ac.rs
[2] Optimal Systems GmbH, Berlin, Germany
milanovic@optimal-systems.de

Abstract. Mapping elements of various interfaces is one of the most complex tasks in enterprise integration. Differences in the ways that these interfaces represent data in lead to the need of conflict detection and resolving. We present an approach where a structural model of the interfaces can be annotated with a semantic model and used together to (semi-)automate this process. A domain-specific language (DSL) is proposed that can be used to specify criteria for interface element mapping, define conflicts with steps for their resolution if possible, and how the resulting mappings will be translated into expressions needed for code generation. This DSL is intended to give the user the possibility to customise a prototype tool (which we have presented earlier) enabling us to practically test our approach and yield a real-world runnable implementation. Code generated by this tool is deployable to an enterprise service bus (ESB).

Keywords: Enterprise integration · Domain specific language · Ontology · Semantic conflicts · ESB · Model-based

1 Introduction

In [18] we have proposed a framework that can be used to automate mapping of interfaces involved in an enterprise integration scenario by adding semantic description (in form of ontologies) to the structural model of involved systems. There are many criteria that can be used to determine mappings in such a model, some of which are shown here (see section 3) and semantic conflicts exist that can occur in the mapping process. It would be extremely difficult to foresee all such possible criteria or conflicts in the context of any integration scenario. This is why we have made our framework extendible. New components for the framework (interface element matchers, conflict detectors and output expression builders) can be defined by means of traditional object oriented programming. In this paper we present a language called SAIL: Semantic-Aided Integration

© Springer International Publishing Switzerland 2015
I. Ciuciu et al. (Eds.): OTM 2015 Workshops, LNCS 9416, pp. 97–106, 2015.
DOI: 10.1007/978-3-319-26138-6_13

Language. This language allows the mentioned components to be described, generated and used in the solution without having to be implemented in a general purpose programming language and are available without having to rebuild the entire application. We test the language by writing a specification for previously manually implemented components.

The architecture overview of the automatic mapper is shown in 4. The framework is implemented as an extension and modification of an open source tool Talend Open Studio for ESB[1] (TOS) evaluated in [12]. The tool itself allows the user to model an integration scenario (called a *job* in TOS). The job can be used to generate code that is runnable directly in TOS or deployable to a standalone ESB runtime. We have customized one of the transformation components available in TOS. This component, the *tXMLMapper*, is used to map elements of one or more input interfaces to one or more output interfaces. Our implementation enhances the Auto Map feature of this component that was originally able to make mappings automatically only if the interface elements have the same name. We let the user annotate system interfaces that otherwise lack semantic description with elements of an ontology. We then use this semantically enhanced model to automate the mapping and conflict resolution process.

We note that modelling ontologies themselves is not the scope of our work. We treat ontologies as a source of semantics for involved systems, but we assume that the ontology modelling process has already been performed, including potential reasoning and merging, and that there is a single ontology describing all of the involved systems.

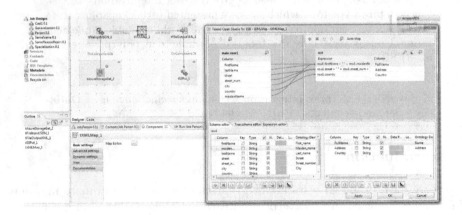

Fig. 1. A TOS job showing automatically established mappings

2   Related Work

A survey in [6] shows the architectures and technologies for integrating distributed enterprise applications, illustrating their strengths and weaknesses, and

---

[1] http://www.talend.com/products/talend-open-studio

identifies research trends and opportunities in this increasingly important area. In [11] a framework is given for conflict analysis and composition on the component level. Components that originate in object oriented middleware are represented canonically on common denominator basis. The framework is model based. A classification of semantic conflicts is given in [15]. Three dimensions are used for classification: naming, abstraction and level of heterogeneity. One (meta)model-based platform for integration is given in [10] along with the accompanying methodology. It allows for a tight cooperation with the domain expert. The platform enables semi-automatic conflict analysis. An approach called ODSOI (Ontology-Driven Service-Oriented Integration) was proposed in [7] to address some problems of enterprise integration for large, dynamic enterprises requiring scalability. They have suggested a topology of web services and ontologies along with a vision of an integration framework. Following Model-Driven Architecture and using a Domain Specific Language (DSL) was proposed in [17]. A DSL called Guaraná was proposed for design and automatic deployment of integration solutions. Another DSL for EAI called Highway is presented in [9]. It is based on Apache Camel and Clojure. An executable DSL that is platform-independent and message-based is described in [16]. In [3] chapter 10 discusses using Ontology Architectural Patterns for semantic enterprise interoperability. A look at detecting semantic conflicts in Web services and Service Oriented Architecture in general when heterogeneous data is exchanged is given in [1]. A step-by-step methodology that explains how to achieve enterprise integration, taking into account different interoperability views like business, process, human resources, technology, knowledge and semantics is described in [2]. In [8] the NEGOSEIO framework is presented, enabling service-based interoperability with semantics and business understanding. It uses reference ontologies for achieving this goal. In [14] it is shown how to integrate Big Data using Talend Open Studio. An ontology-based information integration with a local to global ontology mapping in order to solve semantic problems when integrating heterogeneous data sources is proposed in [4].

3   The Mapping Process

First, we ask the user to annotate the model of the integration scenario with elements from the ontology which describes involved systems. Each element of the involved interfaces (schema column in TOS) may be annotated with one or more ontology elements. In this way the structural model is enriched with a semantic description. We allow multiple input and multiple output schemata to be involved in each mapping. The automatic mapping process in our approach is divided into following phases: finding mapping candidates, conflict detection and resolution, output expression building and code generation.

Mapping Criteria. The process of finding possible mappings consists of traversing each output element of each output interface and examining the possibility of mapping it to each input element of each input interface. Determining if these pairs should constitute a mapping candidate is done by subjecting it to criteria such as described in Table 1. Each pair may suffice zero, one or more of these criteria. If more than one match is found, their interaction will be examined in the conflict resolution phase.

Table 1. Mapping criteria overview

Name	Short description
Equal name	Interface elements have the same name (case ignored)
Same annotation	Interface elements are annotated with the same ontology element
Aggregation	Two or more output interfaces are annotated with ontology elements that are part_of an ontology element by which an output interface element is annotated
Generalisation	Input interface elem. is annotated with a ont. elem. that is subclass_of the ont. elem. annotated to the output interface elem.
Specialisation	Output interface elem. is annotated with a ont. elem. that is subclass_of the ont. elem. annotated to the input interface elem.
Splitter	Two or more output interface elements are annotated with ont. elements that are part_of an ont. element by which an input interface element is annotated
Rejection	Input and output interfaces are annotated by elements that are marked as distinct in the ontology

Conflict Detection and Resolution. When all the mapping candidates are found, they are then inspected against each other in order to detect and attempt to resolve mapping conflicts. These are some of such conflicts that are detected:

- Multiple mappings for the same reason - mapping candidates are the result of the same criterion and the reasons within that criterion are the same for all mappings
- Specialisation ambiguity - an output element is annotated with an ontology element that is more general than that of the input element. In the opposite case, we may always want to make the mapping, but here it isn't certain that they should remain mapped.
- Different types - elements have been mapped whose types cannot be assigned to each other. A conversion should be performed if possible.

Expression Building. After mappings have been found and conflicts resolved, expressions need to be built that describe the final format of each output interface element. These expressions will be inserted as assignment to the attribute representing the output interface element in the code generation phase. This means that expressions need to conform to Java syntax, but also that the expression has access to the entire object structure that represents the involved interfaces and their data. TOS offers a bundle of utilitarian functions that can be inserted in the expressions:mathematical, string operations, type conversion and data generation.

4   Framework Architecture and Implementation

Talend Open Studio is an application on the Eclipse Rich Client Platform described in [13]. Such an application consists of plug-ins communicating on an OSGi [5] infrastructure. The tMap and tXMLMap components that we have modified are implemented as such plug-ins.

A simplified class diagram of the automatic mapper is given in Fig. 2. Each interface element (*column* in TOS) is a TreeNode. Each TreeNode can be annotated with one or more ontology elements, represented by the Jena framework[2] Resource class. Each of the matching criteria described in section 3 is represented by a class implementing the *Matcher* interface. Its *match()* method will take two tree nodes and determine if they should be mapped to each other, returning a *MatchedEntryPair* if so. To support rejection criteria, a *MatchedEntryPair* can be disabled by another. List of pairs that have disabled a pair is available via *disabledBy()* method.

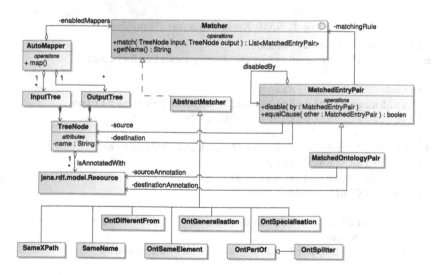

Fig. 2. Matcher class diagram

---
[2] Apache Jena framework: http://jena.apache.org/

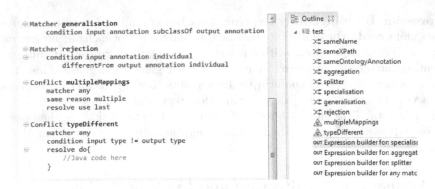

Fig. 3. SAIL editor and outline

5   Parametrisation Using SAIL

The goal of this DSL is to provide a way to specify how each of the steps of the automated mapping process (see Sect. 3) will be performed in the context of an integration scenario. This specification is then used to generate the needed framework components (see Sect. 4). Listing 2 illustrates how the proposed language constructs allow this. This example results in generated components that have equal behaviour as those that have been manually implemented in Java.

Since the framework runs inside an Eclipse RCP application, we have chosen to implement the language using Xtext[3], which gives us the benefit of easily getting an editor (shown in Fig. 3) and other supporting infrastructure that can be integrated with the existing environment.

Listing 1. SAIL Xtext grammar (simplified)

```
Model:     elements+=Element*;
Element:     Matcher | Conflict | ExpressionBuilder;
//...
Matcher:     'Matcher' name=ID
    (fullName=MatcherFullName)? condition=Condition
    (continuation=ContinuationExp)?
//...
Conflict:     'Conflict' name=ID matcher=ConflictMatcher
    (condition=Condition)?
    (causeMul=ConflictCauseMultiplicity)?
    resolve=ConflictResolve;
//...
ExpressionBuilder:     'OutExpression'     matcher=
    ConflictMatcher
    (condition=Condition)?   'out' out=OutputExp;
//...
```

---

[3] Xtext is a framework for development of programming languages and domain specific languages, https://eclipse.org/Xtext

Property Accessors. Where needed, it is possible to reference `input` and `output` interface elements, their properties: `name`, `type`, `length`, `count` and semantic `annotations`. Ontology elements can also be accessed via their their uniform resource identifier using the `ontURI()` construct.

Conditional Expressions. A conditional expression is formed by the keyword condition followed by property accessors, literals (strings, numbers) and comparison operators. Conjunction and disjunction are also supported (keywords `and`, `or`).

Matchers. Definition of a matcher begins with the keyword `Matcher` followed by its identifier. A descriptive name can be specified by writing `full name` followed by a quoted string. Next, the `condition` is specified that will be used when comparing input and output elements according to this matcher. If a match is found for a pair the matcher can go to the next input/output element pair, or keep looking for other matches in the current pair (e.g. this is possible when interface elements are annotated with multiple ontology elements), which is the default behaviour. This is determined by the keyword `when found` followed with either `continue [looking]` or `next [pair]`.

Conflict Detectors. Conflict detector definition begins with `Conflict`, followed by the detector's identifier. A detector can be instructed to only look at matches made by certain Matchers. This is done by listing matcher names after the keyword `matcher`. Alternatively, the detector can look at all matched pairs by specifying `matcher any`. Detection of multiple mappings for the same reason (see Sect. 3) is achieved by stating `same reason multiple`. Next, the `condition` of the conflict is specified. Finally, it is determined how to `resolve` the conflict if detected. Currently, possible resolution options are: `ignore` the conflict; `disable` the offending *MatchedEntryPair*; `use` only some of the multiple matches: `first`, `last`, or `user choice` (through a selection dialogue); or finally by specifying Java code inside a `do` block.

Expression Builders. Output expression builders begin with `Out Expression`. Like with the conflicts, the `matcher` and `condition` keywords may be used to specify when the builder will be used. Each output interface element may have only one expression builder defining it. If more than one builder is a candidate, the one which was defined last will be used. If no expression builder is found for an output element that has multiple mappings, the framework will fall back to the default behaviour where input element values are converted to strings and concatenated using space as delimiter. The output expression is described using the `out` keyword, followed by: `concatenate` - to merge multiple output interfaces inserting the delimiter specified as a string after `with`; `split` - to split a single input element using the specified delimiter and assign the result to multiple output elements; or `function` - to use one of the built in TOS functions like `SUM()` or `AVG()`. When using concatenate or split, the order in which interface

elements will be inserted can be specified by listing their names after the `order`
keyword. This also gives us the ability to `ignore` some of the elements. Missing
values may be mended using `null substitute`.

Listing 2. An example SAIL definition

```
Matcher sameName
    full name "Same name"
    condition input name = output name
    and input type = output type
Matcher sameOntologyAnnotation
    condition input annotation = output annotation
Matcher aggregation
    condition output annotation partOf input annotation
Matcher splitter
    condition input annotation partOf output annotation
Matcher specialisation
    condition input annotation
        superclassOf output annotation
Matcher generalisation
    condition input annotation subclassOf output annotation
Matcher rejection
    condition input annotation individual
        differentFrom output annotation individual
Conflict multipleMappings
    matcher any
    same reason multiple
    resolve use last
Conflict typeDifferent
    matcher any
    condition input type != output type
    resolve do{
        System.out.println("Java code here"); }
OutExpression
    matcher specialisation, rejection
    condition pair count > 1
        and every pair type = "String"
    out concatenate input name with " "
OutExpression
    matcher any
    condition pair count > 1
    and every pair type = "Number"
    out function SUM(output name)
OutExpression
    matcher aggregation
    condition output name = "address"
    out concatenate input name with "\n"
    order "street", "number", "zip" ignore, "city"
OutExpression
    matcher splitter
    out split with "," null substitute ""
```

6   Conclusion and Future Work

We have shown a language that can be used to specify components of an automated interface mapper. A specification written in this language was successfully used to generate components that behave like those previously manually implemented. Since those components were tested earlier with several real-world integration scenarios, we are confident that those who deal with enterprise integration tasks can benefit from using SAIL and the associated auto-mapping framework. To further improve their usefulness, research is needed for even more complex scenarios with adjustments to the language and framework accordingly. In contrast to the present implementation where a single output expression builder is responsible for each output interface element, we plan to devise a way to allow several of them to be responsible for parts of the output expression and then specify how they will interoperate. Use of regular expressions may be useful when stating element names. The splitter use case provides a variety of research topics, with respect to element order and input data validity. Semantic validators for the SAIL editor should be developed to further aid the user.

References

1. Al-Baltah, I.A., Ghani, A.A.A., Ab Rahman, W.N.W., Atan, R.: Semantic conflicts detection of heterogeneous messages of web services: Challenges and solution. Journal of Computer Science **10**(8), 1428 (2014)
2. Chalmeta, R., Pazos, V.: A step-by-step methodology for enterprise interoperability projects. Enterprise Information Systems **9**(4), 436–464 (2015)
3. Charalabidis, Y.: Revolutionizing Enterprise Interoperability through Scientific Foundations. IGI Global (2014)
4. Gagnon, M.: Ontology-based integration of data sources. In: 2007 10th International Conference on Information Fusion, pp. 1–8. IEEE (2007)
5. Gu, T., Pung, H.K., Zhang, D.Q.: Toward an osgi-based infrastructure for context-aware applications. IEEE Pervasive Computing **3**(4), 66–74 (2004)
6. He, W., Da, X., Da Xu, Y.: Integration of distributed enterprise applications: a survey. IEEE Transactions on Industrial Informatics **10**(1), 35–42 (2014)
7. Izza, S., Vincent, L., Burlat, P.: A framework for semantic enterprise integration. In: Interoperability of enterprise software and applications, pp. 75–86. Springer (2006)
8. Jardim-Goncalves, R., Coutinho, C., Cretan, A., da Silva, C.F., Ghodous, P.: Collaborative negotiation for ontology-driven enterprise businesses. Computers in Industry **65**(9), 1232–1241 (2014)
9. Kovanovic, V., Djuric, D.: Highway: a domain specific language for enterprise application integration. In: Proceedings of the 5th India Software Engineering Conference, pp. 33–36. ACM (2012)
10. Kutsche, R., Milanovic, N., Bauhoff, G., Baum, T., Cartsburg, M., Kumpe, D., Widiker, J.: Bizycle: model-based interoperability platform for software and data integration. In: Proceedings of the MDTPI at ECMDA **430** (2008)
11. Leicher, A., Busse, S., Süß, J.G.: Analysis of Compositional Conflicts in Component-Based Systems. In: Gschwind, T., Aßmann, U., Wang, J. (eds.) SC 2005. LNCS, vol. 3628, pp. 67–82. Springer, Heidelberg (2005)

12. Majchrzak, T.A., Jansen, T., Kuchen, H.: Efficiency evaluation of open source ETL tools. In: Proceedings of the 2011 ACM Symposium on Applied Computing, pp. 287–294. ACM (2011)
13. McAffer, J., Lemieux, J.M., Aniszczyk, C.: Eclipse rich client platform. Addison-Wesley Professional (2010)
14. Millham, R.: Integrating heterogeneous data for big data analysis. Handbook of Research on Cloud Infrastructures for Big Data Analytics p. 263 (2014)
15. Naiman, C.F., Ouksel, A.M.: A classification of semantic conflicts in heterogeneous database systems. Journal of Organizational Computing and Electronic Commerce 5(2), 167–193 (1995)
16. Shtelma, M., Cartsburg, M., Milanovic, N.: Executable domain specific language for message-based system integration. In: Schürr, A., Selic, B. (eds.) MODELS 2009. LNCS, vol. 5795, pp. 622–626. Springer, Heidelberg (2009)
17. Sleiman, H.A., Sultán, A.W., Frantz, R.Z., Corchuelo, R.: Towards automatic code generation for EAI solutions using DSL tools. In: JISBD, pp. 134–145 (2009)
18. Vuković, Ž., Milanović, N., Bauhoff, G.: Prototype of a framework for ontology-aided semantic conflict resolution in enterprise integration. In: Society for Information Systems and Computer Networks, ICIST 2015, pp. 257–260 (2015)

Propelling SMEs Business Intelligence Through Linked Data Production and Consumption

Barbara Kapourani[1], Eleni Fotopoulou[2], Dimitris Papaspyros[3],
Anastasios Zafeiropoulos[2]([⊠]), Spyros Mouzakitis[3], and Sotirios Koussouris[3]

[1] Critical Publics, 4 Flitcroft St., London WC2H 8DH, UK
barbara@criticalpublics.com
[2] Ubitech, Thessalias 8 & Etolias 10 15231 Chalandri, Athens, Greece
{efotopoulou,azafeiropoulos}@ubitech.eu
[3] DSS Lab, National Technical University of Athens, 9 Iroon Polytechniou str.
15780 Zografou, Athens, Greece
{dpap,smouzakitis,skous}@epu.ntua.gr

Abstract. The introduction of the linked data concepts to SMEs, coupled with sophisticated analytics and visualizations deriving through an integrated environment, called the LinDA Workbench, reduces the effort of specific workflows within a company, by almost 50% in terms of time, while its major benefit is the introduction of new, innovative, business models and values in the SMEs' service provisioning. In this manuscript, the initial findings of the Business Intelligence Analytics (BIA) pilot operation of the LinDA project is discussed, which concerns the examination of the effects of Over-The-Counter (OTC) medicines liberalisation in Europe. The analysis aims at identifying correlations between pharmaceutical, healthcare, socio-economic and political parameters and introduces several research questions, which the present paper aims to answer, such as: Are the linked data useful for SMEs? Which are the benefits of integrating them in its operational environment? Are the analysis results of such a scenario meaningful for the SME service provisioning?

1   Introduction

The information era of the last years gave its place to the data analytics era (today known as Analytics 3.0) [5], which require from SMEs that want to process and extract intelligence from the huge amount of data and information available over the Internet, to invest on innovative solutions that integrate a variety of easy-to-use tools for data storage and processing, information extraction and analysis, visualization and presentation. The LinDA project [2] aims to address these specific requirements and support the SMEs' efforts to effectively adopt Linked Open Data (LOD) [8] in their pursuit of competitiveness, by providing a complete bouquet of tools, so-called LinDA Workbench. The tools under this umbrella support various important LOD operations such as publication, consumption, analysis and visualization and the novelty of the approach is not only the close integration of these tools, but also their user-friendliness and practicability, which is one of the major identified obstacles in the LOD research agenda [4].

I. Ciuciu et al. (Eds.): OTM 2015 Workshops, LNCS 9416, pp. 107–116, 2015.
DOI: 10.1007/978-3-319-26138-6_14

Specifically, by using LinDA, the enterprise users and developers not familiar with LOD can easily transform their data sources to the RDF format as well as connect to any available public linked data mart. Thereafter the generation of queries, visualizations and analytics on these pre-processed data pieces is performed very easily, by using an open source engine that delivers advances analyses and visualization, alongside with advanced but easy to construct queries. Making use of the LinDA framework and of its tools, SMEs are able to renovate their data management pipeline and share artefacts with collaborators through public or private data sources. The target audience of this framework are SMEs that usually do not afford built-in data warehouses, in order to easily setup business intelligence systems internally, towards gaining significant competitive advantage. The introduction of Linked Data through the use of the LinDA tools aids enterprises to create and consume high-quality linked data, faster.

The paper at hand presents briefly the tools composing the integrated LinDA environment (Section 2) through a step-by-step presentation of a real life scenario, which concerns the Over-The-Counter (OTC) medicines (medicines which are not prescribed by doctors and can be freely bought by consumers in pharmacies) liberalization in Europe that has been implemented as a Business Intelligence pilot within the project (Section 3). Next, Section 4 discusses the added-value identified for SMEs, while Section 5 concludes the paper, listing the major benefits from the usage of the LinDA Workbench, in comparison to other alternative solutions.

2   A Glimpse at the LinDA Workbench

The LinDA Workbench [3] is the integrated environment, consisting of a set of tools that facilitates the manipulation of the linked data and is the major output of the LinDA project. In an easy, straightforward and user friendly way, a user may follow a simple 3-step process for transforming raw data to RDF data, linking (and querying) them with public and private endpoints, and as a last step, analysing and/or visualising the resulted information. In more detail, the LinDA Workbench consists of (a) the LinDA Transformation engine, a lightweight transformation to linked data tool, the (b) LinDA Vocabulary repository for increasing the semantic interoperability of the data, (c) the LinDA RDF2Any, a tool for converting RDF to conventional data structures in order to be used by legacy applications, (d) the LinDA Query Builder and Query Designer to easily navigate and query the data, (e) the LinDA Visualization to perform smart visualizations on linked data out-of-the box, and finally, (f) the LinDA Analytics package for running analytic processes against the data [6].

LinDA enables SMEs to accelerate their learning process of semantic technologies and harvest the potential of linked data in an intuitive and cost-effective manner, demonstrated from the initial results of the running pilot (presented in the next sections). LinDA is in a position to aid SMEs to publish and consume high-quality linked data faster, and more importantly, to introduce new business values and steams of revenues.

3   Real-Life Scenario – Linked Data for the Pharmaceutical Sector

In this real-life scenario, an SME which is operating in the Business Intelligence (BI) sector, by providing consultation services in a wide range of national and multinational enterprises, organizations and governments, helping them to build their communication strategy and uphold their decision making processes, is testing out the LinDA tools. The pre-LinDA status included employing a large group of consultants that gather and assess huge amount of data, often time-sensitive information, in a daily basis, from different sources, in different formats and by using a variety of tools. For this reason, political, economic, regulatory, social, industry and market data are collected for composing the conceptualization map of the clients' domain, aiming at monitoring and analysing each part of it, that might affect the SME's clients.

As one can easily notice, the volume, variety, velocity, the time-sensitivity, the heterogeneity and non-interoperability of the data to be handled is a great burden for the SME, in terms of effort, time, resources and complexity. These are some of the reasons that a challenging domain, such as the pharmaceutical one has been selected for the LinDA BIA pilot; so that to identify the potentials and whether a set of tools like LinDA Workbench would facilitate some of the aforementioned tasks, and add more value in the service provisioning of the SME.

The pilot scenario is about the Over-The-Counter (OTC) medicines liberalization in Europe, in terms of price, retail and entry. It aims at investigating the OTC liberalization impacts by studying and analysing the countries where the liberalization has already taken place, and by combining this information with the unique parameters of the rest European countries of interest (e.g. Greece), where the liberalization has not been yet implemented. The goal is to drive conclusions and obtain insights on whether the OTC liberalization is beneficial, for whom (public and/or private sector) and how is related to critical socioeconomic and political factors.

The importance and the challenges of the OTC domain are clearly demonstrated in [1], where it is stated that despite of the global financial crisis, OTC medicines sales have continued to rise and this market is nowadays a key source of business expansion and competitive edge, where powerful dynamics are driving new potential for growth; however, challenges abound and identifying the best opportunities will not be easy. Various studies have been conducted for the OTC market, focusing only in a subset of the correlated parameters that affects or are being affected by the OTC liberalization, which basically reveals the complexity of the domain. LOD offers the option to compose a complete, cumulative map of all the correlated parameters for the OTC market. Based on such a map, and by using the LinDA Workbench, we have tried to identify the indicators playing a prominent role in the OTC liberalization, find their correlations and analyse their impact, with the ambition for intelligence extraction of the trends to be emerge in the nearby future.

Through the LinDA Workbench we revealed quite interesting insights concerning the OTC scenario. Moreover, we have detected the benefits of the linked data usage for the SME and their great potentials, in comparison to the "business as usual" state, which reflects the current workflows followed by the company to do its business.

3.1   Pharmaceutical Scenario Implementation

Figure 1 delivers the steps followed for the implementation of the OTC scenario within the LinDA framework. As a result of research and intelligence-gathering activities, conducted manually by the involved actors, spanning from health advisors to business intelligence consultants, the conceptualization map of the OTC scenario has been crafted, becoming the basis of the data needed for composing the full map of the correlated parameters for the OTC market. The identified public and private datasets have been classified into five main categories: (a) healthcare indicators [e.g. healthcare expenditures, pharmaceutical market], (b) OTC indicators [e.g. OTC liberalization, out-of-pocket expenditures], (c) economic indicators [e.g. GDP per capita, inflation rate], (d) political indicators [e.g. political stability, government effectiveness] and (e) social indicators [e.g. unemployment, corruption].

Overall, this map contains more than twenty unique indicators, half of which represents private datasets of the SME that have been created for the purpose of the OTC scenario. Furthermore, the indicators are spanning in various time ranges [some of them from 1980 until 2014] and across different European countries [e.g. EU-28], comprising in that way a set of more than 200 datasets. Most of these datasets are in excel or csv format, while some of the public sector datasets have SPARQL endpoints to be retrieved from (e.g. Eurostat, World Bank, Transparency.org).

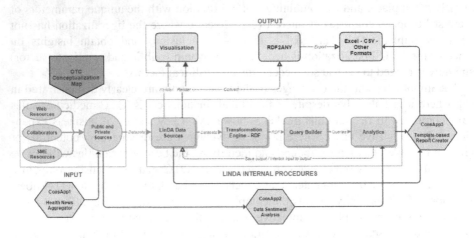

Fig. 1. OTC scenario implementation steps in LinDA.

Two major interlinking directions have been followed in the BIA pilot's scenario; in the 1st case (Figure 2) all the private datasets have been interlinked with the World Factbook/Eurostat [7], both by country and by year property. The World Factbook contains approximately 195 properties (such as: demographics, GDP, debt, budget, investment, population, labour force, etc.), which are valuable source of instant information fetching to be mixed and matched with the OTC and healthcare indicators and output meaningful presentations and analysis for the scenario, and in the long run for supporting the clients' consultation services. In the 2nd interlinking case (Figure 3) some of the identified private and public datasets have been interlinked together, so as to formulate valuable questions for the OTC scenario [such as: Which are the most significant correlations of the OOP expenditures with the rest of the healthcare, social and economic-political indicators? What's the relationship between the Out-Of-Pocket (OOP) expenditures with the GDP per capita?], to be answered through the analytic processes of the LinDA tools.

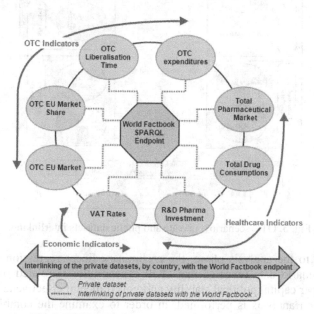

Fig. 2. OTC scenario – private datasets interlinking.

After the datasets recognition and interlinking, the SME can use the LinDA tools (e.g. Data Sources, Transformation, Query Designer) for registering public SPARQL endpoints, uploading RDF dumps, transforming tabular data in RDF format and for-mulating the interlinking questions to be used next, into the analysis phase. The LinDA Analytics package is being used for drilling down to the study (by applying algorithms such as, linear and multiple linear regressions, forecasting [arima] and clustering [clustersNumber, K-means]) of the OTC scenario, which is the fundamen-tal step towards the intelligence extraction.

Prior to initiating the analysis phase, a set of visualisations are produced aiming at getting preliminary insights regarding trends or correlations among specific parame-ters. Such a visualization is depicted in Figure 4, where the trends in the relationship between the OOP expenditures and the government effectiveness parameter are shown. A bubble chart is provided for this purpose, where it can be seen that low OTC values correspond to high governmental effectiveness values.

A similar trend is also shown in Figure 5, where a "bar plot" is produced with the same parameters. In this case, it is also evident the existence of a set of outliers in the dataset that provide indications to the business intelligence analyst to apply appropriate filters in order to remove outliers prior to the analysis and receive more accurate results.

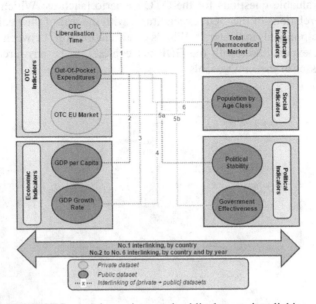

Fig. 3. OTC scenario – private and public datasets interlinking.

Moving on to the analysis phase, the preliminary linear regression analysis over part of the scenario data revealed that OOP expenditures is related with indicators such as GDP per capita, political stability and governmental effectiveness. A multiple linear regression analysis is performed, in order to examine the combined effect of governmental effectiveness, political stability and GDP per capita to the OOP expenditures. Based on the results, the overall analysis is considered statistical significant, however the correlation between the OOP expenditures and the variables of political stability and governmental effectiveness is not very evident.

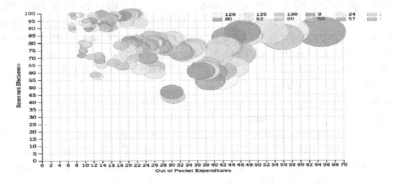

Fig. 4. Relationship among OOP expenditures and governmental effectiveness (bubble chart).

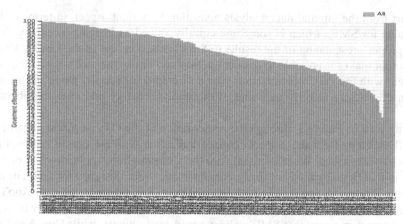

Fig. 5. Relationship among OTC and Governmental Effectiveness (barplot).

Next, a clustering algorithm has been used to check whether the formulation of well-defined non-overlapping clusters is possible. By executing a clustering algorithm (ClustersNumber) over the aforementioned interlinked dataset, it seems that a selection of number of clusters in the range of 3 or 4 leads to the formulation of such clusters. The next step deals with the execution of a k-means clustering algorithm [7] for partitioning the overall observations in three clusters. Three really well defined clusters with no overlapping among each other are produced.

Cluster 1 refers to countries with low political stability, low governmental effectiveness and low GDP per capita that tend to have high OOP expenditures. Cluster 2 includes countries with medium-to-high political stability, high governmental effectiveness and high GDP per capita that tend to have low OTC expenditures. Cluster 3 is grouping together countries with medium political stability, low governmental effectiveness and low GDP per capita that tend to have medium to low OTC expenditures. In order to reveal, for example, the positioning of country "Greece" in one of these clusters, one has to link the produced k-means clustering output with the initial dataset denoting the OOP expenditures per country. Upon authoring the corresponding query and performing the necessary linking one can witness that "Greece" belongs to the cluster 1 (along with participation from "Cyprus" and "Bulgaria" and partial from "Lithuania" and "Latvia").

Finally, a multiple linear regression is realised specifically for the countries that belong to cluster 1, where the analysis is rather statistically significant (low p-value) with a high Adjusted R-squared value (0.5928). The coefficients for the government effectiveness and the GDP per capita seem to be more significant in this case, in comparison with the trends already presented for all the EU-28 countries. From all the countries in cluster 1, that seem to follow the same levels in terms of political stability, government effectiveness and GDP per capita, the only country that has proceeded to liberalization of OTC market is "Bulgaria", leading to a significant reduction of the OOP expenditures. Thus, it can be assumed that similar effect could be possibly produced in the case of "Greece".

Apart from the internal data analysis a similar, important aspect, in terms of business value for SMEs which is sometime equally valued as insights' accuracy, is that of the proper presentation of the results to the clients. The use of the LinDA Visualizations tool makes it possible to extract quickly and easily the analysis results, correlate them with the OTC liberalization year and graphically depict them, so that a client can effortlessly identify the trend of the analysis before and after the liberalization.

Going back to Figure 1, through the presentation of the OTC scenario implementation, all the steps from the scenario conceptualization until the output retrieval have been briefly described. What is missing are the Consumption Applications (ConsApp) shown in that figure, which are small, custom-made tools, designed for facilitating the SME job, through its interaction with the platform. For example, the ConsApp3 prepares and publishes custom reports based on a predefined template, in order to present the final report in a way that SME's client could easily digest, while ConsApp2 deals with Sentiment Analysis on the acquired data for providing even more intelligent information based on crowd sourced data.

4   Delivering the Real Value of Linked Data to SMEs

Evaluation of the business value introduced to the SME by the usage of the LinDA Workbench, has been performed by comparing the generation of similar business intelligence reports including four parameters (e.g. GDP per capita, OOP expenditures, Unemployment and Political Stability) with and without the LinDA tools, where in turn the processes of acquiring, transforming analysing and visualising data on a weekly basis happened both in a manual and in an automatic (using LinDA) fashion. The evaluation considered aspects such as execution time, human capital and the tools employed. Figure 6 showcases in detail the SME's four core business phases, as well as the tasks, resources and effort needed when the example is implemented "as usual" and then, when implemented with the help of LinDA.

One can easily notice that the necessary time-to-result, when using LinDA, is reduced; ranging from 19min to 3,42hours (e.g. almost 50%). Moreover, the number of executed tasks is also reduced from 11 to 9. As for the involved experts, some changes have been recorded; LinDA introduces a new actor called "data analyst", while the "designer" needed in the "as usual" case is taken out of the scene. The change is quite significant as it is closely related to the reduction of the outsourcing costs of the report's visual design (done now by ConsApp3). Furthermore, what is quite vital, is that with LinDA all tasks are realised within a unified environment offering to the SME a "one-stop-shop", with a quite user friendly and straightforward UI, sidestepping the need of hopping between different tools and distributed, autonomous working environments.

Overall, it is crystal clear the added-value coming from the usage of LOD and of the LinDA Workbench. It has been calculated that the LOD concept could definitely assist and improve SMES to reach to more and instant information, while the usage of the LinDA Workbench has proven to facilitate the SME's current workflow, reducing the effort required for specific tasks both in terms of time and resources. More importantly, LinDA introduces new business values and operations to the SME (e.g. analytic process which were not implemented before, due to, e.g. lack of experience or time), which can boost the provided services to new levels of completeness and analysis, supporting SMEs also to refine parts of their business model by opening up new horizons and options that were not accessible before due to resources constrains. During this 1st round of the BIA pilot operation, the business processes in place were transformed into processes running in a faster, simplest, more effective and user friendly way, while supplementary and enhanced insights were served to SME's clients too.

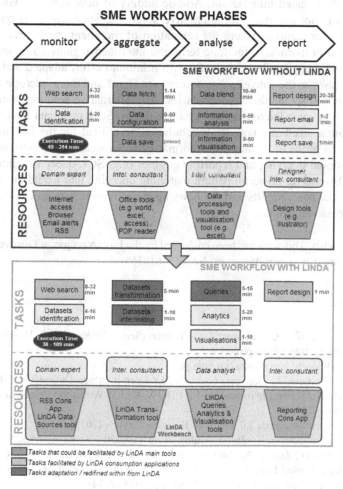

Fig. 6. SME workflow, with and without LinDA.

5   Conclusions

In this paper we have tried to present briefly a linked data analysis pilot case, focusing on the workflows followed by an SME, providing consultation services to its clients, with and without the usage of the LinDA Workbench, so as to derive insights about the usefulness of the linked data concepts, if adopted by an SME. Based on the produced results, it can be claimed that –compared to LinDA- alternative solutions (relational databases tools for storage and consumption) would require manual updates of data or the development of custom harvesters. On the other hand, relying on linked data endpoints will remove the need for manual updates of data, saving many man-hours for daily updated information. Ad-hoc adding of new metadata without database changes is not possible with alternative solutions. Such feature is quite critical for this particular scenario, where the reputation of the client can be evaluated on a dynamic set of properties. In the long term, the intelligence gathered by the business intelligence company can be ad-hoc and with minimum effort adapted and offered to other clients also, as the outcome data sources are "live" and more interoperable, since they are based on standardized vocabularies. Any alternative solution would not endorse, by design, such interoperability characteristics. Such metadata interoperability, based on standardized and popular vocabularies, is critical for the interlinking of a great variety in terms of metadata and format of news sources. Furthermore, in contrast to traditional querying and reporting engines (e.g. SQL query in relational databases), LinDA enables powerful pattern matching querying that would allow complex queries over the news reports and the news agencies with minimum effort, providing further business value to the company.

Acknowledgments. This work has been co-funded by the LinDA project, a European Commission research program (Grant Agreement No. FP7-610565).

References

1. The Rising Tide of OTC in Europe, Andy Tisman (Senior Principal, IMS Health) (2010)
2. LinDA website: http://linda-project.eu/
3. LinDA Workbench: http://linda.epu.ntua.gr/
4. Davies, S., Hatfield, J., Donaher, C., Zeitz, J.: User Interface Design Considerations for Linked Data Authoring Environments. In: LDOW, CEUR Workshop Proceedings, vol. **628**. CEUR-WS.org (2010)
5. Davenport, T.H.: Analytics 3.0. Harward Business Review (2013)
6. Hasapis, P., Fotopoulou, E., Zafeiropoulos, A., Mouzakitis, S., Koussouris, S., Petychakis, M., Kapourani, B., Zanetti, N., Molinari, F., Virtuoso, S. & Rubattino, C., Business Value Creation from Linked Data Analytics: The LinDA Approach. In: eChallenges e-2014 Conference, Belfast, Northern Ireland, 29-31 October 2014 (2014)
7. Hartigan, J.A.: Clustering Algorithms. John Wiley & Sons, Inc., New York (1975)
8. W3C What is Linked Data (2015). http://www.w3.org/standards/semanticweb/data

A Domain Specific Language for Organisational Interoperability

Georg Weichhart[1,2](✉) and Christian Stary[2]

[1] Profactor GmbH, Steyr, Austria
Georg.Weichhart@profactor.at
[2] Deptartment of Business Informatics - Communications Engineering,
Johannes Kepler University Linz, Linz, Austria
{Christian.Stary,Georg.Weichhart}@jku.at

Abstract. In the SUDDEN (SMEs Undertaking Design of Dynamic Ecosystem Networks) project a web-based environment has been researched supporting automotive SMEs (Small and Medium Sized Enterprises) with respect to organisational interoperability using performance measurement systems. Using a CAS (Complex Adaptive Systems) point of view, we have implemented a Domain Specific Language and interoperability support services implementing the SUDDEN frame of reference. Extending interoperability support to the process and data level, this environment enables simulating processes and data transfers.

Keywords: Enterprise interoperability · Complex adaptive systems · Scala · Domain specific language

1 Introduction

In the project SUDDEN (SMEs Undertaking Design of Dynamic Ecosystem Networks) an organisational-learning frame of reference supported by a web-based platform for organisational interoperability in automotive supply networks has been developed [15]. That framework extends the intra-organisational learning approach by Heftberger and Stary [7] towards networks of automotive suppliers. It approaches learning rather from a process and experience point of view than from an outcome or result point of view [10]. The frame of reference and learning support tool facilitates the process of learning on the organisational, the supply chain, and the supply network level [15].

With respect to organisational interoperability, the SUDDEN framework supports groups of organisations to collaboratively develop performance measurement systems (PMS). These PMSs are used to measure a supply chain's targeted and actual performance. Evaluation of the SUDDEN approach showed that modelling of key performance systems of suppliers starting a supply chain has positive impact on the communication and planning process due to deeper understanding of the addressed qualities by these systems.

© Springer International Publishing Switzerland 2015
I. Ciuciu et al. (Eds.): OTM 2015 Workshops, LNCS 9416, pp. 117–126, 2015.
DOI: 10.1007/978-3-319-26138-6_15

118   G. Weichhart and C. Stary

Fig. 1 shows the above discussed frame of reference. Marked with (1) is the individual learning cycle [10]. Organisational members are observing their environment. They individually assess observed situations. If response to a situation is needed according to their analysis a plan for acting is designed. It is then implemented, and the impact of this implementation is again observed and assessed by the respective individual.

Within an organisation such individual learning cycles result in information which can be stored in the organisation's repository (2). A typical example are reports capturing performance assessments. Usually, organisations do not have a single repository but many, including automatically captured and processed data in databases. In organisations, repositories can take different forms, and are distributed across organisational units [4]. Such an exchange among organisational members and/or organisational information systems supports sharing and the transfer of knowledge, and thus learning - labelled (3) in fig. 1.

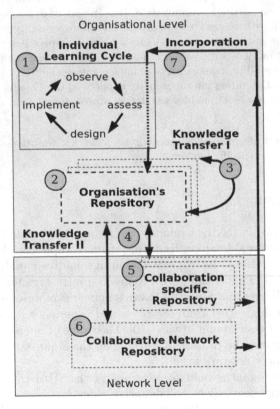

Fig. 1. SUDDEN Frame of Reference for Learning using Performance Measurement Systems in Supply Networks

On the network level, the SUDDEN project has identified and supported two kinds of repositories, collaboration (supply chains in this case) -specific ones (wikis) (5), and a SUDDEN network-wide repository (6). Members of participating organisations provide the knowledge that is kept in these repositories (4). When further organisations need or want to gain access to that knowledge the SUDDEN repository can be incorporated in different organisations by its members (7). In this way, a learning cycle across multiple organisations can be triggered.

SUDDEN supports an interoperability approach which is based on performance indicators. Ensuring interoperability on business level, it supports the creation of supply chains. A web-based tool allows a single or small group of SUDDEN network partners designing a performance measurement system for a (planned) supply chain. The system enables partners to estimate expected performance of a collaborative effort, and allows comparative analyses of candidate supplier. Performance information is acquired by asking each supply network participant to fill in a questionnaire. A corresponding online tool supports collecting organisational data along 12 dimensions. This data is matched against the requirements for a specific collaboration. As the repositories can be accessed by organisation's member according to his/her profile, individual learning cycles can be triggered by performance data.

Business interoperability, as used so far, is based on static performance indicators. It has to be enriched meeting dynamic enterprise interoperability requirements. Interoperability on process level, requires estimating the behaviour of individual suppliers and simulating interactions between suppliers. In this papers the existing approach is extended to support dynamic organisational development capabilities.

In the following section we discuss the conceptual foundation of this systemic approach to Enterprise Interoperability. Section 3 details the developed infrastructure, consisting of a multi-agent system and a domain specific language supporting different levels of enterprise interoperability. The final section presents our conclusions and the next steps in research.

2   CAS Extended Ontology of Enterprise Interoperability $(OoEI^{CAS})$

In this section the conceptual elements for designing the SUDDEN system including modelling participants' behaviours is discussed. Fig. 2 shows the systemic core of the ontology of enterprise interoperability [11,6] extended by concepts from the complex adaptive systems theory [17].

A system consists of system elements which have structural and behavioural relationships. System elements are interacting and have interfaces.

A Complex Adaptive System (CAS) in $OoEI^{CAS}$ is a system which places particular emphasis on its dynamics and evolution. System dynamics is captured by a special type of system element called *agent*. An Agent is an active element which has its own memory and is in control of its own behaviour (i.e. its autonomous). Multiple agents co-exist and all system elements co-evolve in an unpredicted manner due to the interaction of the agents.

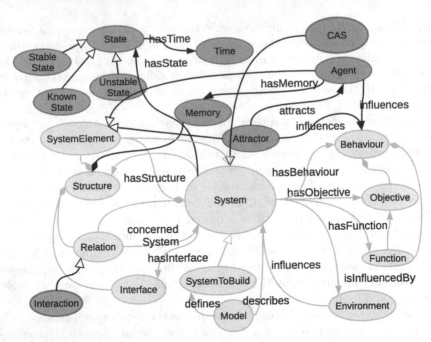

Fig. 2. Elements of the Ontology of Enterprise Interoperability, extended with CAS related concepts. [16,17]
Legend: Ovals: Light-blue ... OoEI systemic concepts; Dark-blue ... CAS concepts
Arrow-heads: Empty triangle ... subclass / subsumption; Diamond-shaped ... partof;
Black triangle and no label ... has;

The Ontology of Enterprise Interoperability follows the framework of enterprise interoperability and defines four levels of concern: Data, Service, Processes, Business [2,6] and identifies three solution strategies:

Integrated Interoperability: A common, agreed exchange-format for all system elements exists.

Unified Interoperability: A common meta-level exchange-format exists. This provides the means for mutual mapping heterogeneous models and systems.

Federated Interoperability: In this case no common format exists. Nothing is imposed on the system by a single system element. It is the most challenging approach - interoperability needs to be managed in an ad hoc manner.

Apparently, the latter approach has minimal a-priori assumptions and provides the highest flexibility.

3   A $OoEI^{CAS}$ Domain Specific Language Supporting the SUddEN Frame of Reference

The initial SUDDEN approach supports interoperability with respect to business performance. Providing means for collaboratively working on supply chain performance measurement systems, SUDDEN allows prospective supply chain participants understanding interoperability requirements using performance indices. The SUDDEN system uses supplier performance indicator values as input to the supply chain specific performance measurement system to find the most suitable supplier for a position in the supply chain. SUDDEN did not address interoperability concerns for processes, services and data from its very beginning.

In order to support a federated approach, we have designed and partially implemented a domain-specific language, including fundamental services which help to model and execute the models of supplier behaviours and their interactions. This approach to interoperability supports the process of maintaining interoperability in a dynamic system [16].

The Domain Specific Language (DSL) approach was chosen, as it allows to combine ontology (as concepts in the DSL) with agent behaviours and agent-system services in a single software model. These elements provide a simple meta-model which can be refined and enhanced depending on the situation. It is rather established at runtime using the development environment with the base implementation provided. It is used to connect system elements specific for a supply chain. Interoperability concepts may be defined a-priori enabling targeted management of interoperability problems.

A generic interoperability system for federated interoperability allows discovering suitable solutions on the fly. A common minimal understanding for operational purposes is ensured through a meta-level ontology. For the researched interoperability environment, we have extended the systemic core of the Ontology of Enterprise Interoperability with CAS concepts ($OoEI^{CAS}$). It specifies the concepts relevant to this common understanding [17]. The Domain Specific Language approach to interoperability then allows capturing and simulating processes in order to understand whether behaviours of agents are interoperable.

3.1   Scala Implementation

The $OoEI^{CAS}$ Domain Specific Language for developing enterprise interoperability solutions is realised using the **Scala** language and its associated development infrastructure.

Scala is a programming language which adheres to two paradigms [14,13]:

Object Orientation: **Scala** is based on the Java programming library, which allows utilizing the existing Java ecosystem. In **Scala** everything is an object.
Functional Programming: **Scala** supports parallel computing and functions as first-class elements.

Scala supports programmatic abstractions based on both paradigms and additionally a flexible way for defining domain-specific languages (DSL) [14]. **Scala** provides also a basic infrastructure for implementing agents. Its these properties that have made the authors choose this particular language. However, no evaluation against other programming languages have been conducted.

3.2 Multi Actor Systems

Due to the focus on dynamics and evolutionary aspects of a system where several agents are interacting, the $OoEI^{CAS}$ DSL does not only implement an ontology for communication. It additionally provides an infrastructure where independent agents are able to interact and communicate.

The Scala development ecosystem includes libraries to build an *actor* based infrastructure. An *actor* in Scala is the basic class to implement an agent. However, in contrast to multi agent systems theory, the actor implementation lacks certain features and infrastructure services [17]. In the following we use the term *agent* to refer to the theoretical concept, and the term *actor* to refer to concrete implementations. The Akka library [1] provides the default actor implementation in the current version of Scala [8].

Actors, as well as agents, are conceptualisations that allow accurate distributed and concurrent computing. In akka, everything is an actor [1]. The multi-actor infrastructure is organised in a hierarchical way. An application's "root" actor starts its children and will receive some notification about the death of a child. Each child in turn may have children.

Agents in a multi-agent system rely on necessary services that support their life-cycle and agent-interactions. The IEEE FIPA (Foundation for Intelligent Physical Agents) standards serve as a general reference for multi agent system architectures [3]. This standard provides platform service specifications for multi agent systems. A FIPA compliant platform provides three important infrastructure services. The agent management system (AMS), the directory facilitator service (DF), and the message transport service [2]. Out of the box, although not FIPA compliant, akka provides an agent management service through the hierarchical organisation of actors, and a message transport service allowing communications across machines. However, there is no directory facilitator supporting the search for agents providing certain functionalities or services.

3.3 Multi Agent System Infrastructure

The description of the implementation of the directory facilitator in the following exemplifies the implementation of actor behaviours. Each actor reacts to messages received. Through interaction protocols, the behaviours of multiple actors get tangled.

The DF actor is a yellow page service on network level, which allows identifying organisations capable to provide a particular function. Interaction protocols which enable registering and de-registering with the DF have been designed and implemented as part of the interoperability infrastructure. The DF actor answers requests concerning actors being able to provide a certain functionality. In order to be discovered by other actors, every actor has first to register the functionality it provides.

---

[1] http://akka.io/
[2] http://fipa.org/specs/fipa00023/SC00023K.html

Listing 1. Parts of the Directory Facilitator comprising the implementation of the query-actors-by-function *query-response type* protocol

```
case class QueryActorsByFunction(functionname: String)
    extends QueryMessage[QueryResponseProtocol](Some(new
    QueryResponseProtocol))
case class InformActorsByFunction(functionname: String,
    descriptions: Seq[ActorServiceDescription], responseTo:
    Some[QueryMessage[QueryResponseProtocol]]) extends
    ReplyMessage[QueryResponseProtocol](responseTo.get.
    protocol, responseTo.get.messageID)
// ... some more protocols ...
class DirectoryFacilitator extends Actor with
    ActorServiceRegistry with InteroperabilityActorBehaviour {
    override def receive = receiveDF orElse
        receiveInteroperabilityDefaultBehaviour

    def receiveDF: Receive = {
        case message: QueryActorsByFunction =>
            val actorsFound = functionRegistry get message.
                functionname
            if (actorsFound != None)
                sender() ! new InformActorsByFunction(message.
                    functionname, actorMap.filterKeys(name =>
                    actorsFound.get.contains(name)).values.toList,
                    Some(message))
            else
                sender() ! new InformActorsByFunction(message.
                    functionname, Nil, Some(message))
```

In Scala messages may be implemented as `case classes`. These type of classes are used in *switch* like statements. When a case class is received by an actor it may implement different functions, depending on type and content of the received message.

The FIPA standard also provides some interaction protocols, which prescribe message types and allowed return answers. These are missing in the akka actor environment.

The interaction protocols used by the DF are implemented as simple Query-Response protocols. Sending a query message to the DF will result in a response message. One of the implemented interaction protocols and a part of the implementation in the DF are shown in listing 1.

The two messages `QueryActorsByFunction` and `InformActorsByFunction` define one interaction protocol. The reply message (Inform) contains the original message to which the DF replies for supporting message routing and handling of asynchronous response messages with respect to identifying the original query message.

The Directory Facilitator class shows the overridden Actor `receive` method. That method is triggered when an actor receives a message. The receive method

highlights the effect of using `case classes` for the actor interaction protocols. The receive function is a partial function which may be chained (i.e. where multiple functions of a particular type are called one after the other - not shown in the snapshot). This makes the implementation of chains of protocols a straight-forward task. In listing 1 the case part of the function
`case message: QueryActorsByFunction =>` handles the situation when the Directory Facilitator receives a message of type `QueryActorsByFunction`. The DF searches the list of registered actors for all actors that have registered with that particular function. The DF returns a `InformActorsByFunction` message (eventually with an empty list (`Nil`)).

The description of the implementation of the directory facilitator exemplifies the definition of dynamic aspects of actors through the implementation of protocols and behaviours. A behaviour is the execution of actor internal process, the protocols specify the behaviour of a set of actors.

$OoEI^{CAS}$ DSL allows encoding artificial representatives of SUDDEN ecosystem participants (suppliers). Models of interacting suppliers may be used to simulate different processes and workflows in order to verify interoperability on the process level. It has to be distinguished between agents and the roles they take within a particular process. Each agent is capable of taking multiple roles (aka. subjects in S-BPM [5,9]). As the interaction is based on sending messages between agents (taking a particular role) and agents have the responsibility to execute tasks that allow them to send a reply message according to the protocol.

3.4   Process Simulation for Interoperability

The environment can be used in several ways to improve interoperability in supplier networks. It is assumed that model components are made available in the SUDDEN repositories. Suppliers use protocol specifications from the repositories to provide refined descriptions how they would like to interact. Making the interfacing processes public (through source code as reference models) allows potential partners adopt to these specifications, e.g., by changing its own processes. In this case, interoperability is established by integrating processes.

The protocols may also be used to map internal processes to the protocols resulting in an unified interoperability approach. Again, by using model components from the repositories the suitability of the protocol can be determined by modelling both sides of the interaction. The flexible DSL approach allows to model the internal behaviour of suppliers and allows to simulate the overall behaviour of the supply network. Internal processes may be modelled in abstract manner, mapping the individual interface processes to the interaction protocol (cf. [12]). Depending on the details modelled performance of supply networks may be simulated along different dimensions.

Of relevance to the SUDDEN eco-system is the possibility of chaining such mappings in order to simulate nested and interacting protocols of multiple supply chains.

4   Conclusions

Organisational sustainability requires structural flexibility on the process and data level (agility), in particular for operating distributed business networks. As domain-specific languages are promising candidates to accurately capture organisationally relevant ontologies and behaviours in a single environment, they can be utilised handling agility issues. In this paper we have demonstrated the conceptual and practical benefits building on achievements interfacing organisational structures and implementing a Complex Adaptive Systems' perspective. Targeting the automotive industry an organizational development environment has been implemented ensuring continuous adaptation of processes and domain ontologies.

Our initial implementation allows manually specifying and checking organisational interoperability on the process level by promoting network partners to specify interface processes and interaction protocols. In order to fully combine the process interaction approach presented here with performance measurement systems, such as developed in the SUDDEN project, features enabling the simulation of processes are required while establishing performance indicators.

Support to specify performance indicators beyond time-related issues is still needed. In this context, performance indicators like costs, or number of produced items may be recorded in the course of simulating processes. With respect to time, the total duration of production processes may also be recorded. However, for event-based, stochastic simulations, in particular a global time management system is required for simulating time-dependent performance parameters like the bullwhip effect that occurs once multiple customers order the same product at the same time.

Using a generic programming language provides a high level of flexibility on what and how to model. On the other hand, the proposed approach requires users to be capable of programming Scala. This clearly limits the use of the approach. Providing code modules through repositories allows re-use within the organisations participating in a network. This implies the requirements for good documentation of the modules.

The proposed language and approach needs to be evaluated by users according to usefulness and usability principles. Suitability for user tasks and ease of modelling support are considered crucial in order to achieve organisational acceptance. Once the language and environment provide sufficient conceptual elements for modelling supply networks and interactions between suppliers, organisations can easily build on these results to increase their agility and implement corresponding requirements.

Acknowledgement. This work has been partially funded by the Austrian Federal Ministry for Transport, Innovation and Technology within the NgMPPS-DPC project.

References

1. Bonér, J., Klang, V., Kuhn, R., Nordwal, P., Antonsson, B., Varga, E.: Akka scala documentation. Tech. rep., Typesafe Inc. (2014). http://akka.io/docs/
2. Chen, D.: Framework for enterprise interoperability. In: Panetto, H., Boudjlida, N. (eds.) Proc. of IFAC Workshop EI2N, pp. 77–88. Interoperability for Enterprise Software and Applications, Bordeaux, March 21, 2006
3. FIPA - Foundation for Intelligent Physical Agents: Standard fipa specifications (2005). http://fipa.org/repository/standardspecs.htmlhttp://www.fipa.org
4. Firestone, J.M., McElroy, M.W.: Doing knowledge management. The Learning Organization **12**(2), 189–212 (2005)
5. Fleischmann, A., Schmidt, W., Stary, C., Obermeier, S., Börger, E.: Subject-Oriented Business Process Management. Springer (2012)
6. Guédria, W.: A contribution to enterprise interoperability maturity assessment: Towards an automatic approach. LAP LAMBERT Academic Publishing (2012)
7. Heftberger, S., Stary, C.: Partzipatives organisatorisches Lernen. Ein prozess-basierter Ansatz. Deutscher Universitäts-Verlag / GWV Fachverlage GmbH, Wiesbaden (2004)
8. Jovanovic, V., Haller, P.: The scala actors migration guide. Tech. rep., Programming Methods Laboratory of École Polytechnique Fédérale de Lausanne (EPFL) (2013). http://docs.scala-lang.org/overviews/core/actors-migration-guide.html (accessed on December 09, 2014)
9. Kannengiesser, U.: Agents Implementing Subject Behaviour: A Manufacturing Scenario, chap. 12, pp. 201–216. Springer International Publishing (2015)
10. Kolb, D.A.: Experiential Learning: Experience as the Source of Learning and Development. Prentice Hall Inc., Englewood Cliffs (1984)
11. Naudet, Y., Latour, T., Guédria, W., Chen, D.: Towards a systemic formalisation of interoperability. Computers in Industry **61**, 176–185 (2010)
12. Norta, A., Grefen, P., Narendra, N.C.: A reference architecture for managing dynamic inter-organizational business processes. Data & Knowledge Engineering **91**, 52–89 (2014)
13. Schinz, M., Haller, P.: A scala tutorial for java programmers. Tech. rep., École Polytechnique Fédérale de Lausanne (EPFL) (2014). http://docs.scala-lang.org/tutorials/scala-for-java-programmers.html
14. Wampler, D., Payne, A.: Programming Scala: Scalability = Functional Programming + Objects. O'Reilly, 2nd edn. (2015)
15. Weichhart, G., Feiner, T., Stary, C.: Implementing organisational interoperability-the sudden approach. Computers in Industry **61**(2), 152–160 (2010)
16. Weichhart, G., Guédria, W., Naudet, Y.: Supporting interoperability in complex adaptive enterprise systems: A domain specific language approach. Data and Knowledge Engineering (2015) (submitted)
17. Weichhart, G., Naudet, Y.: Ontology of enterprise interoperability extended for complex adaptive systems. In: Meersman, R., et al. (eds.) OTM 2014 Workshops. LNCS, vol. 8842, pp. 219–228. Springer, Heidelberg (2014)

Understanding Personal Mobility Patterns for Proactive Recommendations

Ruben Costa(✉), Paulo Figueiras, Pedro Oliveira, and Ricardo Jardim-Goncalves

CTS, Uninova, Dep.ª de Eng.ª Electrotécnica, Faculdade de Ciências e Tecnologia, FCT,
Universidade Nova de Lisboa, 2829-516 Caparica, Portugal
{rddc,paf,pgo,rg}@uninova.pt

Abstract. This paper proposes an innovative methodology for extracting and learning personal mobility patterns. The objective is to award daily commuters in a city with personalized and proactive recommendations, related with their mobility habits on a daily basis. In currently approaches, users have to explicitly provide their routes (origin, destination and date/time) to a routing engine in order to be notified about traffic events. The proposed approach goes beyond and learns daily mobility habits from the users, without the need to provide any information. The work presented here, is currently being addressed under the EU OPTIMUM project. Results achieved establish the basis for the formalization of the OPTIMUM domain knowledge on personal mobility patterns.

Keywords: Intelligent transport systems · Mobility patterns · Data acquisition · Machine learning

1 Introduction

Intelligent Transport Systems were envisaged to bring about optimization of travel through synergies of various technologies in particular information and communication technologies [1]. The main philosophy has been employing a wide range of devices which were able to provide information of the status and whereabouts of components in a transportation system, in order to control the various parts including vehicles, people, etc. towards an optimum versus a limited set of criteria, e.g., inter-urban traffic management systems.

Nowadays with the proliferation of smartphones and tablets on the market, almost everyone has access to mobile devices, which offers better processing capabilities and access to new information and services. Taking this into account, the demand for new and more personalized services which aid users in their daily tasks is increasing. Current navigation systems lack in several ways in order to satisfy such demand, namely, accurate information about urban traffic in real-time, possibility to personalize the information used by such systems and also the need to have a more dynamic and user friendly interactions between device and traveller. In short, the current navigation systems were not designed to be intelligent enough to process humans' needs

© Springer International Publishing Switzerland 2015
I. Ciuciu et al. (Eds.): OTM 2015 Workshops, LNCS 9416, pp. 127–136, 2015.
DOI: 10.1007/978-3-319-26138-6_16

effectively, and they are not intelligent enough to understand humans' attempts to satisfy those needs.

We recognize how the proliferation of social media access to transport and traffic system's information via mobile broadband services, and the availability of information of smartphones as sensors, have changed the landscape in terms of our ability to deploy cooperative systems. Google was early to catch on this trend with their traffic information system which built on principles of crowd-sourcing [2], enabling participants in the system to contribute and benefit from shared information. Information being disseminated by social networks can have an important role in providing accurate and personalized evidence about urban traffic in real-time. Although analysis and detection of traffic events from social networks is not part of the work presented here, such efforts are part of the mobility framework being addressed by the same authors. Preliminary findings regarding mining traffic events from twitter are published in [3].

GPS-enabled devices such as smartphones and tablets, allow people to record their location histories with GPS traces, which imply human mobility habits and preferences related to personal journeys. Recently people started recording their outdoor movements using smartphones apps, such as travel experience sharing and sports activity analysis, just to name a few. Due to the exponential increase of social networks devoted to such activities, several online communities started to emerge, where users upload their GPS signals and manage their experiences over the web and share them among others.

Before understanding why personal mobility patterns are so important, first it is necessary to know what human mobility patterns are. According to the authors in [4], mobility patterns are defined as: "Human trajectories showing a high degree of temporal and spatial regularity, where each individual is characterized by a time-independent characteristic travel distance and a significant probability to return to a few highly frequented locations". Uncovering the statistical patterns that characterize the trajectories humans follow during their daily activity is not only a major intellectual challenge, but also of importance for public health, city planning, traffic engineering and economic forecasting. For example, quantifiable models of human mobility are indispensable for predicting the spread of biological pathogens or mobile phone viruses [5].

The approach addressed here, tackles mobility which is supported by vehicles (private owned vehicles), where the main objective is to proactively interact with daily commuters, by providing personalized notifications/suggestions each time an unexpected event occurs, which could influence usual traffic behaviour. In order to cope with this main objective, first it is essential to know where commuters are and predict where they are moving. i.e. to analyse their typical mobility movements (patterns) in a non-intrusive way.

In order to understand personal mobility patterns, first we need to understand where people are; how, when and where they move. To achieve that, it is essential that the access to the user location history is granted and accurate. An approach able to collect GPS data from smartphones presents several challenges. First, the approach should adopt a non-intrusive philosophy. Smartphones users are likely to stop using a mobile app in an early stage, if it demands frequent interactions between app and user. Meaning that, the approach presented, must provide users with an app which collects data from users in a non-intrusive way. Secondly, GPS signals acquired from smartphones present several irregularities, which implies that its acquisition tends to be quite complex. GPS data used under this work presents various inconsistencies/noise, which needed to be addressed. Noise can be influenced by: (i) the type of the mobile device being used to capture data; (ii) the nature of the geography itself, and; (iii) weather conditions. Also, the noise found in GPS data can be manifested into two distinct ways: (i) randomly (occasionally stationary points are interrupted by GPS signals acquired several meters away from the exact physical location of person) and; (ii) repeatedly (GPS signal is continuously being acquired several meters away from the exact physical location of person).

The idea here is to basically take GPS data streams generated by users' phones as input and create a personalized profile of typical locations and activities. The approach should be supported by novel algorithms for trajectory clustering of massive GPS signals from a baseline in parallel to compute the most typical locations of a user. Considering users' travel experiences and location interests as well as transition probability between locations, we mine the classical travel sequences from multiple users' location histories.

The innovative aspects concerning the work tackled here are related with: (i) the need to have a better guess (prediction/forecasting) of the conditions of different trajectories; and (ii) to propose better alternatives and calculate the ETA (Estimated Time of Arrival) more precisely. This means, to develop a step-wise approach which is able to acquire: (i) frequent locations; (ii) frequent trajectories; and (iii) individual urban mobility, in a non-intrusive way.

This paper is structured as follows: section 2 describes the related work, which is considered relevant for support the development of the work presented here. Section 3 presents the initial methodological approach for achieving personalized mobility. Section 4 describes some examples of the proposed approach using real data. Section 5 highlights the results collected from the extraction of frequent locations. Finally, Section 6 concludes the paper and points out future achievements.

2 Related Work

From a more high-level perspective, the overall mobility framework encompasses several branches from different areas within Intelligent Transportation Systems (ITS) and knowledge acquisition (KA). In fact, the OPTIMUM project aims to be an agglomerate enabler in terms of ITS technologies, integrating several research topics into one single system. The objective is to cover several technology branches which present great research efforts, as is the case of Traffic Prediction and Simulation [6], [7], Smart Parking [8], User Context-based Navigation Systems [9]. The objective is simple: to improve traffic and road conditions and flow, while lowering carbon emissions and pollution within the road network. Some research regarding these topics is already taking place, as evidenced in [10], and ITS generic platforms are already being developed [11]. Moreover, the above mentioned research endeavours use different types of data sources, from sensor data to floating car data, social networks, and infra-structure-gathered data.

Location-based services suggest new locations that match a user's inferred interests and preferences, making use of content-based or collaborative recommendation techniques. In most cases, distance is used as the main criteria for inclusion in recommendations. As argued by Mokbel et al. [12], location-based services usually only take the current location into account. However, apart from visiting new locations, users often visit places that they visited before [13]. These revisited places include home and work locations, but also less frequently visited places, such as specialty stores, hiking areas, friends, relatives and business partners. Several studies confirmed the intuition that human mobility is highly predictable, centred on a small number of base locations. This opens a wide range of opportunities for more intelligent recommendations and support of routine activities. Such recommendations may serve as reminders for activities or locations to be included in the user's schedule, and may be used to minimize traveling time between the destinations that a user is likely to visit. In the literature, one can find only a few studies on common travel patterns, or on locations that are typically visited on certain hours during the week or during the weekend. Such insights are expected to be useful for selecting techniques for predicting a user's travel activity and likely destinations. In this work, we analyse, visualize and discuss patterns found in a dataset of GPS trajectories. Further, we compare and analyse the performance of common prediction techniques that exploit the locations' popularity, regularity, distance and connections with other locations.

González et al. [4] studied people movements, based on a sample of 100,000 randomly selected individuals, covering a six-month time period. The results show that human mobility patterns have a high degree of spatial and temporal regularity. Further, individuals typically return to a few highly frequented locations and most travel trajectories are rather short in terms of distance and travel time.

Song et al. [5] found that 93% of human mobility is predictable; how predictable an individual's movements are, depends on the entropy of his patterns. However, for predictability it did not make a difference whether an individual's life was constrained to a 10-km neighbourhood or whether he travels hundreds of kilometres on a regular basis.

Zheng et al. [14] used GPS data for mining interesting locations and `classical sequences', based on the number of visits and the individual visitors' location interests. The outcomes are reported to be useful for tourists, who can easily discover landmarks and popular routes.

The most relevant works rely on data which is acquired by GPS devices, meaning that, the data is more accurate than the data acquired from a smartphone. Some of the challenges addressed by this work as for example, noise caused from GPS reception and semantic annotation of frequent locations, are still an open problems being addressed by the research community.

3   Methodology for Extracting Frequent Locations

This section describes the approach developed for extracting and learning personal frequent locations. Acquiring personalized mobility patterns, involves obtaining the physical locations for a person's places and typical routes that matter to his/her daily life and routines. This problem is driven by the requirements from emerging location-aware applications, which allow a user to pose location queries and obtain information in reference to places, e.g., "home", "work" or "gas station".

The proposed approach comprises three main steps: (i) extraction of frequent locations; (ii) extraction of frequent trajectories; and (iii) predicting individual urban mobility. Although this is still part of an ongoing work, results regarding the extraction of frequent locations were achieved and will be presented.

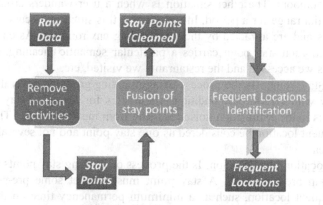

Fig. 1. Approach overview

The extraction of user frequent locations consists of the following sequential steps:

<u>Remove motion activities</u>: Is the process of removing data (gps coordinates) which indicates that commuter is moving. This is done to eliminate what movement points. If the user is on movement, it means that the point it is not stationary, therefore not a frequent location. The input is GPS raw data collected from smartphone, the output will be a collection of stay points.

The user location history is a composition of several GPS logs with different time-stamps describing the user mobility patterns. A GPS log, is basically a collection of GPS points $P=\{p1, p2,..., pn\}$. Each GPS point pi $\in$ P contains latitude (pi.Lat), longitude (pi.Lngt) and timestamp (p_i.T).

It is possible to sequentially connect GPS points into a curve based on their time serials, and split this curve into GPS trajectories (Traj) if the time interval between consecutive GPS points exceeds a certain threshold ΔT. Thus, $Traj = p_1 \rightarrow p_2 \rightarrow ... \rightarrow p_n$, where $p_i \in$ P, $p_{i+1}.T > p_i.T$ and $p_{i+1}.T - p_i.T < \Delta T$ ($1 \le i < n$).

A stay point s stands for a geographic region where a user stayed over a certain time interval. The extraction of a stay point depends on two scale parameters, a time threshold (T_{threh}) and a distance threshold (D_{threh}). A single stay point s can be regarded as a virtual location characterized by a group of consecutive GPS points $P=\{p_m, p_{m+1}, ... , p_n\}$, where $\forall m < i \le n$, $Distance(p_m, p_i) \le D_{threh}$ and $|p_n.T - p_m.T| \ge T_{threh}$.

Formally, conditioned by P, D_{threh} and T_{threh}, a stay point $s=(Lat, Lngt, arvT, levT)$, where

$$s.Lat = \sum_{i=m}^{n} p_i \cdot \frac{Lat}{|P|} \qquad (1)$$

$$s.Lngt = \sum_{i=m}^{n} p_i \cdot \frac{Lngt}{|P|} \qquad (2)$$

respectively stand for the average latitude and longitude of the collection P, and $s.arvT=p_m.T$ and $s.levT=p_n.T$ represent a user's arrival and leaving times on s.

Typically, these stay points occur in the following two situations. One is that an individual remains stationary exceeding a time threshold. In most cases, this status happens when people enter a building and lose satellite signal over a time interval until coming back outdoors. The other situation is when a user wanders around within a certain geospatial range for a period. In most cases, this situation occurs when people travel outdoors and are attracted by the surrounding environment. As compared to a raw GPS point, each stay point carries a particular semantic meaning, such as the shopping malls we accessed and the restaurants we visited, etc.

Fusion of Stay Points: Is the process of aggregating/grouping several stay points which comply with certain pre-conditions (heuristics for fusion of stay points) and also contributes to the elimination noise resulting from inaccurate data. This is so one plausible frequent location be considered as one stay point and not several stay points in a certain area.

Frequent Location Identification: Is the process of filtering stay points which comply with certain pre-conditions. A stay point must respect some pre-conditions to become a frequent location, such as a minimum permanency time on that location, and is a place visited a minimum number of times.

4   Extracting Frequent Locations

This section depicts an instantiation of the method for extraction frequent locations from raw GPS data acquired from smartphone. The dataset used, takes into account the period from 29-11-2013 to 12-09-2014, which corresponds to total of 140.246 GPS points from a single user.

Fig. 2, depicts a subset of the data source using Google Maps overlay.

Fig. 2. GPS raw data

Fig. 3 highlights a heatmap for the GPS data. From the heatmap, it is possible to detect where the highest concentration of GPS data is located. This analysis is considered useful, because it allows visualizing where are the most frequent locations. Blue color (cold) indicates low concentration of GPS points, where on the other hand, red color (hot) indicates high concentration of GPS points.

Fig. 3. Heatmap of GPS data

Fig. 4, illustrates the process of fusion stay points. The figure on the left, describes a situation where several stay points where identified. The process starts by calculating the center of the cluster for such stay points, if the distance of center of each stay point to the center of the cluster is less than a predefined threshold (δ), than the stay point can be grouped (fused). The figure on the right highlights the distance of each stay point to the center of the cluster.

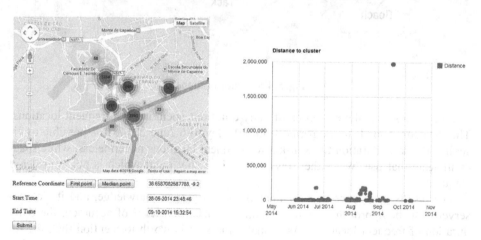

Fig. 4. Fusion of Stay Points

5   Assessment

The objective of the assessment was to validate against human judgement, how accurate were the extracted frequent locations. In order for a region in the map be considered a frequent location, the concentration of GPS points in that region must be higher a predefined threshold (γ). For now, we are taking into account the regions where the number of GPS points is higher or equal to 125 points, as in the heatmap. This threshold can be better tuned in order to obtain more accurate results.

Fig. 5, depicts the final result of the frequent locations extraction, where frequent locations are semantically identified. Despite the step related to semantic identification of a frequent location is still in development phase, it is worth to illustrate what should be the final result of this process. Basically, the idea is to match (geographically speaking) a frequent location to known locations available in social media (ex. google places, foursquare). From a general perspective, the results indicate that the approach is able to detect all frequent locations (higher recall), but at the same time, some locations were badly identified as frequent locations (lower precision). This means that, additional tuning regarding the process of fusion stay points, the γ threshold, and the process of semantically identify frequent locations, need to be addressed.

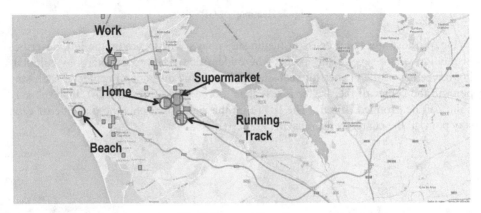

Fig. 5. Frequent Locations

Fig. 6, illustrates the extraction of daily durations spent in each frequent locations. The data corresponds to the period from 29 May to 6 June 2014. It is possible to visualize the daily duration for well-known frequent locations nevertheless, white spaces indicate that user was either traveling or in a stay point which is not considered frequent.

The results were once again validated against human knowledge, and it was observed that the approach is able to identify with a high level of accuracy, the daily duration of frequent locations. As a final remark, it is worth to mention that, the results achieved led us to conclude that the proposed methodology for extracting frequent locations is sound and presents promising results. Some minor work still needs to be carried out for better fine tune, but the principles where the methodology relies upon, are well established.

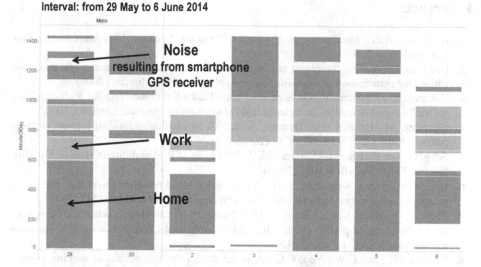

Fig. 6. Daily duration (min.) in Frequent Locations

6   Conclusions and Future Work

This paper, describes an approach for detecting and learning individual mobility plans from daily commuters. The vision is to be able to predict a frequent travel movement from point A to point B. User-generated GPS trajectories do not only connect locations in the physical world but also bridge the gap between people and locations. In this work, we are able understand most frequent locations and trajectories from users.

We observed that human mobility patterns contain strong regularities: people typically spend most of their time at and between a small number of locations. We also found that most people have a relatively regular schedule for traveling from one location to another (eg. commuting on weekdays, fixed weekend activities). The mobility patterns that we observed can be modelled with different basic methods for visitation prediction; as future work, we propose a Markov model which makes it a suitable technique for predicting individual common locations taking into account the hour of the day and the day of the week. Considering the results achieved, we believe that this work provides the first step towards understanding personal mobility patterns. The next steps are related with: (i) Identification of frequent trajectories; and (ii) Trajectory forecasting for each individual commuter.

Acknowledgment. The authors acknowledge the European Commission for its support and partial funding and the partners of the research project: H2020–644715 OPTIMUM.

References

1. IEEE.org: IEEE Intelligent Transportation Systems Society. http://sites.ieee.org/itss/ (accessed April 7, 2014)
2. Brabham, D.: Moving the crowd at iStockphoto: The composition of the crowd and motivations for participation in a crowdsourcing application. First Monday (2008)
3. Gutiérrez, C., Figueiras, P., Oliveira, P., Costa, R., Jardim-Goncalves, R.: Twitter mining for traffic events detection. In: Science and Information Conference, London (2015)
4. González, M., Hidalgo, C., Barabási, A.-L.: Understanding individual human mobility patterns. Nature **453**(7196), 779–782 (2008)
5. Song, C., Qu, Z., Blumm, N., Barabási, A.-L.: Limits of Predictability in Human Mobility. Science **327**(5968), 1018–1021 (2010)
6. Lee, W.-H., Tseng, S.-S., Tsai, S.-H.: A knowledge based real-time travel time prediction system for urban network. Expert Systems with Applications **36**, 4239–4247 (2009)
7. Tseng, P.-J., Hung, C.-C., Chang, T.-H., Chuang, Y.-H.: Real-time urban traffic sensing with GPS equipped probe vehicles. In: 12th International Conbference on ITS Telecommunications, Taipei, Taiwan (2012)
8. Chen, C.H., Hsu, C.W., Yao, C.C.: A novel design for full automatic parking system. In: 2th International Conference on ITS Telecommunications, Taipei, Taiwan (2012)
9. Hung, J.C., Lee, A.M.-C., Shih, T.K.: Customized navigation systems with the mobile devices of public transport. In: 12th International Conference on ITS Telecommunications, Taipei, Taiwan (2012)
10. Chueh, T.-H., Chou, K.-L., Liu, N., Tseng, H.-R.: An analysis of energy saving and carbon reduction strategies in the transportation sector in Taiwan. In: 12th International Conference on ITS Telecommunications, Taipei, Taiwan (2012)
11. Chen, I.-X., Wu, Y.-C., Liao, I.-C., Hsu, Y.-Y.: A high-scalable core telematics platform design for intelligent transport systems. In: 12th International Conference on ITS Telecommunications, Taipei, Taiwan (2012)
12. Mokbel, M., Bao, J., Eldawy, A., Levandoski, J., Sarwat, M.: Personalization, socialization, and recommendations in location-based services 2.0. In: PersDB 2001 Workshop, Seattle (2011)
13. Krumm, J., Brush, A.: Learning time-based presence probabilities. In: Lyons, K., Hightower, J., Huang, Elaine M. (eds.) Pervasive 2011. LNCS, vol. 6696, pp. 79–96. Springer, Heidelberg (2011)
14. Zheng, Y., Zhang, L., Xie, X., Ma, W.-Y.: Mining interesting locations and travel sequences from gps trajectories. In: 18th International Conference On World Wide Web, Madrid (2009)

A Real-Time Architecture for Proactive Decision Making in Manufacturing Enterprises

Alexandros Bousdekis[1], Nikos Papageorgiou[1], Babis Magoutas[1],
Dimitris Apostolou[2(✉)], and Gregoris Mentzas[1]

[1] Information Management Unit, National Technical University of Athens,
9 Iroon Polytechniou Str. 157 80 Zografou, Athens, Greece
{albous,npapag,elbabmag,gmentzas}@mail.ntua.gr
[2] Department of Informatics, University of Piraeus, 80 Karaoli & Dimitriou Str.
185 34 Piraeus, Greece
dapost@unipi.gr

Abstract. We outline a new architecture for supporting proactive decision making in manufacturing enterprises. We argue that event monitoring and data processing technologies can be coupled with decision methods effectively providing capabilities for proactive decision-making. We present the main conceptual blocks of the architecture and their role in the realization of the proactive enterprise. We illustrate how the proposed architecture supports decision-making ahead of time on the basis of real-time observations and anticipation of future undesired events by presenting a practical condition-based maintenance scenario in the oil and gas industry. The presented approach provides the technological foundation and can be taken as a blueprint for the further development of a reference architecture for proactive applications.

Keywords: Proactivity · Decision-making · Event-driven computing · Condition-based maintenance

1 Introduction and Motivation

The emergence of the Internet of Things paves the way for enhancing the monitoring capabilities of enterprises by means of extensive use of physical and virtual sensors generating a multitude of data. The sensing enterprise concept can influence a wide range of industries. For example, manufacturing companies can utilize sensors to enable the identification of deviations from production plans as soon as they appear; logistics networks can identify delays about in the delivery time in real-time through sensor-generated events. The main driving concept in sensing enterprises is the use of multi-dimensional data captured through physical and virtual sensors generating events and providing added value information that enhances context awareness. Consequently, the large amount of data generated by sensors leads to a strong demand for data-driven, real-time systems capable of efficiently processing data in order to get meaningful insights about potential problems.

Event monitoring and data processing accompanied with enabling real-time systems are essential for managing problems in complex, dynamic systems. Advanced

© Springer International Publishing Switzerland 2015
I. Ciuciu et al. (Eds.): OTM 2015 Workshops, LNCS 9416, pp. 137–146, 2015.
DOI: 10.1007/978-3-319-26138-6_17

monitoring capabilities should provide the basis for a new level of sensing performance that not only observes current problems, but also senses that the problem might appear, that is, by focusing on a proactive approach. Indeed, observing a delay is very useful information, but anticipating that there will be a delay is even more important from the business point of view. The capability to anticipate leads to the possibility to decide and act ahead of time, i.e., to be proactive in resolving problems before they appear or realizing opportunities before they become evident and be able to recover and support continuity.

Proactive, event-driven decision-making has been recently introduced in the literature as a conceptual model for deciding ahead of time about the optimal action and the optimal time for its implementation [1]. A proactive enterprise decision support architecture should integrate different sensor data, provide large-scale and real-time processing of sensor data and combine historical and domain knowledge with current data streams in order to facilitate proactive decision-making. In this paper we focus on proactive decision making in the manufacturing domain where the challenges associated with the provision of decision support based on predictions become significant, especially when dealing with maintenance where several factors should be considered such as costs of maintenance actions as a function of time, safety issues and degradation of equipment.

Despite the plethora of existing works for and prognosis in maintenance, most of them do not examine the integration with real-time, data-processing platforms and the automation of decisions by providing recommendations for maintenance actions, while the supported level of proactivity is typically low [2], [3]. Further, there is no support for switching easily between available decision methods or selecting a preferred method among the available ones since decision methods may address different challenges in terms of the availability of data and domain knowledge.

The integration of various decision methods in a real-time platform that would allow users to select appropriate methods based on the available data and the desired proactive decision support is the research objective for our work. Technically, the challenge is to develop a real-time architecture that would support the development of decision support applications enabling the business analyst to select decision methods and configure them so that they are operable for the problem at hand. In this paper we present such an architecture for decision making that enables the transition from sensing to proactive enterprise.

The rest of the paper is organized as follows. Section 2 discusses enabling technologies and works related to real-time architectures for enterprise decision making with an emphasis on supporting proactivity. Section 3 outlines the proposed architecture for realizing proactive enterprise decision making. Section 4 presents a scenario in which proactive decision making in maintenance is enabled with the proposed architecture. Section 5 discusses the main findings of our work and our future plans.

2   Enabling Technologies and Related Work

In the context of the sensing enterprise, physical and virtual sensing devices such as sensors, actuators and controllers can detect state changes of objects or conditions and create events, which can then be processed by a system or service. From the point of view of communication, the use of a web-service communication paradigm allows sensors to be easily integrated into a complex architecture. To this end, the Service-Oriented Architecture (SOA) paradigm strongly contributes to the development of monitoring and control infrastructures, enabling interconnectivity at an object level. Moreover, the Event Driven Architecture (EDA) provides an architectural computing paradigm that has the ability to react to changes by processing events [4], [5]. EDA can complement SOA because services can be activated by triggers fired on incoming events[6], [7]. Building on EDA, proactive event-driven computing is a new paradigm where a decision is neither made due to explicit requests nor as a response to events, but is triggered by real-time predictions of an event. Therefore, the decisions are taken under time constraints and require the exploitation of large amounts of historical and streaming data [6-8].

In the manufacturing domain, sensors have the capability of measuring a multitude of parameters frequently and collecting plenty of data. Analysis of Big Data, both historical and real-time, can facilitate predictions on the basis of which proactive maintenance decision making can be performed. The e-maintenance concept can significantly address these challenges [9-11]. DYNAMITE 'Dynamic Decisions in Maintenance' research project has examined e-maintenance [12], [13]. It developed the TELMA 'TELeMAintenance platform' which provides intelligent agents directly implemented at the shopfloor level into the PLCs and decision-making services in front of the degraded situation process performance, including assessment of the degraded process performance, prognostic of the future situation and decision to be taken to control the process in its optimal performance state. The WelCOM project developed an e-maintenance architecture exploiting the following key relevant technological factors: web-based maintenance services, wireless sensing and identification technologies, data and services integration and interoperability, as well as mobile and contextualized computing [14]. Within such a framework, the authors proposed a layered e-maintenance architecture, leveraging upon the strengths of smart and wireless components in order to upgrade the maintenance-services from the low level of operations to the higher levels of planning and decision making. For an overview of other e-maintenance platforms, both from academia and industry, please refer to [12], [13], [15], [16] and [17].

E-maintenance can be leveraged with EDA and proactive event-driven computing in order to enable proactive decision making about optimal maintenance actions and the optimal time for their implementation. To do this, e-maintenance should be extended in order to handle real-time, data-driven predictions and coupling them with domain knowledge and decision methods. Several decision methods, ranging from operational research to machine learning and statistical ones, have been proposed in the literature in support of proactive maintenance decision making. Nevertheless, decision methods have not been integrated in e-maintenance platforms yet and are rarely validated in an industrial environment.

3   A Conceptual Architecture for Decision Making in the Proactive Manufacturing Enterprise

In this section we outline the proposed architecture for proactive enterprise decision-making, its main conceptual blocks as well as the main functionality implemented by each block. The role of the architecture depicted in Figure 1 is two-fold. *Configuration role:* to allow business analysts create decision method instances addressing anticipated problems and configure them by adding, removing or changing possible mitigating actions as well as other domain knowledge required by the underlying decision methods. Domain knowledge can include the list of alternative actions, their costs, their delays (corresponding to the time period from its implementation until it starts taking effect), the time-to-undesired event after their implementation as well as the next planned maintenance. *Processing role*: to support decision-making ahead of time on the basis of real-time observations and anticipation of future undesired events, by coupling decision methods to a real-time processing environment. The proposed architecture consists of a user interaction and a real-time processing layer, along with a *data layer* which houses a relational database engine where all information needed by the two other layers is stored and retrieved.

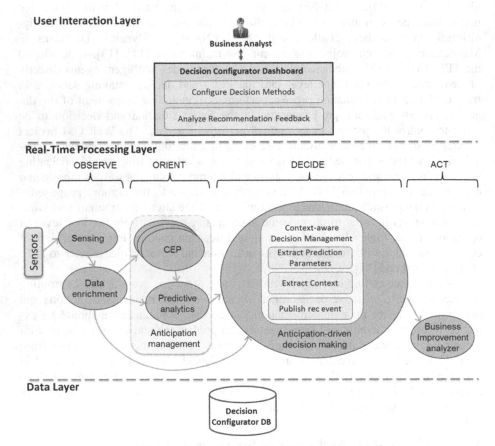

Fig. 1. Proactive Decision Making Architecture

The *user interaction layer* occupies the top level of the architecture and includes a web-based application that supports the configuration of the architecture, by allowing business analysts to select the most appropriate decision method for mitigating predicted undesired events, on the basis of functional and non-functional requirements, as well as to embed domain knowledge with the aim to define and configure the various parameters of the decision method instances. Examples of decision methods incorporated in the aforementioned decision configurator dashboard include Markov Decision Process (MDP) [1] and Cost Optimization [18], while more details are provided in [3]. Decision method instances are specific instances of decision methods, corresponding to specific equipment or other subject of a predicted undesired event. As can be seen in Figure 1, another functionality exposed by the decision configurator to the business analyst is related to the visualization of feedback received by the recipients of the recommendation with respect to the implementation of the recommended actions. This feedback aims to support business analysts in the process of refining the recommendation generation process on the basis of such feedback.

The *real-time processing layer* fulfills the processing role of the proposed proactive decision making architecture and is based on the Observe, Orient, Decide, Act (OODA) model of situational awareness [19]. This model sees decision-making occurring in a recurring cycle of unfolding interaction with the environment, oriented via cues inherent in tradition, experience and analysis. These cues inform hypotheses about the current and emerging situation that, in turn, drive actions that test hypotheses. The real-time processing layer deals with the continuous processing of sensor data by applying OODA principles and subsequent sending of notifications/recommendations to relevant people or systems. The sensor data are collected from sensors and they are injected into the real-time processing layer, where they are handled by the OODA information-processing pipeline as follows:

- (Observe) The *sensing service*, deals with data acquisition, transformation (including cleaning) and publishing. It is responsible for sensing relevant sources and transforming data in a format useful for further analysis. The sensing service is followed by the *data enrichment service* that enables semantic enrichment of real-time streams (events) with background knowledge.
- (Orient) The orient phase includes services for anticipation management, which enable the generation of real-time, data-driven predictions of future undesired events through the *predictive analytics service*. Predictions are triggered on the basis of unusual situations discovered on the basis of complex enriched events identified by the *Complex Event Processing (CEP) service*.
- (Decide) The decide phase includes services enabling anticipation-driven decision-making, in the sense that the predictions of undesired events generated by the services of the Orient phase are taken into account. More specifically, based on a "prediction" event, which predicts the probability distribution for the occurrence of a future undesired event as a function of time, the *context-aware decision management service* generates proactive recommendations of actions that mitigate or eliminate this event along with the recommended activation time. The recommended actions and action activation times are calculated by enacting the decision method instances that are defined and configured through the decision configurator. The generated proactive recommendations are further propagated within the OODA information-processing pipeline through the *publish recommendation event service*, until they reach the relevant enterprise

stakeholders. Prediction parameters and contextual elements needed by the context-aware decision making service are made available by auxiliary services responsible for *extracting* (i) *prediction parameters* from received prediction events and (ii) *contextual parameters* that are important for the enterprise decision problems considered, from enriched sensed data carrying out contextual information, respectively.

- (Act) The act phase includes the business improvement analyzer, a component which deals with the visualization of anticipation-driven recommendations, the monitoring of their success, as well as the definition and monitoring of KPIs and corresponding adaptation of the whole OODA cycle, closing the feedback loop and leading to the continual proactive business optimization.

The real-time processing layer of the architecture has been implemented as a Storm[1] topology. Storm is a distributed data processing system whose processing is based on elements organised in a topology and called spouts and bolts. Spouts, which are the entry points into the real-time processing layer, poll relevant data sources such as sensors and distribute the data further in the topology. Bolts, which are the processing elements, implement the OODA information-processing services described above. Bolts are interconnected with an internal pub/sub mechanism and communicate through messages called tuples. The Decision Configurator Dashboard of the User Interaction Layer has been implemented as a Python web-application developed using the web2py[2] framework. Web2py is an open-source web framework (released under the LGPL version 3 license) for agile development of secure database-driven web applications, written also in Python. Finally, the Data layer of the architecture includes a Database Abstraction Layer (DAL) that generates SQL statements, transparently to the developer, for many databases engines such as SQLite, MySQL, PostgreSQL, MSSQL, FireBird, Oracle, IBM DB2, Informix and Ingres.

4   Envisaged Scenario

In this section we present a practical application of the proposed architecture for proactive event-driven decision-making, in the oil and gas industry. We describe the practical role and use of the proposed architecture focusing on how it can support decision-making ahead of time on the basis of real-time observations and real-time data-driven predictions of future undesired events, through an indicative scenario of proactive Condition-Based Maintenance (CBM). The practical application is illustrated through a decision configurator dashboard that receives prediction events and enables the embodiment of domain knowledge given by an expert in order to provide recommendations for the proactive enterprise.

CBM in the oil and gas industry employs various monitoring means to detect deterioration and failure in some critical drilling equipment. Equipment failure situations can be forecasted based on observations of events related to this equipment or the surrounding environment; e.g monitoring engine temperature indicators, monitoring electric indicators (measuring change in the engine's electric properties) and perform-

---

[1] https://storm.apache.org
[2] http://web2py.com/books/default/reference/29/web2py

ing oil analysis [20]. In reality, several different patterns will imply various failure distributions. In this scenario, we focus on the gearbox drilling equipment and consider as indicators the rotation speed of the drilling machine's main shaft in Rounds Per Minute (RPM), along with the lube oil temperature of the drilling machine's gearbox [21].

The OODA model - on which the real-time processing layer of the proposed architecture is based - deals first with real-time smart sensing of RPM and lube oil temperature of the drilling machine's gearbox (Observe). In the Orient phase, a prognostic model is developed in order to estimate Remaining Useful Life (RUL) and the probability distribution of the occurrence of a gearbox breakdown. This prognostic model is triggered by detecting in real-time abnormal friction losses on the basis of observed data. The friction losses detection deals with complex patterns of oil temperature and RPM events characterized by an abnormal oil temperature rise (10% above normal) measured over 30% of the drilling period when drilling RPM exceeds a threshold. This pattern, learned at the offline phase, is a strong indication that a gearbox equipment failure starts to occur. Decide phase deals with online provision of proactive recommendations of maintenance actions (take the equipment down for full maintenance, perform lubrication of metal parts, shift drilling to lower pressure mode) and suggested activation time that maximize the utility for the manufacturing enterprise. Finally, the Act phase defines and monitors related KPIs such as downtime and cost.

The decision configurator dashboard addresses the Decide phase and enables the expert to insert domain knowledge that is needed for the provision of recommendations as it is included in the user interaction layer of the proposed architecture. The Decide phase receives a prediction event from the Orient phase and utilizes domain knowledge to provide optimal solutions for maintenance. We have selected MDP method as the most suitable for the current scenario as it is a method that can provide recommendations about the optimal action and the optimal time of applying it and therefore, it covers the user requirements [22]. The user is able to create a new decision making instance for the use of MDP method in order to provide recommendations based on the gearbox breakdown prediction. Then, the user inserts the list of actions (take the equipment down for full maintenance, perform lubrication of metal parts, shift drilling to lower pressure mode) accompanied with the cost as a function of time for each action, the delay of the action (corresponding to the time period from its implementation until it starts taking effect) and the time-to-breakdown after the implementation of each action. Moreover, the user specifies the time of next planned maintenance.

The cost of each action can be either fixed (e.g. 1000 euros) or variable as a function of time (e.g. 800 euros / day due to production loss).The duration of the delay for each action increases in proportion to the complexity of the action (e.g. full maintenance requires a longer delay in comparison to lubrication). The time-to-breakdown after the implementation of each action is related to the extent of the maintenance action. For example, full maintenance transforms the equipment to good-as-new, while lower pressure and lubrication are actions for imperfect maintenance [1], [23]. Finally, the time of next planned maintenance corresponds to the end of decision epoch parameter of MDP. So, a recommendation about a maintenance action should belong to the time period between now and the end of decision epoch in order to be valid [1]. This means that, since any defective part of equipment will be identified during the planned maintenance, the predicted gearbox breakdown will not be valid anymore after that time.

The business added value of proactive event-driven decision-making in this scenario is huge. With a typical day rate for a modern oil rig being around USD 500 000, reducing undesired downtime, with its associated high cost (one hour of saved downtime is typically worth USD 20 000) is of outmost importance in the oil drilling industry. Therefore, we expect that the proposed architecture, which supports the provision of proactive recommendations about optimal decisions on the basis of utility, cost and other factors, will allow enterprises in the oil and gas industry to gain a strong competitive advantage based on reduced downtimes and optimized performance.

5   Conclusions and Future Work

We outlined a visionary approach for a new architecture supporting proactive decision making in enterprises. The main novelty of our approach lays on the integration of state-of-the-art decision methods into an event-driven real time environment which can handle big data generated by a multitude of enterprise sensors. Although the concept of proactive decision-making in not completely new, there are still many challenges associated with its application in large scale, big data-based enterprise environments. A major challenge is the treatment of anticipation as a first class citizen: supporting the whole life-cycle of the anticipation, from sensing and generating anticipations till validating the reactions based on them, through the Observe-Orient-Decide-Act loop.

Our work has several implications for both practitioners and researchers. Practitioners need to design and implement physical (such as smart sensors and actuators, location-aware sensors, cyber-physical systems) and virtual sensors (such as agents in customer transaction and relationship systems) in virtually every aspect of their enterprise that has an impact on the end result. Moreover, practitioners should be ready to select and apply decision methods that will leverage business performance through the proactive realization of actions in anticipation of predicated enterprise challenges and opportunities. There is a need for new business methodologies that will enable recognition of possible opportunities for application decision methods in the enterprise environment, design of actions for responding to such situations as well as benchmarks for comparison real performance measurements and identified KPI's.

Researchers will be able to build on top of the proposed real-time platform new algorithms to model the data that overcome the deficiency of traditional analytic methods by fixing the granularity (resolution) of the analytic problem ahead of time. Additionally, new methods for semantic enrichment of the data with the background knowledge from ontologies describing the data domain and its contextual environment will improve the capabilities of the platform to react intelligently. Finally, new situational awareness methods for inferring users' situational state and approaches to model situational probabilistic influences on user needs as well as new data-driven and knowledge-based recommender algorithms based on streaming data can be researched so that business users are provided with the most relevant support based on rich landscape of sensed data.

Regarding future work, we aim to follow a multi-aspect approach for validating the main blocks of the proposed architecture which are currently under development in the ProaSense project. We will pursue validation in diverse enterprise settings with different technical constraints and user requirements so that the impact is leveraged. Validation will be performed on a technical level, covering system-related metrics such as performance, and on a business level, covering the benefits for end-users from the leveraged business decisions. Specifically for the maintenance perspective, validation will be focused based on performance in terms of decreased maintenance costs, decreased equipment deterioration and better quality of products that are leaving the assembly line. On the other hand, domain experts will validate the results based on factors which are usually hard to measure such as increase in safety, decrease of environmental impact and the accessibility and adaptability of the system in order to support the needs and expectations of beneficiaries. Validation of the approach will be performed in the context of the ongoing EU project ProaSense (http://www.proasense.eu/) in two main use cases: proactive manufacturing in the area of production of lighting equipment, and proactive maintenance within the oil and gas sector.

Acknowledgments. This work is partly funded by the European Commission project FP7 STREP ProaSense "The Proactive Sensing Enterprise" (612329) http://www.proasense.eu/.

References

1. Engel, Y., Etzion, O., Feldman, Z.: A basic model for proactive event-driven computing. In: 6th ACM Conf. on Distributed Event-Based Systems, pp. 107–118. ACM (2012)
2. Peng, Y., Dong, M., Zuo, M.J.: Current status of machine prognostics in condition-based maintenance: a review. J. Advanced Manuf. Technology **50**(1–4), 297–313 (2010)
3. Bousdekis, A., Magoutas, B., Apostolou, D., Mentzas, G.: A Proactive Decision Making Framework for Condition Based Maintenance. Industrial Management & Data Systems **115**(7), 1225–1250 (2015)
4. Luckham, D.: Power of events. Reading: Addison-Wesley (2002)
5. Dunkel, J., Fernández, A., Ortiz, R., Ossowski, S.: Event-driven architecture for decision support in traffic management systems. Expert Systems with Applications **38**(6), 6530–6539 (2011)
6. Engel, Y., Etzion, O.: Towards proactive event-driven computing. In: Proceedings of the 5th ACM International Conference on Distributed Event-Based System, pp. 125–136. ACM (2011)
7. Fournier, F., Kofman, A., Skarbovsky, I., Skarlatidis, A.: Extending event-driven architecture for proactive systems. In: Event Processing, Forecasting and Decision-Making in the Big Data Era (EPForDM), EDBT 2015 Workshop (2015)
8. Feldman, Z., Fournier, F., Franklin, R., Metzger, A.: Proactive event processing in action: a case study on the proactive management of transport processes. In: Proceedings of the Seventh ACM International Conference on Distributed Event-Based Systems (DEBS 2013), pp. 97–106 (2013)

9. Muller, A., Suhner, M.C., Iung, B.: Formalisation of a new prognosis model for supporting proactive maintenance implementation on industrial system. Reliability Engineering & System Safety **93**(2), 234–253 (2008)
10. Lee, J., Ni, J., Djurdjanovic, D., Qiu, H., Liao, H.: Intelligent prognostics tools and e-Maintenance. Computers in Industry, Special Issue on e-Maintenance **57**(6), 476–489 (2006)
11. Muller, A., Crespo Marquez, A., Iung, B.: On the concept of e-maintenance: review and current research. Reliability Engineering & System Safety **93**(8), 1165–1187 (2008)
12. Levrat, E., Iung, B.:TELMA: a full e-maintenance platform. In: Proceedings of the Second World Congress on Engineering Asset Management (WCEAM 2007) (2007)
13. Irigaray, A.A., Gilabert, E., Jantunen, E., Adgar, A.: Ubiquitous computing for dynamic condition-based maintenance. Journal of Quality in Maintenance Engineering **15**(2), 151–166 (2009)
14. Pistofidis, P., Emmanouilidis, C., Koulamas, C., Karampatzakis, D., Papathanassiou, N.: A layered e-maintenance architecture powered by smart wireless monitoring components. In: Proceedings of the 2012 International Conference on Industrial Technology (ICIT 2012), pp. 390–395. IEEE (2012)
15. Iung, B., Levrat, E., Marquez, A.C., Erbe, H.: Conceptual framework for e-Maintenance: Illustration by e-Maintenance technologies and platforms. Annual Reviews in Control **33**(2), 220–229 (2009)
16. Campos, J., Jantunen, E., Prakash, O.: A web and mobile device architecture for mobile e-maintenance. The International Journal of Advanced Manufacturing Technology **45**(1–2), 71–80 (2009)
17. Macchi, M., Crespo Márquez, A., Holgado, M., Fumagalli, L., Barberá Martínez, L.: Value-driven engineering of E-maintenance platforms. Journal of Manufacturing Technology Management **25**(4), 568–598 (2014)
18. Elwany, A.H., Gebraeel, N.Z.: Sensor-driven prognostic models for equipment replacement and spare parts inventory. IIE Transactions **40**(7), 629–639 (2008)
19. Boyd, J.R.: The Essence of Winning and Losing. Unpublished lecture notes (1996)
20. Jagadish, H.V., Gehrke, J., Labrinidis, A., Papakonstantinou, Y., Patel, J.M., Ramakrishnan, R., Shahabi, C.: Big data and its technical challenges. Communications of the ACM **57**(7), 86–94 (2014)
21. Magoutas, B., Stojanovic, N., Bousdekis, A., Apostolou, D., Mentzas, G., Stojanovic, L.: Anticipation-driven architecture for proactive enterprise decision making. In: CAiSE 2014, pp. 121–128 (2014)
22. Bousdekis, A., Magoutas, B., Apostolou, D., Mentzas, G.: Supporting the selection of prognostic-based decision support methods in manufacturing. In: Proceedings of the 17th International Conference on Enterprise Information Systems (ICEIS 2015), pp. 487–494 (2015)
23. Jardine, A.K., Lin, D., Banjevic, D.: A review on machinery diagnostics and prognostics implementing condition-based maintenance. Mechanical Systems and Signal Processing **20**(7), 1483–1510 (2006)

Osmotic Event Detection and Processing for the Sensing-Liquid Enterprise

Artur Felic[1(✉)], Spiros Alexakis[1], Carlos Agostinho[2], Catarina Marques-Lucena[2], Klaus Fischer[3], and Michele Sesana[4]

[1] CAS Software AG, CAS-Weg 1-5, 76131 Karlsruhe, Germany
{artur.felic,spiros.alexakis}@cas.de
[2] Centre of Technology and Systems, CTS, Uninova, 2829-516 Caparica, Portugal
{ca,cml}@uninova.pt
[3] DFKI GmbH, 66123 Saarbrücken, Germany
klaus.fischer@dfki.de
[4] TXT e-solutions, 20126 Milan, Italy
michele.sesana@txtgroup.com

Abstract. The Sensing-Liquid Enterprise paradigm enhances sensing capabilities of the Sensing Enterprise with fuzzy boundaries of the Liquid Enterprise by interconnecting real, virtual and digital worlds through semi-permeable membrane behavior. Shadow images of the different worlds need to be kept consistent. Osmotic data flows between the real, digital and virtual world allow events to break out of their inner world behavior and to advance to inter-world events.

This paper combines semantic web technologies and complex event processing to enable osmotic event detection and processing for the Sensing-Liquid Enterprise. Events are enriched with semantic information and examined for inter-world relevance. The presented approach is accompanied with its application in the OSMOSE Project.

Keywords: Sensing Enterprise · Sensing-Liquid Enterprise · Semantic web · Complex event processing

1 Introduction

The Sensing-Liquid Enterprise paradigm combines the characteristics of the Sensing Enterprise and the Liquid Enterprise [1]. The Sensing Enterprise has the capability to sense and react to business stimuli while the intelligence is decentralized in connected environments. Active cooperation of things with advanced networking and processing capabilities form a sort of nervous system connecting the real and virtual world. The Liquid Enterprise is characterized by fuzzy and blurred enterprise boundaries. The 'inside' and 'outside' is difficult to distinguish leading to cloudiness of the enterprise. The characteristics of the Sensing and the Liquid Enterprise combined cause the necessity to handle real, virtual and digital assets as well as their interaction and behavior. The main objectives of the OSMOSE Project [2] is to interconnect the real,

I. Ciuciu et al. (Eds.): OTM 2015 Workshops, LNCS 9416, pp. 147–156, 2015.
DOI: 10.1007/978-3-319-26138-6_18

virtual and digital world osmotically, i.e. the same way a semi-permeable membrane permits the flow of liquid particles through itself, in order to keep background consistency of shadow images in the worlds.

Events that occur in any of the worlds need to be analyzed and distinguished regarding their relation to the other worlds. Semantic descriptions of entities enable reasoning about the belonging to the worlds. Queries for event properties allow to detect whether the event needs to be osmotic, i.e. be processed between the worlds, or not. Thus, new challenges for Event-Driven Architectures, business process modelling and semantic web technologies appear to deal with multiple representations of the same object in each world automatically.

The paper is structured as follows: Section 2 will introduce the OSMOSE framework and the metaphor from biology. In Section 3, a state-of-the-art analysis of (semantic) complex event processing is provided. Section 4 presents the main approach and Section 5 gives a brief example from the OSMOSE Project. The conclusion and future work can be found in Section 6.

2   Osmotic Sensing-Liquid Enterprise Framework

2.1   The OSMOSE Metaphor

The liquid enterprise can be considered as an enterprise having fuzzy boundaries, in terms of human resources, markets, products and processes. Its strategies and operational models will make it difficult to distinguish the 'inside' and the 'outside' of the company [1]. The liquid enterprise concept can be better explain adopting a metaphor from physics. Thus, let us imaging that the Sensing-Liquid Enterprise is a pot internally subdivided into three sectors by means of three membranes and forming the real/digital/virtual sector [3] [4]. If the membrane is totally impermeable, the population of the three liquids (worlds) will never mix together and, if they want to communicate, they need to send blind messages across the membranes. This meets the classical definition of interoperability, which is defined as the ability of disparate and diverse organizations to interact towards mutually beneficial and agreed common goals, involving the sharing of information and knowledge between them [5]. However, in those interoperability scenarios, enterprises, organizations, or even people and objects are from different worlds (liquids) and act as totally independent entities.

On the other hand, if the membranes are semi-permeable, by following the rules of osmosis, each of the world's population could pass through the membrane and influences the neighboring world, so that in reality in the real world is possible to find a shadow (interoperability) ambassadors of the digital/virtual world and similarly for the other worlds. Such feature enable the user to experience multiple views (perspectives) on the same entities, events and associated processes, etc. Thus, using a three world interface and the osmose membrane the user can seamlessly move from one world to the other, accessing information from different worlds, and consequently have control over manufacturing processes execution. As an example, if mistakes are made during the manufacturing process and validation will result in large expenses to the manufacturer. However, it may occur that parts were correctly produced and the problems detected by the user are consequences of bad usage. In that case, a concrete proof that the part was correctly built is needed. It can be facilitated by the archival of detailed 3D model of the part, corresponding to the exact copy of the delivered product. This enables the virtual (RW → VW) recalling to the moment the part came out of the warehouse.

2.2   Osmotic Event-Driven Architecture and Implementation

The conceptual architecture follows the OSMOSE metaphor, in which the three worlds, namely the real, digital and virtual world, are separated from each other and bound by a semi-permeable membrane. The overall OSMOSE architecture is illustrated in Figure 1. Communication between the three worlds has to pass the membranes between the worlds, which is incorporated in the OSMOSE middleware. Event processing is a key aspect in the OSMOSE architecture. The requirement to provide background consistency among the worlds and to enable osmotic behavior led to the need of a new Event-Driven Architecture for the OSMOSE Project.

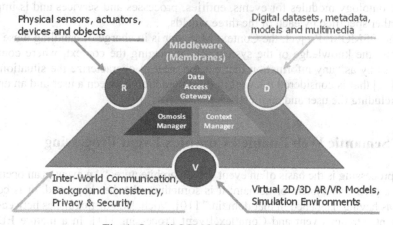

Fig. 1. Overall OSMOSE Architecture

Events are the most important entities the membrane is directly concerned with. In each world a complex event processing engine is actively detecting events. When events are detected the context manager, which is responsible for semantic analysis of events, is responsible for deciding on whether this event is osmotic, i.e. needs to be passed to another world, or whether it will stay local.

As an example we can take a look at the aeronautics pilot. A lamp of a beamer in a flight simulator might have a temperature which is too high for a longer period. When this event is detected the context manager reasons on it and comes up with the decision that it is necessary to trigger the scheduling of a maintenance procedure for the beamer lamp. The event is passed to the digital world where it results in the process of scheduling the maintenance procedure for the lamp.

2.3   Osmotic Knowledge and Context Management Approach

Major objectives of knowledge management are knowledge creation, sharing and reuse [6]. In the OSMOSE Project, knowledge is created inside each of the worlds and shared in and outside of each world. Hence, it is extremely important to consider the special requirements that come along with the Sensing-Liquid Enterprise paradigm. Semantic Web technologies, i.e. ontologies have been widely adopted in knowledge management to structure knowledge in a machine-readable manner. They enable proper communication and collaboration in physically or virtually distributed environments where knowledge is heterogeneous [7].

The differentiation of real, virtual and digital assets complicate the application of classic knowledge management approaches. On the one hand it would be eligible to implement a centralized knowledge base for the three worlds, on the other hand separated knowledge bases allow each of the world to manage knowledge independently. The latter case implies a loss of a shared meaning of knowledge which is inevitable for proper inter-world communication. Modular ontologies [8] allows to separate the ontologies of the worlds from each other while adhering to a greatest common divisor of knowledge also known as upper ontology. The upper ontology module incorporates generic ontology modules for events, entities, processes and services and is imported and further specified by each of the three worlds.

In the OSMOSE Project, the Context Manager is in charge of handling these ontologies and the knowledge of the system, i.e. managing the context, where context is described by as "any information that can be used to characterize the situation of an entity [...] that is considered relevant to the interaction between a user and an application, including the user and applications themselves" [9].

3   Semantic Web Enabled Complex Event Processing

Event processing is the basis of an event driven architecture. "An event is an occurrence within a particular system or domain; it is something that has happened, or is contemplated as having happened in that domain." [10]. Michelson distinguishes between Simple Event, Stream Event and Complex Event Processing [11]. In a mature EDA the three basic styles are most of the time used together. OSMOSE's aim is to define from a methodological point of view how to deal with existing concepts and tools.

The main interest of OSMOSE is to investigate osmosis processes where events are passed between the real, digital, and virtual worlds. In the first place this means that event processing needs to take place in all three worlds and events have to be classified according to whether they trigger an osmosis process. Therefore, only a simple envelope is defined to pass on information between the different worlds. The following example shows an instance of such an event envelope:

```
<domain> Aeronautics </domain>
<worldID> Real World </worldID>
<eventType> Critical Error </eventType>
<timeStamp> Time </timeStamp>
<eventResourceURI> URI </eventResourceURI>
<dataURI> URI </dataURI>
```

We combined the ontologies from the BPMN 2.0 event package and linking open descriptions of events (LODE) [12] to classify and describe the events in the three different worlds. The osmosis processes which transfer the events from one world into another are themselves described in BPMN 2.0 [13].

The Semantic Web takes its name from the idea of a World Wide Web that is meaningfully described for humans and machines [14]. Meaning and relation between terms can be described by Ontologies. Semantic Complex Event Processing [15] combines the power of Complex Event Processing described in the previous section with semantic descriptions of events.

In the OSMOSE Project, knowledge can be accessed via the Context Manger. A SPARQL [16] query interface enables the Complex Event Processor of the middleware to query for semantic information about events and thus decide on the basis of knowledge inside the knowledge base. Hence, events that are related to entities, services, processes or other events of other worlds than the source world the event has arisen can be detected. These events are called osmotic events and break through the semi-permeable membrane.

4   Osmotic Event Detection and Processing

4.1   Osmotic Process Modeling

The progressive adoption of Business Process Management (BPM) paradigm by organizations puts the spotlight on the business process lifecycle and on tools and technologies to support each stage of process modeling [17]. Moreover, large-scale organizations need to connect thousands of variables when modeling their processes. These processes can change several times after the process first model, being continuously improved and adapted to the organization needs. Thus, it is important to keep trace of the business requirements that originated a change in the process and the impact that it will have in terms of specific technologies.

In the case of the OSMOSE Sensing-Liquid Enterprise paradigm, osmosis processes are a special type of business processes used to moderate the information exchanged among the worlds. Since the notion of osmosis processes is conceptual, they can be modeled using the same strategies of regular business processes. In the scope of the OSMOSE project, six processes were considered, corresponding to every possible transition between the three worlds. These processes are [4]: Digitalization, Actuation, Enrichment, Simulation, Virtualization and Augmentation.

It is assumed that the adoption of model driven practices and standard notation are able to facilitate the interoperability and communication at both the modeling and technical levels [18]. Research in Enterprise Interoperability (EI) suggests that organizations can seamlessly interoperate with others at all stages of development, as long as they keep their business objectives aligned, software applications communicating, and the knowledge and understanding of the domain harmonized [19].

The Model Driven Service Engineering Architecture (MDSEA) architecture proposed by Ducq et al. [20] supports services and processes modeling stage and guides the transformation from the business requirements (Business Service Model, BSM) into detailed specification of components that need to be implemented (Technology Specific Models, TSM). The MDSEA approach implies that the different models, obtained via model transformation from the upper-level ones, should use dedicated service/process modeling languages that represent the system at ICT, Human and Physical levels with the appropriate description [21].

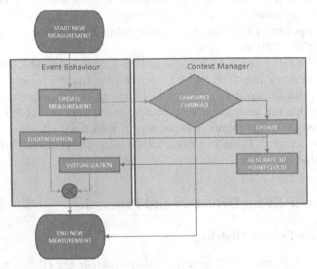

Fig. 2. Osmotic Event Behavior Exemplified

4.2   Semantic Event Detection and Decision Making

The osmotic processes are instantiated when appropriate events are detected, i.e. when they are classified as relevant for other worlds. Such events need to pass the middleware. Therefore, they are caught by the Complex Event Processor. The Context Manager provides semantic descriptions comprising (inferred) information about the entities involved in inter-world communication and is used for decision making about further event processing. In case that it is detected that an event has a direct or indirect relation to another world, the appropriate osmotic process described in the previous section is instantiated for inter-world transition.   Figure 2 gives a shortened example of the osmotic event behavior. When a new measurement arrives at the middleware, the corresponding part is checked for changes since the last measurements and updated in the digital world via the digitalization process and in the virtual world via the virtualization process if a change was identified. Otherwise, no osmotic process needs to be instantiated.

4.3   Runtime Osmotic Event Processing

CEP evaluates a confluence of events to derive actions to take. Events may cross event types and occur over a long period of time. OSMOSE builds on the complex event processing engine Esper [22] which uses a relational data models and the Event

Processing Language (EPL) as a query language. EPL is quite similar to the query language SQL for relational databases but allows additionally to define time intervals in which the matching objects popped up. With EPL it is possible to define complex rules for event detection. In case events are detected new tuples/object might be inserted into the database of the CEP engine which might result in a cascade of detected events or outside processes are triggered which are designed to deal with the events. Events can consult the Context Manager, a Semantic Web service based on Apache Jena [23]. Its API allows to query for event properties that makes inter-world communication necessary. The queries are set up on the (inferred) knowledge bases. Once an event is detected it triggers a process in the respective world. Processes are described in BPMN 2.0 and executed in the jBPM [24] process execution engine. The process might just run locally in the world in which the event originally arose or trigger an osmotic process that decides on whether the event needs to be passed to a different world and, if yes, to which world. Figure 3 shows an example for an osmotic process from the Manufacturing pilot. In the process of tracing the life-cycle of a part, a deviation map is produced in the digital world. In a deviation map the difference between the physical part and its digital CAD data is computed with the help of a 3D laser scan of the physical part. The deviation map is evaluated in the digital world.

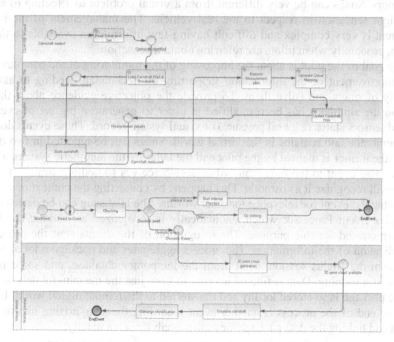

Fig. 3. BPMN Process Description of an Osmotic Process.

5   Sensing-Liquid Enterprise Application in the OSMOSE Project

Into the aeronautics pilot the events are correlated to the monitoring of a complex system identified in a Full Flight Simulator. The simulator is used for the training of pilots and it is composed by different components. First of all it has the perfect replica of the real command cabin and cockpit of the real helicopter. The complementary part is related to the software simulating the flight that is a dynamic simulation system taking inputs from the cockpit interactions, simulating the flight including weather conditions and/or injected vehicle malfunctions and providing output to the hardware proper of the simulator including the projection of the visual on the dome, the motion system and the cockpit again. The simulator is the basis of the real world together with the pilot, the instructor pilot and the maintenance technician. The digital world is composed by the software managing the simulator, including the scheduling, the configuration control and the snag management. The whole picture is complemented by the virtual word in which the configuration control heuristic are placed. Being the simulator a complex and dynamic system occasionally snags can happen. A snag is a difference perceived from the actual behavior of the simulator and the supposed right behaviors. Snags can be very different, from a visual problem to a feeling of a different flight sensation in respect to the real vehicle. The management of the snag assessment is very complex and difficult having few information available to the technician, especially when pilots are referring about a sensation.

The goal of the pilot is about the improving of the monitoring of the complex system and improvement of the information supporting the technician needing to assess the validity of snags and solve them. To provide the objective evidence about the flight session the simulator has been modified in order to generate a big set of events like virtual sensors status (e.g.: oil pressure) or visual system record. Those events don't pass the membrane and remains in the virtual world. Snags can be reported in two different ways: the former is manual by the pilot and the latter by the automatic system. The pilot send a snag event to the membrane when sees/perceives something strange, the membrane will recognize it as osmotic. This happens by contacting the context manager and analyzing the event for relevance for other worlds. The HW snag can be detected by the Complex Event Processor which automatically is recognized as osmotic due to rules that are created for this purpose. The recognition of the events start the processes of digitalization of the information. The process aggregates and package a lot of information from the flights session, some from the temporary database, and some from the system still running. Data is filtered in order to keep just the meaningful data and, finally, the package is so stored locally and transferred to the remote digital world. In particular the end of the process is another event recording the snag arising into the digital world and linking the data package for further analysis semantically.

6   Conclusion and Future Work

The present paper presents an approach for detection and processing of osmotic events between the real, virtual and digital world. Semantic information can be analyzed and processed automatically. Event behavior may be directly interpreted from the event descriptions, or indirectly queried by reasoning of the event ontology taking domain knowledge about the context of the event into account. Next steps comprise further evaluation of the architecture and conceptual framework as well as finalization of the architecture, implementation and deployment into the proof of concept scenarios of the OSMOSE Framework. In its current form the approach is limited to transactional processes with no real-time requirements on the communication technology. Domain processes and with this also osmosis processes might run over hours or even days where the number of events arising for a specific process is reasonably small. However, massive amount of events for a specific process depending on how long the process is active is still possible. But event processing with high frequency data input is not in the scope of the OSMOSE project.In the presented effort for modelling processing and reasoning over events is rather high. It is therefore highly desirable that models can be shared between different projects. With this an ecosystem of process and event models could arise which in the end would include best practice processes and events for different application domains.

Acknowledgments. Authors would like to acknowledge the European funded Project OSMOSE (FP7 610905) that supported the development of various ideas, concepts and use case presented.

References

1. FInES Research Roadmap Force: FInES Reasearch Roadmap 2025 (2012). http://cordis.europa.eu/fp7/ict/enet/documents/fines-research-roadmap-v30_en.pdf (accessed January 1, 2015)
2. OSMOSE Consortium: The OSMOSE Project (2013). http://www.osmose-project.eu (accessed July 24, 2015)
3. Agostinho, C., Jardim-Goncalves, R.: Sustaining interoperability of networked liquid-sensing enterprises: A complex systems perspective. Annu. Rev. Control (2015)
4. Agostinho, C., Sesana, M., Jardim-Gonçalves, R., Gusmeroli, S.: Model-driven service engineering towards the manufacturing liquid-sensing enterprise. In: 4th Int. Cce Model. Softw. Dev. (2015)
5. ISA Interoperability Solutions for European Public Administrations: European Interoperability Framework (EIF) for European public services (2010). http://ec.europa.eu/isa/documents/isa_annex_ii_eif_en.pdf
6. Meihami, B., Meihami, H.: Knowledge management a way to gain a competitive advantage in firms (evidence of manufacturing companies). In: Int. Lett. Soc. Humanist. Sci., Nr. 14, pp. 80–91 (2014)
7. Leung, N.K., Lau, S.K., Fan, J.: An ontology-based collaborative knowledge management network to enhance the reusability of inter-organizational knowledge. In: Commun. IIMA, Nr. 9/1, pp. 61–78 (2009)
8. Ben Abbès, S., Scheuermann, A., Meilender, T., d'Aquin, M.: Characterizing modular ontologies. In: Proc. of the 6th International Workshop on Modular Ontologies (2012)

9. Abowd, G.D., Dey, A.K., Brown, P.J., Davies, N., Smith, M., Steggles, P.: Towards a better understanding of context and context-awareness. In: Gellersen, H.-W. (ed.) HUC 1999. LNCS, vol. 1707, pp. 304–307. Springer, Heidelberg (1999)

10. Etzion, O., Niblett, P.: Event Processing in Action. Manning Pub. Co (2011)

11. Michelson, B.M.: Event-Driven Architecture Overview. Patricia Seybold Group 2 (2006)

12. Shaw, R., Troncy, R., Hardman, L.: LODE: linking open descriptions of events. In: Gómez-Pérez, A., Yu, Y., Ding, Y. (eds.) ASWC 2009. LNCS, vol. 5926, pp. 153–167. Springer, Heidelberg (2009)

13. Natschläger, C.: Towards a BPMN 2.0 ontology. In: Dijkman, R., Hofstetter, J., Koehler, J. (eds.) BPMN 2011. LNBIP, vol. 95, pp. 1–15. Springer, Heidelberg (2011)

14. Berners-Lee, T., Hendler, J., Lassila, O.: The Semantic Web (2001). http://iir.ruc.edu.cn/pdf/The%20Semantic%20Web.pdf

15. Schaaf, M., Grivas, S.G., Ackermann, D., Diekmann, A., Koschel, A., Astrova, I.: Semantic complex event processing. In: Recent Researches in Applied Information Science (2012)

16. W3C: SPARQL (2008). http://www.w3.org/TR/rdf-sparql-query/

17. Delgado, A., Ruiz, F., García-Rodríguez de Guzmán, I., Piattini, M.: MINERVA: model drIveN and sErvice oRiented framework for the continuous business process improVement and relAted tools. In: Dan, A., Gittler, F., Toumani, F. (eds.) ICSOC/ServiceWave 2009. LNCS, vol. 6275, pp. 456–466. Springer, Heidelberg (2010)

18. Larrucea, X., Díez, A.B.G., Mansell, J.X.: Practical model driven development process. In: Proc. 2nd Eur. Work. Model Driven Archit. with an Emphas. Methodol. Transform (2004)

19. Berre, A., Elvesæter, B., Figay, N., et al.: The athena interoperability framework. In: 3rd Int. Conf. Interoperability Enterp. Softw. Appl. (2007)

20. Ducq, Y., Chen, D., Alix, T.: Principles of servitization and definition of an architecture for model driven service sys-tem engineering. In: 4th Int IFIP Work Conf Einterprise Interoperability (IWEI 2012)

21. Agostinho, C., Bazoun, H., Zacharewicz, G., et al.: Information models and transformation principles applied to servitization of manufacturing and service systems design. In: Proc. 2nd Int. Conf. Model Eng. Softw. Dev. (2014)

22. EsperTech: EsperTech – Esper (2015). http://www.espertech.com/esper/ (accessed August 26, 2015)

23. Apache Software Foundation: Apache Jena (2015). https://jena.apache.org/ (accessed August 24, 2015)

24. Red Hat Inc.: jBPM - Open Source Business Process Management (2015). http://www.jbpm.org/ (accessed August 24, 2015)

PiE - Processes in Events: Interconnections in Ambient Assisted Living

Monica Vitali and Barbara Pernici[✉]

Politecnico di Milano, Milano, Italy
{monica.vitali,barbara.pernici}@polimi.it

Abstract. In the era of Internet of Things (IoT), sensors distributed in the environment can provide essential information to be exploited. In this work we propose to exploit the advantage of a sensor-enriched environment for supporting the processes of several cooperating organizations. Our approach, PiE (Processes in Events), aims to identify and exploit interconnections between processes, without demanding the restructuring of their inner structure. Starting from a set of events generated by sensors and business processes (BPs), we propose a methodology for multiple process annotation. From the analysis of the events correlations, we can discover interconnections among processes of several organizations involved in the same goal and derived additional information about the processes being executed. An example within an Ambient Assisted Living (AAL) scenario is studied, where several organizations cooperate to provide social and health care to a subject.

1 Introduction

Nowadays, organizations cooperate in order to provide a better service to their customers, by combining their expertise. Most of the time, they act separately, without any high level coordination, following an independent process to provide their contribution. This approach is problematic from several points of view. First of all, the information items over which the processes of the different organizations work are not independent, and the data used and produced by each of them should be shared to provide a better service. Another relevant aspect is that these processes, even if independently executed by different organizations, are not actually independent. In fact, they are implicitly related to each other and this relation should be exploited in order to provide a better global service.

In addition, several sensors could be available in the environment, not necessarily related to the process execution: also events generated by these sensors can be exploited to provide additional useful information on the processes and their possible implicit dependencies.

In this work, we aim to discover implicit relations among processes and events, and to exploit this knowledge to provide additional information about the global process. To achieve this goal, we propose the PiE (Process in Events) methodology: starting from a set of business processes (BPs) and from a set of events recorded during the execution of the processes, we aim to provide a deeper

© Springer International Publishing Switzerland 2015
I. Ciuciu et al. (Eds.): OTM 2015 Workshops, LNCS 9416, pp. 157–166, 2015.
DOI: 10.1007/978-3-319-26138-6_19

knowledge about the global process, analyzing relations between processes and events, between events, and between processes. This knowledge, acquired in an automatic way, can also be exploited for conducting advanced analysis about the behaviour of the involved processes. As an example, we show how PiE can be applied to a case of health and social care of elderly people in an Ambient Assisted Living (AAL) scenario.

The paper is organized as follows. In Sect. 2 we discuss related work. In Sect. 3 we describe a running example. Sect. 4 illustrates the events being considered in the analysis. Sect. 5 describes the first phase of the methodology, in which relationships between different types of events events are discovered. In the second phase, illustrated in Sect. 6, possible ways of analyzing global processes through mining information from events are discussed.

2   State of the Art

The need of living in a sensitive and interacting environment has brought to the study of technologies needed to realize such an environment, e.g. Ambient Intelligence (AmI) and Internet of Things (IoT). One of the first definitions of AmI can be found in [3] where it is described as a developing technology to enhance the sensitivity and the reactivity of the environment to the human presence. In [6] authors envision the future as a non perceivable integration of technology in the environment to ease and improve human life. The six features of this enriched environment are defined in [5]: sensitive, adaptive, reactive, transparent, ubiquitous, and intelligent. This environment produces a big amount of information that has to be managed for getting advantage of its richness.

Information gathered by AmI and IoT can be also used to support business processes of several kinds. An event-based approach has been proposed as a basis of business process modelling by several authors. A summary of the main approaches is described in Weske's book [11]. In particular, many approaches are based on events related to the start and end of processes and activities, and on other significant events for the process, such as incoming and outgoing message exchanges, time outs, exceptions, cancellation and termination. In the area of business process analysis, first workflow mining [1] and, later, process mining [2] have been proposed to derive process models from logs of events, with different purposes: reconstructing actual process models from events of activities, to avoid the complex and error-prone manual design activities; comparing actual flows with the designed ones in order to check for compliance; discovering new flows in addition to the ones which have been originally designed. The recent challenges mentioned in [10] are being considered also for analysing the relation between processes and events. The challenge presented in BPI 2015[1] asks to identify how changes in the organization or in the procedures or regulations have affected the processes in general, to identify possible improvements, or the impact of some changes. In [8], the authors started to propose a systematic approach to analyze sets of events originating from a process not only for process mining, but also to

---

[1] http://www.win.tue.nl/bpi/2015/challenge

derive some additional information to relate the events occurring in a process. It is possible, for instance, to uncover bottlenecks or other problems, by adding to the original events log trace other information related to event derived from the process log, such as associating the duration of an activity to its starting event, or the next activity in the trace. In this way it is possible to build decision trees to answer questions about possible process characteristics. In [9], the proposal to extend process logs with events from supplementary sources is focused on recognizing missing events with the support of other traces. In our paper, we want to extend the possibility of analyzing related events examining not only internal events or information within a process, but also external events derived from other processes and from sensors.

3   Running Example

Nowadays, the assistance at home of elderly and non sufficient people is an important topic from a social and care perspective. Moreover, it can significantly benefit from the support of technologies. We consider a typical context in which AAL can be employed. The subject lives in an environment enriched with sensors and devices to collect useful information about his social and health care status. Several organizations can interact to provide assistance to the subject, each of them with its own processes to follow. These organizations, even if not directly coordinated, need to share common information and to be aware of important events related to the subject. This information may be composed of different kinds of data, such as data coming from sensors inside the house of the subject, or data produced by the BPs. From the collection and the analysis of these data, useful information can emerge to help in providing assistance.

The technological infrastructure to provide such an environment is being developed within the Attiv@bili project, centred on a middleware realised to exchange events between all operators in home care [7]. In the running example, we consider two BPs, part of the Attiv@bili scenario: (i) the *Operator Process* models the activities performed by an operator involved in the assistance process and the interactions with the subject (Fig. 1(a)); (ii) the *Administration Process* models a process performed by the administration in order to decide the activities needed for the subject and to manage reports and payments to the operators (Fig. 1(b)). The environment is enriched with sensors which monitor the environment and create events: devices installed in the house of the subject allow the registration of the exit and entrance of operators; wearable devices, in the specific case a wrist watch, monitor physiological parameters and activities of the subject (fall and stillness detection, exit and entrance in the house). Finally, other events may be manually created and inserted in the system through a web interface by operators, such as the registration of a health service or the approval of a plan for health and social care for a new subject.

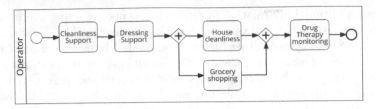

(a) The operator process

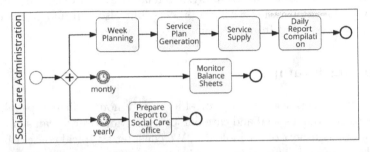

(b) The administration process

Fig. 1. Attiv@bili: two examples of social/health care processes

4 Events Classification

In the proposed approach, events are information captured and recorded in the system, coming from several sources. Through events it is possible to detect important phases of the processes and to collect information generated by sensors and/or devices belonging to the observed environment. According to this definition, an event is a generic container of information with a well-specified structure. The description of the structure of events goes beyond the scope of this paper, since whichever format is adopted, it is not a limitation for the approach. The only constraint is to have a shared structure for all the events and that the system is designed in order to capture relevant information. In the methodology we distinguish between two categories of events:

- *Process Events* (P): they are generated during the execution of one of the processes of the organizations. In this category we find start/end events generated by the activities, together with information generated during the activity execution. This kind of events is directly connected to the process and can be easily mapped to the execution of a specific activity. In this category we distinguish between *internal* and *external events*. Internal events are directly connected to a specific process, while external events may have a relation with events being generated by other processes.
- *Environmental Events* (E): these events are generated by sensors distributed in the environment or placed in devices provided to the subject in order to monitor physiological activities. This information is not directly linked to the processes, but can have an indirect relation with some of them.

Table 1. Events classification in the Attiv@bili platform

ID|Name	|Cat.|Description
T_1 |Operator Entrance |E	|Records when an operator enters into the subject house
T_2 |Operator Exit	|E	|Records when an operator exits from the subject house
T_3 |Service Registration|P	|Records a service performed by an operator
T_4 |Expense Report	|P	|Records a cost paid for offering a service to the subject
T_5 |Drugs Report	|P	|Generation of a report about the drug therapy of the subject
T_6 |Payment Emission |P	|Records a payment addressed for a service by the social care
T_7 |Week Plan Creation|P	|Records when a week plan is created for a subject
T_8 |Subject Fall	|E	|Detects the fall of the subject
T_9 |Subject Immobility |E	|Detects a lasting absence of movement for the subject

For each category, several types of events can be defined by providing a description of their structure and the kind of information carried by them. Every time a specific event is recorded, we call it an event instance.

Definition 1. *An event instance e_i is the recording of an event detected in the observed environment. It is defined by a tuple $e_i = < c, T_j, ts >$, where c is the information recorded in the event (content), T_j is the type to which it belongs, and ts is the timestamp at which it has been recorded.*

Tab. 1 contains a classification of events recorded in the Attiv@bili platform that are useful for our case study.

5   Multiple Process Annotation

In PiE we exploit the availability of information contained in the events to acquire a deeper knowledge about the processes involved in the global scenario and about their hidden interrelations. We claim that this knowledge can be important to better understand each of the systems involved and to improve the way each organization operates in the described scenario. The proposed PiE methodology consists of two main phases: (i) multiple process annotation; (ii) process mining (see Sect. 6). In this section we describe the first phase. The idea is to start with a set of processes described in a notation representing the set of activities composing the process and the order in which they are executed. Given this information, we imagine to immerse the process in the pool of events, obtaining a set of annotated and interconnected processes. The annotation procedure consists of three steps:

1. *Events to Processes Mapping*: events are analysed to find a relation between them and the activities of each of the involved processes (Sect. 5.1);

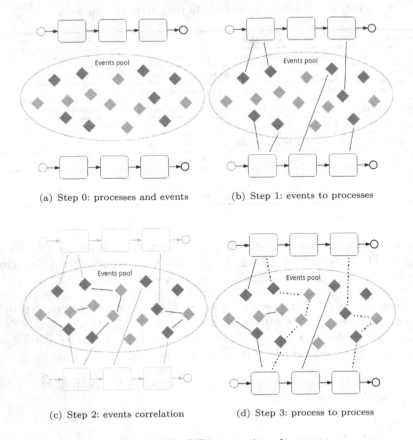

(a) Step 0: processes and events   (b) Step 1: events to processes

(c) Step 2: events correlation   (d) Step 3: process to process

Fig. 2. The PiE annotation phase

2. *Events Correlation Discovery*: the pool of event instances is analysed to find implicit relations among event types, building a network of events describing the discovered interconnections (Sect. 5.2);
3. *Process to Process Interconnection*: events interconnections and the mapping of events to processes are used to find indirect relations among processes, discovering hidden dependencies. (Sect. 5.3).

Fig. 2 shows a graphical representation of the approach. In Fig. 2(a) two processes are represented together with their pool of events: process events are shown using a darker colour and environmental events in lighter colour. In the rest of this section we analyse each of these steps in more detail.

5.1   Events to Processes Mapping

The first step of the annotation process consists in associating process events to the BPs activities. Given a process, the events recorded during the execution of its instances are analysed in order to detect relations with the execution of the activities. In this step, the approach links the internal process events to the process, obtaining an annotated process. As described in Sect. 4, internal events are process events that are intrinsically connected to one or more processes, and this connection is expressed in the event definition. In order to create the links, the body c of the event is analysed. The discovered relation is a link $L(A_p, e_i)$ connecting an activity of a process to an event instance. This first step is represented in Fig. 2(b), where some of the activities of the two processes depicted in the figure are linked with one or more process events.

5.2 Events Correlation Discovery

The second step investigates relations between events, both of process and environmental kind. Given the pool of event instances $E = \{e_i\}$, relations are analysed in order to detect hidden dependencies. The analysis is performed considering the temporal distribution of the event types T_j looking for patterns according to the timestamp at which the event has been recorded ts. The analysis that can be performed over the events are of different kinds and depend from the kind of relations that are to be investigated. Examples are:

- *Pattern Matching*: this technique analyses the temporal succession of events in order to detect regular patterns. These patterns are connected to the temporal distribution of the event instances registration. Pattern matching techniques enable the detection of regular sequences of event types in a specific or in an arbitrary order. The set of patterns detected by the pattern matching analysis is scored according to the number of times the pattern has been identified in the data set;
- *Association Rules*: this technique is used to detect causal relations among events which occur in the same time frame. An association rule is expressed as a premise and a consequence, meaning that when a premise (the detection of a specific set of event types in a time range) is true, then the consequence (another set of event types) is going to be verified too [4]. Association rules are scored using two metrics: support and confidence. Support measures the proportion of events recording which contain the association rules. Confidence measures the proportion of the events that contain the premise which also contain the consequence.

This step is shown in Fig. 2(c), where the pool of events is enriched with links connecting both process and environmental events. The output is a set of links $L(T_j, T_k)$ between event types, each one associated with a score expressing the reliability of the detected relation.

5.3 Process to Process Interconnection

After the focus on the events relations, the third step consists in expanding the vision to the global view in order to find interconnections among processes of different organizations. These interconnections derive directly from the two steps already defined. The detection of the interconnections is performed by analysing possible paths existing between two activities passing through a set of interconnected events:

Definition 2. *An interconnection between two processes P_a and P_b is detected when it exists a path $\mathcal{P}$ between two activities $A_a \in P_a$ and $A_b \in P_b$:*

$$\mathcal{P}(A_a, A_b) = T' \subseteq T \mid \forall\, T_j \in T' \,\exists\, T_k \mid \exists\, L(T_j, T_k) \tag{1}$$

A threshold can be applied for considering only strong relations among events. Also, given a set of possible paths between two activities, the most reliable one is selected. In Fig. 2(d) two paths are detected (highlighted with dashed lines) linking activities of the first and the second process.

5.4   The AAL Example: Interconnections Between Processes

The methodology described in this section is illustrated considering the running case study introduced in Sect. 3 considering the events described in Tab. 1. Events have been connected to the activities of the two processes and relations among them have been exploited to discover interconnections among processes. The discovered paths link the activities of the operator related to the providing of a service or the registration of expenses to the management of the balance sheets in the administration process. Events relations and paths are shown in Fig. 3.

6   Process Analysis: Mining Information from Events

In the second phase of the PiE methodology, we propose to exploit the results of the first phase for mining useful information about the processes execution. We start from the methodology proposed in [8], that allows mining information from relating different types of events generated by processes. The approach can be extended considering all the relationships derived in the first phase of the methodology, therefore relating events in processes or environmental events which are not necessarily related to each other by design. Information that can be mined can be general and use-case specific:

- *General Information* is about conformance and coverage of the processes. *Conformance* evaluates if the processes observed through the generated events reflect the structure provided by the several organizations or if there are inconsistencies between the modelled and the real processes. *Coverage* measures the total number of activities which are observable through events. In fact, some activities are not sensed by any of the collected events and their execution is not verifiable.

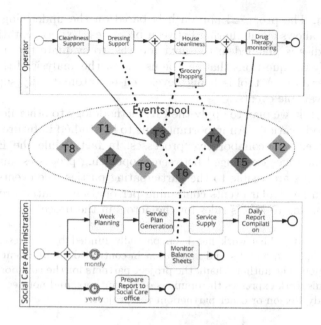

Fig. 3. PiE annotation applied to the Attiv@bili use case

- *Use-case Specific Information* enables to perform complex reasoning about the specific use case. Through mining the information obtained by the PiE framework about interconnections among processes, it can be possible to answer questions about the execution of the processes. In the AAL example considered in this work, possible questions are: (i) Which are the assistance activities followed by the production of a report? (ii) How many activities require a payment and how often they are executed? (iii) Which is the average duration of the cleaning and dressing activities for a specific subject? Is it regular? Does it change with operator? Is it in line with the duration of the same activities on other subjects? (iv) Which is the average cost of the grocery shopping for a specific subject and from what this cost is dependent? Answering these questions can provide an additional knowledge useful for analysing the efficiency and effectiveness of the social and health care service provided to the subject and can help in improving its quality.

7 Final Remarks

In this work we presented a first proposal of the PiE methodology that allows understanding interconnections existing between several BPs of cooperating organizations, starting by available process and environmental events. Processes are first annotated correlating them with events. This additional knowledge enables complex reasoning about the behaviour of the considered processes (process mining). We have illustrated a possible application of the methodology in the AAL field. The proposed approach is based on the underlying Attiv@bili platform that allows event sharing between processes. Experimentation on running case studies is planned in the next months, to evaluate the methodology and to identify the questions that can be useful for the analysis of the processes under consideration. A tool is being developed to automatically support these analyses on available events.

In future work, we plan to apply the PiE methodology to other fields without substantial modifications. An important issue to be studied in future work is the visibility of events in collaborative processes. In fact, while the BPs models may include messages exchanged between cooperating processes, and therefore the related events are visible to the participating parties, the events related to sensors, and in particular events containing personal information, require to be managed according to access rules for the actors in the processes.

Acknowledgments. This work has been partially funded by the research project Attiv@abili - digital care and social innovation in controlled environments, funded by Lombardy Region. The authors thank the project partners for the collaboration within the project. This work expresses the opinions of the authors, and not necessarily those of the Lombardy Region or other partners in the project.

References

1. Van der Aalst, W., Weijters, T., Maruster, L.: Workflow mining: Discovering process models from event logs. IEEE Transactions on Knowledge and Data Engineering **16**(9), 1128–1142 (2004)
2. der Aalst, W.M.P.V.: Process Mining - Discovery, Conformance and Enhancement of Business Processes. Springer (2011)
3. Aarts, E.: Ambient intelligence: a multimedia perspective. IEEE MultiMedia **11**(1), 12–19 (2004)
4. Agrawal, R., Imieliński, T., Swami, A.: Mining association rules between sets of items in large databases. In: ACM SIGMOD, vol. 22, pp. 207–216. ACM (1993)
5. Cook, D.J., Augusto, J.C., Jakkula, V.R.: Ambient intelligence: Technologies, applications, and opportunities. Pervasive and Mobile Computing **5**(4), 277–298 (2009)
6. Crutzen, C.K.: Invisibility and the meaning of ambient intelligence. International Review of Information Ethics **6**(12), 52–62 (2006)
7. Fugini, M., Cirilli, F., Locatelli, P.: Integrated care solutions. ERCIM News 102, 42, July 2015
8. de Leoni, M., Maggi, F.M., der Aalst, W.M.P.V.: An alignment-based framework to check the conformance of declarative process models and to preprocess event-log data. Inf. Syst. **47**, 258–277 (2015)
9. Mannhardt, F., de Leoni, M., Reijers, H.A.: Extending process logs with events from supplementary sources. In: Fournier, F., Mendling, J. (eds.) BPM 2014 Workshops. LNBIP, vol. 202, pp. 235–247. Springer, Heidelberg (2015)
10. Santucci, G., Martinez, C., Vlad-Calcic, D.: The sensing enterprise. Tech. rep., European Commission DG CONNECT 02 (2012)
11. Weske, M.: Business Process Management - Concepts, Languages, Architectures, 2nd edn. Springer (2012)

International Workshop on Fact Based Modeling (FBM) 2015

FBM PC Co-Chairs' Message

The first question of most enterprises is: what does fact based conceptual modeling bring me in practical terms? Why should we adopt it?

FBM is not alone. There are many existing systems running every day using various modeling techniques to express a certain perspective such as BPMN, UML, ER, XSD, DMN, OWL, RDF, SBVR to mention the most widely used.

The FBM 2015 Workshop Theme: perspective integration, has as its main objective to review the challenges of an enterprise from an integrated conceptual point of view. An enterprise wants practical solutions that have the support of many stakeholders. Hence an important topic in business practice is how to build sufficient consensus. The FBM 2015 workshop is the first FBM workshop to focus on the perspective of integration. The call for papers for the FBM 2015 workshop lead to a high number of high-quality submissions of which 12 have been selected for presentation at the 2 day workshop. The submissions come from a wide array of practitioners and researchers of FBM. We want to thank all authors for their efforts in writing the submitted papers, and we want to congratulate the authors of those papers that have been selected for the workshop.

September 2015

Peter Bollen
Robert Meersman
Hans Mulder
Maurice Nijssen

Developing and Maintaining Durable Specifications for Law or Regulation Based Services

Diederik Dulfer[1(✉)], Sjir Nijssen[2], and Mariette Lokin[1]

[1] Ministry of Finance, John F. Kennedylaan 8, 7314 PS Apeldoorn, The Netherlands
dph.dulfer@belastingdienst.nl, m.h.a.f.lokin@minfin.nl
[2] PNA Group, Heerlen, The Netherlands
Sjir.Nijssen@pna-group.com

Abstract. The Netherlands has enacted many laws. The responsibility for the execution of associated services and enforcement of this legislation is assigned to a substantial number of governmental bodies. Where possible, the associated services are performed digitally. The interaction between citizens/businesses and government as often implicitly described in legislation is the basis for the durable specifications of these services. One of the organisations in charge of developing and delivering these services is the Dutch Tax and Customs Administration (DTCA). DTCA is facing several challenges in developing and maintaining durable specifications for these services. This paper proposes to combine FBM with the case based semantics of rules for durable specifications. The need was established to extend the work of Hohfeld with a clear distinction between legal relations and legal acts, add time travel and the strong connection between the expected and actual cases with the laws and regulation.

Keywords: Regulation based services · Legal relations · Legal acts · Time travel · Case and rule connection · Fact based modelling (FBM)

1 Introduction

The Netherlands has a substantial number of governmental bodies responsible for the execution and enforcement of the Dutch legislation. This legislation is the basis for interaction between citizens / businesses and the government. The interaction is designed and realized by the government in cooperation with society. The laws are at some points very precise and at other points intentionally ambiguous. The legislation describes roughly speaking which rights and duties are applicable for a specific citizen or business and under which circumstances.

There are different kinds of laws, from laws covering more than one domain to very specific laws, covering exactly one domain. One example of a multi-domain law is the General Administrative Law Act (Algemene wet bestuursrecht, abbreviated Awb). This law prescribes many of the interactions between government and citizens / businesses and vice versa in a standardized and systematized way applicable in many domains. This law describes in outline the rights and duties of citizens /

© Springer International Publishing Switzerland 2015
I. Ciuciu et al. (Eds.): OTM 2015 Workshops, LNCS 9416, pp. 169–177, 2015.
DOI: 10.1007/978-3-319-26138-6_20

businesses and government regarding decisions on permits, benefits, administrative fines, and the objection and appeal against such decisions. Specific laws in the field of the DTCA are Income Tax Law 2001 and the Law on VAT (Value Added Tax) 1968.

When designing the implementation of a specific tax law, like the Income Tax Law, attention has to be paid to other multi-domain regulations, one could say more general laws such as the State Tax Act (Algemene wet inzake rijksbelastingen, abbreviated Awr), which sets out the general framework for levying tax described in various tax domain laws.

2   Dutch Tax and Customs Administration

The Dutch Tax and Customs Administration (DTCA) is a part of the Ministry of Finance. DTCA is responsible for services covering benefits, customs and the collection of taxes.

The IT-department of DTCA has extensive experience in the development and exploitation of rule based systems. Rule based systems are used to deal with an enormous number of different situations and complex calculations. DTCA's biggest system is covering the income tax and is executing over 3000 rules for several different purposes. The rules are executed in different environments, some in a custom-built rule engine and some in a COTS (Commercial Of-The-Shelf) rule engine. Other rules are implemented in programming code.

Besides specifications of rules DTCA makes use of process models, a data model and specifications for (electronic) forms. For instance the specifications for the tax forms for income tax cover more than 500 pages, containing more than 1000 variables. The specification of the calculation rules for income tax cover more than 100 documents. DTCA faces several challenges in maintaining the specifications of their legacy systems:

a. Ensuring the integrity of the process models, data models, rules and concept definitions is becoming more complex which each change in legislation.
b. Drawing up and changing the specifications to be in line with new legislation seems to take longer each time.
c. Validating the specifications by legal experts is a process, which is difficult to manage.
d. Traceability of the specifications to the underlying legislation is often lacking.

In the quest to search for solutions for these challenges, DTCA defined a new approach in creating and maintaining specifications. This approach is called 'Wendbare wetsuitvoering' (Agile execution of legislation) [13].

2.1   DTCA's Approach 'Agile Execution of Legislation'

The approach consists of four steps that must be executed for the design of services necessary to implement a specific piece of legislation. The approach aims to provide greater flexibility and agility in the implementation of changes in laws and/or regulations.

Since the spring of 2012, a number of people from DTCA, other government organisations, the academic world and businesses are working together, under the name 'The Blue Chamber', an example of co-creation [2, 3, 4, 5, 6]. The group is named after the room in a castle where the first ideas around this cooperation were developed. The members of 'The Blue Chamber' are collaborating in their quest to develop a protocol for creating and maintaining durable and tested specifications directly based on legislation.

Figure 1 shows the conceptual architecture of the Blue Chamber. It shows the complete development of services from initial idea (left) to their actual delivery (right). The approach of DTCA focusses on the yellow part in the middle. This is the creation and maintenance of durable specifications for services that can be tested by the various stakeholders.

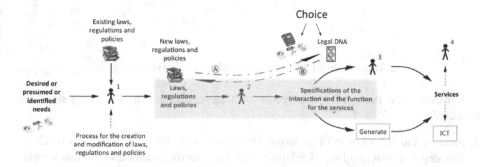

Fig. 1. Conceptual architecture of the Blue Chamber

DTCA's approach aims to create a traceable "translation" of the applicable legislation (the union of laws, government decrees and ministerial decrees) into durable specifications that are the complete basis for designing processes and information systems [8, 9, 10, 13]. The term translation, in the previous sentence, has to be interpreted in a broad sense. The "translation" includes explication, detailing and extending. Developing these durable and tested specifications is performed in a multidisciplinary group. Hence the symbol of actor with the number 2 attached represents a group of actors from various disciplines.

In the approach described, we assume that frequent changes occur in laws, regulations, policies and objectives of the organization. To be promptly informed as service provider of these changes and have the possibility to anticipate, the environment (including the legislative process) is constantly monitored for possible changes by the service organisation.

An overview of the complete approach is depicted in the figure below.

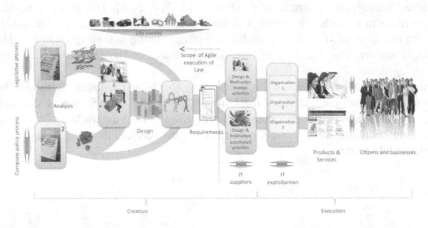

Fig. 2. Overview of the approach 'Agile execution of legislation'

For every new piece of, or change in existing legislation, the following steps are executed:

1. Analyse the (changes in) legislation and implementation policies. Main result of this step is a structured set of references for the specifications based on this legislation.
2. Analyse goals and objectives of the organization itself. These steps give a structured set of references for the specifications based on internal policy documents.
3. Design the specifications for the services of the organization and the interaction with citizens and businesses.
4. Design the specifications for the derivation of legal consequences.

The results of the analysis of legislation and internal policies consist of structured descriptions of rights, duties, legal concepts, fact patterns, concept descriptions, legal actions, legal actors, legal documents and legal rules. They also include integrity rules, which are often left implicit in legislation. The results of the design steps consist of services, events, actors, fact patterns and various kinds of rules [1, 11]. They are brought together in knowledge models, which can be used in developing or generating service applications.

After these steps implementation of the specified services can be assigned to specific business units, based on their expertise. This will ensure that services are implemented as efficiently as possible.

Although the approach suggests a sequence, the steps can be executed in parallel and will often have an iterative pattern. After these steps the specifications are ready for the design, realization and implementation of services in the form of processes and information systems.

3   Case "Tax Assessment"

3.1   Analysis of Legislation

Legislation is purposely formulated as independent as possible of the structure of the service organization that has to implement it. Laws and regulations leave some and well defined possibilities to the implementing organizations to make decisions regarding implementation and enforcement. These choices are often enshrined in implementation policies of the organization that has to deliver the services. The implementation policies will, within the framework of the law, lead to tightening or adjustment of the original requirements.

Legislation and implementation policies are formulated in natural language. A natural language, as opposed to a formal language in general, does not directly support the unambiguous formulation of specifications. In order to create durable, clear, valid and testable specifications [1, 11], we will need to translate legislation and implementation policies into a formal yet understandable language in which the specifications can be expressed and documented, as well as traced back via an annotation to the original legislation [13], and can be tested in a multi-disciplinary group on a reasonably representative set of foreseeable cases, in terra juridica called ex-ante. This understandable language is necessary to enable the different expert's to work together and to effectively validate the specifications, a very crucial step. This translation process is for a very long time, at least tens of years, to come the work of a human expert.

The analysis includes the clearing of elements in legislation and internal policies that have been left implicit, such as relations to general legislation that is applicable in the specific domain we are working on.

Three of the categories of rules we distinguish during the analyses of legislation are:

- Rules regarding legal relations
- Rules regarding legal actions
- Derivation rules.

Rules regarding legal relations are legal rules, which determine the legal situation of a kind-of-right party and the associated kind-of-duty party and are intended to guide the behaviour of legal actors. Legal actions are actions by one single party, performed within the context of a legal relation the acting party is part of. Derivation rules are the rules that describe how to derive legal consequences from legal facts.

In this case we will focus on the rules regarding legal relations and legal actions. Rules regarding legal relations describe the legal relations that exist between two parties [7, 11] and legal rules describe in our case the intended interaction between the government and the citizens. The valid rules are determined by evaluating the actual legal relations. These actual legal relations determine the legal status of the legal role. Based on the valid rules regarding legal relations the legal actor is allowed or obliged to perform these legal actions. Performing a legal action will result in a new set of legal relations and one or more new legal facts. The new legal relations determine the new legal status or situation of the two actors involved in each legal relation. Based on the new legal status and the new set of legal facts a new set of valid rules regarding legal relations can be determined.

Two examples of rules regarding legal relations are shown below:

Article 6, of the Income tax law, first section, first sentence.
1. With respect to taxes levied by assessment or by payment on declaration, the inspector may invite the person, who in his opinion is likely to have to pay tax, to file a tax declaration.

Please be aware that the meaning of the term invitation is not the same as commonly understood. It actually results in a duty. This is one of the kinds of things that make automatic generation of specifications only possible in an ivory tower. Developing durable specifications is a human task of the highest order. Of course a well developed and tested protocol is also here welcome. Representative scenarios or cases, an essential part of Fact Based Modelling, are also an essential part of this protocol [12].

Article 6, second section.
2. The person who submits a request for an invitation to the inspector is in any case invited to declare tax.

The first section of article 6 describes that the actor, 'the inspector', is empowered to execute a legal action (fundamentally creating a duty!) 'invite to declare tax' towards the indirect object, 'the person, who in his opinion likely to have to pay tax'. There is no obligation on the part of the inspector to do so. The inspector may execute the legal action.

The second section of article 6 describes two possible legal actions. The first legal action describes that the actor 'the person' is allowed to execute the legal action, 'request for an invitation' towards the indirect object 'inspector'. The second legal action describes that the inspector shall execute the legal action 'invite to declare tax' towards the actor 'person'.

In rules, like the one above, we find actors and a legal action. The rules also have a kind of legal relation in the sense that e.g. an actor has the right or obligation to execute the legal action. Hohfeld [7] described the first comprehensive classification of different types of rights and duties from actors towards each other was.. In this way the first and second section of article 6 describe the possible interactions between the inspector and citizens/businesses and the government. Rules regarding legal relations consist of the following elements[1]:

- The party that holds the kind-of right side of the legal relation.
- The party that holds the associated kind-of-duty side of the legal relation.

---

[1] Norm [2] is a synonym for rule regarding legal relation.

- The condition; the legal facts, which should be met before the legal relation comes into existence.

In this case we have limited our analysis to assessment taxes (aanslagbelastingen), a specific type of tax. This specific type of tax is used in the Netherlands for income tax, corporation tax, inheritance and donation tax. The general procedural rules for assessment tax are described in the State Tax Act, a multi-domain law. These rules apply to all tax legislation and describe the possible interaction between the tax inspector and the taxpayer. We have analysed possible legal relations and legal relations described in articles 6 until 11.

The concept of legal relations is the same as jural relations [7]. A legal relation is a legal relation between two parties. The relations describe the rights and duties of the parties towards each other. The legal actions are assigned to the following classification:

1. Actions that are requested by a legal actor from another legal actor that is liable to that request are classified as legal acts that may be done (e.g. request a postponement for declaring tax). These actions are classified as 'power/liability'.

2. Actions required from a legal actor are classified as legal acts that must be done (e.g. declare tax). These actions are classified as 'claim/duty'.

This classification is necessary to be able to define the services. This way of analyzing the legislation resulted in important questions regarding the meaning in the possible scenarios of several legal relations and associated legal actions. One of those questions was whether granting postponement was the same as extending the period for declaring tax. Actually one should know from every phrase if is it is the same as another. Like whether 'to file a tax declaration' (Article 6, first section) is the same as 'to declare tax' (Article 6, second section). In the end we discovered that the meaning of these rules and the phrases in it is not only derived from the legislation itself but is also determined by the real world cases or scenarios.

The rules that describe the legal actions that must or may be performed by the legal actor. When a legal action is performed, the corresponding legal relation is created. Based on this legal relation the valid rules regarding possible legal relations are determined. Based on this valid rules the possible legal actions can be determined.

For instance the legal relation 'invitation' can be written as the following fact pattern [5]:

```
The taxpayer <taxpayer number> is invited on date <invi-
tation date> to declare tax in the period from <date
from> to <date to> by tax inspector <tax inspector num-
ber>.
```

The variables in these fact types or patterns can be referred to in rules to derive other legal consequences if necessary.

The time at which the action is performed is the 'invitation date' of the fact pattern 'invitation'. After the action 'Declare tax', the corresponding fact with the pattern 'invitation' is considered not to be applicable any more.

A state transition diagram can be created, representing a well known perspective of the model. The state transaction diagram is depicted in figure 3.

We present a state transition diagram, as this is for many a well known diagramming technique. We are aware that we need more legal semantics to represent case diagrams as have been introduced in [2, 7, 11].

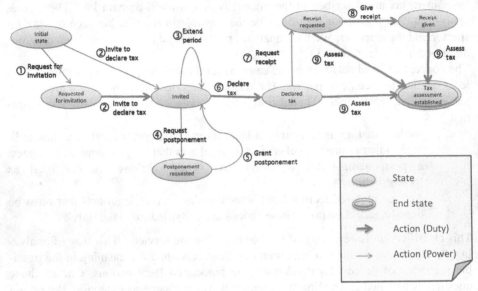

Fig. 3. State transaction diagram from a part of assessment tax

This state transition can be used to develop a citizen portal containing actions that have to be done by the citizens (duties) and actions that can be done by citizens (powers).

4   Conclusions and Future Work

The combination of modelling the interaction with legal relations in combination with fact based modelling gives DTCA the possibility to have a complete set of durable specifications which are more manageable, testable (validatable) [1, 11] and from which the traceability to the legislation is ensured [13].

Just recently the management of DTCA announced a large reorganization. This reorganization will take several years and will eliminate more than 5000 jobs. Massive investments will be made to speed up the development of digital services. One of the ambitions is to create a portal for Dutch citizens and companies with integrated information regarding all their aspects of taxes and benefits. Other ambitions are to renew all of the legislation based back office applications. The approach 'Agile execution of legislation' should be able to support this de-juridification of the information provided by the back office systems in order to provide integrated information for Dutch citizens and companies.

Acknowledgement. This paper wouldn't have been possible without the support of several colleagues from the Ministry of Finance and the Dutch Tax Administration. The members of the Blue Chamber gave a lot of inspiration. The Dutch Tax Administration will continue to improve the development and maintenance of durable specifications in the future, which will result the future developments of the approach 'Agile execution of legislation'.

References

1. Brattinga, M., Nijssen, S.: A sustainable architecture for durable modeling of laws and regulations and main concepts of the durable model. Paper Accepted at the FBM 2015 Workshop of the OnTheMove 2015 Conference, Rhodos, Greece, October 29–30, 2015. Springer
2. Engers, T.M., van Nijssen, S.: Bridging social reality with rules. Paper Presented at IRIS2014, Das Internationale Rechtsinformatik Symposion, Salzburg, Austria, February 21, 2014
3. Van Engers, T., Nijssen, S.: Connecting people: semantic-conceptual modeling for laws and regulations. In: Janssen, M., Scholl, H.J., Wimmer, M.A., Bannister, F. (eds.) EGOV 2014. LNCS, vol. 8653, pp. 133–146. Springer, Heidelberg (2014)
4. Engers, T.M., van Nijssen, S.: From legislation towards service development – an approach to agile implementation of legislation. Paper Accepted for Presentation at EGOVIS 2014 in München, September 1–5 and to be Included in the Proceedings
5. Engers, T.M., van Doesburg, R.: First steps towards a formal analysis of law. In: Malzahn, D., Conceição, G. (eds.) eKNOW 2015, pp. 36–42. IARIA (2015)
6. Engers, T.M., van Doesburg, R.: At your service, on the definition of services from sources of law. In: Proceedings of the 15th International Conference on Artificial Intelligence and Law (ICAIL 2015), pp. 221–225. ACM, New York (2015)
7. Hohfeld, W.N.: Fundamental legal conceptions as applied in judicial reasoning. In: Cook, W.W.(ed.) (2010). ISBN-13: 978-1-58477-162-3
8. ISO TR9007: Concepts and Terminology for the Conceptual Schema and the Information Base, ISO Technical Report (1987)
9. Kleemans, F., Saton, J.: Developing the uniform economic transaction protocol a fact based modeling approach for creating the economic internet protocol. Paper Accepted at the FBM 2015 Workshop of the OnTheMove 2015 Conference, Rhodos, Greece, October 29–30, 2015. Springer
10. Lemmens, I., Pleijsant, J.M., Arntz, R.: Using fact-based modeling to develop a common language - a use case. Paper Accepted at the FBM 2015 Workshop of the OnTheMove 2015 Conference, Rhodos, Greece, October 29–30, 2015. Springer
11. Lokin, M., Nijssen, S., Lemmens, I.: CogniLex a legal domain specific fact based modeling protocol. Paper Accepted at the FBM 2015 Workshop of the OnTheMove 2015 Conference, Rhodos, Greece, October 29–30, 2015. Springer
12. Nijssen, S., Valera, S.: An Architecture Ecosystem for the Whole Systems Perspective, Including System Dynamics, Based on Logic & Set Theory and Controlled Natural Languages. Working paper for the OMG Architecture Ecosystem SIG (2012)
13. Straatsma, P., en Dulfer, D.: Wendbare Wetsuitvoering. DREAM (2014)

Fact Based Legal Benefits Services

Gert Veldhuijzen van Zanten, Paul Nissink, and Diederik Dulfer[✉]

Ministry of Finance, John F. Kennedylaan 8, 7314 PS Apeldoorn, The Netherlands
{ge.veldhuijzen.van.zanten,plhm.nissink,dph.dulfer}
@belastingdienst.nl

Abstract. One of the organisations in charge of developing and delivering legal services in the Netherlands is the Dutch Tax and Customs Administration (DTCA). Next to Tax and Customs, DTCA is also responsible for benefits (like housing allowance, health care insurance allowance, childcare allowance). The benefits services of DTCA were one the first services which were based on a fact based approach. This paper shows how the benefits services of DTCA are designed, tells about the current challenges and future plans.

Keywords: Legal services · Benefits · Fact based modelling (FBM)

1   Introduction

The Netherlands has several governmental bodies responsible for the execution and enforcement of the Dutch legislation. This legislation is the basis for interaction between citizens / businesses and the government. The interaction is designed and realized by the government in cooperation with society. The laws are at some points very precise and at other points intentionally ambiguous. The legislation focusses on which rights and duties are valid for a specific citizen and under which circumstances.

There are different kinds of laws, from laws applying to more than one domain to very specific laws. One example of a multi-domain law is the General Administrative Law Act (Algemene wet bestuursrecht, abbreviated Awb). This law prescribes many of the interactions between government and citizens / businesses and vice versa in a standardized and systematized way. This law describes in outline the rights and duties of citizens / businesses and government regarding decisions on permits, benefits, administrative fines, and the objection and appeal process against such decisions.

When designing the implementation of a specific tax law, like the Income Tax Law, attention has to be paid to aforementioned more general laws like the State Tax Act (Algemene wet inzake rijksbelastingen, abbreviated Awr), which sets out the general framework for levying tax.

2   Dutch Tax and Customs Administration

The Dutch Tax and Customs Administration (DTCA) is a part of the Ministry of Finance. DTCA is responsible for services covering benefits, customs and the collection of taxes.

© Springer International Publishing Switzerland 2015
I. Ciuciu et al. (Eds.): OTM 2015 Workshops, LNCS 9416, pp. 178–187, 2015.
DOI: 10.1007/978-3-319-26138-6_21

Every year DTCA needs to change their services based on the changes in legislation. The changes in legislation cover more than 100 pages each year. DTCA faces several challenges in maintaining the specifications of their legacy services:

a. Ensuring the integrity of the process models, data models, rules and concept definitions is becoming more complex with each change in legislation.
b. Drawing up and changing the specifications to faithfully be in line with new legislation seems to take longer each time.
c. Validating the specifications by legal experts is a process which is difficult to manage.
d. Traceability of the specifications to the underlying legislation is often lacking.

In the quest to search for solutions for these challenges, DTCA defined a new approach in creating and maintaining specifications. This approach is called 'Wendbare wetsuitvoering' (Agile execution of legislation).

2.1   DTCA's Approach 'Agile Execution of Legislation'

DTCA is working on an approach to create specifications for the services they deliver. The main requirements for the results of the approach are:

- Durable specifications, which are independent from information technology.
- Traceable to legislation and internal policies.
- Understandable and can be validated by various domain experts

The approach consists of four steps which must be executed for the design of services necessary to implement a specific piece of legislation. The approach aims to provide greater flexibility and agility in the implementation of changes in laws and/or regulations [1].

2.2   Collaboration with 'The Blue Chamber'

Since the spring of 2012, a group of professionals from government organisations, the academic world and businesses are working together, under the name 'The Blue Chamber'. The group is named after the room where the first ideas around this cooperation were developed. The members of 'The Blue Chamber' are collaborating in their quest to develop a protocol for creating and maintaining durable and tested specifications directly based on the intention of the legislation.

Figure 1 shows the conceptual architecture as envisioned by the Blue Chamber. It shows the complete development of services from initial idea to their actual delivery. The approach of DTCA focusses on the yellow area which is about the creation and maintenance of durable specifications for services.

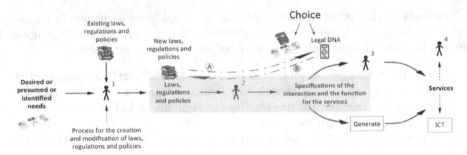

Fig. 1. Conceptual architecture of the Blue Chamber

This paper describes the approach of the benefits department to create specifications which can be used to generate ICT, which deliver services to citizens and businesses(right lower part of figure 1). ICT (Information and Communication Technology) is the Dutch term for what is internationally referred to as IT.

DTCA's approach aims to create a traceable "translation" of the applicable legislation into durable specifications that are useful for designing processes and information systems to provide services. The term "translation" in the previous sentence has to be interpreted in a broad sense. The "translation" includes explication, detailing and extending, Developing these durable and tested specifications is done in a multidisciplinary group.

2.3   An Overview of the Approach

In the approach described we assume that frequent changes occur in laws, regulations, policies and objectives of the organization.

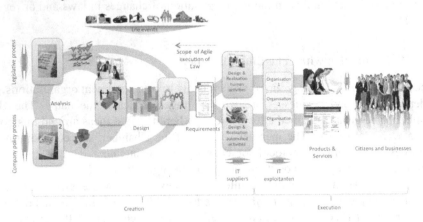

Fig. 2. Overview of the approach 'Agile execution of legislation'

To be promptly informed of these changes and have the possibility to anticipate, the environment (including the legislative process) is constantly monitored and advised on the impact of possible changes.

An overview of the complete approach [1] is depicted in figure 2. For all new legislation, or changes in existing legislation, the following analysis and design steps are executed:

The Analysis of Legislation and Internal Policies

1. Analyse the (changes in) legislation and implementation policies. The main result of this step is a structured set of annotations on this legislation.
2. Analyse internal policies, goals and objectives. These steps give a structured set of annotations on internal policy documents.

The Design of the Services

3. Design the services specifications of the organization and the interaction with citizens and businesses.
4. Design the derivation of legal consequences.

The results of the analysis of legislation and internal policies (result of step 1 and 2) consist of structured descriptions of rights, duties, legal concepts, fact patterns, concept descriptions, legal actions, legal actors, legal documents and legal rules. They also include integrity rules, which are often left implicit in legislation. The results of the design steps (3 and 4) consist of services, events, actors, fact patterns and rules. They are brought together in knowledge models, which can be used in manually developing or generating service applications. During the development of these knowledge models knowledge engineers are working closely together with the legislators and service experts.

After these four steps, implementation of the specified services can be assigned to specific business units, based on their expertise.

Although the approach suggests a sequence, the steps can be executed in parallel and will often have an iterative pattern. After these steps the specifications are ready for the design, realization and implementation of services in the form of processes and information systems.

3   The Benefits Services

Next to Tax and Customs, DTCA is also responsible for benefits. Examples of benefits handled by DTCA are housing allowance, health care insurance allowance, childcare allowance. The benefits legislation is relatively new compared to the tax legislation. That is why the services executing this legislation are also relatively new and developed based on current knowledge with the latest technology.

The services landscape of the benefits department roughly consist of 3 major services:

- The portal service
- The service for determining facts
- The service for determining legal consequences

The figure below shows a screenshot of the citizens portal. The citizen's landing page shows an overview of the benefits which have been claimed , the possibility to inform the benefits department on new live-events, like change of address, change of income, new child is born or change of composition of the household. It also shows the status and results of the processing of the last life events from this citizen or from other sources like other governmental departments.

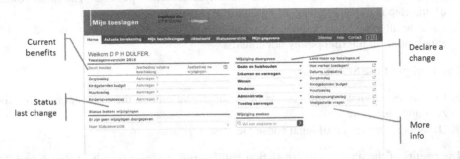

Fig. 3. The customer portal for benefits.

Each of these services have their own administration, with respectively:

- Assertions
- Facts
- Legal Facts

The definitions of these three terms are as follows:

- An assertion is a claim on an actual state of affairs or a value judgment, which can be true or false.
- A fact is a claim on an actual state of affairs or a value judgment, which is true according to DTCA. So a fact is a subtype of an assertion.
- A legal fact is defined as a fact to which a legal rule is applied to derive legal consequences. So a legal fact is a subtype of a fact.

An example covering all three is as follows:

- Assertion: Benefit applicant A claims that his income will be € 35.000 in 2016.
- Fact: According to DTCA, the income of benefit applicant A in 2016 is €40.000.
- Legal fact: The fact above was used to determine that applicant A is entitled to a health care insurance allowance of €900 in 2016. This use turns the fact into a legal fact.

An overview of the major services and administrations is presented in figure 4. Customers makes assertions in the Customer Portal. Based on internal risk rules DCTA determines the facts, based on the assertions available. The DCTA applies the relevant legal rules and the result is one or more facts describing the legal consequences.

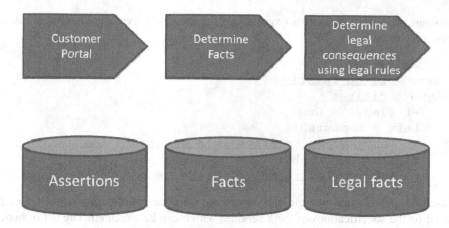

Fig. 4. Overview of the major benefits services.

The benefits department faces several challenges in maintaining the specifications of these services:

a. Ensuring the integrity of the overall specifications of the portal service, the service for determining the facts and the service for determining legal consequences.
b. Drawing up and changing the specifications in conformance with new legislation seems to take longer each time.
c. Managing the process of validation of the specifications by legal experts is difficult.
d. Traceability of the specifications to the legislative source is often lacking.

3.1 The Derivation of the Legal Consequences

The service which supports the derivation of the legal consequences is specified with a high level domain specific language. An example of such a high level specification is shown below in two classification rules which are specified relative to a given citizen:

```
A blood relative is a citizen who
is a blood relative in a straight line or
is a blood relative in the second degree sideline.

A blood relative in straight line is a citizen who
is a descendant or who
is an ancestor.
```

Definitions of the concepts blood relative in the second degree sideline, descendant and ancestor are defined similarly but omitted here. In the concrete syntax of the rules above, the names of concepts are underlined in order to distinguish them from other language elements. The abstract syntax tree for the first previously mentioned rule is presented below:

```
Set definition
  name = blood relative
  type = citizen
    Set Clause = Or
      Left = Membership
        Set = blood relative in a straight line
      Right = Membership
        Set = blood relative in the second degree sideline
```

Based on specification like the once above source code generators produce C# code based on the specifications of the 8 services which can be executed. The list of benefits services is presented in Table 1.

Table 1. List of benefits services.

Service (Dutch description)	Service (English description)
AWIR-service	Multi benefits service
Betalen Toeslagen service	Benefits payment service
Huur-service	Housing allowance service
Kantoortoedeler service	Office work dispatcher service
Kinderopvang-service	childcare allowance service
Kindgebonden Budget-service	Child-related budget allowance service
Signalering Kindgebonden Budget service	Child-related budget allowance signaling service
Service Zorg-service	health care insurance allowance service

The specification environment for this service is recently migrated to Jetbrains MPS (https://www.jetbrains.com/mps/). MPS (Meta Programming System) is a configurable language workbench for creating Domain Specific Languages. This language workbench has functionality to generate source code like Java. Functionality to generate source code can be created to generate rules for a rule engine or other programming languages like C[3]. In an FBM conference the question will arise: how are the facts, fact patterns, associated rules and descriptions managed? In MPS definitions rule type patterns and fact type patterns are defined at language level and rules and fact types are defined at language level. An example of the new way of creating specifications in MPS is shown in figure 5.

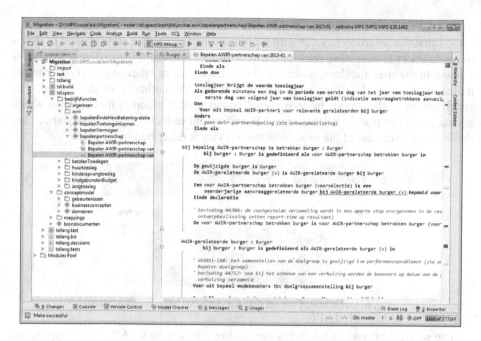

Fig. 5. Example of the specifications in MPS.

The specifications of the service for determination of the legal consequences are never the bottleneck in changes of the benefits legislation. The main reasons for this are:

- Specifying is developing, if it is specified there is no need for coding software. The source code is generated and 'correct by construction'.
- There is a strong correlation between legislation and the specifications, formal and understandable to modelling experts, which makes updating the specifications relatively easy.

Domain experts are able to validate the specifications, since the specifications look very much like natural language. Due to the fact that MPS supports multiple notations of the same concept[2], it possible to adjust the notation based on the preferences or language of the domain expert.

The specifications in the functional language 'conceal' date and time operations. In the information model date and time concepts are avoided. Instead in the specifications generic operations are used to handle changes of facts. For instance 'date of birth' is not in the information model. Instead a fact is known 'citizen is alive'. This fact is changed when the events 'birth' and 'death' occur. So the fact 'citizen is alive' is true from 'date of birth' until 'date of death'.

Using generic date and time operations in the specifications allows us to abstract from the maintenance of the history of facts. This reduces the amount and complexity of the specifications. Specification like 'the income of you and your partner may not exceed € 32.655 per year' means a sum of all your incomes of each month added to the sum of all the incomes of each month of your partner. (Or partners in case of changing partners in one year).

All assertions received have a start date and some have an end date, else it is assumed that the assertion is valid until a point in the future. The service used to determine the facts is executing rules to create a single truth from the different assertions known. In the specifications, assertions from life-events or other sources (government partners, etc.) are classified based on for instance the authority of the source. The specification of the service to derive legal consequences assumes that all facts which are received are true in a legal sense. Based on these facts, legal consequences are derived. An overview of the process in this service is described in figure 6.

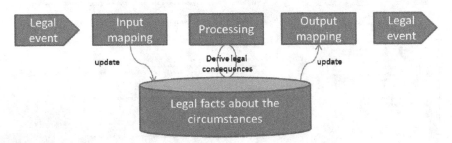

Fig. 6. Overview of the service for deriving legal consequences

The service receives legal events containing the new facts. After the mapping the legal rules to derive legal consequences are applied on these facts, resulting in new facts. These facts are mapped on output events that represent the results. The resulting legal events may trigger other services to process the effects of other legislation or to start a payment service or messaging service to inform the citizen.

4   Conclusions and Future Work

The specification process described here delivers DTCA traceable, verifiable and easily maintainable specifications of its legislation. These specifications are fully automated converted by MPS into source code that is correct by construction.

DTCA will investigate whether the specification environment of the benefits services can be extended toward the other areas like the portal and the determination of facts from life events or other sources.

Mid 2015 the management of DTCA unfolded plans to renew its business processes, applications and infrastructure. Substantial investments will be made to speed up the development of digital services. One of the ambitions is to create a portal for Dutch citizens and companies. The portal provides an integrated information view regarding all aspects of taxes and benefits.

Another ambition is to renew all of the back office applications, which execute legislation. The 'Agile execution of legislation' approach should be able to support a less formal interaction between government and citizens and companies and a less formal defined shared information position.

Acknowledgement. This paper wouldn´t have been possible without the support of several colleagues from the Ministry of Finance and the Dutch Tax Administration. Also the members of the Blue Chamber gave a lot of inspiration. The Dutch Tax Administration will continue to improve the development and maintenance of specifications in the future, which will result in future developments of the approach 'Agile execution of legislation'.

References

1. van Engers, T., Nijssen, S.: From legislation towards the provision of services. In: Kő, A., Francesconi, E. (eds.) EGOVIS 2014. LNCS, vol. 8650, pp. 163–172. Springer, Heidelberg (2014)
2. Voelter, M., Lisson, S.: Supporting diverse notations in MPS' projectional editor. In: 2nd International Workshop on The Globalization of Modelling Languages at MODELS (2014)
3. Voelter, M., Ratiu, D., Schaetz, B., Kolb, B.: mbeddr: an extensible C-based programming language and IDE for embedded systems. In: Proceedings of the 3rd Annual Conference on Systems, Programming, and Applications: Software for Humanity (SPLASH 2012), pp. 121–140. ACM, New York (2012). doi:10.1145/2384716.2384767, http://doi.acm.org/10.1145/2384716.2384767

Integrating Modelling Disciplines at Conceptual Semantic Level

Inge Lemmens

PNA Group, Heerlen, The Netherlands
Inge.Lemmens@pna-group.com

Abstract. For an organization to maintain (or achieve) a competitive edge and to be continuously compliant with ever changing regulations, it is necessary that it can react in a timely and cost-effective fashion to changes in the immediate environment which affects its business. This can only be achieved if the organization has an effective grip on its total body of knowledge.

In order to get grip on its knowledge, an organization needs insight and control in the way the overall goals of the organization and the associated laws and regulations are translated into an operational way of working. As new technologies are introduced frequently, it is of great interest to have a sustainable knowledge description of the operational way of working, independent of any physical realization, including a two-way audit trail (from source to implementation and back).

In this paper we explain that for an organization to gain true insights in its operations, it is not enough to create independently conceived process, information and rules models, but that it is of importance to gain insight in (and thus understanding of the relationships between these different models.

Keywords: Integration · Fact-based model · Conceptual · Semantic

1 Introduction

In today's business environment, the challenges an organization has to face, have increased in both number and complexity. Not only competition has become tougher, organizations also have to fulfil an increasing number of regulations imposed by external organizations and have to become more and more cost-effective.

For an organization to maintain (or achieve) a competitive edge and to be continuously compliant with ever changing regulations, it is necessary that it can react in a timely and cost-effective fashion to changes in the immediate environment which affects its business. This can only be achieved if the organization has an effective grip on its total body of knowledge.

In order to get grip on its knowledge, an organization needs insight and control in the way the overall goals of the organization and the associated laws & regulations are translated into an operational way of working. That is, the operational way of working of the organization needs to be defined before physical realization in, for example, IT systems or mechanization.

© Springer International Publishing Switzerland 2015
I. Ciuciu et al. (Eds.): OTM 2015 Workshops, LNCS 9416, pp. 188–196, 2015.
DOI: 10.1007/978-3-319-26138-6_22

As new technologies are introduced frequently, it is of crucial interest to have a sustainable knowledge description of the operational way of working (independent of any physical realization in a specific technology), preferably including a two-way audit trail (from source to realization/implementation and back).

In particular, the organization needs insight in:

1. The services and products it delivers in order to achieve its business goals,
2. The processes it executes in order to deliver its services and products,
3. The information (fact types, object types, including terms and definitions) it needs for executing its processes, and
4. The rules it has to obey (use) for proper execution of its processes.

These form together the body of knowledge and can be subject to (partial) automation.

In section 2, the major pitfall of the disconnected approach is discussed. Section 3 specifies the structural framework of the proposed approach by identifying the knowledge classes and their meaning, while in section 4 a small meta model fragment for the complete approach is given. In section 5, a conclusion and further research issues are provided.

2   Major Pitfall of the Disconnected Approach

Process modelling, information modelling and rules modelling are the disciplines that aim to provide insight into a specific aspect or perspective of the body of knowledge of an organization. For each of them, standard languages exist that are intended to provide the best fit for the modelling goal or perspective at hand. Think for example of BPMN (Business Process Modelling and Notation) [1] for business process modelling, DMN (Decision Model and Notation) [2] for (derivation) rule modelling and SBVR (Semantics of Business Vocabulary and Rules) [3] for rules and (to a certain extent) information modelling.

While all of these types of models have their own merits, it is argued in [4] that: *"if left unconnected and uncontrolled, instead of integrated and interconnected, they can result in a fragmented perspective on the enterprise and thereby can negatively affect the overall coherence of models as well as the performance of the organization"*. In particular, within organizations, each discipline is due to historical organizational reasons approached from its own perspective, using standards that provide the best fit for the desired modelling viewpoint and the purpose at hand, thereby overlooking integration aspects.

2.1   Insight and Understanding Requires a Semantic Approach

In order for an organization to gain *true* insight in its operation and long term possibilities, and thus providing the necessary and sustainable grip on its body of knowledge, it is not enough to create independently conceived process, information and rule models. It is necessary to gain insight in the relation between these different models, and in particular to understand how, during execution, rules, information and processes influence each other.

The term "insight" implies "understanding". It is therefore required that processes, information and rules as well as the interactions between these model types are represented in such a manner that they are communicable and understandable to all stakeholders involved. This requires a definition at the conceptual (semantic) level void of any implementation details, focusing on the semantics.

3   A Fully Integrated Modelling Approach

The fully integrated modelling approach suggested in this paper consists of a framework based on the fact-based modelling methodology, covering the process, information and rule perspectives. For this, the knowledge triangle as depicted in Figure 1 is introduced.

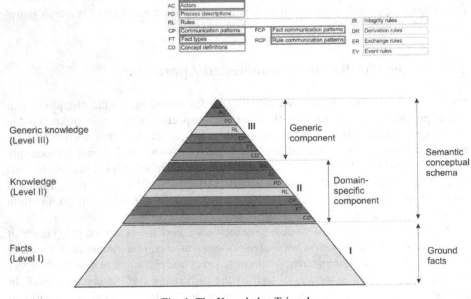

Fig. 1. The Knowledge Triangle.

Level I: The Ground Facts or Assertions

The assumption of fact-based modelling methodologies is that the most concrete level in any structured knowledge description or business communication consists of *ground facts*. It is observed that these comprise the vast majority in business, engineering or technical communication.

A ground fact is defined as "*a proposition taken to be true by a relevant community*" and is expressed as an assertion that either simply predicates over individual objects or simply asserts the existence of an individual object. Examples are:

"Marie Curie received the Nobel prize in Physics in 1903".
"Linus Pauling received the Nobel prize in Chemistry in 1954".

Ground facts, expressed by means of sentences, describe factual, planned or imagined situations, in the past, current time or future; they do not prescribe any grammar aspect.

Level II: The Domain Specific Component of the Knowledge Triangle

Level II of the knowledge triangle consists of the domain specific conceptual schema. It consists of knowledge categories to which the ground facts of level I must adhere as well as concept definitions to understand the ground facts; it could be said it provides interpretation semantics. In other words, level II specifies the rules that govern the ground facts at level I and defines the concept definitions of the terms used in the facts, when there is the slightest doubt they could be misunderstood. Moreover, the usage of ground facts is also described at this level. Level II is expressed by means of a series of knowledge categories, namely:

1. *Concept definitions*, which have as function to describe the meaning of every term or group of terms in the ground facts for which it is assumed that the meaning is not fully known to the intended audience and common understanding of the meaning is required. In case the meaning of a term is assumed to be known it is good practice to state this explicitly in order to avoid any confusion.
2. *Fact types*, which provide the functionality to define which kinds of ground facts are considered to be within *scope* of the system, subject or domain of interest. A fact type is either:
   (a) variable-based fact type, i.e. a fact type seen as a populatable construct, generalizing level I ground facts on the basis of common properties, using fact-communication patterns.
   (b) A role-based fact type, i.e. a fact type seen as a construct that generalizes level I ground facts on the basis of common properties, using rule-communication patterns.
   The boundary (scope) of the system, subject or domain is determined by the set of fact types.
3. *Communication patterns*, whereby there is a distinction between:
   (a) *Fact communication patterns*: their function is to act as communication mechanism to be used as a template to communicate ground facts in a language and using terms the subject matter expert is familiar with, and
   (b) *Rule communication patterns* , whose function is to act as communication mechanism for communicating the rules, listed in point 4 below, of the conceptual schema.
   Both types of communication patterns use community-specific terminology.

4. *Rules*, distinguishing between:
   (a) *Integrity* or *validation rules*, also known as constraints. These have as function to restrict the set of ground facts and the transitions between the permitted sets of ground facts to those that are considered useful. In other words, integrity rules have the function to restrict populations as well as transitions between populations to useful ones.
   (b) *Derivation rules*, which are used to derive or calculate new information (ground facts) on the basis of existing information. That is, derivation rules describe how to derive new ground facts on the basis of existing ground facts.
   (c) *Exchange rules,* which have as function to move ground facts from the domain under consideration into the administration of that domain and vice versa, or to remove ground facts from the administration. In other words, they specify how ground facts are added and/or removed from the knowledge base such that the knowledge base stays in sync with the communication about the outside world.
   (d) *Event rules*, which specify when to update the set of ground facts by a derivation rule or exchange rule in the context of a process description.
5. *Process descriptions*, specifying the fact consuming and/or fact generating activities (the exchange and/or derivation rules) to be performed by the different actors for that process, as well as the event rules invoking those exchange and derivation rules in an ordered manner.
6. *Actors* identifying the involved participants and their responsibilities in the processes (in terms of the exchange and derivation rules they need to execute).
7. *Services*, identifying the realizations of the process descriptions in terms of information products to be delivered.

Level III: The Generic Component of the Knowledge Triangle
The third level of the knowledge triangle, the generic component, independent of any specific domain, consists of the knowledge categories to which each conceptual schema of level II must adhere. In other words, Level III of the knowledge triangle consists of the generic conceptual schema, expressed in the same knowledge categories as any domain-specific conceptual schema. Each element in the generic component of the knowledge triangle or the generic conceptual schema is independent of any specific part of the domain or system. Interestingly enough, the generic conceptual schema is a population of itself.

4   Processes as an Ordering of Rules

At the highest level of abstraction, a process is nothing more than a fact-generator (a derivation): based on input facts, new facts, the output facts, are generated in order to provide a (requested) service. Typically, several steps have to be undertaken to achieve the output. That is, in most process-views, a process consists of a series of steps that together generate the output on the basis of the input, triggered by an event. From an integrated perspective, these steps correspond to exchange rules and derivation rules in combination with event rules.

While derivation rules are well-known within the fact-based modelling community, exchange rules have been only recognized in the CogNIAM variant of fact-based modelling. These rules are however of importance since only through exchange rules it is possible to ensure communication between the system to be realized and the outside world.

The main reason for considering processes as an ordering of exchange and derivation rules in combination with event rules is that it aids in identification of the granularity of the possible actions as well as to enable a consistent way of using the Business Process Model and Notation.

4.1   Exchange Rules

Exchange rules are the mechanism to bring facts into the system, to remove them from the system, to update them or to report on them. Exchange rules always work on combination of related fact types. That is, exchange rules always apply to so-called conceptual structures. A conceptual structure is a grouping of fact types and object types whereby the grouping is determined through the existence-dependency of the fact types and object types on the object type under consideration. Determination of a conceptual structure is part of the FAMOUS-2 research performed with ESA and is described in [5].

Create rules are exchange rules that bring facts into the knowledge base from the outside world. A creation rule can only be performed if all the integrity rules that are part of the conceptual structure are fulfilled. This means that, in a BPMN-representation of an activity that corresponds to an exchange rule, there is always a conditional boundary event associated to the activity that is triggered when not all constraints are fulfilled. Consider the following use case text:

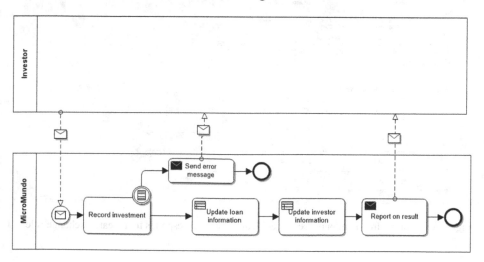

Fig. 2. An example BPMN collaboration view.

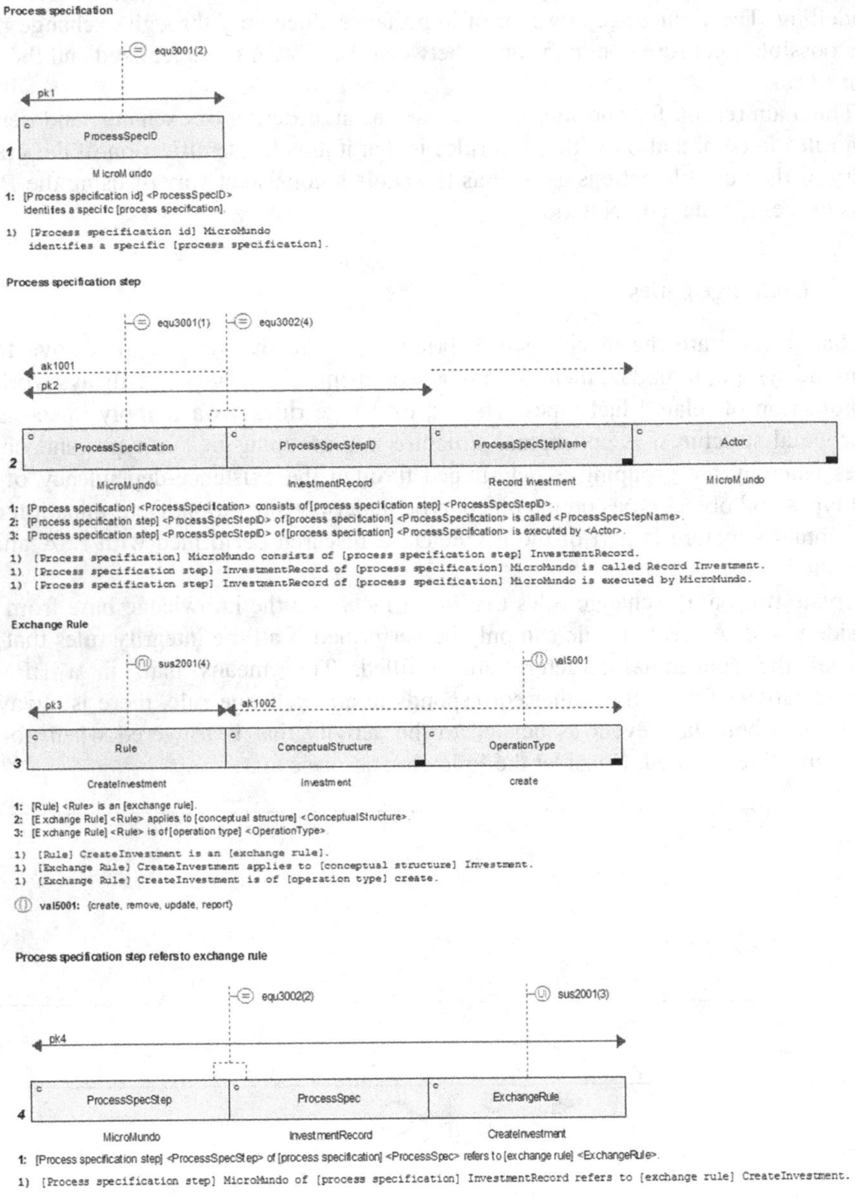

Process specification

1: [Process specification id] <ProcessSpecID> identifies a specific [process specification].

1) [Process specification id] MicroMundo identifies a specific [process specification].

Process specification step

1: [Process specification] <ProcessSpecification> consists of [process specification step] <ProcessSpecStepID>.
2: [Process specification step] <ProcessSpecStepID> of [process specification] <ProcessSpecification> is called <ProcessSpecStepName>.
3: [Process specification step] <ProcessSpecStepID> of [process specification] <ProcessSpecification> is executed by <Actor>.

1) [Process specification] MicroMundo consists of [process specification step] InvestmentRecord.
1) [Process specification step] InvestmentRecord of [process specification] MicroMundo is called Record Investment.
1) [Process specification step] InvestmentRecord of [process specification] MicroMundo is executed by MicroMundo.

Exchange Rule

1: [Rule] <Rule> is an [exchange rule].
2: [Exchange Rule] <Rule> applies to [conceptual structure] <ConceptualStructure>.
3: [Exchange Rule] <Rule> is of [operation type] <OperationType>.

1) [Rule] CreateInvestment is an [exchange rule].
1) [Exchange Rule] CreateInvestment applies to [conceptual structure] Investment.
1) [Exchange Rule] CreateInvestment is of [operation type] create.

val5001: {create, remove, update, report}

Process specification step refers to exchange rule

1: [Process specification step] <ProcessSpecStep> of [process specification] <ProcessSpec> refers to [exchange rule] <ExchangeRule>.

1) [Process specification step] MicroMundo of [process specification] InvestmentRecord refers to [exchange rule] CreateInvestment.

Fig. 3. Meta model fragment: a process specification step corresponds to a create exchange rule.

"An investment is a transaction where money is transferred from the account of an investor to a loan of a business. Each investment is assigned a unique investment number by MicroMundo, in order to provide an identification for each specific investment within the collection of all investments performed at MicroMundo.

The investor and the invested amount of each investment are recorded. Furthermore, the loan for which an investment is made and the date of each investment are recorded. Regarding the investments of investors in loans the following applies: an investment amount of an investment may not exceed the non-collected capital at the time of the investment of the loan that is invested in. The collected capital and non-collected capital of a loan are updated after each investment made."

In the BPMN collaboration diagram of Figure 2, the activity "record investment" corresponds to a creation rule that creates an investment. The boundary event associated with the activity is a conditional event that is triggered when the integrity rules associated with an investment, as described above, are not fulfilled. For example, if the investor is not known, or if the date of the investment is not recorded, or if any of the other rules is not fulfilled, the boundary event will be triggered, resulting in the sending of an error message that describes which integrity rules have been violated.

The result of the creation rule is that facts are added to the system under consideration.

The meta model fragment associated with the above is given in Figure 3. As is depicted, through populating the associated model fragment, it is shown that a BPMN activity, called a process specification step in the meta model fragment, refers to an exchange rule that creates an instance of a conceptual structure, namely the conceptual structure associated with the object type 'investment'.

5   Conclusions and Future Research

In this paper, we showed a small fragment of the integrated approach to business modelling at semantic level. In this fragment, it is demonstrated that a process can be seen as an ordering of rules, each of which are grounded in fact types.

The integrated approach, of which a portion is illustrated in this paper, complies to the following ISO principles [6]:

The Helsinki Principle: "Any meaningful exchange of utterances depends upon the prior existence of an agreed set of semantic and syntactic rules. The recipients of the utterances must use only these rules to interpret the received utterances, if it is to mean the same as that which was meant by the utterer."

The Conceptualization Principle: "A conceptual schema should only include conceptually relevant aspects, both static and dynamic, of the universal discourse, thus excluding all aspects of (external or internal) data representation, physical data organization and access as well as all aspects of particular external user representation such message formats, data structures, etc."

The 100 % Principle: "All relevant general static and dynamic aspects, i.e. all rules, laws, etc., of the universe of discourse should be described in the conceptual schema. The information system cannot be held responsible for not meeting those described elsewhere, including in particular those in application programs.

Moreover, it complies to a fourth principle, namely the principle of "early valida-tion" which implies that the development process builds on a representative set of examples that is used to validate the model throughout the development of the model, not only afterwards.

Using this approach, the author believes that through this approach, greater flexi-bility and agility in the implementation (of changes) can be achieved. That is, the author considers an integrated approach as a prerequisite for the realization of cus-tomer-oriented services and for securing the collaboration between organizations (interoperability).

References

1. Object Management Group: Business Process Model and Notation (BPMN) version 2.0 (2011). http://www.omg.org/spec/BPMN/2.0/PDF
2. Object Management Group: Decision Model and Notation (DMN) version 1.0 (2014). http://www.omg.org/spec/DMN/1.0/Beta2/PDF
3. Object Management Group: Semantics of Business Vocabulary and Business Rules (SBVR) Version 1.0 (2008). http://doc.omg.org/formal/08-01-02
4. Bjeković, M., Proper, H.A., Sottet, J.-S.: Enterprise modelling languages. In: Shishkov, B. (ed.) BMSD 2013. LNBIP, vol. 173, pp. 1–23. Springer, Heidelberg (2014)
5. Lemmens, I., Valera, S.: Achieving interoperability at semantic level. In: PV 2013, Ensuring Long-Term Preservation and Adding Value to Scientific and Technical Data (2013)
6. ISO, ISO/TC97/SC5/WWG3 - TR9007 Information Processing Systems - Concepts and Terminology for the Conceptual Schema and the Information Base (1987)

Using Fact-Based Modelling to Develop a Common Language

A Use Case

Inge Lemmens[1](✉), Jan Mark Pleijsant[2], and Rob Arntz[3]

[1] CogNIAM Finance, Amsterdam, The Netherlands
Inge.Lemmens@cogniamfinance.com
[2] ABN AMRO, Amsterdam, The Netherlands
Jan.Mark.Pleijsant@nl.abnamro.com
[3] I-refact, 's Hertogenbosch, The Netherlands
Rob.Arntz@i-refact.com

Abstract. In today's business environment, the challenges an organization has to face have increased in amount and complexity. Not only competition has become tougher, organizations, and in particular financial institutions have to fulfil an increasing amount of regulations imposed by external organizations. To fulfil these legal obligations, a common understanding is required to remove ambiguities within the organizations and to ensure correct reporting.

A common understanding is achieved through the use of a common language in which each relevant term is foreseen of a single Definition that contains no ambiguity such that the risk of misinterpretation is reduced drastically and the time spent on research in case of a new reporting query coming from a (change of) legislation decreases. In this paper, it is explained how fact-based modelling is used to develop the common understanding, by using the fact types as the basic building blocks for the Definitions.

Keywords: Fact-Based Model · Common language · Concepts and definitions

1 Introduction

In today's business environments, the challenges an organization has to face have increased in amount and complexity. Not only competition has become tougher, organizations, and in particular Financial Institutions, have to fulfil an increasing amount of regulations imposed by external organizations like the "National Central Bank", the "National Financial Authority", and the "European Central Bank".

For an organization to be compliant to ever changing regulation it is of importance to understand the regulation and to have an unambiguous translation of the language of the regulation into the language used within the organization. This is a challenge if there is no common language that is used in an organization. And even if the common language exists, without a common understanding of the terms used in the common language, there are no guarantees that compliance is achieved.

© Springer International Publishing Switzerland 2015
I. Ciuciu et al. (Eds.): OTM 2015 Workshops, LNCS 9416, pp. 197–205, 2015.
DOI: 10.1007/978-3-319-26138-6_23

Developing a common language is often thought of as developing a lexicon (an alphabetic list of words with information about used in a given field). However, if not done properly, the risk of misinterpretation due to ambiguities and inconsistencies in the lexicon remains. All too often, a lexicon is developed by defining the terms in a specific context, isolated from the other terms and their Definitions. That is, developing a lexicon is tackled as a "writing exercise". In this paper, a modelling approach to the development of a lexicon is introduced. This approach is currently in use within a large Financial Institution as the means to come to a common understanding of the terminology used within the organization.

The Semantic Information Model plays a central role in the Financial Institution's goal of model-driven development. This role of the SIM, as conceived by the organization, is explained in section 2. In section 3 we introduce the Semantic Information Model (SIM) and its elements. To develop this Semantic Information Model, a development approach is developed to cater the specific requirements of the organization. This development approach is explained in section 4. To assure that the resulting lexicon is of the correct quality, quality requirements with respect to the terms and Definitions are identified, which are based on ISO/IEC 11179-1 [1]. This leads to a four-level qualification schema, which is introduced in section 5. In section 6, the future development of the SIM and associated relationships is explained.

2   The Role of the Semantic Information Model

The development of an organization-specific lexicon that is the single source of reference for the semantics associated with the Business Terms that are used in communication with the stakeholders is realized by developing a *Semantic Information Model (SIM)*, which is an information model that consists of Business Concepts, their associated Business Terms and Definitions as well as the Relationships between the Business Concepts such that the information structure of the organization is represented at semantic level. The Semantic Information Model aims to be the trusted source of information for all Business Concepts, associated terms and Definitions and Relationships. The Financial Institution also intends to use the Semantic Information Model to map all the data sources containing the actual data regarding the Business Concepts to the associated Business Terms such that lineage from Business Terms to data elements in all sources is achieved.

In the frame of model-driven development, the Financial Institution associates the following purposes to the Semantic Information Model:

1. It serves as the basis for the lexicon of Business Terms and associated Definitions, describing the common language of the organization.
2. It provides insight in the Relationships between the Business Concepts that are represented through the Business Terms such that dependencies between Business Concepts become insightful.
3. It serves as the central point of reference whereby external terms provided by e.g. legislative organizations, are matched against.

4. It serves as the central point of reference for all mappings to IT-related data models such that traceability throughout the complete chain of development (i.e. from Term as used in external glossaries like e.g. laws and regulations, to realization in IT application) is achieved.
5. It serves as communication mechanism from Business to Business, from Business to IT and from IT to Business.

3   The Elements of the Meta Model of the Semantic Information Model

One of the main purposes of the Semantic Information Model is to form the basis for the lexicon of the Financial Institution. That is, in early phases, the Semantic Information Model and the lexicon were considered to be the same thing. Therefore, the focus was on the Business Concepts, their associated Terms and Definitions. Later, the Relationships between Business Concepts were introduced as an important element, differentiating between the lexicon and the Semantic Information Model.

In the frame of "practicing what you preach", the meta model Semantic Information Model is defined together with the Subject Matter Experts, on the basis of the protocol that is developed and which is explained in section 4. As said, central elements of the meta model of the Semantic Information Model are Business Concept, Business Term, Definition and Relationship.

3.1   Business Concepts and Business Facts

In order to determine the elements of the meta model of the Semantic Information Model, inspiration is taken from the CogNIAM framework [2, 3]. Thereby, a selection is made by looking at the FIBO Foundations [4], the Financial Industry Business Ontology Foundations meta model.

The central element in the meta model of the Semantic Information Model is the Business Concept. A Business Concept is defined as "*a Thing that is important enough to the Business that Business Facts about the Thing are necessary to run the Business*". This definition implies that Business Concepts are only limited to those Things that are used to run the Business. This aids in the classification of Business Concepts versus not-so- relevant concepts. For example, in the case of the Financial Institution, through the definition of Business Concept, the Thing denoted by the Term "Credit risk" would be denoting a Business Concept while the Thing denoted by the Term "Housecat" would not be denoting a Business Concept.

In the definition of Business Concept, there is a reference to "Thing" and "Business Fact". For defining "Thing", the definition as stated in FIBO is taken, namely: "*a Thing is a set of elements which are defined according to the facts given for that kind of things.*". In fact-based modelling terminology, a "Thing" as defined above represents an Object Type.

A Business Fact is defined as a "*fact that describes a Business Concept*". For example, "first name" would be a "business fact" about the Business Concept

"Individual". It should be noted that the term Business Fact might be confusing since it represents a *type of fact*, not a specific fact. However, the term "fact type" is not accepted by the Business users while the term "fact" is acceptable.

The Financial Institution has a need to distinguish between "Characteristics" and "Relationships", whereby a business fact either represents a Characteristic or a Relationship. This distinction is introduced because not only "Characteristic" and "Relationships" are terms that the business is acquainted with, it is also used for the mapping to the underlying technical models.

A Characteristic is defined as: "*a Business Fact that represents an aspect of a Business Concept*", while a Relationship is defined as: "*a Business Fact that represents a meaningful link between two or more Business Concepts*".

The model fragment associated with the elements of the meta model of the Semantic Information Model introduced above, are given in Figure 1.

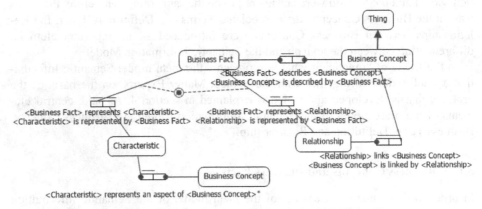

Fig. 1. Model fragment for Business Concept and Business Fact.

3.2   Business Terms

A Business Concept can only be talked about if there is a Business Term that denotes the Business Concept. Therefore, it is stated that each Business Concept is denoted by at least one Business Term. A Business Term is defined as: "*a word or phrase that designates a Business Concept*". Moreover, the Financial Institutions has also realized the potential need for using a term to denote a Business Fact.

From an enterprise-wide common language perspective, the Financial Institution has decided that for each Business Concept, there is exactly one Preferred Business Term. Synonyms are allowed, but they are only allowed as reference to the Preferred Business Term associated with the Business Concept. For example, if the Business Term "Customer" is the preferred term to denote the Business Concept, then the Definition of the synonym "Client" is a mere reference to the Business Term "Customer", by stating in the Definition of "Client": "*see Customer*". Figure 2 depicts the model fragment of the Semantic information Model that captures the above.

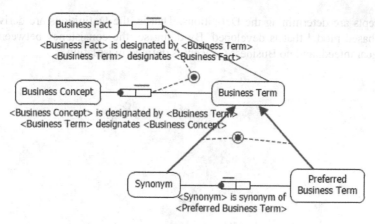

Fig. 2. Model fragment associated with Business Term.

3.3   Definitions

Associated with a Business Concept is a Definition. That is, for each Business Concept, there is exactly one Definition. However, in order to tailor for the option to specify in the Definition of a synonym the reference to the preferred Business Term, the choice has been made to state that with each Business Term exactly one Definition is associated. A Definition is thereby defined as: *"a phrase that states the exact meaning of a Business Term"*.

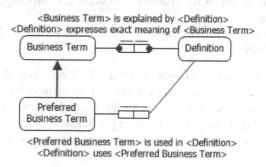

Fig. 3. Model fragment associated with Definition.

As shown in Figure 3, in a Definition, preferred Business Terms are used. This to fulfil one of the quality criteria for Definitions that are described in section 5.

4   The Protocol

To "populate" the meta model of the Semantic Information Model structure as defined above (i.e. to develop the Semantic Information Model), the Financial Institution has developed a protocol that aids in developing correct and consistent Definitions. As the observant reader can deduce from above, the identification of the Relationships between the concepts are determining the Definitions. That is, the Definitions are derived from the fact-based model that is developed. By doing so, the consistency between Definitions is guaranteed, and no Business Concept is defined in isolation.

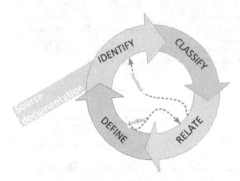

Fig. 4. The 4 phases of the overall development process.

As can be seen in Figure 4, the overall process for the development of the Semantic Information Model can be split in 4 main phases, namely:

1. The *identify* phase in which Business Concepts are identified and foreseen of a preliminary meaning and context.
2. The *classify* phase in which Business Concepts are formally placed in an overall hierarchy.
3. The *relate* phase in which the Business Concepts are formally placed in relationship to each other.
4. The *define* phase in which the Definition is created based on the outcome of the three previous phases.

Each of the phases identified consists of a set of activities that have to be performed in order to result in a concise, correct and understandable Semantic Information Model. These activities are inspired by the CogNIAM protocol as described in [2]. The use of concrete examples to illustrate the business concepts and Relationships has shown to be of a great advantage to come to a common understanding of the Business Terms.

4.1   Definition Development and Validation Process

To implement the protocol, the cooperation of the subject matter experts (SMEs) is important. Therefore, the protocol is supported by a development and validation process that is implemented in the organization to ensure the correct quality of Definitions. This process consists of:

1. A development phase, in which the Semantic Information Model is developed in accordance to the protocol. In this phase, 3 workshops with the SMEs are identified, namely:

(a) The clarification workshop in which clarification of context, meaning and purpose of the Business Concept is given by the subject matter experts. In this workshop, a sketch of the Relationships between the Business Concepts is the major outcome.
(b) The Definition workshop in which the Business Concepts are classified, the Relationships identified in the previous workshop are fine-tuned and the Business Concepts are defined in accordance to the identified Relationships.
(c) The confirmation workshop in which the Definitions are fine-tuned and confirmed by the subject matter experts.
2. A challenge phase, in which the Definitions of the Business Concepts and their Relationships are challenged by other subject matters experts to ensure that the intended meaning is correct. This is considered to be a quality check on usefulness, comprehensiveness and consistency of the Business Concepts.
3. A review phase in which the common understanding is reviewed by a broad community throughout the different business domains that use the Business Terms.
4. An approval phase in which the bank-wide Data Definition Board is responsible for approving the identified Business Concepts and their associated Definitions and Relationships.

This overall development and validation process is implemented to ensure that the developed Semantical Information Model is a consistent and coherent model, whereby the Definitions constructed fulfil the quality requirements listed in the next section.

5   Quality Criteria

In [1], ISO has identified several quality criteria for data definitions. These quality criteria have been taken as the basis for developing quality criteria for the Definitions of the Business Concepts. Thereby, the criteria are organized to differentiate between different levels of quality. The aim of the Financial Institution is to get the Definitions to level 3.

The quality criteria themselves are defined as follows:

1. Level I criteria – from incoherent to ambiguous:
   (a) A Definition is a descriptive phrase or sentence.
   (b) A Definition does not contain a reference to itself.
   (c) A Definition follows the following pattern: "a <Business Term> is a <more general Business Term in hierarchy> that/which/what/who <discriminating reasons>.".
2. Level II criteria – from ambiguous to unambiguous
   (a) A Definition states what the concept is, not only what it is not.
   (b) A Definition states the essential meaning.
   (c) A Definition is unambiguous.
   (d) A Definition does not introduce a second-order circular reference.
   (e) A Definition does not introduce a contradiction with or between other Definitions.

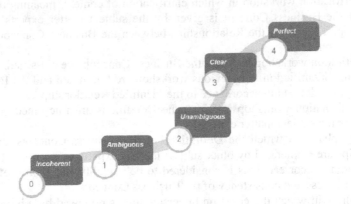

Fig. 5. The different levels of quality of the Definitions.

3. Level III criteria – from unambiguous to clear:
  (a) A Definition is stated in the singular.
  (b) A Definition contains only common understood abbreviations and terms.
  (c) The form of a Definition is such that it can replace the term in context.
  (d) A Definition uses the same terminology and consistent logical structure as related Definitions.
  (e) A Definition does not require additional explanations or other references to understand the meaning.
  (f) A Definition follows the writing guidelines of the Financial Institution.
4. Level IV criteria – from clear to perfect:
  (a) A Definition is expressed without embedding Definitions of other data or underlying concepts.
  (b) A Definition is expressed without embedding rationale, functional usage or procedural information.
  (c) A Definition consists of a single phrase specifying the concept.

6   Conclusions and Future Work

The development of a common understanding is gaining more and more interest from organizations, in particular from organizations that have to comply to all kinds of external regulations. This in turn has attracted interest of those organizations in semantic modelling. What distinguishes the Financial Institution whose way of working is described in this paper from other organizations is their well-defined way of working.

This way of working has not come about in a week's time. It has taken the Financial Institution many months to come to this structure for the Semantic Information Model and the associated protocol. Earlier versions of the protocol did not emphasize the use of Relationships to define the Business Concepts. Only by practicing the way of working together with CogNIAM experts has given them the insight to use the Relationships between the concepts (the so-called Business Facts) as the basis for the

Definition. Also, the identification of quality criteria and associated quality levels has come about only in the last month but has already proven to be very useful in the governance process.

The work has not finished. In the process of building the Semantic Information Model, the Financial Institution realizes that defining Business Concepts and their Relationships is not enough. For a good understanding, it is also required to identify data integrity rules, like uniqueness, mandatory and referential integrity, as well as derivation rules. The latter are in particular of relevance for defining reporting terms that are derivations of data that conforms to the Business Concepts.

In the near future, the current version of the Semantic Information Model will be extended by adding rules that ensure the integrity of the data associated with the Business Concepts. This as a first step to use the Semantic Information Model as a means to aid in solving data quality issues.

The Semantic Information Model is only one of the business models and does not stand in isolation. As part of business architecture, the Relationships between the Business Information Model and other types of business models, like the business process model and business rules model will be further developed. By doing so, an integrated way of working can be developed and true model-driven development can be achieved.

References

1. ISO/IEC.: ISO/IEC 11179-1 Information technology – Metadata registries (MDR) – Part 1: Framework (2004)
2. Nijssen, S., Valera, S.: An Architecture Ecosystem for the Whole Systems Perspective, Including System Dynamics, Based on Logic & Set Theory and Controlled Natural Languages. Working paper for the OMG Architecture Ecosystem SIG (2012)
3. Lemmens, I., Valera, S.: Achieving interoperability at semantic level. In: PV 2013, Ensuring Long-Term Preservation and Adding Value to Scientific and Technical Data (2013)
4. Object Management Group: Financial Industry Business Ontology Foundations Version 1.0 – Beta 1 (2014). http://www.omg.org/spec/EDMC-FIBO/FND/1.0/Beta1/

Achieving Interoperability at Semantic Level

Inge Lemmens[1(✉)], Jean-Paul Koster[1], and Serge Valera[2]

[1] PNA Group, Heerlen, The Netherlands
{Inge.Lemmens,Jean.Paul.Koster}@pna-group.com
[2] European Space Agency, ESTEC, Noordwijk, The Netherlands
Serge.Valera@esa.int

Abstract. Developing and operating Space Systems involves complex activities, involving many parties distributed in location and time. This development requires efficient and effective interoperability during the overall Space System development and operations lifecycle.

Interoperability is often described from a syntactic viewpoint, focusing on data exchange formats. While syntactic interoperability is required, the prerequisite for any successful information exchange is to ensure that all actors involved share a common understanding of the information that will be exchanged. This aspect of interoperability is known as semantic interoperability. Semantic interoperability focusses on "what" is being exchanged, while syntactic interoperability focuses on "how" it is being exchanged.

The need for semantic interoperability is described in [1], which is developed by the European Cooperation for Space Standardization (ECSS). In this technical memorandum, the concept of a "global conceptual data model" as a means to achieve the required semantic interoperability is introduced. Fact-based modelling is introduced as the means to develop a global conceptual data model.

In this paper, we address the issues of semantic interoperability and describe the developments on-going at the European Space Agency (ESA) for fully supporting semantic interoperability.

Keywords: Semantic interoperability · Fact-based modelling · Global conceptual data model

1 Introduction

Interoperability, the ability of systems and organizations to work together, is often described in terms of data exchange according to specific data formats and communication protocols; i.e., from the syntactical viewpoint. While syntactic agreements on how to interoperate are required for interoperability, syntactic agreements alone are not sufficient to guarantee a complete understanding of the information that is exchanged. Semantic interoperability, addressing the "what" in the exchange is also required.

I. Ciuciu et al. (Eds.): OTM 2015 Workshops, LNCS 9416, pp. 206–215, 2015.
DOI: 10.1007/978-3-319-26138-6_24

Interoperability typically focuses on the physical data model (e.g., the structures, the data format, i.e. the syntax) used in the exchange as described, for example, in an interface control document. Semantic interoperability addresses the conceptual knowledge that has been used for producing the physical model. Semantic interoperability focuses on ensuring that all parties involved in the exchange share the same semantic understanding of the information carried by the physical data model. This implies formalization of that knowledge, i.e. the production of the conceptual data model focusing on the semantics, e.g. removing any technology-dependent requirements.

As depicted in Figure 1, usually and unfortunately, the limited perception that many users have on exchange consists of the following steps:

- Depending on who is in charge, i.e.:
  - The *supplier:* identify the subset of the supplier data that needs to be transferred to the customer, or
  - The *customer:* identify the subset of the customer data that needs to be supplied by the supplier,
- Produce an interface control document that exposes this subset under the structural form that is most adequate for the party in charge of the data subset identification.

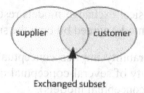

Fig. 1. Common understanding – supplier and customer "share" a subset.

This approach is insufficient, especially due to historical reasons, i.e. the vocabularies used by the supplier and customer rarely match in "meaning". For example, homonymous forms might exist which heightens the risk of misunderstanding and wrong information.

What is depicted as a subset in Figure 1 is not necessarily a subset. Closer to reality, at physical level, the need exists to map the supplier model to the exchange model and the exchange model to the customer model as depicted in Figure 2. This mapping results in transforming the data contained within the supplier's system in data compliant with the exchange model and transforming the exchanged data into data compliant with the customer's system.

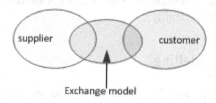

Fig. 2. Exchange model as the basis for exchange.

Semantic interoperability formally addresses these mapping issues providing the means to formally express how to convert the supplier conceptual model used to produce the supplier physical data model into the customer conceptual model used to produce the customer physical data model. Semantic interoperability requires conceptual modeling, i.e., the means to formally develop solutions capturing the "what" and transforming the what into a "how" that is technology-dependent, i.e. transforming the conceptual data model into a logical data model (e.g., relational, object oriented) and a physical data model that is tool specific.

Addressing the exchange from a semantic perception implies removing any ambiguity, any risk of misunderstanding. To achieve this, the development of the exchange shall be formalized, resulting in interface control documents that:

- Specify the exchange model at conceptual level,
- Map the exchange conceptual model to the conceptual model of the supplier (for the part that is exchanged). This assumes that the conceptual model is effectively available at supplier level (else it needs to be produced),
- Map the exchange conceptual model to the conceptual model of the customer (for the part that is exchanged). This also assumes the existence of the customer conceptual model,
- Specify the logical and physical exchange models resulting from the transformation of the conceptual exchange model agreed by both the supplier and the customer.

Addressing semantic interoperability implies conceptual modeling and means to address the semantic compatibility of several conceptual models (e.g. mapping the supplier, exchange and customer conceptual models).

In this paper, we address the concept of the "global conceptual data model" as introduced in [1] as a means to achieve semantic interoperability. To develop this global conceptual model, fact-based modelling is promoted as the means to create and specify the conceptual models that are used in exchange. Fact-based modelling is a modelling methodology that applies modelling, based on logic and controlled natural language (formal), whereby the semantics of the relevant (part of the) domain of interest is captured in the resulting fact-based conceptual data model. This resulting fact-based conceptual data model captures these semantics by means of fact types (kind of facts), together with the associated concept definitions, the fact- and rule communication patterns as well as the rules applying to these fact types.

In section 2, the knowledge triangle that is used in the context of the development of the global conceptual model is introduced. Section 3 specifies what is meant by the global conceptual model. In section 4 we introduce FAMOUS-2, the tool that is meant to support semantic interoperability.

2   Fact-Based Modelling

Fact-based modelling is a modelling methodology for modelling information at conceptual level. Conceptual is to be understood as completely independent of any software implementation technology; that is, the concepts used and means of expression do not refer in any way to a possible implementation strategy like e.g. relational, object-oriented or hierarchical. The methodology applies formal modeling based on logic and controlled natural language. The resulting conceptual model captures the semantics of the relevant domain of interest are captured by means of fact types (kind of facts), together with the associated concept definitions – the terms and definitions, the communication patterns as well as the rules applying to these fact types – the system requirements related to the information model.

One of the distinguishing factors of fact-based modeling (compared to other modeling notations) is the fact that validation and testing is integrated in every step of the conceptual modeling process associated to the system requirements production. That is, all intermediate results are validated with the stakeholders before any implementation activity starts. This validation is performed by the use of concrete examples of fact type populations and associated verbalizations in a notation and language the stakeholder is familiar with.

2.1   The Knowledge Triangle

The Knowledge Triangle is a three-level knowledge framework that over the years has proven to be very productive for developing fact-based conceptual models. It can be considered as an additional stratification of knowledge categories in which logical reasoning is applied. The Knowledge Triangle is also a visual aid in the development of fact-based conceptual modelling. The Knowledge Triangle is depicted in Figure 3.

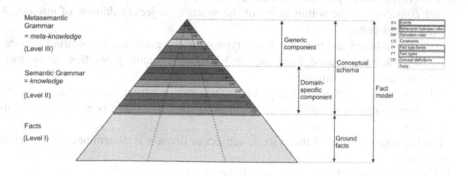

Fig. 3. The Knowledge Triangle.

Level I: The Ground Facts or Assertions

The assumption of fact-based modelling methodologies is that the most concrete level in any structured knowledge description or business communication consists of ground facts. It is observed that these comprise the vast majority in business, engineering or technical communication.

A ground fact is defined as "a proposition taken to be true by a relevant community" and is expressed as an assertion that either simply predicates over individual objects or simply asserts the existence of an individual object. Examples are: "The launch attempt performed by launcher Ariane 5", "Flight number VA212 took place on February 7th 2013" and "Launcher Ariane 5 exists".

Ground facts, expressed by means of sentences, describe factual, planned or imagined situations, in the past, current time or future; they do not prescribe any grammar aspect.

Level II: The Semantic Grammar of the Domain

Level II of the knowledge triangle consists of the domain specific conceptual model. It consists of knowledge categories to which the ground facts of level I must adhere as well as concept definitions to understand the ground facts; it could be said it provides interpretation semantics. In other words, level II specifies the rules that govern the ground facts at level I and defines the concept definitions of the terms used in the facts, when there is the slightest doubt they could be misunderstood. Moreover, the usage of ground facts is also described at this level. Level II is expressed by means of a series of knowledge categories, namely:

1. *Concept definitions*, which have as function to describe the meaning of every term or group of terms in the ground facts for which it is assumed that the meaning is not fully known to the intended audience and common understanding of the meaning is required. In case the meaning of a term is assumed to be known it is good practice to state this explicitly in order to avoid any confusion.
2. *Fact types*, which provide the functionality to define which kinds of ground facts are considered to be within *scope* of the system, subject or domain of interest. A fact type is either:
   (a) variable-based fact type, i.e. a fact type seen as a populatable construct, generalizing level I ground facts on the basis of common properties, using fact-communication patterns.
   (b) A role-based fact type, i.e. a fact type seen as a construct that generalizes level I ground facts on the basis of common properties, using rule-communication patterns.
   The boundary (scope) of the system, subject or domain is determined by the set of fact types.
3. *Fact type forms*, whereby there is a distinction between:
   (a) *Fact communication patterns*: their function is to act as communication mechanism to be used as a template to communicate ground facts in a language and using terms the subject matter expert is familiar with. A fact communication pattern is a template whereby the placeholders (denoted by angle brackets can be instantiated by ground level fact values. A fact communication pattern associated with one of the example above would be: *"The launch attempt performed by launcher <Launcher name> and flight number <Flight number> took place on <Launch date>*, and

(b) *Rule communication patterns*, whose function is to act as communication mechanism for communicating the rules, listed in point 4 below, of the conceptual model. The rule communication pattern associated with the example is: *"[Launch attempt] took place on [Date]"*. Instantiation might result in the following rule: "Each *[Launch attempt] took place on* exactly one *[Date]"*.

Both types of communication patterns use community-specific terminology.

4. *Constraints*, also known as "integrity rules" or "validation rules", have as function to restrict the set of ground facts and the transitions between the permitted sets of ground facts to those that are considered useful. In other words, integrity rules have the function to restrict populations as well as transitions between populations to useful ones.

5. *Derivation rules*, which are used to derive or calculate new information (ground facts) on the basis of existing information. That is, derivation rules describe how to derive new ground facts on the basis of existing ground facts.

6. *Behavioral business rules*, which have as function to move ground facts from the domain under consideration into the administration of that domain and vice versa, or to remove ground facts from the administration. In other words, they specify how ground facts are added and/or removed from the system such that the system stays in sync with the communication about the outside world.

7. *Events*, which specify when to update the set of ground facts by a derivation rule or behavioral rule. That is, an event specifies under which circumstances the set of facts corresponding to the fact types is updated.

Level III: The Generic Component of the Knowledge Triangle
The third level of the knowledge triangle, the generic component, independent of any specific domain, consists of the knowledge categories to which each conceptual model of level II must adhere. In other words, Level III of the knowledge triangle consists of the generic conceptual model, expressed in the same knowledge categories as any domain-specific conceptual model. Each element in the generic component of the knowledge triangle or the generic conceptual model is independent of any specific part of the domain or system. Interestingly enough, the generic conceptual model is a population of itself.

3   Fact-Based Modelling and Semantic Interoperability

Semantic interoperability is tackled by "bi-directional mapping" of different models. This only works if he models are expressed in a modelling language that is formal and unambiguously defined. Unfortunately not many modeling methods fulfill these criteria. The unified modeling language (UML), for example, lacks a formal representation of its meta model, resulting in the fact that models expressed in UML are not unambiguous nor clear. For example, the meaning of an "aggregation" is not formally defined in UML. Even in the UML 2.5 standard it is specified that: "precise semantics of shared aggregation varies by application area and modeler" [2].

For semantic interoperability to be successful, it is necessary to model using a conceptual modelling methodology that is completely implementation-independent, unambiguous in interpretation and formal in representation. That is why fact-based modelling is promoted in [1] as the modelling methodology to be used for developing models at the conceptual level.

3.1   Conceptual Model at Global Level

In [1], the way forward promoted to solve the interoperability issues at semantic level consists of:

- Standardizing at global level the "what",
- Offering means to tailor that "what" recursively where tailoring means adding the specific needs and selecting the subset of interest of the global conceptual model.

This approach has the benefit to only model at local level (e.g. a supplier) what that local level needs. The semantic interoperability is addressed at global conceptual level where the semantic required for a safe exchange is captured, e.g. by means of synonyms, community specific fact type readings, derivations rules, etc. That is, each party involved in the exchange can extract its own "local" conceptual model from the global conceptual model by:

1. Identifying within the existing global conceptual model those conceptual definitions of interest to the local view,
2. Potentially tailoring the identified conceptual definitions to establish the local view on the global conceptual model for the local view, and
3. Extracting the tailored view on the global conceptual model for further development of the local conceptual model, whereby the link with the global conceptual model is maintained for traceability purposes.

This principle is depicted in Figure 4.

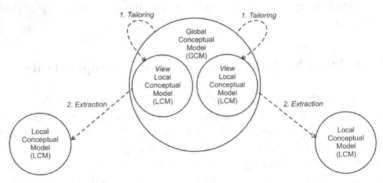

Fig. 4. The process of selecting, tailoring and extracting the local model from the global.

3.2   Achieving Interoperability

To achieve the overall objective of efficient and effective information exchange, two functions need to be combined, namely the following functions:

1. The function to support the production of physical models of the supplier and customer's information systems that are used in the exchange, and
2. The function to support the exchange of data on the basis of the global conceptual model that comprises the globally-consistent conceptual definitions and of which the local conceptual models are a (potentially tailored) subset.

The combination of these two functions support interoperability between different local systems both at semantic as well at syntactic level. This principle is depicted in Figure 5.

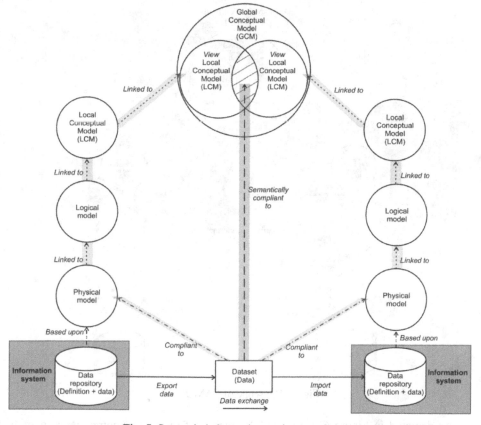

Fig. 5. Semantic information exchange support.

As illustrated in Figure 5, the dataset exchanged between two data repositories of local information systems is compliant to the physical model of both applications. These physical models are based upon their respective logical models which are derived from the local conceptual model that is an extracted view from the global conceptual model. Because of this compliance to the physical model and the linking all the way up to the global conceptual model it is accomplished that the information exchanged between the local information systems is semantically compliant to the global conceptual model. Hence, semantic interoperability is achieved.

4   FAMOUS-2 as Supporting Tool

The support of the complete process, from global conceptual model to implementation in local information system views, is the subject of the FAMOUS-2 research project at ESA. This research project aims to develop the complete specification to support all aspects of semantic interoperability as described above.

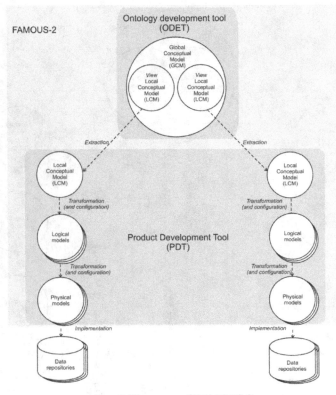

Fig. 6. The scope of FAMOUS 2.

As depicted in Figure 6, FAMOUS-2 consists of two major components, namely the Ontology Development Tool (ODET), which has as aim to support the development of a global conceptual model and the extraction of the local conceptual models.

The extracted local conceptual models can, in the Product Development Tool (PDT) of FAMOUS-2, be transformed into different kinds of logical (relational,

UML, and hierarchical) and physical models (amongst others SQL, XSD, XMI). The physical models can be implemented creating data repositories which are based upon the physical models.

5   Conclusions

In this paper it is mentioned that reliable information exchange during the whole life-cycle of a Space System implies that the information has to be exchanged between the sharing parties without any mismatch of meaning or loss of semantics. This semantic interoperability between sharing parties can be achieved if the involved information systems implement globally-consistent conceptual definitions. The approach suggested in this paper is to develop a global conceptual model whose scope embraces the complete Space System lifecycle. Each individual information system shall implement a subset of this global conceptual model, being the local conceptual models for these information systems. The global conceptual model can be established using a fact-based modeling method, which is a method for modeling information systems at the conceptual and completely implementation independent level, capturing the semantics of the relevant (part of the) domain of interest. The local conceptual models, being a subset of and linked to the global conceptual model, can be transformed into corresponding logical and physical models, with a linking between the semantically equivalent elements from the physical models via the logical models and the local conceptual model all the way up to the global conceptual model. With an information exchange that complies to the physical models of the information systems that exchange this information and the linking of the physical models of these information systems all the way up to the global conceptual model, where that global conceptual model embraces the scope of these information systems, it is accomplished that the information exchanged between the local information systems is semantically compliant to the global conceptual model. Hence, semantic interoperability between the local information systems is achieved.

References

1. ECSS, ECSS-E-TM-10-23A: Space Engineering – Space system data Repository, Noordwijk, The Netherlands (2011)
2. OMG, OMG Unified Modeling Language™ Version 2.5 FTF – Beta 1
3. ESA/ESTEC, Fact based Modeling Unifying System Toward Implementation Solutions for ECSS-E-TM-10-23A, Contract No. 4000107725/13/NL/GLC/al (2013)
4. Nijssen, G.M.: A Framework for Discussion in ISO/TC97/SC5/WG3 and comments on 78.04/01 and 78.05/03 (1978)
5. Lemmens, I., Sgaramella, F., Valera, S.: Development of tooling to support fact-oriented modeling at ESA. In: Meersman, R., Herrero, P., Dillon, T. (eds.) OTM 2009 Workshops. LNCS, vol. 5872, pp. 714–722. Springer, Heidelberg (2009)

The Great Work of Michael Senko as a Part of a Durable Application Model

Peter Bollen[(✉)]

Maastricht University, Maastricht, The Netherlands
p.bollen@maastrichtuniversity.nl

Abstract. This paper defines a language for expressing a durable semantic application model as major part of the specifications for business applications This language consists of the modeling constructs from Natural Language Modeling (NLM). It will be shown in this article how these modeling constructs constitute a hierarchy within any durable semantic application model.

Keywords: Semantic-conceptual modeling · Natural Language Modeling · Michael senko

1   Introduction

As the number of information services (e.g. web-services, application service providers and e-commerce applications) continues to grow, in a globalized economy and the need for interoperability between those services becomes apparent in the context of organizational resilience, the availability of a durable modeling language that enables analysts to capture a changing and evolving application business communication is necessary. This language therefore must be able to establish links with common business vocabularies and data in applications and should be easy to understand by the various groups of stakeholders including non-expert users. Such a language must be very close to the natural language that is used by people in their daily business communications.

Some people assert that an ontology can serve as a semantic-conceptual model. In the literature a number of definitions for ontology can be found " an ontology is a description of the concepts and relationships for an agent or a community of agents." [1] , " shared understanding of a domain that can be communicated between people and application systems." [2]. "an ontology is a formal conceptualization of a real world, sharing a common understanding of this real world." [3: p.155]. [4] distinguish four types of material ontologies: *application, domain*, *generic* and *representation* ontologies. We conclude that the unqualified term ontology is a first class homonym that we recommend to avoid.

In the context of the diffusion of IT for organizational resilience, we will furthermore, require that a language for a durable application model allows for fast adaptation to ever changing organizational environments, in terms of products and services delivered, changing market regulations and so forth.

I. Ciuciu et al. (Eds.): OTM 2015 Workshops, LNCS 9416, pp. 216–225, 2015.
DOI: 10.1007/978-3-319-26138-6_25

The application modeling constructs in NLM are based upon the axiom that all verbalizable information (computer screens, reports, note-books, traffic signs and so forth) can be translated into *declarative natural language sentences* [5]. It means that it is *neither* a real *nor* an abstract world that is the object described in the model, but the *communication about* such a real or abstract world. This will require the feasible modeling constructs to provide those constructs that enable analysts to model what in the seventies and eighties was called natural language sentences and today more often is referred to as facts. Since the early 1970's a number of conceptual semantic models approaches have emerged. A NLM based model was the fact based modeling approach. The most widely used, by far, is the entity-relationship (ER) approach. The first definition of the ER constructs can be found in Chen [6]. This approach has been developed and extended further in [7] and [8]. The first fact based modeling approach had the name ENALIM, Evolving Natural Language Information Model. As the name implies Natural Language Information modeling was at the very beginning in the seventies. Soon thereafter Control Data decided to call the then as a professional service offered modeling NIAM, later explained as Natural language Information Modeling. From this ORM emerged in the nineties, as well as FCO-IM and DOGMA.

The rest of this paper is structured as follows: section 2 gives an introduction of the NLM modeling constructs for expressing a durable application model; in section 3 the concepts for the durable application modeling are given; in section 4 conclusions regarding the construct hierarchy in durable semantic modeling will be drawn.

2   The Modeling Constructs in NLM for Capturing the Durable Application Model

In this section, the modeling constructs for natual language modeling will be introduced. The first modeling construct is the *name*.

A name in human communication is used to refer to a concept or a thing in a real or abstract world [9]. A *name* is a sequence of words in a given language that is agreed upon to refer to *at least* one concept or thing in a real or abstract world, for example, *Jake Jones*, *567893AB*, *General Electric*. We will call the union of all names the *archetype*.

The choice of names used in communication is constrained by the reference requirement for effective communication. For example, the university registration office will use a *student ID* for referring to an individual *student*. The use of names from the name class *last name* in the university registration subject area for referring to individual students, however, will not lead to effective communication because in some cases two or more students may be referenced by *one* name instance from this name class. This is one of the reasons why not all names can be used for referencing entities, things or concepts in a specific part of a real or abstract world. On the other hand, it is evident that knowledge workers that are involved in activities in an application subject area have knowledge of the reference characteristic of the potential name classes for the different groups of "things" in a real or abstract world. This means that they should be able to tell an analyst whether a name from a specific name class can be used to identify a thing or concept among the union of similar things or similar concepts (in a specific part of a real or abstract world).

2.1   The Natural Language Axiom

In every (business) organization many examples of communication can be found. These examples can be represented on a computer screen, a worldwide web page, a computer report or even a formatted telephone conversation. Although the outward appearance of these examples might be of a different nature every time, their content can be expressed using natural language. We will refer to this class of examples of communication as *verbalizable* information.

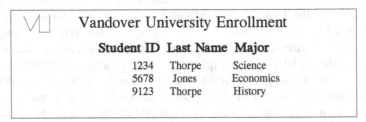

Fig. 1. Example Vandover University Enrollment.

Now that we have defined the possible application areas for NLM we can start defining modeling constructs for durable application models that can take natural language sentences or facts as a starting point. In figure 1 an example of a *university enrollment document* is given. In this example the Vandover University wants to record information about the major for each of its students. It is assumed that the *student ID* can be used to identify a *specific* student among the *union* of students that are (and have been) enrolled in the Vandover University, and that a *major name* can be used as identifier for a *specific* major among the *union* of majors that are offered by the Vandover University. The application of the natural language axiom on the example of communication from figure 1 leads to facts 1.1 through 1.6.

student 1234 majors in Science..*(fact 1.1)*

student 5678 majors in Economics... ....*(fact 1.2)*

student 9123 majors in History..*(fact 1.3)*

student 1234 has last name Thorpe..*(fact 1.4)*

student 5678 has last name Jones...*(fact 1.5)*

student 9123 has last name Thorpe... *(fact 1.6)*

2.2   Variables and Roles: Both are Needed

If we analyze example facts 1.1 through 1.6 that have resulted from verbalizing the university enrollment example in figure 1, we can divide them into two groups according to the type of sentence predicate (..majors…, respectively ..has last name..). If we focus on the first group we can derive two fact group templates in which we have denoted the predicate as text, and the variable parts as text between brackets: *Student <enrolled student> majors in major <chosen major>* and *Student <enrolled student> has chosen the major <chosen major>*. We will refer to the variable parts as *roles, when we abstract from the naming convention*. However for modeling the communication we need to include the naming convention and then we speak of a variable. Figure 2 shows a graphical representation of the two fact groups in the University Enrollment example. Each role in the role representation is represented by a "box", e.g. *enrolled student*. Each abstract fact group is represented by a combination of role boxes. Fact group *Sg1* is represented by the combination of role boxes *enrolled student* and *chosen major*. Fact group *Sg2* is represented by the combination of "role" boxes *registered student* and *last name*. For each fact group one or more fact group templates are positioned underneath the combination of role boxes that belong to the fact group. In the diagram of figure 2, factgroup templates 1 and 2 belong to fact group *Sg1*. Fact group template 3 belongs to fact group *Sg2*.

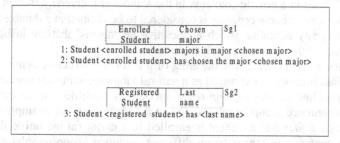

Fig. 2. Roles, fact group and fact, group template(s) for university enrollment

If we examine figure 2 we will see that a fact group template can reveal additional information about the type of things that can be "inserted" into a *role*. For example, the word "student" specifies what type of thing (or concept) is allowed to play the role "enrolled student" but also what type of thing (or concept) is allowed to play the role "registered student". We will call the "student" part in the fact groups in figure 2 the *intension* of the roles "enrolled student" and "registered student". We will now illustrate how such a list of terms or concept definitions can help us capture a durable *application-* or *domain model*.

To make a durable application model explicit, we need to incorporate a definition of the concepts or pronouns in the fact group templates including the intensions. For example, the definition of the concept *Student*: *A student is a person that studies at a University*. The names of things or concept instances to which such a definition of intension applies within a *specific* application subject area at a *specific* point in time is called the *extension*. We can now give an example extension for the intension *Student*: *{1234, 5678, 9123}*. In the remainder of this paper we will use the term *intension* to denote the *type* of thing or concept to which a *specific* thing or concept belongs. For every application area we will document the relevant concepts and their definitions in a list. In the following illustration we have given an example of such a list for the university enrollment UoD (see table 1).

Table 1. List of definitions for university enrollment example

Concept	Definition
Student	*a person that studies at Vandover University*
Student ID	*an ID that identifies a specific student at Vandover University*
Major	*a course program offered to <student>s by Vandover University*
Major name	*a name class , instances of which can be used to identify a <major> among the union of <major>s offered by Vandover University*
Last name	*a characteristic of a student, namely his or her last name*

Such a list of concepts and their definitions should contain a definition for *each* intension in the UoD. The definition of an intension should specify how the knowledge forming the intension (*definiendum*) is to be constructed from the knowledge given in the definition itself and in the defining concepts (*definiens*). A defining concept should either be an intension or a different concept that must be previously defined in the list of concepts or it should be defined in a generic ontology. In the Vandover University student enrollment example the concept *course program* is considered to be defined in a durable application model for university education which implies that all 'agents' that are involved in this UoD have attached the same meaning to this concept.

The construct for modeling the meaning of a a surface structure sentence is a *fact instance*. A fact instance is expressed as a natural language sentence instance of a one of its corresponding *sentence group template(s)*. It is possible that the extensions of two different sentence group templates refer to the same *fact*. For example we can say that there exists a *fact* that a student is enrolled in a major (at the university of Vandover). Two sentence instances (from different sentence group templates) for communicating this *fact instance* can be:

Student 1234 has chosen the major Science
Student 1234 majors in major Science.

We need to make a distinction into the concept of *fact* (the deep structure sentence) and the concepts that we use to *represent a fact (surface structure sentence)*. A specific fact instance can be represented as one or more sentence instances from one or more sentence group templates. We can now conclude that an abstract fact type is a set of roles that can be represented by one or more sentence group template(s) in which these roles are contained. The roles that are contained in these sentence group templates are *identical* although they can have a different sequence.

2.3   Naming Convention Fact Types

In this section we will further formalize the outcome of the process of the selection of a name class for referring to things in a real or abstract world. The outcome of such a naming process will result in the utterance of sentences or facts for example facts 2.1, 2.2, 2.3 and 2.4.

1234 is a name from the student ID name class that can be used to identify a student within the union of students at Vandover University......................................(fact 2.1)

5678 is a name from the student ID name class that can be used to identify a student within the union of students at Vandover University....................   ....*(fact 2.2)*
Science is a name from the major name name class that can be used to identify a major within the union of majors at Vandover University.......................   ...*(fact 2.3)*
Economics is a name from the major name name class that can be used to identify a major within the union of majors at Vandover University ....*(fact 2.4)*

We see that facts 2.1 through 2.4 express that a certain *name* belongs to a certain *name class* and that instances of the name class *student ID,* can be used to identify an instance of a *student,* and an instance of the name class *major name,* can be used to identify an instance of a *major* within the UoD of Vandover University. We can give, for example, the definition of the concept *Student ID: Student ID is a name class.* The 'intension' of the names in fact sentences 2.1 through 2.4 is a *name class* and NOT a type of *thing, entity* or *concept* in the real world. We will, therefore, refer to facts 2.1, 2.2, 2.3 and 2.4 as *naming convention facts.* The corresponding fact type will then be called a *naming convention fact type.*

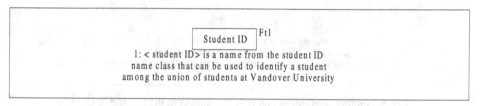

Fig. 3. Naming convention fact type for *Student*

A role representation is the preferred one if one is interested in formulating rules; a variable representation is the preferred one if one is interested in performing validation with realistic examples.

2.4   Compound Reference Schemes

In the Vandover University example the intension student has a "simple" reference scheme, namely: the single role "enrolled student" or "registered student". In many cases, however, a *simple* reference scheme will not be sufficient for referencing instances of a given intension as many people prefer to agree on names within a selected context, like city within a country, or street within a village, within a municipality within a province within a country. In those cases we will need *compound* reference schemes.

We can apply compound reference schemes in NLM in the same way as the simple reference schemes. To illustrate this we will first adapt our example UoD. We will assume that Vandover University has merged with Ohao University. In order to streamline the enrollment operations, it is decided to centralize them. This means that after the merger, a student can no longer be identified by the existing student ID because a given *student ID* can refer to a student in the (former) Ohao University, *and* to a different student in the (former) Vandover university. To capitalize on the existing naming conventions it is decided to add the qualification *O* (for Ohao) or *V* (for Vandover) to the existing student ID. This extension is the *university code.* The sentence group templates and the corresponding fact types in which such a compound reference scheme is implemented are given in figure 4.

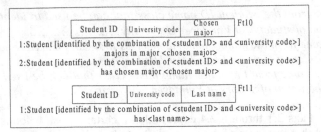

Fig. 4. Fact types and sentence group templates with compound reference scheme for student

We have introduced the [ ] ('brackets') symbol for capturing the definition of the compound reference scheme (see figure 4). For example, the reference scheme for student in fact type Ft10 consists of the roles *student ID* and *university code* and is defined as follows: *Student [identified by the combination of <student ID> and <university code>].*

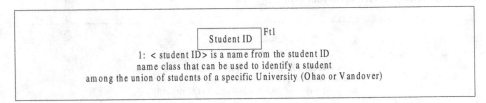

Fig. 5. Naming convention fact type for student in the integrated UoD

The case of a simple reference scheme is actually a special case of the compound reference scheme in which the brackets and description within (except for the role name used in the reference) are left out. In addition to this we need to adapt the naming convention fact types for the constituting intensions of the compound reference scheme. For example, the naming convention fact type for *student* should be adapted to reflect the application subject area in which it can be used to identify a specific student. In this case a student can be identified by his/her student ID within a *specific* University (Ohao or Vandover).

The unification of simple reference schemes and the different types of compound reference schemes into one uniform way of referencing, and the capability to capture the precise semantics of naming conventions are improvements in NLM to the predecessor methodologies.

2.5   The Basic Durable Application Model

A *basic durable application model* (DAM) for a Universe of Discourse U is defined by a list of concepts and their definitions applicable to that UoD, a set of roles, a set of variables, a set of fact types, and a set of sentence group templates for every fact type. The *extension* of a DAM his the union of the extensions of the fact types that are contained in that basic durable application model.

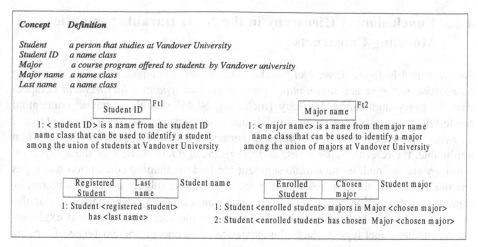

Fig. 6. Basic durable application model for University enrollment example

3   The NLM Representation Ontology

In this section we will narrow down the "real" or "abstract" world of interest (Universe of Discourse) to the UoD of NLM application ontology modeling or the NLM representation ontology [4]. First, the list of concepts for NLM representation ontology is provided (see table 2).

Table 2. List of concepts for NLM's durable application modeling language

Concept	Definition
Sentence (instance)	The result of the verbalization and qualification of a piece of verbalizable information by a domain user
Sentence group	The variable abstraction of a set of < sentence>s
Sentence group template	The ordering of fixed and variable parts of a group of < sentence>s that reflect domain semantics
Role	a variable part in one or more <sentence group template>s
Role code	a name class, instances of which can be used to identify a <role> among the union of <roles> in the application ontology
Intension	the meaning of a concept in a real or abstract world
Intension name	a name class, instances of which can be used to identify a <intension> among the union of <intensions> in the application ontology
Extension(of intension)	the set of names of things or concepts to which the definition of its < intension> applies
Verb	the parts of a < sentence group template> that are not variable
Fact type	a set of < role>s
Fact type code	a name class, instances of which can be used to identify a <fact type> among the union of <fact types> in the application ontology
Basic information model	a list of concepts and their definitions, a set of <role>s, a set of <fact type>s and a set of < sentence group template>s for each <fact type>
Extension (of fact type)	a set of < sentence instances> for that <fact type>

4   Conclusion: A Hierarchy in the NLM Durable Semantic Modeling Constructs

As illustrated in figure 7, we can put the concepts of *archetype, name class, naming convention fact type* and *non-naming convention fact type* in a *hierarchical* perspective. In every application ontology (including NLM' durable semantic conceptual modelling language) we can distinguish three segments in an application ontology. The *top* segment consists of the world of names in which the *archetype,* (and, when applicable, the relevant *scale types)* and the *relevant name classes* for the application ontology are defined. In the *middle* segment we find the naming convention fact types for the intensions that are relevant for the application subject area. This hierarchy replaces the distinction between *concepts* and *names* by considering names as populations of fact types in the hierarchy. The verbs in the fact types then will explicitly show whether a fact type declares the existence of a concept, the existence of a name that can be used to identify a concept or a semantic relationship among concepts. The application of NLM for capturing an application's ontology will improve the organization's resilience, because changes, in products, services, product-life cycle, customers, regulations and other external conditions can be easily adapted in the application's ontology, by adding or redefining a concept and naming convention and/or adding or deleting a semantic relationship.

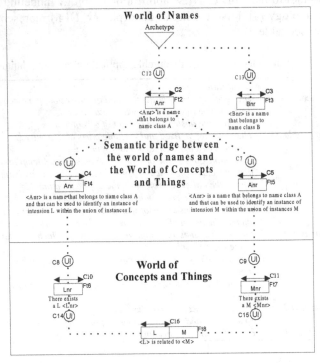

Fig. 7. Hierarchy in semantic conceptual modelling constructs.

References

1. Gruber, T.: A translation approach to portable ontologies. Knowledge Acquisition **5**(2), 199–220 (1993)
2. Fensel, D.: Ontologies: Silver Bullet for Knowledge Management and Electronic Commerce. Springer verlag (2001)
3. Lammari, N., Metais, E.: Building and maintaining ontologies: a set of algorithms. Data & Knowledge Engineering **48**, 155–176 (2004)
4. Burton-Jones, A., Storey, V., Sugumaran, V., Ahluwalia, P.: A semiotic metrics suite for assessing the quality of ontologies. Data & Knowledge Engineering **55**(1), 84–102 (2005)
5. Nijssen, G.: A Framework for discussion in ISO/TC97/SC5/WG3 and comments on 78.04/01 and 78.05/03 (1978)
6. Chen, P.: The entity-relationship model: Towards a unified view of data. ACM Transactions on Database Systems **1**(1), 9–36 (1976)
7. Teory, T., Yang, D., Fry, J.: A logical design methodology for relational databases using the extended E-R model. *ACM Computing Surveys* **18**(2) (1986)
8. Markowitz, V., Shoshani, A.: Representing extended entity-relationship structures in relational databases: A modular approach. ACM Transactions on Database Systems **17**(3), 423–464 (1992)
9. Senko, M.: DIAM as a detailed example of the ANSI/SPARC architecture. In: Nijssen, G. (ed.), *Modeling in Database Management Systems*, North-Holland (1976)

The Evolution Towards a Uniform Referencing Mode in Fact-Based Modeling

Peter Bollen[✉]

Department of Organization & Strategy, School of Business and Economics,
Maastricht University, Maastricht, Netherlands
p.bollen@maastrichtuniversity.nl

Abstract. Since its inception in the 1970's, fact-based modeling has evolved. In this article we will sketch this evolution mainly from the referencing mode's point of view. In this article we compare referencing modes from the N-ary 1989 NIAM model to the contemporary incarnation of fact-based modeling known as CogNIAM.

1   Introduction

Fact-based modeling (FBM) is a durable modeling approach that has been pioneered by Falkenberg [1, 2, 3] and Nijssen [4, 5] and in the 1970's was referred to as a conceptual modeling approach. Over the years the FBM approach has seen many incarnations and many (sometimes competing) dialects have evolved over time. Many of these dialects were characterized by being *binary* or *N-ary* (among other distinctive characteristics). The first-generation of fact-based modeling dialects, i.e. ENALIM [6, 7, 8] was N-ary and was soon converted to NIAM [9] that was restricted to *binary* fact types. The limitations of the binary dialects in terms of being able to capture 'N-ary' domain semantics has led to the introduction of multiple referencing modes [11].

In subsequent fact-based dialects additional ways of referencing objects or concepts have been introduced and some of these referencing modes have evolved over the years. In [11] these referencing modes have been evaluated with respect to the *conceptualization principle*, the principle *of semantic stability* and *ease of validation*. In this article we will follow-up on the results of [11]. In sub-section 1.1. we will present our running example that we will use in this article. In sub-section 1.2 we will show the conceptual schema for the running example using the NIAM 1989 N-ary FBM dialect. In section 2 we will summarize the results of the assessment of referencing modes in 'classic' FBM. In section 3 we will introduce a further development in referencing modes within the 'contemporary' CogNIAM incarnation of fact-based modeling. Finally in section 4 conclusions will be given.

1.1   The Running Example: University Staff Languages Spoken Abroad

We will illustrate the evolution of the referencing modeling concepts in this article by a running example (based on [10]) that we will introduce here. In this communication example we are interested in the language that university staff members have spoken abroad. We will give examples of instances of ground facts in this domain:

I. Ciuciu et al. (Eds.): OTM 2015 Workshops, LNCS 9416, pp. 226–234, 2015.
DOI: 10.1007/978-3-319-26138-6_26

```
Staff member Peter B. has spoken English in the United States
      Staff member Peter B. has spoken English in Canada
Staff member Peter B. has spoken Spanish in the United States
Staff member Thijs M. has spoken English in the United States
```

These four ground facts constitute a significant set of instances with respect to the permitted states of the fact base. The communication pattern for this example can be generalized as follows:

```
AT1: Staff member <staff member name> has spoken <language>
                    in <country>
```

In combination with the following naming convention fact types:

```
AT2: Staff member name <staff member name> identifies a
specific member of the University staff among the group of
             all University staff members
```

```
AT3: Language name <language name> identifies a specific
      language among the group of all languages
```

```
AT4: Country name <country name> identifies a specific
      country among the group of all countries
```

1.2 The N-ary 1989 NIAM Model

In figure 1 we have shown the durable model of our running example using the N-ary fact modeling conventions from the N-ary version of NIAM 1989 [12]. We will call this way of referencing 'flat', since we will implicitly use the abbreviated referencing scheme for every entity type that plays (a) role(s) in the fact type.

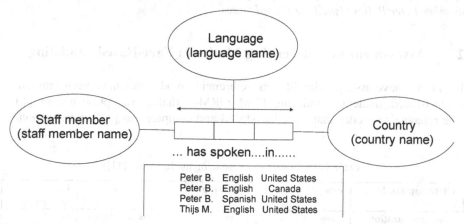

Fig. 1. Durable model of running example expressed in NIAM 1989 using flat referencing mode

Another modeling feature that was introduced in NIAM 1989 was the concept of *nesting* (or *nominalization*). An example of nominalization is the situation in which the initial user verbalization is as follows:

```
Staff member Peter B. has visited the United States.
During that (those) visits he has spoken English.
```

Applying the conceptual schema design procedure (CSDP) on these verbalized sentence instances will lead to a 'nominalized' (or nested) NIAM 1989 durable model in figure 2.

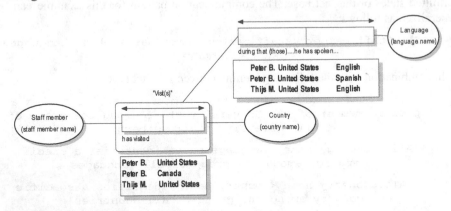

Fig. 2. Durable model expressed in NIAM 1989 using nesting (or nominalization).

We note that the application of the nesting modeling construct is user-driven, i.e. the domain user explicitly acknowledges the existence of the nested or nominalized concept (i.e. *visit*) in the domain. So the application of the nesting concept in this way is in line with the conceptualization principle. It should also be noted that the nested 'object type' is information-bearing, e.g. it can be phrased as a sentence, e.g. *Staff member Peter B. has visited the United States.*

2   Assessment of Referencing Modes in Fact-Based Modeling

In [11] we have assessed the different referencing modes that have been introduced in fact-based modeling until the FBM ORM-2 dialect (as presented in [13]). The referencing modes that were introduced and compared in [11] were: *flattening,*

Table 1. Evaluation of referencing modes (from [11])

Criterion\mode	Flat	Nesting	Co-referencing
Conceptualization principle	*Complies*	*Complies, as long as objectifications are not forced upon users that communicate in a 'flat' way*	*violates*
Semantic stability	*Complete additivity*	*nesting in retrospect might be required, when some domain experts adapt the objectified concept.*	*complete additivity*
Ease of validation	*Very good: efficient*	*good*	*not possible*

nesting and *co-referencing[1]*. These referencing modes haven been evaluated on the extent to which they comply to the *conceptualization principle, semantic stability* and *ease of validation* [11]. In table 1 we have summarized the main findings of [11].

From table 1 we can conclude that the 'flat' referencing mode and under certain conditions, the 'nesting' referencing mode comply to these evaluation criteria. The co-referencing referencing mode violates the conceptualization principle and does not enable the application of validation steps.

3   Further Evolution of Fact-Based Modeling

In parallel to the evolution from referencing modes from the binary 1982 NIAM to ORM-2 (2008) that was described in [11], another evolutionary path in the development of fact-based modeling can be distinguished. Developed and applied in hundreds of projects in the Netherlands the approach is now known under the name Cog-NIAM (an acronym for 'cognition enhanced natural language information analysis method'). In CogNIAM [14] and its pre-decessors [15], the focus is on a generic knowledge architecture that also covers the process and behavioural perspectives in durable modeling.

In this article we will illustrate the application of the fact-based approach by using CogNIAM's knowledge architecture and notational convention for semantic grammars. A theoretical foundation for CogNIAM can be found in [16, 17, 18].

In fact-based modeling we will use tangible documents or 'data-use cases' as a starting point for the modeling process. In most, if not all cases, a verbalizable knowledge source is a document that often is incomplete, informal, ambiguous, possibly redundant and possibly inconsistent. As a result of applying the fact-based knowledge extracting procedure (KEP), we will yield a document that only contains structured knowledge or a semantic grammar which structures verbalizable knowledge into the following elements (*semantic grammar* or *knowledge reference model(KRM)*)[19]:

1. Knowledge domain sentences
2. Definitions and naming conventions for concepts used in domain sentences
3. Knowledge domain fact types including sentence group templates
4. Population state (transition) constraints or validation rules for the knowledge domain
5. Derivation rules that specify *how* specific domain sentences can be derived from other domain sentences.
6. Rules that specify *what* fact instances can be inserted, updated or deleted.
7. Event rules that specify *when* a fact is derived from other facts or when a fact must be inserted , updated or deleted.

The CogNIAM knowledge extracting procedure (KEP) specifies *how* we can transform a possibly informal, mostly incomplete, mostly undetermined, possibly redundant and possibly inconsistent description of business domain knowledge into the following classes: *informal comment, non-verbalizable knowledge* and *verbalizable knowledge* to be classified into types 1 through 7 of the semantic grammar (or KRM).

---

[1] In co-referencing (compound) reference schemas are modeled as (a collection of) binary fact types that are not populatable.

We note that the knowledge extraction procedure that is needed to instantiate the elements 1 through 5 (of the KRM) is an extension of N-ary NIAM's conceptual schema design procedure (CSDP) [12]. In business domains, furthermore, we can capture the dynamic aspects by defining the exchange rules (element 6 of the KRM) and the event rules (element 7 of the KRM).

3.1   Running Example Expressed in CogNIAM

In this section we will analyze the types of reference modes that exist in CogNIAM and we will relate these referencing modes to the criteria in section 2. First we will give the CogNIAM semantic grammar for our running example. In CogNIAM's semantic grammar we first list the definitions of concepts (see table 2).

Table 2. CogNIAM's list of concept definitions of running example (element 2 of the KRM)

Country
Definition: Political division of a geographical entity, a sovereign territory, most commonly associated with the notions of state or nation and government
Language
Assumed to be known
Staff member
Definition: A Person that has a labour contract within a department of a University and who is assigned to teach and/or perform research.
Has spoken..in..
Assumed to be known

Elements 1,3,4,5,6 and 7 of the semantic grammar (or KRM) of the running example are given in figure 3

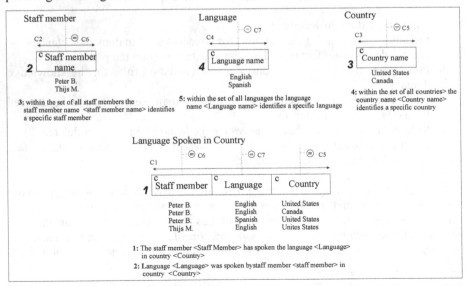

Fig. 3. CogNIAM semantic grammar of running example.

In CogNIAM there is no longer a graphical distinction into roles (or fact types) and objects. In principle CogNIAM uses elementary fact types that can have 1, 2 or N (≥3) place-holders. The reference to the object types (entity types or value types) as we find in the earlier fact-based dialects no longer takes place in a graphical way by connecting roles to entity types (and an abbreviated reference scheme) or value types, but takes place via a hierarchy of subset (or equality) constraints (e.g. see [18]) that ends in a naming convention fact type for the object type that is referenced in the place-holder. If we compare the CogNIAM information grammar from figure 3 with the equivalent 'flat' NIAM 1989 conceptual schema from figure 1 we get the mapping as is given in table 3.

Table 3. Mapping model elements from NIAM 1989 and CogNIAM

NIAM 1989 durable model (figure 1)	CogNIAM semantic grammar(figure 3)
Fact type predicate: ..has..spoken in..	Fact type form 1 of fact type 1
Entity type Staff member	Naming convention fact type 2
Declaration of name class staff member name as identifier for entity type staff member	Fact type form 3 of fact type 2
Entity type Language	Naming convention fact type 4
Declaration of name class language name as identifier for entity type Language	Fact type form 5 of fact type 4
Entity type Country	Naming convention fact type 3
Declaration of name class country name as identifier for entity type Country	Fact type form 4 of fact type 3
Uniqueness constraint spanning the fact type	Uniqueness constraint C1
Declaration that the entity type Staff member plays the left-hand role of the fact type	Equality constraint C6
Declaration that the entity type Language plays the middle role of the fact type	Equality constraint C7
Declaration that the entity type Country plays the right-hand role of the fact type	Equality constraint C5
(implied) Mandatory role of Entity type Staff member in fact type	Equality constraint C6 (instead of subset)
(implied) Mandatory role of Entity type Country in fact type	Equality constraint C7 (instead of subset)
(implied) Mandatory role of Entity type Language in fact type	Equality constraint C5 (instead of subset)

We will now illustrate how an adaption of our running example will be implemented in CogNIAM. We will first of all illustrate how CogNIAM will handle an initial verbalization in a nominalized format:

```
Staff member Peter B. has visited the United States.
During that (those) visits he has spoken English.
```

In table 4 and figure 4 we have given the CogNIAM semantic grammar for our adapted running example in which the concept of *visit* is used in the nominalized verbalization.

Table 4. CogNIAM's list of concept definitions of adapted running example

---

Country
Definition: Political division of a geographical entity, a sovereign territory,
               most commonly associated with the notions of state or nation and
               government
Language
               Assumed to be known
Staff member
Definition: A Person that has a labour contract within a department of a Univer-
               sity and who is assigned to teach and/or perform research.
 Has spoken..in..
               Assumed to be known
Visit
Definition: To reside temporarily at a place

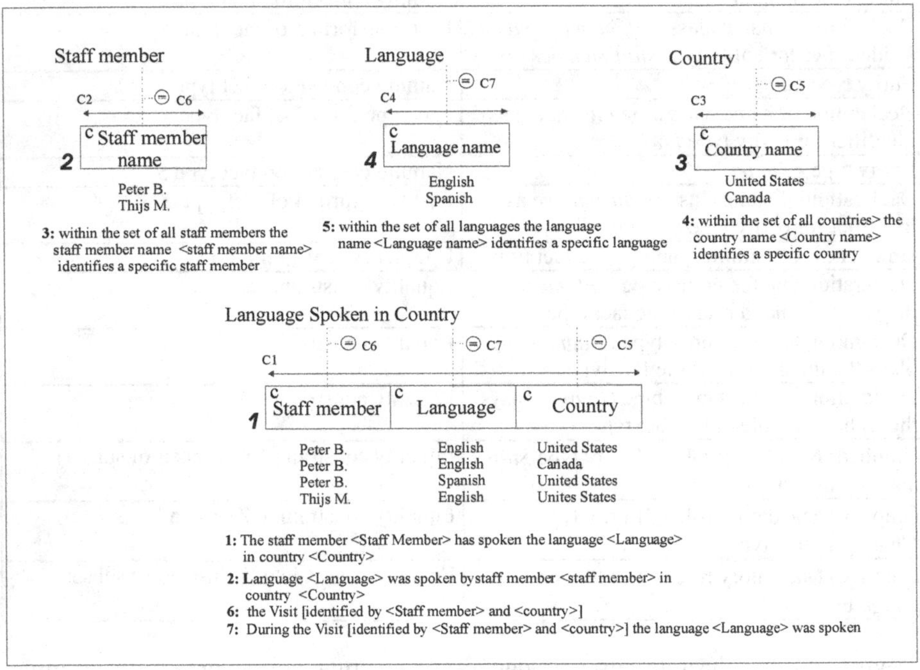

Fig. 4. CogNIAM semantic grammar of adapted running example

In fact type form 7 in figure 4 we have captured the nested or nominalized verbalization for fact type 1. In fact type form 6 in the CogNIAM semantic grammar in figure 4 we see that a nominalized verbalization can be transformed into an object-verbalization [18]:

```
The visit [identified by <Staff member> and <Country>]
```

We can easily add a fact type form that contains such an objectified verbalization for a target group that uses this verbalization in their communication. We note that by using the objectification symbols [ ], CogNIAM captures the name of the objectification while allowing to use non-objectified communication patterns for different target groups.

With respect to the explicit declaration of naming convention fact types in CogNIAM (i.e. fact types 2,3 and 4 in the semantic grammar of figure 4) we notice that the fact type forms explicitly capture a description of the 'name-space' within which a name can identify an instance of a concept (or object). We note that these explicit referencing semantics could not be captured in earlier fact-based dialects (e.g. NIAM 1989).

4   Conclusion

In this paper we have summarized the results of a comparison of the three most important referencing formats in 'classic' Fact-Based Modeling: *flat*, *nested* and *co-referencing*. In the second part of the paper the evolution of the referencing modes into CogNIAM have been demonstrated. Being able to define multiple fact type forms for any fact type in CogNIAM allows us to incorporate nesting (or nominalization) and the flat referencing mode into the same uniform fact type structure in FBM and at the same time allow different stakeholder communities to use their preferred 'local' way of referencing in a 'global' model. With respect to the overarching objective of this article we can conclude that in CogNIAM on a diagrammatic level there is only one way to reference objects. However, CogNIAM allows for adding multiple fact type forms to one diagram, thereby making it possible to record nominalized and flat fact type verbalizations at the same time for a given fact type. A major advantage of the CogNIAM naming convention fact types is the ability to capture 'name space' semantics in an explicit way.

References

1. Falkenberg, E.: Strukturierung und Darstellung von Information an der Schnittstelle zwischen Datenbankbenutzer und Datenbank-Management-System, Ph.D thesis, University of Stuttgart (1975)
2. Falkenberg, E.: Significations: the key to unify data base management. Information Systems **2**, 19–28 (1976)
3. Falkenberg, E.: Concepts for modelling information. In: Modelling in Database Management Systems (1976)
4. Nijssen, G.: A brief introduction to common data base languages DDL-DML. Codasyl Base Task Group Report (1972)
5. Nijssen, G.: Present and future possibilities of database technology. In: Medinfo, pp. 1–4 (1974)
6. Nijssen, G.: On the gross architecture for the next generation database management systems. In: Information processing, IFIP 1977 (1977)

7. Nijssen, G.: A gross architecture for the next generation database management systems. In: Nijssen, G. (Ed.) Modelling in Database Management Systems, North-Holland, pp. 1–24 (1976)
8. Nijssen, G.: A framework for discussion in ISO/TC97/SC5/WG3 and comments on 78.04/01 and 78.05/03 (1978)
9. Verheijen, G., van Bekkum, J.: NIAM: an information analysis method. In: IFIP TC-8 CRIS-I conference, North-Holland, Amsterdam (1982)
10. Nijssen, G.: The first increment of the SIMF proposed by the SIMF EU response group (2012)
11. Bollen, P.: referencing modes and ease of validation within fact-based modeling. In: Meersman, R., et al. (eds.) OTM 2014. LNCS, vol. 8842, pp. 289–298. Springer, Heidelberg (2014)
12. Nijssen, G., Halpin, T.: Conceptual schema and relational database design: a fact oriented approach, New-York: Prentice-hall. 337 (1989)
13. Halpin, T., Morgan, T.: Information Modeling and Relational Databases; from conceptual analysis to logical design 2nd edn., San-Francisco, California. Morgan-Kaufman (2008)
14. Nijssen, G., Le Cat, A.: Kennis gebaseerd werken: de manier om kennis productief te maken. PNA Publishing, Heerlen (2009). (in dutch)
15. Lemmens, I.M., Nijssen, M., Nijssen, S.: A NIAM 2007 conceptual analysis of the iso and omg mof four layer metadata architectures. In: Meersman, R., Tari, Z. (eds.) OTM-WS 2007, Part I. LNCS, vol. 4805, pp. 613–623. Springer, Heidelberg (2007)
16. Bollen, P.: On the applicability of requirements determination methods, in Management and Organization, University of Groningen, Groningen, p. 219 (2004)
17. Bollen, P.: The natural language modeling procedure. In: Halevy, A.Y., Gal, A. (eds.) NGITS 2002. LNCS, vol. 2382, p. 123. Springer, Heidelberg (2002)
18. Bollen, P.: Natural Language Modeling for Business Application Semantics. Journal of Information Science and Technology 2(3), 18–48 (2005)
19. Nijssen, M., Lemmens, I.M.: Verbalization for business rules and two flavors of verbalization for fact examples. In: Meersman, R., Tari, Z., Herrero, P. (eds.) OTM-WS 2008. LNCS, vol. 5333, pp. 760–769. Springer, Heidelberg (2008)

CogniLex

A Legal Domain Specific Fact Based Modeling Protocol

Mariette Lokin[1], Sjir Nijssen[2(✉)], and Inge Lemmens[2]

[1] Ministry of Finance, The Hague, The Netherlands
m.h.a.f.lokin@minfin.nl
[2] PNA Group, Heerlen, The Netherlands
{sjir.nijssen,inge.lemmens}@pna-group.com

Abstract. The Dutch Government has decided to provide services and enforcement actions based on laws and decrees. The vast majority of these services and actions are IT-based. The union of laws and decrees, both government and ministerial, are collectively called regulation hereafter. So far the large regulation based projects often have been running in the hundreds of millions over budget. Of course the Dutch parliament has held more than one investigation how to avoid this overspending, but there is still a lot to be improved. A number of government services organizations, academia and innovative companies has decided in 2012 to establish a co-creation with the aim to develop a national protocol to "translate the regulation" into a durable model that can better be used in intelligent work than the conventional textual representation. The co-creation, called "The Blue Chamber", has so far issued two reports in Dutch and presented 5 papers at international conferences. In this paper we describe the conceptual architecture of The Blue Chamber and how the CogNIAM variant of Fact Based Modeling has been used to develop a protocol that is tuned to this specific but extremely large domain of legislation.

Keywords: Durable modeling for regulation based services · Legal services · Jural relations · Fact Based Modeling (FBM) · Legal domain specific protocol

1 Introduction

The Netherlands, like many other countries, has a number of governmental bodies responsible for the execution and enforcement of the applicable legislation. Legislation is the union of laws, government decrees, ministerial decrees and several other regulations, including decisions by the courts. This legislation is the basis for interaction between citizens or enterprises on the one hand and the government service providers or enforcement organizations on the other hand. The intent of the legislation needs to be faithfully applied in all practical scenarios or cases. Legislation is at some points very precise and at other points intentionally ambiguous. The legislation describes very roughly speaking which rights and duties are applicable for a specific citizen or enterprise and under which circumstances. For a faithful application of the legislation in all practical scenarios it is needed to model explicitly all the semantics

© Springer International Publishing Switzerland 2015
I. Ciuciu et al. (Eds.): OTM 2015 Workshops, LNCS 9416, pp. 235–244, 2015.
DOI: 10.1007/978-3-319-26138-6_27

intended in the legislation applicable to the practical scenarios or cases. There is a need for a protocol such that a durable model can be used as solid basis for all the stakeholders involved as the formal and tested model of the associated services and enforcement actions.

In section 2 the current situation with the development of services based on regulations is described. From the quote of the first report by the Blue Chamber it is clear that we have a very interesting challenge in front of us. This is the AS-IS situations.

In section 3 we present the desired situation, the TO-BE.

In section 4 we present the durable architecture of the Blue Chamber for the TO-BE situation. In the architecture of the Blue Chamber, the three major actor groups are presented and the facts and rules they read or write are included.

In section 5 we present the three principles of ISO TR9007 which are the basic requirements that the presented architecture fulfils.

In section 6 we present the legality principle, that requires a faithful representation of the intended semantics for all relevant practical cases

In section 7 we present the knowledge microscope principle which is used to identify which knowledge elements are needed to fulfil the legality principle.

In section 8 we present the clear connection between facts at knowledge level I and the fact patterns at knowledge level II, an essential part of CogNIAM [17].We discuss the advantages of this strong connection and the fact that in the legal services world, testing at level I has been used since a very long time, long before IT arrived. It is called in that community *ex-ante*.

In section 9 we present the essential aspects of CogniLex, a CogNIAM based protocol for the legal domain.

In section 10 we present a summary and suggestions for the road ahead.

2   The AS-IS for Regulation Based Services

The first effort of the Blue Chamber was to take stock. What was the situation with respect to producing a durable model for regulation in 2012?

The best answer is to quote part of the first report of the Blue Chamber.

"In recent decades, public administration has changed under the influence of digitization. These changes affect the processes of implementing public services. Both the large-scale processes for handling cases of large groups of citizens, and processes for the treatment of individual cases in complex situations are affected. Examples can be found in the area of benefit provision, granting of subsidies, licensing and taxation. Central government, provincial governments and municipalities strive, as much as possible, to process applications for licenses, benefits and the provision of other public services electronically."

Successive governments have been working on a response to this development. Among other things, this has resulted in a government-wide vision of the provision of services to citizens and businesses. This vision is based on the customer-driven public services viewpoint in which there is a central focus on the requests of citizens and businesses. The implementing bodies are expected to design their processes and services in such a way that they can meet the needs and perspectives of their customers. In other words, efficacy is central. A prime challenge will be to offer the desired effective processing of customer requests in an affordable and efficient manner.

The effective and efficient handling of customer requests requires cooperation between different organizations. This helps to diminish the boundaries between layers of government and government organizations.

In order to play their part for and on behalf of citizens, it is necessary for the government organizations to design their processes and services in such a way that they can respond to changing conditions, changing stakeholder demands and changes in cooperation with other organizations in an efficient and cost-effective manner.

What is still lacking however is a uniform and coherent method to analyze and interpret sources of law that would achieve integrated information, rules and process models with which the desired flexibility and agility in the provision of information can be realized. Such an approach is therefore a prerequisite for the realization of a customer-oriented service and for securing collaboration between organizations (interoperability). The observations below from daily implementation practice illustrate the lack of a 'clear and coherent method of analysis for the interpretation of legislation by implementing bodies':

- Translating legislation into customer-driven service and product requirements for the implementation of processes and applications is usually quite time-consuming.
- The (contents of) services and processes are not sufficiently traceable to the legislation.
- Up till now, the translation of legislation into service and product requirements has often proved to be a process difficult to control. The procedure is not clear, is in part implied and depends on the individual 'translator'. Analysis usually takes place from this translator's own discipline (legal, implementation, information science or IT). The required expertise is scarce.
- Adequate support which allows for intelligent searching of the corpus of legislation is currently lacking and there is only limited support for adequately managing the results in conjunction." [6]

The AS-IS situation contains enough aspects that are considered in need of substantial improvement.

3   The Goals for the TO-BE Situation

The TO-BE situation is in the first report of the Blue Chamber described as follows: "In legislation rights and obligations are defined: among citizens, citizens towards the government and vice versa. Legislation contains concepts, rules and conditions that directly affect the actions of citizens, businesses and government organizations. These concepts, rules and conditions form the basis for the services and processes of public implementing bodies. For the following reasons, it is important to be able to distill concepts, rules and conditions from the legislation in an unambiguous and repeatable manner:

A. It promotes legal certainty for citizens and prevents unnecessary disputes and proceedings in court.
B. It enhances the transparency of government. The government can show that what they are doing is in accordance with the democratically established legislation. This includes providing insight into the rules that give the authorities a margin of discretion to do justice in special cases.
C. It simplifies implementation of legislation in services and processes. Thus, orders from politics and public demands can be accommodated more rapidly.
D. It improves an implementing body's capacity to, as part of ex ante feasibility tests, to provide feedback on proposed changes in legislation. This contributes positively to the effectiveness and efficiency of the implementation.
E. It provides insight into the coherence of the complex of legislation. Consequently, generic and specific elements in processes and services can more easily be distinguished. This offers possibilities for reuse, not only within an organization, but also between organizations.

In short, the added value of a repeatable approach to the organization of the implementation of legislation comes from the ability to transform legislation into legitimate and meaningful services for citizens and businesses and to perform this in a truthful, efficient, multidisciplinary and timely fashion." [6]

4   The Durable Architecture Developed by the Blue Chamber for the TO-BE Situation

In the diagram below the three main actor groups are presented [1].

The first actor group consists firstly of law makers, government and ministers. When they observe desired or presumed or identified needs, they start a new law and later on associated decrees, or start to modify an existing law and associated decrees. The government service organization can also modify or introduce a new operational policy.

But there is a third and very important subset of actors in this group and that are the judges in the various courts at the various levels. Their decisions have a clear effect on similar cases or scenarios.

It is the combination of all the actors that determines the entirety of the regulation.

In figure 1 below, the dotted arrow below actor group 1 indicates that actor group 1 executes a process for the creation and modification of the regulations. An actor group is represented with the familiar actor symbol.

Regulations are produced to provide services for the citizens and enterprises, or require them to perform certain duties. These services are primarily IT-based.

The traditional textual representation of the law, (by the second author considered jewels, given the limited tools that the lawmakers have available,) is not adequate to be used as drawings for the IT-builders or precise instructions for civil servants.

What is needed is a complete specification that takes the (new) laws, decrees and policies as input and produces a testable specification of the interaction between the government service providers and the citizens or enterprises. This is a multidisciplinary effort and in principle independent of IT such that new IT technologies can be based on the durable specifications or model. Actor group 2 in the diagram below consists of legal experts, service experts and architects.

Actor group 2 also provides the two-way references between the durable model and the regulations. This is needed for impact analysis and certification. Often this is also referred to as annotation services. As can be seen, the specifications of the durable model can be represented with traditional Word, PDF or Excel documents, or by the so-called juridical DNA, a representation that can be consulted with a logical language. An organization has a choice. No matter what the choice is, there is a need to know which requirement is based on which pieces of texts in the regulations. This is represented by the arrows with the A and B in a circle.

Actor group 3 consists of the builders of the services. The builders take as input the specifications of the interaction and the function of the services (the durable model) just like a builder of a large office block receives as input the drawings of the architect, and build the services. In some cases there is a functionality that provides the automatic mapping from the durable specifications into an executable service.

Actor group 4 consists of the citizens or enterprises that receive the services of the government service provider or the duty dispatching service.

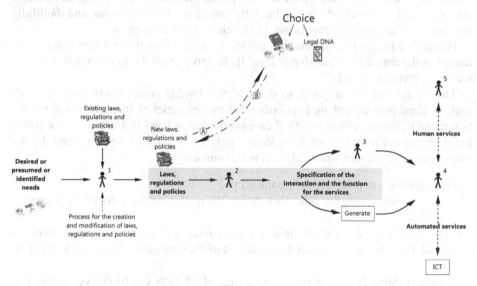

Fig. 1.

5   The Three Principles of ISO TR9007

In 1987, after ten years of work by an international expert group in modeling, consisting of 43 persons, ISO issued a technical report with the tittle Concepts and terminology for the Conceptual Schema and the Information Base, with code ISO TR9007 [13, 16]. The three principles from this ISO report are applicable for the protocol that the Blue Chamber has developed. A summary of the three principles is:

1. The Helsinki principle: "Any meaningful exchange of utterances depends upon the prior existence of an agreed set of semantic and syntactic rules. The recipients of the utterances must use only these rules to interpret the received utterances, if it is to mean the same as that which was meant by the utterer."
2. The conceptualization principle: "A conceptual schema should only include conceptually relevant aspects, both static and dynamic, of the universal discourse, thus excluding all aspects of (external or internal) data representation, physical data organization and access as well as all aspects of particular external user representation such message formats, data structures, etc."
3. The 100 % principle: "All relevant general static and dynamic aspects, i.e. all rules, laws, etc., of the universe of discourse should be described in the conceptual schema. The information system cannot be held responsible for not meeting those described elsewhere, including in particular those in application programs."

6   The Legality Principle

One of the requirements for which the law makers are not willing to compromise, is that the services provided should be fully based on the regulation and faithfully represents the intent of the regulation in all relevant practical cases.

Hence that means that the durable model must represent the full semantics as intended in the regulation (knowledge level II) to apply to all the foreseen cases or scenarios (knowledge level I).

This means that the language to describe the durable model (knowledge level II) must be capable of describing **explicitly** what the semantics as specified in the regulation mean in the associated practical cases (knowledge level I). Here we see a strong link between the level I of the knowledge triangle (the level of the facts) and the domain specific regulation, knowledge level II, consisting of

1. Fact patterns, to precisely define the scope,
2. The associated integrity rules that define the quality of the facts of the scenarios (at level I),
3. The associated concept definitions that provide a description of each term for which there is any doubt that the members of the community have no clear definition,
4. The associated derivation rules, specifying which facts can be derived from other facts,
5. The associated behavioral rules, specifying which actor can assert which facts according to which guidelines,
6. The associated fact communication patterns, providing a tool to communicate the deep structure of a fact in any surface structure selected by a community,
7. The associated rule communication patterns, providing a tool to communicate the deep structure of any rule in any surface structure selected by a community,
8. The associated events, specifying the conditions that start the execution of a derivation rule or behavioral rule,

9. The concept of context, specifying one or more pieces of text within one or more different regulations together forming a context, within which a concept definition is valid for a specific term and

10. The concept of relevant regulations (relreg) introduced by Robert van Doesburg under the term "script" [8, 9], specifying all the pieces of regulations from one or more different regulations that are involved in the often many scenarios that follow a certain legal act until all the specific scenarios come to an end.

Please note the concept of context is used to define the boundaries within which a certain term has a certain definition, while the concept of relevant regulations contains a set of pieces of (often) various regulations that define the rules applicable to a prototypical legal act [19].

7   The Knowledge Microscope Principle

One of the unique principles of the Blue Chamber is based on a well-accepted principle in some natural sciences: "Use a microscope, describe what you see and generalize towards a consistent theory".

The Blue Chamber has accepted this principle and makes use of a so called knowledge microscope. Hence put a sufficient set of regulation texts under the knowledge microscope and conclude which knowledge elements are needed to fully describe the semantics for all relevant practical cases.

Applying this principle means that neither with OWL, nor RDF, nor UML, nor SBVR, nor BPMN, nor DMN one can satisfy the legality principle. They all lack the functionality to represent 100% of the integrity rules, an ISO TR9007 principle; hence the quality of the associated facts is not guaranteed.

We have used the knowledge microscope principle on some regulations as used in the Netherlands or EU directives and indeed the conclusion is that none of the above listed standards is powerful enough to satisfy the legality principle.

The knowledge microscope is operated by a durable knowledge modeler (2nd and 3rd author) who submits questions on concrete scenarios to a legal expert (1st author). Specifying a durable model is a multi-disciplinary task, not a durable modeler as a hermit.

Fig. 2.

8   Strong Connection between the Scenario Level and the Regulation Level

One of the interesting experiences of working with the above listed principles is that the strong connection between level I (scenario) and level II (regulation) made many things much clearer [17]. The level I is well known in the legal world, although under represented in the legal text books. Before a regulation is put into practice a so-called ex-ante is performed. That means that before the actual implementation a number of relevant scenarios, often called cases, are lived through. This can be well accomplished by the cooperation between the operator of the knowledge microscope and the law expert. The authors have played these roles and that has resulted in substantial insight into the deep structure of elements in regulations and the clarity.

9   CogniLex, a CogNIAM Based Protocol for the Legal Domain

Although fact based modeling has been around as an industrial service since the late seventies (Control Data Corporation, Information Analysis Services) it has not so far been a mainstream product like ER, UML or BPMN [18].

A series of papers could be dedicated to the why of that phenomenon. For too long Fact Based Modeling was too abstract and at the same time too precise. In recent years we observe that FBM is more accepted as an industrial service if the user is given options to only use a subset of the FBM arsenal [12, 13, 14, 15]. Users do not want to be told to use a too precise and too abstract way of communication. This is a major challenge for FBM in the coming years.

FBM is by many considered too abstract. It is not tied into one or more specific domains. The domain of laws, decrees, regulations and directives is very large. When the experts from that domain expressed three years ago their requirements for a durable modeling protocol, it became clear that it was worth trying to specialize CogNIAM for an application domain as it was assumed that the experts in that domain would experience such a domain adaption as more helpful as a tool for that specific domain.

This approach was tried in the Blue Chamber and it turned out to be a good step forward.

The regulation domain specific extensions of CogNIAM are called CogniLex. CogniLex started with the assumption that Hohfeld [10 (original publication was in 1913)] was a good basis to include in that extension [2, 3, 4, 5, 7].

When applying the knowledge microscope to Dutch laws, while respecting the legality principle, it appeared that extensions were needed to Hohfeld. These are described in separate papers.

It also became clear in professional multi-disciplinary practice that a graphical support for scenarios was very welcome and therefore CogniLex contains a scenario level graphical support such that an entire scenario, consisting of a series of scenes, can be graphically represented in line with the way a scenario unfolds in the world people experience a scenario in time.

It is the multi-disciplinary way of working that is used in CogniLex. CogniLex uses the concepts of CogNIAM as well as Hohfeld and its extensions as basis, as structure, upon which CogniLex as a protocol is build. This is the beginning of a long road of continuous development and feedback from industrial practice. Please feel invited to join.

10   Conclusions and Future Work

The Blue Chamber has adopted the knowledge microscope principle. That means that the regulation is the primary object of study. This dictates which concepts are needed in a durable model. There is at the time of writing no single ISO, OMG or W3C standard modeling language that has the representational power required by the legality principle. Hence one needs a smart combination of various standards and of course some interfaces between the various standards. It is not to be excluded that the Blue Chamber will publish a proposal for such a standard language if ISO, OMG and W3C continue to fail to fill this gap.

Acknowledgements. The authors gratefully acknowledge the many discussions in the Blue Chamber since June 2012. The Blue Chamber a multi-disciplinary group with the principle that each member brings more sandwiches to the lunch than he intends to eat and users are the ultimate decision makers whether or not a modeling approach is accepted. The authors express their thanks to the colleagues of the Blue Chamber for their inspiring sessions; in particular they are thankful to Diederik Dulfer, Rani Wierda and Robert van Doesburg for extensive suggestions on this paper . The Blue Chamber will continue to improve the development and maintenance of regulation based specifications for services in the future.

References

1. Brattinga, M., Nijssen, S.: A Sustainable Architecture for Durable Modeling of Laws and Regulations and Main Concepts of the Durable Model. Paper accepted at the FBM 2015 Workshop of the OnTheMove 2015 Conference, Rhodos, Greece, October 29–30. Proceedings by Springer (2015)
2. Corbin, A.: Legal Analysis and Terminology. Yale Law School (1919)
3. Corbin, A.: Jural Relations and Their Classification. Yale Law School (1921)
4. Dulfer, D., Lokin, M., Nijssen, S.: Developing and maintaining durable specifications for law or regulation based services. Paper accepted at the FBM 2015 Workshop of the OnTheMove 2015 Conference, Rhodos, Greece, October 29–30. Proceedings By Springer (2015)
5. Engers, T.M. van Nijssen, S.: Bridging Social reality with Rules. Paper presented at IRIS2014, Das Internationale Rechtsinformatik Symposion, Salzburg, Austria, February 21, 2014
6. Engers, T.M., van Nijssen, S.: Connecting People: Semantic-Conceptual Modeling for Laws and Regulations. Paper accepted for Presentation at and to be Included in the Proceedings of the IFIP EGOV2014 Conference, to be Held in Dublin, Ireland, September 1–4

7. van Engers, T.M., Nijssen, S.: From Legislation towards Service Development – An Approach to Agile Implementation of Legislation. Paper accepted for Presentation at EGOVIS 2014 in München, September 1–5 and to be Included in the Proceedings

8. van Engers, T.M., van Doesburg, R.: First Steps Towards a Formal Analysis of Law. In: Malzahn, D., Conceição, G. (eds.) eKNOW 2015, pp. 36–42. IARIA (2015)

9. van Engers, T.M., van Doesburg, R.: At your service, on the definition of services from sources of law. In: Proceedings of the 15th International Conference on Artificial Intelligence and Law (ICAIL 2015), pp. 221–225. ACM, New York (2015)

10. Hohfeld, W.N.: Fundamental Legal Conceptions as Applied in Judicial Reasoning, edited by Walter Wheeler Cook (2010). ISBN-13: 978-1-58477-162-3

11. ISO TR9007, Concepts and terminology for the Conceptual Schema and the Information Base, ISO Technical Report (1987)

12. Kleemans, F., Saton, J.: Developing the Uniform Economic Transaction Protocol A Fact Based Modeling approach for creating the economic internet protocol. Paper accepted at the FBM 2015 Workshop of the OnTheMove 2015 Conference, Rhodos, Greece, October 29–30. Proceedings by Springer (2015)

13. Lemmens. I., Pleijsant, J.M., Arntz, R.: Using Fact-Based Modeling to Develop a Common Language - a use case. Paper accepted at the FBM 2015 Workshop of the OnTheMove 2015 Conference, Rhodos, Greece, October 29–30. Proceedings by Springer (2015)

14. Lemmens, I., Koster, J.-P., Valera, S.: Achieving Interoperability at Semantic Level. Paper accepted at the FBM 2015 Workshop of the OnTheMove 2015 Conference, Rhodos, Greece, October 29–30. Proceedings by Springer (2015)

15. Moberts, R., Nieuwland, R., Janse, Y., Peters, M., Bouwmeester, H., Dieteren, S.: Business Object Model: a Semantic-Conceptual Basis for Transition and Optimal Business Management. Paper accepted at the FBM 2015 Workshop of the OnTheMove 2015 Conference, Rhodos, Greece, October 29–30. Proceedings by Springer (2015)

16. Nijssen, G.M.: A Framework for Discussion. In: ISO/TC97/SC5/WG3, 78.09/01 (1978)

17. Nijssen, S., Valera, S.: An Architecture Ecosystem for the Whole Systems Perspective, Including System Dynamics, Based on Logic & Set Theory and Controlled Natural Languages. Working paper for the OMG Architecture Ecosystem SIG (2012)

18. Nijssen, S., Piprani, B.: 1975-2015: 1975-2015: Lessons Learned with Applying FBM in Professional Practice. Paper accepted at the FBM 2015 Workshop of the OnTheMove 2015 Conference, Rhodos, Greece, October 29–30. Proceedings by Springer (2015)

19. Straatsma, P., Diederik, D.: Wendbare Wetsuitvoering. In: DREAM (2014)

Business Object Model: A Semantic-Conceptual Basis for Transition and Optimal Business Management

Roel Moberts[1], Ralph Nieuwland[1], Yves Janse[1], Martijn Peters[2], Hennie Bouwmeester[2], and Stan Dieteren[2(✉)]

[1] Obvion, Heerlen, The Netherlands
{roel.moberts,ralph.nieuwland,yves.janse}@obvion.nl
[2] CogNIAM Finance, Amsterdam, The Netherlands
{martijn.peters,hennie.bouwmeester,
stan.dieteren}@cogniamfinance.com

Abstract. Obvion is a residential mortgage loans provider operating on the Dutch market. A recent internal Obvion study into the target architecture of their services recommends to provide further elaboration of an Obvion Business Object Model (BOM). This model comprises the business terms used within Obvion, their meaning, interconnections and related regulations. This model would offer the upcoming transition projects – where new designs are created for existing applications – a reliable and sufficiently detailed starting point. This has significant positive effects on the reduction of errors, time and costs in the implementation.

A proven approach was chosen for the implementation of the Obvion BOM. For the model the CogNIAM variant of Fact Based Modeling is used that allows the knowledge present in documentation, applications and people's minds to be elicited and represented in a completely structured fashion. To capture the knowledge in a model the OMG's open knowledge standard SBVR is applied.

Keywords: Residential mortgage loans · Customer interaction · Business Object Model · Transition projects · Customer intimacy · Fact Based Modeling (FBM)

1 Introduction

Obvion is a residential mortgage loan provider operating on the Dutch market. Obvion believes everyone has a right to their own personal place to live. Therefore, Obvion wants to make and keep home ownership attainable. Today and in the future. To achieve this, it offers sound financing solutions for the residential needs of its customers. The strategy of Obvion is: The customer is leading in our thinking and acting. Obvion puts the customer's perspective first in their vision of the mortgage market of the future. The strategy to achieve this implies a transition from a product-driven organization to a customer-driven organization and brings along changes for almost every business unit. An important aspect is the renewal of core business applications for which a target architecture was adopted to meet the future needs.

© Springer International Publishing Switzerland 2015
I. Ciuciu et al. (Eds.): OTM 2015 Workshops, LNCS 9416, pp. 245–253, 2015.
DOI: 10.1007/978-3-319-26138-6_28

Under the program called 'Customer' Obvion addresses the design of these applications. In this program the target situation as requested by the business should be leading, not the existing design of the applications. Although at issue in a number of different projects, the design of the various applications will have to be consistent. In order to achieve this Obvion will have to provide its suppliers, but also its internal stakeholders accurate and understandable information [10, 11] with respect to the meaning of concepts, their interrelations, rules and the link to the implementation. Obvion faces the challenge to precisely determine and capture this information together with the stakeholders, as a starting point for the various transition projects. One of the components suggested to address this considerable challenge is the creation of an Obvion Business Object Model. In designing the Obvion Business Object Model three preconditions were identified in advance, namely:

1. The composed model must be complete, correct, consistent and understandable, based on a sound validation.
2. It must be possible to communicate the captured model in a comprehensible manner with all transition projects.
3. It must be possible to maintain the captured model in an efficient manner, allowing it to be kept up-to-date.

CogNIAM Finance has relevant experience with this type of activity and uses its own proven approach for both the composition and validation of the semantic-conceptual model as well as for capturing it. For the composition and validation of the model the CogNIAM variant of Fact Based Modeling is used that allows the knowledge present in documentation, applications and people's minds to be elicited and represented in a completely structured fashion. This ensures a high level of quality and understandability of the Obvion Business Object Model. Capturing is done in a model that is based on the open knowledge standard SBVR which subsequently functions as Single Point of Reference (SPOR).

The manner of capturing of the model ensures that the knowledge can automatically be presented in views for specific target groups. In addition, after relevant training, users can update the knowledge by themselves. Within a short turnaround time of 8 weeks the section of the Obvion Business Object Model related to the Customer Interaction domain was delivered in the form of a SPOR. The delivery included representations in various forms for the different stakeholders in the transition projects. As a result, all those involved in the transition projects can make use of the implementations based on a shared set of source terms, represented in a way which is comfortable and understandable for the various target groups.

CogNIAM Finance has in recent years facilitated various financial institutions with assignments in the areas of data management, process optimization, IT issues, (business) rules management, simplification of conditions and related topics. It always involves providing the necessary insight into complexity and optimizing the communication about it with different experts. The CogNIAM variant of Fact Based Modeling has proven itself in these situations as an approach that offers practical solutions and leads to desired results.

2 Outline

The previously mentioned target architecture is intended to prepare Obvion's digital environment for the way customers want to be served in the near future. In the short term this leads to 5 major change projects, which have a high level of coherence and result in a new application portfolio:

1. New Online environment;
2. New Mid-Office environment;
3. Continuation CRM application;
4. New Special Management application;
5. New Data warehouse and BI environment.

These applications exchange and edit a substantial amount of data. Everyone should be able to rely on the accuracy and consistency of this data and the rules applied in the various applications [8]. This is of paramount importance for reliable services to customers by way of the Online Platform, but also for transparent reporting to internal and external stakeholders, traceable to the source applications [2, 9, 12].

To achieve this, the different transition projects within Obvion will need to have a common starting point, which means further elaboration of the current target architecture. All relevant information, rules and concept definitions contained in the various applications should be identified and given proper definitions [3, 4, 5]. This leads to a rich integration, which in turn will result in the acquisition of (new) insights and experiences. Therefore at this stage we no longer talk about mere information, but call the ensemble 'knowledge'. This knowledge should subsequently be captured in the Obvion Business Object Model and supplemented with the additional concepts used in business and customer communications.

That model concerns a common conceptual framework equal interpretation of rules and the underlying information model. Take for example the concept of 'Customer', which already exists in different applications and in different capacities and whose precise definition must be translated to the new frameworks as a starting point for the design of the various applications.

3 Challenges

Completeness, Consistency, Understandability and Correctness. Obvion's first challenge is to create a starting point that satisfies all four elements, namely: completeness, consistency, understandability and correctness. Knowledge elicitation often involves information that cannot be found at a single source, is largely present in people's minds and which needs further agreement among the various stakeholders. In addition, such a high level of detail (information richness) is both desirable and necessary that the meaning of information must be open for just a single interpretation [6, 7].

Communication with Transition Projects. Obvion's second challenge is that the Obvion Business Object Model needs to be communicated with the applications' implementation partners and other stakeholders, all of whom typically utilize their own templates and diagrams. Only when these translations exhibit a one-to-one connection to the established understanding and agreements, can errors in the implementation and in the final customer communications or in reports be avoided.

Maintenance and Management. The third challenge is how the captured knowledge will be managed and maintained so that it retains its value for the organization; also after subsequent changes. Capturing in Word and/or Excel does not provide enough structure for good overview and efficient management of knowledge. Furthermore, this makes the work error-prone, creating a risk for the reliability and causing part of the work to be redone after subsequent changes.

4   Solution and Approach

In a broad sense CogNIAM Finance applies structure to complex, knowledge-intensive environments in the financial sector thereby utilizing the CogNIAM variant of Fact Based Modeling. This approach provides for both a protocol-based elicitation and analysis of data, rules, concepts and – if desired – processes, and also for the structured capturing of the knowledge in an integrated knowledge model. A model in which everyone can subsequently retrieve and view the total perspective, or if so desired, a specific part perspective (e.g. only the definitions, just the fact model, or the combination of definitions and fact model). In this way, both the quality of the model, as well as the (re)usability of the knowledge are ensured and facilitated [1, 4. 5].

This project was specifically started by way of a kick-off session with all directly involved stakeholders. During this session, the 30 concepts identified by Obvion domain experts as being key concepts, were tested on level of importance and prioritized. Also, all directly involved stakeholders were informed about the technical approach and methodology of the project.

Producing the Obvion Business Object Model. The CogNIAM expert has analyzed in advance the received input documentation on the basis of the CogNIAM protocol. Subsequently, at weekly interview sessions a group of Obvion domain experts were questioned based on the CogNIAM protocol. This implies that use is made of concrete, practical examples in a repetitive fashion, according to protocol. The CogNIAM expert subsequently compiled a list of specific questions based on these examples and in this way the domain experts could contribute their knowledge in a targeted and structured fashion and where necessary, they could make decisions based on full insight and clarity about the consequences.

The validation of elicited and captured knowledge is addressed in dual fashion. First of all, the elicited knowledge is integrally verified during interview sessions using again the aforementioned concrete representative examples. The manner of representation of the examples conforms to the specific business preferences and makes use of the natural language of the stakeholders. In addition, the interim results have been shared with a larger group of stakeholders who have – partially from a distance – monitored the developments and have been offered the opportunity to provide feedback. The interviewed domain experts and the review group represented a wide and varied range of insights and expertise from within the organization. The interviewed domain experts and reviewers hold such functions as project manager, enterprise architect, IT architect, business consultant, or senior sales representative.

In addition to the interview session a steering committee meeting also took place fortnightly. Within the steering committee the client management, project management, account management and content experts were involved. Within the steering committee both the progress in the areas of content and budget were reported and discussed. In this formation scope related issues could also be determined in a quick and clear way as well as any, associated follow-up actions. Furthermore, relevant issues such as connection to the transition projects and the emerging data governance issue were also on the agenda during these meetings.

Organized Capturing and Communication. The result of the analysis, review and interview sessions is captured in an organized fashion in a Single Point of Reference (SPOR). From there, the knowledge is presented to the transition projects, each party involved in its own preferred form, fully synchronous with the determined starting point. As a result, work is performed by everyone involved without any differences in interpretation and based on the same principles both when working within and between the transition projects. The elements in the model are, wherever desired by the domain experts, enhanced with the underlying justification and the reference to the source. In addition, relevant reflections on future developments are captured in the model on a fine-grained, per element basis.

Management and Reuse of the Knowledge. Safeguarding the use of the Obvion Business Object Model in transition projects proceeds via the project manager and participants who are actively involved in both the Obvion BOM process as well as in one or more transition projects.

The created Obvion Business Object Model is a knowledge base that thanks to the structured method of capturing, after appropriate training, can be managed and maintained by Obvion so it remains current and retains its value. It can be reused in many ways, for example in the design of reports or in the impact assessment for future changes.

The model also forms the basis for the modeling of processes, which can be incorporated in full into the model. In this way it is possible to make use of simulations, both in the validation process as well as in process optimization. In addition, the possibility arises to fully include working instructions for employees.

A concrete example is shown in the illustration below (see Fig. 1), which was extensively used during the interview sessions. It depicts the individuals Jaap and Ria, who together have a house in mind and want to take out a mortgage at Obvion in order to be able to buy the house. Apart from Jaap and Ria, Jaap's father Hans is also involved: he will move into the house as well. In addition, Jaap has an uncle named Kees. Kees is a successful businessman who is more than willing to make available a portion of his assets to finance the mortgage.

Now suppose that the Marketing department comes up with the idea to send all new customers a welcome gift and consults the Operations department to discuss this. In many organizations the ensuing dialog will go along the following lines:

Marketing: "We would like to send all new customers a welcome card, starting next month. Can you arrange that?"

Operations: "That's possible, but we do need some additional information. If you send us the text to be put on the card, then we will arrange it."

Marketing: "We'll do. Thanks!"

This seems like a simple question, and in principle it should be. In such a situation in everyday practice, however, it remains doubtful whether all the 'correct' individuals will receive the welcome card. In principle that has nothing to do with technical (im)possibilities, but everything with the right conceptualization and shared views. Who do you think will be given a welcome card, given the example described and provided of course that the mortgage application is approved? One card each for Jaap and Ria, as separate customers? Or are they just a single customer? And what about Hans and Kees? Are they to be treated as 'customers', possibly just within this context?

Jaap   Ria   Hans   Kees

Fig. 1.

Within the Obvion Business Object Model a clear definition and clear data structure of the term 'Customer' were determined, in cooperation with the domain experts. These elements were determined on the basis of concrete examples, expressed in facts such as shown above [10]. In this way a validated and accepted definition is composed that is clear for all departments and under all circumstances. It is thus ensured that in this case Marketing and Operations mean exactly the same thing in such a practical scenario and that the execution is based on a single shared image. This approach even allows for the possibility to have different coexisting definitions, as long as each party involved in the communication is aware of any possible differences in the definitions. For Obvion, this is particularly the case when they have contact with external parties, which have their own, distinct definition of the term 'Customer'.

5   Deliverables

The delivered product is the Obvion Business Object Model on the subject of the Customer Interaction domain. This model was captured using supporting software. From this model the following derivatives and views were subsequently delivered:

1. Concept definitions
   A list of all relevant terms plus their definition. In this context relevant means every term that occurs in the model, including additional terms that are necessary to define a term.
2. Fact Type Diagrams (FTDs)
   A diagrammatic representation of the Obvion Business Object Model (including completed and articulated example populations).
3. Articulated Fact Type Diagrams
   An automatically generated textual representation of the Obvion Business Object Model, expressed in natural language (Dutch), using sentence patterns.
4. HTML view (Obvion BOM Web)
   A web-based version of the Obvion Business Object Model (Obvion BOM Web).
5. Overview Diagram
   An overview of the relationships between entities (including their properties).
6. Example case concerning the concept 'Suspect'
   One of the prominent concepts explained in narrative form, including the link to the Obvion BOM.
7. The relevant rules.

6   Results

With the aid of this approach and the broad commitment, a complete, consistent, understandable and correct semantic-conceptual foundation has been laid for the various transition projects within Obvion, which is supported by the business and is transferable towards implementation. With the completion of the model in its different output formats Obvion's primary requirement has been met, namely mapping the major entities around the concept of 'Customer', including associated information and rules and concept definitions. All those involved in the transition projects receive validated, unambiguous, complete and coherent information. This entails for the various transition projects that the participants can fully focus on the challenges of the projects themselves and no more time and energy needs to be put into previously defined concepts. These concepts can be transferred and, whenever necessary, a request can be made to provide specific enhancements to the concepts.

It is noteworthy to mention that this project was finished on time and within budget and with the required quality.

7   Experiences

Remarks from domain experts who took part in the interview sessions, as collected on the evaluation forms:

"Especially the diversity of representations and the mechanism of controlled increase of the number of entities has exceeded my expectations."

"The ability to apply a fairly abstract and theoretical method in a way that was understood and appreciated by all participants."

"Very good skills to unearth the right information."

"The approach is very practical and Obvion staff is actively involved in the sessions."

8   Conclusions and Future Development

Within a short timespan an Obvion Business Object model has been created for the Customer Interaction domain. For the short term a semantic-conceptual basis for the transition projects in this domain has been established in this way. For the long term a foundation has been laid that can be extended in order to accommodate the business operations in a broad sense.

A major reason why we can talk about the foundation being project or organization-wide lies in the fact that this Obvion Business Object Model came about through the combined effort of staff with a wide range of functions. Such a multidisciplinary approach avoids a biased picture of the knowledge in the organization and ensures that the result and the product will be relevant to many disciplines. This in turn contributes positively to the experience, capacity and applicability in other projects and in the line organization.

The CogNIAM variant of Fact-Based Modeling has proven to be an excellent way to facilitate such a multidisciplinary approach, due to the protocol-based elicitation and objective composition based on concrete examples from practice [3].

However, the Obvion Business Object Model will only retain its value if the knowledge is kept up-to-date. If interim changes are incorporated, the Obvion BOM in its current form will retain its function for knowledge and information requirements within the Customer Interaction domain. The maintenance and management issue therefore calls for clarity on procedures surrounding the maintenance and management and ownership. This problem can be classified under data governance. Setting up and structuring of data governance is one of the next steps Obvion will take.

The accumulated Obvion Business Object Model provides a solid starting point for extensions towards other challenges. This includes both process optimization, business-IT alignment, product development, external regulations, (internal) business rules management, but also the other content areas within Obvion.

Acknowledgements. CogNIAM Finance would like to thank Obvion staff for their candor and their positive contributions to the meetings, in the review sessions and in the evaluation. The quality and success of a project is to a great extent determined by the willingness, professionalism and expertise of the domain experts. These characteristics were highly represented within this project. This in combination with a proven approach and a solid protocol, resulted in the creation – in close cooperation – of an outstanding product.

References

1. Brattinga, M., Nijssen, S.: A Sustainable Architecture for Durable Modeling of Laws and Regulations and Main Concepts of the Durable Model. Paper accepted at the FBM 2015 Workshop of the OnTheMove 2015 Conference, Rhodos, Greece, October 29–30. Proceedings by Springer (2015)
2. Dulfer, D., Lokin, M., Nijssen, S.: Developing and maintaining durable specifications for law or regulation based services. Paper accepted at the FBM 2015 Workshop of the On-TheMove 2015 Conference, Rhodos, Greece, October 29–30. Proceedings by Springer (2015)
3. van Engers, T.M., Nijssen, S.: Bridging Social reality with Rules. Paper presented at IRIS 2014, Das Internationale Rechtsinformatik Symposion, Salzburg, Austria, February 21, 2014
4. Van Engers, T., Nijssen, S.: Connecting people: semantic-conceptual modeling for laws and regulations. In: Janssen, M., Scholl, H.J., Wimmer, M.A., Bannister, F. (eds.) EGOV 2014. LNCS, vol. 8653, pp. 133–146. Springer, Heidelberg (2014)
5. van Engers, T.M., Nijssen, S.: From Legislation towards Service Development – An Approach to Agile Implementation of Legislation. paper accepted for presentation at EGOVIS 2014 in München, September 1–5 and to be Included in the Proceedings (2014)
6. Hohfeld, W.N.: Fundamental Legal Conceptions as Applied in Judicial Reasoning, edited by Walter Wheeler Cook (2010). ISBN-13: 978-1-58477-162-3
7. Kleemans, F., Saton, J.: Developing the Uniform Economic Transaction Protocol A Fact Based Modeling approach for creating the economic internet protocol. Paper accepted at the FBM 2015 Workshop of the OnTheMove 2015 Conference, Rhodos, Greece, October 29–30. Proceedings by Springer (2015)
8. Lemmens, I., Pleijsant, J.M., Arntz, R.: Using Fact-Based Modeling to Develop a Common Language - a use case. Paper accepted at the FBM 2015 Workshop of the OnThe-Move 2015 Conference, Rhodos, Greece, October 29–30. Proceedings by Springer (2015)
9. Lokin, M., Dulfer, D., Straatsma, P.: Wetsanalyse voor wendbare wetsuitvoering; Voor het bouwen van bruggen tussen wet- en regelgeving en beleid en de informatievoorziening van de overheid (2013). versie 2013-05-13-0755, 057
10. Nijssen, G.M.: A Framework for Discussion. In: ISO/TC97/SC5/WG3, 78.09/01 (1978)
11. Nijssen, S., Valera, S.: An Architecture Ecosystem for the Whole Systems Perspective, Including System Dynamics, Based on Logic & Set Theory and Controlled Natural Languages. Working paper for the OMG Architecture Ecosystem SIG (2012)
12. Straatsma, P., Dulfer D.: Wendbare Wetsuitvoering, DREAM 2014

A Sustainable Architecture for Durable Modeling of Laws and Regulations and Main Concepts of the Durable Model

Marco Brattinga[1] and Sjir Nijssen[2(✉)]

[1] Ordina, Utrecht, The Netherlands
marco.brattinga@ordina.nl
[2] PNA Group, Heerlen, The Netherlands
sjir.nijssen@pna-group.com

Abstract. The authors have been involved in durable modeling of laws and regulations to be used as the formal, testable and in a multi-disciplinary group understandable requirements for law and regulation based services. At least one co-creation initiative in the Netherlands has decided to develop an extended protocol for durable modeling of laws and regulations. The vast majority of these services and actions are information-intensive and require a substantial IT effort. The main ideas underlying the protocol developed in the last three years in the Blue Chamber are described. Durable modeling of laws and regulations can only be practically applied, whenever the result is recognizable by stakeholders and can be used for the modelling of services based on these laws and regulations. To test this assumption, we illustrate the protocol using the new Dutch environment planning act.

Keywords: Durable modeling for regulation based services · Legal services · Environment law · Case histories · Fact Based Modeling (FBM) · Legal domain specific protocol

1   Introduction

Legislation is the basis for all public services. Legislation is the union of laws, government decrees, ministerial decrees and several other regulations, including court decisions. The legislation describes very roughly speaking which rights and duties are applicable for a specific citizen or enterprise and under which circumstances. To deliver the intended services, governmental organizations face the challenge of understanding the intended semantics of the legislation and of transforming these intentions to durable and tested specifications.

The development of durable and tested specifications is considered the major obstacle for delivering the actual services within time and budget [8]. The intent of the legislation needs to be faithfully applied in all practical cases [14]. There is a need for a protocol such that a durable model can be used as solid basis for all the stakeholders involved as the formal, tested and accepted model of the associated services and

© Springer International Publishing Switzerland 2015
I. Ciuciu et al. (Eds.): OTM 2015 Workshops, LNCS 9416, pp. 254–265, 2015.
DOI: 10.1007/978-3-319-26138-6_29

enforcement actions [5]. In this paper we propose an architecture that uses fact based modeling as the main part of this protocol and the durable model.

In section 2 we describe the key characteristics of the desired situation. In section 3 we propose a sustainable architecture for the desired situation. The architecture relates the three major actor groups and the facts and rules they use or produce. The architecture provides a solution for the fundamental problem: a fact based durable model between legislation and the actual services. In section 4 we describe the requirements for such a durable model. In section 5 we discuss what we can learn from biology when we apply the durable model. In section 6 we present the key characteristics of the elements of the durable model, using the legality principle that requires a faithful representation of the intended semantics in practical cases. We present the clear connection between the facts at the scenario level and the fact patterns at the regulation level, an essential part of fact based modeling with CogNIAM [17]. In section 7 we discuss the advantages of this strong connection and the fact that in the legal services world, testing at the scenario level has been used since a very long time, long before IT arrived. It is called in that community *case histories* as part of a regulation impact analysis. In section 8 we present two cases associated with the new environment act. We use these cases to exemplify how our sustainable architecture can be the bases for a durable model of law and regulations. In section 9 we present a summary and suggestions for the road ahead.

2   The Key Characteristics for the Desired Situation

To achieve the desired situation for the durable modeling of laws and regulations, a co-creation initiative "Blue Chamber" was started in The Netherlands in 2012, consisting of government institutions, universities and innovative companies. In the spring of 2013 the Blue Chamber published its first report regarding regulation based services in The Netherlands. [8]. It concluded that the current situation is far from ideal. The key characteristics for the desired situation have been described in this report as follows: "In legislation rights and obligations are defined: among citizens, citizens towards the government and vice versa. Legislation contains concepts, rules and conditions that directly affect the actions of citizens, businesses and government organizations. These concepts, rules and conditions form the basis for the services and processes of public implementing bodies. For the following reasons, it is important to be able to distill concepts, rules and conditions from the legislation in an unambiguous and repeatable manner:

A. It promotes legal certainty for citizens and prevents unnecessary disputes and proceedings in court.
B. It enhances the transparency of government. The government can show that what they are doing is in accordance with the democratically established legislation. This includes providing insight into the rules that give the authorities a margin of discretion to do justice in special cases.
C. It simplifies implementation of legislation in services and processes. Thus, orders from politics and public demands can be accommodated more rapidly.

D. It improves an implementing body's capacity to, as part of ex ante feasibility tests, to provide feedback on proposed changes in legislation. This contributes positively to the effectiveness and efficiency of the implementation.

E. It provides insight into the coherence of the complex of legislation. Consequently, generic and specific elements in processes and services can more easily be distinguished. This offers possibilities for reuse, not only within an organization, but also between organizations.

In short, the added value of a repeatable approach to the organization of the implementation of legislation comes from the ability to transform legislation into legitimate and services for citizens and businesses that they experience as meaningful and to perform this in a truthful, efficient, multidisciplinary and timely fashion." [8]

3   A Sustainable Architecture for the Desired Situation

In this section we present the major actor groups in the entire process from initial wish for a law or regulation or modification of a law or regulation up till and including the running service. In the diagram below the three main actor groups are presented as well as which information or rules they read and/or which information or rules they write. [1, 7, 8, 10]

The first actor group consists of law makers, government and ministers. When they observe desired or presumed or identified needs, they start a new law and which are followed by associated decrees, or start to modify an existing law and associated decrees. The government service organizations can also modify or introduce a new operational policy. Judges are an important subset of actors in this group. Their decisions can have an effect on the service execution with regard to similar cases (jurisprudence). It is the combination of the work of these actors that determines the effective regulation.

To give all stakeholders due credit: although actor group 1 executes a process for the creation and modification of the regulations, this actor group doesn't undertake this process alone. Stakeholders like citizens, business and governmental organizations take part in the process, and in the end it is the corresponding legal authority that formally takes the decision (for example: cabinet and parliament for laws, town counsel for municipally rules).

Regulations are produced to provide services for the citizens and enterprises, or have them perform certain duties. These services are information-intensive and often heavily supported by IT. The traditional textual representation of law performs a more than excellent job in creating legal security, along with all the legal authorities. However, a textual representation lacks the necessary "hooks" and explicitly depicted relations between these "hooks" to be used as support for the specification of services.

What is needed is a complete specification that takes the (new) laws, decrees and policies as input and produces a well-tested and by the various stakeholders agreed and therefore accepted specification of the interaction between the government service providers and the citizens or enterprises. This is a multidisciplinary effort [9, 14] and in principle independent of IT or in case of human processes, the specific implementation of these human processes such that new IT technologies and other organizational structures can be based on the durable specifications or model.

Actor group 2 also provides the two-way references between the durable model or specifications and the regulations. The group consists of legal experts, service experts and architects. A two-way reference is needed for impact analysis [19]. Often this is also referred to as annotation services. As can be seen, the specifications of the durable model can be represented with traditional Word, PDF or Excel documents, or by the so-called juridical DNA, a representation that can be consulted with a logical language. An organization has a choice. No matter what the choice is, there is a need to know which requirement is based on which pieces of texts in the regulations. This is represented by the arrows with the A and B in a circle.

Actor group 3 consists of the service builders. Such services can be processes performed by humans or by machines. At the current state of affairs, the majority of services are heavily based on IT services. The builders can use the specifications depicted in the durable model in the same way as a builder of a large office block uses the blue prints of the architect. We have already seen cases in which this building process has been automated, creating IT services directly from specifications.

Actor group 4 consists of the citizens or enterprises that receive the services of the government service provider or the duty dispatching service. Actor group 5 consists of civil servants offering human services.

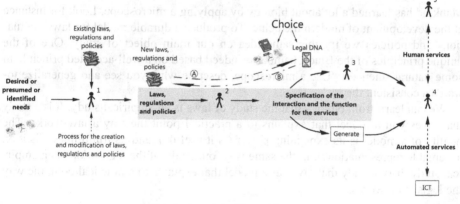

Fig. 1. A sustainable architecture

The validity of the sustainable architecture is supported by the fact that a number of Dutch governmental organizations have already implemented parts:

- The Dutch Taxation Office has issued a European tender in late 2013 under the name Annotation Services, to provide the starting point of two-way links between the durable model and the original laws, decrees and regulations [19].
- The Dutch Land Registry has published the two-way links between registration facts and the corresponding legislation at http://tax.kadaster.nl.

- The Ministry of Infrastructure and Environment has stated[1] that the success of the new environment planning act depends upon the availability of a durable model as a link between legislation and public services.

4   The Requirements for a Durable Model

One of the requirements for which the law makers are not willing to compromise, is that the services provided should be fully based on the regulation and faithfully represents the intended semantics in cases. This is referred to as the legality principle. Only services that are described in the laws, regulations and policies are legally permitted. Commercial organizations can do anything but what is not prohibited, governmental organizations services are rooted in laws and regulations. [8, 14]

Hence that means that the durable model must include a two-way link between the services and the (textual) representation of the legislation, and represent the full semantics as intended in the legislation (regulation level) to apply to all the foreseen cases (scenario level).

5   What can Modelers Learn from Biology?

Mankind has learned a lot about biology by applying a microscope. Look for instance at the development of modern medicine. To produce a durable model for laws, regulations and policies we try this same idea on our main object of study. One of the unique principles of the Blue Chamber is indeed based on a well-accepted principle in some natural sciences: "Use a microscope, describe what you see and generalize towards a consistent theory".

We can learn from biology that the study of laws is an empirical study. It is a study that gives you a model that explains to a practical point the way a law works. The quality of a model is its explaining power (is it useful?), and its truthfulness (is it an acceptable representation?). In the same way, our study of the legislation is an empirical study. It is a study that gives us a model that explains to a practical point the way the legislation works.

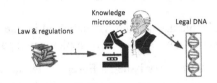

Fig. 2. The knowledge microscope

---

[1] This statement can be found in the administrative covenant regarding the implementation of the environment planning act: bijlage bij kamerstukken II 2014/2015 33118, nr. 19, https://zoek.officielebekendmakingen.nl/blg-546306.

The Blue Chamber has accepted this principle and makes use of a so called knowledge microscope. Hence put a sufficient set of regulation text under the knowledge microscope and conclude which knowledge elements are needed to fully describe the semantics for all relevant practical cases. We use the knowledge microscope as a way to have a truthful model (step 1). But we won't present our microscopic observations as-is: an abstraction is necessary to give an acceptable an understandable explanation of the observations (step 2). In the analogy of biology: after the discovery over a certain type of bacteria under the microscope, the doctor announces that the patient has the common flu. The observation is "bacteria type". The acceptable explanation is the abstraction to a human level of a particular decease.

The knowledge microscope is operated by a durable knowledge modeler who submits questions on concrete cases to a legal expert or an experienced service provider or architect. It is used by actor group (2) as depicted in the architecture: a multi-disciplinary group that works together in co-creation to specify the durable model or as we call it: intelligent specifications.

6   Key Characteristics of the Durable Model

The language to describe the durable model (regulation level) must be capable of describing **explicitly** what the intended semantics of the regulations are in the associated practical cases (scenario level). Here we see a strong link between the scenario level (the level of the facts) and the domain specific regulation level [16, 17].

How do we find out which constructs are needed in durable specification language? By applying the knowledge microscope to a representative set of regulations, se have applied the microscope to a number of regulations and this has resulted in the following list of constructs:

1. Fact patterns, to precisely define the scope;
2. The associated integrity rules that define the quality of the facts of the cases;
3. The associated concept definitions and the references to the legal sources, that provide a description of each term for which there is any doubt that the members of the community have no clear definition;
4. The associated derivation rules, specifying which facts can be derived from other facts (including the derivation of institutional facts from brute facts);
5. The associated behavioral rules, specifying which actor can assert which facts according to which guidelines, following an extended Hohfeld typology (see end of this section);
6. The associated fact communication patterns, providing a tool to communicate the deep structure of a fact in any surface structure selected by a community;
7. The associated rule communication patterns, providing a tool to communicate the deep structure of any rule in any surface structure selected by a community;
8. The associated events, specifying the conditions that start the execution of a derivation rule or behavioral rule;

9. The concept of context, specifying one or more pieces of text within one or more different regulations together forming a context, within which a concept definition is valid for a specific term and

10. The concept of relevant regulations (relreg) introduced by Robert van Doesburg under the term "script" [9], specifying all the pieces of regulations from one or more different regulations that are involved in the often many cases that follow a certain legal act until all the specific cases come to an end.

11. The domain of regulations specific concepts of legal relations and legal actions (extensions to Hohfeld) which can be expressed with the previous 10 constructs.

Please note the concept of context is used to define the boundaries within which a certain term has a certain definition, while the concept of relevant regulations contains a set of pieces of (often) various regulations that define the rules applicable to a prototypical legal act.

The Hohfeld [2, 3, 12] typology is basically a typology of the right-duty pair. He called such a pair in which one party has the kind of right and another party the associated kind of duty a legal relation. Hohfeld had studied before 1913 a number of decisions by various courts, or cases. We could see he used the knowledge microscope principle already over 100 years ago. He came to the conclusion that four different pairs were needed, the claim-duty, the liberty(=privilege)-noright, the power-liability and the immunity-disability. His two publications are landmarks and recommended reading for every one that is concerned with modeling of laws [11, 18, 19].

Hohfeld used his typology of legal relations in the context of court decisions. His model didn't include the creation of new legal relations. In the Blue Chamber we have accepted Hohfeld as a solid basis, to be extended with requirements to include the creation of new legal relations and to use the Hohfeld typology in the context of Dutch legislation.

Creation of legal relations is possible by a solid distinction between a legal relation and a legal act [5]. A legal relation is a state between two parties, having a start time and possibly an end time. A legal act is an act by one party related to a legal relation the party is part of. A legal act can take place at one moment in time or a period in time.

In the Blue Chamber we have come to the conclusion that applying the knowledge microscope principle to Dutch laws and regulation we need to extend Hohfeld with at least one new pair to properly represent the pair DutchClaim-DutchDuty. This will be described in a forthcoming paper.

7   Strong Connection between the Scenario Level and the Regulation Level

In the Blue Chamber we have come to the conclusion that cases are first class citizens. Without expected cases there is no need for a law or regulation. Hence we have come to the conclusion that there is a strong bond between the domain specific level of the rights and duties extended with concepts described above. A case consists of a set of facts. A fact is an event or circumstance which is considered real. In the brute reality brute facts occur. All actions of people, business and governmental organizations are facts that take place in brute reality. But some of these facts are considered "special": those facts result in corresponding institutional facts: facts that correspond to institutional regulations. These regulations (regulation level) dictate which institutional facts can occur.

Legal relations and legal acts are institutional rules. How do rules at the regulation level relate to facts at the scenario level? A fact shares a part of a fact pattern at the regulation level, namely the part that is constant for all fact instances belonging to a fact pattern. And every rule refers to one or more variables in a fact pattern. Voila, the connection between the facts at the case or scenario level and the rules at the domain specific durable model level have the common link of the constant part of a fact and the corresponding part of the fact pattern, sometimes referred to as fact type [17].

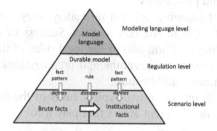

Fig. 3. The knowledge triangle

One of the interesting experiences of working with the principles listed above is that the strong connection between the scenario level and the regulation level makes many things much clearer. The scenario level is well known in the legal world, although underrepresented in the text books.

Before a regulation is put into practice so-called *case histories* are tested as part of an *ex-ante* (Latin for "beforehand") regulation impact analysis. That means that before the actual implementation of the regulation, a number of relevant cases are investigated. We can imagine that the durable model can actually be used during this phase. Although we are very careful not to impose a (different) formal model on the process of lawmaking, we have found that the feedback that such a model gives can be useful in playing with the different scenarios at the scenario level. We have played such roles in collaboration with a number of law experts and this has resulted in substantial insight into the deep structure of elements in regulations and the understanding of legislation by non-legal professionals.

8   Two Related Cases for the New Environment Planning Act

We will now describe two related cases. The physical environment includes constructions, infra-structure, water, soil, air, landscapes, nature and cultural heritage. Citizens, businesses and governments conduct activities that affect change in the physical environment or habitat. Such activities change the usability, health or safety of the physical environment for others. Conflicts of interests can easily occur, due to the fact that parties have different stakes with regard to the same (piece of) environment. These conflicts were prompted to propose rules on activities in the physical environment.

The current environmental law is fragmented and spread across dozens of laws. There are separate laws for land, building, noise, infrastructure, mining, environment, heritage, nature, spatial planning and water management. This fragmentation leads to tuning and coordination problems and reduced recognizability and usability for all users. Initiators of activities are struggling with many different laws, each with its own procedures, plans and rules. Authorities assess an initiative not always in coherence and an integrated policy (set of rules) for one particular piece of the environment is hard to achieve. The proposed Environment Planning Act[2] integrates the area-specific parts of the current laws in one act with one coherent system of planning, decision-making and procedures.

The new environment planning act will ultimately integrate no less than 26 acts and parts of other legislations in one coherent act. Success of the environment planning act can only be achieved if and only if the legal rules of the Act can be successfully translated to the services of governmental organizations. A very realistic and timely case for our sustainable architecture!

In this section, we will introduce two typical cases of the environment act. These scenarios will introduce the different actors that play a role in the environment planning act:

- *Initiators* are parties that want to initiate a certain activity in the environment;
- *Affected parties* are parties that are affected by the proposed activity of the initiator. Affected parties could be neighbors or environmental stakeholders.
- *Authorities* are parties that have the power (Hohfeld) to create the legal situation in which the initiator is granted the liberty (Hohfeld) to initiate the activity, and corresponding the situation in which the affected parties are restricted by the no-right (Hohfeld) to interfere, but granted the power to go to court (case #1). Authorities also have the power to create rules by which first mentioned powers and liberties are restricted (case #2).

Case #1

"Bert" wants to open a restaurant. For the location of the restaurant, Bert has chosen an old building on a river dike at the border of a town in the municipality of "Rivierenland" (Riverland). Bert needs to rebuild and extend the building.

---

[2] At the time of writing of this article, the act is being discussed in the Dutch parliament. The current proposal can be found at: kamerstukken II 2014/2015, 33962, nr. A: https://zoek.officielebekendmakingen.nl/kst-33962-A.html.

The Act prohibits the activity of building, unless Bert has a permit which gives him the liberty[3] to build his restaurant (Article 5.1 under 1 sub a). Bert files a request for the permit with the authorities (according to Article 5.8: the executive board of the municipality Rivierenland).

"Hans" is a civil servant of the municipal of Rivierenland. He is authorized by the executive board to decide on requests for environmental permits in their name.

The activities for which Bert asks a permit are handled according to the "regular procedure" (Article 16.60). The core of this regular procedure is dictated by the rules stipulated in the general administrative act (Awb). The request of Bert is published so affected parties are informed of the activities that Bert wants to undertake.

Bert wants to build his restaurant, but also wants to make a playground in the area between the dike and the river. Hans informs Bert that this isn't allowed with respect to the environmental rules in place. Although Bert could file a request for just such an activity (Article 5.1 under 1 sub b), Bert chooses not to file such a request, but to postpone his desire for a playground.

"Annie" is a neighbor of Hans. Annie is concerned about the activities that Hans wants to undertake. Although Annie likes the idea of a restaurant, she doesn't like the idea of a long building period. She gets in contact with Bert. She shares her concerns, and Bert reassures her that it's also in his interest to have a short building period.

Bert has given Hans all the information that Hans needs to make his decision. Hans decides to grant Bert the permit, and thereby the liberty[4] to start building after the period in which affected parties can object against the decision of Hans.

Although Annie has the power to object against the decision of Hans, she has been reassured by Bert, and won't object. After a short building period, Bert opens his restaurant and welcomes Annie as a regular customer.

Case # 2

In the municipality of Rivierenland, Hans also takes part in the formulation of the environmental plan. In the current plan, the area between dike and river can only be used for the function of agriculture. But, more and more, requests are made to use this piece of land for different functions. It is decided that the environmental plan should change, to also allow the functions of recreational activities.

According to Article 16.28, this corresponds to the extended procedure, described by Section 3.4 of the general administrative act. In this case, the end result is not a particular right or duty of an individual civilian or organization, but the act of law in itself creates new rules. In this way, a fact at the scenario level will introduce a new

---

[3] The observant reader might notice that we use the Hohfeld categorization of rights and duties. This is actually another part of research done by the Blue Chamber, partly published in [5, 6, 7, 8, 14, 19].

[4] This is actually a simplified description of the legal rights that are the result of the permit. The permit not only grants Bert a liberty, but may impose certain duties, powers and other rights. Almost every legal act results in a complex of Hohfeld relations. This will be the topic of further study at the Blue Chamber.

rule and fact patterns at the regulation level. From case #2 we observe that not only legal facts are the result of certain brute facts, but actually all regulation is the result of certain brute facts. This needs further research.

9   Conclusions and Future Work

The case descriptions of the previous section make clear how the concepts of knowledge level II (as descripted by the articles of the environmental planning act) are linked with the concrete facts at knowledge level I (as descripted by the actors Hans, Bert and Annie, the acts they perform or want to perform, and the rights and duties that correspond with these acts). But it isn't by far a model that conforms to the requirements formulated in section 6.

The Blue Chamber has adopted the knowledge microscope principle. That means that the regulation is the primary object of study. This dictates which concepts are needed in a durable model. There is at the time of writing no single ISO, OMG or W3C standard modeling language that has the representational power required by the legality principle. Hence one needs a smart combination of various standards and of course some interfaces between the various standards. It is not to be excluded that the Blue Chamber will publish a proposal for such a standard language if ISO, OMG and W3C continue to fail to fill this gap. In other words, within the metaphor of biology: at a certain time in history, mankind thought that all matter was made up out of fire, earth, water and air [4]. This clouded their judgement with regard to the explanation of natural laws. After the discovery of the model in which matter is made up out of molecules that are made up out of elemental elements, the resulting descriptions of the characteristics of matter were more durable and sustainable. We propose a similar sustainable architecture that results in a durable model for services based on legislation. A model that is understood and accepted by all stakeholders, and rooted in a precise understanding of the semantics of legislation.

Acknowledgements. The authors gratefully acknowledges the many discussions in the co-creation the Blue Chamber.

References

1. Bouwman, H., van Houtum, H., Janssen, M., Versteeg, G.: Business Architectures in the Public Sector: Experiences from Practice. Communications of the Association for Information Systems **29**, Article 23 (2011)
2. Corbin, A.: Legal Analysis and Terminology. Yale Law School (1919)
3. Corbin, A.: Jural Relations and Their Classification. Yale Law School (1921)
4. Crosby, A.W.: The Measure of Reality: Quantification and Western Society, 1250-1600, 245p. Cambridge University Press (1997)
5. Dulfer, D., Lokin, M., Nijssen, S.: Developing and maintaining durable specifications for law or regulation based services. Paper Accepted at the FBM 2015 Workshop of the OnTheMove 2015 Conference, Rhodos, Greece, October 29–30. Springer (2015)

6. Engers, T.M., van Nijssen, S.: Bridging social reality with rules. Paper Presented at IRIS2014, Das Internationale Rechtsinformatik Symposion, Salzburg, Austria, February 21, 2014
7. Van Engers, T., Nijssen, S.: Connecting people: semantic-conceptual modeling for laws and regulations. In: Janssen, M., Scholl, H.J., Wimmer, M.A., Bannister, F. (eds.) EGOV 2014. LNCS, vol. 8653, pp. 133–146. Springer, Heidelberg (2014)
8. Engers, T.M., van Nijssen, S.: From legislation towards service development – An approach to agile implementation of legislation. Paper Accepted for Presentation at EGOVIS 2014, München, September 1-5 and to be Included in the Proceedings (2014)
9. Engers, T.M., van Doesburg, R.: First steps towards a formal analysis of law. In: Malzahn, D., Conceição, G. (eds.) eKNOW 2015, pp. 36–42. IARIA (2015)
10. Engers, T.M. van Doesburg, R.: At your service, on the definition of services from sources of law. In: Proceedings of the 15th International Conference on Artificial Intelligence and Law (ICAIL 2015), pp. 221–225. ACM, New York (2015)
11. Hart, H.L.A.: The Concept of Law, 3rd edn. Oxford University Press (2012). ISBN 978-0-19-964470-4 (First edition 1961)
12. Hohfeld, W.N.: Fundamental legal conceptions as applied in judicial reasoning. In: Cook, W.W. (ed.) (2010). ISBN-13: 978-1-58477-162-3
13. Lemmens, I., Pleijsant, J.M., Arntz, R.: Using fact-based modeling to develop a common language – A use case. Paper Accepted at the FBM 2015 Workshop of the OnTheMove 2015 Conference, Rhodos, Greece, October 29–30. Springer (2015)
14. Lokin, M., Nijssen, S., Lemmens, I.: CogniLex a legal domain specific fact based modeling protocol. Paper Accepted at the FBM 2015 Workshop of the OnTheMove 2015 Conference, Rhodos, Greece, October 29–30. Springer (2015)
15. ISO TR9007: Concepts and terminology for the Conceptual Schema and the Information Base, ISO Technical Report (1987)
16. Nijssen, G.M.: A Framework for Discussion in ISO/TC97/SC5/WG3, 78.09/01 (1978)
17. Nijssen, S., Valera, S.: An architecture ecosystem for the whole systems perspective, including system dynamics, based on logic & set theory and controlled natural languages. Working paper for the OMG Architecture Ecosystem SIG (2012)
18. Singer, J.W.: The legal rights debate in analytical jurisprudence from Bentham to Hohfeld. Wisconsin Law Review (1983)
19. Straatsma, P., Dulfer, D.: Wendbare Wetsuitvoering, DREAM 2014, The Netherlands (2014)
20. Thomson, J.J.: The Realm of Rights. Harvard University Press (1990). ISBN-0-674-74949-9

1975-2015: Lessons Learned with Applying FBM in Professional Practice

Sjir Nijssen[1(✉)] and Baba Piprani[2]

[1] PNA-Group, Heerlen, Netherlands
sjir.nijssen@pna-group.com
[2] MetaGlobal Systems, Ottawa, Canada
baba@metaglobal.ca

Abstract. Around 1975 the first FBM conceptual modeling services were introduced in Europe. A few years later Control Data Corporation introduced Information Analysis Services in North America. What have the various professionals introducing or applying FBM learned in that period? In this paper we will focus on the experiences obtained in The Netherlands and Belgium in Europe and Canada and USA in North America. What do business persons ask? What do they like in FBM? What do they dislike in FBM? This paper summarizes the experiences of two FBM practitioners during the period 1975-2015.

Keywords: Application development · Systems development life cycle · Analysis techniques · NIAM · ORM · FCO-IM · CogNIAM · Fact Based Modelling · Experience with FBM in business practice · Fact-Based Model · How to introduce FBM · How to apply FBM

1 Introduction

The hype goes on....for the search for the holy grail in the streamlining of the development of computer applications. We have seen a variety of analysis techniques, coding techniques, programming languages, database structures, and application development techniques, architectural isolation techniques through tier-ing, loosely coupled, service oriented---and including the streamlining of project management techniques from waterfall, structured, agile and so on. But the philosophy is, and has been, as a legacy, more or less a video-game technique---If you crash, push the button and start over again, this time faster but use a different approach.

The success rate for applications development has flat-topped at near 50 percent since 2004 [11,27] and, in fact getting worse. Sure, any coded application can be made to work---courtesy of bubble-gum and chicken wire with spaghetti coding, akin to a Saturday afternoon dart throwing exercise to get at the target. The success rate for applications development has been flat-topped at near 50 percent since 2004. Whereas the success track record from the use of Fact Based Modelling (FBM) techniques for analysis has consistently shown a considerable leap in the success rate (near 100%) of these applications---build it once and turn away, with a guarantee for success. So why

© Springer International Publishing Switzerland 2015
I. Ciuciu et al. (Eds.): OTM 2015 Workshops, LNCS 9416, pp. 266–275, 2015.
DOI: 10.1007/978-3-319-26138-6_30

has FBM not become the panacea for mainstream development? What have the various professionals introducing or applying FBM in professional business practice learned in that period?

In this paper we will focus on the experiences obtained in The Netherlands and Belgium in Europe, and Canada and US in North America. What do business persons ask? What do they like in FBM? What do they dislike in FBM? This paper summarizes the experiences of two FBM practitioners. Fact Based Modelling (FBM) is a methodology, a protocol for modeling the semantics of a subject area in a language that the various stakeholders understand [18, 20, 21, 22]. FBM applies first and for all the knowledge that the various stakeholders use every day like concrete examples of communication, expressed in their preferred notation. FBM is also based on logic [19] and controlled natural language, whereby the resulting fact based model captures the semantics of the domain of interest by means of fact types, together with the associated concept definitions and the integrity rules and a model populated with examples [21].

The roots of FBM go back to the 1970s. NIAM, a FBM notation style, was one of the candidate notations used for expressing conceptual schemas as defined in ISO TR9007:1987 Concepts and Terminology for the Conceptual Schema and the Information Base [13]. Subsequently, several developments have taken place in parallel, resulting in several fact based modeling "dialects", including NIAM, ORM2, Cog-NIAM, DOGMA and FCO-IM.

Fact Based Modeling was introduced in the mid-s70's in Europe by Control Data Corporation, first in Belgium and The Netherlands, then later in Norway, Sweden, Germany and France. Control Data Corporation introduced a few years later the next version of FBM under the name Information Analysis Services in the USA, Canada and Mexico. The two authors have been involved since the beginning of introducing FBM services in business practice.

In section 2 we describe the first 20 years of NIAM, Natural language Information Analysis Method.

In section 3 we describe FCO-IM, a further development of NIAM.

In section 4 we describe ORM as a further development of NIAM.

In section 5 we describe CogNIAM, Cognition enhanced NIAM as a further development of NIAM.

In section 6 we describe what we have learned from business practice what users consider the essential aspects of FBM. Hence viewed from the perspective of a business that wants to use FBM to solve a practical communication problem. What are customers asking for?

In section 7 we describe the experiences obtained in Canada and US.

In section 8 we describe the experiences obtained in The Netherlands.

In section 9 we present our conclusions and recommendations.

2   The First 20 Years of NIAM

With computing technology rapidly evolving in the late sixties propelled by the race to land a man on the moon, data processing software was rapidly playing catchup in the early seventies. Database technology, being able to address all relevant information, was in its nascent state with identified data modeling approaches like hierarchical, network, CODASYL sets [3], relational [25], and information modelling (aka putting semantics into structures). The pace was rapid, with new database vendors coming and going. Rapid scene changes occurred with CODASYL trying to establish some semblance of standardization, hierarchical models going down the sunset path, and relational based database systems gaining foundation----and saw the early establishment of semantic modelling or information modelling.

It is interesting to note that on the information modelling front the evolution was driven in 2 directions---semantics i.e. the meaning of the data vs. attribute based data modelling. Attribute models essentially resembled grouped attributes in some form of mapped 'entity type' or 'table type' data structures. Some called this semantic modelling, driven by the US Air Force efforts at Integrated Computer Aided Manufacturing (ICAM)---giving birth to modelling techniques like IDEF0, IFDEF1X, IDEF2 (subsequently IDEF3) morphing into FIPS standards.

Meanwhile, emphasis on the *meaning* of the data was being espoused by some schools in Europe and parts of North America, essentially based on the clear separation between the type and instance of data, with elementary relationships between modelled in binary or n-ary forms.

While this paper is not going into a repetition of the various actors involved (please see reference [21]), suffice it to say that the initial acceptance of Fact Based Modelling techniques for information modelling established its roots in mid-70's, and starting to be used in industrial strength projects. The natural-language based affinity of NIAM [21] —an industrial strength realization of FBM---was being embraced by the developer and analyst communities. Control Data Corporation, then headquartered in Minneapolis, USA, led the initial foray of the commercialization of FBM, including training, support tools, and successful implementation across several projects.

2.1   The NIAM Foundation and Protocol

NIAM---originally called Nijssen's Information Analysis Method by the employer of Sjir Nijssen, Control Data Corporation, subsequently renamed by Sjir Nijssen to Natural language Information Analysis Method---was first introduced by Control Data in Europe. The development group was based in Brussels. The group consisted of more than 20 professionals. They had three missions: develop a practical protocol that persons can use to apply NIAM in business practice; develop a tool to support these services and develop a DBMS to support the high business volume transactions.

Before Control Data Corporation introduced the term NIAM, the term ENALIM (Evolving Natural Language Information Modeling) was introduced by the first author to stress the point that such a modeling protocol would require a long time period during which the fist foundation would be tested in practice and adjusted taking the feedback from practice into account. Thereafter the second version of the foundation would be set up and tested in business practice and so on. The publications associated with this early period can be found in references [2, 21].

The services offered by Control Data Corporation were information analysis and training in information analysis.

NIAM was based on the following principles:

"Each communication between a human being and an information system, as well as each communication between any two information systems can be considered to consist of a set of natural language sentences." [21]

"INSYGRAM (Information Systems GRAMmar: 100 % of the prescription [of integrity rules] is in one (conceptually) central contract and 0 % in the application program." [21]. This principle was later adopted in ISO TR9007 and renamed to the 100 % principle.

A conceptual schema as defined in the ENALIM and INSYGRAM approach is a set of rules specifying the set of allowable information base states and the set of allowable transitions (a transition is the difference between the successor information base state and the information base state). It is obvious that in such a conceptual schema one has abstracted from programming or computer considerations. When further abstracting from the naming conventions with respect to object instances, one then no longer deals with sentences but ideas or propositions with objects. he grammar including the naming conventions is given the name significational schema, the grammar in which from the naming convention is abstracted is called the ontological schema." [18]

All schemata can be described in a meta schema. Michael Senko's work has had its positive influence on the early thinking in DIAM [25] as a detailed example of the ANSI SPARC Architecture.

The absence of an available standardized DBMS implementation vehicle with the capability to implement the 100% declared rules may have hurt the promulgation of FBM techniques. Hence, the realization of the FBM-based analysis had meagre automation support for the rule based schemas to be transformed to rule driven DBMS for industrial strength applications.

The 80's saw even more thrusts of NIAM based projects gaining foothold, along with Entity Relationship (ER) techniques offering instant gratification to the attribute-based modelling community---especially with the onslaught of early relational database management systems. Like the Betamax-VHS battle engagement, the VHS-style camp of ER started gaining footholds with support tools being made available, and that would directly feed the quasi-relational based systems of the day. At about the same time, in an effort to standardize the FBM concepts and approach, the ISO Working Group on Conceptual Schemas and Terminology published the ISO Technical Report TR9007 that established a pronounced footprint in the information modelling space [13]. TR9007, in no uncertain terms, laid the path ahead for information modelling techniques, clearly identifying and separation of the fact based vs. attribute based modelling approaches.

Fast forward to the late 80's and 90's saw the refinement and various avatars of NIAM in ORM, FCO-IM and others. At the same time, the staunch foundation vehicle i.e. Control Data , supporting the NIAM integrated fabric space consisting of support resource personnel, training, software tools and implementations, sailed onwards into its sunset, leaving behind NIAM-boomers to carry the ball.

2.2   ISDIS: Information System Design Information System, and EDMS

The group at Control Data Europe in Brussels developed ISDIS, an information system to support the NIAM version of FBM. It was developed using a meta schema approach. It used its own DBMS called EDMS, Evolutionary Database Management System

The group at Control Data Europe in Brussels also developed a DBMS with both a relational and CODASYL DDL and DML interface, above referred to as EDMS. The system was written in itself using a meta schema approach and had therefore to be bootstrapped; the system was specified in ISDIS.

3   FCO-IM as a Further Development

Guido Bakema and his team used NIAM in the early nineties in the Information Systems curriculum at the HAN University of Technology. Guido developed interesting improvements to NIAM which he gave the term Fully Communication Oriented Information Modeling, FCO-IM. Guido and his team have made substantial contributions to the introduction of FBM in the educational institutions in The Netherlands; he also travelled extensively to other countries and gave well received introductions in FCO-IM.

4   ORM : The Formalization of NIAM

In 1989 Terry Halpin finished his PhD at the University of Queensland. His major contribution was the formalization of NIAM. Later on Terry introduced various extensions to the NIAM notation that he gave the name ORM (Object Role Modeling). Terry has produced over a hundred articles and several books on ORM [12, 19].

5   CogNIAM as a Further Development

Starting in 1989 a company was set up in The Netherlands to market FBM services to customers. The goal of the company was to have a substantial group of expert FBM modelers while continuously improving and extending the CogNIAM protocol. It was in this period that first derivation rules and events were added. In the late nineties concept definitions were added to FBM. A few years later the process perspective was added to CogNIAM.

It was in this period that the original idea of NIAM came to fruition: most businesses want to manage their business communication in an effective way. The systematic use of examples in the form of facts became an essential part of the protocol.

6   What has FBM Learned from Business Practice?

Professional business practice has taught FBM many many useful lessons.

The most interesting experience with FBM services in business practice is that customers are primarily interested in getting the business communication within the business, with customers and with various authorities as productive as possible.

Employing as much as possible examples represented in natural language facts is the most appreciated feature of FBM in combination with agreed concept definitions among the various stakeholders.

Hence FBM has more and more evolved into the application of a multi-disciplinary effort to obtain agreement on which facts are within scope, which integrity rules apply to these fact populations and transitions, while having available an agreed list of concept definitions.

Most customers provide a limited budget and this often means that the modeler has to produce only a subset, or at times, none of the integrity rules; working with a limited budget means different subsets of the overall conceptual model.

Modeling laws and regulations means that business practice also demands the derivation rules, behavioral rules and events [1, 4, 5, 6, 7, 8, 9, 16].

In nearly all FBM services for customers they want to have the process perspective included in the overall conceptual model.

7   Experience Obtained in Canada and US

Initially, in the late 70's, NIAM was applied in the 'background' to design and develop applications for the clients of the consulting service arm of Control Data Canada—meaning, the analysts would use the NIAM methodology to derive ER diagrams and eventually to arrive at the database design for implementation using early relational DBMSs. Some of the managers observed that nearly all NIAM-based implementations were profitable as they were not extended in resources or budget, unlike most of the non-NIAM based implementations which generally were in the red for the Control Data balance sheet. This was sufficient to convince more investment in NIAM for the training of analysts and also bringing in clientele at various Control Data sites. The 80's saw more NIAM successes, and even as a vehicle for marketing of mainframe hardware. On a project with the Canadian Department of National Defense, NIAM was set up as the language of communication amongst nearly 56 team personnel made up of six or more 4 person teams. Each team consisted of up to 2 military personnel and 1 civilian analyst and 1 civilian developer.

Reference [28] documents this project, and highlights the experiences of these personnel in establishing the necessary framework for requirements definition and specification. Instead of presenting application requirements using narrative text for contractors as a basis to develop applications this large project used NIAM in formalizing its application functional specifications for presentation to contractors. The reference [26] also defines the framework of models that were used in establishing the set of system specifications and its associated problems with people, skills, time and resources---in terms of Conceptual Schemas, Database Semantics, and Databases---to handle a mix of classified and unclassified data, including supporting hardware and software. This is the first time that a large government project in North America had approached industry with a formal specification suite based on a comprehensive set of integrated models consisting of NIAM constructs and generated ER and relational table definitions towards delivery of a complete solution based on formal FBM models.

NIAM had a following at NIST(National Institute of Standards and Technology--- now NBS) from 1984 on. NIST worked with the US ANSI standards mirror commit- tees to draft a proposal for a New Work Item into ISO on a "standard for the exchange of conceptual schemas". The proposal included a model of NIAM using NIAM. But somewhere in the religious modelling war---with opposition from other National Bo- dies---the proposal did not materialize [23,24].

There were also major projects at Sandia, Boeing and Honeywell.

After Control Data's exit from computer manufacturing, the NIAM-boomers con- tinued to successfully apply NIAM in the background in applications across Banking, Finance, Defense, Transport, Universities etc., with applications winning bronze medals [28], gold medals [10]. There are examples of user-analyst joint sessions wherein the business clients are given a crash course in selected basic FBM concepts and notations. The subsequent walkthroughs increased client-analyst interaction to nearly 90-95% common agreement using natural language sentences. The mapping from natural language sentences to the NIAM graphical notation enabled rapid con- firmation of rules. The use of population diagrams helped gain a 'meeting of the minds'. However, on large projects, the user was often inundated with massive sets of natural language sentences. Also, due to lack of updated support tools, non- availability of a formal dictionary/registry style interface, the synchronization of NIAM models, thru to SQL schemas was found to be quite taxing.

More importantly, the NIAM-boomers are reaching their retirement age (or already have and continue to FBM!). So, an impetus is born to promote and popularize FBM to the main stage, and this is what is going onin Europe in new application fields [1, 14, 15, 17].

8   Experience Obtained in The Netherlands

PNA was set up in 1989 to offer FBM modeling services in The Netherlands. It has gradually grown to 30+ employees. PNA has performed modeling services for various customers, banks, insurance companies, university management and law and regula- tion based government service organizations.

PNA has put a lot of emphasis on the actual testing of the model with examples expressible in natural language facts. This has lead PNA to the conclusion that there is a clear need for a variable based model to get the communication in facts right. There is also a clear need for a role based model as that model is more adequate to support the formulation of rules.

PNA nearly always is asked by customers to help with the development of concept definitions for the new and/or existing systems of the various departments in an organization and to make links with the many existing systems and enhance the semantics of these systems.

Another major lesson that PNA has learned from offering conceptual modeling services is to provide different perspectives to different groups of stakeholders. Indeed there are several well respected professions that do not like any of the FBM graphical notations!

9   Conclusions and Further Recommendations

A most important conclusion is that FBM has to work together with various other modeling disciplines.

Another important conclusion is that most customers want to start small with FBM and when satisfied with the results, want to cover more. Hence it is necessary for professional modelers to understand that most customers prefer to work with fixed budgets and a consequence is often that only a part of an entire FBM model can be produced.

The authors recommend to listen more to the needs of customers when it comes to the further development of FBM.

PNA has come to the conclusion that many customers consider FBM too abstract and too far away from their domain. PNA has developed in the last three years in co-creation with others [1, 4, 16, 5, 6, 7], a domain specific version of FBM for the legal and regulation domain. The experience is that such a domain dependent version is more acceptable to customers of that domain.

The authors hope that business experience will be freely exchanged in future FBM workshops such that customers and FBM developers can jointly further develop an FBM version that most businesses feel comfortable with.

Acknowledgement. The authors express their thanks to Dr. Ed Barkmeyer, previously of NIST, for his useful information of FBM in the USA.

References

1. Brattinga, M., Nijssen, S.: A sustainable architecture for durable modeling of laws and regulations and main concepts of the durable model. Paper Accepted at the FBM 2015 Workshop of the OnTheMove 2015 Conference, Rhodos, Greece, October 29–30. Springer (2015)
2. Bubenko, Jr., J.: From information algebra to enterprise modelling and ontologies—A historical perspective on modelling for information systems. In: Krogstie, J., Opdahl, A., Brinkkemper, S. (eds.) Conceptual Modelling in Information Systems Engineering. Springer(2007)

3. CODASYL Data Description Language Committee, Journal of Development, Materiel Data Management Branch, Dept. of Supply and Services, Canadian Govt., Hull, Que., Canada, January 1978

4. Dulfer, D., Lokin, M., Nijssen, S.: Developing and maintaining durable specifications for law or regulation based services. Paper Accepted at the FBM 2015 Workshop of the OnTheMove 2015 Conference, Rhodos, Greece, October 29–30. Springer (2015)

5. Van Engers, T., Nijssen, S.: Bridging social reality with rules. Paper Presented at IRIS2014, Das Internationale Rechtsinformatik Symposion, Salzburg, Austria, February 21, 2014

6. Van Engers, T., Nijssen, S.: Connecting people: semantic-conceptual modeling for laws and regulations. In: Janssen, M., Scholl, H.J., Wimmer, M.A., Bannister, F. (eds.) EGOV 2014. LNCS, vol. 8653, pp. 133–146. Springer, Heidelberg (2014)

7. Van Engers, T.M., Nijssen, S.: From legislation towards service development– An approach to agile implementation of legislation. Paper Accepted for Presentation at EGOVIS 2014 in München, September 1-5 and to be Included in the Proceedings

8. Engers, T.M., van Doesburg, R.: First Steps Towards a Formal Analysis of Law. eKnow 2015

9. van Engers, T., van Doesburg, R.: At your service, on the definition of services from sources of law. Presented at the 15th International Conference on Artificial Intelligence & Law — San Diego, June 8–12, 2015. as research abstract

10. Government Technology Exhibition and Conference (GTEC) Distinction award Gold for Transport Canada for Transport Object Dictionary project for conceptual design, GTEC 2010, Canada (2010)

11. Gartner Group Report: Gartner Press Release, Gartner Website – Media relations (2005). http://www.gartner.com/press_releases/pr2005.html

12. Halpin, T., Morgan, T.: Information Modeling and Relational Databases, 2nd edn. an imprint of Elsevier. Morgan Kaufmann Publishers, San Francisco (2008). ISBN: 978-0-12-373568-3

13. ISO TR9007, Concepts and terminology for the Conceptual Schema and the Information Base, ISO Technical Report (1987)

14. Kleemans, F., Saton, J.: Developing the uniform economic transaction protocol a fact based modeling approach for creating the economic internet protocol. Paper Accepted at the FBM 2015 Workshop of the OnTheMove 2015 Conference, Rhodos, Greece, October 29–30. Springer (2015)

15. Lemmens, I., Pleijsant, J.M., Arntz, R.:Using fact-based modeling to develop a common language - A use case. Paper Accepted at the FBM 2015 Workshop of the OnTheMove 2015 Conference, Rhodos, Greece, October 29–30. Springer (2015)

16. Lokin, M., Nijssen, S., Lemmens, I.: CogniLex a legal domain specific fact based modeling protocol. Paper Accepted at the FBM 2015 Workshop of the OnTheMove 2015 Conference, Rhodos, Greece, October 29–30. Springer (2015)

17. Moberts, R., Nieuwland, R., Janse, Y., Peters, M., Bouwmeester, H., Dieteren, S.: Business object model: A semantic-conceptual basis for transition and optimal business management. Paper Accepted at the FBM 2015 Workshop of the OnTheMove 2015 Conference, Rhodos, Greece, October 29–30. Springer (2015)

18. Nijssen, G.M.: Current issues in conceptual schema concepts. In: Nijssen G.M. (ed) Proc. 1977 IFIP Working Conf. on Modelling in Data Base Management Systems, Nice, France, pp. 31–66. North-Holland Publishing, Oxford (1979)

19. Nijssen, G.M., Halpin, T.A.: Conceptual Schema and Relational Database Design. Prentice Hall, Victoria (1989)

20. Nijssen, G.M.: An overall model for information systems design and associated practical tools. In: Proceedings of the IFIP TC 8.1 Conference Formal Models and Practical Tools for Information System Design, Oxford, England, April 18–20, North-Holland Publishing Company (1979)
21. Nijssen, G.M.: A Framework for Discussion in ISO/TC97/SC5/WG3, 78.09/01 (1978)
22. Nijssen, S., Valera, S.: An architecture ecosystem for the whole systems perspective, including system dynamics, based on logic & set theory and controlled natural languages. In: Working paper for the OMG Architecture Ecosystem SIG (2012)
23. NIST Special Publication 500-292, The NIST Cloud Computing reference Architecture, September 2011
24. NIST special Publication 800-145, The NIST Definition of Cloud Computing, September 2011. Senko, M: DIAM as a detailed example of the ANSI/SPARC architecture. In: Modelling in Data base Management Systems, North Holland, Amsterdam (1976)
25. Piprani, C., Morris, C.R.B.: A multi-model approach for deriving requirements specifications for a mega-project. In: Rolland, C., Cauvet, C., Bodart, F. (eds.) CAiSE 1993. LNCS, vol. 685, pp. 199–220. Springer, Heidelberg (1993)
26. Standish Group International, Inc.: Chaos Chronicles and Standish Group Report (2003). http://www.standishgroup.com/sample_research/index.php
27. TC Express, a Transport Canada publication referencing Government of Canada Technology Week (GTEC) bronze medal awarded towards the implementation of a strategic information management application e-Directory at Transport Canada (2002). http://www.tc.gc.ca/TCExpress/20021112/en/fa05_e.htm

Developing the Uniform Economic Transaction Protocol

A Fact Based Modeling Approach for Creating the Economic Internet Protocol

Johan Saton[1(✉)] and Floris Kleemans[2]

[1] CogNIAM Finance, Amsterdam, The Netherlands
johan.saton@cogniamfinance.com
[2] Focafet, Amsterdam, The Netherlands
floris.kleemans@focafet.org

Abstract. The global economy faces a growing number of interfaces for economic transactions to take place. As more and more types of transactions occur in the information age, more regulations, guidelines and IT approaches are created to handle these transactions. This results in increasing costs, cumbersome processes and higher entry barriers for small and new players. The Uniform Economic Transaction Protocol (UETP) is a free, open source protocol for an open global network for economic transactions; the economic internet. A uniform economic language will enable an aligned, real time connectivity which increases trust, decreases costs and the number of needed connections. It makes it possible for all economic parties (buyer, seller, banks, fiscal authorities, logistics providers etc.) to speak the same economic language and connect to the online economic transaction. In this paper we describe UETP and how the cogNIAM variant of Fact Based Modeling has been used to develop UETP.

Keywords: Economic internet · Uniform Economic Transaction Protocol (UETP) · Fact Based Modeling (FBM)

1 Introduction

The standardization of shipping containers has given an enormous boost to the economic growth in the world. Is a similar standardization possible for economic transactions? The Uniform Economic Transaction Protocol (UETP) is a proposed solution.

An economic transaction is comprised by several separate processes like product selection by the buyer, stock availability check by the supplier, identification of buyer and method of payment, payment execution, delivery, tax payment, invoicing, book keeping etc. What remains constant in these processes is the data contained in them. For example the price of a product in any given purchase; the amount remains the same throughout the processes needed for the purchase to be executed. However, each process requires and each stakeholder demands that this amount is to be filled in its own form, format and description. The more parties involved in a transaction, the more interfaces are required, which spurs complexity and increases the possibility of errors.

© Springer International Publishing Switzerland 2015
I. Ciuciu et al. (Eds.): OTM 2015 Workshops, LNCS 9416, pp. 276–285, 2015.
DOI: 10.1007/978-3-319-26138-6_31

In order to generate a message that can be understood by all parties involved, regardless of their role in the transaction, a language (UETP) that consists of single, interpretable and relatable definitions is being developed. UETP is created by means of a FBM approach, the cogNIAM method.

In section 2, the current situation for economic transactions is described. In section 3, an overview is given of UETP and its main components. UETP is based on three main requirements, which are described in section 4. The core of UETP is formed by four principles; the semantic GUID principle (section 5), the decentralized envelope in envelope principle (section 6), the group chat principle (section 7) and the smart transaction receipt principle (section 8). Section 9 describes the overall architecture for developing UETP by using the cogNIAM method and the three-layered approach (durable, logical and physical). In section 10 (durable model), section 11 (logical message model) and section 12 (physical model and protocol documentation) the different stages of the knowledge model and its outputs are described in more detail. In section 13 we present the experiences with this approach to this challenge and our conclusions about the use of FBM in a highly connected and complex domain like UETP.

2   The Current Situation for Economic Transactions

A transaction is the act of transferring something from one party to another party. The term 'transaction' is ambiguous to start with; it is used in so many different contexts (financial, IT, legal) with different meanings that a specialization of the term is inevitable for meaningful communication or else the context must be added each time to avoid misunderstanding. Hence, for the development of the UETP domain we started with defining the term economic transaction:

"An economic transaction is the whole of transfer of products, the rendering of services and transfers of money which are needed to complete a purchase or any other economic trade. An economic transaction can be seen as the complete economic session from start to finish between two or more parties."

When we apply this definition to the current situation, we see that *different* communication models exist for specific types of transactions that occur during an economic transaction. A financial transaction that is handled by financial institutions uses a three or a four corner model [Ref. 1] for communicating the facts of the transaction between the parties involved. The corners represent the buyer, seller and the buyer's bank in a three corner model. In a four corner model, the seller's bank is added. A transition is already made by SWIFT from the three corner model to the four corner model to amongst others limit the number of interfaces and to be able to communicate with known parties [Ref. 1]. Of course, a financial transaction in its simplest form is a two corner model; the buyer and seller exchange information, products and money between each other without the involvement of other parties.

Similar communication models exist for the transferring of products (with product we mean both goods and services). A product can be transferred directly between buyer and seller (two corner model), by means of a carrier (goods) or subcontractor (service) (three corner model) or by the combination of a logistics service provider and one or more carriers (four corner model).

Fig. 1. Examples of 2, 3 and 4 corner models

An interesting situation occurs in communicating tax information and transferring payments between a fiscal authority and the taxed party. Although the tax of one transaction can influence both the seller and the buyer directly, both parties have their own private communication line with the fiscal authority.

Thus, in the current situation transactions within one economic transaction are done between a small number of parties (the number of parties determines the communication model) and are specific for that type of transaction. Also, these are typically unconnected transactions and a lot of time and money can be saved by connecting transactions that belong together e.g. to connect payments to invoices which improves automatic reconciliation. This can be done automatically when the payment includes an invoice number or a payment reference, however reconciliation becomes more difficult when multiple payments and/or multiple invoices exist within one economic transaction. It also slows down innovative product solutions since we are bound to the current framework.

3   The Goal of UETP

The main goal of UETP is to provide a free and open source protocol for the exchange of information between all parties in the economic ecosystem.

We would like to improve all the current 'standalone' communication models for economic transactions and use one protocol instead of an array of different communication models. The core vision of Focafet (the foundation behind UETP) is that non-dualistic propositions (unity, alignment and connectivity) outcompete dualistic propositions (separated, unaligned, and disconnected). All parties in an economic transaction can share and access data real time about the transaction between each other on a level playing field basis.

The real time component is an important aspect of the non-dualistic approach as is the addition of location services. For example, the current 'internet of information' solved the disconnectivity issue of information; before the internet, it was considered normal to study in another country of city where libraries were present that had books with specific information. This is inconceivable anno 2015. To be able to connect to information from anywhere on the world brought an enormous amount of new information. We think that the same applies to the economic situation. Although we are moving towards a global economy, some hurdles still need to be taken. The disconnectivity in an economic context between services, organizations, industries and countries is at least as large as the disconnectivity of information until the 1980s.

We have identified 12 major subdomains in UETP which are depicted in Figure 2. Each subdomain can be used in one economic transaction, but this is not a necessity. In version 1.0 we focus primarily on the domains Identification and Authentication, Delivery Billing and Shipping, Taxation and Payment Clearing and Settlement.

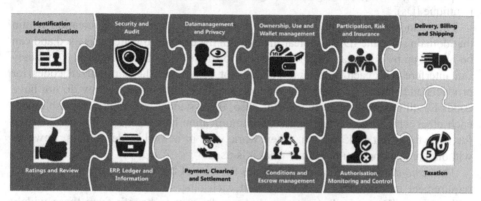

Fig. 2. The UETP ecosystem divided into 12 subdomains and the focus domains for UETP version 1.0.

4   The Three Main Requirements of the Economic Internet

UETP can be compared to what HTTP is for the 'regular' or 'information' internet. The economic internet is not a complete new internet, it is merely a part of the evolution of the internet to the next level: Web 3.0 or most commonly known as the Semantic Web. In the Semantic Web, the third stage of web development introduced in 2001, one of the goals was to increase the meaning of content and the understanding of this content by computers, enabling machine-to-machine interaction to facilitate rapid transaction and effective filtering of information. [Ref. 2]. The Semantic Web is defined as a "mesh of information linked up in such a way as to be easily processable by machines on a global scale" [Ref. 3]. It uses 'common and minimal language to enable large quantities of existing data to be analyzed and processed' [Ref. 2, 4].

In our opinion the economic internet is part of the evolution to web 3.0. This evolution is already taken place at this moment. We have stated three main requirements for the economic internet. UETP is created to facilitate these three requirements:

1. Connect; to connect people, organizations, things, machines, money, assets, data, rules, information, messages and transactions (so basically everything) with each other in (near) real time.
2. Understand: to express and interpret in a uniform way, who, what, how much, where, when, and how in economic transactions.
3. Transact: to instruct and execute in a uniform way, identification, authentication, delivery, reporting, taxation, subsidies, authorization, conditions, payments, reviews, ratings, insurance and participation and more in economic transactions.

5   The Semantic GUID Principle

To be able to connect people, organizations, things, machines, money, assets, data, rules, information, messages and transactions in (near) real time, *identification* is key. There are multiple standards and best practices available for IDs, however they either focus on a specific ID (e.g. harmonized codes for products [Ref. 5], UNSPSC codes for products [Ref. 6]) or are generic (e.g. IETF RFC 4122 [Ref. 7] for creating globally unique IDs).

The main benefit of domain specific IDs is that they ease communication within that domain since the ID has a clear meaning in the context in which it is used and can be looked up by other parties. The drawback of these type of ID standards is that they can interfere with each other and / or are not complete. The harmonized codes for products and UNSPSC codes for products are both not complete: they do not have codes for all the products in the world. Also, these standards are not compatible with each other which make unambiguous communication hard. Generic IDs can be used for everything but lack context. They work well in a worldwide domain, however without context one cannot tell for what it is used.

The *semantic* GUID principle combines the best of both worlds. In UETP the first requirement is to connect everything with each other. We do not want to interfere with existing ID standards / systems, but we do want to benefit from these widely adopted standards, hence we want to interoperate with them. Also, in accordance with the nature of the Internet, we want a decentralized system for creating the IDs without losing the ability to exactly know what an ID represents in analogy with the identification of a website by using Uniform Resource Locators (URL).

The semantic GUID principle is a three step approach:

1. Generate a unique ID
2. Provide that unique ID with meaning (and / or references to other IDs), so that it relates to a person, thing, message, piece of information, etc.
3. Place that unique ID with meaning in a directory service so it can be found and understood or connected with.

To make sure the GUID is truly unique and to make sure security and privacy demands are met, the semantic GUID principle is implemented by means of the combination of a certificate authority, a public key infrastructure and the IETF RFC 4122 [Ref. 7] standard.

6   The Decentralized Envelope in Envelope Principle

The second main requirement is amongst others met by the decentralized envelop in envelop principle. In section 2 already a definition of an economic transaction is described. In each economic transaction multiple messages are sent between the parties involved.

In UETP the first message in the economic transaction also creates an envelope for the economic transaction itself. An economic transaction can be seen as a dossier.

Each message is exactly between two parties and is placed in its own envelope with its own header and content. This envelope is put into the economic transaction envelope. Depending on the properties set by the sender, the envelop can be opened by all parties that are involved in the economic transaction or only by the recipient. In the latter, the message content is also encrypted by means of a public – private key pair using the latest SHA encryption methods.

UETP shall create a set of standardized messages for version 1.0. but shall also make it possible in this version or the next version to be able to construct own messages. Every time a message is added to the economic transaction envelop, each party receives a new version of the economic transaction envelop including all messages. Thus, an audit trail of all messages and the complete dossier are always present for each party real time. Although some messages cannot be opened by a specific party, this principle also has an extra advantage; if a party would tamper with a message, this can be detected by checking all the economic transaction copies. This check is done during sending of the new copy, which makes it impossible to alter the truth. Even encrypted messages can be easily checked; even the slightest change in a message results in a different hash string and hash strings can be easily compared. The decentralized envelope in envelope principle improves security by its design and enables communication and privacy based on the sender's needs.

7   The Group Chat Principle

In section 2 we described the different communication models (2, 3 and 4 corner) that currently exist. The Group Chat principle is an n-corner model in which n is the number of parties involved in the economic transaction. All parties have access to the economic transaction and can see all messages as described in section 6 like in a social media group chat. There is a slight difference in this metaphor; some information can be held back by encryption for the group, which cannot be done on a social media group chat. Due to privacy laws and regulations like the E-Privacy act [ref. 8], the Data Protection Directive 1995 and the Privacy and Electronic Communications Directive 2002 ("ePrivacy Directive") [ref. 9], we have to provide the possibility to encrypt the content of a message. The header is always visible for the other parties.

8   The Smart Transaction Receipt Principle

The smart transaction receipt principle was basically the starting point for determining which data we need to support in UETP. The receipt is the natural endpoint of the purchase phase of an economic transaction, by which most economic transactions end (of course some economic transactions continue in case of e.g. returning of goods or payment in installments). In Figure 3 the smart transaction receipt principle is depicted. It basically contains the who (relevant information about all parties involved), what (product), how much (amount), where (although not visible here, we add geotags to amongst others transactions to determine the legal and fiscal jurisdiction(s) and the consequences of these jurisdictions for the transaction), when (date time), and how (based on the legal and contractual agreements of the transaction) in a specific economic transaction.

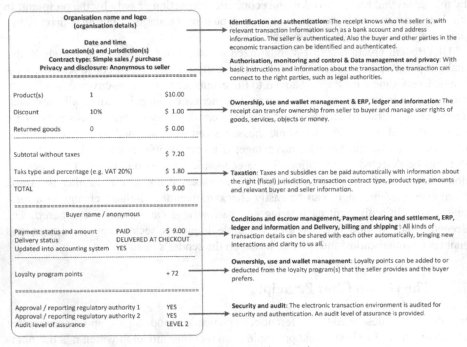

Fig. 3. A smart transaction receipt

9   FBM and the Overall Architecture for Developing the UETP

To create the UETP protocol we have defined an architecture that is based on the three layered approach for the conceptual, logical and physical data model. This architecture is depicted in Figure 4.

We chose to use a FBM approach because the main purpose of FBM is to capture as much of the semantics as possible of the communication between parties, to validate intermediate and final results with the subject matter expert in his preferred language, preferably systematically using concrete illustrations and to remain independent of the representation for a specific implementation, hence durable. FBM provides the means to capture the knowledge of the domain experts in terms of "what" (i.e. the user requirements). FBM is conceptual, hence free of any software implementation bias. FBM adheres to the Conceptualization and 100% principle of ISO TR9007. [Ref. 10]

We have to point out that we intended to use the term durable instead of conceptual because of semantics. Our durable model is a detailed description of the concepts in the UETP Universe of Discourse. It contains terms and their definitions, concepts, the relations between these concepts, variables of the facts of concepts we want to communicate, communication patterns and integrity rules that restrict those variables. However, the term conceptual model is most commonly used for a high level description and that does normally only include the concepts and the relations between them. In our durable model no implementation specific facts are stored. Since we use a far more detailed description, we prefer to use the term durable instead of conceptual.

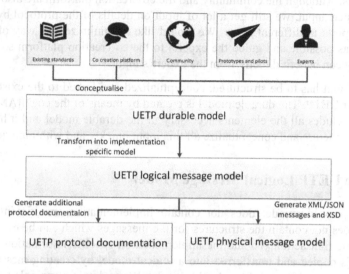

Fig. 4. Overall architecture for developing the UETP

10 The UETP Durable Model

The UETP Universe of Discourse is quite large in contrast to regular Universes of Discourse. Dozens of standards already exist today that describe parts of what we intend with UETP. We want to reuse the knowledge in those standards, hence we want to interoperate. To get input for the durable model we identified 5 sources:

1. Existing standards and protocols like ISO standards, UBL (Unified Business Language), GS1 standards for barcodes, different country originated e-invoicing standards etcetera.

2. A co-creation platform which is open for everyone to discuss new ideas and existing functionalities of the UETP protocol. The output of the co-creation platform is structured into use case descriptions. We created a use case format which basically describes all the elements in a durable model in a natural language format. In this way, the community on the co-creation platform is pre structuring and pre conceptualizing their input for the UETP durable model. The co-creation platform can be found via www.focafet.org.

3. A community of small, medium and large organizations that join to help developing the UETP. Also, we are setting up different hubs on all continents to set up local communities.

4. Prototypes and pilots. We do not believe in creating a standard purely based on theory. A standard needs testing in practice, what is called ex-ante in the development of laws and regulations. The protocol is tested before release by means of pilots and prototypes. This also directly improves the traction of the protocol within and outside the community.

5. Experts. Although the community and the co-creation platform are also means to get expert input, we still get a lot of input on details of the protocol by consulting experts in different areas. We would like to minimize this way of input as much as possible and guide the experts to the co-creation platform so the community can benefit directly from the expert's input.

All this input has to be structured, conceptualized and linked to the existing durable model of UETP. The durable model is created by means of the cogNIAM method, because it includes all the elements necessary in the durable model and it has a solid protocol to structure and conceptualize all this input quickly and with high quality.

11   The UETP Logical Message Model

The UETP durable model does not contain implementation specific information. Hence, it does not contain the structures for the messages which can be exchanged in the economic transaction. To add the implementation specific information, the durable model is copied and transferred into a logical model by creating message structures based on the concepts of the durable model. We maintain one single list of terms and definitions for both the durable model as the logical message model to improve efficiency and to lower maintenance. Each version of a durable model has one or more versions of a logical model. These models are loosely coupled to quickly implement alterations while maintaining the links between the models.

12   The UETP Physical Model and the Protocol Documentation

The UETP logical message model is used for generating the output in the physical layer. Typically, a protocol is communicated to the public by means of a series of documents and output files in a specific technical language. The main downside of these output formats is that they cost a lot of time and effort to create and to update. By using cogNIAM we are able to generate 95% of the physical model output files which are XSD, XML instance examples, JSON files based on the XSD and the XML instance examples and an Excel overview of all messages. The JSON files can be improved further to reduce the payload of the transaction. We use JSON files currently as a starting point for the communication with the first UETP implementers.

Due to the fact that natural language is embedded in the cogNIAM method, we are able to generate the basic protocol documentation which can be further altered for reading purposes. We are investigating the use of linked data output, amongst others for translation purposes and to enhance the connectivity of the UETP dataset with the rest of the world.

13   Conclusions and Future Work

Our biggest challenge in this project is communication and the unambiguous transfer of knowledge. FBM is the key element for determining the What instead of the How. In our opinion no other approach is suitable to address our demands of durability. We are still further creating and refining the UETP protocol and its output, however we are already recognized by other standards bodies like the W3C, because of the high quality of detail we deliver due to FBM. In our opinion FBM can be further combined with the three layered approach in one standard. We gained a lot of efficiency because we described the logical model in a FBM way.

We aim to have UETP 1.0 version ready for testing at the end of 2015. Currently we are working in several projects to develop UETP and let the exchange protocol interact with (crypto)currency networks, identity frameworks and taxation models. Earlier versions are added to www.focafet.org.

Acknowledgements. The authors would like to acknowledge the UETP community and experts who provide us with all the knowledge we need. A special acknowledgement to the UETP core team members Berry de Boer, Job ten Bosch, Hans Cremer, Cynthia van Drie, Hans van Ingen, Sander van Loosbroek and Caren Wolferink. Your good intentions and energy help us to keep pushing our limits and to complete this major task.

The authors would like to thank the FBM community for their feedback and suggestions. A dedicated paper about the cogNIAM analysis in the durable model of UETP will be submitted for the FBM 2016 conference.

References

1. http://www.swift.com/assets/swift_com/documents/about_swift/WP_SWIFT_Supply_Chain_Finance_Apr2013.pdf
2. http://buhalis.blogspot.nl/2012/03/semantic-web-in-tourism-new-era.html
3. Siau, K., Tian, Y.: Supply Chains Integration: Architecture and Enabling Technologies. The Journal of Computer Information Systems 44(3), 67–72 (2004)
4. Gutierrez, C., Hurtado, C., Mendelzon, A., Perez, J.: Foundations of Semantic Web databases. Journal of Computer and System Sciences 77(3), 520–541 (2011)
5. http://unstats.un.org/unsd/tradekb/Knowledgebase/Harmonized-Commodity-Description-and-Coding-Systems-HS
6. http://www.unspsc.org/
7. https://www.ietf.org/rfc/rfc4122.txt
8. https://epic.org/crypto/legislation/eprivacy.html
9. http://www.infosecurityeurope.com/__novadocuments/21997
10. http://www.factbasedmodeling.org/

Workshop on Industrial and Business Applications of Semantic Web Technologies (INBAST) 2015

INBAST 2015 PC Co-Chairs' Message

Semantic and knowledge-based technologies provide a consistent and reliable basis to face the challenges for organization, manipulation and visualization of the data and knowledge, playing a crucial role as the technological basis of the development of a large number of intelligent information systems. Knowledge in information systems is becoming more crucial because the domains of software applications are inherently knowledge-intensive. These technologies draw on standard and novel techniques from various disciplines within Computer Science, including Knowledge Engineering, Natural Language Processing, Artificial Intelligence, Databases, Software Agents, etc. The methods and tools developed and integrated for this purpose are generic and have a very large application potential in a large amounts of fields like Information Retrieval, Semantic Searches, Information Integration, Information Interoperability, Bioinformatics, eHealth, eLearning, Software Engineering, eCommerce, eGovernment, Social Networks, etc.

After the first edition of the workshop, INBAST 2011 in Crete, the following series of the workshop were held in Rome 2012 and in Amantea 2014. INBAST 2015 is now the fourth edition of the Industrial and Business Applications of Semantic Technologies and Knowledge-based information systems workshop series. The goal of the workshop is the feasibility investigation of advanced Semantic and Knowledge-based methods and techniques and their application in different domains.

The workshop attracted a number of submissions, of which a total of 8 papers was accepted for presentation. The topics of the accepted papers cover a wide range of interesting application areas of semantic web technologies, such as Linked Data, Dialogue systems, Semantic integration, Ontology Mapping, Data access, Knowledge management, Machine Translation and Business Process Modeling.

We would like to take this opportunity to thank the Program Committee members who agreed to review the manuscripts in a timely manner and provided valuable feedback to the authors. Finally, we want to thank the authors for their valuable contributions and insights.

September 2015

Rafael Valencia-García
Miguel Ángel Rodríguez García
Ricardo Colomo-Palacios
Thomas Moser

Benchmarking Applied to Semantic Conceptual Models of Linked Financial Data

José Luis Sánchez-Cervantes[1], Lisbeth Rodríguez-Mazahua[1], Giner Alor-Hernández[1],
Cuauhtémoc Sánchez-Ramírez[1], Jorge Luis García-Alcaráz[2],
and Emilio Jimenez-Macias[3]

[1] Division of Research and Postgraduate Studies, Instituto Tecnológico de Orizaba
Av. Oriente 9, 852. Col. Emiliano Zapata, 94320, Orizaba, México
isc.jolu@gmail.com, {lrodriguez,galor,csanchez}@itorizaba.edu.mx
[2] Department of Industrial Engineering, Universidad Autónoma de Ciudad Juárez
Av. del Charro, 450 Norte. Col. Partido Romero, 32310, Ciudad Juárez, México
jorge.garcia@uacj.mx
[3] Department of Electrical Engineering, University of La Rioja,
C/Luis de Ulloa, 20, 26004 Logroño, La Rioja, Spain
emilio.jimenez@unirioja.es

Abstract. Semantic modeling plays a central role in knowledge-based systems where information sharing and integration is a primary objective. Ontology and metadata description languages such as OWL (Web Ontology Language) and RDF(S) (Resource Description Framework Schema) are commonly the most used for representing semantic models and data. The graph-like structure adopted for semantic metadata representation allows simple and expressive queries by using SPARQL-based subgraph matching. While performance of such knowledge-based systems depends on multiple factors, in this work we present a mechanism to properly choice a semantic modeling pattern in order to significantly reduce the data query execution time. Based on this understanding, this work proposes a comparative analysis of different conceptual modeling approaches on the basis of financial domain. In order to show the efficiency/accuracy of our approach, an evaluation of SPARQL-based queries was performed against different modeled datasets.

Keywords: Conceptual modeling · Linked Data · Performance · Semantics; SPARQL

1   Introduction

Nowadays the Financial domain is a source of a great amount of data, as enterprises periodically publish information relative to their financial statements. However, there are multiple ways for representing this information. In financial environments, finding the right information at the right time is the key issue for decision-making process [1]. From this perspective, the importance of performance is twofold. On the one hand, finding information in a fast way could be critical for making an important decision

© Springer International Publishing Switzerland 2015
I. Ciuciu et al. (Eds.): OTM 2015 Workshops, LNCS 9416, pp. 289–298, 2015.
DOI: 10.1007/978-3-319-26138-6_32

and, on the other hand, due to the great volume of information, it is necessary to optimize the process. For this reason, an appropriate representation model could provide
a common way for efficiently representing and retrieving financial information. This
work is based on the hypothesis that the use of the appropriate semantic modeling
pattern might reduce the data retrieval time through the SPARQL-based queries execution, and therefore the process of finding data and decision-making process can be
more efficient. To confirm this hypothesis, a process for the extraction and processing
of XBRL (eXtensible Business Reporting Language) financial statements published in
the EDGAR (Electronic Data Gathering, Analysis, and Retrieval system)[1] repository
using semantic technologies, such as RDF(S), OWL and SPARQL, was performed,
with the aim of generating a financial knowledge base inspired on Linked Data principles [2] that is conformed of two different graphs assigned at Mixed and Entity-
Attribute-Value (EAV) semantic models. Through these semantic models, we have
designed and run a set of SPARQL-based queries with the aim of identifying which of
these semantic models provides the acquisition of financial data faster.

This paper is organized as follows: Section 2 summarizes the Literature review;
Section 3 presents the financial taxonomy and the two models (EAV and Mixed) used
as basis of this research; Section 4 describes the experiment set up and Section 5
presents and discusses the obtained results; finally Section 6 presents conclusions and
future work.

2   Literature Review

In the literature, there are many initiatives related with applying benchmark testing on
RDF (Resource Description Framework) datasets corresponding to several domains.
Some of these initiatives have obtained interesting results, which are briefly described
below. Fundulaki et al. [3] presented the Linked Data Benchmark Council (LDBC)
project with the aim of providing a solution to the following problems: a) the lack of a
comprehensive suite of benchmarks that encourage the advancement of technology
by providing both academia and industry with clear targets for performance and functionality; and b) the need for an independent authority for developing benchmarks and
verifying the results of RDF engines. The solution to these problems was timely and
urgent because non-relational data management is emerging as a critical need for the
new data economy based on large, distributed, heterogeneous, and complexly structured datasets. Our proposal intends to contribute providing a benchmark to measure
the time for information retrieval from the comparison of two models for semantic
representation of financial data.

The Berlin SPARQL Benchmark (BSBM) for comparing the performance of several semantic systems, such as native RDF stores, systems that map relational databases into RDF, and SPARQL wrappers around other kinds of data sources across
architectures, was presented by Bizer and Schultz [4]. FedBench, a comprehensive
benchmark suite for testing and analyzing both the efficiency and effectiveness of
federated query processing on semantic data was presented by Schmidt et al. [5].

---

[1]   https://www.sec.gov/edgar/searchedgar/companysearch.html

An evaluation of FedBench, which is considered as the most comprehensive SPARQL testbed up to now, was presented by Montoya et al. [6]. The creation of a generic procedure SPARQL benchmark applied to the DBpedia base knowledge was proposed by Morsey et al. [7]. SRBench, a general-purpose benchmark primarily designed for streaming RDF/SPARQL engines, completely based on real-world data sets from the Linked Open Data cloud was introduced by Zhang et al. [8]. A benchmark for comparing the expressivity as well as the runtime performance of data translation systems, trough the design of LODIB (Linked Open Data Integration Benchmark) was presented in the work of Rivero et al. [9]. Bail et al. [10] presented FishMark, a Linked Data application benchmark to compare the performance of the native MySQL application, the Virtuoso RDF triple store, and the Quest OBDA system on a fishbase.org like application.

Unlike the initiatives [4-10], in this work several datasets are not compared. In our proposal, we have established a comparison between the EAV and Mixed models to represent financial information. Such comparison involves the execution of a set of SPARQL-based queries in order to measure the runtime of data retrieval in both models.

A classification methodology for federated SPARQL queries and a heuristic called SPLODGE for automatic generation of benchmark queries that is based on this methodology and takes into account the number of sources to be queried and several complexity parameters were presented by Görlitz et al. [11]. The RDF benchmark to model a large scale electronic publishing scenario was presented by Tarasova and Marx [12]. Unlike these initiatives, in our work, we propose a comparative analysis of two different conceptual modeling approaches on the basis of financial domain. The first contribution of the work presented by Aluç et al. [13] is an in-depth experimental analysis which shows that existing SPARQL benchmarks are not suitable for testing systems for diverse queries and varied workloads. To address these shortcomings, their second contribution is the Waterloo SPARQL Diversity Test Suite (WatDiv) that provides stress-testing tools for RDF data management systems. Our contributions are 1) Propose two semantic models inspired in Linked Data principles [2] in order to publish financial information from multiple sources; 2) Provide a benchmark that allows the definition of which financial Linked Data model presented is the most appropriate to publish, search and calculate financial information.

Some of previously works described have obtained outstanding results by applying benchmark tools over several datasets. A key challenge for the semantic Web is to acquire the capability to effectively query large knowledge bases. From this perspective, unlike these works, we describe two Semantic data models (EAV and Mixed models) with their respective benchmarking in order to compare their performance for data retrieval in a financial data context.

3   Description of Semantic Data Models

The overall objective of semantic data models is to capture more meaning of data by integrating relational concepts with more powerful abstraction concepts known from the Artificial Intelligence field in order to facilitate the representation of real world situations [14], [15]. For benchmark purposes, we evaluated two data models, the

EAV model and the Mixed model. Such models include public companies' financial statements reporting such as balance sheets, cash flow and income statements. This is an entry point for the general evaluation of the modeling techniques oriented at query performance and data retrieval. Each model semantically represents the interaction between classes and subclasses that integrate it, basing on a simplified financial taxonomy, generated from published Balance sheets under the US-GAAP principles, through the EDGAR repository.

3.1   Entity Attribute Value Model

The Entity-Attribute-Value (EAV) approach is popular for modeling highly heterogeneous data by using a relatively simple physical database schema (in database literature, alternative terms for entity and attribute are object and parameter, respectively) [16].

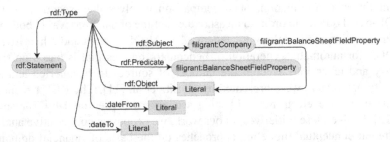

Fig. 1. Entity-Attribute-Value (EAV) Financial data model with reification

As shown in the Fig. 1, the EAV data model representation is as follows: *Entity* is the company name; *Attribute* corresponds to the financial ratio and; *Value* is the value assigned to financial ratio. Furthermore, this model uses the reification [17], [18] in order to attaching as properties the period (start and end dates) of publication of the balance sheets. Unlike the Mixed semantic model, the financial data transformation to RDF notation, following the EAV data model, uses the ratios of the taxonomy as properties (Attributes).

3.2   Mixed Model

The Mixed model (see Fig 2.) developed for the analysis of its performance in the data retrieval through the execution of SPARQL-based queries, is sustained in the EAV model, and in the canonical data model, also named Common Data Model (CDM), that allows defining the entities relevant for a specific domain, including their attributes, associations, and their semantics [19].

In the Mixed model, the data transformation to RDF notation uses the financial ratios specified in the simplified taxonomy as a class hierarchy, representing the inherent nature and characteristics of the financial data, its structure and how the different parts (classes, subclasses and values) are related to each other. The aim of this transformation is to provide a normalized model that is adjusted in a "natural way" in the simplified financial taxonomy, but keeping the features of the EAV model.

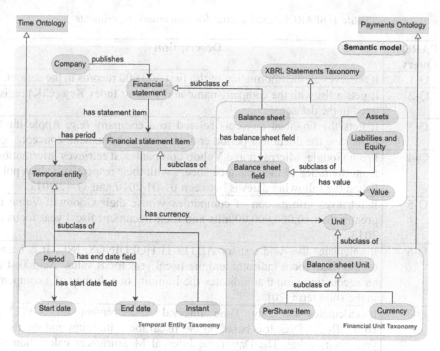

Fig. 2. Mixed Financial data model

4   Benchmark Experiments Design

We have provided two financial data collections; each one consists of a number of interlinked datasets. It is important to underline that we do not assess repositories per se nor we analyze them in terms of query complexity (such as Berlin Benchmark [4] and DBPedia SPARQL Benchmark [7]), but we focus on how semantic data modeling strategies can affect the performance of data retrieval. The experiment starts with the creation of semantic graphs of each semantic model for representing the same financial information. The data is obtained in the information extraction process from financial fillings corresponding to 830,321 XBRL files published by US companies in the EDGAR system. We performed the conceptual modeling part and we created two semantic schemas that they were later used to represent XBRL 10-Q reports data. As a result, we obtained two distinct RDF data graphs that represent the same information as the original data source, but structured after different semantic models. The graphs were loaded to separate semantic repositories, and some series of prepared SPARQL-based queries typical of the financial domain (see Table 1) were issued to measure the execution time that each model takes for data retrieval.

Table 1. SPARQL-based queries for benchmark experiments

SPARQL Query	Description
Q-1	It retrieves all the information of the first 500,000 records in the dataset.
Q-2	It gets a list with the company name and Central Index Key (CIK) registered in the dataset.
Q-3	It gets the financial concepts related to a company (e.g. Apple Inc.), indicating the document period end date for each financial concept.
Q-4	From Google, Microsoft and Yahoo companies, it retrieves information from the ratios of their balance sheets with their respective values published the following dates is between 01/01/2010 and 31/12/2012.
Q-5	It retrieves information of companies whose their Goodwill Value is greater than 10,000,000,000dlls and their document fiscal year focus is 2013.
Q-6	It calculates the Acid test for ABTECH HOLDINGS, INC. It is based on the fiscal focus indicator and the fiscal year focus value. Acid Test is an accounting ratio that indicates the liquidity or solvency of a company in the short term [20].
Q-7	It calculates the Day Time Interval Measurement for ABTECH HOLDINGS, INC. It is based on the fiscal focus indicator and the fiscal year focus value. The Day Time Interval Measurement calculation allows getting the number of days in which a company can continue operating, if for some reason, the company stops its daily activities [20].

The experiments have been carried out under the following technological capabilities: a computer of 64 bits with Operating System Windows Server 2008 R2 Standard, Service Pack 1,8 GB of RAM, a processor AMD Phenom(tm) II X6 1090 3.20GHz and Virtuoso Open-Source Edition (version 7.2.1) as support platform to the RDF triplets.

We decided to use Virtuoso Open-Source because we believe that it is the platform for management, access and integration of Linked Data more convenient to perform our experiments. Our decision is based on the results of benchmark tests for the execution of SPARQL-based queries performed by other authors, such as Bizer and Schultz [4] and Morsey et al. [7], which compared various systems for managing data based on Linked Data, and their obtained results indicated that Virtuoso was the fastest. The results obtained after the execution of the set of SPARQL-based queries for both models are described in the next section.

5   Results

First, we have considered to measure the loading time of the triples in Virtuoso Open-Source for both models. The mixed model obtained a loading time of 3,9 hours with 4,76 GB of files with triples, while the EAV model obtained a loading time of 5,18 hours with 5,84 GB of files with triples. The loading process of the triples in the dataset generated a total of 138, 675, 457 triples, of which 89,977,851 correspond to the

EAV model and 48,697,606 triples to the graph of Mixed model. For both models, the set of SPARQL-based queries was executed five times with the purpose of finding the same information and to calculate the average runtime of the data retrieval. These SPARQL-based queries were executed through the iSQL tool of Virtuoso Open-Source, and the results were dumped into .txt files. The records stored in these files allow analyzing the data retrieved. The main metric used to compare the obtained results of the EAV and Mixed models is the runtime of data retrieval (measured in milliseconds/ms). These results are shown in the Table 2 and are available (.zip) on the following URL:

https://drive.google.com/file/d/0B1dT-T9E25tTUVJLc2hYeTFHQnM/view?usp=sharing

Table 2. Benchmark time of data retrieval for EAV and Mixed models

MODEL	Time to data retrieval (ms)						
	Q1	Q2	Q3	Q4	Q5	Q6	Q7
EAV	37737	920	748	3198	826	2870	550
	38095	858	733	3213	827	3447	560
	38048	890	764	3042	1404	3588	550
	35210	874	827	3183	780	3354	550
	37690	874	734	3214	780	3292	560
Mixed	47705	499	47	3261	827	952	484
	31808	1529	31	3276	624	967	515
	35990	1560	31	2121	889	936	468
	35990	1653	16	3276	687	936	499
	36083	1279	31	3183	827	952	483
Averages (ms)							
EAV	37356	883,2	761,2	3170	923,4	3310,2	554
Mixed	37515,2	1304	31,2	3023,4	770,8	948,6	489,8

The following program listing is an example of a SPARQL-based query executed for the Mixed model

```
SELECT DISTINCT ?companyName ?goodwillValue ?documentFiscalYearFocus
WHERE { ?s flgrant:EntityRegistrantName ?companyName .
    ?s flgrant:hasBalanceSheetField ?BalanceSheetField .
    ?s flgrant:DocumentFiscalYearFocus ?documentFiscalYearFocus .
    ?BalanceSheetField flgrant:hasMonetaryValue ?monetaryValue .
    ?monetaryValue flgrant:value ?goodwillValue .
    ?BalanceSheetField a ?bsclass .
    ?bsclass rdfs:label ?BalanceSheetFieldLabel .
    FILTER (?BalanceSheetFieldLabel = "Goodwill")
    FILTER (xsd:integer(?goodwillValue) >= 10000000000)
    FILTER (xsd:integer(?documentFiscalYearFocus)="2013"^^xsd:integer)};
```

The above SPARQL-based query is an example of obtaining the results of Q5 corresponding to the Mixed model. For simplicity, we skipped the prefixes in this example.

The initial experiments were performed to the EAV model and its average results favor to the Q2, Q3, Q5 and Q7 queries with values of less than 1000ms for each query. Q2, Q3 and Q5 are medium complexity queries that require retrieving data based on one or two search criteria. Q5 is slightly more complex because it requires searching those values corresponding to the Goodwill ratio with value of more than 1000,000,000dlls. In contrast, Q7 requires a series of calculations for the Daytime interval measurement based on a particular Document Fiscal Focus and a Focus Document Fiscal Year. Moreover, Q1 and Q4 are queries that require retrieving a considerable amount of data. The first one requires retrieving the general information of the first 500,000 records of all triples generated in this model, while the second one requires obtaining data within a date range. The times obtained for these queries are reasonable, considering that the subject of triples generated for this model serves as an index, which is the retrieval path for the desired data during the search process. However, the time obtained in Q7, compared to Q6, is very good, indicating that this model is useful for certain calculations.

If the results of each model are analyzed one by one in the Table 2, we can find two notable differences; the first one indicates that the average time for data retrieval in Q2 is higher in the Mixed model compared with the EAV model. However, it is not the same case for Q6. Other queries have certain similarities in both models, for example queries Q1 and Q4 exceed 1000ms, while Q3, Q5 and Q7 remain this value. The average times presented in Table 2 show that the Mixed model scored the best times for data retrieval in processed queries, with exception of Q1 and Q2. However, the difference between the two models does not exceed the 500ms. The overall average time for EAV model is 6708,285,714ms, and on the Mixed model is 6297,571,429ms, with a difference of 410,714,285ms. Therefore, we deduce that the Mixed model is the most optimal for the execution of queries processed in these experiments.

6   Conclusions and Future Work

Knowledge representation is the basis for sharing and knowledge reuse. In this way, Ontologies and Linked Data provide the structure and the tools for representing and sharing knowledge allowing information retrieval based on common vocabularies. These characteristics are especially relevant for the financial domain where the data sources are diverse and appropriate semantic models are necessary for representing and retrieving information. Based on this understanding, the calculation of rations in the financial domain is particularly relevant. However, performance issues must be taken into account in order to provide the right information at the right time. For this reason, in this paper two conceptual modeling approaches for the financial domain have been presented.

Both conceptual models are based on the simplified US-GAAP Balance Sheet Taxonomy. These models allow the representation of financial ratios as well as perform searches. Despite that the EAV model is optimal for directly browsing and finding information, the Mixed model proposed favors the financial calculations and the search of ratios. This model is especially relevant for the financial domain where information is usually result of calculations based on data not directly accessible. Thus, the results of the benchmark analysis of both approaches showed that the Mixed model is the most optimal for the execution of the SPARQL-based queries corresponding to the context of our work.

Based on the results of this study, future research will include the execution of more experiments with the processing of SPARQL-based queries, as well as the calculating of Student's T-distribution to corroborate statistically if the Mixed model continues acquiring the financial data faster. Furthermore, we pretend adding an extension of the Mixed Model in order to provide a Linked-Data based framework for representing the financial data of enterprises which publish their results in order to provide an efficient environment for sharing financial information. Such Linked Data approach will connect the financial data with other data sources in order to enrich the information and provide efficient added value services.

Acknowledgement. The authors are very grateful to National Technological of Mexico for supporting this work. Also, this research paper was sponsored by the National Council of Science and Technology (CONACYT), as well as by the Public Education Secretary (SEP) through PRODEP.

References

1. O'Riain, S., Curry, E., Harth, A.: XBRL and open data for global financial ecosystems: A linked data approach. Int. J. Account. Inf. Syst. **13**(2), 141–162 (2012)
2. Berners-Lee, T.: Linked Data - Design Issues. Linked Data (2009). http://www.w3.org/DesignIssues/LinkedData.html (Accessed October 08, 2013)
3. Fundulaki, I., Pey, J.L., Dominguez-Sal, D., Toma, I., Fensel, D., Bishop, B., Neumann, T., Erling, O., Neubauer, P., Groth, P., Van Harmelen, F., Boncz, P.: The Linked Data Benchmark Council (LDBC). Proc. First Eur. Data Forum **877**, 6–8 (2012)
4. Bizer, C., Schultz, A.: The Berlin SPARQL Benchmark. Int. J. Semant. Web Inf. Syst. **5**(2), 1–24 (2009)
5. Schmidt, M., Görlitz, O., Haase, P., Ladwig, G., Schwarte, A., Tran, T.: FedBench: a benchmark suite for federated semantic data query processing. In: Aroyo, L., Welty, C., Alani, H., Taylor, J., Bernstein, A., Kagal, L., Noy, N., Blomqvist, E. (eds.) ISWC 2011, Part I. LNCS, vol. 7031, pp. 585–600. Springer, Heidelberg (2011)
6. Montoya, G., Vidal, M.-E., Corcho, O., Ruckhaus, E., Buil-Aranda, C.: Benchmarking federated sparql query engines: are existing testbeds enough? In: Cudré-Mauroux, P., Heflin, J., Sirin, E., Tudorache, T., Euzenat, J., Hauswirth, M., Parreira, J.X., Hendler, J., Schreiber, G., Bernstein, A., Blomqvist, E. (eds.) ISWC 2012, Part II. LNCS, vol. 7650, pp. 313–324. Springer, Heidelberg (2012)
7. Morsey, M., Lehmann, J., Auer, S., Ngonga Ngomo, A.-C.: DBpedia SPARQL benchmark – performance assessment with real queries on real data. In: Aroyo, L., Welty, C., Alani, H., Taylor, J., Bernstein, A., Kagal, L., Noy, N., Blomqvist, E. (eds.) ISWC 2011, Part I. LNCS, vol. 7031, pp. 454–469. Springer, Heidelberg (2011)
8. Zhang, Y., Duc, P.M., Corcho, O., Calbimonte, J.-P.: SRBench: a streaming RDF/SPARQL benchmark. In: Cudré-Mauroux, P., Heflin, J., Sirin, E., Tudorache, T., Euzenat, J., Hauswirth, M., Parreira, J.X., Hendler, J., Schreiber, G., Bernstein, A., Blomqvist, E. (eds.) ISWC 2012, Part I. LNCS, vol. 7649, pp. 641–657. Springer, Heidelberg (2012)
9. Rivero, C.R., Schultz, A., Bizer, C., Ruiz, D.: Benchmarking the performance of linked data translation systems. In: Linked Data on the Web (LDOW 2012) workshop (2012)
10. Bail, S., Alkiviadous, S., Parsia, B., Workman, D., Van Harmelen, M., Concalves, R.S., Garilao, C.: FishMark: A linked data application benchmark (2012)

11. Görlitz, O., Thimm, M., Staab, S.: SPLODGE: systematic generation of SPARQL benchmark queries for linked open data. In: Cudré-Mauroux, P., Heflin, J., Sirin, E., Tudorache, T., Euzenat, J., Hauswirth, M., Parreira, J.X., Hendler, J., Schreiber, G., Bernstein, A., Blomqvist, E. (eds.) ISWC 2012, Part I. LNCS, vol. 7649, pp. 116–132. Springer, Heidelberg (2012)
12. Tarasova, T., Marx, M.: ParlBench: a SPARQL benchmark for electronic publishing applications. In: Cimiano, P., Fernández, M., Lopez, V., Schlobach, S., Völker, J. (eds.) ESWC 2013. LNCS, vol. 7955, pp. 5–21. Springer, Heidelberg (2013)
13. Aluç, G., Hartig, O., Özsu, M., Daudjee, K.: Diversified stress testing of rdf data management systems. In: Mika, P., Tudorache, T., Bernstein, A., Welty, C., Knoblock, C., Vrandečić, D., Groth, P., Noy, N., Janowicz, K., Goble, C. (eds.) ISWC 2014, Part I. LNCS, vol. 8796, pp. 197–212. Springer, Heidelberg (2014)
14. Klas, W., Schrefl, M.: Semantic data modelling. Metaclasses Their Appl. Data Model Tailoring Database Integr, 71–81 (1995)
15. NIST-FIPS: Integration definition for information modeling (IDEF0-IDEF1X) (1993)
16. Nadkarni, P.M., Marenco, L., Chen, R., Skoufos, E., Shepherd, G., Miller, P.: Organization of Heterogeneous Scientific Data Using the EAV/CR Representation. J. Am. Med. Informatics Assoc. 6(6), 478–493 (1999)
17. Alexander, N., Ravada, S.: RDF object type and reification in the database. In: Proceedings of the 22nd International Conference on Data Engineering, ICDE 2006, p. 93 (2006)
18. Manola, F., Miller, E., McBride, B.: RDF primer. W3C Recomm. 10, 1–107 (2004)
19. Dell, M., Dell, S.: Canonical Data Model Design Guidelines (2010)
20. Montero, J.M., Fernández-Aviles, G.: Enciclopedia de economía, finanzas y negocios. Editorial CISS (Grupo Wolters Kluwer), Madrid (2010)

Ontology-Driven Instant Messaging-Based Dialogue System for Device Control

José Ángel Noguera-Arnaldos[1], Miguel Ángel Rodriguez-García[2(✉)],
José Luis Ochoa[3], Mario Andrés Paredes-Valverde[4], Gema Alcaraz-Mármol[5],
and Rafael Valencia-García[4]

[1] Proyectos Y Soluciones Tecnológicos Avanzadas, SLP (Proasistech) Edificio CEEIM,
Campus de Espinardo, 30100 Murcia, Spain
jnoguera@proasistech.com

[2] Computational Bioscience Research Center, King Abdullah University of Science
and Technology, 4700 KAUST, P.O. Box 1608, 23955-6900 Thuwal, Kingdom of Saudi Arabia
miguel.rodriguezgarcia@kaust.edu.sa

[3] Department of Industrial Engineering, Universidad de Sonora,
Blvd. Rosales Y Transversal, 83000 Hermosillo, Sonora, Mexico
joseluis.ochoa@industrial.uson.mx

[4] Department of Informatics and Systems, Universidad de Murcia, Murcia, Spain
{marioandres.paredes,valencia}@um.es

[5] Department of Modern Philology, University of Castilla-La Mancha,
Castilla-La Mancha, Spain
gema.alcaraz@uclm.os

Abstract. The im4Things platform aims to develop a communication interface for devices in the Internet of the Things (IoT) through intelligent dialogue based on written natural language over instant messaging services. This type of communication can be established in different ways such as order sending and, status querying. Also, the devices themselves are responsible for alerting users when a change has been produced in the device's sensors. The system has been validated and it has obtained promising results.

Keywords: Dialogue systems · Natural Language Interfaces · Ontologies · The Internet of Things

1 Introduction

The Internet of things refers to the connection of physical things to the Internet in order to make it possible to access remote sensor data and to control the physical world from a distance [1]. The incorporation of an electronic system into these physical things requires a certain amount of expertise for programming and control of the hardware and software elements. Nowadays, it is important to increase the access to technology and the development of tools that allow all kind of users to carry out tasks such as maintaining a comfortable temperature or programming the coffee maker, among others, thus enhancing the quality of their lives.

© Springer International Publishing Switzerland 2015
I. Ciuciu et al. (Eds.): OTM 2015 Workshops, LNCS 9416, pp. 299–308, 2015.
DOI: 10.1007/978-3-319-26138-6_33

On the other hand, the semantic Web aims to provide Web information with a well-defined meaning and make it understandable not only for humans but also for computers [2]. In the Semantic Web, the ontologies are the main vehicle for domain modeling. An ontology is defined as a formal and explicit specification of a shared conceptualization [3]. Nowadays, data stored in ontology-based knowledge bases have significantly grown, becoming an important component in enhancing the Web intelligence and in supporting data representation. Indeed, ontologies are being applied to different domains such as biomedicine [4], finance [5], innovation management [6], Cloud computing [7] [8], medicine [9], and Human Perception [10], among others. In the context of Internet of Things, the ontologies play an important role in device and service interoperability as not only do they provide semantics for the data to be exchanged, but also for describing the devices themselves [11], thus allowing these components to communicate unambiguously with each other [12].

In this work, we describe the im4Things platform which represents an effort to provide users a mechanism for control and query different devices such as electrical appliances or industrial systems in a distributed scenario. The im4Things platform provides an ontology-based natural language dialogue system which allows users to interact with different devices through instant messaging services in a fast and intuitive way, improving the performance and comfort of smart environments, thus enhancing the quality of users' lives. This paper is structured as follows: Section 2 outlines the state of the art on NLI development and device control applications. Section 3 describes the architecture design, modules and interrelationships of the suggested approach. Section 4 thoroughly describes the evaluation of the suggested platform. Finally, conclusions and future work are presented.

2   Related Works

Nowadays, there are prominent efforts to provide NLI (*Natural Language Interfaces*) for ontology-based data sources in different contexts such as rehabilitation robotics [13], finances systems [14], among others. Also, there are research efforts to provide ontology-driven NLI in different domains, some examples of these works are SWSNL [15] and FREyA [16]. Despite the aforementioned works obtained promising results, they are not focused on the control and query of devices such as electrical appliances or industrial systems.

There are research efforts to use ontologies for describing real Ambient Intelligence environments [17]. The suggested ontologies aim to solve several key challenges such as application adaption, automatic code generation and code mobility. Despite this work seems very interesting, it does not offer natural language interfaces that allow users to interact with this kind of environments. On the other hand, in [18] the authors presents a survey of semantic-based approaches for reasoning about the context in Ambient Intelligence.

In the context of device control, the number of mobile applications for the control of electronic devices has dramatically increased. Thanks to these applications users can manipulate domotic systems by means of mobile devices such as smartphones and tablets. Among the device control applications we can highlight those systems that allow interaction with different devices by means of both written and oral natural language dialogues. An example of this is found in Mayordomo [19], a multimodal dialogue system which allows interaction with an Environmental Intelligence context in a house through speech. Another example of this kind of application is AmIE [20] a system which aims to provide an intelligent environment able to improve the quality of life of elderly people.

Most of those systems have focused on controlling domotic devices in a centralized way, by using domotic connection technologies such as EIB-KNX [21], X10 [22] or proprietary systems. In contrast, the im4Things platform provides users a mechanism for controlling and querying different devices in a distributed scenario. Besides, the use of ontologies has two main objectives: (1) to describe every action, function, sensor, and state of devices through a domain ontology, which incorporates linguistic information of all these features, (2) to retrieve all semantic information from the user query in order to translate it to commands that can be executed by the devices. In the next section, the architecture design, modules and interrelationships of the proposed approach are described in detail.

3   Platform Architecture

The system suggested here is composed of three main modules: im4Things app, im4Things cloud service and the device (see Fig. 1). The im4Things app implements an instant messaging chat through which users can send and receive messages from

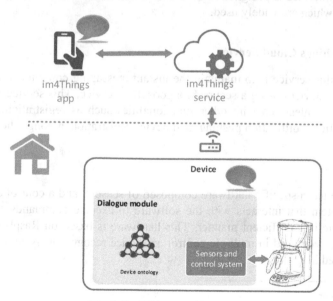

Fig. 1. Im4Things architecture

the im4Things cloud service. The im4Things cloud service is in charge of securing and managing the instant messaging communication between the im4Things app and the devices. Inside each device there is a dialogue module that permits to execute commands and query the current state on the device. This module also permits to detect alerts from the device in order to transform these alerts into natural language and send them through the system (i.e.: the command execution has finished). Every action, function, sensor and state of devices are represented through a domain ontology that incorporates linguistic information of all these features. Taking into account that the ontology creation and management related processes are very important to define and develop semantic services [23] the ontology used in this work was designed by a group of experts on domotic devices programming.

Next, each module is described in detail.

3.1   im4Things App

This app permits instant messaging communication between users and devices in real time. This communication is done using the XMPP[1] protocol that allows to manage a very secure instant messaging session.

Users need to register into the platform in order to start using this application. Then the user can add other users and devices that incorporate to the cited hardware. The app registers devices through a unique code that is printed in each device. Users can identify each device by means of an identifier and password. Besides, the app has other functionalities such as sending files or creating groups composed by other users and devices.

The user interface is designed to be intuitive and it is similar to other instant messaging apps which are widely used.

3.2   im4Things Cloud Service

The aim of this service is to maintain the instant messaging communication between the users and devices using a secure MongooseIM[2] service. This service was adapted in order to be integrated with other functionalities such as registration, messaging, synchronization, notification pushing, and device registration, among others.

3.3   Device

Each device has a specific hardware composed of sensors, and a control and communication system that interacts with the software to execute commands and send the device's state in an efficient manner. This hardware is based on Raspberry as it has successfully been used in multiple control and voice recognition systems such as the one presented in [24].

---

[1] http://xmpp.org/

[2] https://www.erlang-solutions.com/products/mongooseim-massively-scalable-ejabberd-platform.

The device also implements a version of the chat app which is managed by the dialogue module that is in charge of managing the conversation between the device and the user.

Next the dialogue module is explained in detail.

3.3.1   Dialogue System

Traditionally, written dialogue systems implement three different natural language tasks: natural language understanding, dialogue management, and language generation. In our approach it is also necessary to include a new module that permits the communication with the devices to query its current state, execute commands or manage the communication between the user and the device.

Fig. 2 shows the dialogue system architecture. As it can be observed, the dialogue system is based on a device ontology that represents and formalizes the information and knowledge of the device such as the action that can be executed, the sensors it contains, the services and alerts that can be executed by the device, its possible states and other devices that can be integrated in this device.

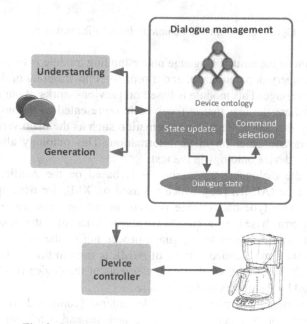

Fig. 2. Ontology-based dialogue system architecture

Fig. 3 shows an example of an ontology that represents a coffee maker device. In this example the coffee maker can adopt up to six different states (CoffeeEmpty, DrinkReady, Off, MakingDrink, SelectDrink, WaterEmpty and Paused). Besides, coffee maker has three sensors (WaterLevel, Temperature, CoffeeLevel) that alert when there is no more water or coffee, and when the drink is ready. Finally, three different actions can be executed in the device (DrinkSelection, Start, and Stop).

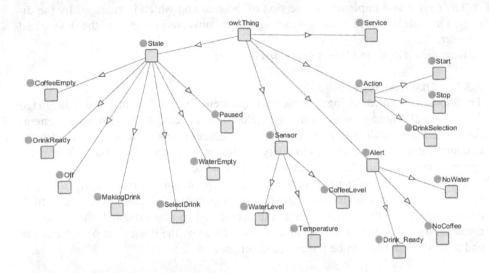

Fig. 3. An excerpt of an ontology for a coffee maker device

The main aim of the natural language understanding module is to analyze if the received text is a query or a command, and it processes the meaning of the text in order to handle this message. This module is based on previous works of our research group such as [25], where the text that is received is represented by means of a question model ontology that stores linguistic information such as the main verb, the question focus, modifiers and other linguistic information. This ontology also contains the references to the device ontology in the text.

As regards the dialogue management, it is based on the Artificial Intelligence Mark-up Language (AIML) [26], which is based on XML for developing conversational systems. This type of language is used for defining pattern templates which produce a response based on a simple correspondence of entry tokens. However, AIML has not been designed for language processing or the understanding of sentences. That is why an extended version of AIML is used in this study, where tokens are not used. Instead of that, we deal with elements of the device ontology and information provided by the understanding module.

The dialogue module obtains the possible patterns (commands or queries) which are more accurate for the received text. It also analyses and checks whether it is possible to carry out that command or query, and it executes it by changing the state and communicating with the device controller and the generation module.

When it comes to a command, it is executed by the device controller, which indicates whether this command has been correctly executed. Then the dialogue management module would establish communication with the generation module so that a natural language response can be generated and sent to the user.

It is important to remark here that not only does the device controller execute the commands, but it also monitors the alerts sent from the device and manages their state. In this case, the controller warns the dialogue management system to alert the user.

4   Evaluation

We have conducted an evaluation in order to know the effectiveness of the im4Things platform to provide control over different devices from the user environment by means of written natural language expressions. This evaluation involved the participation of a group of five people which have no knowledge or experience on devices programming within smart environments. This group represents potential real-word end users. The evaluation was performed as described below.

1. The devices involved in this evaluation were a coffee maker, a washing machine and a watering system.
2. In order to avoid questions out of the context, the people received a description of the functionalities that the devices are able to perform, as well as their possible states.
3. The participants were asked to express 20 messages in natural language concerning commands and states of the involved devices.
4. The natural language expressions provided by the non-expert users were executed through the im4Things app.
5. The response provided by the im4Things platform was compared to the expected behavior of each device.
6. In this evaluation we employed the *precision* metric, which is commonly applied by researchers in the context of NLI development [27] [28] [29]. In this context, the precision metric refers to the proportion of messages that were successfully executed by the corresponding device. This score was obtained by dividing the number of messages successfully executed by the im4Things platform by the total of messages provided by the group of end-users.

The accuracy obtained was 0.92%, which means that 92 of 100 questions and commands were correctly handled by the system. Despite the fact that these results seem promising, there are still some issues to be solved. On the one hand, the ontology does not have many labels representing synonyms, however we cannot guarantee that all knowledge entities contained in this knowledge base are correctly annotated. On the other hand, it is difficult to detect some of the commands to be executed in the device. Besides, some of these commands were unable to be executed because the device does not provide this functionality.

5   Evaluation

There is a first functional version of the prototype and all the components have been developed. What is more, the prototype has been configured for the control of a coffee machine, a washing machine and a watering system. Future research lines will consist in improving how modules work. Most of the improvement work will focus on the dialogue and sensor systems. Around 50 potential users will be selected for the validation of the system by means of a graphic questionnaire which does not affect them about their use of language to interact with the devices. This study will measure the accuracy of the system. Besides, this dialogue system will be improved so that language can be generated, since nowadays it just obtains a set of parameterized patterns to respond to the user.

The authors are also working on a device configuration assistant which allows the semi-automatic, ontology-based generation of most part of configuration and defined patterns found on the platform, so that device configuration will be easier for the user.

The authors are also contemplating the possibility of interacting with devices through speech, by using VoiceXML technology, in a similar way to [30].

Finally, prototypes for the control and consulting of complex industrial facilities are being designed. They are based on the technology that has been developed in this work.

Acknowledgements. Mario Andrés Paredes-Valverde is supported by the National Council of Science and Technology (CONACyT) and the Mexican government.

References

1. Kopetz, H.: Internet of things. In: Kopetz, H. (ed.) Real-Time Systems, pp. 307–323. Springer, US (2011)
2. Berners-Lee, T., Hendler, J., Lassila, O.: The Semantic Web. Sci. Am. **284**(5), 28–37 (2001)
3. Studer, R., Benjamins, V.R., Fensel, D.: Knowledge Engineering: Principles and Methods. Data and Knowledge Eng. **25**, 161–197 (1998)
4. Ruiz-Martínez, J.M., Valencia-García, R., Martínez-Béjar, R., Hoffmann, A.: BioOnto-Verb: A top level ontology based framework to populate biomedical ontologies from texts. Knowl.-Based Syst. **36**, 68–80 (2012)
5. Lupiani-Ruiz, E., García-Manotas, I., Valencia-García, R., García-Sánchez, F., Castellanos-Nieves, D., Fernández-Breis, J.T., Camón-Herrero, J.B.: Financial news semantic search engine. Expert Syst. Appl. **38**(12), 15565–15572 (2011)
6. Hernández-González, Y., García-Moreno, C., Rodríguez-García, M.Á., Valencia-García, R., García-Sánchez, F.: A semantic-based platform for R&D project funding management. Comput. Ind. **65**(5), 850–861 (2014)
7. Rodríguez-García, M.Á., Valencia-García, R., García-Sánchez, F., Samper-Zapater, J.J.: Ontology-based annotation and retrieval of services in the cloud. Knowl.-Based Syst. **56**, 15–25 (2014)
8. Rodríguez-García, M.Á., Valencia-García, R., García-Sánchez, F., Samper-Zapater, J.J.: Creating a semantically-enhanced cloud services environment through ontology evolution. Future Gener. Comput. Syst. **32**, 295–306 (2014)
9. Rodríguez-González, A., Alor-Hernández, G.: An approach for solving multi-level diagnosis in high sensitivity medical diagnosis systems through the application of semantic technologies. Comput. Biol. Med. **43**(1), 51–62 (2013)
10. Prieto-González, L., Stantchev, V., Colomo-Palacios, R.: Applications of Ontologies in Knowledge Representation of Human Perception. Int. J. Metadata Semant. Ontol. **9**(1), 74–80 (2014)

11. Roelands, M., Plomp, J., Mansilla, D.C., Velasco, J.R., Salhi, I., Lee, G.M., Meersman, R.: The DiY Smart Experiences Project. In: Uckelmann, D., Harrison, M., Michahelles, F. (eds.) Architecting the Internet of Things, pp. 279–315. Springer Berlin, Heidelberg (2011). http://link.springer.com/chapter/10.1007/978-3-642-19157-2_11

12. Tang, Y., Debruyne, C., Criel, J.: Onto-DIY: A Flexible and Idea Inspiring Ontology-Based Do-It-Yourself Architecture for Managing Data Semantics and Semantic Data. In: Meersman, R., Dillon, T., Herrero, P. (eds.) OTM 2010. LNCS, vol. 6427, pp. 1036–1043. Springer, Heidelberg (2010)

13. Doğmuş Z., Patoğlu, V., Erdem, E.: Ontological query answering about rehabilitation robotics. In: IROS 2014 Workshop: Standardized Knowledge Representation and Ontologies for Robotics and Automation, Chicago (2014)

14. Valencia-García, R., García-Sánchez, F., Castellanos-Nieves, D., Fernández-Breis, J.T.: OWLPath: an OWL ontology-guided query editor. IEEE Transactions on Systems, Man, Cybernetics 41(1), 121–136 (2011)

15. Habernal, I., Konopík, M.: SWSNL: Semantic Web Search Using Natural Language. Expert Syst. Appl. 40(9), 3649–3664 (2013)

16. Damljanović, D., Agatonović, M., Cunningham, H., Bontcheva, K.: Improving habitability of natural language interfaces for querying ontologies with feedback and clarification dialogues. Web Semant. Sci. Serv. Agents World Wide Web 19, 1–21 (2013)

17. Preuveneers, D., Van den Bergh, J., Wagelaar, D., Georges, A., Rigole, P., Clerckx, T., Berbers, Y., Coninx, K., Jonckers, V., De Bosschere, K.: Towards an extensible context ontology for ambient intelligence. In: Markopoulos, P., Eggen, B., Aarts, E., Crowley, J.L. (eds.) EUSAI 2004. LNCS, vol. 3295, pp. 148–159. Springer, Heidelberg (2004)

18. Bikakis, A., Patkos, T., Antoniou, G., Plexousakis, D.: A survey of semantics-based approaches for context reasoning in ambient intelligence. In: Mühlhäuser, M., Ferscha, A., Aitenbichler, E. (eds.) Constructing Ambient Intelligence, pp. 14–23. Springer, Berlin Heidelberg (2008)

19. Espejo, G., Ábalos, N., López-Cózar Delgado, R., Callejas, Z., Griol, D.: Sistema Mayordomo: uso de un entorno de inteligencia ambiental a través de un sistema de diálogo multimodal. Procesamiento del Lenguaje Natural 45, 309–310 (2010)

20. Kantorovitch, J., Kaartinen, J., Abril, L.C., Martín, R. de las H., Cantera, J.A. M., Criel, J., Gielen, M.: AmIE - towards ambient intelligence for the ageing citizens. In: Proceedings of the 2nd International Conference on Health Informatics. ANDITEC, pp. 421–424, Portugal (2009)

21. Ruta, M., Scioscia, F., Sciascio, E.D., Loseto, G.: Semantic-based enhancement of ISO/IEC 14543-3 EIB/KNX standard for building automation. IEEE Transactions on Industrial Informatics 7(4), 731–739 (2011)

22. Cuevas, J.C., Martínez, J., Merino, P.: El protocolo x10: una solución antigua a problemas actuales. In: Actas del Simposio de Informática y Telecomunicaciones, SIT 2002, pp. 87–96. Universidad de Málaga, España (2002)

23. García-Peñalvo, F.J., Colomo-Palacios, R., García, J., Therón, R.: Towards an ontology modeling tool. A validation in software engineering scenarios. Expert Systems with Applications 39(13), 11468–11478 (2012)

24. Haro, F.D., Córdoba, R., Rojo Rivero, J.I., Diez de la Fuente, J., Avendano Peces, D., Bermudo Mera, J.M.: Low-Cost Speaker and Language Recognition Systems Running on a Raspberry Pi. Latin America Transactions IEEE (Revista IEEE America Latina) 12(4), 755–763 (2014)

25. Paredes-Valverde, M.A., Rodríguez-García, M.A., Ruiz-Martínez, A., Valencia-García, R., Alor-Hernández, G.: ONLI: An Ontology-Based System for Querying DBpedia Using Natural Language Paradigm. Expert Systems with Applications **42**(12), 5163–5176 (2015)
26. Wallace, R.: The elements of AIML style. Alice AI Foundation (2003)
27. Cimiano, P., Haase, P., Heizmann, J., Mantel, M., Studer, R.: Towards Portable Natural Language Interfaces to Knowledge Bases - The Case of the ORAKEL System. Data Knowl. Eng. **65**(2), 325–354 (2008)
28. Erozel, G., Cicekli, N.K., Cicekli, I.: Natural Language Querying for Video Databases. Inf. Sci. **178**(12), 2534–2552 (2008)
29. Minock, M., Olofsson, P., Näslund, A.: Towards building robust natural language interfaces to databases. In: Kapetanios, E., Sugumaran, V., Spiliopoulou, M. (eds.) NLDB 2008. LNCS, vol. 5039, pp. 187–198. Springer, Heidelberg (2008)
30. Griol, D., García-Jiménez, M., Molina, J.M., Sanchís, A.: Desarrollo de portales de voz municipales interactivos y adaptados al usuario. Procesamiento del Lenguaje Natural **53**, 185–188 (2014)

Ontology-Based Integration of Software Artefacts for DSL Development

Hele-Mai Haav[✉], Andres Ojamaa, Pavel Grigorenko, and Vahur Kotkas

Laboratory of Software Science,
Institute of Cybernetics at Tallinn University of Technology, Tallinn, Estonia
{helemai,andres.ojamaa,pavelg,vahur}@cs.ioc.ee

Abstract. This paper addresses a high level semantic integration of software artefacts for the development of Domain Specific Languages (DSL). The solution presented in the paper utilizes a concept of DSL meta-model ontology that is defined in the paper as consisting of a system ontology linked to one or more domain ontologies. It enables dynamic semantic integration of software artefacts for the composition of a DSL meta-model. The approach is prototypically implemented in Java as an extension to the DSL development tool CoCoViLa.

Keywords: Semantic interoperability · Semantic integration · Ontology-based modelling · DSL meta-models · DSL development

1   Introduction

Domain Specific Languages (DSLs) have been used for a long time in order to shorten the software development lifecycle and make it cost effective in a particular domain of interest. There are many well-known DSLs available like XML for describing data, HTML to mark-up web documents, Structured Query Language (SQL) for querying relational databases, etc. There are also DSLs that are more specific like WebDSL [4] and the Modelica modelling language [2]. In order to create a DSL, several tools have been developed. For example, Xtext[1], MS Visual Studio[2], Metaedit[3], and CoCoViLa[4] are tools that enable the development of a DSL. However, issues related to the integration of these tools and the corresponding DSL meta-models are not entirely solved.

Currently, tools are in many cases integrated on the basis of XML or UML profile SysML or via given transformations of different software artefacts related to DSL models so that models can be imported or exported among tools. However, these representations of software artefacts or corresponding metadata do not formally and explicitly capture semantics of described artefacts. Although model transformations represent semantics, it is encoded into the set of transformation rules.

---

[1]   http://www.eclipse.org/Xtext
[2]   https://www.visualstudio.com/
[3]   http://www.metacase.com/mep/
[4]   http://cocovila.github.io/

© Springer International Publishing Switzerland 2015
I. Ciuciu et al. (Eds.): OTM 2015 Workshops, LNCS 9416, pp. 309–318, 2015.
DOI: 10.1007/978-3-319-26138-6_34

In this paper, we provide a new approach to integration of software artefacts for DSL development using the semantic representation of software artefacts in the form of linked formal ontologies described in Ontology Web Language (OWL) [9]. The role of OWL is to serve as a common language for representation of semantics of software artefacts.

Novelty of our approach is twofold: the semantic integration of distributed software artefacts into a coherent DSL meta-model as well as the simplification of the development lifecycle and evolution of a DSL. In addition, our method also facilitates the semantic integration between DSL meta-models created by different DSL development tools in the case there exists a commitment by software developers to use a common top level system ontology or to explicitly define and make available the system ontology of their tool.

The approach presented in this paper is prototypically implemented as an extension to the DSL development tool CoCoViLa [7]. It allows an automatic generation of executable Java programs according to a DSL meta-model and a specification of an application expressed in the corresponding DSL. In this paper and in CoCoViLa, the term DSL is used to denote a specific type of DSLs i.e. Domain Specific Modelling Languages. However, our approach is general enough to be applied for the development of different kinds of DSLs.

The rest of the paper is structured as follows. Section 2 is devoted to the related work and Section 3 provides background knowledge about the DSL development process with CoCoViLa. In Section 4, our new approach for semantic integration of software artefacts is presented. Section 5 provides an overview of a system architecture supporting the approach. Section 6 concludes the paper.

2   Related Work

Ontologies are used in the existing ontology driven software engineering methodologies in several ways. In general, they are mostly used for the consistency checking of software models and as tools for representing model transformations [13, 14]. Another trend is to integrate ontologies to the OMG meta-pyramid of MDA [15] and to the Ecore meta-meta-model of the Eclipse Modelling Framework [5] in order to provide meta-meta-model for modelling DSL languages [14, 16].

Research that is tightly related to the approach provided in this paper express two views. From the modelling point of view, semantic search and composition of models of software components [6] are important. From the technical point of view, integration of OWL and Java is essential. For example, a hybrid modelling approach that enables software models partially developed in Java and in OWL is given in [12].

However, to the best of our knowledge we do not know the DSL development approaches that use linked ontologies for semantic integration of software artefacts and for dynamic building of DSL meta-models as presented in this paper.

3   Background: the DSL Development Process with CoCoViLa

The CoCoViLa system supports the CoCoViLa modelling language that consists of visual and declarative languages for developing DSLs for domains, where scientific and engineering computations play an important role. Expected users of the CoCoViLa modelling language are DSL designers, who create a meta-model of a DSL for a particular domain. The syntax of the full CoCoViLa modelling language is presented in [3]. The CoCoViLa tool was successfully used for the development of different DSLs in the domains of simulation of hydraulic systems as well as simulations of security measures for banking and communication networks [7].

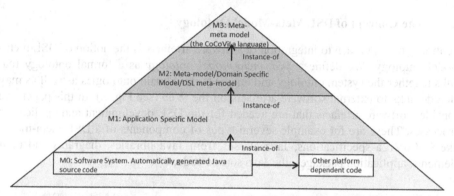

Fig. 1. The meta-pyramid of models based on the CoCoViLa language and tool

In Fig. 1, the current DSL development process with the CoCoViLa system is explained using the OMG MDA terminology [11] and its modelling pyramid. Extensions that constitute the core of this paper are presented in the next sections.

The CoCoViLa modelling language (on the level M3 in Fig. 1) enables to describe meta-models that define DSLs for various domains. Application specific models are created by DSL users. These models of the level M1 are automatically transformed to the corresponding valid logical representation in order to use the method of automatic construction of algorithm of a program [8] and for efficient generation of the corresponding Java source code. The CoCoViLa tool is implemented in Java; therefore the system by default allows generating the Java code directly from an application specific model. Other platform dependent code can be generated from the Java source code.

In Fig. 1, a DSL is created manually taking into account users' requirements and domain knowledge. This corresponds to the previous method of DSL development with CoCoViLa that did not include any special requirements concerning the representation of domain models to be used. In practice, informal methods were used.

Recently, (in [10]) we have presented a method that allows formal domain ontologies presented in OWL to automatically transform to design templates of a DSL meta-model in order to partially automate the DSL development process with CoCoViLa. The current paper takes these transformations into account when extending the original architecture of the CoCoViLa tool.

4   Semantic Integration of Software Artefacts

In order to semantically describe software artefacts used for the development and implementation of a DSL and its meta-model, we use OWL ontologies that are widely utilized in semantic web technological space and supported by well-known standards by W3C. One of the effects of using semantic web standards is an opportunity to semantically describe DSL artefacts and to link software artefacts developed by one modelling tool to artefacts developed by other modelling tools or systems in a distributed way over the Web. Another effect is possibility to use Description Logics (DL) reasoning facilities [1] as ontologies are represented in OWL [9].

4.1   The Concept of DSL Meta-Model Ontology

Central to our approach to integration of software artefacts is the notion of DSL meta-model ontology. We define a *DSL meta-model ontology* as a formal ontology that links together the system ontology and one or more domain ontologies as well as may include links to external software artefacts on the Web (see Fig. 2). In this paper, we consider software artefacts that are needed for the DSL development and application processes. These are for example several types of components of a DSL meta-model like CoCoViLa specifications, Java classes from Java libraries, diagrams and their elements, application packages, the Java source code, etc.

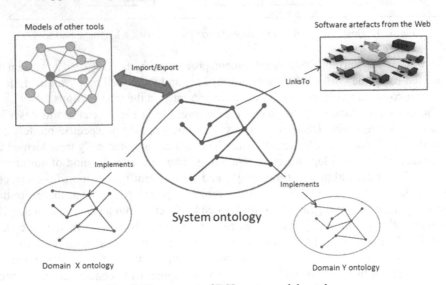

Fig. 2. The concept of DSL meta-model ontology

The *System ontology* formally describes concepts of a particular modelling language and the corresponding software system as well as relationships among them. For example, the CoCoViLa system ontology includes concepts like JavaClass, MetaClass, ConceptSpecification, etc.

The *Domain ontology* provides a specification of a conceptualization of a domain. For example, the geometry domain ontology may contain concepts like 2DimShape, Rectangle, etc.

The DSL meta-model ontology facilitates semantic integration of software artefacts for DSL development and implementation. As shown in Fig. 2, concepts of the system ontology may be related to the concepts of domain ontology via the implementation relationship or they may provide links to external resources used for DSL development. In addition, a part of system ontology concepts may refer to components of models created by the other DSL development tools. This case requires availability of the system ontology of these external tools. In order to ensure the consistency of a DSL meta-model ontology, DL reasoning services are used.

4.2   The CoCoViLa System Ontology

We now explain how the previously described general ontology-based integration approach is implemented for a particular system i.e. the CoCoViLa modelling tool.

The CoCoViLa system ontology formally describes the CoCoViLa modelling language and system concepts (see Fig. 3 for a part of this ontology). The current version of this ontology includes OWL descriptions of 40 classes, 21 object properties and 16 data properties.

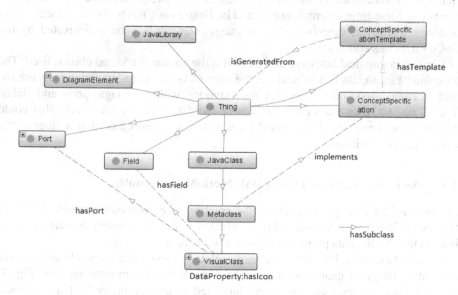

Fig. 3. A fragment of the CoCoViLa system ontology

The ConceptSpecification class represents a collection of concept specifications that are textual specifications in the CoCoViLa modelling language. The latter includes definitions of variables, constants, and relations. Concept specifications are used to facilitate automatic composition of an application. Individuals of the

ConceptSpecification class are related to the automatically generated ConceptSpecificationTemplate class instances via the hasTemplate object property.

Concept specification templates are restricted forms of concept specifications that do not include specifications of dynamic parts of a DSL meta-model like relations (except equality relation). These templates are automatically generated from class descriptions of domain ontology using transformation rules given in [10]. The corresponding relationship is represented in ontology by the isGeneratedFrom object property that provides links to domain concepts used in a DSL meta-model. Concept specification templates can be later manually extended with the CoCoViLa language statements that could not be covered by transformations (e.g. equations and relations).

Individuals of the MetaClass class are implemented on the basis of individuals of the ConceptSpecification class and Java. The corresponding relationship is expressed by the implements object property whose domain is the class MetaClass that is a subclass of the class JavaClass collecting instances that are Java classes. The MetaClass class collects individuals that are Java classes and may contain Java methods that are realizations of relations described by the ConceptSpecification class individuals.

It is possible to use diagrammatical elements for a DSL development. Therefore, the CoCoViLa system ontology includes several classes for representing diagram elements as subclasses of the DiagramElement class. Individuals of these elements can come from external sources and be linked via URIs to the DSL meta-model ontology. However, diagrammatical language elements can be also created by the CoCoViLa class editor.

For diagrammatical language of CoCoViLa the notion of a visual class is used. The VisualClass class is a subclass of the MetaClass class. Its individuals are the MetaClass class individuals that are extended with an image, ports and fields. The VisualClass class individuals have the data property hasIcon that could be URI to an image of an icon used for denoting a visual class on a toolbar of the CoCoViLa DSL window.

4.3   An Example: the Geometry DSL Meta-Model Ontology

Let us consider a simple example of the creation of a meta-model ontology for the Geometry DSL. In the following Fig. 4, a fragment of the geometry domain ontology is depicted. All the data property ranges in Fig. 4 are xsd:double.

In order to create a DSL for calculations related to geometric shapes from the given domain ontology of geometric shapes, the CoCoViLa system ontology (see Fig. 3) and domain ontology (see Fig. 4) are imported to the Geometry DSL meta-model ontology. For each (or selected) domain ontology class a corresponding instance of the ConceptSpecificationTemplate class is created and linked to it via the isGeneratedFrom object property value. This object property value indicates from what domain ontology class the template is automatically generated. For example, the following templates in Fig. 5 are generated from the OWL class Rectangle and its super-classes.

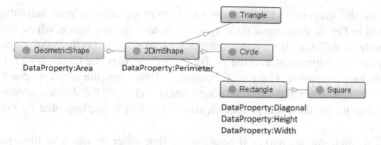

Fig. 4. Domain ontology of geometric shapes (a fragment)

The generated concept specification template of the concept `Rectangle` can be manually completed by corresponding equations for calculating for example a value of the variable `Diagonal`. After that the template becomes the complete concept specification for the concept `Rectangle` that is related to its template via the `hasTemplate` object property value.

```
specification GeometricShape {
        double Area; }

specification _2DimShape super GeometricShape {
        double Perimeter; }

specification Rectangle super _2DimShape {
        double Height, Width, Diagonal; }
```

Fig. 5. A part of a concept specification template in the CoCoViLa textual modelling language.

```
SubClassOf( sys:MetaClass sys:JavaClass )
SubClassOf( sys:VisualClass sys:MetaClass )
DataPropertyDomain( sys:hasIcon sys:VisualClass )
DataPropertyRange( sys:hasIcon xsd:anyURI )
SubClassOf( geo:Rectangle geo:2DimShape )

Individuals and their relationships

ClassAssertion( sys:ConceptSpecificationTemplate meta:CST1 )
ClassAssertion( sys:ConceptSpecification meta:CS1 )
ClassAssertion( sys:VisualClass meta:VC1 )
ClassAssertion( geo:Rectangle meta:Rectangle )

ObjectPropertyAssertion( sys:isGeneratedFrom meta:CST1 meta:Rectangle )
ObjectPropertyAssertion( sys:hasTemplate meta:CS1 meta:CST1 )
ObjectPropertyAssertion( sys:implements meta:VC1 meta:CS1 )

DataPropertyAssertion( sys:hasIcon meta:VC1
"http://www.cs.ioc.ee/cocovila/icons/rectangle.png"^^xsd:anyURI )
```

Fig. 6. The DSL meta-model ontology classes and instances (a fragment)

Some of the Geometry DSL meta-model ontology classes and individuals are represented in Fig. 6. Functional style syntax[5] is used in this figure, where the prefix "sys" denotes the CoCoViLa system ontology elements, the prefix "geo" denotes the geometry ontology elements and the prefix "meta" denotes the Geometry DSL meta-model ontology elements. The Fig. 6 basically shows that the concept specification template CST1 is generated from the Rectangle class of the domain ontology and it is the template for the concept specification CS1 that is implemented by the visual class VC1.

The DSL meta-model makes it possible to link other domains in the analogous way. The consistency of the DSL meta-model ontology is checked by using ontology inference provided by Apache Jena[6].

5   The System Architecture and its Prototypical Implementation

In order to implement a DSL, the original CoCoViLa required a domain expert to transfer the knowledge and a programmer able to convert such informal representation of knowledge into Java classes and annotate these classes with concept specifications. Concept specifications include besides variables also functional dependencies related to concepts. The realizations of functional dependencies can be equations or Java methods implemented in corresponding Java classes. Steps related to the DSL application for solving a particular problem are mostly done automatically by the tool.

The following Fig. 7 depicts the architecture of the CoCoViLa extension that is mainly related to the improvement of a DSL development while components of the previous system (about 80% of the whole system) are used for a DSL application.

The CoCoViLa extension provides facilities for DSL designers to carry out the ontology-based DSL development process that enables the usage of existing formal domain ontologies in combination with the system ontology for a DSL construction.

When loading a DSL, its meta-model ontology (created by DSL designers) is loaded and SPARQL[7] queries are used to dynamically collect and semantically integrate all metadata about artefacts of a DSL meta-model for instantiation of the computational model. Afterwards, the DSL is ready to be used by application developers.

Application developers build the problem specification using the DSL and translate it into the computational model with the help of the CoCoViLa tool. Applying a set of Jena rules enables to extend the computational model with additional relations between concepts in the model. Components (re)used from the previous system are the following: a computational model, the planner, an algorithm and the generated Java code. For more details we refer to [7].

---

[5]   http://www.w3.org/TR/2012/REC-owl2-syntax-20121211/
[6]   https://jena.apache.org/
[7]   http://www.w3.org/TR/sparql11-query/

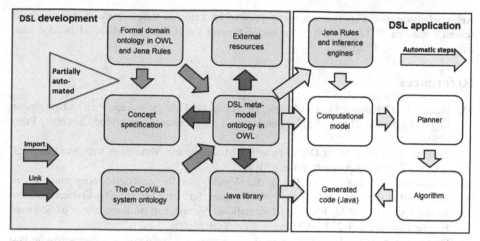

Fig. 7. The CoCoViLa architecture extended with ontology-based DSL development facilities

Computational model is an internal representation of the computational problem and concept specifications. It is used as an input for the planner, a theorem prover, which considers the computational model as a logical theorem with axioms derived from the functional dependencies defined in the specification. Since the prover is based on intuitionistic logic, the solution to the specified computational problem, an algorithm, is extracted from the constructive proof. CoCoViLa generates the Java source code from the algorithm, compiles and executes it at runtime and immediately presents the result of the computation to the user. The generated code can be later (re)used, as it can be saved into the file system.

6   Conclusion

This work demonstrates applicability of formal ontologies for semantic integration of software artefacts for building DSL meta-models. Representing domain models and the system model as OWL ontologies and linking them together to form a unified DSL meta-model ontology makes it possible to effectively integrate software artefacts that constitute a DSL meta-model as well as link it with external resources over the Web. This facilitates dynamic loading (instantiation) of software artefacts of DSL meta-models to a DSL development tool. We have prototypically implemented our approach as an extension to the CoCoViLa DSL modelling tool.

Using the DSL meta-model ontology makes it possible to automatically check its consistency using DL reasoning facilities used for debugging DSL meta-models. It is also easy to incorporate the domain terminology into the DSL at the early development stages due to formalization of domain ontology. Our approach makes it is easy to capture the evolution of a domain in the DSL via automated transformations [10]. However, for semantic integration of artefacts from external tools and models, the approach requires the commitment to a common system ontology or availability of system ontologies of these tools.

Acknowledgements. This research was supported by Estonian Research Council institutional research grant no. IUT33-13, and by the ERDF through the ICT project MBJSDT and Estonian national CoE project EXCS.

References

1. Baader, F., Calvanese, D., McGuiness, D., Nardi, D., Patel-Schneider, P.: The Description Logic Handbook: Theory, Implementation and Applications. Cambridge University Press (2003)
2. Fritzson, P.: Principles of Object-Oriented Modeling and Simulation with Modelica 3.3: A Cyber-Physical Approach. Wiley (2014)
3. Grigorenko, P., Saabas, A., Tyugu, E.: Visual tool for generative programming. In: ESEC/FSE-13: Proceedings of the 10th European Software Engineering Conference Held Jointly with 13th ACM, SIGSOFT International Symposium on Foundations of Software Engineering, pp. 249–252. ACM Press, New York (2005)
4. Groenewegen, D.M., Hemel, Z., Kats, L.C., Visser, E.: WebDSL: a domain-specific language for dynamic web applications. In: Harris, G.E. (ed) Proceedings of OOPSLA 2008, pp. 779–780. ACM (2008)
5. Gronback, R.: Eclipse Modeling Project: A Domain-Specific Language (DSL) Toolkit. Addison-Wesley Professional (2009)
6. Katasanov, A.: Ontology-driven Software Engineering: Beyond Model Checking and Transformations. Int. J. Semantic Computing **06**, 205–242 (2012)
7. Kotkas, V., Ojamaa, A., Grigorenko, P., Maigre, R., Harf, M., Tyugu, E.: CoCoViLa as a multifunctional simulation platform. In: Proc. of the 4th Int. ICST Conference on Simulation Tools and Techniques (SIMUTools 2011), pp. 198–205. ICST, Brussels (2011)
8. Mints, G., Tyugu, E.: Propositional Logic Programming and the Priz System. J. Log. Program **9**(2&3), 179–193 (1990)
9. Motik, B., Patel-Schneider, P.F., Horrocks, I.: OWL 2 Web Ontology Language: Structural Specification and Functional-Style Syntax. http://www.w3.org/TR/owl2-syntax
10. Ojamaa, A., Haav, H.-M., Penjam, J.: Semi-automated generation of DSL meta models from formal domain ontologies. In: Bellatreche, L., Manolopoulos, Y., Zielinski, B., Liu, R. (eds.) MEDI 2015. LNCS, vol. 9344, pp. 3–15. Springer, Heidelberg (2015)
11. OMG: MDA Guide 1.0.1 (June 2003). http://www.omg.org/mda
12. Puleston, C., Parsia, B., Cunningham, J., Rector, A.L.: Integrating object-oriented and ontological representations: a case study in java and OWL. In: Sheth, A.P., Staab, S., Dean, M., Paolucci, M., Maynard, D., Finin, T., Thirunarayan, K. (eds.) ISWC 2008. LNCS, vol. 5318, pp. 130–145. Springer, Heidelberg (2008)
13. Roser, S., Bauer, B.: Automatic generation and evolution of model transformations using ontology engineering space. In: Spaccapietra, S., Pan, J.Z., Thiran, P., Halpin, T., Staab, S., Svatek, V., Shvaiko, P., Roddick, J. (eds.) Journal on Data Semantics XI. LNCS, vol. 5383, pp. 32–64. Springer, Heidelberg (2008)
14. Staab, S., Walter, T., Gröner, G., Parreiras, F.S.: Model driven engineering with ontology technologies. In: Aßmann, U., Bartho, A., Wende, C. (eds.) Reasoning Web. LNCS, vol. 6325, pp. 62–98. Springer, Heidelberg (2010)
15. Walter, T., Parreiras, F.S., Staab, S., Ebert, J.: Joint language and domain engineering. In: Kühne, T., Selic, B., Gervais, M.-P., Terrier, F. (eds.) ECMFA 2010. LNCS, vol. 6138, pp. 321–336. Springer, Heidelberg (2010)
16. Walter, T., Parreiras, F.S., Staab, S.: An ontology-based framework for domain-specific modeling. Software & Systems Modelling **13**, 83–108 (2014)

Towards an Adaptive Tool and Method for Collaborative Ontology Mapping

Ramy Shosha[✉], Christophe Debruyne, and Declan O'Sullivan

CNGL Center for Global Intelligent Content, Knowledge and Data Engineering Group,
School of Computer Science and Statistics, Trinity College Dublin, Dublin, Ireland
{shoshar,debruync,declan.osullivan}@scss.tcd.ie

Abstract. Linked Data makes available a vast amount of data on the Semantic Web for agents, both human and software, to consume. Linked Data datasets are made available with different ontologies, even when their domains overlap. The interoperability problem that rises when one needs to consume and combine two or more of such datasets to develop a Linked Data application or mashup is still an important challenge. Ontology-matching techniques help overcome this problem. The process, however, often relies on knowledge engineers to carry out the tasks as they have expertise in ontologies and semantic technologies. It is reasonable to assume that knowledge engineers should require help from the domain experts, end users, etc. to contribute in the validation of the results and help distilling ontology mappings from these correspondences. However, the current design for the ontology-mapping tools does not take into consideration the different types of users expected to be involved in the creation of Linked Data applications or mashups. In this paper, we identify the different users and their roles in the mapping involved in the context of developing Linked Data mashups and propose a collaborative mapping method in which we prescribe where collaboration between the different stakeholders could, and should, take place. In addition, we propose a tool architecture based on bringing together an adaptive interface, mapping services, workflow services and agreement services that will ease the collaboration between the different stakeholders. This output will be used in an ongoing study to constructing a collaborative mapping platform.

Keywords: Semantic Web-Based Knowledge Management · Semantic mashups · Ontology mapping · Ontology Mapping Engineering · Collaborative mapping

1 Introduction

The Linked Data (LD) initiative is making available a huge amount of data on the Web of which some of are sharing, to some extent, parts of their (application domain) [1]. The LinkedMDB[1] and DBpedia[2], for instance, have different ontologies to state things about movies, actors, directors and so forth. Since Linked Data datasets do not

---

[1] http://www.linkedmdb.org/
[2] http://dbpedia.org/

© Springer International Publishing Switzerland 2015
I. Ciuciu et al. (Eds.): OTM 2015 Workshops, LNCS 9416, pp. 319–328, 2015.
DOI: 10.1007/978-3-319-26138-6_35

necessarily use the same ontologies, one is faced with the problem of managing heterogeneity in meaning and representation when information from different sources need to be merged, integrated or combined. Ontology matching is concerned with tackling the problem of this semantic heterogeneity by proposing solutions to find correspondences between semantically related entities of ontologies [2]. These correspondences are then curated and refined to create mappings that prescribe how , instances of, one ontology's concepts relate to, instances of, another ontology's concepts. Mapping management methodologies are concerned with the activities related to the creation of ontology mappings from the identification of the ontologies to be aligned and the discovery of correspondences to rendering the mappings in artifacts that computer-based systems can execute [3].

Though rooted in related work in the fields of, amongst others, database [4] and XML schema [5] matching, ontology matching has its own peculiarities such as the assumptions adopted on the Semantic Web and the ontology languages adopted for reasoning tasks. Ontology matching has been around for over a decade and yet still has many challenges to overcome [6]. Some of these challenges include finding appropriate matchers or configuration thereof fit for particular tasks, designing ways to involve users in the matching process that reduce the burden involved, and supporting interactions between users to support social and collaborative matching and mapping and the managing of the created mappings.

The engineering of ontologies and the engineering of ontology mapping processes are very similar in that both are cognitive intensive activities and in that both artifacts are created for a particular purpose. Furthermore, that purpose will further influence various variables in the process and is driven by a community of stakeholders with varying degrees of expertise in knowledge engineering, IT literacy and (application) domain expertise. In addition, similar to (collaborative) ontology engineering, the tools for ontology matching and mapping are often developed for users with expertise in knowledge engineering [7].

In this paper, we propose to leverage user involvement in collaborative ontology mapping to tackle the social and collaborative matching problem [6]. We can benefit from the collaboration to enhance the matching results. The user input in the matching process will help in generating results that are more accurate and speed the process in the same time. This will be achieved by focusing on adapative interfaces tailored for the different types of stakeholders. We start by identifying the various types of stakeholders in Section 2 and by introducing a collaborative ontology mapping lifecycle in Section 3. We will also indicate in which activities the stakeholders are involved and where collaboration could and should take place. The cross referencing of user types and tasks helps us identify where different perspectives (i.e., interfaces) on the tasks are needed, which in turn motivates the adoption of an adaptive user interface for use in the collaborative ontology-mapping environment. Section 4 presents the proposed tool framework behind the ideas proposed in this paper. Our ideas will be exemplified with the use case of finding correspondences between datasets on the Linked Data Web for the creation of mashups. Section 5 compares our approach with the current state of the art and, finally, Section 6 concludes our paper by indicating next steps. Where necessary, we integrate background information in the relevant sections.

2   Stakeholders in Collaborative Ontology Mapping

The Linked Data Web is available for all and allows for innovative and creative application be developed on top of very simple, standardized technologies such as URIs, RDF, SPARQL and the HTTP platform. The Linked Data Web is actually a complex socio-technical environment in which various types of participants are important. Take, for instance, the creation of semantic mashups, which are application that combine multiple LD datasets, use RDF as the data model and SPARQL to support task execution [8]. In this setting, we not only have knowledge engineers, but also (web) developers, domain experts, and end users. We already stated that ontology-matching tools help find similarities and differences between ontologies and knowledge bases by identifying potential correspondences. In [9], however, the authors considered a fully automated mapping impracticable. Human intervention will be crucial to guarantee a certain quality in the mapping process. User involvement in the mapping process is still however considered a challenge [6], even more so since ontology-matching tools are typically designed for use by knowledge engineers [7].

Knowledge engineers have expertise in knowledge modeling and the technical skills needed to use the ontology-matching tools and execute the process. Knowledge engineers are, however, not necessarily completely familiar with the universe of discourse. Domain experts, on the other hand, have that domain knowledge, but are not necessarily familiar with knowledge modeling or programming. This makes it typically hard for domain experts to participate in the mapping process without the help of a knowledge engineer. In addition, in the context of creating Linked Data mashups the following types of users are also of concern: web developers and end users. Web developers are acquainted with developing applications and, though not necessarily acquainted with the domain or semantic technologies, can provide valuable input by their knowledge gained while developing the application. It will also be the developer that will execute the created mappings. End users will use the mashup, but who are not necessarily "tech savvy".

In this paper, we thus distinguish four types of stakeholders who can contribute to the mapping process. Again, similar to ontology engineering, the creation of mappings is not a trivial task. From scoping the mapping project to the creation of an executable mapping, all are driven by the social interactions within the *community* of stakeholders that lead to the necessary *agreements* and decisions to proceed from one-step to another. Since ontology mappings are created to suit a need of a particular community of stakeholders, we need to promote those stakeholders as first class citizens in the matching and mapping processes. Designing the mapping engineering process as a collaborative effort necessitates the formulation of tasks (the method) and the creation of adequate tools and interfaces tailored to each of the different types of users (tools). By doing so, we are able to leverage both matching and mapping tasks for all stakeholders. To aid that community in reaching those agreements, one has to prescribe and orchestrate the different steps, activities and tasks that need to take place. In our LD mashup scenario, each type of stakeholder will have a specific set of tasks to perform in the mapping process, some of which are collaborative in nature. A method for collaborative mapping engineering will be proposed in the next section.

3   A Collaborative Ontology Mapping Engineering Method

Here, we propose a collaborative mapping method that allows different types of users to work in collaborative settings to discover correspondences between data ontologies to build and enrich the data model in the semantic mashups applications. Our approach differs from the state of the art (see Section 5) in that it addresses the problem of user involvement by looking for adequate means to leverage participation. We do this not only by defining the mapping and matching process explicitly as a collaborative undertaking, but also by addressing specific usability requirements by developing interfaces that are tailored for each type of user for each specific task. We will thus propose an ontology mapping workflow in which we prescribe the different activities and link those to the different user types. Whenever different user types are linked to an activity or different user types are involved between two subsequent activities, some form of collaboration will be necessary.

The mapping process as shown in Fig. 1 has two scenarios when dealing with mappings between the ontologies: creating a new set of mappings and reusing an existing mapping. The creation of a mapping starts with defining data sources that need to be combined. After grouping these sources, a feasibility study is then conducted to identify the set of requirement for the mashups applications.

The next set of activities in the mapping process is to look for and assess reusable mappings in order to force reuse. Two alternative types of reuse can take place in the process; the first type is to use the mapping *as is* (which is a decision that is taken when the retrieved mapping fits the application requirement); the other type is to feed those mappings to the matchers in order to produce better results. Following on this, the process continues if the mapping were found to be reusable (to feed to the matchers) or if they were created from scratch. The activity set starts by retrieving matchers, assessing those matchers, finding a suitable set for execution, configuring the matchers and then running them.

The next set of activities will be dedicated to evaluating correspondences generated by the matchers, reconfiguring matchers for better results and amending results in order to proceed with the mapping creation or to be used as an input for the matchers.

After that, the flow starts with rendering the mapping to the stakeholders for assessment and evaluation and reaching an agreement as to whether to proceed with the creation or going back to certain a particular step for generating better results. The roles of the different stakeholders in this collaborative method are as follows:

- The knowledge engineer (K) is involved in all the process activities as he has expertise in ontology mappings and thus his input is valuable. In the first activity in the process, knowledge engineers are able to look for (additional) data sources to be merged, integrated or aligned. Following on the knowledge engineer is able to assess whether the project is actually a semantic heterogeneity problem. In addition, the knowledge engineer is involved in all the data modeling tasks including matchers' retrieval, selection and configuration, and mapping curation, storage and publish.

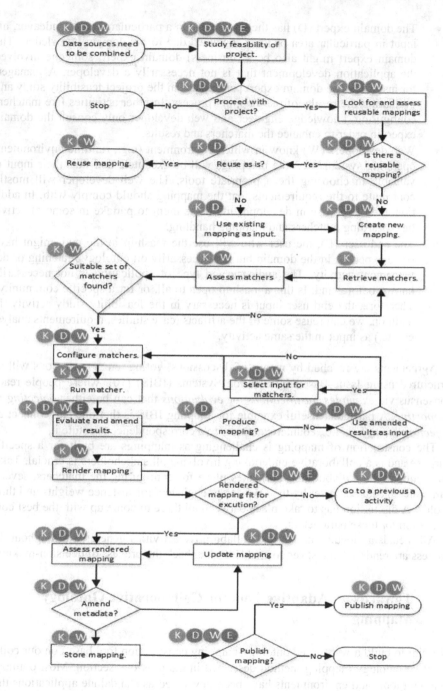

Fig. 1. The collaborative mapping process. Each activity is annotated with symbols that represent knowledge engineers (K), web developers (W), domain experts (D) and end users (E). Whenever an activity has two or more types of stakeholders, collaboration should take place.

- The domain expert (D) has the knowledge in a particular area of endeavor, his input in particular area or topic is valued due to his domain knowledge. The domain expert might also be a (business) domain expert; someone involved the application development that is not necessarily a developer. A manager, for instance. The domain expert participates in the project feasibility study and evaluating the results of the mapping process. In other activities like matchers configuring, knowledge engineer and web developer only consult the domain expert in order to enhance the matchers and results.
- Web developers (W) know in which environment (e.g., runtime environment, operating system, etc.) the mappings will be executed, and thus their input is valuable in choosing the appropriate tools. The web developer will mostly contribute to the requirements that the mapping should comply with. In addition, their expertise in development allows them to partake in some of activities regarding matchers and mapping handling.
- The end user (E), the user who will use the mashup in the end, might have some expertise in the domain but not necessarily on ontology matching or development activity. The audience and type of application is not necessarily known beforehand. Is this a mashup open to all, or for a specific community? Therefore, the end user input is necessary in the feasibility study activity. In addition, we can reuse some of the artifacts (case studies, requirements analyses, etc.) as input in the same activity.

Agreements are reached by means of discussions, voting, etc. Discussions will be structured using Issue-Based Information Systems (IBIS) [10], where people reach consensus via *examples*, *justifications*, or *evaluations* that can be either *objecting* or *supporting*. A particular useful example for adopting IBIS is that one can connect an *objecting example*, – i.e., counterexample – to a correspondence to refute it.

The construction of mapping is challenging as mappings are built for a specific purpose and is a collaborative undertaking involving all stakeholders is crucial. Take, for example, the collaboration that takes place for configuring the matchers, several parameters needs to be set by the knowledge engineers for instance weights and thresholds. A discussion has to take place between all three to come up with the best configuration for these parameters.

All metadata, documentation and collaborative activities generated throughout the process are rendered and saved to enable tracing back the process of decision-making.

4   Towards an Adaptive Tool for Collaborative Ontology Mapping

We aim to build a web-based ontology-mapping construction tool based on our collaborative ontology mapping method described in the previous section. Most ontology mapping tools and environments have been developed as standalone applications that need to be installed on one's machine. Web-based applications have the benefit that one only needs to have a browser installed. There are exceptions activities. [11], for instance, created a web-based environment for sharing and discovering mappings.

Another challenge with current design of the ontology-matching tools is that it often appears cluttered, presenting irrelevant and relevant information together, which makes mapping construction difficult even for knowledge engineers as asserted in [7],[9], Cluttered interfaces negatively affect user usability [12, 13]. Knowledge engineers and web developers are usually working with development environments and are used to process a lot more information on one screen. In order to involve domain experts as well as end users in the mapping process, however, we believe that usability needs to be significantly improved. We argue that interfaces of mapping-development tools need to be adaptive in order to provide better support for the range of stakeholder users that will be involved.

Thus, the tool under development aims to enhance the matching process from two perspectives: enhanced usability and support for a collaborative mapping. By designing the mapping process in a way that makes it a collaborative undertaking and by adapting (the interfaces of) the tasks to the expertise and role of users, we aim to leverage the expertise of the different stakeholders and reduce the cognitive load overall.

An adaptive user interface will solve the problem of clutter and will facilitate the involvement of different users in the ontology development tasks. An overview of the design is presented in Fig. 2. The User Interface layer interacts with the Adaptation Engine to generate an interface based on the user's profile, role being played and tailored to the particular task involved. The Adaptation Engine thus orchestrates the activities and relies on or mediates between the users and the following components: 1) Mapping services constituting all the tools needed for identifying correspondences (with the matchers), and creating and managing mappings.2) Workflow services, which is responsible for orchestrating and monitoring the tasks (not the interfaces) and the generation of metadata concerned with each task in the ontology mapping process. 3) Agreement services, which are components that will aid and capture the agreements, and thus decisions, made by the community of stakeholders while constructing a mapping.

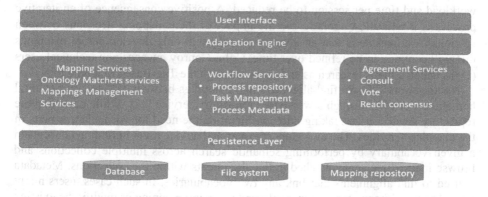

Fig. 2. The tool's architecture

Note that capturing the interactions not only renders the process more traceable, but also more transparent. Decisions are linked to the different parts of an ontology mapping and can thus be looked up for inspection.

The intended key benefit of the adaptive tool is that it will stand out as a collaborative mapping environment that allows domain experts, web developers, and end users to be involved in the mapping process.

5   Related Work

Ontology matching is an important part of ontological engineering activities, and should thus be supported by adequate methods and tools. Yet, at present, most of the approaches to ontology-matching lack support for collaboration at both the level of method and tool. Few approaches have focused on methodology [14]. There are some methodological guidelines proposed for ontology matching [15], but those guidelines do not treat the ontology mapping process as a collaborative undertaking and only focuses on the creation and management of mappings; the guidelines do not take into account activities such as feasibility studies when the need for creating an ontology mapping arises. As for the state of the art, throughout sections 1 to 3 we have stated that most methods either do not take into account collaboration or focus only on a few of the activities (e.g., discovery and sharing [11]).

Collaboration has been studied in, for instance, in [16] the focus was in circulating the correspondences between communities. The shared correspondences will have information about the author's name, application domain and trust in a community. This approach is mainly designed for domain experts validating the produced correspondences, edit and share them. It does not take into consideration other types of users that might be take place in the mapping process.

There is also the work done by Colm Conroy, reported in [17–19], in converting the mapping process from a one-time task to one performed over several sessions in an iterative manner. Mapping occurs in smaller sessions over time that allows the workload and time per session to be reduced. A positive consequence of an iterative process is it will allow users to see the impact of their mapping decisions between sessions. A downside is that an iterative process will only develop partial mappings that will continue to be refined over time. Colm Conroy engages non-technical users (Or as denoted in his research as end users) through the Tag-Based Mapping tool.

Another work done to find alignment and mappings between vocabularies cultural heritage collections through a web based repository service [11]. While designing the repository service, it was taking into consideration the need for vocabulary experts in the mapping activities. The tool support expert and novice users in finding concepts in a given vocabulary by performing semantic search across multiple collections and browse indexed metadata attached to the alignments within the collections. Metadata is used to find alignments that link any two vocabularies. In such cases, users might amend some of mapping result manually, add missing mapping or modify the existing ones, this raises a conflict between users that can be solved through some given agreement mechanisms, which is missed in this tool.

6   Conclusions and Future Work

The creation of ontology mappings on the Linked Data Web is not a trivial task as such mappings are the result of numerous agreements between different types of stakeholders each with their own skill sets and valuable input. The stakeholders in building a Linked Data mashups are knowledge engineers, domain experts, web developers and end users. In this paper, we have identified several gaps in the state of the art. Firstly, user engagement is a big challenge as tools are often created for knowledge engineers. Another reason that user engagement is a challenge is that tools are often created as standalone applications, which limits collaboration. Secondly, tools that do provide a (web-based) tool often only look a few activities of the ontology mapping lifecycle. Thirdly, a collaborative tool is not sufficient. In order to accommodate and engage the different users in the collaborative undertaking, the different stakeholders will need different perspectives on the same tasks. The challenge here is to define how these interfaces and tasks should be orchestrated. Adoption of adaptive interfaces would be suitable to tackle this challenge that lead to ease the involvement of other stakeholders besides the knowledge engineer. This will allow distributing the workload between users and give the opportunity to enhance what others have done.

Finally, to encourage traceability and render the ontology mapping process transparent, one needs to structure the interactions between the stakeholders so that one can relate parts of the ontology mapping with the discussions; e.g. to explain why certain choices were made.

Next to identifying the challenges, we proposed a collaborative method supported with adaptive interfaces in which we relate the different stakeholders to the different activities. This exercise identified which activities should be collaborative in nature and hence adaptive interfaces could play a role. A general idea of the tool is presented in which the different components are identified. This tool would bit in a broader Linked Data mashup method (agile, unified process, etc.). Future work consists of using and validating the adaptive tool in a realistic Linked Data mashup creation scenario.

Acknowledgements. This research is supported by the Science Foundation Ireland (Grant 07/CE/I1142) as part of the CNGL Centre for Global Intelligent Content (www.cngl.ie) at Trinity College Dublin.

References

1. Bizer, C., Heath, T., Berners-Lee, T.: Linked data-the story so far. Semantic Services, Interoperability and Web Applications: Emerging Concepts, 205–227 (2009)
2. Euzenat, J., Shvaiko, P.: Ontology matching. Springer, Heidelberg (2007)
3. Bellahsene, Z., Bonifati, A., Rahm, E.: Schema matching and mapping. Springer, Heidelberg (DE) (2011)
4. Batini, C., Lenzerini, M., Navathe, S.B.: A comparative analysis of methodologies for database schema integration. ACM Computing Surveys (CSUR) **18**, 323–364 (1986)
5. Bernstein, P.A., Madhavan, J., Rahm, E.: Generic schema matching, ten years later. Proceedings of the VLDB Endowment **4**, 695–701 (2011)

6. Shvaiko, P., Euzenat, J.: Ontology matching: state of the art and future challenges. IEEE Transactions on Knowledge and Data Engineering **25**, 158–176 (2013)

7. Falconer, S.M.: Cognitive support for semi-automatic ontology mapping. Doctoral dissertation, University of Victoria (2009)

8. Heath, T., Bizer, C.: Linked data: Evolving the web into a global data space. Synthesis Lectures On The Semantic Web: Theory And Technolog **1**, 1–136 (2011)

9. Noy, N.F.: Semantic integration: a survey of ontology-based approaches. ACM Sigmod Record **33**, 65–70 (2004)

10. Kunz, W., Rittel, H.W.J.: Issues as elements of information systems. University of California Berkeley, California, Institute of Urban and Regional Development (1970)

11. van der Meij, L., Isaac, A., Zinn, C.: A web-based repository service for vocabularies and alignments in the cultural heritage domain. In: Aroyo, L., Antoniou, G., Hyvönen, E., ten Teije, A., Stuckenschmidt, H., Cabral, L., Tudorache, T. (eds.) ESWC 2010, Part I. LNCS, vol. 6088, pp. 394–409. Springer, Heidelberg (2010)

12. Dahl, Y., Svendsen, R.-M.: End-user composition interfaces for smart environments: a preliminary study of usability factors. In: Marcus, A. (ed.) HCII 2011 and DUXU 2011, Part II. LNCS, vol. 6770, pp. 118–127. Springer, Heidelberg (2011)

13. Wesson, J.L., Singh, A., van Tonder, B.: Can adaptive interfaces improve the usability of mobile applications? In: Forbrig, P., Paternó, F., Mark Pejtersen, A. (eds.) HCIS 2010. IFIP AICT, vol. 332, pp. 187–198. Springer, Heidelberg (2010)

14. Mochol, M.: The methodology for finding suitable ontology matching approaches. Doctoral dissertation, Freie Universität Berlin, Germany (2009)

15. Euzenat, J., Le Duc, C.: Methodological guidelines for matching ontologies. In: Ontology Engineering In A Networked World, pp. 257–278. Springer (2012)

16. Noy, N.F., Griffith, N., Musen, M.A.: Collecting community-based mappings in an ontology repository. In: Sheth, A.P., Staab, S., Dean, M., Paolucci, M., Maynard, D., Finin, T., Thirunarayan, K. (eds.) ISWC 2008. LNCS, vol. 5318, pp. 371–386. Springer, Heidelberg (2008)

17. Conroy, C., O'sullivan, D., Lewis, D.: Ontology mapping through tagging. In: International Conference on Complex, Intelligent and Software Intensive Systems, CISIS 2008, pp. 886–891. IEEE (2008)

18. Conroy, C.: Towards semantic mapping for casual web users. In: Sheth, A.P., Staab, S., Dean, M., Paolucci, M., Maynard, D., Finin, T., Thirunarayan, K. (eds.) ISWC 2008. LNCS, vol. 5318, pp. 907–913. Springer, Heidelberg (2008)

19. Conroy, C., Brennan, R., Sullivan, D.O., Lewis, D.: User evaluation study of a tagging approach to semantic mapping. In: Aroyo, L., Traverso, P., Ciravegna, F., Cimiano, P., Heath, T., Hyvönen, E., Mizoguchi, R., Oren, E., Sabou, M., Simperl, E. (eds.) ESWC 2009. LNCS, vol. 5554, pp. 623–637. Springer, Heidelberg (2009)

Data Access in Cloud HICM Solutions. An Ontology-Driven Analytic Hierarchy Process Based Approach

Ricardo Colomo-Palacios[1](✉), Eduardo Fernandes[2], and Juan Miguel Gómez-Berbís[3]

[1] Faculty of Computer Sciences, Østfold University College,
B R a Veien 4, 1783 Halden, Norway
ricardo.colomo-palacios@hiof.no
[2] Meta4 Spain, Calle Rozabella, 8, 28290 Las Rozas, Madrid, Spain
eduardofer@meta4.com
[3] Department of Computer Science, Universidad Carlos III de Madrid,
Av. Universidad 30, 28911 Leganés, Madrid, Spain
juanmiguel.gomez@uc3m.es

Abstract. Data federation and virtualization in SaaS environments is one of the issues present in cloud environments. Within human resource management information systems, there is a huge amount of data that other corporate applications are needed to access and manipulate. Meta4 is one of the leaders in Human and intellectual capital sectors both in SaaS and on premise scenarios. This paper presents a framework to select the best option for data access in SaaS environment from the developer side using the Analytic Hierarchy Process enriched by an ontological representation of it. This framework would be useful for all SaaS service providers willing to open SaaS data to their customers.

Keywords: Human Intellectual Capital Management · Cloud computing · Multitenant · Monotenant · Analytic Hierarchy Process

1 Introduction

Computing is facing commoditization. Now, cloud computing, the long-held dream of computing as a utility, has the potential to transform a large part of the IT industry, making software even more attractive as a service and shaping the way IT hardware is designed and purchased [1]. However, and in spite of the attractiveness of cloud solutions, literature, and more precisely, the work of Subashini and Kavitha [2] has detected a set of benefits and potential challenges. On the benefits we can find, according to these authors, fast deployment, pay-for-use, lower costs, scalability, rapid provisioning, rapid elasticity, ubiquitous network access, greater resiliency, hypervisor protection against network attacks, low-cost disaster recovery and data storage solutions, on-demand security controls, real time detection of system tampering and rapid re-constitution of services. On the challenges side we can also find a long list of potential issues including accessibility vulnerabilities, virtualization vulnerabilities, web application vulnerabilities such as SQL injection and cross-site scripting, physical access issues, privacy and control issues arising from third parties having physical

© Springer International Publishing Switzerland 2015
I. Ciuciu et al. (Eds.): OTM 2015 Workshops, LNCS 9416, pp. 329–338, 2015.
DOI: 10.1007/978-3-319-26138-6_36

control of data, issues related to identity and credential management, issues related to data verification, tampering, integrity, confidentiality, data loss and theft, issues related to authentication of the respondent device or devices and IP spoofing.

The services that can be offered by cloud computing can be listed in the following three main areas [3]: Infrastructure as a Service (IaaS). IaaS is the delivery of computer infrastructure as a service; Platform as a Service (PaaS). Services provided by the traditional computing model which involved teams of network, database, and system management experts to keep the system up and running (e.g., operating systems, databases, middleware, Web servers, ..); Software as a Service (SaaS) that is a multi-tenant platform that uses common resources and a single instance of both the object code of an application as well as the underlying database to support multiple customers simultaneously [4].

Scientific literature has underlined the importance of cloud technology for all kind of environments [5–9] including human resource management scenarios [10, 11]. Human and intellectual capital (HICM) software vendors are not of the cloud shift. Thus, according to [12] the SaaS HICM market is growing as more HR and applications delivery professionals recognize the need to move to more agile and engaging HR systems; SaaS is a viable option as the deployment model of choice, and vendors leverage SaaS to deliver more rapid innovation in processes and user experiences. Other recent report underlines that HICM market is moving from a product perspective and that the integrated HICM market is maturing as all vendors embrace SaaS delivery and service out of European datacentres, and offer subscription pricing [13]. Moreover, according to [12], SaaS provides to HICM solutions adopters the opportunity to advance their processes with new levels of flexibility, usability, and insight rather than being constrained by customization, technical complexity, and deferred software upgrades. Finally, SaaS is becoming the default deployment model for human resources management systems, as it already has for learning and talent solutions [12].

However, daily operation of SaaS environments leads to several issues. After some years in production, this paper presents one of these real problems: the need to access central data by SaaS customers operating in multitenant as they were using this on a monotenant basis. Many of these customers are willing to access data and manipulate that data using their own means on a local server and there are not automatic procedures to perform this task in a secure and reliable way. This paper illustrates main options and strategies to tackle this problem and an evaluation of such options by means of a multi-criteria tool as the Analytic Hierarchy Process (AHP),

The remaining of the paper is structured as follows. Section 2 describes Meta4 as a company illustrating its main facts, figures and aims. Section 3 illustrates SmartTenant4all as a project including its objectives and main outputs. And finally, conclusions are drawn and future development work is presented in the final section.

2   META4: The Company

Meta4 was founded in Madrid, Spain back in 1991. More than twenty five years ago, Meta4 started out as a provider of Windows-based payroll solutions, and moved into core HR and later talent management. Meta4 is now one of the world's leading providers of solutions for the management and development of HICM solutions. Meta4 presents 1,300 clients in 100 countries and manages more than 18 million people worldwide. 60% of the incomes in 2014 are coming from outside Spain (35% of these incomes are coming from the rest of Europe and America 25%).

Meta4's is able to market its product, PeopleNet, in three different scenarios: traditional behind-the-firewall on premise, SaaS and fully outsourced. Since the second decade of the XXI century, the traditional on premise model is giving way to a cloud-based SaaS offer. Thanks to this, its line of HR solutions in the cloud has driven growth in the group last year. Meta4 saw a 50% increase in revenue in this line of business; their cloud offering already represents 25% of the total revenue of the group, as compared to a 15% share in 2011 and 21% in 2012. The number of contracts has also raised 50% from 2013 and in 2014 using this cloud model, Meta4 manages around 250000 people in 100 countries.

Apart from this, Meta4 is one of two Spanish software vendor companies included in the well-regarded report: Truffle 100 Europe 2014 index of the top 100 companies in Europe, where the company has appeared in the last four years. Meta4 received ISO 27001:2005 certification for information security management, has branches in eleven countries, although the headquarters of the company is located in Madrid, Spain. Meta4 invest, at least 20% of the turnover in R&D activities. Not in vain, Meta4 R&D and innovation centers in Europe and the Americas with around a hundred professionals devoted to R&D develop HICM solutions on premise and cloud solution. As a result of their activity, its presence in the literature is remarkable [14–17] in the few last years.

3   SmartTenant4all: The Project

3.1   Aims and Overall Description

The overall objective of the project is the evolution of the SaaS platform by Meta4 in order to let multitenant users to use mono tenant configurations via the use of a specific procedure to be defined, designed and implemented in the project. However, this task is not trivial, given that it must deal with the complexity of the multitenant architecture of the Meta4 SaaS solution and the panoply of options available in the mono-tenant side.

Given the set of customers that demand this feature, Meta4 faces a redesign in its cloud service with regard to data access options. The description of the SaaS architecture can be found in [14]. An overall view on the data access problem is depicted in Figure 1.

In order to tackle this complexity, it is schedule a task devoted to perform a study on the integration options by means of the AHP. This paper is the initial step towards this goal.

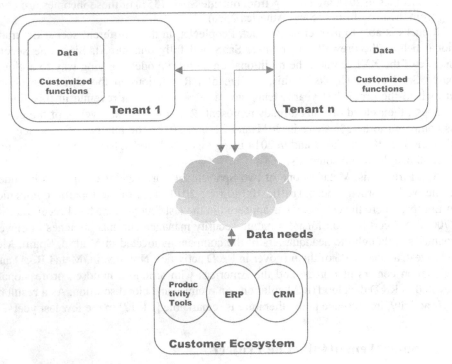

Fig. 1. SaaS Access Neds

3.2   Data Needs: Evaluation Using AHP

Data access is one of the key issues in all SaaS implementation. According to [18], the different strategies for data access in SaaS environments are as follows:

1. SQL access. Users are granted to access data directly to the cloud database using multi-tenant ODBC or JDBC drivers and SQL.
2. Data export. User downloads data from cloud server either on-demand or on a planned basis typically by means of files in Excel or CSV formats.
3. Web service access. A Web Service API for data access is provided and managed by the SaaS service.
4. Staged Database. The last solution is to export data from the cloud into a relational database.

Once options are presented, the process for assessment must be presented. AHP was developed by Saaty back in 1980 [19]. In a nutshell, AHP It is a multi-criteria decision-making method which permits the relative assessment and prioritization of alternatives [20]. Given its importance, it has been employed in several environments including information systems scenarios. Examples on the use of this technique in these environment include critical success factors of executive information systems [21], open source CRM tools [22], intellectual capital management tool selection [23], IT staff behavior analysis [24], and IT automation decisions [25] citing the most relevant and recent cases.

Literature reported some enrichments of this priority assessment methods suing ontologies to extract and represent the important concepts and their relationships from the AHP method itself [26]. Authors decided to use this ontological approach to enrich the model and map relationships found in the domain. The main objective of ontologies is to establish ontological agreements, which serve as the basis for communication between either human or software agents, hence, reducing language ambiguity and knowledge differences between agents, which may lead to errors, misunderstandings and inefficiencies [27]. The use of semantic technologies in both industry and academia is widespread and literature have witnessed an important increase in the number of works devoted to the topic e.g. [7, 8, 28–34].

In our case, and focusing again on the AHP model, the overall goal is the ranking of alternatives 1-4. Once defined, main criteria must be defined and further decomposed into sub criteria. Figure 2 shows the structure of SaaS data access options hierarchy with the overall goal, different criteria, sub-criteria and alternatives.

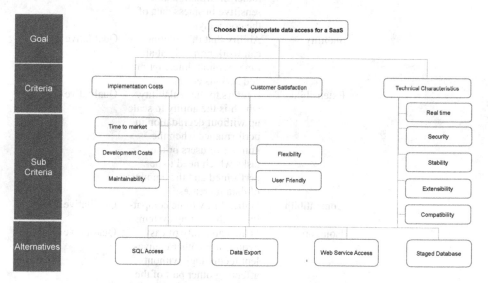

Fig. 2. Hierarchy of the SaaS data access options

The overall goal, that is choosing the appropriate data access option for a SaaS is accomplished through three criteria that satisfy it. These criteria are Implementation Costs, Customer Satisfaction and Technical Characteristics. Considered sub-criteria including meaning and proposed indicator typology are proposed and explained in terms of meaning and type of indicator to assess the value in Table 1:

Table 1. Criteria, Sub-Crieria and Indicators

Criteria	Sub-Criteria	Meaning	Indicator
Implementation Costs	Time to market	Time to get the solution working.	Quantitative
	Development Costs	Cost of implementation.	Quantitative
	Maintainability	The ease with which the solution can be maintained.	Qualitative
Customer Satisfaction	User Friendly	Measures to what extent the solution is easily applicable and configurable.	Qualitative
	Flexibility	Capacity to adapt to different needs and requirements on the customer side.	Qualitative
Technical Characteristics	Real time	The ability to retrieve real time data.	Dichotomous
	Security	This refers to the ability to ensure the privacy of customer information and sensitive business data of the company.	Qualitative
	Stability	Ability that the solution can work normally at all times without interruption and serious errors.	Qualitative
	Extensibility	It refers to the scalability, which is the ability to scale up without degradation in performance when the number of users or the tasks which need to be performed and the amount of data increases.	Qualitative
	Compatibility	Is the ability to be compatible with existing systems	Qualitative
	Isolation	Is the capability of easy evolution to other equivalent technology without affecting other part of the system	Qualitative

AHP weights calibration was carried out starting from a specific survey carried out in the company. Respondents were recruited from a sample of engineers (n=11) by means of an interview. Expert Choice was used for the calculation of the priorities and the sensitivity analysis. Criteria and sub-criteria weights are coded in Table 2:

Table 2. Criteria and Sub-Criteria Weights

Criteria	Weight	Sub-criteria	Weight
Implementation Costs	0.28	Time to market	0.27
		Development Costs	0.33
		Maintainability	0.40
Customer Satisfaction	0.41	User Friendly	0.58
		Flexibility	0.42
Technical Characteristics	0.31	Real time	0.19
		Security	0.26
		Stability	0.20
		Extensibility	0.12
		Compatibility	0.14
		Isolation	0.09

According to the weights shown in Table 2 for the three main criteria, the criterion "Customer Satisfaction" is the most important one reaching 0.41 while "Technical Characteristics" is the second most important with 0.31. Finally, "Implementation Costs" is the least important factor with 0.28. In any case, all criteria are highly ranked presenting low differences among them.

Among the sub-criteria, taking into account that under customer satisfaction there are just two sub-criteria, both present a high priority (User Friendly: 0.58 and Flexibility: 0.42). When properly weighted, these two are also the most crucial factors in the assessment (User Friendly: 0.238 and Flexibility: 0.172). Other important factor, this time behind Implementation Costs is Maintainability with a relative importance of 0.4 and a weighted score of 0.112.

Finally, the proposed framework was implemented to compare different data access options. Table 3 shows the final score for each of the alternatives by weighting according to their global priorities. According to that, Staged DB is the most valuable option with a value of 0.304 points. It is followed by SQL Access with 0.273 points and Web Service raising 0.222 points and, finally, Data Export with 0.203 points

Table 3. Overall priorities for the four alternatives

Sub criterion	SQL Access	Data Export	Web Service	Staged DB
Time to market	0.015	0.038	0.008	0.015
Development Costs	0.028	0.028	0.009	0.028
Maintainability	0.022	0.022	0.045	0.022
User Friendly	0.071	0.048	0.024	0.095
Flexibility	0.052	0.017	0.052	0.052
Real time	0.024	0.006	0.024	0.006
Security	0.024	0.008	0.016	0.032
Stability	0.012	0.012	0.012	0.025
Extensibility	0.011	0.007	0.011	0.007
Compatibility	0.011	0.011	0.011	0.011
Isolation	0.003	0.006	0.011	0.011
TOTAL	0.273	0.203	0.222	0.304

4   Conclusions and Future Works

Data virtualization and federation is one of the hot topics in cloud scenarios. In an arena in which cloud applications from different vendors bring their services to several companies by means of multitenant solutions, accessing to data among these applications and for traditional on premise solutions is an issue for customers and service providers alike.

In this paper, authors present an AHP-based multi-criteria decision model has been designed and developed. This model provides a holistic consideration in the selection of data access approaches for all kinds of SaaS providers but especially for HICM service providers, like Meta4. However, this model, properly adapted, is also valid for customers to assess SaaS offerings from the providers focusing these assessment on data access options, one of the most important factors in the implementation of a SaaS solution.

The model is based on a set of factors that have been systematically identified, defined and deployed following a defined hierarchy. The model has been applied to the problem of data access in multitenant environments for the four available and pertinent solutions: SQL Access, Data Export, Web Service and Staged DB. Through experts' evaluation of these alternatives, the readers can gain a closer look at the alternatives in terms of their specific features and potentialities for SaaS solutions.

Future works include performing of a sensibility analysis to test the responsiveness of the outcome when making changes in the priorities of the major criteria as well as the sub-criteria. Apart from that and as a part of the project authors aim to test solutions in a production environment and later conduct research on the acceptation of a specific subset of these options.

Acknowledgements. This work supported by "Ministerio de Industria, Energía y Turismo" under the program "Acción Estratégica Economía y Sociedad Digital 2/2014" grant number TSI-100105-2014-214, project "Plataforma para la interacción entre entornos en la multitenant y monotenant en la gestión del capital humano e intelectual".

References

1. Armbrust, M., Fox, A., Griffith, R., Joseph, A.D., Katz, R., Konwinski, A., Lee, G., Patterson, D., Rabkin, A., Stoica, I.: others: A view of cloud computing. Communications of the ACM **53**, 50–58 (2010)
2. Subashini, S., Kavitha, V.: A survey on security issues in service delivery models of cloud computing. Journal of Network and Computer Applications **34**, 1–11 (2011)
3. Sultan, N.A.: Reaching for the "cloud": How SMEs can manage. International Journal of Information Management **31**, 272–278 (2011)
4. Rimal, B.P., Jukan, A., Katsaros, D., Goeleven, Y.: Architectural Requirements for Cloud Computing Systems: An Enterprise Cloud Approach. J. Grid Comput. **9**, 3–26 (2011)
5. Stantchev, V., Colomo-Palacios, R., Soto-Acosta, P., Misra, S.: Learning management systems and cloud file hosting services: A study on students' acceptance. Computers in Human Behavior **31**, 612–619 (2014)

6. Petruch, K., Stantchev, V., Tamm, G.: A survey on IT-governance aspects of cloud computing. International Journal of Web and Grid Services **7**, 268–303 (2011)
7. Rodríguez-García, M.Á., Valencia-García, R., García-Sánchez, F., Samper-Zapater, J.J.: Ontology-based annotation and retrieval of services in the cloud. Knowledge-Based Systems **56**, 15–25 (2014)
8. Rodríguez-García, M.Á., Valencia-García, R., García-Sánchez, F., Samper-Zapater, J.J.: Creating a semantically-enhanced cloud services environment through ontology evolution. Future Generation Computer Systems **32**, 295–306 (2014)
9. Colomo-Palacios, R., Soto-Acosta, P., Ramayah, T., Russ, M.: Electronic markets and the future internet: from clouds to semantics. Electron Markets **23**, 89–91 (2013)
10. Stone, D.L., Deadrick, D.L.: Challenges and opportunities affecting the future of human resource management. Human Resource Management Review
11. Cascio, W.F.: Leveraging employer branding, performance management and human resource development to enhance employee retention. Human Resource Development International **17**, 121–128 (2014)
12. Hamerman, P.D.: The Forrester Wave™: SaaS HR Management Systems, Q4 2014 (2014)
13. Lykkegaard, B.: IDC Market Scape: Western Europe Integrated Talent Management 2013 Vendor Analysis (2013)
14. Colomo-Palacios, R., Fernandes, E., Sabbagh, M., de Amescua Seco, A.: Human and Intellectual Capital Management in the Cloud: Software Vendor Perspective. Journal of Universal Computer Science **18**, 1544–1557 (2012)
15. Colomo-Palacios, R., Fernandes, E., Soto-Acosta, P., Sabbagh, M.: Software product evolution for Intellectual Capital Management: The case of Meta4 PeopleNet. International Journal of Information Management **31**, 395–399 (2011)
16. Colomo-Palacios, R.: The Expert Opinion: An Interview with Marc Sabbagh, R&D Vice President, Meta4. Journal of Global Information Technology Management **14**, 70 (2011)
17. Colomo-Palacios, R., Fernandes, E., de Amescua-Seco, A.: M-PeopleNet: mobile human and intellectual capital management based on the cloud. In: Proceedings of the First International Conference on Technological Ecosystem for Enhancing Multiculturality, pp. 215–218. ACM, New York (2013)
18. Sarkar, S.: Is your data access strategy blocking adoption of your SaaS application?. https://blogs.datadirect.com/2013/06/big-trend-saas-data-federation-gateways.html
19. Satty, T.L.: The analytic hierarchy process. McGraw-Hill New York, New York (1980)
20. Vidal, L.-A., Marle, F., Bocquet, J.-C.: Using a Delphi process and the Analytic Hierarchy Process (AHP) to evaluate the complexity of projects. Expert Systems with Applications **38**, 5388–5405 (2011)
21. Salmeron, J.L., Herrero, I.: An AHP-based methodology to rank critical success factors of executive information systems. Computer Standards & Interfaces **28**, 1–12 (2005)
22. Lee, Y.-C., Tang, N.-H., Sugumaran, V.: Open Source CRM Software Selection using the Analytic Hierarchy Process. Information Systems Management **31**, 2–20 (2014)
23. Carlucci, D., Kujansivu, P.: Using an AHP Rating Model to Select a Suitable Approach to Intellectual Capital Management: The Case of a Not-for-Profit Welfare Service. International Journal of Information Systems in the Service Sector **6**, 22–42 (2014)
24. Stantchev, V., Petruch, K., Tamm, G.: Assessing and governing IT-staff behavior by performance-based simulation. Computers in Human Behavior **29**, 473–485 (2013)
25. Iskin, I., Daim, T.U., Noble, S., Baltz, A.: Approaching IT Automation Decisions using Analytic Hierarchy Process (AHP). International Journal of Information Technology Project Management **5**, 77–89 (2014)

26. Liao, Y.X.: Rocha Loures, E., Canciglieri, O., Panetto, H.: A Novel Approach for Ontological Representation of Analytic Hierarchy Process. Advanced Materials Research **988**, 675–682 (2014)
27. Blanco, C., Lasheras, J., Fernández-Medina, E., Valencia-García, R., Toval, A.: Basis for an integrated security ontology according to a systematic review of existing proposals. Computer Standards & Interfaces **33**, 372–388 (2011)
28. Hernández-González, Y., García-Moreno, C., Rodríguez-García, M.Á., Valencia-García, R., García-Sánchez, F.: A semantic-based platform for R&D project funding management. Computers in Industry **65**, 850–861 (2014)
29. Colomo-Palacios, R., González-Carrasco, I., López-Cuadrado, J.L., Trigo, A., Varajao, J.E.: I-Competere: Using applied intelligence in search of competency gaps in software project managers. Inf. Syst. Front. **16**, 607–625 (2014)
30. Beydoun, G., Low, G., García-Sánchez, F., Valencia-García, R., Martínez-Béjar, R.: Identification of ontologies to support information systems development. Information Systems **46**, 45–60 (2014)
31. García-Peñalvo, F.J., Colomo-Palacios, R., García, J., Therón, R.: Towards an ontology modeling tool. A validation in software engineering scenarios. Expert Systems with Applications **39**, 11468–11478 (2012)
32. Piedra, N., Tovar, E., Colomo-Palacios, R., Lopez-Vargas, J., Chicaiza, J.A.: Consuming and producing linked open data: the case of OpenCourseWare. Program: Electronic Library and Information Systems **48**, 16–40 (2014)
33. Valencia-García, R., García-Sánchez, F., Casado-Lumbreras, C., Castellanos-Nieves, D., Fernández-Breis, J.T.: Informal learning through expertise mining in the social web. Behaviour & Information Technology **31**, 757–766 (2012)
34. Colomo-Palacios, R., Casado-Lumbreras, C., Soto-Acosta, P., Misra, S.: Providing knowledge recommendations: an approach for informal electronic mentoring. Interactive Learning Environments **22**, 221–240 (2014)

Knowledge Management for Virtual Education Through Ontologies

Ana Muñoz[1,2(✉)], Victor Lopez[3], Katty Lagos[2], Mitchell Vásquez[2],
Jorge Hidalgo[2], and Nestor Vera[2]

[1] CEMISID Los Andes University, Mérida, Venezuela
amunoz@uagraria.edu.ec
[2] Computer Science Department, Agrarian of Ecuador University, Guayaquil, Ecuador
{amunoz,klagos,mvasquez,jhidalgo,nvera}@uagraria.edu.ec
[3] GIISIC, Technological of Panamá University, Panama, Panama
victor.lopez@utp.ac.pa

Abstract. Current knowledge management focuses on knowledge acquisition, storage, retrieval and maintenance. E-Learning systems technology today is used primarily for training courses about carefully selected topics to be delivered to students registered for those courses. Knowledge management is used to rapidly capture, organize and deliver large amounts of corporate knowledge. The practice of adding value to information by capturing tacit knowledge and converting it into explicit knowledge is known as Knowledge Management. Ontologies can represent an existing knowledge from a domain, in this work; ontologies allow to model different aspects of knowledge management for virtual education in higher education. Universities, from the perspective of knowledge management, provide an updated concept of higher education where knowledge is considered a product, and the customers are students. This paper explains an ontological framework, used to model and integrate knowledge management processes and technological architecture for knowledge management in virtual education.

Keywords: Knowledge Management · Virtual Education · Ontology · Higher Education

1 Introduction

Knowledge management is the practice of adding value to information by converting tacit knowledge into explicit knowledge, through storage, retrieval, filtering and spreading of knowledge, and the creation and testing of new knowledge [2].

Currently, knowledge management is perhaps the most commonly used term in the literature of management and although it is widely used in the management area, in higher education it is rarely mentioned. However, it is in higher education where future knowledge workers are being prepared and also knowledge workers are already present as professors. Knowledge is an important resource in the knowledge society and knowledge workers play an important role in it; therefore knowledge management

© Springer International Publishing Switzerland 2015
I. Ciuciu et al. (Eds.): OTM 2015 Workshops, LNCS 9416, pp. 339–348, 2015.
DOI: 10.1007/978-3-319-26138-6_37

and best practice solutions in the business world can be extended and used for its application in modern higher education.

Ontology represents existing knowledge in a domain. In this case ontology represents a different model for higher education knowledge management. An ontology is "A formal explicit specification of a shared conceptualization" [10]. Ontologies are generally defined as a representation of a shared conceptualization of a particular domain. It is anticipated that Ontologies and Semantic Web technologies will influence the next generation of e-learning systems and applications. The role of ontology consists on facilitating the construction of a model domain. It provides a vocabulary of terms and relationships in a specific domain.

In this research we present a knowledge management for virtual education through ontology, focusing on academic processes carried out in universities. It is aimed to create a knowledge representation through ontology and engineering methodology to support both dimensions of knowledge. Ontology is used as the primary mechanism for representing information and knowledge. It defines the meaning of the terms, as well as the languages and relationships used in the knowledge management system.

2   Background

György Kende [12] show knowledge as a key asset for higher education and define knowledge management according to Davenport & Prusak [7]. They apply a business model as a plus point of the organization to achieve competitive advantage, as well as supporting tools to promote knowledge management and evaluation, utilization, creation, expansion, protection, division and intellectual equity of the organization. The model of Intellectual Capital and its structure as the INTELECT model [4]. This definition is related to the business world, but it is updated in association with higher education concepts, where knowledge is considered the product and students are the customers.

Knowledge creation refers to the activity that modifies organizational knowledge resources through socialization, internalization, externalization and combination of knowledge. The spiral of knowledge [18] shows how to extend individual knowledge, working groups into and across the organization. The authors explain the transformation of knowledge between individuals and between organizations and individual.

Paniagua et al. [20], describes how universities can develop these requirements under the vision of universities as knowledge bases. These new dimensions see universities as innovation centers to produce and distribute knowledge as a product. Every process of knowledge management for virtual education will be developed using this vision.

3   State of the Art

Marla Corniel et al. [5] stand for an ontological model that provides support for decision making in the selection of educational opportunities for the Venezuelan higher education subsystem (SES). The model makes the standardization of the vocabulary used in the domain. The prototype shows four elements: knowledge area, career, agency, region, and possible relationships established among them.

Aggarwal et al. [1] defines a knowledge management framework for curriculum development and research in universities. They define knowledge management factors that enhance the curriculum: curriculum design, faculty development and knowledge repositories, counseling techniques and lessons learned, relationships with companies and support of technologies to knowledge management.

Huang et al. [11] present an e-learning semantic framework that considers both technical and pedagogical aspects in an integrated environment. They present a generic model for semantic representation of context, both static and dynamic, considering the interoperability between XML / RDF and e-learning technologies on the WWW. The key feature of this framework is that it is sensitive to information management services supporting context-enabled learning model for knowledge representation and personality of the learner.

This research proposes a guiding model of quality standards for each one of the virtual education processes defined though ontologies. These different abstraction levels besides resembling the knowledge on the different processes of e-learning, will allow to deduce new knowledge through the business rules established on the knowledge management system. Knowledge processes are established at diverse levels of abstraction supported by a technological framework.

4   Ontological Model for Virtual Education

The Ontological Model Architecture for knowledge management is shown in Figure 1. It is formed by three layers: Model, Process and Technology. Those layers are all seen from the ontologies at different levels: general, domain and task. In the following figure the architecture of knowledge model shown consists of three layers: the knowledge management layer, the educational processes layer, and the technology layer. Acquisition of knowledge is done through ontologies, representing each of the layers of the model, from the general, domain and task view.

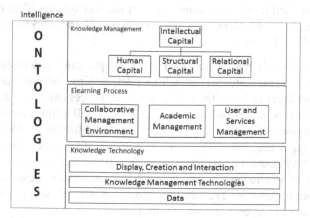

Fig. 1. Knowledge Management Model for Virtual Higher Education through Ontologies.

Knowledge Management Layer. The knowledge management layer describes the intellectual capital model consisting of 1) human capital, which is composed by the roles performed by students, professors, researchers and training personnel; 2) structural capital, made of policies and procedures to carry out the various academic processes existing in higher education, such as curriculum development, knowledge transfer service to community, technology development, and research and innovation; 3) relational capital is found, representing customer relationships. In this case we refer to students, professors, alliances and other institutions.

Educational Process Layer. The educational process layer consists of three modules: the collaborative environment module, the learning management module, and the user and services management module. These modules describe how processes are run in a virtual educational organization. The collaborative environment module describes the activities to be performed by professors, students and researcher in a virtual environment. We are using ontologies for collaborative learning management as described in this model (the first version was developed in Muñoz, et al., [15, 16, 17]). The learning management module is defined according to different instructional teaching models through the knowledge management. The users and service management module describe the different processes and activities undertaken to support users in an educational system, as well as the different types of users and services.

Technology Layer. Knowledge Technology Management involves the vision, mission, business models, and strategies which solve global managing of information and knowledge in virtual education. This platform has three layers: the creation, display and sharing of knowledge layer, the knowledge management layer and the data layer. The creation, display and sharing of knowledge layer would be shown to users through a Knowledge Portal and supported by elements such as the Semantic Web and technologies providing descriptions of the business model. All that has been shown above allows the conversion process of tacit to explicit knowledge and vice versa [19]. The technological elements that support the knowledge layer include: knowledge bases (as organizational memory and semantic repository of learning objects), information systems (like learning management systems, knowledge management content, knowledge-based systems, decision support systems, data mining, etc.). The information retrieval system, document management and workflow management support organizational memory.

Ontology Layer. In this transversal layer the concepts can be defined through the general, domain and task ontology as well as relationships and instances of the elements of different layer of Knowledge Management, Process and Technology Layers of academic processes in Virtual Education. This layer will allow showing the know-how of the processes of virtual higher education, establishing standards, from the view of knowledge management. From the perspective of the processes a model to be followed is the development of activities through existing and new knowledge, which can be provided by ontologies: also, viewing the ontologies on technology as agents of application and integration. The ontology model, in general, will guide the integration process among the layers that from the framework.

Some concepts used to describe the ontologies are: Intellectual Capital, Human Capital and Structural Capital and Technological Layer. Relationships can be: is a; part of; have. Axioms that construct the ontology are described in Table 1.

Table 1. Axioms that support the General Ontology Process Knowledge Management for Virtual Education.

Sentences	First-Order Logic (FOL)
Virtual Education Models have Knowledge Managemnt layer and Educational Process layer and Knowledge Management Technology Layer	∀ x VirtualEducationModel(x) → have (x, KnowledgeManagementLayer) ∧ have (x, EducationalProcess) ∧ have (x, TechnologyLayer)
The Knowledge Management layer have intellectual Capital	∀ x KnowledgeManagementLayer(x) → have (x, IntellectualCapital)
Intellectual Capital has Human Capital, Structural Capital and Relational Capital	∀ x Intellectual Capital (x) → have (x, HumanCapital) ∧ have (x, StructuralCapital) ∧ have (x, RelationalCapital)
Human Capital has Roles, Work Capacity Leadership and Training	∀ x Human Capital (x) → have (x, Roles) ∧ have (x, WorkCapacity) ∧ have (x, Leadership) ∧ have (x, Training)
Roles are employees performing different organizational processes and they have salary	∀ x Role (x)→ is_a (x, Employees) ∧ have (x, Salary) ∧ performs (x, OrganizationalProcess)
Capacity Working assessments are performance Role	∀ x CapacityWorking (x) → is_a (x, Performance Evaluation)
Leadership has management skills	∀ x Leadership (x) → have (x, ManagementSkill)
The training phases have Training Needs Detection, Identify Training Resources, Training Plan Design, Implementation Training Program, Evaluation, Control and Monitoring	∀ x Training (x) → have (x, TrainingNeedsDetect) ∧ have (x, ResourcesTrainigIdenfy) ∧ have (x, TrainigPlanDesign) ∧ have (x, TrainingProgram) ∧ have (x, TrainingProgramImplementation) ∧ have (x, TrainingProgramEvaluation) ∧ have (x, TrainingProgramControlMonitoring)
Structural capital has organizational structure, organizational culture, technological Systems, Research and Innovation	∀ x Structural Capital (x) → have (x, OrganizationalStructure) ∧ have (x, OrganizationalCulture) ∧ have (x, TechnologicalSystems) ∧ have(x, Research) ∧ have (x, Innovation)
The organizational structure has processes, Coordination and Control Areas, Rules and Procedures (degree of standardization of activities)	∀ x OrganizationStructure (x) → have (x, Processes) ∧ have(x, CoordinationandControl) ∧ have (x, RulesandProcedures)
The organizational cultures have values, vision, standard, working language, systems, symbols, beliefs and habits	∀ x OrganizationalCulture (x) → have (x, Values) ∧ have (x, Vision) ∧ have (x, Standards) ∧ have (x, WorkingLanguage) ∧ have (x, Systems) ∧ have (x, symbols) ∧ have (x, Beliefs) ∧ have (x, Habits)
Organizational Systems have structure, procedures and organizational processes	∀ x OrganizationalSystem (x) → have (x, Structure) ∧ have (x, Procedures) ∧ have (x, OrganizationalProcess)
The Technological System has Communication Networks, Hardware and Software that support an organization	∀ x Technological System (x) → have (x, ComunicationNetworks) ∧ have (x, Hardware) ∧ have (x, Software)
Research and development activities are aimed to acquire more knowledge. These activities can be: Basic Science Research, Technological Development for Problem Solving, Product or Process Development	∀ x ResearchandDevelopment (x) → is_a(x, ResearchBasicScience) V is_a (x, TechnologicalDevelopment) V is_a (x, ProductDevelopment) V is_a (x, ProcessDevelopment)
Innovation is a technological innovation or service innovation, or innovation in business models, or design innovation, or social innovation	∀ x Innovation(x) → is_a (x, Tecnologicalinnovation) V is_a (x, Serviceinnovation) V is_a (x, BussinesModelinnovation) V is_a (x, Designinnovation) V is_a (x, Socialinnovation)
The Relational Capital has Users, Conventions and Alliances	∀ x Relational Capital (x) → have (x, Users) ∧ have (x, Conventions) ∧ have (x, Alliances)
The Educational Process layers has Management Learning, Collaborative Working and User and Services Management	∀ x ProcessEducationalLayer (x) → have (x, ManagementLearning) ∧ have (x, CollaborativeWorking) ∧ have (x, ManagementUserServices)
The Management Learning have Teaching Module and Learning Module	∀ x ManagementLearnig (x) → have (x, TeachingModule) ∧ have (x, LearningModule)
The Learning Module is a Visual or Auditory or Reading/Writing or Kinesthetic	∀ xLearningModule (x) → is_a (x, Visual) V is_a (x, Auditory) V is_a (x, ReadingWriting) V is_a (x, Kinesthetic)
The Teaching Module is a direct instruction or inquiry-based learning or cooperative learning	∀ x TeachingModule (x) → is_a (x, Directinstruction) V is_a (x, InquireBasedLearning) V is_a (x, CooperativeLearning)
The technology layer has creation, presentation and sharing layer, knowledge management layer, and network and data layer	∀ xTechnologicalLayer (x) → have (x, CreationPresentationSharingLayer) ∧ have (x, ManagementKnowledgeLayer) ∧ have (x, NetworkandData)

These three layers are modeled using ontologies to represent knowledge, processes and technology layers. The Ontologies will be developed in three levels: General, Domain and Tasks. The general Ontology is shown in Figure 2.

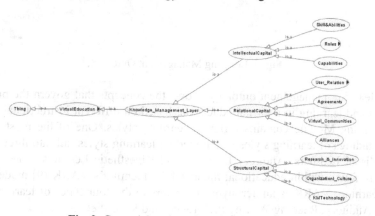

Fig. 2. General Ontology for Virtual Education.

The Ontology for Collaborative Module describes the activities to be performed in a collaborative environment for the learning management for both student-to-student and student-to-teacher interaction. To describe this model we are using ontologies for collaborative learning in management, which first version was developed in Muñoz et al., [17] it is shown in figure 3.

Fig. 3. Ontology for collaborative learning, Muñoz et al., [17]

The learning Management Model describes the instructional model of students and teachers through knowledge management as shown in Figure 4.

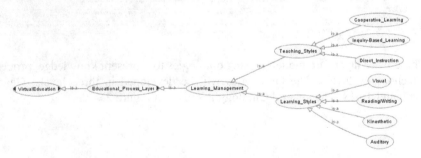

Fig. 4. Learning Management Ontology.

The learning management ontology shows the concepts that govern the process of teaching and learning in a virtual education, based on different instructional theories. The Learning Module contains different learning styles. One of the most accepted understandings of learning styles is that student learning styles fall into three "categories:" Visual Learners, Auditory Learners and Kinesthetic Learners. These learning styles are found within educational theorist Neil Fleming's VARK [9] model of Student Learning. VARK is an acronym that refers to the four types of learning styles: Visual, Auditory, Reading/Writing Preference, and Kinesthetic.

The Teaching module refers to the general principles, pedagogy and management strategies used for classroom instruction. There are three main teaching styles in educational pedagogy: direct instruction, inquiry-based learning and cooperative learning.

Direct instruction is the general term that refers to the traditional teaching strategy that relies on explicit teaching through lectures and teacher-led demonstrations. Direct instruction is the primary teaching strategy under the teacher-centered approach, in that teachers and professors are the sole supplier of knowledge and information. Direct instruction is effective in teaching basic and fundamental skills across all content areas.

Inquiry-based learning is a teaching method that focuses on student investigation and hands-on learning. In this method, the teacher's primary role is that of a facilitator, providing guidance and support for students through the learning process. Inquiry-based learning falls under the student-centered approach, in that students play an active and participatory role in their own learning process.

Cooperative Learning refers to a method of teaching and classroom management that emphasizes group work and a strong sense of community. This model fosters students' academic and social growth and includes teaching techniques such as "Think-Pair-Share" and reciprocal teaching. Cooperative learning falls under the student-centered approach because learners are placed in responsibility of their learning and development. This method focuses on the belief that students learn best when working with and learning from their peers.

The users and services management module is just being developed and should describe the different processes and activities to support users in the learning management model, as well as the different types of users and services. Knowledge Management Technology is the vision, mission, business models, and strategies which solve globally managing information and knowledge in higher education.

The Technology Management layer is an adaptation of the architecture proposed by Paniagua et al. [20], and describes the technological elements that must support the model, as shown in figure 5.

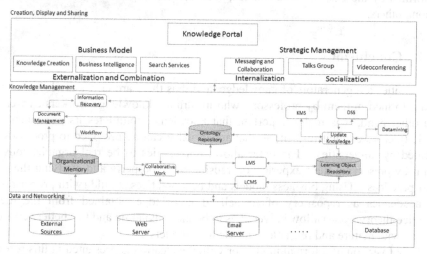

Fig. 5. Technology Platform Knowledge Management Virtual Higher Education

Ontology describing these three layers as shown in figure 6. The presentation layer shows the business model and strategic management to the users through a Knowledge Portal and supported by elements such as the Semantic Web. All these activities allow the conversion process of tacit to explicit knowledge, according to Nonaka &Takeuchi [19], for example the transformation of tacit knowledge to explicit knowledge occurs while recording knowledge in the repositories, and new knowledge can be deduced from ontologies. The presentation layer shows the business model and strategic management to the users through a Knowledge Portal and supported by elements such as the Semantic Web. All these activities allow the conversion process of tacit to explicit knowledge, according to Nonaka &Takeuchi [19].

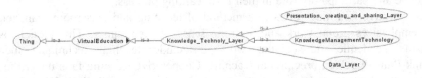

Fig. 6. Technology Knowledge Ontology for Virtual Education.

The knowledge management layer describes the technological elements that support the presentation layer such as: the creation and management of knowledge bases like organizational memory and semantic sources of learning objects, these are supported by ontologies that allow integration of learning management systems and knowledge management objects. Knowledge-based systems, decision support systems and data mining allow updating of knowledge. The information systems, document management and workflow management support organizational memory. Ontologies for integration process to both systems and ontologies. The data and networking layer is formed by the external data sources, Web servers, email and domain repositories, among others.

5   Conclusions

Universities are generators of knowledge, and thus there are new knowledge workers being formed in them by professors, who in turn are knowledge workers as well. On the other hand, it is really important that knowledge completes its permanent vital cycle (tacit-to-explicit-to-tacit) so that added value can be provided to processes performed by universities. The latter allows universities to be real organizations that learn by preserving their experiences, reusing them properly and evolving them into best practices. Using business models and best practices should (with proper respect to academics as repository of formalized knowledge obtained from the theory-practice-theory cycle) allow universities to be more dynamic and to better serve their clients with mature and reusable "knowledge products".

A first version of a formal model for virtual education is presented in this research, using first-order logic (FOL). It is modeled through ontologies, which describe the semantic architecture of a knowledge management system. We have been able to establish rules and meaning of behaviors through the different ontologies of the processes that comprises it. The ontologies describe the intelligent behavior of the model. General ontologies describe the superior level of processes, while domain ontologies describe the different processes in the education domain such as collaborative learning, teaching, etc. Finally, task ontologies will describe different tasks of the model, for example creation of learning objects.

General Ontology is the element that represents the management of knowledge which guides the model; this ontology is formed by concepts that allow to integrate the diverse layers that form the model, as well as the rules and axioms that domain the framework from a general view. This is apparent when we describe the structural capital, containing the learning management processes and collaborative work, such as found on the processes and technologies on the third layer. General ontology (shown in figure 2) integrates different layers of the model done through axioms of behavior described on table 1. For instance a rule states that "integrations include the human capital, which includes professors, students and researchers."

Each one of the ontologies describes the processes of integration and re-use of knowledge given on the different processes; this is a work in development using Neon methodology.

Future research will be conducted on the development of intelligent agents that support recommended activities to establish processes standards. Agents whom would allow to consult on the activities of measurement of quality which will be communicated to users, as well as other Agents who will allow the creation of users' profiles.

References

1. Aggarwal, P.D., Ravi, K., Anil K.V.: Enhancing Curriculum and Research in Higher Education with a Strategic Use of Knowledge Management. Global Journal of Management and Business Research 11(12) (2011)
2. Anvari, A., et al.: Analysis of Knowledge Management within Five Key Areas. Journal of Knowledge Management. Economics and Information Technology 1(6) (2011)
3. Benjamins, R., Dieter, F., Asunción, G.-P.: Knowledge management through ontologies. In: CEUR Workshop Proceedings (CEUR-WS. org) (1998)
4. Bueno, E., Azúa, S.: Medición del capital intelectual: modelo Intelect. Instituto Universitario Euroforum Escorial, Madrid (1998)
5. Marla, C., Luis, R., Ana, M.B., Leonardo, C., Richard, G.: Ontological model to support decision making in educational opportunities. Rev. FacEng UCV. v.25 n.3. (2010)
6. Chandrasekaran, B., John R.J., Benjamins, V.R.: The ontology of tasks and methods (1998)
7. Davenport, T.H., Laurence, P.: Working knowledge: How organizations manage what they know. Harvard Business Press (1998)
8. Fernández-López, M., Asunción, G.-P., Natalia, J.: Methontology: from ontological art towards ontological engineering (1997)
9. Fleming, N., Baume, D.: Learning Styles Again: VARKing up the right tree!. Educational Developments 7(4)(2006)
10. Gruber, T.R.: The role of common ontology in achieving sharable, reusable knowledge bases. KR 91, 601–602 (1991)

11. Huang, W., et al.: An intelligent semantic e-learning framework using context-aware Semantic Web technologies. British Journal of Educational Technology **37**(3), 351–373 (2006)
12. Kende, G., Erzsébet, N., György, S.: Role of the knowledge management in modern higher education–the e-learning. EDUCATION **6**(4), 559–573 (2007)
13. Knublauch, H., Fergerson, R.W., Noy, N.F., Musen, M.A.: The protégé owl plugin: an open development environment for semantic web applications. In: McIlraith, S.A., Plexousakis, D., van Harmelen, F. (eds.) ISWC 2004. LNCS, vol. 3298, pp. 229–243. Springer, Heidelberg (2004)
14. Loh, B., et al.: Applying knowledge management in university research (2003)
15. Muñoz A., Lamolle M., Pérez J., Ramirez Y., Uzcátegui M., Angarita D.: ontological model to interactive distance education since knowledge management. In: JIISIC, The Latin American Conference on Software Engineering and Knowledge Engineering (2012)
16. Muñoz A., Sandia, B.: Knowledge Management System CEIDIS. Quality Interactive Distance Education Virtual Iberoamerican Congress on Distance Education Quality. Eduq @ (2008)
17. Munoz, A., Lamolle, M., Le Duc, C.: Un modèle ontologique pour l'apprentissage collaboratif en formation interactive à distance". 1er congrès National de la Recherche en IUT, Tours, France (2012)
18. Nonaka, I.: A dynamic theory of organizational knowledge creation. Organization Science **5**(1), 14–37 (1994)
19. Nonaka, I., Takeuchi, H.: The knowledge-creating company: How Japanese companies create the dynamics of innovation. Oxford university press (1995)
20. Paniagua, E., et al.: Knowledge Technology Management. Technical Report. Murcia University. (2007)
21. Sureephong, P., et al.:An ontology-based knowledge management system for industry clusters. In: Global Design to Gain a Competitive Edge. Springer, London, pp. 333–342 (2008)

Semantic Model of Possessive Pronouns Machine Translation for English to Bulgarian Language

Velislava Stoykova[✉]

Institute for Bulgarian Language, Bulgarian Academy of Sciences,
52, Shipchensky Proh. Str., Bl. 17, 1113 Sofia, Bulgaria
vstoykova@yahoo.com

Abstract. The paper presents technique to interpret possessive pronouns for English to Bulgarian language syntax-based machine translation. It uses Universal Networking Language (UNL) as a formal framework to present possessive pronouns grammar features by employing semantic networks for both English and Bulgarian language. The technique includes also use of statistically-based estimation of accuracy of translation by measuring precision and recall of both training and controlled electronic text corpora and by improving related grammar rules.

Keywords: Knowledge representation and reasoning · Semantic data models · Knowledge-based natural language processing

1 Introduction

The problem of correct machine translation of inflected forms of Bulgarian possessive pronouns into English was interpreted as a problem of proper inflectional and syntactic rules representation of related grammar features and their semantic correlation for both languages. One of its solutions is to use common formal framework to present grammar features of possessive pronouns for both languages, so to relate them semantically.

The approach is based on the use of semantic translation for the source language and then to use that translation to generate output for the targed language. The methodology allows improvement of accuracy of received translation by improving related grammar rules and their coreference.

2 Related Approaches

Generally, approaches to machine translation can be regarded as of two basic types. The first approach uses pairs of languages for which formal grammar and lexical resources are developed for both languages. The second approach require development of core grammar and lexical resources for one language – English for example – and then to localize them for several languages allowing multilingual machine translation.

Further, we are going to describe application using secound approach and to extend its methodology of machine translation for "The Little Prince Project" which uses the text of related book.

© Springer International Publishing Switzerland 2015
I. Ciuciu et al. (Eds.): OTM 2015 Workshops, LNCS 9416, pp. 349–356, 2015.
DOI: 10.1007/978-3-319-26138-6_38

3   The Electronic Text Corpora Search Results

We use two electronic text corpora consisting of text of the book "The Little Prince" – in English and in Bulgarian language. Both corpora use the Sketch Engine (SE) [3,4] software for processing electronic text corpora which allows different types of search procedure including for aligned multilingual corpora. Various types of queries can be generated by using statistical search. For example, we can generate concordances of English possessive adjective *my* and for its related Bulgarian possessive pronoun *moj*.

The results presented at Fig. 1 and Fig. 2 show that for the English adjective we have obtained several different morphologically and syntactically related word forms from Bulgarian corpus. Thus, the main problem to resolve is to relate semantically all Bulgarian possessive pronouns word forms to their English correlates by using proper grammar rules and common formal multilingual framework. For that, we have used Universal Networking Language (UNL).

- Query my **172** (7,742.9 per million)

file1629466	to see a light break over the face of	my	young judge: "That is exactly the
file1629466	to find out more on this subject. "	My	little man, where do you come
file1629466	to unscrew a bolt that had got stuck in	my	engine. I was very much worried,
file1629466	a sigh, he took his leave. "I made you	my	Ambassador," the king called out,
file1629466	; one never knows). It is of some use to	my	volcanoes , and it is of some use to
file1629466	for your rose..." "I am responsible for	my	rose," the little prince repeated, so
file1629466	I reached the wall just in time to catch	my	little man in my arms; his face was
file1629466	you have known me. You will always be	my	friend. You will want to laugh with
file1629466	colored pencil I succeeded in making	my	first drawing. My Drawing Number

Fig. 1. The electronic corpus concordance of English possessive adjective *my*.

- Query мой **82** (543.9 per million)

file1629532	се изненадах, когато лицето на	моя	млад съдник светна: - Тъкмо това
file1629532	да узная още: - Откъде идваш,	мое	малко момче? Къде е това "при теб"?
file1629532	един прекалено стегнат болт на	моя	мотор. Бях угрижен, защото повредата
file1629532	и тръгна. - Назначавам те за	мой	посланик - бързо викна подире му
file1629532	Човек никога не знае. За	моите	вулкани и за моето цвете е полезно, че
file1629532	роза... - Аз съм отговорен за	моята	роза... - повтори малкият принц, за да
file1629532	навреме, за да поема в ръцете си	моя	мъничък принц, блед като сняг. - Това
file1629532	си ме познавал. Винаги ще бъдеш	мой	приятел. Ще ти се иска да се смееш
file1629532	цветен молив първата си рисунка.	Моята	рисунка номер 1. Тя беше такава:

Fig. 2. The electronic corpus concordance of Bulgarian possessive pronoun *moj*.

4   The Universal Networking Language

In the UNL approach, information conveyed by natural language is represented as a hypergraph composed of a set of directed binary labeled links (referred to as "relations") between nodes or hypernodes (the "Universal Words" (UWs)), which stand for concepts. UWs can also be annotated with "attributes" representing context information [11].

Universal Words (UWs) represent universal concepts and correspond to the nodes to be interlinked by "relations" or modified by "attributes" in a UNL graph. They can be associated to natural language open lexical categories (noun, verb, adjective and adverb). Additionally, UWs are organized in a hierarchy (the UNL Ontology), are defined in the UNL Knowledge Base and exemplified in the UNL Example Base, which are the lexical databases for UNL. As language-independent semantic units, UWs are equivalent to the sets of synonyms of a given language, approaching the concept of "synset" used by the WordNet.

Attributes are arcs linking a node onto itself. In opposition to relations, they correspond to one-place predicates, i.e., function that take a single argument. In UNL, attributes have been normally used to represent information conveyed by natural language grammatical categories (such as tense, mood, aspect, number, etc). Attributes are annotations made to nodes or hypernodes of a UNL hypergraph. They denote the circumstances under which these nodes (or hypernodes) are used. Attributes may convey three different kinds of information: (i) The information on the role of the node in the UNL graph, (ii) The information conveyed by bound morphemes and closed classes, such as affixes (gender, number, tense, aspect, mood, voice, etc), determiners (articles and demonstratives), etc., (iii) The information on the (external) context of the utterance. Attributes represent information that cannot be conveyed by UWs and relations.

Relations, are labeled arcs connecting a node to another node in a UNL graph. They correspond to two-place semantic predicates holding between two UWs. In UNL, relations have been normally used to represent semantic cases or thematic roles (such as agent, object, instrument, etc.) between UWs.

UNL-NL Grammars are sets of rules for translating UNL expressions into natural language (NL) sentences and vice-versa. They are normally unidirectional, i.e., the enconversion grammar (NL-to-UNL) or deconversion grammar (UNL-to-NL), even though they share the same basic syntax.

In the UNL Grammar there are two basic types of rules: (i) Transformation rules - used to generate natural language sentences out of UNL graphs and vice-versa and (ii) Disambiguation rules - used to improve the performance of transformation rules by constraining their applicability.

The UNL offers universal language-independent and open-source web-based platform for multilingual applications [2]. The UNL applications for English and French languages [6] are available but some applications for other languages like Russian [1] and Bulgarian [7,8] are available as well.

The UNL web-based platform also offers UNL-NL Grammar deconversion system EUGENE and NL-UNL Grammar enconversion system IAN which allow multilingual representation and localization of grammars for Natural-language generation and Natural-language analysis tasks for machine translation applications.

5   Multilingual Representation of Possessive Pronouns in UNL

Possessive pronouns exist in almost all European languages and they share similar semantics. In fact, the semantic relation of possession is accepted as a semantic universal and it varies depending on whether it is referred to the possessor or to the thing being possessed. However, for different languages there exist different grammar features to express above semantic relations.

For English language, we differentiate for possessive pronouns and possessive adjectives which differs with respect to their syntactic positions. For Bulgarian language, we differentiate possessive pronouns' grammar features of gender, number, definiteness (which are inflectional) and person (which is not inflectional). Also, we differentiate between their syntactic positions as modifiers and specifiers. A detailed description of Bulgarian UNL possessive pronouns inflectional morphology representation is given at [9] with related principles and presented inflectional rules. A comparative multilingual UNL possessive pronouns representation for English and Bulgarian languages also is described at [10].

Both applications are based on the idea to represent possessive pronouns grammar features (inflectional and syntactic) for both languages as relations with subsequent graph representation using semantic networks. Further, we need to correlate that representation as semantically equivalent by localizing developed English grammar for Bulgarian language grammar features adopting it with related inflectional and syntactic grammar rules.

5.1   Developing UNL Grammar for Possessive Pronouns

For our approach, we adopt the methodology described in [5]. We use UNL-NL Grammar deconversion system EUGENE and NL-UNL Grammar enconversion system IAN to represent and localize English grammar and dictionary and we extend them with Bulgarian grammar and dictionary. Generally, the process starts with NL-UNL enconversion of English sentences and is followed by UNL-NL deconversion of Bulgarian sentences. The sentences from both languages are represented as language-independent UNL relations which have to be semantically equivalent.

Thus, the sentence from English text corpus (Fig. 1) *I am responsible for my rose* is represented into UNL graph using relations *ben(am:03.@present, my rose:0C.@for)* and *obj(am:03.@present, responsible:05)*. The visual representation of related UNL graph is given at Fig. 3 and its correlated Bulgarian translation is given at Fig. 4, respectively.

Alternatively, the English text corpus sentence *Something was broken in my engine* is represented as UNL graph by using relations *plc(was:03.@past,*

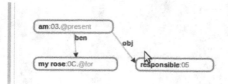

Fig. 3. The UNL graph representation of the sentence *I am responsible for my rose.*

Fig. 4. The Bulgarian translation of the sentence *I am responsible for my rose.*

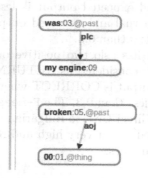

Fig. 5. The UNL graph representation of the sentence *Something was broken in my engine.*

my engine:09) and *aoj(broken:05.@past, 00:01.@thing)*. The related visual UNL graph representation is given at Fig. 5 and its Bulgarian language translation is given at Fig. 6.

5.2   Measuring Accuracy of Translation

The UNL web-based platform allows statistically-based measurement of accuracy of translated texts by estimation of precision and recall. For that, F-measure

```
[S:11]
{org}

{/org}
{bul}
Нещо беше счупено в моя мотор
{/bul}
{eng}
broken
{/eng}
{unl}
plc("was":03.@past, "my engine":09)
 aoj("broken":05.@past, 00:01.@thing)
{/unl}
[/S]
Dictionary Lookup Time 0 seconds, 5 milliseconds.
Disambiguation Time 0 seconds, 0 milliseconds.
Transformation Time 0 seconds, 626 milliseconds.
Total Time 0 seconds, 631 milliseconds.
```

Fig. 6. The Bulgarian translation of the sentence *Something was broken in my engine.*

score is used. It considers both precision and recall of grammar. *Precision* is the number of correct results divided by the number of all returned results. *Recall* is the number of correct results divided by the number of results that should have been returned.

The NL-UNL enconversion has two types of positive outcome – RETURNED and CORRECT. For RETURNED output it is needed that result must be UNL graph or UW. For CORRECT output it is needed that: (i) the discrepancy of relations between actual and expected output is less than 0,3 and (ii) the discrepancy of UWs between actual and expected output is less than 0,3 and (iii) the overall discrepancy is less than 0,3.

The UNL-NL deconversion has aslo two positive outcome – RETURNED and CORRECT. The output is considered as RETURNED when it is a list of natural language words. The output is CORRECT when the difference between actual and expected output is less than 0,3. The F-measure score of English to UNL enconversion and related direct UNL to Bulgarian deconversion translation is given at Fig. 7. It is evaluated as not very high and needs to be improved by improving accuracy of grammar rules.

5.3 Improving Bulgarian Grammar with Inflectional and Syntactic Rules

Generally, the incorrect translations can be found where it is possible to have more than one translation (ambiguity rules) or in case of missing grammar rules for the target language. For Bulgarian possessive pronouns, we have found more than one possible translation for the inflected forms which function as modifiers. That cases have been considered as RETURNED but not CORRECT. The number of incorrect translations of inflected forms of possessive pronouns which function as specifiers was much less. Thus, we have improved grammar accuracy by adopting mainly inflectional and syntactic rules.

The UNL specifications offer types of formal grammar rules particularly designed to present pronouns grammar features of person, number and gender

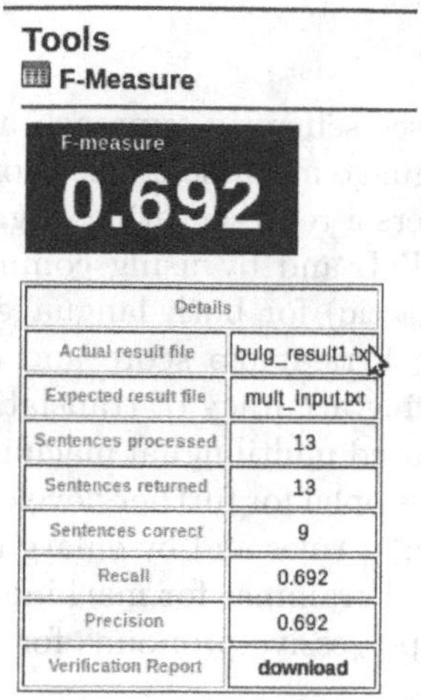

Tools

F-Measure

F-measure

0.692

Details	
Actual result file	bulg_result1.txt
Expected result file	mult_input.txt
Sentences processed	13
Sentences returned	13
Sentences correct	9
Recall	0.692
Precision	0.692
Verification Report	**download**

Fig. 7. The *F-measure* of direct English-UNL-Bulgarian syntax-based translation.

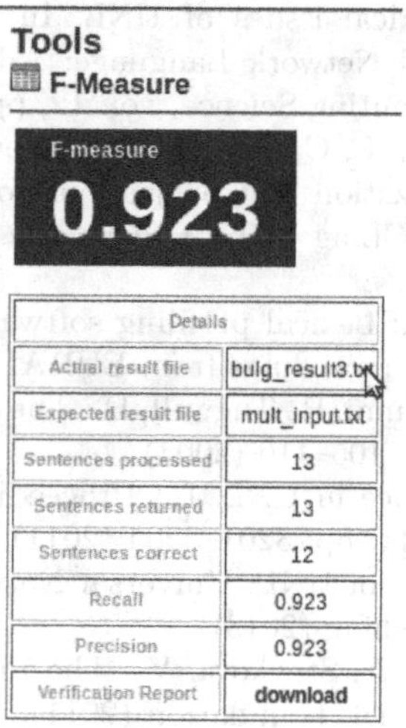

Tools

F-Measure

F-measure

0.923

Details	
Actual result file	bulg_result3.txt
Expected result file	mult_input.txt
Sentences processed	13
Sentences returned	13
Sentences correct	12
Recall	0.923
Precision	0.923
Verification Report	**download**

Fig. 8. The *F-measure* after improvment of Bulgarian grammar accuracy.

which are interpreted as inflectional features (like gender, number and definiteness). The inflection can be represented with respect to prefixes, suffixes, infixes, and to the sound alternations. Also, we have developed transformation syntactic rules to differentiate possessive pronouns as modifiers from that as specifiers.

Repeating improvement of grammar accuracy by adopton of new grammar rules we have obtained a higher **F-measure** score presented at Fig. 8 and have significantly improved accuracy of translation.

6   Conclusion

The applied methodology uses semantic approach and syntax-based technique for English to Bulgarian language machine translation of all possessive pronouns in Bulgarian language. It offers a representation of grammar knowledge by common formal framework of UNL and by using common semantic relations and grammar rules (mostly syntactic) for both languages. The resulting grammars can be tested by estimating **F-measure** score and can be extended with new disambiguation rules improving accuracy of translation.

The model uses syntax-based multilingual machine translation approach and web-based UNL platform. It is open for further development and improvement by introducing additional grammar rules and by enlarging database. Further, it will be interesting to test improved grammar for machine translation between several related languages including possessive pronouns for more Slavonic languages.

References

1. Boguslavsky, I.: Some lexical issues of UNL. In: Cardenosa, J., Gelbukh, A., Tovar, E. (eds.) Universal Network Language: Advances in Theory and Applications. Research on Computing Science, vol. 12, pp. 101–108 (2005)
2. Boitet, C., Boguslavskij, I.M., Cardeñosa, J.: An evaluation of UNL usability for high quality multilingualization and projections for a future UNL++ language. In: Gelbukh, A. (ed.) CICLing 2007. LNCS, vol. 4394, pp. 361–373. Springer, Heidelberg (2007)
3. Kilgarriff, A., Rundell, M.: Lexical profiling software and its lexicographic applications: a case study. In: Proceedings from EURALEX 2002, pp. 807–811 (2002)
4. Kilgarriff, A., Rychly, P., Smrz, P., Tugwell, D.: The Sketch Engine. In: Proceedings from EURALEX 2004, pp. 105–116 (2004)
5. Martins, R.: Le Petit Prince in UNL. In: Proceedings from Language Resources Evaluation Conference 2011, pp. 3201–3204 (2011)
6. Martins, R.: Lexical Issues of UNL: Universal Networking Language 2012 Panel. Cambridge Scholars Publishing (2013)
7. Noncheva, V., Stancheva, Y., Stoykova, V.: The Little Prince project - Encoding of Bulgarian grammar. UNDL Foundation (2011). www.undl.org
8. Stoykova, V.: Bulgarian inflectional morphology in Universal Networking Language. In: Kay, M., Boitet, C. (eds.) Proceedings of 24th International Conference on Computational Linguistics (COLING 2012): Demonstration Papers, pp. 423–430 (2012a)
9. Stoykova, V.: The inflectional morphology of Bulgarian possessive and reflexive-possessive pronouns in Universal Networking Language. Procedia Technology 1, 400–406 (2012b). Elsevier
10. Stoykova, V.: Representation of possessive pronouns in Universal Networking Language. In: Iliadis, L., Papadopoulos, H., Jayne, C. (eds.) EANN 2013, Part II. CCIS, vol. 384, pp. 129–137. Springer, Heidelberg (2013)
11. Uchida, H., Zhu, M., Senta, T.D.: Universal Networking Language. UNDL Foundation (2005)

Machine-Assisted Generation of Semantic Business Process Models

Avi Wasser and Maya Lincoln[✉]

University of Haifa, Haifa, Israel
maya.lincoln@processgene.com

Abstract. Generic reference models are based on the assumption of similarity between enterprises - either cross industrial or within a given sector. The research suggests a machine assisted methodology and tools for the design and generation of individualized business process models based on generic repositories. An empirical evaluation is included to assess the effectiveness of the proposed method.

Keywords: Business processes · Industry blueprints · Reference models · Enterprise-specific

1 Introduction

Modern enterprise management focus has shifted to integrate and manage the process-centered enterprise [2] using tools such as Business Process Management (BPM) and Enterprise Resource Planning (ERP) [3]. These tools form the basis for enterprise operation planning, optimization, and assessment.

Most business process management works have focused on the study of structural frameworks and IT related execution patterns [14], putting little emphasis on the *content layer* that adds the operational data to these frameworks. "Real life" business process models, which represent practical "how to" content, have been somewhat disregarded except in illustrative examples [13]. Few scientific researches have addressed the topic of designing business process content [4,7,10,12] aiming to develop theories, empirical studies and supporting tools. The lack of suggestions for standard structure, terminology and tools for the process content layer has restricted the development of "reference modeling content science," leaving it mostly to vendors and commercial organizations [13].

Currently, most of the generic business process repositories are provided by industrial organizations, developed on the basis of experience accumulated through analyzing business activity and implementing IT systems in a variety of industries. These repositories are presented as generic – i.e. typical for an industrial sector (e.g. SAP's "aerospace industry" business solutions[1] or Oracle's "retail solutions"[2]).

---

[1] SAP. Business Maps and Solution Composer, http://www.sap.com/solutions/businessmaps/composer/, 2015.

[2] Oracle. [12] www.oracle.com/industries/retail/index.html, 2015.

© Springer International Publishing Switzerland 2015
I. Ciuciu et al. (Eds.): OTM 2015 Workshops, LNCS 9416, pp. 357–366, 2015.
DOI: 10.1007/978-3-319-26138-6_39

The generation of enterprise-specific, or *individualized* process models is conventionally based on manual customization of sectorial models. Since a typical generic process repository constitutes thousands of processes and tens of thousands of activities, this enterprise-specific customization is considered a manual, labor intensive task. It requires significant domain expertise and is prone to errors or inconsistencies due to reliance on human, without the assistance of a machine.

Aiming to confront the above concern, the objective of this research is to suggest a structured methodology for automating the construction of enterprise-specific business process models based on the operational characteristics of the implementing organization.

After a review of related work (Section 2), we present a framework for business process classification (Section 3). Based on this framework we then present the methodology for the design and generation of enterprise-specific process models (Section 4). In Section 5 we present an empirical evaluation of the proposed method effectiveness. Section 6 includes conclusions and directions for future work.

2   Related Work: Application of Reference Process Models

2.1   Commercial Reference Models

Commercial reference process models are usually developed by vendors such as SAP[3] and Oracle[4]; by system integrators such as HP[5], IBM BCS (Business Consulting Services)[6], and Accenture[7]; and by BPM specific companies.

ERP vendor reference process models include, for example, SAP's industry and cross-industry Business Solution Maps, INFOR/Lawson's ERM (Enterprise Reference Models)[8], and Oracle's OBM (Oracle Business Models) library. From these models vendors and integrators develop a suite of processes, reflecting what an enterprise does, or needs to do, in order to achieve its objectives [9].

These models are based on the assumption of significant similarity between enterprises that operate within a certain industry. SAP, for example, offers Business Solutions for 24 industrial branches.

In summary, research into commercial business process models has introduced the following concepts: (a) the idea of generic industry-related process models; and (b) the idea that a specific enterprise process model is a sub-set of a generic

---

[3] SAP. Business Maps and Solution Composer, http://www.sap.com/solutions/businessmaps/composer/, 2015.

[4] Oracle. Business Models (OBM), http://www.oracle.com/consulting/offerings/implementation/methods_tools/, 2015.

[5] EDS. EDS web-site, URL=www.eds.com, 2015.

[6] IBM. IBM web-site. URL=ww1.ibm.com/services/us/bcs/html/bcs_index.html?trac=L1, 2015.

[7] Accenture. Accenture web-site. URL=www.accenture.com/, 2015.

[8] Intentia. Enterprise Reference Models, http://www.intentia.com/WCW.nsf/pub/tools_index, 2015.

reference business process model, and can be generated by scoping-out non-relevant elements.

2.2 Derivation of Individualized Process Models

While academia has devised novel notions regarding model-driven structural process configuration of enterprise systems [1,5,11], the prevailing practitioner procedure for generating individualized process models content is a top-down customization of generic sectorial models.

According to this approach, sectorial classifications reflect the end-product of the enterprise, rather than its modus operandi. Hence, focusing on what the enterprise produces (or supplies), instead of how this production is carried out, can be misleading and may result in inappropriate business process models [14].

2.3 Machine Assisted Approach in Business Process Modeling

BPM science has presented in recent years some works that focus on the automation of modeling tasks [7,8,12]. Yet, these methods and tools have not been applied on machine-assisted generation of organizational business process models- which is the focus of this work.

To sum-up: this research suggests an alternative, machine-assisted, approach for generating individualized process models, based on the correlation between the operational characteristics of the organization and a set of corresponding business processes.

3   Business Process Classification

According to [9], in a complete repository, processes are divided into five operational classes: (a) business functionalities: (1) basic business processes, (2) business support processes; (b) industrial functionalities: (3) basic manufacturing processes, (4) manufacturing support processes, (5) service processes. These classes can be considered separable (i.e. no overlapping of processes within classes). In addition, most business functionalities were found to be common to all enterprises. Therefore, according to this work, enterprises are differentiated mainly by their industrial functionalities – the degree to which each of the manufacturing and service sub-classes are implemented.

As a result, the authors of [9] proposed a general typological representation of enterprises that overcomes the necessity to distinguish between production and service industries, seeing that both types of activities occur in most organizations. Their typology characterizes industrial functionality by two codes: M(*) and S(*). M(*) defines goods production functionality (oriented along product development through manufacturing), whilst S(*) defines service provision functionality (oriented towards the proximity between the provider and customer). The scale of functionalities ranges from "pure goods production" (M(4)) through "pure service provision" (S(4)) (See Fig. 1, where the M and S classifications are marked by "*").

This presentation implies that an enterprise implementing "full production" functionality (R&D, product engineering, configuration management and production), with no service functionality, would be coded as $M(1+2+3+4)S(0)$. An enterprise implementing "full service" functionality (front office, contact office, mobile office and remote office), with no goods functionality, would be coded as $M(0)S(1+2+3+4)$. All other enterprises can be characterized within this spectrum in accordance with their tendency to be oriented towards manufacturing or service. For example: a ticket sales office that is a "pure" service enterprise would be coded as $M(0)S(1+2+3+4)$ (sales of tickets via the web, through agents in the field, via a call center, and person-to-person at the enterprise offices). A software company oriented both towards creating software and providing services would be coded as $M(2+3+4)S(2+3)$ (development of customized software reusing modules; providing a help desk in the field and through a call center).

#	Operational Characteristic	Code		#	Operational Characteristic	Code
1	Production/operations (MtS)	M(4)*		10	Front office service (provider)	S(4)*
2	Configuration management (AtO)	M(3)*		11	Multi-subsidiary enterprise	B(1)
3	Product engineering (EtO)	M(2)*		12	Self management of internal IT	B(2)
4	Research and development (DtO)	M(1)*		13	Substantial holdings of fixed assets	B(3)
5	No significant goods production	M(0)*		14	Project based work	B(4)
6	No significant service provision	S(0)*		15	Working in shifts	B(5)
7	Remote office service (web/vending)	S(1)*		16	Care for environmental safety	B(6)
8	Mobile office service (field)	S(2)*		17	A public company	B(7)
9	Contact office service (call center)	S(3)*		18	Teleworkers	B(8)

Fig. 1. Operational Classification of Enterprises.

In this work we have elaborated the functional code suggested in [9] by further analyzing the business functionalities that were previously considered generic. The goal was to find differentiating business characteristics that will enable us to refine the operational classification and by that generate more accurate enterprise specific models.

To do that we used the ProcessGene process repository[9] as follows. The ProcessGene repository consists of 4,531 processes comprising 17,608 activities. Processes are interconnected to each other and therefore the repository can be represented as a general graph. We have analyzed 63 enterprise specific process models that were created based on the ProcessGene repository as part of a BPM

---

[9] ProcessGene Ltd., http://processgene.com/business-process-repository/, 2015.

project each organization carried out. Therefore, each specific model represented a subset, or a sub-graph of the generic repository.

The analysis was carried out in a bottom-up manner. First, all business processes in the repository were linked to those organizations in the sample in which they were found to be implemented. Then, by analyzing the 63 enterprises we have defined a list of 48 candidate business characteristics that can influence the enterprise operations (e.g. "a public company", "project based work", and "field work"). Then, a statistical regression analysis was carried out to find significant correlations between processes and business characteristics. The processes were found to correspond to a high degree with eight out of 48 of the predefined business characteristics. It was found that (a) the probability is high that companies are significantly associated with the same number and content of processes corresponding to each of the eight classifying characteristics; and (b) the degree of separation between clusters (processes related to each characterizing class) is almost absolute. Thus the business classes can be considered separable (i.e. no overlapping of processes among classes).

These findings also support two significant conclusions: (a) an enterprise model can be constructed by a separable and additive set of business processes; (b) if an enterprise is characterized by a business class, it most likely implements all of the corresponding processes. These properties enable us to extend the former industrial classification suggested by [9] and extend the utilization of the process repository systematically for the design of individualized business process models. The additional business classes are presented in Fig. 1, marked by "B."

The rest of the business processes that were not related to any business classification were marked as "general." The inclusion probability of each such process in an arbitrary process model was calculated according to its number of occurrences among the sample of 63 organizations. For example, the process "Fill supplier questionnaire" belongs to the "business functionalities" group. It was marked "general" since it was not correlated to any of the classes B(1)-B(8). Since it was found in 58 out of 63 examined organizations, its probability to be included in a newly designed process model is 92%.

4   Generating Individualized Process Models

In this section we present a method for generating enterprise specific process models by: (1) using the refined business process classification (Section 3); (2) fine-tuning the enterprise specific model using content validation methods.

The enterprise-specific model generation method (the "modeling assistant") relies on an underlying process repository and encompasses five main stages, as illustrated in Fig. 2. The design process starts when a process designer defines the operational characteristics of the enterprise. This is done by selecting additive characteristics from a pre-defined characteristics list (see Fig. 1). For example, a multi-subsidiary, public company implementing "full production" functionality (R&D, product engineering, configuration management and production), with no service functionality, would be coded as M(1+2+3+4)S(0)B(1+7). The user also

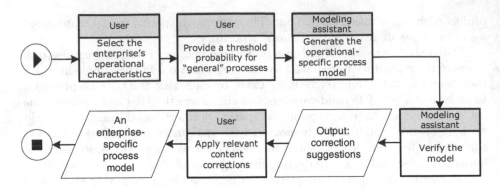

Fig. 2. The modeling assistant mechanism.

provides a threshold probability for adding "general" processes to the specific model (see Section 4.2).

Based on the process designer inputs, the modeling assistant combines the enterprise-specific model (see Section 4.3). The generated model content is then being verified using NLP methods (see Section 4.4), aiming to assure that the logic of the model is complete and sound (e.g. that there are no contradicting activities, and that activities are presented in the right execution order). This stage outputs a list of correction options. The designer then reviews the correction suggestions and fine-tunes the model accordingly (see Section 4.5). Finally the modeling assistant outputs a full-fledged process model that reflects the enterprise specific modus-operandi.

4.1 Phase #1: Determination of the Operational Classification of an Enterprise

At this stage the user (process designer) is presented with the list of enterprise operational classifications as presented in Fig. 1. In response, she selects the classifications compatible to the currently modeled organization in an additive manner.

4.2 Phase #2: Provision of a Threshold Probability for "General" Processes

At this stage the process designer specifies the threshold for adding general business functions. This threshold indicates the level of tolerance the organization has towards redundant vs. missing processes at the final, output model. Low threshold (e.g. 40%) means that general business processes will be added to the organizational-specific model even if on average they are present only in 40% of the enterprises. This increases the probability of redundant processes that the organization will have to review and delete at the final refinement stage. On the other hand, a high threshold (e.g. 90%) may prevent the inclusion of general business processes that might be required at the enterprise specific model.

4.3   Phase #3: Generation of the Individualized Business Process Content Model

The procedure for generating an individualized business process model is as follows.

1. Automatically generate a reduced model, encompassing only those processes constituting the top-level operational characteristics of the enterprise, according to the user's input at phase #1.
2. Based on the general threshold probability provided by the process designer (Step #2), automatically retrieve and add "general" business processes, having a probability equal to or greater than the threshold value.

For example, a multi-subsidiary plastic seats manufacturer produces and markets a range of mass-produced seats for sale. From the classification questionnaire we learn that its operations are characterized by make-to-stock production, a call center for customer orders, a fleet of tracks for distribution to stores. In addition, the work in this organization is managed in shifts. According to the categorization of operational characteristics (Fig. 1), the enterprise would be classified as M(3+4)S(1+2+3)B(1+5): managing the seat production, distributing customer orders in shifts, and receiving orders from stores. The corresponding set of industrial and business processes can be retrieved top-down from the business process repository, and, as a consequence of the additive property of the process clusters, the operational modules and the general processes that correspond to the given threshold can be easily combined to rapidly establish the plastic seat manufacturer's business process model.

4.4   Phase #4: Specific-Model Verification

Since the individualized model was combined additively by groups of processes, a final "tailoring" phase is required to assure that the business logic expressed in the model is complete and sound. For example, we need to make sure that based on the generated model content, there are no missing activities and that processes are represented at the right execution order. To do that, we used the content validation method suggested in [6]. Using natural language processing (NLP), the method outputs a list of correction suggestions, for the user's review.

4.5   Phase #5: Application of Model Corrections

Finally, the user reviews the correction suggestions and applies the relevant corrections to the suggested process model. In continuous to the above example, the validation mechanism may find out that there is a missing process in the model named: "Locating nearest service provider," due to the fact that the enterprise has multiple subsidiaries and it provides field service. The modeler will then decide if such a process is relevant for her organization and if yes - will add it from the ProcessGene repository to the enterprise-specific model.

The output of this framework is a full-fledged enterprise-specific process model. Naturally, the process modeler will afterwards review the model and fine-tune it manually – usually at the activity (low) level – to ensure that all relevant processes have been included and unnecessary processes eliminated. This may require some time, as the various "key users" in the enterprise become involved at this stage. However, they begin from the specific enterprise model as an initial input, rather than from a generic, all-inclusive, repository. This focuses attention on the enterprise functionality, and can greatly shorten the time to reach agreement on the final model.

5   Experiments

We now present an empirical evaluation of the proposed method effectiveness. First, we present the experimental setup and describe the data sets that were used. Based on this setup we present the implemented methodology. Finally, we present the experiment results and provide an empirical analysis of these results.

5.1   Data

We chose a set of additional 23 enterprise-specific process models that were generated based on the ProcessGene repository for the needs of various organizations. The selected enterprises operate in different industries, are of various company sizes (considering workforce and financial aspects) and different geographical locations.

5.2   Evaluation Methodology

To evaluate the suggested method we conducted 23 experiments. At each experiment, an enterprise-specific model was generated based on the suggested framework (phases #1-#3 only, threshold=50%) and then compared to the model that the current model that organization already constructed. This "machine assisted design" has enabled us to objectively measure the method's effectiveness.

5.3   Results and Analysis

Fig. 3 presents a summary of the experiment results. On average, 4.9% processes from the ProcessGene repository were missing from the generated enterprise-specific model (see column #1). This was the case despite the diversity of the examined enterprises, highlighting the level of accuracy one would expect when automatically generating new process models based on the ProcessGene repository. This percentage was lower for the manufacturing and service parts of the model (2.1% and 3.5% correspondingly) than for the business part of the model (9%). This can be explained due to the fact that manufacturing and service provision may be more standardized and therefore more predictable. These results were produced using a 50% threshold. A higher threshold will reduce the amount of missing processes.

In addition, on average, 6.1% of the processes in the generated model were redundant (see column #2), again, highlighting the level of accuracy of the generated model. This percentage was lower for the manufacturing part (3.6%), medium for the service part (5.7%) and higher for the business part of the model (8.9%). Higher percentage means more diversity in the way the operational classes are being implemented. Therefore, the low percentage that was found for the manufacturing processes means that usually when implementing the different types of manufacturing methods, most of their related processes are required. It should be noted though that these results were produced based on a 50% threshold. A lower threshold will decrease the number of redundant processes.

Finally, on average, each organization added 2.5% unique processes that were not represented in the ProcessGene repository (see column #3). This percentage was lower for the manufacturing and business parts (1% and 2.1% respectively), and higher for the service part (4.3%). This indicates that service processes are more diverse and unique per enterprise.

Column #	1	2	3
Column name	% of missing processes in the generated model	% of redundant processes in the generated model	% of enterprise-specific processes that are not represented in the ProcessGene repository
Avg.-all	4.9%	6.1%	2.5%
Avg.-Manufacturing	2.1%	3.6%	1.0%
Avg.-Service	3.5%	5.7%	4.3%
Avg.-Business	9.0%	8.9%	2.1%

Fig. 3. Experiment results.

To summarize, the experiments have demonstrated the usefulness of the machine-based modeling assistant in constructing enterprise-specific process models. We have also measured and evaluated the effectiveness of the method in the given experimental setup, both in terms of the amount of missing processes and in the amount of redundant processes.

6   Conclusions

We proposed a mechanism for automating the generation of enterprise-specific process models from a predefined process repository. Such a mechanism saves design time and supports non-expert designers in creating new, enterprise specific business process models. The proposed method and experiments provide a starting point that can already be applied in real-life scenarios, yet several research

A. Wasser and M. Lincoln

issues remain open, including: (1) an extended empirical study to further examine the quality of newly generated process models; (2) extending the method to include the activity level as well; and (3) defining a learning mechanism that will take into account previous design outcomes and adjust the modeling assistant mechanism for the next usage.

As a future work we intend to investigate further the sets of generic business processes in order to extend and refine the enterprise operational classification.

References

1. Cai, H., Xu, B., Bu, F.: A conceptual ontology-based resource meta-model towards business-driven information system implementation. Journal of Universal Computer Science **18**(17), 2493–2513 (2012)
2. Davenport, T.H.: Process innovation: reengineering work through information technology. Harvard Business Press (2013)
3. Hatten, K.J., Rosenthal, S.R.: Managing the process-centred enterprise. Long Range Planning **32**(3), 293–310 (1999)
4. Karni, R., Wasser, A., Lincoln, M.: Content analysis of business processes. International Journal of E-Business Development (2014)
5. Leopold, H., Smirnov, S., Mendling, J.: Refactoring of process model activity labels. In: Hopfe, C.J., Rezgui, Y., Métais, E., Preece, A., Li, H. (eds.) NLDB 2010. LNCS, vol. 6177, pp. 268–276. Springer, Heidelberg (2010)
6. Lincoln, M., Gal, A.: Content-based validation of business process modifications. In: Jeusfeld, M., Delcambre, L., Ling, T.-W. (eds.) ER 2011. LNCS, vol. 6998, pp. 495–503. Springer, Heidelberg (2011)
7. Lincoln, M., Golani, M., Gal, A.: Machine-assisted design of business process models using descriptor space analysis. In: Hull, R., Mendling, J., Tai, S. (eds.) BPM 2010. LNCS, vol. 6336, pp. 128–144. Springer, Heidelberg (2010)
8. Lincoln, M., Golani, M., Gal, A.: Machine-assisted design of business process models using descriptor space analysis. Technical Report IE/IS-2010-01, Technion, March 2010. http://ie.technion.ac.il/tech_reports/1267736757_MachineAssisted_Design_of_Business_Processes.pdf
9. Lincoln, M., Karni, R.: A generic business function framework for industrial enterprises. In: CD Proceedings of 17th ICPR Conference (2003)
10. Malone, T.W., Crowston, K., Herman, G.A.: Organizing business knowledge: the MIT process handbook. MIT press (2003)
11. Recker, J., Rosemann, M., van der Aalst, W.M.P., Mendling, J.: On the syntax of reference model configuration – transforming the C-EPC into lawful EPC models. In: Bussler, C.J., Haller, A. (eds.) BPM 2005. LNCS, vol. 3812, pp. 497–511. Springer, Heidelberg (2006)
12. Wasser, A., Lincoln, M.: Semantic machine learning for business process content generation. In: Meersman, R., et al. (eds.) OTM 2012, Part I. LNCS, vol. 7565, pp. 74–91. Springer, Heidelberg (2012)
13. Wasser, A., Lincoln, M., Karni, R.: ERP reference process models: from generic to specific. In: Eder, J., Dustdar, S. (eds.) BPM Workshops 2006. LNCS, vol. 4103, pp. 45–54. Springer, Heidelberg (2006)
14. Wasser, A., Lincoln, M., Karni, R.: Accelerated enterprise process modeling through a formalized functional typology. In: van der Aalst, W.M.P., Benatallah, B., Casati, F., Curbera, F. (eds.) BPM 2005. LNCS, vol. 3649, pp. 446–451. Springer, Heidelberg (2005)

International Workshop on Information Systems in Distributed Environment (ISDE) 2015

ISDE 2015 PC Co-Chairs' Message

Information System in Distributed Environment (ISDE) is becoming a prominent standard in this globalization era due to advancement in information and communication technologies. In distributed environments, business units collaborate across time zones, organizational boundaries, work cultures and geographical distances, to an increasing diversification and growing complexity of cooperation among units. The advent of the Internet has supported distributed information system environment by introducing new concepts and opportunities, resulting in benefits such as scalability, flexibility, interdependence, reduced cost, resource pools, and usage tracking. The number of organizations distributing their software development processes worldwide to attain increased profit and productivity as well as cost reduction and quality improvement is growing. Despite the fact that information system in distributed environment is widely being used, the project managers and software professionals face many challenges due to increased complexity, cultural as well as various technological issues. Therefore, it is crucial to understand current research and practices with researchers and practitioners in these areas.

Following selected papers of ISDE 2015 international workshop in conjunction with OTM conferences present recent advances and novel proposals in this direction.

Claude Moulin, Kenji Sugawara, Yuki Kaeri, Marie-Hélène Abel presented the design and implementation of a distributed digital system supporting participants during co-located collaborative sessions and presented the architecture of a distributed system involving different types of devices and for the main modules a large multi-touch screen.

In their paper Evolving Mashup Interfaces using a Distributed Machine Learning and Model Transformation Methodology, Antonio Jesus Fernandez-Garcia et al. proposed a methodology to allow mashup user interfaces to be intelligent and evolve over time by using computational techniques like machine learning over huge amounts of heterogeneous data, known as big data, and model-driven engineering techniques as model transformations.

Liguo Yu, Alok Mishra, Deepti Mishra reviewed distributed Web services and studied their current status through examining the distributed data centers of several top Internet companies and concluded that distributed services, including distributed data centers, are the key factors to scale up the business of a company, especially, an internet-based company.

Tool Chain in Agile ALM Environment by Saed Imran, Martin Buchheit, Bernhard Hollunder, Ulf Schreier highlights tool integration within the Agile Application Lifecycle Management (ALM) environments. This article addresses the problem faced by practitioners while establishing a tool chain environment, aligned with development process and culture.

One of the most important aspects when designing and constructing an Information System is its architecture. This also applies to complex systems such as System of Information Systems (SoIS). An Architectural Model for System of Information Systems by Majd Saleh, Marie-Hélène Abel, Alok Mishra proposed an architectural model of System of Information Systems (SoIS).

A Software Development Lifecycle Model for Cloud Combining Waterfall, Prototyping and Incremental Models by Tuna Hacaloglu et al. proposed a new conceptual software development life cycle model for cloud software by synthesis of different process models for traditional software development.

Software factories are a key element in Component-Based Software Engineering due to the common space provided for software reuse through repositories of components. Javier Criado, Luis Iribarne, Nicolas Padilla describe a matching process based on syntactic and semantic information of software components.

September 2015

Alok Mishra
Jürgen Münch
Deepti Mishra

Tool Chains in Agile ALM Environments: A Short Introduction

Saed Imran[✉], Martin Buchheit, Bernhard Hollunder, and Ulf Schreier

Faculty of Business Informatics and Informatics,
University of Applied Sciences Furtwangen, Furtwangen, Germany
{saed.imran,martin.buchheit,bernhard.hollunder,
ulf.schreier}@hs-furtwangen.de

Abstract. The article highlights tool integration within the Agile Application Lifecycle Management (ALM) environments. An essential ingredient of an effective agile ALM process is concerned with the techniques used to form the coalitions of tools that support some or all of its activities. This article aims to address the problem faced by practitioners while establishing a tool chain environment, aligned with development process and culture. To provide practical step wise information on the creation of a tool chain, we have explored how the ALM process model can be used for creating a skeleton of specialized tools. We identify a set of proposed criteria for tool selection and show how tools can be set up on different development platforms.

Keywords: Application Lifecycle Management · Software tool chain · Integrated application development tools

1 Introduction

Traditionally, software development was treated as a factory process in which the development activities were mainly aligned in a sequence as were the efforts on their management. This results in longer development time-lines with slower responses to a changing environment and lower user satisfaction rating. As a consequence, software engineering moved into the era of agile software development.

Agile software development is in fact a realisation of agile practices such as Scrum, Extreme Programming etc [1]. These practices advocate iterative learning, development and improvements through earlier and continuous customer feedback. This has led to the recognition of agile practices as being adaptive and people-oriented. In addition, the process of software application development requires experts from a number of software engineering disciplines such as domain knowledge, design and architecture etc. Each of these disciplines involves a different set of specialized development tools that are specific for their particular development phase.

Application Lifecycle Management (Application Lifecycle Management (ALM)) on the other hand provides the capability to integrate, coordinate and

© Springer International Publishing Switzerland 2015
I. Ciuciu et al. (Eds.): OTM 2015 Workshops, LNCS 9416, pp. 371–380, 2015.
DOI: 10.1007/978-3-319-26138-6_40

manage the different phases of software engineering discipline that are related from the initial planning phase of the software product throughout its retirement [2]. In addition, Application Lifecycle Management (ALM) supports an agile environment that allows development teams to adapt agile practices to best fit to their needs, mitigate barriers and risks that could impede the teams progress. According to David Chappell [3], ALM is a business process, which includes the set of activities required to create and run custom applications. He emphasises that "any organization that creates custom software should take the ALM process at least as seriously as it does any other important business process". It is also described as a continuous process of managing the life of an application through platforms that provide a project workspace with an integrated tool set, encompassing all software development activities, such as requirements management, design, coding, testing, and release management [4] [5].

In contrast to the traditional approach of software development, where the initiation of the subsequent activity relies on the completion of the preceding, the performance of the agile approach relies heavily on a tool support, which plays a fundamental role in smoothly running and efficiently managing product development environment [6]. According to Doyle [7], ALM is a set of tools, processes and practices. Therefore, it can be argued that one of the paramount goals of agile ALM is to facilitate integrated tool-sets to support project lifecycle.

Multiple tools have the potential to improve the productivity in the development process, depending on how well they are integrated with each other and their degree of automation. It is important to mention here that the term "integration" refers to the relationship of a tool with other elements in the environment, chiefly other tools, a platform and process [8]. Moreover, tool chains can provide different coverage of the development process and it is widely believed that integrating the tools into an automated tool chain can improve the productivity of development [9]. However, in agile development environment, applying a tool chain can impose great hardship on a software development team, so as to ensure that an arrangement of tools qualify the established development culture, processes and standards. In practice, tools do not interoperate well, which is a common challenge faced by many development teams while exchanging or passing data from one stage of software development to its succeeding in order to facilitate continuous process flow between the activities of development lifecycle.

The importance of this problem derives from the fact when the development teams are not clear on the concept of tools chains, because the lack of knowledge on how to create a fundamental model against which a set of tools can be arranged in chain setup. Thereby, allowing the tasks of the entire agile application development process to be performed more or less in a sequence, that is, from a development activity to the next with minimal manual intervention. Therefore this investigation aims to address this challenge, by providing understanding on the establishment of a fundamental sets of a tools in a chain along with some exemplar tool chain models based on different development platforms, which can be used as a reference model.

The remainder of the paper is structured as follows: In Section 2, the main activities of the ALM process are highlighted and the approach to be undertaken to align software tools along with the activities of the ALM process. In Section 3, we present tabulated data gathered as a result of our limited survey on the availability of software tools from different development platforms, for the different phases of application development. Furthermore, exemplary tool chain models based on different development and technological background are presented to demonstrate the actual implementation of tool chain concepts in a variety of development platforms. Section 4, emphasises on the transparency in software tool chain environment. Section 5 contains a limited discussion and a brief conclusion is provided in Section 6.

2 Approach

2.1 ALM Activities

It is a common misconception to equate ALM with the Software Development Lifecycle (SDLC), where the focus is mainly on application development [3]. In fact, (SDLC) is mainly comprised of application development phases, such as requirement gathering, design, coding etc [2]. On the other hand, ALM is about managing the entire application development lifecycle, that is, from the initial idea to its retirement and everything in between. Figure 1 shows all the main activities involved in ALM, where the existence of version control and change and configuration management plays the key roles.

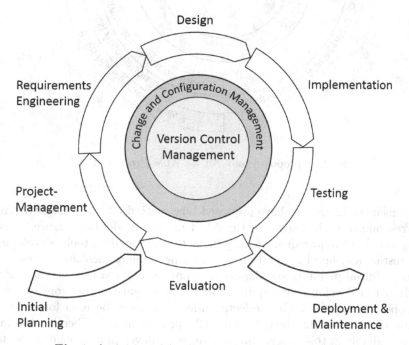

Fig. 1. Activities of Application Lifecycle Management.

2.2   Aligning Tools with ALM Process Model

To establish a streamline tool chain for an agile ALM platform, we need firstly
to identify all of its primary activities. For this purpose, this study aims to
demonstrate a possible combination of tool sets that can align with each activity
of ALM process model as shown in Figure 1. There is no single correct way to
break each activity of ALM process model into sub, as they can vary significantly
based on many factors such as the project requirements, development platform,
and development techniques.

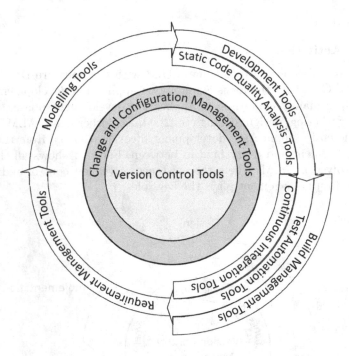

Fig. 2. A proposed tools set for ALM Process Model.

In this investigation we have proposed how specialised tools can be arranged
to correspond to each activity of the ALM process model (see Figure 2), comprising mainly of requirement management tools, modelling tools, development
tools, testing and build integration tools, change management and version control tools. Initial planning and deployment are not covered here, as these stages
of Agile ALM development required further investigation, therefore are out of
the scope of this paper. This collected information can be used for creating a
skeleton of a tool chain aligned with ALM process model. Thereby, the information available in this process model can assist development teams to identify
the proper tools and their arrangement with respect to it corresponding activity. Although, in addition to this, to establish an automated tool chain much

more information would be required, such as the relationship between the data of different tools, its access and flow. However, this process model merely serves as a exemplary structure against which software tools can be aligned.

2.3   Tool Selection

The selection of distinct software development tools is one of the most challenging task in software tool-chain development environment. The criteria on the selection of the tools that can perform specific tasks in an automated software tool-chain environment can vary depending on the technicalities and the requirements of the development platform. Nevertheless, the criteria that have focused on the selected tools for this survey includes: (i) *Purpose*: to serve the purpose, specialised to perform a specific task based on particular conditions; (ii) *Vendor qualification*: market share, maturity of the vendor and the tool; (iii) *Vendor support*: technical assistance, software updates, emergency maintenance, user training and other support services; (iv) *Integration support*: ensures coherent development, that is, capability of weaving together with other tools; (v) *Tool configuration*: To configure the setting for a tool to best perform particular activity in development process; (vi) *Community support*: on-line community support like discussion forums, wikis, podcast etc.; (vii) *Licensing cost*: Cost effectiveness based on variety of influencing factors such as selection of Open Source Software (OSS) or propriety software, maintenance cost, and training cost. In addition, we suggest there can be a number of additional factors such as the business decisions and goals, product requirements and scope and the underlying development lifecycle model.

3   Survey on Tool-Support

A short survey has been conducted by taking into account the selection criteria mentioned in section 2.3 on those tools which can enhance the performance of Agile ALM, as being part of a set of loosely coupled tools realising the integrated solution in strengthening the concept of tool-chain environment. This survey is by no means comprehensive and the main goal of our brief survey was mainly to address the possibilities on the use of a variety of tools in setting up a tool chain support for entire application development lifecycle. Therefore, we have taken a general view on those available software tools or technologies that can carry out distinct tasks on the activities of agile ALM process, which includes: (i) Task or requirement management tools; (ii) Design management tools; (iii) Development tools; (iv) Static code quality analysis tools; (v) Test automation tools; (vi) Build management tools; (vii) Continuous Integration servers (viii) Version Control management systems; (ix) and Change and Configuration Management tools.

3.1   Survey Findings

To demonstrate this survey findings, we have randomly selected a few snippets on the tabulated information, shown in Figure 3. The information provided on these tables has not been prioritised or ranked. The information gathered in these tables is presented by a number of table columns such as the tool provider, language support, versions etc. The information on the tables can vary, subject to the knowledge and experience of the tool selection team. However the information that we have set mandatory is to identify firstly the software tool specialised to perform a specific software development task and its provider. In our survey finding, we have found that the count and the diversity of the available tools can vary depending on the chosen development platform and project's requirements.

ToolName	Provider	Languages S
Checkstyle	Open Source Comm	Java
FindBugs	Open Source Comm	Java
PMD	Open Source Comm	Java
FXCop	Microsoft	.NET
SonarQube	SonarSource SA	Java
JSHint	Open Source Comm	JavaScript
Jtest	Parasoft	Java
dotTest	Parasoft	.NET
sotoarc	hello2morrow	Java/.NET
Squore	Squoring Technolog	Java/.NET
CodeIt.Right	SubMain	.NET

(a) Code Quality Tools

ToolName	Provider	Languages Supp
Maven	Apache Software Fou	Java
Ant	Apache Software Fou	Java
Gradle	Gradleware inc.	Java/Groovy
MSBuild	Microsoft	cross-language
Nant	Open Source Commu	.NET
sbt	Typesafe Inc.	Java/Scala
Buildr	Apache Software Fou	Java/Scala/Groc
FinalBuilder	Vsoft	cross-language
tweaker	Open Source Commu	cross-language
Jam	Perforce	cross-language
Sbuild	Open Source Commu	Scala/Java
sCons	Open Source Commu	cross-language

(b) Build Automation Software Tools

ToolName	Provider	Languages S
Junit	Open Source Com	Java
TestNG	Open Source Com	Java
Selenium	Open Source Com	Web
DBUnit	Open Source Com	Java
NUnit	Open Source Com	.NET
Unit Testing Fram	Microsoft	.NET
arquillian	Red Hat inc.	Java
Cactus	Apache Software I	Java
Abbot	Timothy Wall	Java
JUnitPerf	Clarkware Consult	Java
Jameleon	Christian Hargrave	cross-langu:

(c) Test Automation Tools

ToolName	Provider
Jenkins/Hudson	Open Source Communit
Bamboo	Atlassian
CruiseControl	Thoughtworks/Open So
CruiseControl.NET	Thoughtworks/Open So
Team Foundation Ser	Microsoft
TeamCity	Jetbrain
AnthillPro	IBM
Continuum	Apache Software Found
Gump	Apache Software Found
Buildbot	Open Source Communit
BuildForge	IBM

(d) Continuous Integration Servers

Fig. 3. A snippet of information on the list of Software Tools

3.2   Exemplar Models

In this section, exemplar models (see Figure 4) on software development toolchain are provided in accordance with the process model shown in Figure 2. These models are intended as reference models for creating a software development tool chain on different development platforms. Also, in these exemplar models, non-available (N/A) is indicated where we have not found the tool that fulfils our selection criteria. The first and second tool-chain models as shown in Figures 4a and 4b respectively are for a Java development platform, however, the first model provides information on the use of commercial software tools and the second on the use of OSS. To provide further reference on how software tools can be integrated to support ALM in different development environments, two additional models are presented in Figures 4c and 4d for .NET and JavaScript platform. The purpose of these models is merely to demonstrate how software tools can be integrated together, supporting the tool-chain concept within application development environments.

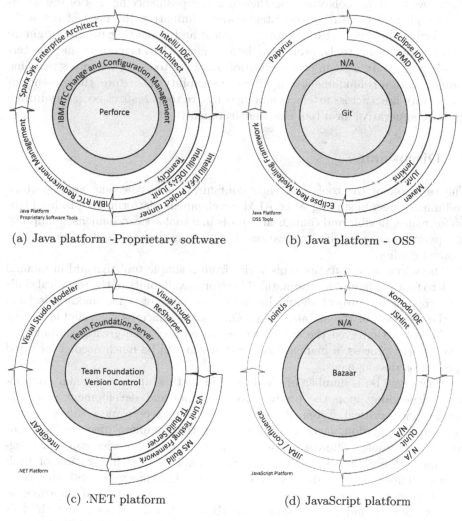

(a) Java platform -Proprietary software   (b) Java platform - OSS

(c) .NET platform   (d) JavaScript platform

Fig. 4. Exemplar tool-chain models for Agile ALM process model

4   Transparency In A Collaborative Tool Chain

To correctly operate the artefacts produced or used in the ALM lifecycle, their linkage to the corresponding requirements is essential to ensure that application meets specification [1]. Therefore, one of the measures of effectiveness on a tool chain is its ability to support requirements tracing in the development process of agile ALM. Traceability ensures the relevance and effectiveness of tools applied for each phase of software development life cycle, hence it is regarded as a key concern in building a tool chain.

However, traceability is an enormous challenge in a collaborative tool chain environment [10] [11]. The term collaboration here can be defined as an activity where two or more tools work together to accomplish specific task of the development phase, by ensuring consistency and eliminating the need of manually transferring the data between tools. Technical and semantic gaps can originate from heterogeneous tools, protocols, data formats, data structures and the terminology that are used in communication between tools [12], where streamline communication is fundamental to adhere traceability. Therefore, the presence of traceability links across artefacts among software tools realizes necessary infrastructure imperative for a tool chain environment.

5   Discussion

The selection of the tools and their configuration has become an important preliminary task in staging Agile ALM development platform. By placing high-performance, flexible and configurable tools in a tool-set can immensely improve the performance of agile application development process and ensure higher product quality.

The selection of software tools varies from a simple tool that aid in manual work to fully configurable automatic. Therefore, availability of the technical skills and scope of the project should be taken into account while making decision on the selection of the suitable tools. One of the concerns that should not be overlooked is that even the automatic advanced tools can greatly simplify the development process, a manual intervention can still be much needed for rapid application development.

There can be a number of challenges in setting up a tool chain environment depending upon the product requirements and development platform. For instance, critical system development, which have to meet safety restrictions and regulation, lacks tool-support for the complete lifecycle [13]. The complexity among different phases of the development cycles can cause significant technical hurdles and it has been realised that integration of tools is not uniform across the all activities of ALM lifecycle, and the manual effort may considerable vary. For example, in our practical implementation we have found that coalitions of IBM Rational Team Concert (RTC)'s Change and Configuration Management (CCM) tool and IBM RTC's Requirement Management (RM) tool, corresponding to requirement management and change and configuration management activities respectively, have taken a minimal manual involvement as compared to setting up IBM RTC CCM tool to work with IntelliJ IDEA corresponding implementation activity. One of the challenges in adopting tool chain environment is dealing with different standards and heterogeneous data models for information exchange and how they can be best reconciled [13]. Furthermore, the adoption of tool chain on different technical platform is an ongoing challenge. The study was not intended to be comprehensive, neither in terms of covering all the topics in setting tool chain in Agile ALM environment nor in terms of covering all the literature needed information on particular aspects. Rather, this study focused on a few aspects relevant to the establishment of software tool chain; thereby attempting to guide the use of the tool chain ALM process model. In addition, in this study the concern is limited within software tools that support the application development lifecycle process and their integration.

6   Conclusion

The proper selection of the suitable tools on setting a tool-chain have shown unquestioned effective interoperability among tools with different standards and data formats, thus providing reliable high-performance alternative to tradition development activities. In this paper, we have investigated the actual implementation aspect of task specific software tools integration with in agile ALM lifecycle environment. We demonstrate how we can set up tool chains on various development environments based on our approach. In conclusion, tool integration in agile ALM environment remains a live research topic. We have based our fundamental approach upon our observation and a limited survey. This study aims to pave the way for more efficient ways towards the establishments and usage of software development tools.

Acknowledgments. This work is supported by the Ministry of Science, Research and Arts of Baden-Württemberg, Germany, within the program "Willkommen in der Wissenschaft" as part of the "Innovations- und Qualitätsfonds (IQF)".

References

1. Hüttermann, M.: Agile ALM. Manning (2011)
2. Rossberg, J.: Beginning Application Lifecycle Management. Apress (2014)
3. Chappell, D.: Application Lifecycle Management as business process, Whitepaper (2008)
4. Fabio, C. Lanubile, F., Sportelli, F.: Can social awareness foster trust building in global software teams? In: Proceedings of the 2013 International Workshop on Social Software Engineering, pp. 13–16. ACM (2013)
5. Fabio, C., Lanubile, F., Ebert, C.: Practice: Collaborative Development Environments. Global Software and IT: A Guide to Distributed Development, Projects, and Outsourcing, pp. 109–123 (2011)

6. Kriinen, J., Vlimki, A.: Impact of application lifecycle management - a case study. In: Enterprise Interoperability III, pp. 55–67. Springer, London (2008)
7. Doyle, C.: The importance of ALM for aerospace and defence (A& D). Embedded System Engineering (ESE magazine) 15(5), 28–29 (2007)
8. Thomas, I., Brian, A.N.: Definitions of tool integration for environments. Software, IEEE 9(2), 29–35 (1992)
9. Biehl, M., Trngren M.: constructing tool chains based on SPEM process models. In: ICSEA 2012, The Seventh International Conference on Software Engineering Advances, pp. 267–273 (2012)
10. Heinonen, S., Kriinen, J., Takalo, J.: Challenges in collaboration: tool chain enables transparency beyond partner borders. Enterprise Interoperability II, pp. 529–540. Springer London (2007)
11. Pesola, J.-P., et al.: Experiences of tool integration: development and validation. Enterprise Interoperability III, pp. 499–510. Springer London (2008)
12. Sunindyo, W. D. et al.: Foundations for event-based process analysis in heterogeneous software engineering environments. In: EUROMICRO-SEAA (2010)
13. Saratxaga, C.L., Alonso-Montes, C., Haugen, O., Cecilia, E., Mitschke, A.: Product line tool-chain: variability in critical systems. In: Proceedings of the Third International Workshop on Product LinE Approaches in Software Engineering, pp. 57–60. IEEE Press (2012)

Scale Up Internet-Based Business Through Distributed Data Centers

Liguo Yu[1(✉)], Alok Mishra[2], and Deepti Mishra[3,4]

[1] Computer Science and Informatics, Indiana University South Bend, South Bend, IN, USA
ligyu@iusb.edu
[2] Department of Software Engineering, Atilim University, Incek, Ankara, Turkey
alok.mishra@atilim.edu.tr
[3] School of IT, Monash University, Subang Jaya, Malaysia
deepti.mishra@monash.edu
[4] Department of Computer Engineering, Atilim University, Incek, Ankara, Turkey
deepti.mishra@atilim.edu.tr

Abstract. Distributed data centers are becoming more and more important for internet-based companies. Without distributed data centers, it will be hard for internet companies to scale up their business. The traditional centralized data center suffers the drawback of bottle neck and single failure problem. Therefore, more and more internet companies are building distributed data centers, and more and more business are moved onto distributed Web services. This paper reviews the history of distributed Web services and studies their current status through examining the distributed data centers of several top Internet companies. Based on the study, we conclude that distributed services, including distributed data centers, are the key factors to scale up the business of a company, especially, an internet-based company.

Keywords: Web service · Distributed Web service · Data centers · Distributed data centers · Cloud computing

1   Introduction

Distributed Web services are becoming a new trend for internet-based business. Companies are considered not aggressive enough if their business is supported by a centralized web service. To improve the service performance, reduce the service cost, secure the data and transactions, and to increase their customer base, more and more companies choose to use distributed Web services, which highly depend on distributed data centers. Therefore, more and more internet-based companies are providing distributed web services through building distributed data centers.

According to Wikipedia [1], Web service is "*a method of communication between two electronic devices over a network. It is a software function provided at a network address over the Web with the service always on as in the concept of utility computing.*" In this paper, we define Web service as a computing service provided remotely by a server over the internet. The service could be in many formats, such as web hosting service, data hosting service, data processing service, or any other specific application service [2].

© Springer International Publishing Switzerland 2015
I. Ciuciu et al. (Eds.): OTM 2015 Workshops, LNCS 9416, pp. 381–390, 2015.
DOI: 10.1007/978-3-319-26138-6_41

Traditionally, web service is centralized or near centralized, which means the service provider has only one or a few servers in adjacent locations. With the increasing demand of business requirement, distributed Web services is becoming a new trend [3]. In the past decade, more and more distributed data centers have been built to support distributed Web services.

In this paper, we review the history and features of distributed Web services. We discuss their benefits and explain why all types of business are aggressively moving their services to distributed Web services. Specifically, we find that for companies to scale up their business they will need to adopt distributed Web services. Using the growth of distributed data centers as an example, we illustrate the direction of the latest and future expansion of internet-based companies.

The remaining of this paper is organized as follows. In Section 2, we briefly review the history of distributed Web services. In Section 3, we describe the features of distributed Web service and its impact on future business models. In Section 4, we analyze distributed data centers of major internet-based companies. Our conclusions are in Section 5.

2   History of Distributed Web Services

Web services evolves from RPC (Remote Procedure Call) [4]. This kind of system has a client/server architecture, where the client sends a request to the server and the server should reply with a result. The first generation of this kind of service allows primitive data to be sent in request and result. Later, distributed object architecture emerged, where both user request and server result could be encapsulated as an object (data structure). Clearly, distributed object architecture is superior to RPC architecture.

However, distributed object architecture suffers the drawback of platform-dependent and language-dependent issue, which means the server and the client must have the same platform and use the same programming language. To solve this problem, the concept of Web services is introduced, where an intermediate data format (such as XML) is proposed. Accordingly (and officially) Web service means the server and the client could be on different platforms and using different languages. This kind of client-friendly services definitely attracted many customers.

If the Web service is deployed in a single server, we call it centralized Web service, even though the clients could be distributed around the globe. Centralized Web service, just like a simple client/server architecture, suffers two drawbacks. First drawback is the bottleneck of the service. Any computing server has a limit on processing power and storage capacity. If the service providers would like to expand their business, they certainly need to deploy more servers. Second drawback is the critical role played by the server. A single point failure either in the network or in the server could result in the meltdown of the entire service. Therefore, a single location service is vulnerable to both malicious attacks and to natural incidents. Figure 1 shows an example of a single location Web service, where the server is located in Europe and the clients could be anywhere in the globe. Figure 2 shows an example of a distributed Web service, where three data centers (servers) are located in North America, Europe, and Asia.

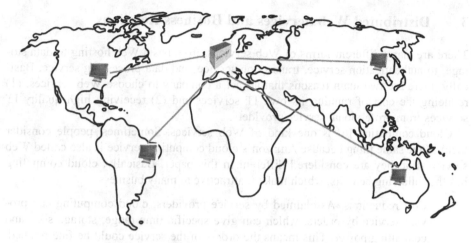

Fig. 1. An example of single location Web service

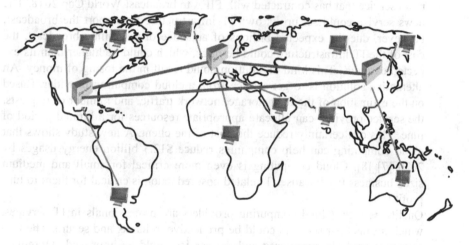

Fig. 2. An example of distributed Web service

Due to the shortcomings of centralized Web services, as described before, distributed web services become the new trend in IT service industry. It is worth noting that in distributed Web service, a client does not need to permanently bind to a specific data center (server). The bindings could be dynamic, which means the servers could be selected based on their locations, current network traffic conditions, and the availability of the data centers. Therefore, distributed Web services solves the two problems of the traditional centralized Web service: bottleneck problem and single point failure problem.

3　Distributed Web Services and Business Relations

There are many different forms of Web services, from basic Web hosting to data storage, to authentication service, transaction service, and data processing service. Basically, there are two main reasons that attract a company to choose Web services: (1) reducing the cost of running its own IT services and (2) receiving high quality IT services from professional service providers.

Cloud computing [6] is one kind of Web services. Sometimes, people consider them as the same thing because Amazon's cloud computing service is also called Web service. But they are considered different in this paper. Basically, cloud computing has the following benefits, which make it attractive to many business.

1. Cost reductions. As claimed by service providers, cloud computing can provide service by orders, which can give specific time range, storage size, and computing power. This means the orders of the service could be fine grained. This could also be interpreted as "buy what you need". Consider an online news service that has contracted with FIFA to broadcast World Cup 2018. The news service could set up its own IT infrastructure to support the broadcast. However, due the expected billions of audience of the online broadcast, the cost of the IT infrastructure could be huge, which could be higher than its expected earnings. This kind of solution could result in the losing of money. An alternative solution is to get service from a cloud computing provider. Based on the estimation of the data storage, network traffic, and number of requests, the service provider can allocate appropriate resources for a limited period of time. This can certainly reduce the cost of the client. A new study shows that cloud computing can help companies reduce $12.3 billion energy usages by 2020 [7] [8]. Cloud computing is even more critical for small and medium sized business [9], because IT related cost reduction is critical for them to turn profit [10].

2. Quality service. Cloud computing providers are professionals in IT services, which means their services could be productive, reliable, and secure. The performance could be monitored and the service could be improved. Moreover, the service is flexible and scalable, which means clients could update their requests based on their business needs [11] [12] [13] [14] [15] [16]. Consider a local healthcare provider. In order for patients to make online payment, the healthcare provider could implement its own online payment system. However, there is a big security risk for this kind of system. A better solution is to contract a third party online payment service, which can provide professional and secure online payment service.

As described before, more and more business are outsourcing their IT service to a third party, and more likely, a Web service. A new trend of the Web service is cloud computing, which is characterized by its distributed services and distributed data centers. Table 1 shows the cloud strategy of large companies with 1000 or more employees (data source: rightscale.com [18] [19]). The data is obtained through surveys of 2014 and 2015.

Table 1. Cloud strategy of large companies [18] [19]

Strategy	Percentage (2014)	Percentage (2015)
Multi-cloud	74%	82%
Single public	13%	10%
Single private	9%	5%
No plan	4%	3%

Although the data in Table 1 is obtained from large companies, we can see a general trend. More companies are choosing cloud services (near 97% for large companies in 2015) and more companies are using multi-cloud services, which means those companies are outsourcing multiple services to cloud providers [20]. Another trend is the reducing use of private cloud and the increasing use of public cloud. Private cloud is a cloud service dedicated to a specific client and public cloud is a cloud service that can be subscribed by any clients. Both public cloud and private cloud have their own benefits [21]. Table 2 shows the most popular public cloud providers and private cloud providers of 2015 [19].

Table 2. Popular cloud providers of 2015 [19]

Public	Private
AWS (Amazon)	VMware vSphere/vCenter
Azure Iaas	VMware vCloud Suite (vCD)
Rackspace Public Cloud	OpenStack
Azure Paas	Microsoft System Center
Google App Engine	Citrix CloudStack
Google Iaas	Microsoft Azure Pack
VMware vCloud Air	
IBM SoftLayer	
HP Helion Public Cloud	

4   Growth of Distributed Data Centers

In this section, we present the evolution and current status of distributed data centers, which are the key infrastructure supporting distributed Web service.

4.1   Google

Google is world's Number 1 search engine, Number 1 most visited web site [22], and Number 4 public corporation by market capitalization [23]. Search requests to Google come from anywhere in the globe. Therefore, it is important for Google to maintain its data centers distributed around the world. Table 3 shows the information of Google data centers. The data is retrieved from [24]. Figure 3 shows the distribution of Google data centers around the world (Map is created using data from [24]).

Table 3. Google data centers [24]

Data Center	Set up year	Location	Continent
Douglas County	2003	Georgia, USA	North America
The Dalles	2006	Oregon, USA	North America
Council Bluffs	2007	Iowa, USA	North America
St. Ghislain	2007	Belgium	Europe
Berkeley County	2007	South Carolina, USA	North America
Mayes County	2007	Oklahoma, USA	North America
Lenoir	2007	North Carolina, USA	North America
Hamina	2009	Finland	Europe
Changhua County	2011	Taiwan	Asia
Singapore	2011	Singapore	Asia
Dublin	2011	Ireland	Europe
Quilicura	2012	Chile	South America
Jackson County	2015	Alabama, USA	North America
Eemshaven	2016 (expected)	Netherlands	Europe

Fig. 3. The distribution of Google data centers

4.2   Facebook

Facebook is world's Number 1 social media platform, Number 2 most visited web site [22], and Number 17 public corporation by market capitalization [25]. As of the first quarter of 2015, Facebook had 1.44 billion monthly active users [26]. To provide service for these users on a 24/7 base, Facebook also has its data centers around the world. Table 4 shows the information of Facebook data centers. The data is retrieved from [27] [28] [29]. Figure 4 shows the distribution of Facebook data centers around the world. With its growing number of users in Asia, Facebook is exploring the possibilities of building a data center in Asia [30].

Table 4. Facebook data centers [27] [28] [29]

Data Center	Set up year	Location	Continent
Prineville,	2010	Oregon, USA	North America
Forest City	2010	North Carolina, USA	North America
Lulea	2013	Sweden	Europe
Altoona	2014	Iowa, USA	North America
Fort Worth	2015	Texas	North America

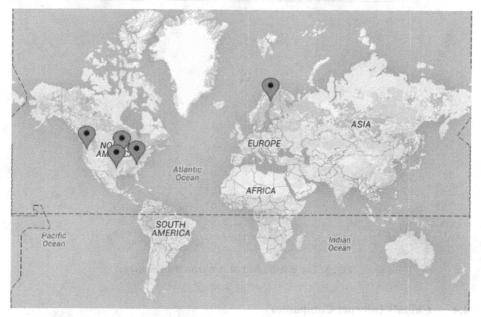

Fig. 4. The distribution of Facebook data centers

4.3   Amazon

Amazon is world's Number 2 E-commerce website, Number 6 most visited web site [22], and Number 34 public corporation by market capitalization [25]. Most importantly, Amazon Web Services (AWS) is the Number 1 public cloud service provider. Its 10 data centers are illustrated in Table 5 and Figure 5 (data is retrieved from [31]). The interesting fact about Amazon is that when this paper is being written, more data centers are being planned, including one in Ohio [32].

Table 5. Amazon data centers [31]

Data Center	Set up year	Location	Continent
US East	2006	Ashburn, Virginia	North America
EU	2007	Dublin, Ireland	Europe
US West	2009	Silicon Valley, California	North America
Asia Pacific	2010	Singapore, Singapore	Asia

Table 5. *(Continued)*

South America	2011	São Paulo, Brazil	South America
US West	2011	Boardman, Oregon	North America
Asia Pacific	2011	Tokyo, Japan	Asia
Asia Pacific	2012	Sydney, Australia	Pacific
China	2013	Beijing, China	Asia
EU	2014	Frankfurt, Germany	Europe

Fig. 5. The distribution of Amazon data centers

4.4   China's Internet Companies

China is world's Number 2 economy. It also has world's Number 1 internet users [33]. For the top 10 internet companies, 3 are in China [34]. They are Alibaba (Number 2), Tencent (Number 5), and Baidu (Number 6). To serve the increasing number of customers of China and around the world, more and more data centers are being built by China's Internet companies. Table 6 shows the current and planned data centers of BAT (Baidu, Alibaba, and Tencent). It should be noted here that data in Table 6 is retrieved from various web sites and might not be complete. When this paper is being written, more and more data centers are being planned by BAT. For example, Alibaba is planning to build more data centers in North America, Europe, Singapore, and Japan [35].

Table 6. BAT (Baidu, Alibaba, and Tencent) data centers

Name	Owner	Location	Continent
Baidu cloud	Baidu	Yangquan, Shanxi, China	Asia
Baidu cloud	Baidu	Beijing, China	Asia
Aliyun	Alibaba	Beijing, China	Asia

Table 6. (*Continued*)

Aliyun	Alibaba	Hongkong, China	Asia
Aliyun	Alibaba	Shenyang, China	Asia
Aliyun	Alibaba	Silicon Valley, California	North America
Aliyun	Alibaba	Dubai, United Arab Emirates	Middle East
Q-cloud	Tencent	Shenzhen, China	Asia
Q-cloud	Tencent	Toronto, Canada	North America
Q-cloud	Tencent	Tianjin, China	Asia
Q-cloud	Tencent	Chongqing, China	Asia
Q-cloud	Tencent	Shanghai, China	Asia

4.5   Discussions

Based on the data presented in this section, we can see that the number of distributed data centers is increasing dramatically in the past decade. Distributed data centers will become the backbone to support distributed Web services. Intel estimates that by 2020, about 85% of the IT applications will be run on cloud [35]. Therefore, we believe distributed Web service supported by distributed data centers will play a significant role in shaping the business structure of the 21st century.

5   Conclusions

In this paper, we studied the history and property of Web services. We found distributed Web services are becoming a new trend in IT industry. Using distributed data centers as an example, we showed that large internet-based companies are expanding aggressively of their Web service (cloud computing) in order to provide more reliable, flexible, and affordable IT services to other companies.

References

1. Web service. https://en.wikipedia.org/wiki/Web_service
2. https://en.wikipedia.org/wiki/List_of_web_service_specifications/
3. Skoutas, D.N., Sacharidis, D., Kantere, V., Sellis, T.K.: Efficient semantic web service discovery in centralized and P2P environments. In: Sheth, A.P., Staab, S., Dean, M., Paolucci, M., Maynard, D., Finin, T., Thirunarayan, K. (eds.) ISWC 2008. LNCS, vol. 5318, pp. 583–598. Springer, Heidelberg (2008)
4. https://www.safaribooksonline.com/library/view/java-web-services/9781449373856/ch01s04.html
5. http://www.tutorialspoint.com/webservices/web_services_examples.htm
6. Cloud computing. https://en.wikipedia.org/wiki/Cloud_computing
7. https://www.cdp.net/en-US/WhatWeDo/CDPNewsArticlePages/cloud-computing-can-dramatically-reduce-energy-costs-and-carbon-emissions.aspx
8. http://www.att.com/gen/press-room?pid=20398

9. http://blogs.technet.com/b/smallbusiness/archive/2013/04/29/blog-how-can-cloud-computing-reduce-business-costs.aspx
10. http://www.computerworld.com/article/2899668/the-obvious-way-to-greatly-reduce-cloud-computing-costs.html
11. He, Q., Han, J., Yang, Y., Jin, H., Schneider, J.G., Versteeg, S.: Formulating Cost-Effective Monitoring Strategies for Service-Based Systems. IEEE Transactions on Software Engineering **40**(5), 461–482 (2014)
12. Katsaros, G., Kousiouris, G., Gogouvitis, S.V., et al.: A Self-adaptive hierarchical monitoring mechanism for Clouds. Journal of Systems and Software **85**(5), 1029–1041 (2012)
13. Mao, M., Humphrey, M.: A performance study on the VM startup time in the cloud. In: The 5th International Conference on Cloud Computing, pp. 423–430. IEEE (2012)
14. Bruneo, D., Distefano, S., Longo, F., Puliafito, A., Scarpa, M.: Workload-based software rejuvenation in cloud systems. IEEE Transactions on Computers **62**, 1072–1085 (2013)
15. Herbst, N.R., Kounev, S., Reussner, R.: Elasticity in cloud computing: what it is, and what it is not. In: ICAC, pp. 23–27, June 2013
16. Islam, S., Lee, K., Fekete, A., Liu, A.: How a consumer can measure elasticity for cloud platforms. In: The 3rd International Conference on Performance Engineering (2012)
17. Distributed cloud. http://www.virtualizationpractice.com/distributed-cloud-31984/
18. http://www.rightscale.com/blog/cloud-industry-insights/cloud-computing-trends-2014-state-cloud-survey
19. http://www.rightscale.com/blog/cloud-industry-insights/cloud-computing-trends-2015-state-cloud-survey
20. Multi-cloud. https://cn.wikipedia.org/wiki/Multicloud
21. http://www.onlinetech.com/resources/references/public-vs-private-cloud-computing
22. Alexa. http://www.alexa.com/topsites
23. https://en.wikipedia.org/wiki/List_of_public_corporations_by_market_capitalization
24. Google data centers. http://www.google.com/about/datacenters/inside/locations/index.html
25. http://www.pwc.com/gx/en/audit-services/capital-market/publications/assets/document/pwc-global-top-100-march-update.pdf
26. http://www.statista.com/statistics/264810/number-of-monthly-active-facebook-users-worldwide/
27. http://www.zdnet.com/pictures/facebooks-data-centers-worldwide-by-the-numbers-and-in-pictures/
28. http://www.datacenterknowledge.com/the-facebook-data-center-faq/
29. http://techcrunch.com/2015/07/07/facebook-announces-fifth-data-center-located-in-fort-worth-texas/
30. http://www.datacenterdynamics.com/news/report-facebook-scouting-asia-data-center-locations/84450.fullarticle
31. http://aws.amazon.com/about-aws/global-infrastructure/
32. http://www.dispatch.com/content/stories/business/2015/05/29/amazon-has-big-plans-in-ohio.html
33. http://www.cnn.com/2015/02/03/world/china-internet-growth-2014/
34. http://www.investopedia.com/articles/personal-finance/030415/worlds-top-10-internet-companies.asp
35. http://www.datacenterknowledge.com/archives/2015/07/23/report-second-alibaba-cloud-data-center-coming-to-us/

Distributed Architecture for Supporting Collaboration

Claude Moulin[1,2](✉), Kenji Sugawara[3], Yuki Kaeri[3], and Marie-Hélène Abel[1,2]

[1] Heudiasyc JR Unit - CNRS 7253, Sorbonne Universités, Compiègne Cedex, France
{claude.moulin,marie-helene.abel}@utc.fr
[2] Centre de Recherche de Royallieu, Université de Technologie de Compiègne,
60205 Compiègne Cedex, France
[3] Faculty of Information and Network Science,
Chiba Institute of Technology,
Chiba, Japan
suga@net.it-chiba.ac.jp, interlude.y@gmail.com

Abstract. The research concerned by this paper is the design and implementation of a distributed digital system supporting participants during co-located collaborative sessions. In many companies, traditional methods are still used. The challenge is to propose a computer supported solution for helping the capitalization of knowledge without impacting the efficiency of such meetings. The paper presents the architecture of a distributed system involving different types of devices for main support a large multi-touch screen. The distributed architecture relies on a multi-agent system whose agents listen events from the applications and exchange messages for performing the functionalities of the system like synchronization and persistence. The technology used for the development of the applications and the agents is also detailed. The last section of the paper introduces experiments that have been achieved thanks to this system.

Keywords: Collaborative activity · Distributed system · Multi-touch device · Synchronous collaboration

1 Introduction

At the very beginning of a project, when teams have to design a new product or define new concepts, they collaborate during several meetings. Main ideas, issues and solutions emerge from discussions between participants. The results of these deep thoughts have to be capitalized and concluding reports must be made. Activities are usually conducted in traditional meeting rooms using pens and paper. Results are written on post-it notes stuck on large surfaces (walls or tables) and then significant efforts are necessary to transcribe hand written notes into a digitally exploitable format.

Previous attempts of computer-supported solutions for helping people in such conditions did not encounter a huge success, mainly because they introduced

I. Ciuciu et al. (Eds.): OTM 2015 Workshops, LNCS 9416, pp. 391–400, 2015.
DOI: 10.1007/978-3-319-26138-6_42

additional instruments that prevent the natural collaboration between participants. Tools can help to collaborative activities, but very few tools are designed
for a group of users working together in the same room.

Trello [2] or Kanban system like the one presented in [1] are good examples of
mono-user collaborative tools. They present a board with different lists of cards.
Lists are designed to show some progress of task achievement (to do, doing and
done lists). Several people can managed separately the cards of the same project.
However, it is the only level of collaboration between people.

Our objective is to design and implement a distributed digital system that
can support participants during co-located team sessions. We call our system
MCB that stands for Multicultural Brainstorming System [9]. Distributed system development is becoming essential due to the necessity of applications
involving different devices and different sources of information. Management
of distributed software development has more challenges and difficulties than
conventional development. [7,6] reviewed some significant management issues
like process management, project management, requirements management and
knowledge management issues in distributed development perspective and show
that often only a scant attention is brought to these problems. When modeling
distributed systems, the true nature of user activities is very important to take
into account. [11] presents some patterns for software modeling. The design of
graphical multi-user interfaces is much more complicated to achieve than mono-
user interfaces. They should result in very dynamic interfaces [13].

We emphasize on the search and organization of ideas during brainstorming
sessions involving simultaneously two distant groups of participants. As traditional work uses a large surface, the main application of our system is intended
to be run on a large multi-touch surface. It allows several people to create cards
(we call them notes) and clusters of cards. Such notes can be directly added and
organized on the large touch screen device but they can be written first on a
tablet pc and then sent to the common display.

The objective of the paper is to present the architecture of our system. We
first describe the types of activities that can be conducted by people alone and
in groups during collaborative sessions (Section 2). Then, Section 3 presents
the different types of resources involving the suite of applications running on
interactive devices (table, whiteboard and tablet pc). In Section 4, we relate an
experiment that has been conducted both at the University of Compiègne (UTC,
France) and at the Chiba Institute of Technology (CIT, Japan).

2   Collaborative Activities

In this section we focus on collaborative activities and their tangible results in
the context of co-located meetings. Generally speaking, collaborative activities
are activities produced by one individual for the benefit of other people. For
example, people insert in a common repository a new document, annotate a
document [3] or a fragment of a document produced by others.

We call brainstorming sessions, the type of meetings where people can progressively agree on some definitions and take decisions. Discussions and argumentation may require the study of external resources. However, results achieved by teams have to be capitalized in some way [10]. We propose that these results take the form of notes (a shortcut for virtual post-it notes) grouped into clusters.

Brainstorming sessions are always sessions where the activities are synchronous. We call co-located brainstorming sessions, the meetings where participants are situated in the same room. At least one surface is designed to be the common support where all the participants can see the resulting notes. Notes can be created directly on this surface or can be created on other devices like tablet pc. However, a note interesting a group must always be visible on the common surface and should be transferred from individual devices.

Marc Weiser, the ubiquitous computing father, proposed twenty years ago that the user-interface paradigm after desktop computers would be tabs, pads, and boards [15]. Today, his prediction proved to be right for tablets, but also for board-size displays. Pieces of software should be designed for these surfaces not for one single user [4], but rather for a group of collocated users working together on one computing system. It is a mandatory condition for a better efficiency of these systems. Group dynamics are altered around interactive devices, engendering a better collaboration. Whiteboards may look like a presenter-audience style of interaction and can stifle collaboration [5], however tabletops have drawbacks regarding the creation of new elements.

We consider that people manipulating virtual notes displayed on a large interactive surface benefit of a good digital support for their activities [8] and bring real advantages (capitalization, reuse, interoperability with other applications, etc.). We claim that digital devices allowing data storing and enhancing the exchanges between participants are a necessary support for teams involved in brainstorming sessions [16,14]. Without this, two many efforts have to be deployed in order to register what have been written on different sheets of papers.

We call remote brainstorming sessions, those where several co-located teams (at least two) participate to the same brainstorming activities. Their actions must be supported by specific software applications [12]. For example, two instances of the same application run on peer systems located in two distant rooms. Teams involved in these sessions interact with the same type of graphical user interface communicating in real time and synchronized, i.e. all the actions on one common surface are reproduced on the common remote surface. A lock system must be installed to prevent concurrent actions on the same element already selected elsewhere. A graphical indication must be added during an action in order to make people understand that somebody else in the remote team has already selected an element.

3   Architecture

We have designed a scalable architecture that brings services for the type of system described in this paper but also for systems having different application

Fig. 1. MCB main module

domains. We use the same basic principles, have defined several formats and implemented reusable components for simplifying the communications between different entities. We define Resources the set of elements manipulated directly or indirectly by participants during collaborative sessions. This set involves three main categories: devices, applications and data. Each category is divided in several sub-categories. Figure 2 details the resources of one team. The other team benefits of the same ones.

Data are produced during sessions and appear concretely under the form of notes. However, it is very important that the conversations can be registered by video cameras. The video may then be consulted because some ideas may not be transcribed into notes during a meeting. Our system produces events for each main activity: creation of a note or a cluster, insertion of a note into a cluster, etc. The events allow to create annotations that are associated with the captured video.

3.1 Devices

We consider two main classes of devices: devices directly supporting users' activities and devices giving access to new modalities or bringing additional services to collaborative sessions.

The first class of devices support people during operations on data and generally people use their fingers for processing these operations. This class of devices involve touch screens and computers attached to these screens. Our system allows to use devices with large touch screens and simultaneously devices with small touch screens (in this case the computer and the screen are components of the same device). Large touch screens (board and tables) are more than sixty inches, allow several people to have interaction with the same application at the same time and support actual collaborative activities. Devices with small touch screens (tablet pcs) are less than twelve inches and are used by participants for complementary activities.

The second class concerns either devices allowing other modalities (microphones, loudspeakers) or devices allowing additional features (cameras, camcorders). For other application domains, this category also involves sensors.

3.2 Applications

Applications are divided into software applications and software entities. There are two subclasses of software applications as there are two classes of devices. The first class involves applications running on computers attached to devices with touch screens, large or small, and support users' interactions. These applications manage user interfaces and produce events that are received by agents. For simplification we call this class "applications". The second class concerns applications managing the second type of devices. We call this class "connectors". They allow for example Speech to text and Text to speech functionalities.

There are two main applications. The first one is the MCB main module running on devices with large touch screen (see Figure 1). It allows the following actions: create/delete notes, create/delete clusters, insert/remove note into/from a cluster, move, zoom, rotate an element, change color of an element, etc. The other application running on a tablet pc is only intended for creating notes more easily. Indeed, it is quite difficult and in some cases impossible, to write texts on a multi-touch surface. That requires the opening of an adapted virtual keyboard.

Software entities or agents insure transverse functionalities. Each application is supported by one or more agents, having their own role, belonging to the same

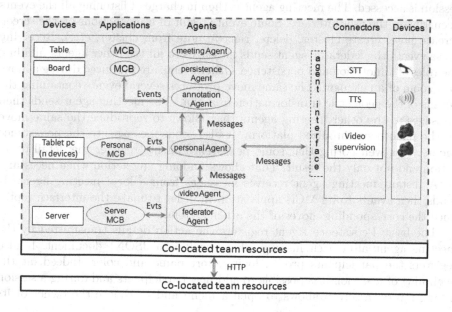

Fig. 2. Details of team resources

multi-agent system and running on the application computer. Agents communicate with other agents exchanging messages, listen events from applications and send events to applications when some data exchanged in the multi-agent system has to be displayed on the user interface. Figure 2 summarizes the resources of each team.

3.3   Agents

In the platform, each agent as a role and is registered in the platform as an agent fulfilling this role. Annotation, persistence are examples of roles. Two agents fulfilling the same role may have different behaviors. Generally a message is sent to all the agents fulfilling specific roles. The system is scalable because it is possible to add new roles without modifying existing behaviors or to add new agents fulfilling an existing role.

The Federator agent runs on the server and is in charge of the connections between platforms. It knows the IP addresses of the platforms it can access. Concretely, a first team has to launch the MCB main application; its platform federator agent is then aware of this event. When launching its MCB, a second team asks to reach an existing MCB and its federator agent looks for existing MCBs from its known IP addresses. It receives the name of the open session and proposes it to its meeting agent.

The Meeting Agent runs on the large screen device and is created as soon as the MCB application is launched. It proposes to open a local session or to reach an already open one. According to the mediator choice, a new, a local or a distant session is accessed. The meeting agent is then in charge of listening all the events occurring in the user interface. Some events result of users' actions on the screen (create note, create cluster, delete, remove note from cluster, etc.). Receiving these events the federator agent sends messages to all the other agents fulfilling the roles of annotation and persistence. Other events are produced during a move or a zoom of an element. The same move produces several events containing the details of the geometric transformation in action. The meeting agent sends then messages to the other meeting agents that allows to reproduce the same move on the remote synchronized platform. It also sends messages to the persistence agents. It is well noting that some persistence agents register the detail of an action and not only the result. That allows undoing any action when necessary.

A distant meeting agent receives messages from a local meeting agent. It sends then events to its MCB application in order to make the interface reproduce the corresponding moves of the other system.

The basic Persistence Agent registers the action details transmitted by the meeting agent after each message. The result is a JSON[1] document. It also registers the participants profile: login, short name and color. Indeed, at the beginning of a session it is possible to add new participants and during a session a long tap on a screen allows to open a menu and to choose the owner of its

---

[1] JSON (JavaScript Object Notation) is a lightweight data-interchange format (http://json.org/).

menu. Such a menu allows to create notes or clusters with default participant colors and to modify later element colors.

The Annotation Agent runs also on the MCB main device and has to produce annotations when it receives action messages from the meeting agent. The details of the actions are not useful for this agent. It is important to know that a note has been created but not the place on the screen where it has been created. Annotations are stored in a database with their occurrence timestamp. The objective is to attach these annotations with the video registering the meetings. We are developing a specific tool that displays the video with the possibility to reach directly the episode where an important event happened during a session.

It is not necessary to create a persistence agent and an annotation agent when a platform reaches another platform. As the meeting agent sends messages after receiving events to the other meeting agent, only one of these types of agents is enough to fulfill the corresponding role.

Each participant to a session may have install on a tablet pc (android or Windows) the MCB personal application creating then a Personal Agent. In this case a participant can write a note and the personal agent allows to send it to the meeting agent. The notes arrive in a hidden box producing only an alert in the MCB main application. They are added to the main display when the moderator of the session decides it. At this moment an event is produced as if the notes had been created directly on the MCB. A participant may also create a note using the speech to text connector. Personal agents have more roles but it is out of the scope of this paper to describe them.

Video supervision and video agents development are an ongoing progress that adds a new functionality to our system. Section 3.5 gives more details about it.

3.4 Technology

Our project started several years ago. Due to the availability of libraries supporting multi-touch applications, multi-agent systems and DLL for devices, we had to combined several technologies. Multi-touch applications are written in Java with the MT4J[2] library. The multi-agent platform is a JADE[3] platform and the connectors are written in C#. However, MT4J, the only available multi-touch library available at the beginning of our project is no more maintained and a future work is planned to rewrite the main applications using Java FX touch features. The integration of JavaFX into Java 8 and thus its compatibility with JADE is also an advantage.

JADE platforms are FIPA[4] compliant. That means they are built according to the standards defined by the FIPA organization. A JADE platform contains three specific agents that provide yellow and white pages services. When two teams are working together, each team system has its own JADE platform. However, it is very simple to exchange messages between agents belonging to two different platforms thanks to an HTTP server that each platform owns.

---

[2] MT4J: Multi-touch for Java. http://code.google.com/p/mt4j/

[3] JADE: Java Agent DEvelopment. http://jade.tilab.com/

[4] FIPA: Foundation for Intelligent Physical Agents. http://www.fipa.org/

3.5   Data and Video Channels

When two remote teams work synchronously using a digital support system, we consider that they are involved in two transverse streams: data produced in one place have to be transferred in the other place and cameras in one place have to transfer video streams towards the other site. For now in our system, these two streams are completely disconnected. We used internal tools to process the data stream and external tools for processing the video stream. However, we have begun to prepare tools for processing the video stream.

We are building a video viewer able to read videos and to place them at any position. In particular, the tool is able to read annotations from a data base and thanks to their timestamps can place the video stream at the right position. After a session, using this tool, it is possible to list the automatic annotations produced by the annotation agent, to choose one of them and to see again what happened some instants before and after. It is very useful for the capitalization of information.

4   Experiment

We continuously experiment our system both at the University of Compiègne (UTC) in France, and at the Chiba Institute of Technology (CIT) in Japan. Two teams, one at the UTC and one at the CIT collaborate on the preliminary design of a website for French travelers in Japan.

Both teams use the system described above. The main tasks are to create and classify ideas about this project. Ideas are written on notes, grouped into clusters and displayed on an interactive device. The actions of one team are transmitted in real time to the devices of the other team.

At the UTC, people can use either an interactive table or an interactive whiteboard. It is possible to test the usability of the main application on both devices. A single camera directed on the audience transmits the scene to the other site. The video stream is received from the CIT with a computer linked to a large screen.

At the CIT, scenes were displayed on an interactive white board but allowing only one interaction point. All moves are possible because we have designed specific zones around the edges of notes representation that allows zoom and rotations with only one finger. One person, as a mediator, stands up near the white board moving and grouping elements according to the discussions with other team members (see Figure 1). In these circumstances, it is not easy and even undesirable for this person to write the content of a note. That means: open a virtual keyboard, type on keys, and so on. Other participants have tablet pcs and, thanks to the personal application running on them, can create notes and send them to the white board.

Researchers at the CIT are more involved in the video channel development. The streams of three cameras are integrated, one for the device where notes are displayed, the second for the Japanese participants and the third one for capturing a particular event.

The experiments with Japanese colleagues have also a multicultural approach. That is why we call the system MCB (Multi-Cultural Brainstorming). Indeed, we consider notes also from a conceptual approach. Discussions are useful in order to explicit some concepts and notes are useful for that. Common sessions generally are about two hours long. Any communication problem between sites is solved. The data channel is still faster than the video channel, however this is not an issue if everybody respects speaking times. After the first results, it seems that people prefer to collaborate on a vertical surface and to interact with a personal device. This point must be confirmed by researches conducted in other places.

5   Conclusion and Future Works

In this paper we have presented the design and implementation of a distributed digital system supporting participants during co-located collaborative sessions. The architecture of the distributed system involves different types of devices and mainly large multi-touch screens. It relies on a multi-agent system whose agents exchange messages for performing the functionalities of the system like synchronization and persistence. The technology used for the development of the applications and the agents is also detailed. The paper also presents an experiment that has been achieved thanks to this system.

Our system is part of an on-going research and we are currently investigating complementary aspects. First, we study how to integrate a vocal interpretation system that does not disturb the participants during collaborative activities and in which it is not necessary to first specify the language in use. The second point is to implement user interfaces in another language because some technologies are no more maintained and to enhance user interaction. The last point is a better integration of the video and data channels.

References

1. Kanbanize web site (2015). https://kanbanize.com
2. Trello web site (2015). https://trello.com/home
3. Brézillon, P.: Explaining for sharing context in communities. In: CSCWD 2011, 15th International Conference on Computer Supported Cooperative Work in Design, Lausanne, Switzerland, pp. 819–826, June 2011
4. Forlines, C., Lilien, R.: Adapting a single-user, single-display molecular visualization application for use in a multi-user, multi-display environment.In: Proceedings of the Working Conference on Advanced Visual Interfaces, AVI 2008, pp. 367–371. ACM, New York (2008)
5. Kendira, A., Gidel, T., Jones, A., Lenne, D., Barths, J.P., Moulin, C.: Conducting preliminary design around an interactive tabletop. In: 18th International Conference on Engineering Design (ICED 2011), Copenhagen, Danmark, vol. 2, pp. 366–376 (2011)
6. Mishra, A., Mishra, D.: Research trends in management issues of global software development: evaluating the past to envision the future. Journal of Global Information Technology Management **14**(4), 48–69 (2011)

7. Mishra, D., Mishra, A.: Distributed information system development: review of some management issues. In: Meersman, R., Herrero, P., Dillon, T. (eds.) OTM 2009 Workshops. LNCS, vol. 5872, pp. 282–291. Springer, Heidelberg (2009)

8. Moulin, C., Jones, A., Barthès, J.P., Lenne, D.: Preliminary design on multi-touch surfaces managed by multi-agent systems. International Journal of Energy, Information and Communications 2(4), 195–210 (2011)

9. Moulin, C., Sugawara, K., Kaeri, Y., Abel, M.H.: Collaborative brainstorming activity results and information systems. In: On the Move to Meaningful Internet Systems: OTM 2014; ISDEWorkshop, Amantea, Italy, pp. 399–407, October 27–31, 2014

10. Piorkowski, B.A., Evans, R.D., Gao, J.X.: Development of a face-to-face meeting capture and indexing process. In: CSCWD 2011, 15th International Conference on Computer Supported Cooperative Work in Design, Lausanne, Switzerland, pp. 4–8, June 2011

11. Raschke, W., Zilli, M., Loinig, J., Weiss, R., Steger, C., Kreiner, C.: Patterns of software modeling. In: Meersman, R., et al. (eds.) OTM 2014. LNCS, vol. 8842, pp. 428–437. Springer, Heidelberg (2014)

12. Sugawara, K., Manabe, Y., Moulin, C., Barthès, J.P.: Design assistant agents for supporting requirement specification definition in a distributed design team. In: 15th Int. Conference on Computer-Supported Cooperative Work in Design (CSCWD), pp. 329–334. IEEE, Lausanne, June 8–11, 2011

13. Vallecillos, J., Criado, J., Iribarne, L., Padilla, N.: Dynamic mashup interfaces for information systems using widgets-as-a-service. In: Meersman, R., et al. (eds.) OTM 2014. LNCS, vol. 8842, pp. 438–447. Springer, Heidelberg (2014)

14. Wallace, J.R., Scott, S.D., MacGregor, C.G.: Collaborative sensemaking on a digital tabletop and personal tablets: prioritization, comparisons, and tableaux. In: CHI 2013, SIGCHI Conference on Human Factors in Computing Systems, New York, USA, pp. 3345–3354 (2013)

15. Weiser, M.: Human-computer interaction. chap. The Computer for the 21st Century, pp. 933–940. Morgan Kaufmann Publishers Inc., San Francisco (1995)

16. Wigdor, D., Fletcher, J., Morrison, G.: Designing user interfaces for multi-touch and gesture devices. In: CHI 2009 Extended Abstracts on Human Factors in Computing Systems, pp. 2755–2758 (2009)

Evolving Mashup Interfaces Using a Distributed Machine Learning and Model Transformation Methodology

Antonio Jesus Fernandez-Garcia[1](✉), Luis Iribarne[1], Antonio Corral[1], and James Z. Wang[2]

[1] Applied Computing Group, University of Almeria, Almería, Spain
{ajfernandez,luis.iribarne,acorral}@ual.es
[2] The Pennsylvania State University, State College, USA
jwang@psu.edu

Abstract. Nowadays users access information services at any time and in any place. Providing an intelligent user interface which adapts dynamically to the users' requirements is essential in information systems. Conventionally, systems are constructed at the design time according to an initial structure and requirements. The effect of the passage of time and changes in users, applications and environment is that the systems cannot always satisfy the user's requirements. In this paper a methodology is proposed to allow mashup user interfaces to be intelligent and evolve over time by using computational techniques like machine learning over huge amounts of heterogeneous data, known as big data, and model-driven engineering techniques as model transformations. The aim is to generate new ways of adapting the interface to the user's needs, using information about user's interaction and the environment.

Keywords: Machine learning · Mashup interfaces · Smart interfaces · Distributed systems · Big data · Model transformation

1 Introduction

The "smart" concept is prominent nowadays. From smart phones to smart TVs by way of classic desktop and laptop computers, the adoption of the word "smart" intends to convey the idea that the devices are no longer simple boxes manipulated by the user but have moved on so far as to add value. New concepts such as the "Internet of Things" [21], which has caused a boom in everyday devices being connected to the Internet, or "smart cities" [17], with the claim that the citizen can actively participate with its urban centre, mean that now, more than ever, devices and systems need to be increasingly "intelligent" and count with better prepared user interfaces.

That leads to today's users to require instantaneous access to information. This information is often simply raw data, but more and more frequently, it is elaborated information that must be processed in order to be offered up. The way users access information may also evolve over time due to different factors.

© Springer International Publishing Switzerland 2015
I. Ciuciu et al. (Eds.): OTM 2015 Workshops, LNCS 9416, pp. 401–410, 2015.
DOI: 10.1007/978-3-319-26138-6_43

This possible development leads to the creation of new interfaces which are capable of responding to the users' demands at the moment they are accessed.

Traditionally, computer systems are defined at the design time according to an architecture and some initial requirements. This means that in many cases, the effect of the passage of time and changes in users, applications and services is that the systems that do not adapt cannot always satisfy the user's requirements. In dynamic and evolving computer systems, where it is intended that the interface adaptation changes intelligently with the needs of users at all times, it can be useful that the implicit architecture evolves in "runtime" to adapt to user's updated needs and their environment.

We propose to evolve distributed information systems using machine learning where algorithms can be applied, analysed and evaluated in order to infer patterns of user behaviour. Through these patterns of behaviour, models which are capable of evolving the user interface at runtime can be created based on the actions performed by users and the system environment, as well as prediction models, capable of deduct users actions and propose a response (adaptation) to them. The interfaces, data and information to be analysed to generate these actions can come from different systems and distributed architectures [15].

In addition to the areas of knowledge already mentioned, the implementation of the proposed methodology for the regeneration of the user interfaces at runtime in an evolutionary way will make use of others such as cloud computing [18], big data [2] or model transformation [1]. Continued access to distributed systems and the data generated by that connection justify the use of cloud computing and big data [16]. The need to adapt the user interface at runtime to new requirements justify the use of model transformation.

The rest of the paper is organized as follows. Section 2 describes related work and the motivation. Section 3 defines in-depth the methodology for developing evolutionary systems. Section 4 explains adaptation methodology to a case study. Finally, Section 5 concludes and provides future directions.

2   Related Work and Motivation

The way people communicate with the devices around them has experienced very rapid change. Much recent work has been on the optimization of user interfaces, using different approaches. For instance, Russis *et al.* [6] focused on optimizing the interaction between users and intelligent environments. Fensel *et al.* [8] modeled interfaces which intelligently manage energy in smart homes. Roscher *et al.* [19], focused on the management of interfaces that dynamically adapt to users in their daily lives within an intelligent environment. In this regard, it is interesting to compare our proposed approach with related work. In our case, we propose the evolution of the dynamic adaptation on distributed information systems, that has not been covered in related work to our knowledge.

For that, dynamic adaptation mashup interfaces [5] are commonly used. Due to their granularity they facilitate the adaptation of their internal structure to new adaptation requirements and they make it easy to study user behavior.

Nowadays, mashup interfaces (or component-based interfaces) are widespread in commercial software, particularly in Web applications [10]. The components forming these mashup interfaces are directly integrated into the system interface according to a component architecture. The use of these components depends on the discovery and access services provided by the system itself. In this type of interface what's important is not only how the interaction occurs, but also what occurs after the interaction.

In work carried out by Iribarne *et al.* [14,12,9] and Criado *et al.* [4], a global method is presented in which component-based architectures are able to compose both dynamically and autonomously in order to best adapt to the user's requirements. It is worth mentioning that all the adjustments made in the system are based on a number of adaptation rules which are defined statically in a rule repository. The system for adapting the interface to the user's needs is achieved by the following processes, as illustrated in Fig. 1.

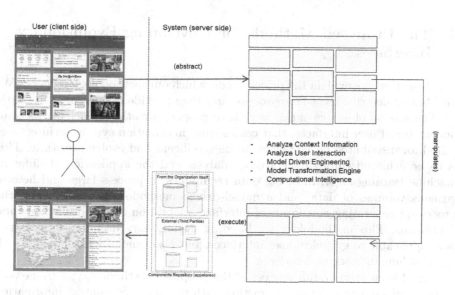

Fig. 1. The process of dynamic user interface adaptation at the runtime.

- *Abstraction of the concrete user interface.* The components which the user is using are identified, isolated and an abstract model is generated based on them.
- *Manipulation of the abstract model.* Analysing the contextual information from the model's environment, the interaction between the user and the interface and using model-driven engineering (MDE) and computational intelligence transformation of the model is produced. The transformation is performed based on the adaptation rules stored in the rule repository.
- *Creation of a new concrete model.* The abstract model is instantiated using the right components in a concrete model thus providing an interface which is better tailored to the needs of the user [14].

As aforementioned, following traditional software architecture development methods, the developed system was designed at a particular time, i.e. "the design time", based on the specific environment and needs identified at that time. The reality is that these requirements are often dynamic and can evolve in the continuous integration and deployment of the distributed system, coming to scene, for instance, with new users and components.

Consequently, it is justified to conclude that this dynamic adaptive behaviour appears to be insufficient. It would be desirable for the user interface to modify its structure at the runtime based on information from the user interaction and the distributed environment, in order to provide users with the components they require. It is even possible to make the form of dynamic adaptation evolve to the user's needs through the discovery of behavioural patterns based on the user's interaction with the interface. That would create prediction models provided by a set of adaptation rules.

3   The Proposed Methods for Developing Evolutionary Interfaces

In this section, we explain the principles on which our methodology is based. We first briefly describe the whole process, and then provide details for each step.

The general objective of this work is to propose a method which allows component based user interfaces, that comes from information system architectures suited for distributed development, to be intelligent and evolve over time. This is to be achieved through the study, analysis and the application of different machine learning algorithms, big data techniques to process large and heterogeneous volumes of data, and a model-driven methodology which allows the process of generating new forms of interface adaptation to be autonomous and continuous. This methodology for building evolutionary user interfaces is not only applicable to graphical user interfaces, but also generally extendable to all types of human machine interfaces.

Fig. 2 shows the overall process of the proposed methodology; a framework scenario which, through user interaction with the interface, context information and information on the environment, allows the creation of intelligent, dynamic and evolving interfaces in distributed systems that modify their structure at runtime.

The process gathers information on how the user handles the interface and its components together with the information about the environment. Due to the size, heterogeneity and speed of data generation, the information gathered is stored using big data techniques in data structures prepared for the purpose.

From this large volume of stored data, different data views are defined. A data view is the result set of structured data drawn from the general database by a stored query for a specific purpose. Unnecessary information is hidden and other information which may be relevant is added.

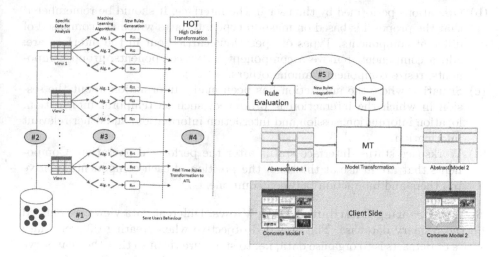

Fig. 2. Dynamic and evolutionary user interface adaptation at the runtime.

Each of these views is focused on a type of study, analysis and evaluation through the use of algorithms and machine learning techniques. Each view is structured to apply different algorithms depending on their nature, as they can be algorithms for clustering, sorting and/or regression. The aim is to infer new knowledge which provides new adaptation rules to the system.

Once the machine learning algorithms have been applied and new rules (which provide the adaptation of the system) generated, a transformation is necessary so that the rules generated have the same format as the rules the user interface use to be adapted to the user's needs. The way the adaptation rules are written can be different for each user interface, and therefore the transformation belongs to the problem domain. Furthermore, it is necessary to define whether the new rules generated are valid or not. For this, a rule evaluation module will be implemented which includes a conflict manager.

Step 1: Distributed Storage of User Behaviour. All the activity generated by the user's interaction with the interface, as well as all the information about the environment during the time in which user interaction occurs is recorded. This information can be:

(a) Information about the user who carried out the interaction. Useful information will be stored like which particular user has made the interaction, what kind of user he is, how is he related to other users, and what characteristics define him. It will be further supplemented, if possible, with other relevant information about the environment, such as cultural information or demographic characteristics.

(b) Operations performed by the user in the interface. It should be remembered that the proposal is based on mashup type interfaces which are composed of different components. Types of operations carried out in the interface are: add a component, remove a component, move components, group components, resize components, among others.

(c) Situation where the interaction has been made. Information about the session in which the interaction is produced, such as temporal information, location information, session and interaction information, and other relevant information.

(d) Workspace status. Interface status after the performed operation. Components that are in use at the time, the position of each components relative to others and interaction between components.

Step 2: Creating Distributed Data Views. Different data views are defined on the primary database. The intended objective when creating different data views or datasets is to organise data, i.e. to structure them so that they can serve as entry elements for the algorithms used in machine learning. Data views are composed with information spread in the whole infrastructure of the distributed information systems. The structure given to data optimises the results obtained during the execution of the experiments as well as to certify that the output of the algorithms generates valid results. In other words, it maximises properly structured relevant information which is able to provide new inferred knowledge susceptible to creating new rules for adaptation of the system, thereby generating evolutionary systems.

Step 3: Application of Machine Learning Algorithms. Different kinds of existing algorithms in the machine learning literature are studied, analysed and applied to the "data views". Experiments are carried out to test and evaluate the correct application of the algorithms, and to determine if valid knowledge can be extracted from the generated outputs. By valid knowledge, it is meant that it can generate new rules capable of improving the user interface adaptation. It is very important to study which algorithm is the most effective in each case and for each data view, depending on its nature. Two groups of algorithms can be identified:

– *Supervised.* Training data is prepared while knowing the right answers. This training data is used to build models which are able to classify new data and, in this way, obtain answers.
– *Unsupervised.* Data is directly entered into the algorithms in the hope of getting some intelligible information through the structuring of data.

Experiments should be performed to identify which algorithm is suited to each situation and how an algorithm can be parameterized to optimize its results. Furthermore, existing algorithms can be modified to achieve the best possible results. Some algorithms of interest are: Clustering, Association Learning, Parameter Estimation, Recommendation Engines, Classification, Similarity Matching, Neural Networks, Bayesian Networks and Genetic Algorithms among others.

Step 4: Conversion Rules. The inferred rules generated by experiments with machine learning algorithms have their own format which is suited to the identity of the data processed and the type of algorithm used.

Using model transformation [13] the outputs of the algorithms are transformed to the format suited to the interface where they will be applied. The way the adaptation rules are written may differ for each user interface and therefore the transformation belongs to the problem domain.

A special kind of transformation exists in which the model transformations (i.e. the transformation models) participate as input or output models in a process called Higher-Order Transformation or HOT [20]. This kind of HOT transformation, described in Fig. 3, is used to rewrite the knowledge generated by the algorithm into an adaptation rule.

Furthermore, it is necessary to define whether the new rules generated are valid or not. For this, a rule evaluation module will be implemented which includes a conflict manager.

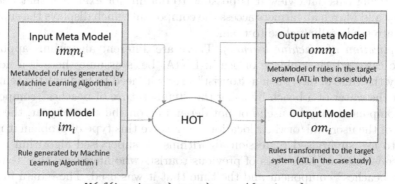

$$H(\,f(im_i, imm_i\,),omm):\ om_i\,/\,\{\forall_i:1\,...\,n\}$$

Fig. 3. Transformation of Rules using a HOT.

Step 5: Evaluation of Rules. The rule evaluation module will define whether a new rule generated should be added to the rule repository or not. It is possible to achieve new rules which contradict existing rules from the repository. For these particular cases, a "conflict manager" should be employed which must resolve how to handle the potential conflicts that may occur with previously established rules.

4   Case Study in the ENIA System

As a case study, the proposed methodology for creating evolutionary mashup user interfaces has been applied to ENIA [7][1] (ENviromental Information Agent),

---

[1] http://www.enia.dreamhosters.com

which is a component-based graphic user interface for environmental management. Different user profiles and various categories of components exist in the ENIA interface. Examples of these components include: natural areas, wetlands, drovers' roads or biosphere reserves, positioned within maps. The application of the methodology to ENIA is described below.

Distributed storage of user behaviour. The following information are stored. Operations carried out on the interface: add component, delete component, move component, resize component; User information: name, category, home region and other personal data; User type: tourist, technician, farmer or politician; Temporal information: date, time, day, month, season; Location information: location, proximity to the coast, proximity to tourist elements amongs others; Session information: duration, operations carried out; Other information: temperature, humidity, precipitation, wind amongs others; State of the workspace: location of components in the workspace, display size of each of the components.

Creating distributed data views. Storing the operations performed by a user type on a component on a certain date could be an example of a data view of ENIA. Using this data view it is possible to obtain, for example, that between January and March all farmers access the component which displays the suppliers of tomato seeds selling close to them.

Application of machine learning. There are different algorithms applied to specific cases which could be of use in ENIA. Let's assume there is a need to identify the time of day when a "tourist" user will need to find out the temperature of the water of a beach by using the "temperature of beaches" component. This component may be useful or not depending on the time of year, the home region of the user and/or their location. To resolve this type of problem it makes sense to use supervised regression algorithms. A supervised algorithm is used because we already have data of previous tourists who have used the "temperature of beaches" component and the time that it was used. These data indicate a priori the right answer to the proposed question, namely, at what time the "temperature of beaches" component was used. A regression algorithm is used because it is designed to predict a continuous value output (time of day) depending on a series of attributes (user type, season, home region or current location among others). There are many other examples where supervised classification algorithms and unsupervised clustering algorithms can be used.

Conversion rules. In order to be able to add a new rule to the rule repository, it is necessary to transform the output of the algorithm into the format of the rules stored in the repository. In this particular case we use model transformation [13] to transform the algorithm outputs and the inferred knowledge to ATL rules [11], which is the format used by ENIA. ATL is a transformation model language which also provides a number of tools for Model Driven Engineering.

Evaluation of rules. Any valid new rule generated is added to the rule repository. If a new rule contradicts an existing rule, the new rule is prioritized. The new rule is considered to have been created in a newer environment and with interactive behavioural data which has been contrasted with more users.

5   Conclusions and Future Work

A methodology is proposed to allow mashup user interfaces in distributed systems to adapt to user requirements at runtime, be intelligent and evolve over time through the use of machine learning and model transformations. The process of applying the methodology is described in the case study of ENIA, an intelligent agent for environmental information.

The creation of an automatic learning system is proposed as future work. Machine learning experiments can be performed in a way that the data is fed automatically from Web services, making the system autonomous and independent. Each new execution of an experiment will have new data collected automatically (updated datasets) which can provide different outputs.

Statistical learning techniques will be used to classify or group different user intentions for individualized interface treatment. Proper integration of learned knowledge with manually-entered preferences is an area of future development. The evaluation with human subjects will be needed to assess the effectiveness and usefulness of dynamic interfaces.

Finally, the optimization and/or improvement of algorithms is also interesting. Areas to be worked on are: defining new algorithms in extending those that already exist in the field of machine learning and customize existing algorithms in both operation and parameterization through statistical programming languages algorithms and statistical analysis as R, Octave or Matlab. It follows that these optimized algorithms should present optimum system results.

Acknowledgments. This work was funded by the EU ERDF and the Spanish Ministry of Economy and Competitiveness (MINECO) under Project TIN2013-41579-R and under a FPI Grant BES-2014-067974 and by the Andalusian Regional Government (Spain) under Project P10-TIC-6114. Wang has been funded by the US National Science Foundation.

References

1. Bollati, V.A., Vara, J.M., Jiménez, A., Marcos, E.: Applying MDE to the (semi-) automatic development of model transformations. Information and Software Technology **55**(4), 699–718 (2013)
2. Chen, C.L.P., Zhang, C.: Data-intensive applications, challenges, techniques and technologies: A survey on Big Data. Information Sciences **275**, 314–347 (2014)
3. Criado, C., Rodriguez-Gracia, D., Iribarne, L., Padilla, N.: Toward the adaptation of component-based architectures by model transformation: behind smart user interfaces. Softw. Pract. Exper. (2014)
4. Criado, J., Vicente-Chicote, C., Iribarne, L., Padilla, N.: A model-driven approach to graphical user interface runtime adaptation. In: 5th International Workshop on Models@run.time, pp. 49–59 (2010)
5. Daniel, F., Matera, M.: Mashups: Concepts, Models and Architectures (2014)
6. De Russis, L.: Interacting with smart environments: Users, interfaces, and devices. Journal of Ambient Intelligence and Smart Environments **7**(1), 115–116 (2015)
7. ENIA Environmental Information Agent. http://www.enia.dreamhosters.com/

8. Fensel, A., Vikash, K., Slobodanka, T.: End-user interfaces for energy-efficient semantically enabled smart homes. Energy Efficiency. Springer (2014)
9. Fernandez-Garcia, A.J., Iribarne, L.: TDTrader: a methodology for the interoperability of DT-web services based on MHPCOTS software components, repositories and trading models. In: 2nd Int. Workshop of Ambient Assisted Living, (IWAAL 2010), pp. 83–88 (2010)
10. Hoyer, V., Fischer, M.: Market overview of enterprise mashup tools. In: Bouguettaya, A., Krueger, I., Margaria, T. (eds.) ICSOC 2008. LNCS, vol. 5364, pp. 708–721. Springer, Heidelberg (2008)
11. Kurtev, I., van den Berg, K., Jouault, F.: Rule-based modularization in model transformation languages illustrated with ATL. Science Computer Programming 68(3), 138–154 (2015)
12. Iribarne, L., Criado, J., Padilla, N., Asensio, J.: Using COTS-widgets architectures for describing user interfaces of web-based information systems. International Journal of Knowledge Society Research 2(3), 61–72 (2011)
13. Iribarne, L., Padilla, N., Criado, J., Asensio, J., Ayala, R.: A model transformation approach for automatic composition of COTS user interfaces in web-based information systems. Information Systems Management 27(3), 207–216 (2010)
14. Iribarne, L., Padilla, N., Criado, J., Vicente-Chicote, C.: Metamodeling the structure and interaction behavior of cooperative component-based user interfaces. Journal of Universal Computer Science 18(19), 2669–2685 (2012)
15. Mishra, D., Mishra, A.: Distributed information system development: review of some management issues. In: Meersman, R., Herrero, P., Dillon, T. (eds.) OTM 2009 Workshops. LNCS, vol. 5872, pp. 282–291. Springer, Heidelberg (2009)
16. Mishra, D., Alok, M.: Research trends in management issues of global software development: evaluating the past to envision the future. Journal of Global Information Technology Management 14(4), 48–69 (2011)
17. Ortner, E., Mevius, M., Wiedmann, P., Kurz, F.: Design of interactional end-to-end web applications for smart cities. In: 24th International Conference on World Wide Web Companion, pp. 551–556 (2015)
18. Richard, K., Deters, L., Deters, R.: Architectural designs from mobile cloud computing to ubiquitous cloud computing - survey. In: IEEE World Congress on Services (SERVICES 2014), pp. 418–425 (2014)
19. Roscher, D., Lehmann, G., Schwartze, V., Blumendorf, M., Albayrak, S.: Dynamic distribution and layouting of model-based user interfaces in smart environments. In: Hussmann, H., Meixner, G., Zuehlke, D. (eds.) Model-Driven Development of Advanced User Interfaces. SCI, vol. 340, pp. 171–197. Springer, Heidelberg (2011)
20. Tisi, M., Jouault, F., Fraternali, P., Ceri, S., Bézivin, J.: On the use of higher-order model transformations. In: Paige, R.F., Hartman, A., Rensink, A. (eds.) ECMDA-FA 2009. LNCS, vol. 5562, pp. 18–33. Springer, Heidelberg (2009)
21. Whitmore, A., Agarwal, A., Xu, L.: The Internet of Things - A survey of topics and trends. Information Systems Frontiers 17(2), 261–274 (2015)

An Architectural Model for System
of Information Systems

Saleh Majd[✉], Abel Marie-Hélène, and Mishra Alok

Sorbonne Universités, Université de Technologie de Compiègne,
CNRS, UMR 7253 Heudiasyc, Compiègne, France
{majd.saleh,marie-helene.abel,alok.mishra}@hds.utc.fr

Abstract. One of the most important aspects when designing and constructing an Information System is its architecture. This also applies to
complex systems such as System of Information Systems (SoIS). Thus, we
aim to propose an architectural model of System of Information Systems
(SoIS). Though Architecture-based approaches have been promoted as
a means of controlling the complexity of systems construction and evolution, what we really look for in this paper is an architectural model
to aggregate services from already constructed systems. Nevertheless,
it would be a good practice to compare the presented architecture of
SoIS to other architecture-based approaches such as Service Oriented
Architecture (SOA). Also, it is beneficial to examine how we can use the
well-established standards of SOA for the designing of SoIS. In this paper
we present an architectural model for System of Information Systems,
and highlight the standards of Service Oriented Architecture that might
help us in this task.

Keywords: System of Systems · System of Information Systems ·
Service Oriented Architecture · Architectural model

1 Introduction

In recent years the work environment is becoming more competitive, as changes
are taking place much faster than before. One of these changes happens with
the services provided by Information Systems employed by companies, as these
systems need to learn how to work and communicate with each other in order to
aggregate services and produce new ones emerged from existing systems. Therefore, securing a competitive advantage does no longer rely only on efficiency,
quality, and customer responsiveness. While each of these factors is important,
the ability to deploy available solution to emergent problems by aggregating
services of existing Information Systems and provide ease of access to these systems is of great importance. This makes innovation, flexibility, coordination,
integration, and speed the new success factors of todays work environment.
Those factors can be achieved through the concept of System of Information
Systems (SoIS). While successful SoIS production provides the basis of great

© Springer International Publishing Switzerland 2015
I. Ciuciu et al. (Eds.): OTM 2015 Workshops, LNCS 9416, pp. 411–420, 2015.
DOI: 10.1007/978-3-319-26138-6_44

potentials, many development activities result in failure. The issue is that while many individual Information Systems work well as an independent system, they fail when incorporated as a component of a SoIS. The desired SoIS needs to connect Information Systems that cross organizational boundaries, come from multiple domains, and generates an overwhelming amount of information. Users struggle to deal with the information produced by each Information System independently by traversing through these systems and keeping track of the generated information separately. A solution might be found in a well-established architectural model of System of Information Systems that provides guidance to produce such solution. The SoIS operates as a single entry point for several Information Systems granting the user access to information produced from multiple Information Systems, and providing the ability to aggregate available services to even create an added value not possible to maintain when those systems were operating separately. Furthermore, this encompassing solution should also work in a distributed environment over a network as the Information Systems composing the SoIS could be geographically distributed. Distributed system development is becoming crucial due to the requirement of applications involving different devices and different sources of information. Management of distributed software development has more challenges and difficulties than conventional development [Mishra and Mishra, 2009] [Mishra and Alok, 2011]. The construction of SoIS, however, requires long-term projects that involve comprehensive organizational changes in terms of new approaches to system usage and different IT governance mechanisms, as well as changes in the roles and responsibilities of employees and Information Systems users in particular. To address this issue we believe that Service Oriented Architecture (SOA) should be utilized as a business transformation tool for solving the needs of SoIS.

This paper is organized as follows: section 2 will provide the definition of the notion of System of Systems (SoS). After that, in section 3, the SoIS architectural model is presented and then discussed by defining the concept of SoIS, and presenting an example following our architectural model of SoIS. Then, a comparison between SoIS and SOA in terms of similarities, differences, and limitations is presented in section 4. Section 5 will present a discussion of the findings of this paper. Finally, we conclude with section 6.

2   Definition of System of Systems

The notion of System of Systems (SoS) can be viewed as an evolution of the standard notion of systems. Many definitions of a SoS exist. An aggregate of systems leads to the creation of new forms of systems which may be either described within the framework of composite systems, or demonstrate additional features which add complexity to the description and may be referred to as System of Systems.

We can summarize the definitions mentioned in [Jamshidi, 2011] [Carlock and Fenton, 2001] [Manthorpe, 1996] [Rechtin and Maier, 2000]. In the light of the definitions mentioned in the literature, we can describe the notion of System of Systems (SoS) as the following; Systems of systems are large-scale integrated systems which are heterogeneous and independently operable on their own, but are networked together for a common goal. The goal, as mentioned before, may be cost, performance, robustness, etc. In other terms, A System of Systems is a super system comprised of other elements which themselves are independent complex operational systems and interact among themselves to achieve a common goal. Each element of a SoS achieves well-substantiated goals even if they are detached from the rest of the SoS.

3   System of Information Systems

In this section we propose a new system that combines the services from different Information Systems. First, we are going to define our new system as a System of Information Systems (SoIS). Then, we are going to present a generic architecture of the SoIS. Finally we propose an intial design for the SoIS that can serve as an example of the architecture

3.1   Definition

The notion of System of Information Systems is defined by [Carlsson and Stankiewicz, 1991] as "networks of agents interacting in a specific technology area under a particular institutional infrastructure for the purpose of creating, diffusing, and utilizing technology focused on knowledge, information, and competence flow." [Breschi and Malerba, 1996] describe SoIS as "the specific clusters of the firms, technologies, and industries involved in the generation and diffusion of new technologies and in the knowledge flow that takes place among them."

Based on the definitions provided we can summaries the features of SoIS as follows:

- SoIS addresses the impact of the interrelationships between different IS.
- SoIS is concerned with the flow of information and knowledge among different information systems.
- SoIS is responsible for generating information from the emergent IS.
- Information interoperability is a key issue when designing a SoIS.

3.2   Architecture

In this part we are going to present the generic architecture of the SoIS. As seen in (Fig. 1), the SoIS will aggregate services from several Information Systems (System A, System B etc.). These systems are working separately. Each of which has its own services and databases. The services of these systems are denoted as solid rectangles inside the system (Service 1A, Service 1B etc.). Information can be represented in different ways within different systems, thus, the SoIS might have trouble access information. Therefore, there is a growing need for

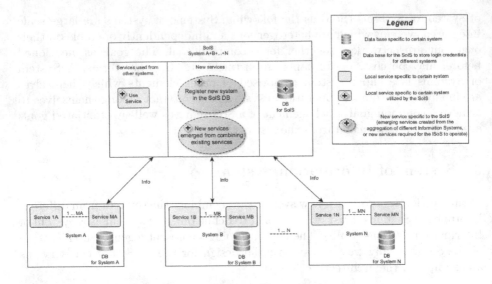

Fig. 1. Architectural model of the SoIS.

a solution to this interoperability issue. A solution to the problem of assuring interoperability within the SoIS is to control the communication medium among the systems. Two methods, outlined by [Bowen and Sahin, 2010], include:

- Creating a software model of each system, where the software model collects data from the system and generates the outputs.
- Creating a common language to describe data, where each system can represent its data such that other systems may interpret.

Due to overhead restrictions on architecture and a required common language, it is not often that individual software models are created for the various systems. Therefore, the most widely used approach to ensure interoperability within a SoIS is to standardize the language of data interpretation throughout the SoIS. The SoIS is represented as a group of services and a database. The services residing in the SoIS can either be utilization of existed services from the Information Systems comprising the SoIS, or emerging services created from the aggregation of different Information Systems. Existing services re denoted with hard lines while emergent services are denoted with dotted lines. In addition, the two headed arrows linking the SoIS with the Information systems represent information path between the SoIS and the different Information Systems.

3.3   Example

As mentioned earlier, the SoIS is composed of several Information Systems. In this part we will take two Information Systems to create a SoIS from them by following the architecture presented earlier in (Fig. 1). These Information

Systems are TiddlyWiki [tid, 2015] and MEMORAe. First we will take a look at each of these systems separately and highlight their functionality as independent systems, before unveiling their role as parts of the SoIS.

TiddlyWiki: Technically, a TiddlyWiki is just an HTML page with a rather large JavaScript section that takes care of displaying all the contents, and provides the interactive tools for their manipulation. The actual text of the page is not immediately visible. It is stored in a set of invisible DIV elements, called tiddlers. The content of the DIV tags is wiki text, i.e. text with a simple markup language, similar to (old) emails. When the user clicks on a tiddler name to show its content, the JavaScript rendering machine translates the wiki text into HTML. The text may also contain macro fragments that trigger the actions of subroutines. Other tiddlers are interpreted as a stylesheet or a JavaScript plugin. When the user asks for a tiddler to be edited, this is replaced inline by a form, and the user is presented with the original text [Bagnoli et al., 2006].

MEMORAe: As defined by [Ala Atrash, 2014], MEMORAe approach is to manage heterogeneous information resources within organizations. The approach is comprised of a semantic model (called MEMORAe-core 2) and a web platform (called MEMORAe) which is based on the semantic model. The model and the platform make together a support to enhance the process of organizational learning. The MEMORAe project uses the Semantic Web standards, therefore, the ontologies occurring in the system are written in OWL. Users registered in the MEMORAe system can access one or more knowledge bases. When a base is chosen, a user can view a semantic map of concepts related to the selected base. Then, a user can create and share resources around the concepts of the map.

After being introduced to the components of the SoIS, the services of both those systems are present in Table 1. Table 2 shows the services available in the SoIS either employed from one of the Information Systems or emerged from the existing services.

Table 1. Available services in the Information Systems comprising the SoIS

	TiddlyWiki (System A)	MEMORAe (System B)
Available Service	Create Wiki pages	Index resources
	Edit Wiki pages	Annotate resources as a whole
	Use macro fragments in Wiki pages	Annotate resources as parts
		Share resources

The idea behind this example is to be able to use MEMORAe system potential in indexing and sharing resources alongside annotating them for the benefit of TiddlyWiki system. Both systems will continue to work autonomously, but new services will emerge from both of them like the ability to index, share, and annotate Wiki Pages.

Table 2. Available services in the SoIS

	SoIS (System A + System B)
	Create Wiki pages
	Edit Wiki pages
	Use macro fragments in Wiki pages
Available Services	Index Wiki Pages
	Share Wiki Pages
	Annotate Wiki Pages as whole
	Annotate Wiki pages as parts

4   System of Information Systems versus Service Oriented Architecture

4.1   Definition of Service Oriented Architecture

The Organization for the Advancement of Structured Information Standards (OASIS) [cov, 2015] defines Service Oriented Architecture (SOA) as the following:

"*A paradigm for organizing and utilizing distributed capabilities that may be under the control of different ownership domains. It provides a uniform means to offer, discover, interact with and use capabilities to produce desired effects consistent with measurable preconditions and expectations.*"

The support of automated business integration by web services developments and standards [Mockford, 2004] [Burbeck, 2000] has driven major technological advances in the integration software space, most notably, the service-oriented architecture (SOA). SOA is designed to allow developers to overcome many distributed enterprise computing challenges including application integration, transaction management, security policies, while allowing multiple platforms and protocols and leveraging numerous access devices and legacy systems [Erl, 2004]. The driving goal of SOA is to eliminate these barriers so that applications integrate and run seamlessly.

The most important aspect of SOA is that it separates service implementation from its interface. Service consumers view a service as an endpoint that respond to a particular request. They are not concerned with how the service goes about executing their requests; they only expect the result [Valipour et al., 2009].

We aim to explore the similarities, differences, and limitation of SoIS and SOA in terms of the following characteristics [Valipour et al., 2009] [Papazoglou and Van Den Heuvel, 2007] [Jian et al., 2010]:

– Service Discoverability: A service consumer that needs a service discovers what service to use based on a set of criteria at runtime.
– Modularity: A service supports a set of interfaces. These interfaces should be cohesive, meaning that they should all relate to each other in the context of a module.

- Loose Coupling: Coupling refers to the number of dependencies between modules.
- Interoperability: The ability to communicate information between different services/systems regardless of the format or presentation of information.
- Location Transparency: Consumers of a service do not need to know the location of the service when they invoke the service.
- Supporting Environment: The technical environment in which services/systems operate.
- Autonomy: The services/systems work independently without interference from outside factors.

Table 3. Comparsion between SoIS and SOA.

Characteristics	SoIS	SOA
Service Discoverability	Fully Supported (Systems and Services level)	Fully Supported (Services level only)
Modularity	Not Supported	Fully Supported
Loose Coupling	Fully Supported	Fully Supported
Interoperability	Fully Supported	Fully Supported
Location Transparency	Fully Supported	Fully Supported
Supporting Environment	Fully Supported	Fully Supported
Autonomy	Fully Supported (Systems and Services level)	Fully Supported (Services level only)

4.2 Similarities

The core strengths of both SoIS and SOA lie in their ability to enhance proper integration, while promoting flexibility. Both of them share similar characteristics, while maintaining different strategies to reach their goals.

In terms of service discoverability, SOA supports the concept of service discovery by providing a registry of services accessible by the service consumer. In SoIS, this registry should be present with the addition to register the whole system and not only its services [Valipour et al., 2009].

Modularity is a key concept in SOA. It is an important concept to take into consideration when creating services. Since the concept of modularity is related to the creation of services in the first place, it is hard to incorporate it with SoIS as the architecture of SoIS is concerned with aggregating services already exist in their respected systems [Jamshidi, 2011].

Both SoIS and SOA provide support for the characteristics of Loose Coupling, Interoperability Location Transparency, and Supporting Environment. All of these characteristics should be found in systems produced by SoIS or SOA [Jamuna and Ashok, 2009].

When it comes to autonomy, SoIS emphasizes on the autonomy of encompassing Information Systems as a whole. In SOA autonomy is enforced on services level [Erl, 2008].

4.3 Differences

The differences between SoIS and SOA lie in their consideration for the building blocks for the system they aim to construct [Erl, 2008]. While SOA consider services to be dependent building blocks that collaborate to deliver functionality, SoIS focuses on Information Systems as black boxes and use them as building blocks. It is also important to note that SOA provides a framework for system development. It is important to plan for interoperability challenges at an early stage. However, for SoIS the systems already exist and the interoperability problems are only addressed at later stages. Therefore, due to overhead restriction on architecture and a required common communication medium, it is often that individual software models are created for the various systems comprising the SoIS.

4.4 Limitations

SoIS engineering faces significant challenges. On one hand, the lack of standards that guide the construction of a complex system constituted of operational independent Information Systems. On the other hand, there is also a lack of standards in regards for evaluation methods for the architecture and performance of the SoIS. However, there is a potential in using SOA as a well-established framework to compensate the lack of standards present currently in the domain of SoIS.

5 Discussion

In the previous section we presented the SoIS with an example that will grant users access to various Information Systems from a single interface. The question here is: How can we evaluate our architecture and the measure the performance of the overall system? Performance optimization of the SoIS architecture in order to achieve a common goal or mission has become the focus of various application areas. In the optimization problem, the most basic work is quantitative objective evaluation of the alternatives [Jian et al., 2010]. For SoIS, objective evaluation confronts several challenges comparing with single system objective evaluation. These challenges are listed as follows:

- SoIS is aiming at future common goal. It consists of heterogeneous component systems which can be divided into as-is and to-be systems. So the components and boundary of SoIS is evolving with time going.
- There exist ad-hoc interconnections and interactions of multiple integrated complex systems as part of the whole SoIS. So its very difficult to find an analytic formulation to measure the objective value of SoIS alternative.

For SOA complex systems there have been established methods for the definition of metrics that can be utilized to evaluate the architecture and performance of the system. It is possible to deploy those methods in order to evaluate the work done under SoIS architecture.

6 Conclusion and Future Work

Our goal was to take current Information Systems and move towards System of Information Systems (SoIS) to aggregate services and exchange information with simplicity and ease. The aim was focused towards providing an architectural model of SoIS to guide such migration. To achieve this goal we undertake this research to determine what is currently known about SoIS and deploy this knowledge to present an example of a SoIS composed of various Information Systems. We found potential to the SoIS to expand and hold new Information Systems. It was also clear that combining services from various Information Systems will result in an added value to users not present when those systems were operating separately.

The next step is to expand our work and introduce new Information Systems to the SoIS based on the example presented in this study and users needs. It should also be tested in a real world experiment. The SoIS should keep simple interface, with all the services as far from the user as a single click, to keep the users experience useful and friendly. Furthermore, we need to apply evaluation metrics used in SOA in the field of SoIS to compensate the absence of such metrics in the newly emerged concept of SoIS.

References

Organization for the advancement of structured information standards (2015). https://www.oasis-open.org/

Tiddlywiki non-linear personal web notebook (2015). http://tiddlywiki.com/

Atrash, A., Abel, M.-H., Moulin, C.: Supporting organizational learning with collaborative annotation. In: 6th International Conference on Knowledge Management and Information Sharing (KMIS), pp. 237–244 (2014)

Bagnoli, F., Jipsen, P., Sterbini, A.: Tiddlywiki in science education (2006)

Bowen, R.M., Sahin, F.: A net-centric xml based system of systems architecture for human tracking. In: 2010 5th International Conference on System of Systems Engineering (SoSE), pp. 1–6. IEEE (2010)

Breschi, S., Malerba, F.: Sectoral innovation systems: technological regimes, Schumpeterian dynamics and spatial boundaries. Università commerciale'Luigi Bocconi', Centro studi sui processi di internazionalizzazione (1996)

Burbeck, S.: The tao of e-business services: The evolution of web applications into service-oriented components with web services. Online document, IBM Software Group (2000)

Carlock, P.G., Fenton, R.E.: System of Systems (SoS) enterprise systems engineering for information-intensive organizations. Systems Engineering 4(4), 242–261 (2001)

Carlsson, B., Stankiewicz, R.: On the nature, function and composition of technological systems. Journal of Evolutionary Economics 1(2), 93–118 (1991)

Erl, T.: Service-oriented architecture: a field guide to integrating XML and web services. Prentice Hall PTR (2004)

Erl, T.: Soa: principles of service design, vol. 1. Prentice Hall, Upper Saddle River (2008)

Jamshidi, M.: System of systems engineering: innovations for the twenty-first century, vol. 58. John Wiley & Sons (2011)

Jamuna, R.S., Ashok, M.S.: A survey on service-oriented architecture for e-learning system. In: International Conference on Intelligent Agent & Multi-Agent Systems. IAMA 2009, pp. 1–3. IEEE (2009)

Jian, X., Ge, B., Zhang, X., Yang, K., Chen, Y.-W.: Evaluation method of system-of-systems architecture using knowledge-based executable model. In: 2010 International Conference on Management Science and Engineering (ICMSE), pp. 141–147. IEEE (2010)

Manthorpe, W.H.: The emerging joint system of systems: A systems engineering challenge and opportunity for apl. Johns Hopkins APL Technical Digest **17**(3), 305 (1996)

Mishra, D., Alok, M.: Research trends in management issues of global software development: evaluating the past to envision the future. Journal of Global Information Technology Management **14**(4), 48–69 (2011)

Mishra, D., Mishra, A.: Distributed information system development: review of some management issues. In: Meersman, R., Herrero, P., Dillon, T. (eds.) OTM 2009 Workshops. LNCS, vol. 5872, pp. 282–291. Springer, Heidelberg (2009)

Mockford, K.: Web services architecture. BT Technology Journal **22**(1), 19–26 (2004)

Papazoglou, M.P., Van Den Heuvel, W.-J.: Service oriented architectures: approaches, technologies and research issues. The VLDB journal **16**(3), 389–415 (2007)

Rechtin, E., Maier, M.W.: The art of systems architecting. CRC Press (2000)

Valipour, M.H., AmirZafari, B., Maleki, K.N., Daneshpour, N.: A brief survey of software architecture concepts and service oriented architecture. In: 2nd IEEE International Conference on Computer Science and Information Technology. ICCSIT 2009, pp. 34–38. IEEE (2009)

A Software Development Process Model
for Cloud by Combining Traditional Approaches

Tuna Hacaloglu[1]([⊠]), P. Erhan Eren[2], Deepti Mishra[3,4], and Alok Mishra[5]

[1] Department of Information Systems Engineering, Atilim University, Ankara, Turkey
tuna.hacaloglu@atilim.edu.tr
[2] Graduate School of Informatics, Middle East Technical University, Ankara, Turkey
ereren@metu.edu.tr
[3] School of Information Technology, Monash University, Subang Jaya, Malaysia
deepti.mishra@monash.edu
[4] Department of Computer Engineering, Atilim University, Ankara, Turkey
deepti.mishra@atilim.edu.tr
[5] Department of Software Engineering, Atilim University, Ankara, Turkey
alok.mishra@atilim.edu.tr

Abstract. Even though cloud computing is a technological paradigm that has been adopted more and more in various domains, there are few studies investigating the software development lifecycle in cloud computing applications and there is still not a comprehensive software development process model developed for cloud computing yet. Due to the nature of cloud computing that is completely different from the traditional software development, there is a need of suggesting process models to perform the software development systematically to create high quality software. In this study, we propose a new conceptual Software Development Life Cycle Model for Cloud Software Development that incorporates characteristics of different process models for traditional software development. The proposed model takes traditional model's specific characteristics into account and also considers cloud's specific nature i.e. advantages and challenges as well.

Keywords: Cloud computing · Software development · Process

1   Introduction

Instead of owning IT assets permanently, Cloud Computing suggests the idea of renting servers, storage, software technologies, tools and applications as utility or service over the internet as and when required [1]. Hence, it is a model being adopted rapidly by both individual and corporate users which targets the software development companies to develop software for cloud. However, as stated in [1] that software development process will include heterogeneous platforms, distributed web services, multiple enterprises located all over the world. The idea of this study emerged with the question of whether the traditional Software Development Life Cycle (SDLC) methodologies can be used in Cloud Computing Environment or not. Software is developed based on functional and non-functional requirements.

© Springer International Publishing Switzerland 2015
I. Ciuciu et al. (Eds.): OTM 2015 Workshops, LNCS 9416, pp. 421–430, 2015.
DOI: 10.1007/978-3-319-26138-6_45

In software development for cloud, there are additional non-functional requirements that play a much more vital role. For example, the non-functional requirements specific to cloud are multi-tenancy, on-demand self-service, resource pooling, rapid-elasticity, measured services are especially the reason why people and organizations choose cloud option to do their businesses. Beside, software development for cloud is not a static activity; software should be evolved continuously to satisfy the need of the users. Even without explicit new requirement statement from the customer, the services should be improved in a proactive way to keep the customer-software interaction alive. Therefore, the software development approach should be formed in a way that it is open to the continuous extensions and improvements. Cloud has also some weaknesses such as security, privacy, data ownership, and vendor lock-in etc. The development model should also be structured in a way that takes these weaknesses into consideration to provide high quality software. Since cloud brings new requirements to consider; available SDLC models cannot be used as is. This issue arise a need for the software development for cloud in a systematic way. In this study, different from available studies, we propose a SDLC model for cloud where we combine the strengths of Waterfall, Prototyping and Incremental model by addressing the new non-functional requirements that cloud brings and critical weaknesses it has.

2   Literature Survey

There are few studies investigating the SDLC in cloud computing applications but there is still not a comprehensive software development process model developed for cloud computing yet [1]. Mwansa and Mnkandla [2] proposed a framework to migrate the Agile software development to the cloud environment. Patidar et al. [3] emphasized the necessity of involving the cloud provider in every stages of the SDLC. They proposed a model that is an extended version of Agile, where they included the cloud-provider in planning, design, development, and testing stages. Raj et al.[4] incorporated security into each phases in the Software development life cycle. Joshi et al. [5] offered a SDLC using semantic technologies and defined new stages such as requirement, discovery, negotiation, composition, and consumption. Different from other studies, Chauhan and Saxena [6] conceptualized a green software development life cycle model incorporating the energy consumption issue to the phases of development life cycle. Song et al. [7] presented a deduced Software as a service (SaaS) Life Cycle model and incorporated cloud provider to the lifecycle as well. Kommalapati and William [8] mentioned that cloud expert (architect or consultant), Tier 1 support lead and Tier 2 escalation lead are taking the roles during the software development. Guha and Al-Dabass [1] suggested a model that extends the XP model and incorporated the cloud provider to the model. It is stated that the software engineering approaches that are available for traditional software development are not adequate for software development on cloud environments therefore the traditional approaches should be adapted keeping in view the cloud environment and its challenges [9].

3   A Software Development Lifecycle Model for Cloud

With the motivation of the absence of a standardized and conventional SDLC for cloud computing [9], we aim to propose a model that combines three available process models namely Waterfall, Prototyping, and Incremental Model iteratively to support continuous evolution of Cloud based software. The role of cloud provider is incorporated to each stage of process model as suggested in [1]. Other cloud actors (cloud auditor, cloud broker, cloud carrier) are also incorporated if they exist in the ecosystem. The difference of our process model is its addressing the specific characteristics, weakness and challenges of cloud-based structure.

3.1   The Challenges of Cloud Computing from SDLC Perspective

Development of the cloud has some challenges compared to the traditional development. Moreover, cloud has some characteristics that are specific to it. Beside, even though it is a very convenient option that many organizations have adopted; it has some weaknesses that should be considered while proposing a software development process for cloud. These challenges are given in the following sub-sections.

New Non-functional Requirements Inherent From Cloud Characteristics. Due to the nature of the cloud structure, the possible circumstances are more varied than traditional software development. Additional non-functional requirements as presented below should be taken into account.

- Multi-tenancy: This characteristic requires a "policy-driven enforcement, segmentation, isolation, governance, service levels and also chargeback/billing models for different usages" [10].
- On-demand self-service/capability: The services should be available when needed in an automatic manner without the interaction of the end-user with the service provider
- Resource pooling: There is always a dynamic assignment of different physical and virtual resources upon the demand of the consumers [10].
- Rapid-elasticity/Scalability: In any time and any quantity the cloud services should be offered to the users [10].
- Measured-Service: It is possible to measure, control and report the usage of the resources for both the cloud provider and consumer [10].

Adaptation to Changing Requirements. In [9], it is also stated that the most important characteristic of cloud-based software, is its ability to adapt to changing requirements and to changing contexts. In software development for cloud environment, the project is not an end task. To respond to the user needs there should be a continuous improvement of the project. Especially, the developers should behave in a proactive manner to satisfy the needs of their customers in advance; not waiting a change or improve request coming from them.

Weaknesses of Cloud Computing Structure. Cloud applications should possess some characteristics and if these are not satisfied it can become to some disadvantages people and organizations consider while adopting it. Some weaknesses of Cloud computing are presented as follows [11][12][13]:

- Control and Reliability: This feature passes to the hands of the cloud provider [11].
- Performance: A service level agreement cannot guarantee performance; it just punishes the bad performance [13]. This issue has the potential of creating a problem when a critical condition is faced.
- Security, Privacy and Compliance: These features are sensitive, since the confidential data of customers are managed by the cloud provider [11]. In [13] it is stated that "Signing a cloud contract without knowing your vendor's security architecture isn't smart"
- Compatibility: Any tool should be "compatible with the Web-based service, platform and infrastructure" [11].
- Unpredicted Costs: There is always an option of unpredicted cost [11].
- Contract and Lock-Ins /Inflexibility: It is stated that in the traditional approach the IT can be downsized, upsized, contracted-in freely by the owner but now cloud provider is the only authority having this power. Moreover, vendor lock-in can also create another problem in future [11].
- Data ownership: There is not a consensus about the "who is the owner of the data". That causes the cloud provider to set up their own rules, terms and conditions [12]. As stated in [13] the vendor can bust out suddenly, therefore it is important to define these rules at the beginning.
- Possible downtime: The service delivery to the clients of the consumer can suffer a lot due to this problem of slowness or unavailability [12].
- Lack of support It is stated in [12] that the support for the customers in cloud-based applications are not so easy and taking a reply to a request or problem statement within 48 hours is not adequate when you do your business over the internet, where 7/24 accessibility is a must.

3.2   Proposed Model Schema

In this section, the proposed schema for SDLC on Cloud Computing to develop software for cloud is presented. The process model we present involves both the activities and the roles of the stakeholders associated with them. To derive a SDLC for cloud environment, we make a synthesis of different process models that are already mature enough for traditional software development. These incorporated models are Waterfall model, Prototyping, Incremental model; by taking their specific characteristics a new model is proposed.

A pictorial description the proposed model is given in Figure 1. Developing software for cloud requires a number of iterations where we keep on adding services when needed. There should always be a continuous improvement and evolution of software which is only possible when a process model supports development in iteration with the possibility of adding new requirements and refining old ones through users' feedback. Moreover, with the time additional services can be incorporated; the users' future demands should be forecasted and these should be proactively incorporated to the system. Therefore we need to adapt the traditional Waterfall Model. Waterfall model is taken as a starting point since it has a formal definition of core phases, a very good standardized documentation that is missing in Agile methods. Main Phases of Waterfall model such as Requirement Analysis, Design, Development, Testing and Maintenance are included. Additionally, a new phase "Planning" is also included because similar to on-premise software development where there is schedule planning, budget planning and risk planning; cloud software development require additional planning where the service planning in terms of contract management is crucial.

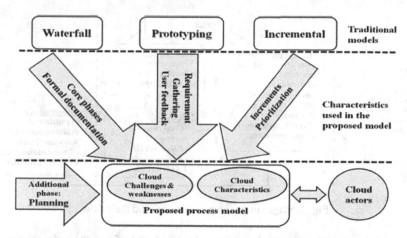

Fig. 1. Synthesis of Waterfall Model, Prototyping and Incremental Model

Prototyping is a model where both the requirements and the user feedbacks can be taken into account during the software development. It also providesa good way to develop system with high usability. Since the usability and aesthetics are very important in web applications, prototyping is a good approach for cloud software development. However, prototyping alone is not sufficient; the reason is that it is not necessary that prototyping model have incremental characteristics. But cloud environment require incremental approach.

We incorporated the Incremental model to the proposed process model since due to the nature of cloud computing applications, at the beginning we may not be eligible to develop all the services. We may prioritize the services and later we can add more. In cloud computing new service will be equivalent to new increment. Even within a single service, some of the features may not be feasible to realize. Beside, as stated previously, the nature of cloud software is prone to changes with additions/ removal / modifications. Therefore, incremental approach should be incorporated.

In contrast with the available studies in the literature, we do not adopt Agile methods. The reason is that even though Agile methods are very flexible and at the same time very product focused approach; in our opinion, it has some characteristics such as absence of formal documentation that are not so convenient for software development for cloud environment. Developing for cloud involves more stakeholders than traditional software development and from our point of view; these stakeholders need to be connected via strict documentation.

3.3   Detailed Description of the Proposed Model

The proposed model includes the requirement analysis, design, development, testing and maintenance of Waterfall model; requirement gathering approach from prototyping; and increments and prioritization from incremental model combined in an iterative manner. The stages order and the work flow among them are shown in the following Figure 2.

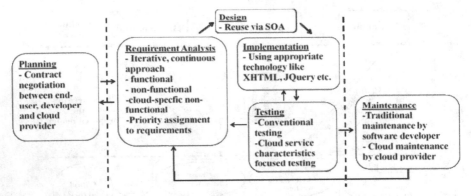

Fig. 2. Stages in the proposed model and their flow

The well-known stages are already standardized, therefore, their descriptions are not provided. We concentrate more on what will differ for cloud case. The stages will be explained in three dimensions which are activity, role and challenges addressed.

Since a cloud based software should be developed in an iterative way, there should be a cyclic structure between requirement gathering and planning to adjust the resources and terms of the agreements. Similarly, since new requirements can be added with the idea of incorporation of new services, the design stage and the requirement stage should be cyclic too. Testing and implementation should be iterative to enhance the development with the testing results. Last but not least, the maintenance in cloud software development is very important and the contract for the maintenance should be planned and updated according to the available and newly introduced requirements. In all these stages the agreement with the cloud actors such as provider, auditor, broker and carrier should be done in a systematic and unbiased manner.

Planning. Planning in software development is a stage where the problem definitions, feasibility analysis, schedule settlement of the project are defined.

Activities are as follows: When we consider a project planning for cloud based software, there are challenges presented in the previous section. Different from the traditional software development, the terms of conditions should be made more carefully. First of all, a cloud project is not a project just between the end-user and the developer team but also between the cloud service provider and the developer team. Therefore, in addition to classical project contracts between developers and the customers, there should be contracts with the service provider.

Consequently, in planning phase there should be two kinds of contracts. The first one is the general contract that specifies the on-time and on-budget completion of the project by stating the conventional codes of ethics. The second contract negotiation is with the service provider or other cloud actors involved in the project ecosystem considering the service offering guarantees. Another activity in this stage is the risk management that addresses both service delivery particularities and operation cost.

Roles are as follows: Here, apart from the developer team and customer (cloud consumers) other the stakeholders such as cloud provider, cloud auditor, cloud broker and cloud carrier are the actors of the environments.

Challenges addressed are as follows: The second contract negotiation addresses the challenges of cloud software development by considering the cloud characteristics. The characteristics of cloud such as on-demand capability, resource pooling, security, privacy and compliance issues, measured services should be defined in that contract negotiation as a part of the project that is independent of the physical system development but instead related to service delivery. As stated in [13] it is not useful to sign a cloud contract without knowing the cloud vendor's security architecture. Besides the control and reliability is another issue open to discussion for the cloud ecosystem where the power is in the hands of cloud provider. The codes of law for this should be defined carefully during the contract negotiation. It is also important to define the data ownership and unpredicted cost. As stated in [12] the cloud provider can have their own rules, terms and conditions and it can disappear suddenly. Therefore, sanctions should be strictly stated in advance to prevent unwanted situations. As stated previously, that in the traditional approach the IT can be downsized, upsized, contracted-in freely by the owner but now cloud provider is the only authority having this power. Moreover, vendor lock-in can also create another problem in future [11] the contract negotiation should address to this challenge.

Apart from above stated issues, performance, possible down-time and lack of support are other issues where the cloud type structure suffers from. Since at the end the clients' business can be affected from even a very less time of service interruption, the sanctions when these problems are occurred should be defined very carefully. These risks should be defined within the risk management activity.

Requirement Analysis. Requirement analysis is one of the key steps of software development.

Activities are as follows: Cloud actors should be incorporated to the process [1]. The cloud software development is not only related to functional requirements of the system. Different from traditional software development, there are also non-functional requirements that are dependent of the cloud service's capabilities. These should be addressed in this phase. Possible activities can be defining user requirements, making a prioritization, defining cloud related non-functional requirements, introducing the initial baseline, consequently developing a prototype including the prioritized services.

Roles are as follows: The development team should gather the requirement from the stakeholders as in the traditional software development but they have to also consult and suggest the cloud actors such as cloud provider, cloud broker, cloud auditor and cloud carrier if they exist in the ecosystem.

Challenges addressed are as follows: In cloud software development, as stated previously the requirement analysis is not a finishing task instead; it is an evolutionary process where the requirements and requests from the customer change over time. Especially, developers should work continuously to add services to satisfy the needs of the customers in a proactive manner. Therefore an iterative and incremental approach should be adopted where it is easy to add new services as increments. Moreover, cloud computing has some characteristics such as multi-tenancy, configurability and on-demand self-service that should be taken into account.

Design. Design for cloud should include flexibility, interoperability and reuse.

Activities are as follows: The service integration should be done without any problem. Moreover in [9] it is stated that there can be two options for SaaS; building from scratch or reengineering the existing web services and legacy software for SaaS. Since as stated in the requirement step that requirements are/can be changing over time, there should be a very flexible and modular design that take into account this issue. The flexible design can be achieved by adopting the service-oriented architecture.

Roles are as follows: In this stage the development team should work in accordance with the cloud actors to get the idea about the cloud service infrastructure such as virtual machine, availability of container approach, data handling method etc.

Challenges addressed are as follows: The proposed design architecture should be addressing the challenge of rapid elasticity and adaptation to changing requirements. Compatibility that is shown as one of the weaknesses of cloud structure should also be taken into account while making a flexible system design.

Implementation. The technologies for web application development can be used for cloud development too. It is suggested in [9] that the technologies appropriate for Cloud such as XHTML, JQuery, Java Script, Python, AJAX, Ruby on Rails and Agile technologies should be incorporated in SDLC for Cloud. As stated in [4], we also suggest Model-Driven approaches; that provides a high-level, platform independent focus to developers which consequently help to overcome the lock-in problems.

Testing. Testing in cloud based software development plays a vital role. Cloud is a very convenient infrastructure to perform the tests. However it has itself to be tested with the provided services.

Activities are as follows: In testing for cloud, the unit testing, integration testing and system testing can be done. But since the difference of cloud based software is the scalability, rapid elasticity these issues should also be tested. Therefore, testers should work with the cloud actors in addition to prepare a requirement test plan, another test plan should be obtained from the cloud actors. Non-functional testing is a key activity due to the requirement of the continuous service delivery of cloud based software.

Roles are as follows: The development team should prepare the requirement test plan, they should work in accordance with the cloud actor for example cloud provider to test the non-functional requirements of the virtual resources. They both prepare a single test at the end to test the system as a whole.

Challenges addressed are as follows: Possible down-time, performance, scalability, security and privacy are the non-functional requirements that are inherent in cloud. Therefore these challenges can be addressed with different testing methods such as stress testing, performance testing and security testing etc.

Maintenance. Management of distributed software development has more challenges and difficulties than conventional development [14]. The maintenance is one of the most critical activities in cloud software development and the criteria should be defined clearly.

Activities are as follows: Different from the traditional software development, the maintenance responsibility does not only belong to the software development team but also it is shared with the cloud providers. In [1] it is stated that a contract that does not violating the software engineering code of ethics should be signed.

Roles are as follows: Software development team responsible for the maintenance of the functional continuity, cloud provider should be responsible for the continuous and high-quality service delivery.

Challenges addressed are as follows: The maintenance activities should manage the possible down-time, the slowness or the unavailability of the system. As stated in [12] the lack-of-support cannot be tolerated by the end-users who do their business on cloud. Therefore, in the maintenance agreement there should be a defined set of duties of the support team and their acceptable response time to user requests as well as the optimum problem resolution time should be contracted to prevent unwanted situations.

To sum up, we have to say that in each activity the challenges of cloud based software development should be addressed, the cloud stakeholders should be part of the software development process with the actual development team. Due to the continuous evolution of cloud-based software an iterative approach should be incorporated.

4   Conclusion

Cloud computing is a paradigm that spread out in a much faster manner among both individual and corporate users. It is seen as the future of the web. Therefore, it is important to draw a formal framework to the software development for cloud environments. However, due to its nature presented in the paper, the software development for a cloud application is not the same as the one for the traditional software development.

In the proposed model, different from the available studies, we tried to benefit from the existing process models' strengths to deal with the cloud-based software development. We took the formal structure and core processes of Waterfall model, combined it with the prototyping to get a good requirement gathering and early user feedback, further combined with the incremental model to prioritize the service development due to the extendable characteristic of cloud computing. Moreover, since cloud based software development is a continuously evolving task; we added the iterative structure to the process model.

As a further study, we aim firstly to perform a theoretical validation considering the other representative studies and our model to investigate the feasibility of this proposed model by comparing it with the available studies in the literature.

References

1. Guha, R., Al-Dabass, D.: Impact of web 2.0 and cloud computing platform on software engineering. In: IEEE Int. Symp. Electron. System Design (ISED), pp. 213–218 (2010)
2. Mwansa, G., Mnkandla, E.: Migrating agile development into the cloud computing environment. In: IEEE 7th International Conference on Cloud Computing (CLOUD), pp. 818–825 (2014)
3. Patidar, S., Rane, D., Jain, P.: Challenges of software development on cloud platform. In: 2011 World Congress on Information and Communication Technologies (WICT), pp. 1009–1013 (2011)
4. Raj, G., Singh, D., Bansal, A.: Analysis for security implementation in SDLC. In: 2014 5th International Conference on Confluence The Next Generation Information Technology Summit (Confluence), pp. 221–226 (2014)
5. Joshi, K.P., Yesha, Y., Finin, T.: Automating Cloud Services Life Cycle through Semantic Technologies. IEEE Transactions on Services Computing 7(1), 109–122 (2014)
6. Chauhan, N.S., Saxena, A.: A Green Software Development Life Cycle for Cloud Computing. IT Professional 15(1), 28–34 (2013)
7. Song, J., Li, T., Jia, L., Zhu, Z.: A deduced SaaS lifecycle model based on roles and activities. In: Advances in Computing and Communications, pp. 421–431 (2011)
8. Kommalapati, Z., William, H.H.: The SaaS Development Lifecycle (2011). http://www.infoq.com/articles/SaaS-Lifecycle (last accessed in May 25, 2015)
9. Baliyan, N., Kumar, S.: Towards software engineering paradigm for software as a service. In: 2014 Seventh International Conference on Contemporary Computing (IC3), pp. 329–333 (2014)
10. http://www.isaca.org/groups/professional-english/cloud-computing/groupdocuments/essentialcharacteristicsofcloudcomputing.pdf (last accessed May 25, 2015)
11. http://www.cloudcomputinginsights.com/management/cloud-computing-advantages-and-disadvantages/?mode=featured (last accessed May 30, 2015)
12. http://sbinfocanada.about.com/od/itmanagement/a/Cloud-Computing-Disadvantages.htm (last accessed May 30, 2015)
13. http://www.informationweek.com/cloud/the-clouds-five-biggest-weaknesses/d/d-id/1089865 (last accessed May 30, 2015)
14. Mishra, D., Mishra, A.: Research Trends in Management Issues of Global Software Development: Evaluating the Past to Envision the Future. Journal of Global Information Technology Management 14(4), 48–69 (2011)

Semantic Matching of Components at Run-Time in Distributed Environments

Javier Criado, Luis Iribarne[✉], Nicolás Padilla, and Rosa Ayala

Applied Computing Group, University of Almería, Almería, Spain
{javi.criado,luis.iribarne,npadilla,rmayala}@ual.es

Abstract. Software factories are a key element in Component-Based Software Engineering due to the common space provided for software reuse through repositories of components. These repositories can be developed by third parties in order to be inspected and used by different organizations, and they can also be distributed in different locations. Therefore, there is a need for a trading service that manages all available components. In this paper, we describe a matching process based on syntactic and semantic information of software components. This matching operation is part of a trading service which is in charge of generating configurations of components from architectural definitions. With this aim, the proposed matching allows us to evaluate and score the possible configurations, thus guiding a search process to build the architectural solution which best fulfills an input definition.

Keywords: Components · Reuse · Trading · Heuristics · Run-time

1 Introduction

Software reuse is a topic of ongoing interest in the construction of applications, especially in the component-based development. In this sense, *Component-Based Software Engineering* (CBSE) provides mechanisms for building applications from the union of pieces [5]. Certain types of component-based software systems have the need of performing a dynamic management of the elements which can be part of the applications [6]. In such cases, components are used for building or adapting software applications at run-time. In this sense, when a new architectural solution is needed, the most appropriate elements are selected from a set of available components. The selection of components involved in this process requires the existence of accessible repositories which can be inspected and queried in order to calculate the best possible configuration.

Repositories can be stored locally or can be intended for public use and shared by different organizations in a distributed environment [15] [16]. This scenario is usual in systems that build their applications using components developed by third parties, for example, based on COTS (*Commercial Off-The-Shelf*) [1]. Thus, these repositories constitute the existing market of components from which

I. Ciuciu et al. (Eds.): OTM 2015 Workshops, LNCS 9416, pp. 431–441, 2015.
DOI: 10.1007/978-3-319-26138-6_46

the software is built. These repositories of components can be managed similarly to a service directory, which are accessed by certain entities for offering services, and by other entities for making use of the available services. With this aim, *trading* techniques are useful to facilitate the execution of export and import operations of services [11]. Furthermore, trading mechanisms can be used to solve component-based architectures from an architectural definition [10].

In this paper, we present a semantic matching mechanism applied in a search algorithm for constructing architectures of software components at run-time. This operation is used as part of a trading service which manages repositories of components developed by third-parties. Specifically, the managed elements are coarse-grained COTS components, which can be specified by the DSL (*Domain-Specific Language*) shown in Figure 1. This language distinguishes between two levels of representation: *abstract* and *concrete*. Abstract components are used for describing architectural definitions (*i.e.*, the set of features that an architecture must include) whereas concrete components are utilized for defining architectural solutions (*i.e.*, the characteristics of an architecture consisting on real software components). Each specification is divided into four parts, with the aim of describing *functional*, *extra-functional*, *packaging* and *marketing* information.

The object implementing this trading service, named as *Semantic Trader*, is in charge of building architectural solutions from the input information contained in architectural definitions. With this regard, matching operations between abstract and concrete components are performed at run-time for scoring and evaluating the different configurations of components that are taken into account as possible solutions. Both, the matching operations and the trading service are part of a methodology for adapting architectures at run-time [3,4].

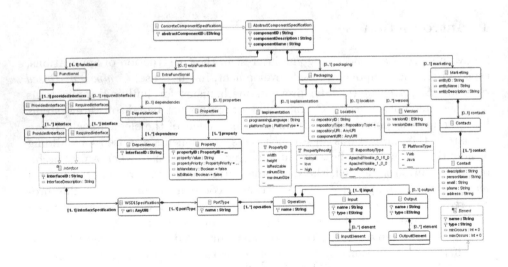

Fig. 1. Specifications of components

The semantic matching of the proposed trading service is based on the following assumption: the possible types that can be used for the description of the inputs and outputs of the interfaces' operations are restricted. Therefore, we propose to create a *namespace* that groups all possible types, which are identified as `trader:typeName`. These types are described using an XML schema syntax, and are referenced from the definition of interfaces, in the corresponding WSDL [8] fragment of the model that contains the specification of the component (see Figure 1). These types are equivalent to complex data types that provide: (a) information about the name, the type and the cardinality of the elements composing the complex data type, and (b) information about the operations using this data type and if it is used as input or output. In addition to the description of interfaces, semantic information is present in the evaluation of components and architectures as part of the heuristics of an A* search algorithm used for generating the architectural solutions.

The remainder of this paper is organized as follows. Section 2 describes the semantic matching approach used for building the architectural solutions at run-time. Section 3 discusses some related work. Finally, Section 4 presents the conclusions and the future work.

2 Semantic Matching of the Trading Service

The final goal of the proposed trading service is to build architectural solutions at run-time. This action is based on a semantic matching between the components of an input architectural definition and the different configurations which are evaluated in a search process. This search is performed using an A* algorithm. In this type of algorithms, a graph represents the search space and its nodes identify the states to advance in the search. The goal is to find the least-cost path to the target node from a starting node. Cost calculation is made using an evaluation function $f(x) = g(x) + h'(x)$. Function $g(x)$ represents a known distance (pre-calculated) between the initial node and the current node. Furthermore, $h'(x)$ identifies the estimated value of an admissible heuristic ($h(x)$) concerning the distance from the current node to the target node. In order to be admissible, the heuristic should not overestimate the real value of the calculated distance.

This type of algorithm always find a solution if one exists. In addition, the search process should not necessarily explore all nodes of the graph to find this solution. The explored search space and, consequently, the complexity of the algorithm depends on the quality of the heuristics. In the worst case, the order is exponential, whereas the order of the best case (where the estimated heuristic is close to the optimal case) is linear. Another reason for choosing this type of algorithm is the run-time nature of the calculation of configurations. The exploration path always moves towards a solution whose distance from the target node is lower than the previous state. Therefore, we can keep a reference to the last 'best solution' and make use of it if the trading service is forced to finish the search (for example, due to time constraints or other restrictions).

In our proposal, each graph node represents a configuration of concrete components, so that, a node is adjacent to another if its configuration differs in one component. Thus, each iteration of the A* search algorithm is executed until a configuration that meets the architectural definition is found. The *Semantic Trader* is in charge of executing this algorithm, evaluating each configuration and building the architectural solution. With this aim, the proposed mechanism for generating the best concrete architecture is based on the following operations: (a) select the candidates, (b) calculate the configurations, (c) close the configurations, (d) calculate the configuration which are compliant with the architectural definition, (e) apply a heuristic function for evaluating the configurations, and (f) build the concrete architecture. Next, such operations are described.

Select the Candidates: Before the execution of the algorithm, candidate components are grouped using the information of the functional part in order to limit the search graph. Each group is related to the operations of a component from the abstract architecture (architectural) and it contains those concrete components which have at least one operation (from provided interface) in common. Thus, graph nodes do not contains more than one component of the same group.

Calculate the Configurations: The pseudocode of the developed algorithm is shown in Figure 2. The algorithm starts from an initial node (*source*) which is adjacent to every node created from the components of one group of candidates. Those are the only existing nodes in the graph and the other nodes are created dynamically when a new node is explored (line 25 of Figure 2). Furthermore, new neighbors are created only if the resulting configurations do not exceed the size of the abstract definition (line 22). These optimizations limit the search space of the algorithm and reduce the number of nodes for which the evaluation function $f(x)$ is calculated. In addition, $f(x)$ is used as a reference for managing the priority queue that stores the set of 'open' nodes. From this priority queue, the nodes explored in each iteration are selected (line 10).

The default value for $g(x)$ is 1, since a node differs from its adjacent nodes in the incorporation of one concrete component. However, after the evaluation of the algorithm, there are situations (*e.g.*, when the number of candidate components is very high) in which the establishment of $g(x) = 0$, allows us to obtain architectural solutions in less time. In such cases, the A* algorithm is equivalent to *greedy* search algorithm. This variation means that implementation of the algorithm does not ensure that the resulting solution is the optimal (*i.e.*, the closest to the starting node). Nevertheless, other operations are responsible for checking the algorithm not to add additional components to those defined in the abstract architecture. Moreover, $g(x)$ is configurable through the *Admin* interface of the *Semantic Trader*.

The value of $h'(x)$ represents the distance between the configuration of concrete components (associated with the current node) and the input abstract architectural model (AAM). This distance must be 0 (lines 13 and 31) to consider that a configuration is a possible architectural solution, and it is calculated from the semantic information of the components' functional interfaces. This decision ensures (at least) the resolution of valid configuration regarding the functional part, and in less time than if all components' part are evaluated. Nevertheless,

```
 1: function ASTAR(source, AAM)
 2:     openSet ← {source}
 3:     pQueue ← {source}
 4:     closeSet ← ∅
 5:     discardedConfigs ← 0
 6:     notDesiredCC ← ∅
 7:     firstSolution ← false
 8:     bestNode ← ∅
 9:     while openSet ≠ ∅ do
10:         currentNode ← pQueue.poll()
11:         if currentNode.getH() < bestNode.getH() then bestNode ← currentNode
12:         end if
13:         if currentNode.getH() == 0 then
14:             if firstSolution == false then firstSolution ← true
15:             end if
16:             bestNode ← currentNode
17:             if evaluateCAM(currentNode, AAM) == true then return bestNode
18:             else discardedConfigs ← discardedConfigs + 1
19:             end if
20:         else
21:             closeSet.put(currentNode)
22:             if checkCAMSize(currentNode) == true then
23:                 if contains(notDesiredCC, currentNode) == false then
24:                     neighbors = ∅
25:                     neighbors ← createNewAdajectNodes(currentNode)
26:                     for each neighbor in neighbors do
27:                         if contains(closeSet, neighbor) == false then
28:                             if contains(openSet, neighbor) == false then
29:                                 h ← heuristics(neighbor, AAM)
30:                                 newNode ← createNode(neighbor, h)
31:                                 if h == 0 then ... // (lines 14–19)
32:                                 else
33:                                     openSet.put(newNode)
34:                                     pQueue.add(newNode)
35:                                 end if
36:                             end if
37:                         end if
38:                     end for
39:                 end if
40:             end if
41:         end if
42:     end while
43:     return bestNode
44: end function
```

Fig. 2. Search algorithm to find the best configuration

when a configuration fulfilling the functional part is found, a full evaluation of the configuration is performed by calculating the distance with respect to the AAM and using all the component parts (including extra-functional information). This evaluation also checks: (a) that configurations are closed, $i.e.$, have no components with additional mandatory required interfaces (with regard to the abstract architecture); and (b) that configurations are compliant with the abstract architecture, $i.e.$, functionality is grouped in the components as determined by the architectural definition.

Apply a Heuristic Function for Evaluating the Configurations: The method in charge of calculating the scores is *heuristics* (line 29 of Figure 2). This operation involved only the functional part of the components, distinguishing between provided and required interfaces. In order to carry out this process, a 'macro' abstract component, containing all information pertaining to the functional specification of the abstract architecture, is created. Similarly, a 'macro' concrete component, which brings together all the functional information of components that are part of the current configuration, is created. In both cases, the union of all provided and required interfaces which are mandatory is produced.

These new specifications are compared with the aim of calculating the distance between both definitions (Figure 3).

Matching of provided and required interfaces (MPI and MRI, respectively) is described by a decimal number between 0 and 1, where 0 indicates no match and 1 means a complete match. This value is calculated by dividing the number of matched by total existing operations in the abstract definition. Furthermore, matching of functional part (MF) is calculated as the average of the matching scores from the two types of interfaces, as shown by the following expressions:

$$MF = \frac{MPI + MRI}{2} \qquad MPI = \frac{matchedProvidedOp}{acProvidedOp} \qquad MRI = \frac{matchedRequiredOp}{acRequiredOp}$$

Evaluation function, which represents the distance between an abstract definition and a concrete specification, is calculated from the obtained matching value: $h'(x) = 1 - matching$. Beside this matching value, it is calculated some specific information about which operations (and belonging to which interfaces) of the configuration solve the operations of the functional interfaces described in the abstract architecture. This data is essential for optimizing the performance in the construction of the concrete architecture model, since the relationships between components (and corresponding dependencies between interfaces) are easily calculated from this information.

Moreover, as supplementary information for pairing analysis, other attributes derived from the comparison are calculated: (a) what type of intersection is produced between sets of interfaces, (b) who owns the largest set of provided and required interfaces, (c) the total number of provided and required operations of the configuration and the abstract architecture, (d) the total number of provided and required interfaces. This data is produced as a result of the comparisons made in the *heuristic* method (line 29 of Figure 2).

Closure of Configurations and Calculation of Compliant Configurations: Both operations are carried out in the *evaluateCAM* function (line 17 of Figure 2). As mentioned above, this method is invoked whenever a configuration is a possible solution, *i.e.*, a configuration whose value of the evaluation function is zero ($h'(x) = 0$). In this function, a new evaluation of matching between the

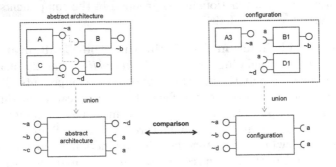

Fig. 3. Comparison between abstract architectures and configurations

abstract architecture and the current configuration is performed. In contrast to the matching of the *heuristics* method (line 29), the comparison is made for each component of the configuration independently, instead of performing an overall comparison. Furthermore, this process of matching takes into account all parts of the component specifications. Therefore, four values, corresponding to each of the main parts of the specification of a component, are calculated:

— *Functional information*: scoring process results in the MF value described for the *heuristics* method.
— *Extra-function information*: the total matching value is the average of the matches of dependencies and properties parts. Additional information is also calculated, as the type of intersection between the sets compared or their relative size. Extra-functional information is divided in: a) *Properties*: firstly, the matching operation checks which properties of the abstract component are fulfilled in the concrete component. Secondly, the matching value is calculated as a weighted sum of the three categories of existing properties (high, normal or low priority). In this sense, the matching of properties with high priority involves higher matching scores than meeting properties with a normal (or low) priority; b) *Dependencies*: for calculating this value of matching, it is necessary to take into account the type of intersection between the sets of dependencies. If there is no intersection, matching is 0.0, provided that both sets are not empty (in which case matching is 1.0). If there is intersection, there may be three possibilities: (1) that all the dependencies of the concrete component (DCC) are within the set of abstract component dependencies (DAC), (2) that DAC is within DCC, and (3) that no set is within the other. Next, the expressions to calculate the value of matching (m), depending on the three possibilities and taking into account the number of dependencies in the intersection ($matchedDep$), are shown:

$$(1)\ m = \frac{matchedDep}{card(DAC)} \qquad (2)\ m = \frac{matchedDep}{card(DCC)} \qquad (3)\ m = \frac{matchedDep}{card(DAC) + card(DCC)}$$

— *Packaging information*: the total matching value is the average of the matches of implementation and location parts. Additional information as the type of intersection between the sets or their relative size is also calculated.
— *Marketing information*: calculated scores represents if the components are developed by the same entity and if same contact people are associated.

Each matching value is described by a decimal number between 0 and 1 (where 0 indicates no match and 1 means that the matching is complete). Thus, total matching between two components is calculated from the matching of the functional part (MF), matching of the extra-functional part (MEF), matching of packaging information (MP), and matching of marketing information (MM). Figure 4 shows a graphical representation of calculated matching scores for three concrete components. On the one hand, we can see that the component which best meets the abstract definition is $CC3$. On the other hand, the representation of the matching score of component $CC1$ has a larger area (determined by the four points of the four components' parts) than the component $CC2$. However, depending on the importance we attach to each part, it can be considered as the component $CC2$ meets better the abstract specification.

In this sense, matching score between two components is calculated from the following expression: $matching = MF * factor MF + MEF * factor MEF + MP * factor MP + MM * factor MM$. By default, the values for $factorMF$, $factorMEF$, $factorMP$ and $factorMM$ are 0.8, 0.15, 0.025 and 0.025, respectively. Therefore, we give more weight to functional and extra-functional properties. Nevertheless, these weight can be modified at run-time using the $Admin$ interface of the trading service (if the condition that the sum of the factors is equal to 1 is satisfied). As a consequence, it is possible to vary the weight given to each of the components' parts for comparison operations.

Resuming the execution of $evaluateCAM$ method, the closure operation verifies there are no additional dependencies (mandatory required interfaces) in concrete components with respect to the abstract definition. With the aim of checking the compliance with the architecture, it is verified that the configuration is made up of the same number of components as the abstract definition. When the trading process is set up, the minimum distances to consider that a configuration meets architecture can be established. In addition, this operations of the $Admin$ interface can be used at run-time to modify the execution policies. For example, it is possible to specify that a ratio of 0.95 for extra-functional properties must be accomplished, thus determining that matching score of that specific part cannot be less than this value. Those configurations that are not closed or do not comply with the architecture, are discarded, continuing the search algorithm until a valid solution is found.

There is another remarkable feature implemented in this process. A maximum value of time that should not be exceeded to obtain a valid solution can be defined. Thus, when this limit is exceeded, the search algorithm stops, although it has failed to reach the final solution. Nevertheless, although several solutions have been discarded, it is highly probable that other configurations have been

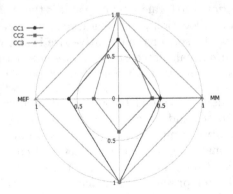

Fig. 4. Example of matching scores

found with a value of $h'(x)$ equal to 0.0. Such configurations are valid solutions in functional terms. Therefore, whenever a configuration of this type is found, a reference to the corresponding node is saved, since it is the best node found up to that point (line 16 of the algorithm shown in Figure 2) In the case that the algorithm must terminate without finding the final solution, this configuration will be returned by the algorithm, to ensure the resolution of the architectural definition (at least at the functional level).

Build the Concrete Architecture: Once the final solution has been obtained, the semantic trading service constructs the concrete architectural model associated with the configuration found by the A* search algorithm.

3 Related Work

In the construction of software architectures, selection and evaluation processes are considered as key operations [14]. An example of work in which these processes are addressed is the Off-The-Shelf Option (OTSO) [12]. In such approach, a hierarchical evaluation criteria analyzes the characteristics of the components based on other factors such as organizational infrastructure or the availability of libraries. In [9], DesCOTS system proposes a methodology based on a quality model which divides the characteristics of the components for their evaluation.

The work presented in [17] evaluates the components and establishes a ranking in terms of performance and according to multiple criteria. In [7], authors perform a management of dependencies between components using goal-oriented models as the basis for component selection. A proposal for selecting COTS components in large repositories is described in [2]. The approach makes use of the 'integrator' concept instead of mediation or trading services. In contrast to our proposal, the approaches mentioned above do not support component selection or calculation of configurations at run-time.

The trading described in [10] is the basis of the work. It presents a mediation process for managing COTS components and building configurations at *design-time*. In contrast, our approach is intended to build architectures at *run-time* based on a semantic matching of components. Algorithms based on heuristic functions are a suitable option for the exploration and evaluation of possible solutions [13]. In addition, other type of algorithms, such as exhaustive search algorithm for building configurations of components [4], results in exponential execution orders because all the nodes in the search space must be evaluated.

4 Conclusion and Future Work

We presented an approach for matching component specifications at run-time. This operation is part of a trading service in charge of dynamically building architectures. This process is responsible for calculating the best architectural solutions starting from their corresponding architectural definitions. In order to address this resolution, matching operations are performed to compare components and obtain scores describing the distance between: (a) an input architectural definition and (b) each of component configurations which are possible solutions of the architecture. Furthermore, these scores are calculated applying an evaluation function that makes use of the syntactic and semantic information described the component specifications. This evaluation function is utilized in an A* algorithm as the heuristic to find the best configuration.

There are identified some lines as future work. We plan to extend the matching information calculated from the comparison of two components or architectures. In addition, we plan to evaluate alternative search algorithms for building architectures at run-time. Furthermore, we plan to improve the performance of the proposed algorithm, for example, parallelizing part of the execution. Moreover, we intend to develop some tools for querying and managing the information of component specifications and their comparisons.

Acknowledgments. This work was funded by the Spanish Ministry MINECO under Project TIN2013-41576-R, the MECD under a FPU grant (AP2010-3259), and the Andalusian Government (Spain) under Project P10-TIC-6114.

References

1. Carney, D., Leng, F.: What Do You Mean by COTS? Finally, a Useful Answer. IEEE Software **17**(2), 83–86 (2000)
2. Clark, J., et al.: Selecting components in large COTS repositories. Journal of Systems and Software **73**(2), 323–331 (2004)
3. Criado, J., et al.: Toward the adaptation of component-based architectures by model transformation: behind smart user interfaces. SPE Jour. (2014). Elsevier
4. Criado, J., Iribarne, L., Padilla, N.: Resolving platform specific models at runtime using an MDE-based trading approach. In: Demey, Y.T., Panetto, H. (eds.) OTM 2013 Workshops 2013. LNCS, vol. 8186, pp. 274–283. Springer, Heidelberg (2013)
5. Crnkovic, I.: Component-based Software Engineering – New Challenges in Software Development. Software Focus **2**(4), 127–133 (2001)
6. Crnkovic, I.: Component-based software engineering for embedded systems. In: 27th ICSE, pp. 712–713. ACM (2005)
7. Franch, X., Maiden, N.A.M.: Modelling component dependencies to inform their selection. In: Erdogmus, H., Weng, T. (eds.) ICCBSS 2003. LNCS, vol. 2580, pp. 81–91. Springer, Heidelberg (2003)
8. Graham, S., et al.: Building Web services with Java: making sense of XML, SOAP, WSDL, and UDDI. SAMS publishing (2004)
9. Grau, G., Carvallo, J.P., Franch, X., Quer, C: DesCOTS: a software system for selecting COTS components. In: 30th Euromicro Conf., pp. 118–126. IEEE (2004)
10. Iribarne, L., Troya, J.M., Vallecillo, A.: A trading service for COTS components. The Computer Journal **47**(3), 342–357 (2004)
11. ISO/IEC 13235-1, ITU-T X.950. Information Technology - Open Distributed Processing - Trading function: Specification (1998)
12. Kontio, J., Caldiera, G., Basili, V.R.: Defining factors, goals and criteria for reusable component evaluation. In: CASCON 1996, pp. 21–32. IBM Press (1996)

13. Korf, R.E.: Real-time heuristic search. Artificial Int. **42**(2), 189–211 (1990)
14. Mohamed, A., Ruhe, G., Eberlein, A.: COTS selection: past, present, and future. In: Engineering of Computer-Based Systems, pp. 103–114. IEEE (2007)
15. Mishra, D., Mishra, A.: Distributed information system development: review of some management issues. In: OTM 2009 Workshops, pp. 282–291 (2009)
16. Mishra, D., Alok, M.: Research trends in management issues of global software development: evaluating the past to envision the future. J. GITM **14**(4), 48–69 (2011)
17. Shyur, H.J.: COTS evaluation using modified TOPSIS and ANP. Applied Mathematics and Computation **177**(1), 251–259 (2006)

Workshop on Methods, Evaluation, Tools and Applications for the Creation and Consumption of Structured Data for the e-Society (META4eS) 2015

META4eS 2015 PC Co-Chairs' Message

The future eSociety, addressed with our workshop, is an e-inclusive society based on the extensive use of digital technologies at all levels of interaction between its members. It is a society that evolves based on knowledge and that empowers individuals by creating virtual communities that benefit from social inclusion, access to information, enhanced interaction, participation and freedom of expression, among others.

In this context, the role of the ICT in the way people and organizations exchange information and interact in the social cyberspace is crucial. Large amounts of structured data – Big (Open) Data - are being generated, published and shared on the Web and a growing number of services and applications emerge from it. These initiatives take into account methods for the creation, storage and consumption of increasing amounts of structured data and tools that make possible their application by end-users to real-life situations, as well as their evaluation. The final aim is to lower the barrier between end-users and information and communication technologies via a number of techniques stemming from the fields of semantic knowledge processing, multilingual information, information visualization, privacy and trust, etc. The applications must be designed in such a way to help people use their knowledge at best and generate new knowledge in return, while keeping intact their privacy and confidentiality.

To discuss, demonstrate and share best practices, ideas and results, the 4th International IFIP Workshop on Methods, Evaluation, Tools and Applications for the Creation and Consumption of Structured Data for the e-Society (META4eS 2015), an event supported by IFIP TC 12 WG 12.7 and The Big data roadmap and cross-disciplinarY community for addressing socieTal Externalities (BYTE) project, with a special focus on cross-disciplinary communities and applications associated with Big Data and their impact on the e-Society, brings together researchers, professionals and experts interested to present original research results in this area.

We are happy to announce that, for its fourth edition, the workshop raised interest and good participation in the research community. After a thorough review process, with each submission refereed by at least three members of the workshop Program Committee, we accepted 5 full papers, 3 short papers and one poster paper covering topics such as ontology engineering, Big Data, smart knowledge processing and extraction, social semantics, software quality, and applied to the fields of education, historical data preservation, e-Health and ambient assisted living.

We thank the Program Committee members for their time and effort in ensuring the quality during the review process, as well as all the authors and the workshop attendees for the original ideas and the inspiring discussions. We also thank the OTM 2015 Organizing Committee members for their continuous support. We are confident that META4eS will bring an important contribution towards the future eSociety.

September 2015

Ioana Ciuciu
Anna Fensel
Christophe Debruyne

Creating and Consuming Metadata from Transcribed Historical Vital Records for Ingestion in a Long-Term Digital Preservation Platform

(Short Paper)

Dolores Grant[1], Christophe Debruyne[2,3(✉)], Rebecca Grant[1], and Sandra Collins[1]

[1] Digital Repository of Ireland, Royal Irish Academy, Dublin 2, Ireland
{d.grant,r.grant,s.collins}@ria.ie
[2] ADAPT Centre for Digital Content Platform Research, Knowledge & Data Engineering Group, School of Computer Science and Statistics, Trinity College Dublin, Dublin 2, Ireland
debruync@scss.tcd.ie
[3] Web & Information Systems Engineering Laboratory,
Department of Computer Science, Vrije Universiteit Brussel, Brussels, Belgium
chrdebru@vub.ac.be

Abstract. In the Irish Record Linkage 1864-1913 (IRL) project, digital archivists transcribe digitized register pages containing vital records into a database, which is then used to generate RDF triples. Historians then use those triples to answer some specific research questions on the IRL platform. Though the triples themselves are a highly valuable asset that can be adopted by many, the digitized records and their RDF representations need to be adequately stored and preserved according to best standards and guidelines to ensure those do not get lost over time. This was a problem currently not investigated within this project. This paper reports on the creation of Qualified Dublin Core from those triples for ingestion with the digitized register pages in an adequate long-term digital preservation platform and repository. Rather than creating RDF only for the purpose of this project, we demonstrate how we can distill artifacts from the RDF that is fit for discovery, access, and even reuse via that repository and how we elicit and conserve the knowledge and memories about Ireland, its history and culture contained in those register pages.

Keywords: Linked data · Metadata · Mapping · Vital records

1 Introduction

The IRL[1] project aims to create a knowledge base containing historical birth-, marriage- and death records translated into RDF and to create a Linked Data platform to analyze those events. In [1], we reported on the semantic architecture in which we separate two concerns: 1) the exact transcription of the register pages from TIFF files (provided by the General Register Office (GRO), Ireland's central civil repository for records relating to births, marriages and deaths in Ireland) by the digital archivists

---

[1] Irish Record Linkage, 1864-1913: https://irishrecordlinkage.wordpress.com/
I. Ciuciu et al. (Eds.): OTM 2015 Workshops, LNCS 9416, pp. 445–450, 2015.
DOI: 10.1007/978-3-319-26138-6_47

transformed into RDF using the Vital Records Ontology[2] and 2) the interpretation thereof by the historians. This requirement resulted in a platform with two distinct knowledge bases where the interpretation refers back to the transcribed register pages, but the knowledge base containing those transcribed register pages cannot be "contaminated" with any other knowledge.

In this paper, we report on the creation of metadata records from the generated RDF to facilitate the exploration of register pages and vital records in an adequate long-term digital preservation platform. We will describe our method to distil Qualified Dublin Core metadata records for each register page and how these can be ingested together with the TIFF and RDF representation. We must note that the terms and conditions of our data sharing agreement with the GRO do not permit us to make public any data that would identify any individual. We will thus obfuscate information concerning individuals where necessary.

2   Related Projects and Initiatives

Though similar practices for ingesting, enriching and preserving metadata exist, such as the Archipel project [5] harvesting data from GLAMS and broadcasters in Flanders (Belgium), we found little related work the transcription, ingestion and preservation of historical vital records. A method for extracting information from vital records transcribed as HTML using ontologies was proposed in [7]. Long-term digital preservation was not an aspect of that study. [6] presented an approach to increase the efficiency of identifying potential links across vital records based on a person's attributes such as names. Their work is situated in the field of record linking databases.

3   Method

The creation of RDF from the transcribed register pages using the Vital Records Ontology was reported in [1]. The creation of the metadata for ingestion into the Digital Repository of Ireland, from now on called the Repository, will be described in this section. The Repository allows one to ingest metadata and related assets in bulk. We adopted the guidelines in [2] for the creation of our Qualified Dublin Core (QDC) metadata records for each register page. We then prepared an RDF file and retrieved the digital surrogate of those register pages (in TIFF format) in such a way that they will be associated with their corresponding QDC file during ingestion.

3.1   DRI Bulk Ingestion

Though technical and not exactly relevant for this paper, we feel it is important to elaborate on the bulk ingestion facilities of the Repository. The Repository includes a web-based user interface to ingest single objects as well as the facility to ingest metadata and their objects in bulk. For the latter, two directories have to be prepared: metadata and data. The first contains the QDC files – one for each object – and the latter

---

[2] http://www.purl.org/net/irish-record-linkage/records

all the digital files associated with the described objects. A file naming convention ensures that the QDC files and digital files are correctly related.

The result of bulk ingesting the files into the Repository is shown in Fig. 1, where one can see the metadata and a surrogate of the asset. The Repository provides means to explore both the TIFF as well as the RDF/XML file. Before one can ingest the files, both the metadata record and RDF/XML files need to be generated. This process will be described in the following sections.

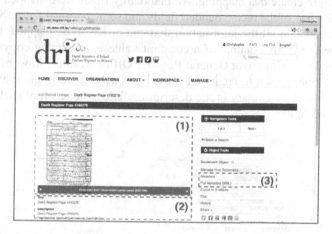

Fig. 1. A register page in the Repository. In (1) we have the assets one can download and for which surrogates are generated. Surrogates are for instance used as thumbnails while browsing collections. In (2), the data provided in the metadata records is shown to the user. The record can also be downloaded as QDC in (3).

3.2   Creation of RDF for Register Pages

The transcribed register pages are transformed into RDF, loaded into a triplestore and made available via a SPARQL endpoint. In order to create an RDF document for each register page, we create an RDF model based on a SPARQL DESCRIBE query for each register page's stamp number. An example of such a query is given below.

```
PREFIX rec: <http://purl.org/net/irish-record-linkage/records#>
DESCRIBE * { ?page rec:stampNumber "4646439"; rec:withRecord ?record. }
```

This query returns descriptions for all variables in the query; in this case a specific register page and its records. We can write the result to an RDF file, but the file does not state which resource is the "topic" of "subject". To solve this problem, we choose to insert an additional triple that explicitly states that the subject of that file is the register page by using the foaf:primaryTopic predicate with the register page's URI. The file is written to the data directory's folder with the Stamp ID as the file name. This folder also contains the digitized register pages with the same name.

3.3   The Creation of Qualified Dublin Core Metadata Records

The guidelines formulated in [5] were aimed at anyone using the Dublin Core metadata standard to prepare content for deposition with the Repository and provides a list of mandatory, recommended and optional fields and, where applicable, suggested controlled vocabularies. In order to create QDC for each register page, we thus have to create and execute a mapping from the RDF to elements in QDC. We adopted XSPARQL [5] to create that mapping. All mandatory fields were mapped and we also covered quite a few of the recommended fields and some optional fields. Note that the RDF does not contain all the information that can or has to be mapped, but constant values can be used. An example of a constant value is attributing copyright, which can be as simple as "Copyright General Register Office Ireland". Most of the register page's information is used to create metadata and each record in the register page is used for a part of the summary in the description field. The result of such a transformation is shown in Fig. 2.

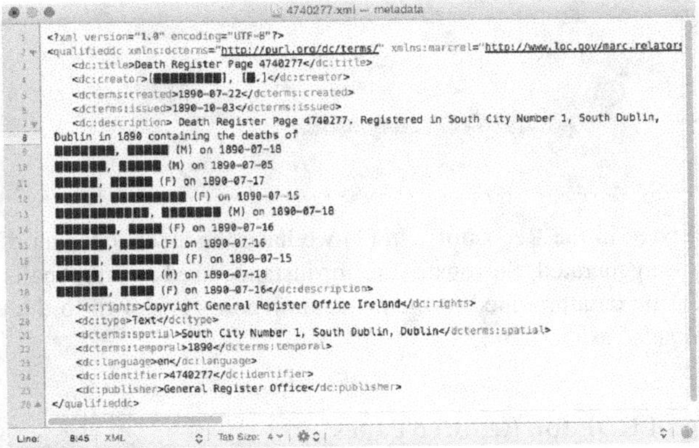

Fig. 2. The result of transforming RDF into Qualified Dublin Core with XSPARQL.

4   Discussion

The work presented in this paper focused on the creation of suitable a mapping from RDF to Qualified Dublin Core for ingestion into a long-term digital preservation platform. One limitation of this study is investigating to what extent the metadata records are adequate for one to find and discover those records not only from the perspective of cataloguers and archivist, but also from the perspective of end users. This limitation is largely due to the sensitive nature of the data, which we hope to address in the future. Due to the sensitive nature of the IRL data, we were also unable to adopt any crowdsourcing mechanisms to leverage the transcription process. Currently, two digital archivists are transcribing the records and quality checking each other's output.

5   Conclusions and Future Work

In the Irish Record Linkage 1864-1913 (IRL) project, digital archivists transcribe historical vital records in register pages, which are transformed into RDF with the Vital Records Ontology. This means that those records are available both as TIFF and RDF. What has not yet been investigated in the project, however, is how these files can be ingested in adequate long-term digital preservation platforms to ensure that this rich information does not get lost. In this paper, we reported on the process of creating RDF files for each register page followed by the creation of a Qualified Dublin Core (QDC) metadata record according to best practices, standards and guidelines. For each register page, we ingested the scan, an RDF file and a DQC file into the Digital Repository of Ireland. We thus demonstrated how the RDF generated in the IRL project was reused to create other structured data that allows one to discover and reuse the information captured in those register pages.

A limitation of this study is the lack of investigating to what extent the mapping of RDF to QDC generates adequate metadata records from a cataloguing perspective and evaluating the to what extent the information in the QDC we generated is rich enough for users to explore. Finally, we are currently investigating the adoption of Encoded Archival Description (EAD) to catalog the register pages, the records as parts of those register pages and the database currently being populated by the digital archivists. The results of this exercise, as well as a comparison with the metadata in QDC is will be reported elsewhere.

Acknowledgements. We thank the Registrar General of Ireland for permitting us to use the vital records for the purposes of this research project. This publication has emanated from research conducted within the Irish Record Linkage, 1864-1913 project supported by the RPG2013-3; Irish Research Council Interdisciplinary Research Project Grant, and within the Science Foundation Ireland Funded Insight Research Centre (SFI/12/RC/2289). The Digital Repository of Ireland (formerly NAVR) acknowledges funding from the Irish HEA PRTLI programme. Christophe Debruyne is supported by the Science Foundation Ireland (Grant 13/RC/2106) as part of the ADAPT Centre for Digital Content Platform Research at Trinity College Dublin.

References

1. Beyan, O., Breathnach, C., Collins, S., Debruyne, C., Decker, S., Grant, D., Grant, R., Gurrin, B.: Towards linked vital registration data for reconstituting families and creating longitudinal health histories. In: KR4HC Workshop (in conjunction with KR 2014), pp. 181–187 (2014)
2. Bustillo, M., Collins, S., Gallagher, D., Grant, R., Harrower, N., Kenny, S., Ní Cholla, R., O'Carroll, A., Redmond, S., Webb, S.: Qualified Dublin Core and the Digital Repository of Ireland (Grant, R. (ed.)). Tech. rep., Maynooth: Maynooth University; Dublin: Trinity College Dublin; Dublin: Royal Irish Academy; Galway: National University of Ireland, Galway (2015)

3. Dell'Aglio, D., Polleres, A., Lopes, N., Bischof, S.: Querying the web of data with XSPARQL 1.1. In: Verborgh, R., Mannens, E. (eds.) Proceedings of the ISWC Developers Workshop 2014, Co-Located with the 13th International Semantic Web Conference (ISWC 2014), Riva del Garda, Italy, October 19, 2014. CEUR Work-Shop Proceedings, vol. 1268, pp. 113–118. CEUR-WS.org (2014)
4. Harris, S., Seaborne, A.: SPARQL 1.1 query language. W3C Recommendation, W3C, March 2013. http://www.w3.org/TR/2013/REC-sparql11-query-20130321/
5. Coppens, S., Mannens, E., Deursen, D.V., Hochstenbach, P., Janssens, B., de Walle, R.V.: Publishing provenance information on the web using the memento date- time content negotiation. In: Bizer, C., Heath, T., Berners-Lee, T., Hausenblas, M. (eds.) WWW 2011 Workshop on Linked Data on the Web, Hyderabad, India, March 29, 2011. CEUR Workshop Proceedings, vol. 813. CEUR-WS.org (2011)
6. Newcombe, H.B., Kennedy, J.M.: Record linkage: making maximum use of the discriminating power of identifying information. Communication of ACM 5(11), 563–566 (1962)
7. Woodbury, C.: Automatic extraction from and reasoning about genealogical records: A prototype. Master's thesis, Brigham Young University (2010)

CoolMind: Collaborative, Ontology-Based Intelligent Knowledge Engineering for e-Society

Ioana Ciuciu^(⊠) and Bazil Pârv

Computer Science Department, University Babes-Bolyai, Cluj-Napoca, Romania
{ioana.ciuciu,bparv}@cs.ubbcluj.ro

Abstract. The paper proposes a collaborative and ontology-based approach for knowledge engineering adapted to e-Society applications. The approach aims to provide intuitive user-system and user-content interaction via processing and visualization of Big Data and the resulting information. Moreover, the approach ensures secured access to personal data via semantic interoperability of security policies. The approach considers large size structured and unstructured contents such as multimedia content (videos, images), web content, video games, sensor data, medical health records, medical databases, etc. We will showcase the concept with an (ongoing) medical decision support system (DS-Med) targeted at real end users and real-world test data from around the city of Cluj-Napoca.

Keywords: Big data · Ontology · Decision support · e-Society · e-Health

1 Context and Motivation

The paper proposes a methodology and its supporting framework – called CoolMind – which aims to bring together communities of users as data providers (e.g., health data, energy data, etc.) on the one hand and data scientists on the other hand. It will ensure, through models and algorithms for processing and interactive visualization of knowledge derived from Big Data, the delivery of services for the e-Society around these data. The proposed approach is centred on the end-user, with the clear objective to solve scientific and technological challenges of the Big Data phenomenon, and to study its impact on the e-Society. The proposed framework is based on:

- novel and non-traditional data storing and data processing methods (e.g., based on NoSQL, graph-based multimodal databases stored in the Cloud, probabilistic methods, etc.) in view of the integration and interpretation of heterogeneous data sources and data flows;
- ontology-based algorithms and tools combining data analysis methods that allow semantic and collaborative annotation of the data, in view of data analysis and information retrieval (e.g., data mining algorithms, advanced machine learning);
- algorithms and methods for the interactive personalized visualization of information. The approach proposes a hybrid representation of the data and the knowledge associated to these data (representation that allows the same information to be interpreted both by the human user and the machine).

© Springer International Publishing Switzerland 2015
I. Ciuciu et al. (Eds.): OTM 2015 Workshops, LNCS 9416, pp. 451–455, 2015.
DOI: 10.1007/978-3-319-26138-6_48

The applications will be conceived in such a way to allow users to efficiently manage and use their knowledge, to generate new knowledge and to keep intact the security and privacy of their (personal) data. The system also integrates a semantic decision support engine, taking into account the user profiles and the user knowledge, observed from human-system interactions in real time.

The approach proposes an integrated model of a connected system. A key factor is represented by the interoperability in e-Society applications (e-Health, e-Learning, e-Commerce, e-Government, etc.), both at national and European level. Interoperability is mainly facilitated by ontologies. In the present approach, the communication among various actors will be facilitated by the creation of a hybrid ontology [1].

The proposed framework is designed as a workplace for data scientists, whether they are data specialists or data analysts, aiming at offering smart applications around huge amounts of data, with high societal impact.

The rest of the paper is composed as follows: Section 2 presents the framework architecture of CoolMind; Section 3 defines evaluation and validation measures; Section 4 introduces DS-Med, an instance of the framework, in order to showcase the concept. Section 5 is the paper conclusion.

2   Framework Architecture – A Conceptual View

The CoolMind framework addresses major ICT Societal challenges, proposing new forms of participation that enable new patterns for value creation based on open and innovative phenomena around a Collaborative and Digital Society. It allows users to play a novel role in the management of their know-how and their virtual and physical resources and encourages them towards increased interaction and participation.

As a result, we propose a secure, robust and flexible system to enable new forms of knowledge engineering. The system is based on a layered architecture consisting of three high-level architectural components, as illustrated in Figure 1.

The CoolMind platform is be based on an architecture that will allow harmonised and cost-effective handling of sensors and other equipment that will be needed in the targeted case studies[1]. The architecture will provide interoperable access to data, information and knowledge across heterogeneous platforms, including web services. This will allow the deployment of the CoolMind software on both new and existing networks of distributed devices. CoolMind will allow for secure, trustworthy and fault tolerant applications through the use of novel security components. The software architecture proposed in this paper subscribes to the Internet of Things (IoT) paradigm, as explained in [2]. As such, it will facilitate the integration of data coming from various data sources and the interoperability between virtual communities and cyber-physical components.

The approach is equally based on a semantic multi-layered architecture and a knowledge base transversal to every layer (see details in [3]). Every layer represents an abstraction of the knowledge so that it will be represented at the highest abstraction

---

[1] For example, in the e-Health domain, for remote monitoring of elder people in view of retrieving personalized medical services.

level accessible to human users of a certain application domain, and then it will be propagated (semantic-wise) towards the lower abstraction layers in order to be processed by the system. Every level is represented with an adapted ontology, and the mapping between the various layers is done via transformation rules (constraints) [3].

At this stage, several modules are already developed (e.g., the security module, or the ontology-based data matching algorithms), others are under development (e.g., the advanced data mining algorithms, user profiling) and there is also a number of future components to be implemented (e.g., the interactive visualization of information, Big Data processing algorithms and scaling).

3   Evaluation and Validation Plans

The proposed approach will adopt two specific validation perspectives: (1) the technical integration of the various components, to ensure that the software is working on real case studies (billions of tuples); the technical validation will ensure that the software operates on clean, correct and useful data and will be able to verify the correctness, meaningfulness and security of new data that are input into the system components; and (2) the socio-technical evaluation of the system, involving human users; in this perspective, we will evaluate the conceptual aspect, i.e., we adopt a *social and community driven approach* to evaluate the technology needed for the creation of communities and their interaction via open and innovative phenomena. In the socio-technical test, the platform will be used by real end-users belonging to specific case study communities in order to validate the platform by analyzing interactions, processes and dynamics within and across communities under social, technical and impact perspectives.

The socio-technical validation is planned with real end-users from the medical landscape in the city of Cluj-Napoca, for interactive and adaptive learning.

4   Case Study

The case study presented in this paper – DS-Med (Medical Decision Support) – is motivated by the biomedical sector, where the problem of data integration from distributed medical data repositories (medical databases, biobanks, hospitals, etc.) is still unsolved in the Romanian setting. Incidentally, this also constitutes a real challenge at European level [4]. DS-Med represents an example of an instance of the CoolMind framework, dedicated to decision support in the medical field.

Three categories of users are identified in this approach:

The **first category** of users is a *user community* represented by users clustered by application domains and common goals (e.g., monitoring their diabetes evolution). This type of user may use the CoolMind environment for the specific purpose of an application, while sharing knowledge with the framework and with the users clustered under the same community (e.g., for the purpose of sharing best practices, news, etc.).

The **second category** of users is represented by *private and public sector institutions* and possibly SMEs. The participating institutions must ensure the (secure) access to their community data (e.g., medical images, sensor data, health records).

The **third category** of users will be formed by the *data analysts and data specialists*. They are the users in charge of analysing the data (provided by the first and second user category) and building appropriate applications (services) for the user communities on top of the CoolMind platform respectively. The applications respond to different functions needed by a community of users. The applications have the role to simulate innovation and the general wealth of the society.

DS-Med will provide secure transmission of sensitive personal data across various heterogeneous medical data repositories and medical records. Moreover, it will adopt the security policy interoperability implemented within the EU TAS[3] project[2].

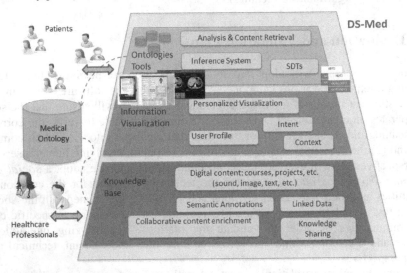

Fig. 1. DS-Med: An e-Health instance of the CoolMind framework.

The main adaptation of the components of the CoolMind framework in the context of this use case concerns the (medical) domain and service ontologies, the visualization (of specific medical data, e.g., medical images) and the data analytics.

Our case study is centred on the end user, which will have full control and visibility over his medical data and the evolution of his medical records. He will be able to set security policies on his digitalised personal data in order to grant or deny access to various medical professionals. Thanks to the CoolMind framework, the patient will be able to identify users with similar medical conditions and exchange information with them. Moreover, users will be able to identify medical specialists and hospitals that suit them best. DS-Med, via the user profiling mechanisms, will be able to recommend best solutions according to patients' needs and conditions. Users will be able to monitor the evolution of their condition and to visualise statistics about their condition and annotated medical results (e.g., CT scans) that will increase their understanding about their own medical condition.

The DS-Med case study is also focused on facilitating data discovery and decision support (via, e.g., semantic decision support tables, SDTs[3]) to researchers and medical

---

[2] http://www.tas3.eu/

[3] https://en.wikipedia.org/wiki/Semantic_decision_table

professionals. In case users wish to anonymise their medical data and make them available to scientific research, their data will be discoverable by data analysis (matching) services. Such services will be available in order to propose appropriate datasets to researchers in view of biomedical studies. Making huge amounts of patient data available to scientists for processing and analysis (e.g., as training data for statistical studies), will provide researchers and medical doctors with better prediction models, benefitting patients from better decision regarding their treatment and better inclusion (for those who are not part of a medical program).

The integration of DS-Med with the University Hospital in Cluj-Napoca in view of creating both an e-Learning platform and clinical studies is work in progress.

5   Conclusion

CoolMind proposes to advance the state of the art of personalized, intelligent knowledge engineering grounded in social processes. The proposed system and methodology are user-centred and user-adaptable, addressing key societal challenges.

As such, CoolMind will impact on the Digital Society, through delivery of personalised services centred on the user knowledge. CoolMind users and other relevant stakeholders are brought into the loop at an early stage of the R&D cycle, to bridge the gap between technologies and their sustainable application and to reach best impacts as possible. CoolMind end users are encouraged to apply these ICT methodologies for better discovering new and emerging behaviors such as "share your health data". The involvement of user communities will ensure that the impact of the Cool-Mind project is for their benefit and that it is being accepted and used in a sustainable way.

The approach will develop and validate all necessary components in order to create a functional prototype with user friendly software and interfaces. The CoolMind communities will to be created and maintained. Most of all, the system has to be adopted by the community members. Future developments will take into account applications of the concept in the Energy Efficiency and Smart Home fields with precise requirements derived from the industrial landscape of the city of Cluj-Napoca.

References

1. Meersman, R., Debruyne, C.: Hybrid ontologies and social semantics. In: Proceedings of 4th IEEE Int. Conf. on Digital Ecosystems and Technologies (2010)
2. Ciuciu, I., Meersman, R., Dillon, T.: Social network of smart-metered homes and SMEs for grid-based renewable energy exchange. In: Proc. of IEEE Int. DEST-CEE 2012, Campione d'Italia, Italy (2012)
3. Ciuciu, I., Meersman, R., Perrin, E., Danesi, F.: Semantic support for computer-human interaction: intuitive 3Dvirtual tools for surface deformation in CAD. In: Meersman, R., Dillon, T., Herrero, P. (eds.) OTM 2010. LNCS, vol. 6428, pp. 645–654. Springer, Heidelberg (2010)
4. Passarani, I.: Patient Access to Electronic Health Records, Report of the eHealth Stakeholder Group (2013)

Improving Software Quality
Using an Ontology-Based Approach

Simona Motogna, Ioana Ciuciu(✉), Camelia Serban, and Andreea Vescan

Computer Science Department 1, Babes-Bolyai University,
M. Kogalniceanu, Cluj-Napoca, Romania
{motogna,ioana.ciuciu,camelia,avescan}@cs.ubbcluj.ro
http://www.cs.ubbcluj.ro

Abstract. The paper aims to define a novel methodology to evaluate the quality of software systems. The methodology is applying the following steps: evaluate object oriented metrics, select quality category, and evaluate quality category. The approach to software quality evaluation is based on an ontology that was defined for the ISO25010 standard. The quality evaluation is enhanced by taking into consideration several object-oriented (OO) metrics and including them into the ontology. A case study is presented regarding the impact of OO metrics on the reliability category. The paper presents preliminary results on the methodology and concludes on the benefits of using an ontology to derive new facts in the context of software quality assessment.

Keywords: Software quality · Object oriented metrics · Ontology

1 Introduction

Why do we choose to use one software application or another, or how do we choose which application to buy, install and use? Is there any method that can predict which application will better serve our purposes? Software quality factors capture different aspects of an application and can offer uniform measurements to compare different applications. These factors refer both to the use of the application (external) and to its development (internal).

Software quality (SQ) models represent a set of factors that offer a complete characterization of the software system. They capture all the features of the product, but also of the development. Several SQ models had been proposed, and some of them had been standardized. The up to date standard of software quality models is ISO 25010 [1], that will be used in our proposal.

In order to be able to measure the quality of a software application, several steps should be followed: establish the software quality model to be used (or define your own model); establish suitable measures, corresponding ranges and measurement methods (preferably automated), and establish evaluation criteria and interpretation of the measurements.

Our approach is based on an ontology, Software Quality Ontology (SQO), in order to accomplish this purpose. The decision of using the ontology is based on the following arguments:

© Springer International Publishing Switzerland 2015
I. Ciuciu et al. (Eds.): OTM 2015 Workshops, LNCS 9416, pp. 456–465, 2015.
DOI: 10.1007/978-3-319-26138-6_49

- The domain of software quality uses several concepts and terms with different definitions and meaning. The ontology allows us to store and use the formal description of these terms;
- The domain of software quality is very variable: even software quality standard models change in time, and terms differ from one issue to another. For example, in ISO 25010 [1], issued in 2011, the term "appropriateness" replaced "suitability" from ISO 9126 [2], issued in 2001. Another aspect to be considered regards the fact that software applications and software development change fast. Software quality models reflect these changes. For example, in the first proposed software quality model [3], security didn't appear. With the appearance and progress of the Web and mobile applications, security had evolved in a software quality factor. An ontology corresponding to software quality domain allows an easier management of these changes, that might be only syntactical or can be also semantic.
- The ontology allows to establish different relations, at different levels. We have noticed that having relations between different subcategories and metrics may influence the overall impact of a certain metric over a category.
- The measures can be properly defined (without ambiguity and in a complete and objective way).
- The flexibility of an ontology is an important argument. Ontologies are well suited to combine information from various sources and infer new facts based on this. Also, the flexibility allows to extend existing ontologies very easy, thus fostering the reuse of existing work.

The distinctive feature captured in our ontology is the fact that we take into consideration object oriented metrics in connection with quality categories. Usually, software quality models suggest specific metrics for evaluating attributes, and object oriented metrics are mostly studied in literature with regard to software design, or only one specific quality attribute. We also consider that the ontology brings a certain level of conceptualization and abstractness that can help us in applying this approach in several aspects regarding software quality such as: estimating software quality factors for different types of software applications, evaluating the impact of object oriented metrics on quality factors, or verifying the consistency of factors.

The major contributions of this paper are: conceptualizing the elements of the ISO25010 software quality model [1] and their relations to object oriented metrics into an ontology, and a proposal for a methodology to software quality assessment based on this ontology.

The paper is organized as follows: Section 2 contains background information about concepts related to metrics and measurements. The Software Quality Ontology (SQO) used for software quality assessment in our approach is described in Section 3. Section 4 introduces the current state of art regarding the application of ontologies in software quality assessment and provides a comparative analysis with our present approach. We conclude our paper and discuss future work in Section 5.

2   Software Quality Assessment

Programs have continuously increased in size and complexity leading to higher development costs and lower productivity.The need for quality in the software system has become more and more obvious on the market. *Quality improvement* is only possible through *quality control.*

In 1977, McCall introduced the first software quality model [3] defining 11 factors characterizing software products, that are further decomposed in criteria. Several notable models followed, including standardized ones [2], [1]. The latest standard [1] used in our approach, is composed of eight *categories*, further divided into *subcategories* related to static and dynamic properties of software systems.

A lot of *metrics* have been proposed so far and new metrics continue to appear in the literature regularly. Marinescu [7] has classified these metrics according to four *internal characteristics* that are essential to object-orientation: - i.e. coupling, inheritance, cohesion and structural complexity.

At this moment, we have included into our ontology a minimal subset of *object oriented metrics* (at least one for each internal characteristic) which we consider that are relevant for our purpose, and in the future we will widen this set. Thus, the selected metrics, considered in our approach are:

- *Depth of Inheritance Tree* (DIT) [4] is defined as the length of the longest path of inheritance from a given class to the root of the tree.
- *Weighted Methods per Class* (WMC) metric [4] is defined as the sum of the complexity of all methods of a given class. The complexity of a method is the cyclomatic complexity.
- *Cyclomatic complexity* (CC) [5] is a measure of a module control flow complexity based on graph theory. CC metric is defined for each module to be $e - n + 2$, where e is the number of edges and n is the number of nodes in the control flow graph.
- *Coupling Between Objects* (CBO) [4] for a class c is the number of other classes that are coupled to the class c. Two classes are coupled when methods declared in one class use methods or instance variables defined by the other class.
- *Tight Class Cohesion* TCC [6] is defined as the ratio between the number of directly connected methods in a class divided by the number of all possible connections between the methods of that class.

A very long standing issue related to interpreting measurements results of any metrics-based approach is that of setting the metrics threshold values [7]. A threshold splits the metrics values having the goal of drawing informed assessment about the measured entity. Consider, for instance we aim to measure the cohesiveness of a class using TCC metric TCC [6] with possible values in [0..1] range. The threshold 0.33 represents a good cohesion. In this respect, all design entities with the value of TCC metric less than 0.33 are considered non-cohesive.

Referring to the selected metrics, we have considered for each of them a recommended threshold value : WMC - threshold value 20 [7]; TCC threshold value 0.33 [7], DIT - threshold value 6 [10], CBO - threshold value 9 [8], CC - 15 [10].

Several studies have sought to establish a correspondence between metric values and *quality categories*, in order to describe how the values of these metrics influence quality categories, namely positive, negative or no influence. We have performed a survey of such studies [9], [11], [12] and included these results into our model (SQ ontology). In some cases, this was not an easy task, since we had to look at the meaning of the factor or category, rather than its name. Table 2 shows a snapshot of the collected information, for the subcategories corresponding to the reliability category. The sign '+' denotes a positive influence, '-' denotes a negative influence, '0' denotes no influence, and an empty cell corresponds to a not known situation. The gathered information about the stated influences may be consulted at this address [14].

3   Software Quality Ontology (SQO)

In this section we describe the Software Quality Ontology (SQO or SQ ontology) inline with the above-mentioned software quality metrics.

The aim of an ontology is to conceptualize the agreed-upon knowledge describing a precise domain, capturing the concepts that describe the domain and the relationships between them. The purpose is that of enabling the semantic interoperability and knowledge sharing between various stakeholders working collaboratively. Semantic interoperability represents the ability of two or more systems to communicate and interpret data. Moreover, an ontology should enable interoperability between computer systems and humans. Our approach adopts the ontology definition of Tom Gruber [13], i.e., "an explicit specification of a conceptualization".

Ideally, an ontology should be represented on several levels (layers) with various levels of abstraction, in order to enable the human-computer interaction [15]. Since the present study is work in progress, we insist on explaining the SQ domain ontology and the approach we adopted in constructing it. However, we are currently working on designing several service (application) ontologies for the proof of concept of our work, such as the e-Learning ontology. In a service ontology the concepts from the domain ontology (i.e., the ontology base) commit to a specific application via several application-specific constraints (example from the e-Learning application and the reliability category).

3.1   Software Quality Assessment Using SQO

Our approach proposes a new method to evaluate the quality of a software systems considering the quality attributes that are important from the perspective of the "actors" involved in the software development (i.e. analyst, developer, QA, end user, etc). The approach uses the ontology, that contains elements of the ISO 25010 quality model and also several OO metrics that are bound to category/subcategory, to automatically establish the quality of the software system being studied.

The methodology that we propose is applying the following steps for quality assessment of an application:

1. Evaluate OO metrics: there are a lot of tools that compute OO metrics corresponding to different programming languages and frameworks. Most of them facilitates export of the results in different formats. Some of the most known tools are Eclipse Metrics [16], NDepend [10], SD-Metrics [17]. These results are compared with the threshold values and a result is produced for each metric. As we have mentioned above, it is not an easy task to establish threshold values for metrics. Depending on the method used in this respect, statistical method or meaningful thresholds values, we can split the metrics values in clusters. If we use statistical based thresholds, these clusters are denoted as Low values, Medium values and High values. Regarding the meaningful thresholds, a value used for each metric splits the metrics values in two clusters: one containing normal values and the other one with values that are too big or too small (depending on the analyzed metric). The decision to select that cluster with metrics values corresponding to design entities that need to be reviewed (suspect entities) depend on the analyzed metric. For instance, a high value of TCC metric means that the class is cohesive, while a high values for CBO metric means that the class is strongly coupled.

2. Select quality category: from the proposed ISO 25010 model, select the categories of interest (which are to be assessed). It is possible to study one quality category in isolation, several categories or even all the categories from the SQ model.

3. Evaluate quality category: The evaluation will take into account the results from step 1 and the relations between metrics and subcategories from step 2. Next, the result for a category is computed based on the results for included subcategories.

More precisely, in order to achieve step 3 - quality category evaluation - in the context of this study, we create the SQ ontology which aims to: (1) define a SQ model following the ISO 25010 standard; (2) link and harmonize the model with other existing approaches and standards in the domain of Software Quality; (3) measure the quality of a software application, architecture or design based on object oriented metrics; (4) ensure the (syntactically and semantically) correct and complete definition of the SQ measures; (5) automate the definition of SQ measures (e.g., inferring new information from incomplete data); (6) ensure traceability of the evolution of SQ (standard) models via correct change management of SQ models.

Following the metrics for SQ assessment described in Section 2, we present the SQ ontology model as illustrated in Figure 1.

The ontology is built around three main concepts: 1) category; 2) subcategory; and 3) metric. A *category* refers to a software quality category from [1]. Thus, we have eight main SQ categories (Compatibility, Functional Suitability, Maintainability, Performance Efficiency, Portability, Reliability, Security and Usability). Each category is split into several *subcategories*, leading to a total of 31 subcategories as identified in Figure 1. Also, categories and subcategories

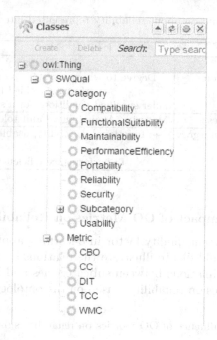

Fig. 1. Software Quality Ontology concepts.

may share a positive, negative, neutral or unknown relation to other categories or subcategories. These relations have been established by different studies [9] [11], [12] and we have tried to collect information from different sources. For example, as shown in Table 1, functional suitability has a positive influence('+') on reliability, in other words if the functional suitability increases then reliability will also increase, while portability has no influence on reliability. Categories and subcategories have associated object oriented *metrics* (see Section 2).

We define rules to infer the influence of each metric on different subcategories and categories. The dependence between an OO metric and a subcategory is computed based on: specificity of the metric (each metric will be treated separately), attribute of the metric (low, medium, high), and influence on subcategory (+,0 or -). The influence of an OO metric on a category will be determined as the average of the influences of that metric on the included subcategories.

The relationships between the ontology concepts, currently under study, will follow closely the above-mentioned rules and dependencies in order to be able to derive from the ontology the hidden (not known) influences that are present in the model, starting from known relations.

Table 1 describes the information stored about reliability (as a category) into our ontology: definition, subcategories, and relations to other categories/subcategories of the quality model. The influences of the considered metrics on reliability are given in Table 2.

Table 1. Information about reliability represented into SQ ontology.

Reliability		
	Type	Category
	Definition	Degree to which a system product or component performs specified functions under specified conditions for a specific period of time.
	Includes	Maturity, Availability, Fault tolerance, Recoverability
	Relation to category	+: functional suitability, usability, maintainability; -: , 0: performance efficiency, portability

3.2   Case Study: Impact of OO Metrics on Reliability

Reliability is an important quality factor in e-learning applications. In the current case study we would like to illustrate the relations between this factor and metrics, and also the relations between subcategories and how to conclude the influence of OO metrics on reliability, based on the ontology and the rules.

Table 2. Influence of OO metrics on reliability subcategories

	Maturity	Availability	FaultTolerance	Recoverability
DIT	-		-	+
WMC	-		+	
CC	-		-	+
CBO			-	-
TCC	+			

Based on the SQ ontology, we can proceed with *Quality category evaluation*: Suppose that we obtain a value 9 for DIT. According to the threshold, we will have a high value for DIT. Based on the collected information, we define the following rule for DIT metric and its impact on subcategories. Such rules will be used to define the relationships from the ontology concepts.

if (DIT = high) and ((influence=-) or (influence = 0) ***then*** *no influence*
if (DIT = high) and (influence=+) ***then*** *influence is negative*
if (DIT = low) and (influence=+) ***then*** *influence is negative*
if (DIT = low) and (influence=-) ***then*** *no influence*

The influence of DIT on reliability will sum up the influences of its composing subcategories, namely (no influence for maturity, not known for availability, no influence on fault tolerance, and negative influence for recoverability, as described in 2), leading to an overall negative influence of a high DIT over reliability.

No information is known about the influence of those metrics regarding other subcategories from the reliability category, i.e. availability. By using the ontology inference we expect to obtain the influence of those metrics also for the availability subcategory. Future case studies would be able to verify our expectations.

4 Related Work and Analysis

This section presents the current state of art regarding the application of ontologies in Software Engineering, particularly for quality measurement.

Most quality models offer a two-level approach, distinguishing externally observable and internally measurable attributes, much effort being devoted to determine which internal attributes influence which external ones. In [18] a scheme that organize attributes according to five ontological levels is proposed. Each level has different types of users and available measurements techniques.

In [19] the authors present several examples of ontology applications throughout the Software Engineering (SE) life cycle, and give a classification on their usage. In their study they have identified the use of an ontology in four stages: analysis and design, implementation, deployment and run-time, and maintenance.

Paper [20] describes the Software Measurement Ontology (SMO) that was initially proposed to address the lack of consensus on Spanish software measurement terms. Three tables were used to represent the elements for the ontology: one with the glossary with the concepts, one with the attributes and one with the relationships.

In [21] an ontology for Software Product Quality Attributes (SWQAs) is proposed. Several experiments were conducted to extract the main concepts for SWQAs: 34 documents, reports and proposals being used to extract various concepts, definitions and terminologies. The papers provides experts, researchers and practitioners in the field of software product quality with an ontology to be considered as the base of a common agreement knowledge.

A very comprehensive survey of the connections between the standard software quality model ISO 9126 [2] and OO metrics is proposed in [9], but it is only in a form of collected information, without the possibility to apply it. However, it has been a very important source of information in constructing the relations between categories/subcategories and metrics in our ontology.

In relation to existing approaches, our aims are similar to:

- paper [18], but our ontology has a hierarchical structure;
- approach from [20], with the difference that our ontology has different levels: category and subcategory, metrics, relations between metrics and subcategories from the ontology;
- study from [21]: compared with it, our ontology also provides an approach to properly define the measurements without ambiguity and in a complete and objective way.

None of the above approaches considered the use of an ontology for the purpose of establishing the impact of OO metrics on quality categories; most studies suggest specific metrics for evaluations of one specific quality category (namely positive, negative or no influence). Because ontologies are well suited to combine information from various sources and infer new facts based on this, we aim to be able to infer new relations between metric values and quality categories by the use of our ontology.

With respect to the state-of-art, the following major aspects characterize the novelty of the approach presented in this paper:

- a methodology to software quality evaluation based on ontology;
- an ontology including ISO25010 quality categories and OO metrics;
- inferring new relations between metrics values and quality attributes, as suggested for DIT metric.

5 Conclusion

The paper presents a methodology for software quality assessment based on a Software Quality Ontology (SQO) that captures relations between main SQ concepts and the influence of object-oriented metrics on them. The approach focuses on the main SQ concepts captured in the model: SQ category; SQ sub-category; and OO metric. The purpose is to prove the influence of OO metrics on the quality of the software applications and to infer new (unknown) relations between metric values and SQ categories in view of SQ assessment. The rules that capture the semantics of the ontology and the results of the inference is ongoing work.

Our future plans consist of: including more OO metrics into the ontology, and validating our proposal, by comparing it with approaches that use empirical studies. Further case studies are needed to better support our empirical results. Another important extension is to build service ontologies that will validate the applicability of the approach to various business domains.

References

1. ISO/IEC 25010:2011-Systems and software engineering. http://www.iso.org
2. ISO 9126–1:2001-Software engineering - Product quality. http://www.iso.org
3. McCall, J., Richards, P., Walters, G.: Factors in Software Quality. Nat Tech. Information Service **1** (1977)
4. Chidamber, S.R., Kemerer, C.F.: A Metric Suite for Object- Oriented Design. IEEE Transactions on Software Engineering **20**(6), 476–493 (1994)
5. McCabe, T.J.: A Complexity Measure. IEEE Transactions on Software Engineering **2**(4), 308–320 (1976)
6. Bieman, J.M., Kang, B.K.: Cohesion and reuse in an object-oriented system. In: ACM Symposium on Software Reusability (1995)
7. Marinescu, R.: Measurement and Quality in Object Oriented Design. Faculty of Automatics and Computer Science, University of Timisoara (2002)
8. Shatnawi, R.: A Quantitative Investigation of the Acceptable Risk Levels of Object-Oriented Metrics in Open-Source Systems. IEEE Transactions on Software Engineering, 216–225 (2010)
9. Compendium of Software Quality Standards and Metrics - v1.0. http://www.arisa.se/compendium/quality-metrics-compendium.html
10. NDepend - Improve your.NET code quality. http://www.ndepend.com/
11. Arcuri, A., Briand, L.: A practical guide for using statistical tests to assess randomized algorithms in software engineering. In: 33rd International Conference on Software Engineering, pp. 1–10 (2011)

12. Gyimothy, T., Ferenc, R., Siket, I.: Empirical Validation of Object-Oriented Metrics on Open Source Software for Fault Prediction. IEEE Trans. Softw. Eng. **31**(10), 897–910 (2005)
13. Gruber, T.R.: Toward Principles for the Design of Ontologies used for Knowledge Sharing. Kluwer Academic Publishers (1993)
14. Software Quality Ontology. http://www.cs.ubbcluj.ro/motogna/research/Factors-metricsInfluence.xlsx
15. Ciuciu, I., Meersman, R., Perrin, E., Danesi, F.: Semantic support for computer-human interaction: intuitive 3Dvirtual tools for surface deformation in CAD. In: Meersman, R., Dillon, T., Herrero, P. (eds.) OTM 2010. LNCS, vol. 6428, pp. 645–654. Springer, Heidelberg (2010)
16. Eclipse Metrics - Source Code Analyzer. https://marketplace.eclipse.org/content/eclipse-metrics
17. SD-Metrics - The Software Design Metrics tool for the UML. http://www.sdmetrics.com/
18. Astudillo, H.: Five ontological levels to descrive and evaluate software architectures. Revista Facultad de Ingenieria - Universidad de Tarapaca **13**, 69–76 (2005)
19. Happel, H., Seedorf, S.: Applications of ontologies in software engineering. In: 2nd International Workshop on Semantic Web Enabled Software Engineering (2006)
20. Garcia, F., Ruiz, F., Calero, C., Bertoa, M., Vallecillo, A., Mora, B., Piattini, M.: Effective use of ontologies in software measurement. The Knowledge Engineering Review Journal **24**, 23–40 (2009)
21. Kayed, A., Hirzalla, N., Samhan, A., Alfayoumi, M.: Towards an ontology for software product quality attributes. In: Fourth International Conference on Internet and Web Applications and Services, pp. 200–204 (2009)

Historical Data Preservation and Interpretation Pipeline for Irish Civil Registration Records

Oya Beyan[1(✉)], P.J. Mealy[1], Dolores Grant[2], Rebecca Grant[2], Natalie Harrower[2], Ciara Breathnach[3], Sandra Collins[2], and Stefan Decker[1]

[1] Insight @ NUIG, National University of Ireland Galway, Galway, Ireland
{oya.beyan,pj.mealy,stefan.decker}@insight-centre.org
[2] Digital Repository of Ireland, Royal Irish Academy, Dublin, Ireland
{d.grant,r.grant,n.harrower,s.collins}@ria.ie
[3] Department of History, University of Limerick, Limerick, Ireland
Ciara.Breathnach@ul.ie

Abstract. Semantic Web technologies give us the opportunity to understand today's data-rich society and provide novel means to explore our past. Civil registration records such as birth, death, and marriage registers contain a vast amount of implicit information which can be revealed by structuring, linking and combining that information with other datasets and bodies of knowledge. In the Irish Record Linkage (IRL) Project 1864-1913, we have developed a data preservation and interpretation pipeline supported by a dedicated semantic architecture. This three-layered pipeline is designed to capture separate concerns from the perspective of multiple disciplines such as archival studies, history and data science. In this study, our aim is to demonstrate best practices in digital archives, while facilitating innovative new methodologies in historical research. The designed pipeline is executed with a dataset of 4090 registered Irish death entries from selected areas of south Dublin City.

Keywords: Knowledge Transformation Pipelines · Civil Registration Records · Linked Data · Digital Archives

1   Introduction

Semantic Web technologies give us the opportunity to understand today's data-rich society and provide novel means to explore our past. Civil registration records such as birth, death, and marriage registers contain a vast amount of implicit information about a society's past, which can be revealed by structuring, linking and combining that information with other datasets and bodies of knowledge. In the Irish Record Linkage 1864-1913 (IRL) project[1], we adopt Semantic Web and Linked Data technologies to create a platform for storing and linking RDF descriptions of birth, death and marriage (BDM) records for Dublin (1864-1913) [1]. The aim of the IRL project is to create a knowledge base which can serve to answer questions about the accuracy of officially reported maternal mortality and infant mortality rates.

---

[1] http://irishrecordlinkage.wordpress.com

© Springer International Publishing Switzerland 2015
I. Ciuciu et al. (Eds.): OTM 2015 Workshops, LNCS 9416, pp. 466–475, 2015.
DOI: 10.1007/978-3-319-26138-6_50

Semantic web and linked data technologies encapsulate the explicit representation of meta-information accompanied by domain theories such as ontologies, which will enable the web to provide a qualitatively new level of services [2]. These technologies have various advantages for capturing and interpreting the civil registration records. RDF metadata enables one to generate different models of data representation for separate concerns or interpretations. Because the linked data is self-describing and explicitly defined in a machine-readable way, it can be linked to external data sets and infer potential relevancies.

1.1   Motivation and Related Work

Our motivation is to develop novel methods to explore and interpret historical data sets with semantic web technologies and Linked Data. Digital repositories provide a central access point for preserving and providing access to data [3]. These repositories may serve diverse interest groups such as archivists, historians, journalists, public researchers and scholars. The developed knowledge infrastructure should satisfy different and potentially conflicting perspectives and concerns, as well as support the privacy of data subjects.

In digital preservation semantic technologies are applied for dynamically discovering and invoking the most appropriate preservation services [4]. XML data standards considered as opportunity in addressing the digital preservation problems [5]. In the Neptuno system, semantic web technologies are applied to create a knowledge base for digital newspaper archives. Archive materials are described using the developed ontologies and semantic search module implemented to use conceptual elements to match information needs against archive contents [6].

In this study, we have developed a three-layer pipeline for storing, exploring and interpreting these Irish civil registration records. We demonstrate our concept with infant deaths as the use case. Infant mortality is an important indicator of human welfare, national wealth and social conditions such as poverty and single motherhood [7,8]. The pipeline will initially include 444 death register pages, which equates to 4090 death entries recorded in two Registrar Districts to the South of Dublin City from the years 1870 and 1890.

2   Methods

In this work we applied semantic web technologies to the digital archival domain. We followed the linked data principles and express the semantic of data with the developed ontologies.

Semantic Web Technologies offers a new approach to managing information and processes, the fundamental principle of which is the creation and use of semantic metadata [9]. Linked data refers to a set of best practices for publishing and connecting structured data on the Web. It creates links between diverse data sources and enables the publishing of data in a machine readable way where its meaning is explicitly defined and linked to the other data sets [10]. A computer-based, shared, agreed formal conceptualisation is known as an ontology [11]. Ontologies are keystone technologies for meaningful and efficient interoperation of information systems. They involve shared concepts and represent externalization of semantics outside of the systems [12].

3   Data Preservation and Interpretation Pipeline

In the IRL project, we have developed a three-layered pipeline to capture, enrich and allow for new interpretations of the historical data.

The aim of the first layer is to preserve the civil registers in their original form and capture the provenance of the archival record. From the digital archivist's point of view, the register pages are the main units to be preserved. The Vital Records Ontology (VRO)[2] is developed to annotate each register page and preserve the authenticity. In this layer, we converted the historical data into Linked Data and preserved them in the original order and without any interpretation.

The second layer is dedicated to creating links between the captured records and identifying the associations between them, for instance, using nominal and geographic data, individuals and familial bonds can be identified and subsequently verified by address. It also includes annotations to other standards or ontologies such as the cause of deaths. The Historical Events Ontology (HEO) was developed to enrich the registers and interlink each archival entry to constitute families.

The third layer is designed for exploring the linked records stored in the second layer from various points of interest. In this layer the data is queried which permits historians to examine the de-identified results from several perspectives. For example, the definition of maternal mortality is historically poorly defined but the pipeline permits historians to reinterpret the data in order to potentially identify additional deaths [13]. This layer permits researchers to apply different definitions, for instance the World Health Organisation's current definition of a direct maternal death is one occurring within 42 days of the delivery or termination of pregnancy [14]. Use case specific ontologies can enable the historical data to withstand multi-factorial queries for example, timeframes for deaths from puerperal sepsis (a common cause of maternal death) can be cross-referenced with the ages of the women involved to reveal patterns in maternal mortality.

4   Results and Implementation

In the IRL project, we have designed and implemented a four steps data preservation and implementation pipeline to answer historians' questions by processing the civil registration records. The proposed pipeline is implemented with linked open data standards and serves over in the JENA Fuseki SPARQL endpoint. Fig. 1 shows the four main steps of the developed pipeline. In the following section, we will describe the role of each layer in detail and present the implementation results.

---

[2]   http://purl.org/net/irish-record-linkage/records

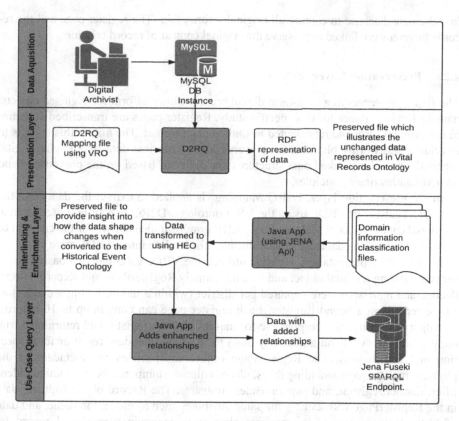

Fig. 1. Implementation of the IRL semantic pipeline.

4.1   Data Acquisition

The project data consists of digitised birth, death and marriage register pages as well as a corresponding database, shared for the duration of the project by the General Register Office of Ireland. As it is presently a closed dataset, access to this data is restricted to IRL team members and no persons can be identified from the project outputs. Each register page may include up to 10 records, each one registering the birth, death or marriage of an individual. The digitised records were analysed by digital archivists and broken down to identify all information captured in a given record and register page.

For the purpose of the project a MySQL database was created to curate a sample of the birth, death and marriage records from the Registrar Districts of Dublin South City 1 and Dublin South City 3. Digital archivists manually transcribed 444 death register page records containing 4090 death records, 15 birth register page records containing 150 birth records, and 28 marriage register page records containing 81 marriage records from 1870 and 1890. Death records have been focused on initially, as the historical research questions examine infant and maternal mortality. Using the original database for reference, as well as manual curation, relevant records were selected and transcribed into the new database to capture all original information. The register page and the records thereon were linked to preserve the original context of record creation.

4.2   Preservation Layer

The first layer serves as a long-term digital preservation platform for digitised objects, namely Register Pages for this specific study. Register pages are transcribed verbatim in the original form and represented in Linked Data format. The aim of this layer is to provide a trustworthy platform for preserving the historical data by applying digital archival principles. Linked data structures are designed based on the provenance and archival authenticity principles.

In the preservation layer, D2RQ Mapping[3] is applied to extract the data from the MySQL database into RDF using the VRO ontology. D2RQ is a system used to treat relational databases as virtual, read-only RDF graphs. It also allows for the creation of custom dumps of the database in RDF formats for loading into an RDF store [16].

In the RDF representation, we have utilized the VRO. VRO has two basic classes for representing a digital object and its data, namely RegisterPage and Record. Births, deaths, and marriages were captured per district (within a union, within a county) as single records in a bound Register. Each register page can contain up to 10 records. The district registrar was responsible for maintaining the register and returning a true copy of all life events on a quarterly basis to the superintendent registrar for inspection and certification. The RegisterPage object encapsulates the metadata of the physical register page including dates, place, volume, stamp number as a unique identifier, district registrar, and superintendent registrar. The Record object captures data in the RegisterPage with exactly the same attributes such as name, forename, and date of birth. Because one of the projects aims is to maintain the original record by minimizing interpretation, we chose to develop a "flat" ontology, which means that most of the information that can be found on such a register page was captured as literals. A RegisterPage and a Record are linked; each record must belong to a register page and each register page can have zero or more records. Fig. 2 presents linked data representation of a registry page and a death record from same page.

In the mappings, special care was taken to preserve the ability to trace information back to the source (the original records). The transcriptions included the original page numbers and unique register stamp numbers, as well as the name of the Registrar and Superintendent Registrar. As presented in Fig. 2, each registry page linked to the death records through 'records:withRecord' property.

4.3   Interlinking and Enrichment Layer

The aim of the interlinking and enrichment layer is to facilitate the exploitation of historical data for various purposes by enabling efficient queries. Hence the data schema of the VRO were designed for preserving digitised objects as they are, it was not particularly effective querying the relations between people and events. Therefore,

---

[3]   http://d2rq.org/ Version: D2RQ v0.8.1 - 2012-06-22

we developed HEO and transform another triple store for exploring the data through generations and gaining insights into longitudinal health histories.

Register Page	Death Record
<http://irl.dri.ie/register_page/D4746422> a records:RegisterPage ; rdfs:label "D4746422" ; records:county "Dublin" ; records:datePageCertified "1890-01-02"^^xsd:date ; records:datePageCertifiedAsTrueCopy "1890-04-14"^^xsd:date ; records:district "South City Number 1" ; records:districtOfSuperintendantRegistrar "South Dublin" ; records:forenameOfRegistrarOnPage "752c4c2bfd8b1a4e7511e7de"records:forename OfSuperintendantRegistrar"2042101ac741bfe43f 3672e67c" ; records:pageNumber "637"^^xsd:int ; records:pageNumberOfManuscript "1"^^xsd:int ; records:quarter "1"^^xsd:int ;records:stampNumber "4746422" ; records:surnameOfRegistrarOnPage"3f6d390dbfd b5ab58b3109f6ba4" ; records:surnameOfSuperintendantRegistrar "76fecf24fdc371ebeb8e459c25d9f373" ; records:union "South Dublin" ;records:volume "2"^^xsd:int ; records:withRecord <http://irl.dri.ie/record/D4746422-67> , <http://irl.dri.ie/record/D4746422-61> , <http://irl.dri.ie/record/D4746422-62> , <http://irl.dri.ie/record/D4746422-66> , <http://irl.dri.ie/record/D4746422-68> , <http://irl.dri.ie/record/D4746422-65> , <http://irl.dri.ie/record/D4746422-70> , <http://irl.dri.ie/record/D4746422-63> , <http://irl.dri.ie/record/D4746422-69> , <http://irl.dri.ie/record/D4746422-64> ; records:yearRegistered "1889"^^xsd:int .	<http://irl.dri.ie/record/D4746422-69> a records:Certificate , records:DeathRecord , records:Record ; rdfs:label "Death of 5bd81ca81adf2879322e0ffd90b771 c6db135761abfeb3b2f79fcb9ccba6 in 1889-12-29" ; records:ageLastBirthday "10 months" ; records:causeOfDeath "bronchitis" ; records:condition "bachelor" ; records:dateOfDeath "1889-12-29"^^xsd:date ; records:dateOfRegistration "1890-01-02"^^xsd:date ; records:deathCertification "Explicitly Certified" ; records:durationOfIllness "8 days" ; records:forename "5bd81ca81adf2879322e0ffd90b771" ; records:forenameOfInformant"341d3faa12b2ccbb5e772e 7be" ; records:forenameOfRegistrar "d005aa409ef3b5c6bf7cb6d8b41" ; records:number "69"^^xsd:short ; records:placeOfDeath "5 Lady Lane" ; records:qualificationOfInformant "present at death" ; records:rankProfessionOrOccupation "labourer's child" ; records:residenceOfInformant "ba5ae2bd62a87e6c9af264a3ef" ; records:sex "M" ; records:surname "c6db135761abfeb3b2f79fcb9ccba6" ; records:surnameOfInformant "c4a8becd037765363048185292" ; records:surnameOfRegistrar "7cb15d9c8b537a241dca387619c" ; records:titleOfRegistrar "Registrar".

Fig. 2. An example linked data entry of Registry Page and Death Record

The interlinking and enrichment layer was implemented with a Java application using JENA API. VRO based linked records were processed and converted to the HEO based linked data. The interlinking creates associations between different pieces of information captured from register pages and allows for the reconstitution of families from the data captured in historical events. This requires the interpretation of the historical data at varying levels. The HEO is developed to represent the structure of the historical event in terms of actors, events and their relations with each other. Metadata for each level of interpretation is held with the HEO and linked to the original record to follow the provenance.

In this layer, we identified the actors of events as they are represented in the civil registration records. Depending on the historical event there are a different number of actors participating in each record. For example in a death event, four different people are identified, i.e. the person who has died, the informant, the district registrar and the superintendent registrar.

The Java app makes use of the Apache Jena API to load the data in RDF from the output of the D2RQ mapping. It works through each record, (death, birth, marriage) and develops a new data model based on the HEO. The resulting linked data contains the object classes detailed in the HEO ontology such as different types of Person (Registrar, Informant, Superintendent) and the various Event types In the next step, the actors are linked with each other according to the role they played in the historical event. Fig. 3 presents the death event and the person extracted from the death record given in Fig. 2.

Death Event:	Dead Person:
<http://irl.dri.ie/record/D4746422-69/deathEvent> a heo:DeathEvent ; heo:InformantQualification "present at death" ; heo:dateOfRegistration "1890-01-02"^^<http://www.w3.org/2001/XMLSchema#date> ; heo:deathCertification "Explicitly Certified" ; heo:eventOf <http://irl.dri.ie/record/D4746422-69/person> ; heo:placeOfDeath "5 Lady Lane" ; heo:registeredBy <http://irl.dri.ie/record/D4746422-69/registrar> .	<http://irl.dri.ie/record/D4746422-69/person> a heo:Person ; rdfs:seeAlso "http://irl.dri.ie/record/D4746422-69" ; heo:AgeAtLastBirthday "10 months" ; heo:AgeAtLastBirthdayInMins "439200" ; heo:CondAtDeath "bachelor" ; heo:dateOfDeath "1889-12-29" ; heo:forename "5bd81ca81adf2879322e0ffd90b771" ; heo:hasAtDeath <http://irl.dri.ie/record/D4746422-69/rank> ; heo:hasCauseOfDeath [heo:classifiedAs "http://purl.org/net/irish-record-linkage/historicalEvents.owl#Bronchitis" ; heo:durationOfIllness "8 days" ; heo:originalText "bronchitis"] ; heo:hasRecordFor <http://irl.dri.ie/record/D4746422-69/deathEvent> ; heo:surname "c6db135761abfeb3b2f79fcb9ccba6" .

Fig. 3. An example linked data entry of Death Even and Person record

We also enrich the original records by adding derived features. An example of these kinds of enhancements is the addition of an ageAtDeathInMinutes field. The original death records contain text in the AgeAtLastBirthday field such as "about 60 years" or "2 years and 3 months". In this form, the data would not lend itself to querying very well, for example, or would not effectively identify children who died under the age of 2. We have employed the PrettyTime:NLP library[4] to process the RDF data text fields such as heo:AgeAtLastBirthday "10 months" and convert it to minutes as heo:AgeAtLastBirthdayInMins "439200".

Another type of interpretation is to enrich the existing data set with standard terminologies and ontologies. Attributes such as place name and cause of deaths can be annotated with related nomenclatures and coding systems. In this study, we examined the cause of death and mapped them to different coding systems. Medical coding systems evolve over time. In 1864 all Irish Registrars were furnished with copies of a standard nosology, which identified 145 causes of death [16]. Reflecting significant advances in medical science, medical coding systems underwent a similar evolution in the period under review 1864-1913. Using the causes of death in the 1890 sample as a guide we explored the coding systems used in that time frame. To supplement the 1864 nosology we selected three available coding systems namely, the International

---

[4]   http://www.ocpsoft.org/prettytime/nlp/

List of Causes of Death, Revision 1 (1900) (ILCD1), the International List of Causes of Death, Revision 2 (1909) (ILCD2), and the International Classification of Causes of Sickness and Death (ICSD) [17,18,19]. The distinct cause of death is selected from the triple store, manually reviewed by the domain experts, and mapped to the available codes in ILCD1, ILCD2, and ICSD.

In HEO, we created CauseOfDeath and identified subcategories for each of them. Each subcategory is annotated with the relevant ILCD1, ILCD2 and ICSD codes. As shown in Fig. 3, in the linked data repository a person object is linked with a blank node, which contains the original cause of death and duration of illness. Then individual causes of death are classified with the defined CauseOfDeath subcategories in HEO. During this process, the HEO records are progressively enhanced to add linkages to allow for identification of individuals and to carry out normalizations such as aligning causes of death with ILCD standards. The Java app loads a custom file, which contains mappings for the domain of causes of death (as found in the data) to a standardized set of international causes of death. As it can be seen from Fig. 4 heo:hasCauseOfDeath relation create a link to relevant cause of death class with heo:classifiedAs object property, and captures heo:durationOfIllness and heo: originalText as data properties of the blank node.

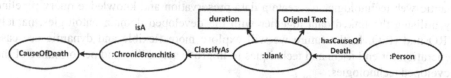

Fig. 4. Enriching the death records with ILCD1, ILCD2, and standards.

4.4   Use Case Query Layer

In the final phase, JENA Fuseki SPARQL endpoint serves to address the use cases and return the query responses. The ultimate aim of the semantic pipeline is to provide historians with tools to analyse historical events and to answer their specific research questions such as "How accurate are historic maternal mortality rates and infant mortality rates for Dublin?" Historic definitions vary for maternal and infant mortality. Infant mortality is currently defined as a death of a child before reaching the age of one, if subject to age-specific mortality rates of that period. Deaths in the first 24 hours and in the following 27 days have specific significance from the historians' perspective.

The use case query layer enables researchers to set their questions and define varying versions of concepts they are interested in. In the infant mortality use case, infant mortality is examined from multiple perspectives including the time frame of death, seasonality, location and the cause of death. Death time frame is defined with four classes; deathIn24hours, deathIn27days, infantDeath, and neoNatalDeath. Fig. 5 presents SPARQL query for the deaths in 24 hours after birth. Results of queries are returned in aggregated form without disclosing any identifiable personal data. The death timeframes correspond with specific diseases and whether or not the infant was weaned too early, which can be indicative of lower socio-economic circumstances.

```
prefix heo: <http://purl.org/net/irish-record-linkage/historicalEvents.owl#>
prefix xsd: <http://www.w3.org/2001/XMLSchema#>
select ?s ?DateOfDeath ?AgeInWords
Where {
    ?s a heo:Person.
    ?s heo:AgeAtLastBirthdayInMins ?ageInMins.
    ?s heo:AgeAtLastBirthday ?AgeInWords .
    ?s heo:dateOfDeath ?DateOfDeath
    FILTER(xsd:integer(?ageInMins) <= 1440) #1440 is 24 hours
    FILTER(xsd:integer(?ageInMins) > 0)    #Ignore records with no recorded age }
```

Fig. 5. Example use case query for deathIn24hours.

5   Discussion and Future Work

Semantic technologies and Linked Data promises many advantage for capturing, exploring and interpreting historical data sets. The developed domain ontologies provide means for separating varying concerns, preserving authenticity and maintaining the provenance of the records. In this study, we present application principles of the semantic web technologies to create a data preservation and knowledge query pipeline by utilising the linked data together with the developed domain ontologies, namely VRO and HEO. In the future we will explore more flexible and dynamic use case generation for end users and techniques to improve scalability and performance of the developed technologies.

Acknowledgements. We thank the Registrar General of Ireland for permitting us to use the rich content contained in the vital records for the purposes of this research project. This publication has emanated from research conducted within the Irish Record Linkage, 1864-1913 project supported by the RPG2013-3; Irish Research Council Interdisciplinary Research Project Grant, and within the Science Foundation Ireland Funded Insight Research Centre (SFI/12/RC/2289). The Digital Repository of Ireland (formerly NAVR) gratefully acknowledges funding from the Irish HEA PRTLI sCycle 5 programme.

References

1. Beyan, O., Breathnach, C., Collins, S., Debruyne, C., Decker, S., Grant, D., Grant, R., Gurrin, B.: Towards linked vital registration data for reconstituting families and creating longitudinal health histories. In: Knowledge Representation for Health Care KR4HC 2014. Organized under the" Vienna Summer of Logic 2014" multi-conference (2014)
2. Davies, J., Fensel, D., Van Harmelen, F. (eds.).: Towards the semantic web: ontology-driven knowledge management. John Wiley & Sons (2003)
3. Harrower, N., Webb, S., Tang, J., Gallagher, D., Kilfeather, E., O'Tuairisg, S., Collins, S.: Developing the Irish National Trusted Digital Repository for the Humanities and Social Sciences: an interdisciplinary approach. OR2013 (2013)

4. Hunter, J., Choudhury, S.: PANIC: an integrated approach to the preservation of composite digital objects using Semantic Web services. International Journal on Digital Libraries **6**(2), 174–183 (2006)
5. Lee, K.H., Slattery, O., Tang, X., Lu, R., McCrary, V.: The state of the art and practice in digital preservation. Journal of Research-National Institute of Standards and Technology **107**(1), 93–106 (2002)
6. Castells, P., Perdrix, F., Pulido, E., Rico, M., Benjamins, V., Contreras, J., Lorés, J.: Neptuno: semantic web technologies for a digital newspaper archive. In: Bussler, C.J., Davies, J., Fensel, D., Studer, R. (eds.) ESWS 2004. LNCS, vol. 3053, pp. 445–458. Springer, Heidelberg (2004)
7. Breathnach, C., O'Halpin, E.: Registered 'unknown' infant fatalities in Ireland, 1916–32: gender and power. Irish Historical Studies **38**(149), 70–88 (2012)
8. Breathnach, C., O'Halpin, E.: Scripting blame: Irish coroners' courts and unnamed infant dead, 1916–32. Social History **39**(2), 210–228 (2014)
9. Sheth, A.P., Ramakrishnan, C.: Semantic (Web) technology in action: Ontology driven information systems for search, integration, and analysis. IEEE Data Engineering Bulletin **26**(4), 40 (2003)
10. Bizer, C., Heath, T., Berners-Lee, T.: Linked data-the story so far. Semantic Services, Interoperability and Web Applications: Emerging Concepts, 205–227 (2009)
11. Meersman, R., Debruyne, C.: Hybrid ontologies and social semantics. In: 2010 4th IEEE International Conference on Digital Ecosystems and Technologies (DEST) (2010)
12. Debruyne, C., Meersman, R.: Semantic interoperation of information systems by evolving ontologies through formalized social processes. In: Eder, J., Bielikova, M., Tjoa, A.M. (eds.) ADBIS 2011. LNCS, vol. 6909, pp. 444–459. Springer, Heidelberg (2011)
13. Kippen, R.: Counting nineteenth-century maternal deaths: the case of Tasmania. Historical Methods: J. of Quantitative and Interdisciplinary History **38**(1), 14–25 (2005)
14. World Health Organization. International Classification of Diseases and Related Health Problems (Geneva) (1992)
15. Great Britain. Lord Lieutenant and Privy Council of Ireland. Registrar General of Ireland Registration of deaths in Ireland: a statistical nosology, comprising the causes of death, classified and alphabetically arranged with notes and observations, Dublin (1864)
16. Bizer, C., Cyganiak, R.: D2R server-publishing relational databases on the semantic web. Poster at the 5th International Semantic Web Conference (2006)
17. Int. List of Causes of Death, Rev.1 (1900). http://www.wolfbane.com/icd/icd1h.html
18. Int. List of Causes of Death, Rev.2 (1909). http://www.wolfbane.com/icd/icd2h.html
19. Department of Commerce and Labor, Bureau of Census. International Classification of Causes of Sickness and Death. Washington Government of Printing Office (1910)

Academic Search. Methods of Displaying the Output to the End User

Svetlana Popova[1,2,3](✉), Ivan Khodyrev[1], Artem Egorov[1], and Vera Danilova[4]

[1] ITMO University, Saint-Petersburg, Russia
svp@list.ru
[2] Saint-Petersburg State University, Saint-Petersburg, Russia
[3] ORION, Saint-Petersburg, Russia
kivan.mih@gmail.com
[4] Russian Presidential Academy of National Economy and Public,
Moscow, Russia
maolve@gmail.com

Abstract. The present paper spans the task of structured representation of search results in developed academic search system. Main contribution of our work is integration into the search process both: 1) structured visualization of search results (clustering and topic graph); 2) providing information about yearly dynamics of topics for query results. The latter makes the system more flexible and suitable for data monitoring. The system can be used not only for academic search, but also for foresight studies.

Keywords: Information retrieval · Academic search · Search output representation · Foresight tools · Natural language processing

1 Introduction and Related Work

The authors of [1] suggest academic search approach based on the construction of keyphrases and their use at the indexing stage. The authors specify such system advantages as the output representation as a list of keyphrases and related texts, the availability of information about keyphrases that are frequently used with another specific phrase. Hence, the system provides data classified with respect to the keyphrases.

Clustering of query results draws much attention of the scientists (e.g., [2,3]). In most cases the following approach is used. The first n snippets obtained by a general search engine are clustered. The most frequent subsequences are extracted from snippets using the suffix tree. These subsequences become cluster topics with respect to which the documents are distributed. Normally, a document is assigned to a topic if it contains a topic-related subsequence.

This research is partially financially supported by the Government of Russian Federation, Grant 074-U01.

I. Ciuciu et al. (Eds.): OTM 2015 Workshops, LNCS 9416, pp. 476–480, 2015.
DOI: 10.1007/978-3-319-26138-6_51

ScienScan [5,6] is academic search tool operates in real time. It discovers topics in the search result and summarizes them in the form of concise hierarchical topic map in which the child nodes represent the subtopics of the parent nodes. System is based on Wikipedia Miner and Microsoft Academic Search API.

In contrast with other works, our contribution is that we not only allow to visualize search results, but also we provide an interactive instrument to analyze themes and their relation changes during time period. Such visualization includes not only graphical representation of links between topics in the search domain, tag cloud and clusters, but also the possibility to track quickly their dynamics in time. Real-time analysis imposes restrictions on algorithms' complexity and a number of additional queries to knowledge storage systems.

There is a difference between the proposed system and the system described in [5,6]: we not only build concepts graph—tree, but we also show which concepts and in which time were used more or less intensively and how do their frequencies relate. To achieve it our system have to analyze thousands query results instead of processing hundreds as other systems do.

2   Characteristics and Capabilities of the System

In proposed approach (test version: http://93.92.203.182/fs) additional knowledge databases are not used. Our goal is to show that indexing of abstracts using keyphrases (concepts) could be enough for a task of interactive concept graph creation. To estimate a size of a concept-node in a graph we are calculating occurrence frequency of a concept in a query result. Links between nodes are weighted proportionally to the number of documents in which these two concepts occur together. We consider two important factors, which affect speed of query processing: each document should be represented by a small number of keyphrases; these keyphrases should be good quality and represent features of a particular paper. We are using two observations which rule our algorithm: 1) scientific papers have important keyphrases aligned to the beginning of the document [8]; 2) usage of one-word keyphrases usually degrade overall quality of keyphrase extraction task, because ratio of good one-word phrases to the whole set of one-word phrases is very low [4]. Based on these observations only multi-words phrases were used in indexing step. We also considered the position of phrase in a document - only abstracts and titles were used to extract keyphrases. In this case we get quite small number of phrases per document with acceptable quality.

Keyphrases were extracted as the longest multi-word sequences of nouns and adjectives directly following each other in the text (details [4,7]). Extracted phrases should not contain punctuation or stop words. Indexing is done using open resources from the web: titles and abstracts of scientific papers. For prototype data about one million abstracts was processed. We are using Apache Solr as a basis for search mechanism.

The main purpose of the developed search system is to create an efficient graphic representation of query results. In order to achieve it, we apply several

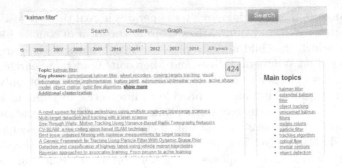

Fig. 1. An example of the interface with clusters

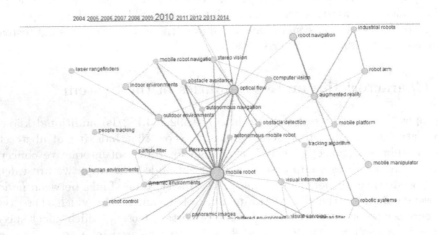

Fig. 2. An example of the interface with clusters

strategies. The results may be represented as a traditional ranking list, as labeled clusters with clusters associated keyphrases or as a graph of relations between keyphrases (concepts). Pic. 1 shows systemś interface. For example, names of the clusters built for the query "robot" according to the data of 2004 2014 years: mobile robotics, humanoid robots, robot manipulator, optical flow, augmented reality, dynamic environment, obstacle avoidance, kalman filter, control scheme, computer vision, outdoor environments e.t.c. We used the idea of year-specific result representation. This representation enables the user to evaluate the dynamics of topic change in the main clusters over the years, which allows to assess the viability of certain topic for the research. Also, system provides a list of most frequent concepts used during the selected year.

Fig. 2 introduces the interface, which represents search results as concept relations in a graph. The vertices are concepts (keyphrases); the thickness of the edges defines the degree of association between the concepts (how many documents contain both concepts). It is possible to visualize the graph of concepts related to certain year or for all years. The node size is proportional to the number of publications that contain a specific concept with respect to the whole number of publications. Green rings around the nodes indicate that the number of publications containing certain concept increased as compared to average of the past two years. Red rings indicate the opposite. The size and the ring of a node change along the years. It allows to evaluate, which topics are more and which are less popular, whether the dynamics of certain topics is similar, and which topics are being developed at the present moment.

3   Conclusion and Future Work

We present a prototype of the system for academic search. The main focus is placed on the representation of search results and its changes in time. The task is approached by means of displaying the main concepts of the query, topic-labeled clusters, graphs of associations between concepts and there dynamic changes in time. We assume that this visualization helps users to quickly analyze the background of the domain, find a specific topic they are interested in, evaluate the trends and exclude unpromising directions.

The system is under development, so it's evaluation has not been presented yet. Only a limited number of articles are currently indexing in the system (approximate one million), making it difficult to assess because of the low Recall. Currently we are working on extending the indexed data-base. On the next step, we plan to perform system evaluation.

References

1. Gutwina, C., Paynterb, G., Wittenb, I., Nevill-Manningc, C., Frankb, E.: Improving browsing in digital libraries with keyphrase indexes // Journal Decision Support Systems - From information retrieval to knowledge management: enabling technologies and best practices archive, Volume 27, Issue 1–2, Nov. 1999, Pages 81–104
2. Bernardini, A., Carpineto, C.: Full-subtopic retrieval with keyphrase-based search results clustering. In: IEEE/WIC/ACM International Joint Conferences on Web Intelligence and Intelligent Agent Technologies, WI-IAT 2009, vol. 1 (2009)
3. Zeng, H.-J., He, Q.-C., Chen, Z., Ma, W.-Y., Ma, J.: Learning to cluster web search results. In: Proceeding SIGIR 2004 Proceedings of the 27th Annual International ACM SIGIR Conference on Research and Development in Information Retrieval, pp. 210–217
4. Popova, S., Khodyrev, I.: Ranking in keyphrase extraction problem: is it suitable to use statistics of words occurrences? In: Proceedings of the Institute for System Programming, vol. 26(4), pp. 123–136 (2014)
5. Mirylenka, D., Passerini, A.: Scienscan – an efficient visualization and browsing tool for academic search. In: Blockeel, H., Kersting, K., Nijssen, S., Železný, F. (eds.) ECML PKDD 2013, Part III. LNCS, vol. 8190, pp. 667–671. Springer, Heidelberg (2013)

6. Mirylenka, D., Passerini, A.: Navigating the topical structure of academic search results via the wikipedia category network. In: Proceeding CIKM 2013 Proceedings of the 22nd ACM International Conference on Conference on Information & Knowledge Management, pp. 891–896
7. Popova, S., Kovriguina, L., Khodyrev, I., Mouromtsev, D.: Stop-words in keyphrase ex-traction problem. In: Proc. FRUCT 2013 Conference, pp. 113–121
8. You, W., Fontaine, D., Barhes, J.-P.: An automatic keyphrase extraction system for scientific documents. Knowl. Inf. Syst. **34**, 691–724 (2013)

Estimating Keyphrases Popularity in Sampling Collections

Svetlana Popova[1,2]([✉]), Gabriella Skitalinskaya[3], and Ivan Khodyrev[1]

[1] ITMO University, Saint-Petersburg, Russia
[2] Saint-Petersburg State University, Saint-Petersburg, Russia
svp@list.ru
[3] Russian Presidential Academy of National Economy and Public,
Moscow, Russia
gabriellasky@icloud.com

Abstract. The problem of structured representation of data has high practical value and is particularly relevant due to growth of data volume. Such methods of data representation as topic graphs, concepts trees, etc. is a convenient way to represent information retrieved from a collection of documents. In this paper, we research some aspects of using a collection of samples for the evaluation of the popularity of concepts. The latter can be used to visualize concept significance and concept ranking in the tasks of structured representation.

Multi-word phrases are considered as concepts. We address the case when these phrases are automatically extracted from the processed document collection. The popularity of a concept (e.g., visually can be presented as the size of the vertex in the topic graph) is judged by the number of documents containing this phrase. We elaborate the case when a sample from the document collection is used to estimate concept popularity. For this case we estimate how permissible is such representation of data, reflecting the proportions of the number of documents containing specific concepts. A frequency-based criterion and the procedure of its calculation is described in the paper. This helps to estimate the expedience of concept popularity representation in respect to the popularity of other concepts. The main aspect here is to establish the criteria when relations between values of concepts popularity in a sample are the same as in the population, and to establish the criterion for selecting n high-frequency concepts which have the same sample rank and frequency distributions as in the population.

Keywords: Key phrase · Topic graph · Search result · Information extraction · Short texts · Sampling

1 Introduction

The problem of structured and visual representation of information is becoming particularly relevant with the rapid growth of data. Such representation allows

This research is partially financially supported by the Government of Russian Federation, Grant 074-U01.

I. Ciuciu et al. (Eds.): OTM 2015 Workshops, LNCS 9416, pp. 481–491, 2015.
DOI: 10.1007/978-3-319-26138-6_52

the end user to find and retrieve the necessary information from large amounts of data quickly. Today there are many ways of presenting data of different nature in a structured way. One approach is to construct thematic maps, conceptual graphs, hierarchy of concepts, annotated clusters etc. Typically, a necessary task in the process of implementation of systems of that kind is to extract main concepts or clusters labels from the dataset which belong or create the dataset's structure. Additional information also can be provided, i.e. number of documents containing this concept or the size of the annotated cluster. In the paper we concentrate on the tasks and applications where this kind of information is used. The second aspect of the paper is the problem of interactive data visualization and data navigation. Real-time processing of the whole textual dataset can be challenging so only a number of samples is processed. We address the question of concept popularity estimation and elaborate a criteria to detect conditions when such estimation is possible/impossible. We hypothesize that concept popularity is directly proportional to the number of documents in the collection having this concept. We consider multi-word phrases as concepts, thus single terms are not taken into account.

To illustrate the problem, we are trying to solve, and to show its relevance consider the following example. For instance we are interested in approaches to the academic search problem, which represent the results of the query as a thematic graph (e.g. Fig.1). The vertices in this graph are concepts found in the query results, the edges are the connections between the concepts. Fast processing and structuring of documents from search results is generally a difficult task in real-time, since the result of the search may be too big. So, we analyze the possibility of using randomly selected data samples from a query for visualizing the thematic graph to show the main keyphrases in the query result, and the proportions between the numbers of documents containing each phrase. The latter allows to specify the size of the vertex in the graph, corresponding to the concept, proportionally to the popularity of the concept. The solution of this problem is interesting, and for example, allows to analyze the dynamics of changes in the popularity of concepts with time, such as the visual trend analysis.

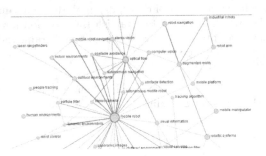

Fig. 1. An example of a part of the thematic graph constructed from the results of processing the search query robot. Result from testing collection

Note that in this paper, we focus only on the information about the popularity of the vertices-concepts and consider only them. As a specific purpose of this study, we consider the presentation of the results from the systems of academic search or from monitoring information in a similar manner as in the example above. The main task of the research is to provide a method of evaluation and assessment of the most frequent concepts to answer the questions 1. if we use a collection of samples instead of the entire result of the query to construct the thematic graph, can we present the popularity of concepts-vertexes, where the popularity of a concept is proportional to the number of documents containing this term; 2. what criterion should we use to identify concepts for which it is reasonable to assess the popularity in relation to the popularity of other concepts.

In other words, we want to answer the question "how many phrases can be selected under condition that their sample rank and frequency distributions are the same as in the population"?

2   Related Work

The problem we are studying is related to the problem of clustering query results [3–5], when the following approach is used for clustering. The first k snippets obtained using general search systems such as Yahoo are chosen, then using the suffix tree from the snippets, the most frequent subsequences are extracted. These subsequences become the topics of clusters, among which the documents are distributed. Expanding these studies, our research can help to evaluate the possibility of samples to identify true proportions between clusters sizes in the search result.

The problem of sampling and faceted search results has been actively studied by researchers (e.g.,[6–9]). Notice that in this study we do not consider the problem of choosing the method of constructing the collection of samples. We used a basic approach - randomly selecting a set of samples.

The problem of key phrase extraction includes several main methods. The first method includes ranking words of the text, selecting the best and constructing phrases from the selected words [10–12]. The other includes: the construction of candidate phrases, followed by the ranking of candidate phrases and selecting of the best of them as keyphrases or making a classification of the candidates [12–18]. Use of information about the parts of speech of words has a significant role [10,12,16]. Thus, it was shown that the use of nouns and adjectives allows to enhance the quality of extracted key terms. We suggested a general algorithm which has shown good results in comparison to the state-of-the-art [18,19]. This algorithm was used in the presented research and is described below.

3   DataSet and Keyphrases Extraction Method

We used a collection of abstracts on different topics (e.g. control systems, robots, semantic technologies and other) which contained: 467512 documents, 2884675 phrases extracted from documents, 7650482 the number of extracted phrases.

Keyphrases were extracted from every abstract separately. During the pre-proccessing all words were stemmed using the Porter stemmer. Punctuation marks and stop words were not removed from the text. We used the Stanford POS-tagger [1] to tag words in each document with parts of speech. All keyphrases were extracted as the longest sequences of words directly following each other in the text during a single pass through a text. Punctuation marks and stop words were used as delimiters. Therefore, keyphrases do not contain punctuation marks or stop words. All single-word keyword phrases were discarded. In our previous studies, we have shown that this approach shows very good results in comparison to the state-of-the-art methods (for details please use [18]). Additionally, a list of stop phrases was used. It consists of common phrases used in abstracts, which do not reflect the topic of the document ("main idea", "important role", "present study", "same time", "promising result", "other method", "experiment result", "different approach", "first stage", "recent work", "previous work" and some other). This list was built manually. Table 1 shows an example of an abstract and keyphrases extracted from it. We did not use extra sources like Wikipedia and WordNet to improve the quality of extracted phrases-concepts. However, the assumption that regardless of the used keyphrase extraction method, concepts are distributed uniformly over the documents in the collection implies that the results may be transferred to other methods of extracting phrases.

In the experiments, we compared the results obtained for the original collection with the results obtained for a collection of a smaller size, a randomly selected sample from the original collection. Two cases were considered: 1) the original collection consists of different-topic documents and 2) the original collection consists of documents containing the query (a single word or a phrase). The following queries were used: "robot", "cluster", "neural network", "control system".

Table 1. Example of Abstract and Extracted Keyphrases

Abstract	Keyphrases
this paper presents basic, yet important, properties that can be used when developing methods for image acquisition, processing, and visualization on the diamond grid. the sampling density needed to reconstruct a band-limited signal and the ideal interpolation function on the diamond grid are derived	ideal interpol function, imag acquisit, diamond grid, sampl densiti, band-limit signal

The following notation has been used: 1. The main collection is denoted MainCollection and contains all the processed documents in the research. MainCollection ("query") - means all the documents containing the word/phrase of query. 2. The collection, obtained by randomly selecting k documents is denoted:

---

[1] Cf. http://nlp.stanford.edu/software/tagger.shtml

1) SmallCollection_k, if the original collection was MainCollection; 2) Small-Collection_k ("query"), if the original collection was MainCollection ("query"). Top-n denotes n phrases with the highest document frequency in the collection taken. In what follows, we assume, that the popularity of the phrase is directly proportional to the document frequency of the phrase.

4 Evaluation

We used the Spearman correlation coefficient value between the number of documents that contain the most n common concepts in the original collection (MainCollection or MainCollection ("query")) and the number of documents that contain the same concepts in the collections of samples (SmallCollection_k, SmallCollection_k ("query")). During the evaluation procedure the Spearman correlation coefficient was not calculated for the first 5 most popular phrases of the original collection to avoid an overrated value of the correlation coefficient. The reason is that the frequency distribution of keyphrases is similar to Zipfian-type distribution. Frequency of the first 5 phrases decreases significantly in both – in the sample collection and in the population. This has significant impact on the correlation value, increasing the value of a positive correlation, thereby concealing the decrease in the correlation of phrases with a lower document frequency.

5 The Structure of the Experiment

All experiments were performed for two types of collections: MainCollection and MainCollection ("query"). We define three sets of experiments. *Group*1: in this set of experiments, we estimated the impact of phrases presented in the top-n most frequent phrases of MainCollection (MainCollection ("query")) but not included in the top-n phrases of SmallCollection_k (SmallCollection_k ("query")). *Group*2: in this set of experiments, we studied the influence of the number of documents k in the collections of samples SmallCollection_k (SmallCollection_k ("query")) gathered from MainCollection (MainCollection ("query")) on the value of the correlation of the frequency of top-n phrases in the MainCollection (MainCollection ("query")) and SmallCollection_k (SmallCollection_k ("query")). *Group*3: in this set of experiments we provide a method of evaluation and assessment of the number of most commonly used concepts to answer the question: if we use a collection of samples instead of the entire result, can we present the popularity of concepts-vertices.

6 Results

Experiment Group 1. The number of phrases from the top-n of MainCollection that are missing in the top-n phrases of SmallCollection_k have been estimated. The problem was considered for cases where for the collections of samples wcrc selected $k-$ 1000, 3000, 5000, 8000, 15000 documents (Table 2, rows All documents). Similar results were obtained for the case of thematic collections MainCollection ("query") and sample collections SmallCollection_k ("query"). But as the size of the collection MainCollection ("query") is about 10000-20000 documents, k is selected as $k=$ 250, 3000, 5000, 8000 (Table 2).

Table 2. The Average Number of Phrases from the Top-n Phrases of MainCollection (MainCollection (query)), Which are not Included in the Top-n Phrases of SmallCollection_k (SmallCollectio_k(query)

SmallCollection_k, SmallCollection_k ("query")	K=250	k=1000	k=3000	k=5000	k=8000	k=15000	Total documents in MainCollection, MainCollection(" query")
				n=50			
All documents	-	22	13	10	8	7	467512
Query "robot"	23	11	5	4	2	-	23008
Query "cluster"	20	11	6	4	3	-	13778
Query "neural network"	22	12	7	5	3	-	13576
Query "control system"	21	11	6.5	5	2	-	8209
				n=100			
All documents	-	47	29	24	19	14	467512
Query "robot"	55	30	18	14	10	-	23008
Query "cluster"	51	27	15	11	5	-	13778
Query "neural network"	50	24	12	9	7	-	13576
Query "control system"	47	24	13	8	1	-	8209
				n=200			
All documents	-	103	64	51	40	30	467512
Query "robot"	114	69	39	28	19	-	23008
Query "cluster"	111	63	34	22	12	-	13778
Query "neural network"	107	56	31	21	15	-	13576
Query "control system"	102	53	26	14	3	-	8209

We also verified (Table 3) the number of the most frequent phrases that should be selected from SmallCollection_5000 (SmallCollection_5000("query")) in order for these phrases to include almost all the phrases of the top-n of MainCollection (MainCollection ("query")). The results show that the loss of phrases in the top-50 for SmallCollection_5000 compared with the top-50 for MainCollection is not critical, since the popularity of such phrases in SmallCollection_5000 almost doesn't decrease, and nearly all such phrases are included in the top-75 phrases of SmallCollection_5000. Though for the top-100 phrases, and at an even greater extent for the top-200 phrases, the number of selected phrases from SmallCollection_5000 must be significantly increased in order not to lose the phrases of the top-100 and top-200 phrases from MainCollection. The situation is similar in thematic collections MainCollection ("query") and SmallCollection_5000 ("query").

Experiment Group 2. In this set of experiments, we studied the influence of the number of documents k in the collections of samples SmallCollection_k from MainCollection on the value of the correlation of the popularity of top-n phrases in the MainCollection and SmallCollection_k. 30 experiments have been conducted for each k, the average results of which are given in Fig. 2, where $n=50$, 100 and 200. The top-n of the keyphrases from MainCollection denoted

Table 3. The average number of phrases based on the results of 30 experiments, included in the top-n most frequent phrases of MainCollection, but not included in the top-s most frequent phrases of SmallCollection_k.The same for MainCollection ("robot") and SmallCollection_k ("robot")

Collection	MainCollection (size: 467512)						MainCollection ("robot") (size: 23008)					
s/n	$n=50$											
s	50	55	60	65	70	75	50	55	60	65	70	75
Mean loss of phrases	6	4	2	2	2	1	4	2	1	1	0	0
	$n=100$											
s	100	120	150	200	250	300	100	120	150	200	250	300
Mean loss of phrases	19	13	7	4	2	1	14	8	3	1	0	0
	$n=200$											
s	200	250	300	500	750	1000	200	250	300	500	750	800
Mean loss of phrases	45	30	21	6	3	1	28	14	6	0	0	0

by Ph(n). Similar results for thematic collections MainCollection ("query") and SmallCollection_5000 ("query") are also shown in Fig. 2.

The results in Fig. 2 show the following observations. Firstly, an increase in the number of phrases leads to a decrease in the correlation value between the document frequencies of phrases in MainCollection and SmallCollection_k. There are several explanations. The frequencies of the first most frequent phrases decrease rapidly. Also phrases with low popularity have a smaller difference between the frequencies of neighboring phrases. These two factors contribute to the fact that the frequency of phrases with high popularity in collections MainCollection and SmallCollection_k correlate stronger than phrases with low popularity.

Next observation is quite expectative: the results indicate that a high increase in the number of documents k in the collection of samples SmallCollection_k leads to a lower increase in quality. Such dependency is observed due to the fact that an increase in the number of documents increases the frequency of phrases. This results in the increase of the difference of frequency between phrases adjacent in popularity. The latter allows to get less errors associated with the order of phrases ranked by their frequency in sample collection vs original collection.

For example, for the collection of samples SmallCollection_1000 the results are low, since the values of frequencies of phrases with high popularity are less than 20, which leads to an increase in noise. It happens because standard deviation of phrase frequent can be significant in comparison to the average.

Also, due to the superimposition of this noise the increasing the number of selected phrases leads to an increase in the number of non-matching phrases in the top-n most frequent phases in MainCollection and SmallCollection_k. As a consequence, in order to select almost all phrases included in the top-n of Main-Collection from the top-s phrases of SmallCollection_k a signifincant increase

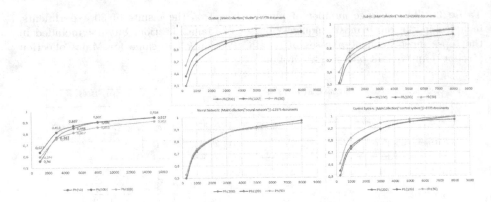

Fig. 2. The correlation of frequent phrases from Ph(50), Ph (100) and Ph (200) in MainCollection and in SmallCollection_k for the case MainCollection and SmallCollection_k (k=1000, 3000, 5000, 8000, 15000). The same results for MainCollection(query) and SmallCollection_k(query), k= 250, 1000, 3000, 5000, 8000. Ph (m) - denotes the number of top-m phrases used, horizontal axis shows the number of documents in the sample collections (SmallCollection_k), the vertical axis indicates the value of the Spearman correlation

in s must be made. But, since the frequencies of phrases in MainCollection for such phrases are relatively close to each other, one can assume the equivalence of their significance. For example: the collection of samples consisting of 5000 documents may be enough to approximate a thematic graph of MainCollection (consisting of 467512 documents) with 30-50 nodes, if we show the popularity of phrases on the graph. Displaying the popularity of remaining phrases-vertices (i.e by making the size of the vertex proportional to the phrases popularity) proves to be useless, because of the high proportion of error.

Experiment Group 3. Due to the fact that documents for the collections of samples SmallCollection_k are selected randomly from the main corpus, the average frequency of each of the phrases in the unit volume of documents should similar. We compare the average frequency of the first 200 phrases per 1000 documents in the MainCollection and SmallCollection_k (k=1000 and 15000). The Result illustrates an obvious dependency: by increasing number of documents in the SmallCollection_k we decrease the error in determining the mean frequency of phrases in comparison with the MainCollection. This fact is the basis of the results of experiments described in the paper.

For a fixed phrase the distribution of its frequency according to the results of 30 experiments is normal (ShapiroWilk test) at a significance level 0,001. So criterion of the optimal number of phrases is based on the comparison of the average frequency of each of the phrases on the results of 30 experiments and calculating the standard deviation.

For the standard deviation in the case of the normal distribution next rule is introduced: according to which, an event is considered to be practically impossible if it lies in the region of values of the normal distribution of a random variable at a distance from its mathematical expectation of more than three times the standard deviation. Approximately 95% of the cases fall into the 2*standard deviation.

When building a thematic graph it is important for us to preserve the proportions between the document-frequency of concepts (document frequencies of phrases) from the MainCollection in SmallCollection_k. This ratio is the less disturbed, the smaller the deviation of the frequency of a phrase in different collections of samples of the same size from the median frequency of the phrase in these sub-collections. In other words, if the average frequency of phrases in 30 sub-collections equals 10, and the values of the frequencies in the sub-collections range from 1 to 20, the possible error in the value of the frequency of phrases may be considered too large.

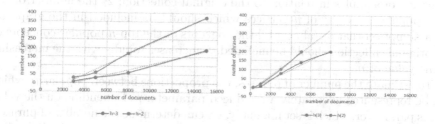

Fig. 3. Dependence of the number of selected phrases for $h - 3$ and $h = 2$ on the number of documents in the collection of samples

Therefore, as a criterion, for number of phrases, that should be selected to calculate the proportions between their frequencies, we used the parameter h=(average frequency of the phrase in 30 collections / (standard deviation* 2)). If the value of h=3 or h=2, then only 2 top phrases from SmallCollection_1000 should be used as nodes with sizes for topic graph. For SmallCollection_15000 these values are 190 and 375. Fig. 3 shows the dependence of the number of selected phrases for h=3 and h=2 on the number of documents in the collection of samples. Fig. 3 shows a similar dependence for the thematic collection MainCollection ("robot") and its corresponding collection of samples SmallCollection ("robot").

Note that for the considered collections minimum frequency of phrases for which $h > 3$ have the approximate value of 35, when h=2 the value is 20. Our assumption is that these values can be used as criterion to estimate the number of phrases, the proportions between document-frequency which can be represented.

6.1   Conclusion and Future Work

The results obtained in this study allow us to make an assumption about the possibility of using randomly selected collections of samples for the approximation a large corpus of texts (abstracts) or query results. The approximation is necessary to solve the problem of thematic graphs online construction when the size of a vertex reflects the popularity of the concept corresponding to the vertex. In this case,it is possible to use a relatively small number of concepts-vertices (e.g., about 30-50 most popular concepts for the collection of 5000 samples for the approximation of a data collection containing 467 512 documents and about 150 most popular concepts for the collection of 5000 samples for the approximation of the thematic collection of a data consisting of 23008 documents). The number of such vertices depends on the size of the collection of samples and the size of the original collection. Our research shows that the document frequency of vertices, for which popularity should be shown on the graph, is in most cases greater than 20 in the collection of samples. The remaining concepts-vertices can be considered relatively equivalent, assessing their popularity and reflecting this information in graphical form is meaningless because of the high noise level.

The number of vertices s, to be included in the graph (built on the basis of a collection of samples) depends on two factors: 1) the ratio of the size of the collection of samples in relation to the original collection; 2) the number of the most popular concepts of n vertices which should be included in the graph on the assumption that all/almost all the concepts of the top-n popular concepts of the original collection should be included. S increases rapidly with the increasing in the value of n.

To estimate the number of phrases, the proportions between popularity which can be represented adequately, we induced parameter h. Depending on the value of this parameter, which is set manually, we can determine the number of phrases, for which it is appropriate to be displayed with its sizes on the graph. According to our observations, we assume that it is advisable to use the value of $h=3$ (or at least $h=2$). In this case, the number of phrases that will be selected using this limit depends on the size of the collection of samples. This dependence is shown in the research. Note that for the considered collections of samples minimum frequency of phrases for which $h>3$ have the approximate value of 35, when $h=2$ the value is 20. Our assumption is that these values can be used as criteria to estimate the number of phrases, the proportions between document-frequency, which can be represented.

Future work implies estimation of relation between number of documents in the population and form of distribution (with the fixed value of parameter h) of number of concepts from number of documents in the sample. We also plan to set the same experiment with the strength of relation between the concepts (strength is calculated as simultaneous occurrence of n concepts in the same document).

References

1. Scaiella, U., Ferragina, P., Marino, A., Ciaramita, M.: Topical clustering of search results. In: WSDM, pp. 223–232. ACM (2012)
2. Mirylenka, D., Passerini, A.: Navigating the topical structure of academic search results via wikipedia category network. In: CIKM 2013 Proceedings of the 22nd ACM International Conference on Information & Knowledge Management, pp. 891–896 (2013)

3. Bernardini, A., Carpineto, C.: Full-subtopic retrieval with keyphrase-based search results clustering. In: IEEE/WIC/ACM International Joint Conferences on Web Intelligence and Intelligent Agent Technologies, WI-IAT 2009, vol. 1 (2009)
4. Zhang, D., Dong, Y.: Semantic, hierarchical, online clustering of web search results. In: Yu, J.X., Lin, X., Lu, H., Zhang, Y. (eds.) APWeb 2004. LNCS, vol. 3007, pp. 69–78. Springer, Heidelberg (2004)
5. Zeng, H.-J., He, Q.-C., Chen, Z., Ma, W.-Y., Ma, J.: Learning to cluster web search results. In: Proceeding SIGIR 2004 Proceedings of the 27th Annual International ACM SIGIR Conference on Research and Development in Information Retrieval, pp. 210–217 (2004)
6. Babcock, B., Chaudhuri, S., Das, G.: Dynamic sample selection for approximate query processing. In: Proc. SIGMOD 2003, pp. 539–550 (2003)
7. Wang, J., Krishnan, S., Franklin, M., Goldberg, K., Kraska, T., Milo, T.: A sample-and-clean framework for fast and accurate query processing on dirty data. In: SIGMOD 2014 (2014)
8. Ganti, V., Lee, M., Ramakrishnan, R.: ICICLES: self-tuning samples for approximate query answering. In: Proc. VLDB 2000, vol. 176, p. 187 (2000)
9. Kong, W., Allan, J.: Extracting query facets from search results. In: Proc. SIGIR 2013, pp. 93–102 (2013)
10. Mihalcea, R., Tarau, P.: Textrank: bringing order into texts. In: Proc. EMNLP 2004, pp. 404–411 (2004)
11. Xiaojun, W., Xiao, J.: Exploiting Neighborhood Knowledge for Single Document Sum-marization and Keyphrase Extraction. ACM Transactions on Information Systems 28(2) (2010)
12. Zesch, T., Gurevych, I.: Approximate matching for evaluating keyphrase extraction. In: Proc. RANLP 2009, pp. 484–489 (2009)
13. You, W., Fontaine, D., Barhes, J.-P.: An automatic keyphrase extraction system for scientific documents. Knowl. Inf. Syst. 34, 691–724 (2013)
14. El-Beltagy, S.R., Rafea, A.: KP-Miner: A keyphrase extraction system for english and arabic documents. Information Systems 34, 132–144 (2009)
15. Kim, S.N., Medelyan, O., Yen, M.: Automatic keyphrase extraction from scientific articles. Language Resources and Evaluation. Springer Kan & Timothy Baldwin (2012)
16. Hulth, A.: Improved automatic keyword extraction given more linguistic knowl-edge. In: Proc. EMNLP, pp. 216–223 (2003)
17. Turney, P.: Learning to extract keyphrases from text. In: NRC/ERB-1057 1999, p. 173 (1999)
18. Popova, S.V., Khodyrev, I.A.: Ranking in keyphrase extraction problem: is it suit-able to use statistics of words occurrences? The Proceedings of ISP RAS 1(2), 2014 (2014)
19. Popova, S., Kovriguina, L., Khodyrev, I., Mouromtsev, D.: Stop-words in keyphrase extraction problem. In: Proc. FRUCT 2013, pp. 113–121 (2003)

Semantic HMC: Ontology-Described Hierarchy Maintenance in Big Data Context

Rafael Peixoto[1,2](✉), Christophe Cruz[2], and Nuno Silva[1]

[1] GECAD - ISEP, Polytechnic of Porto, Porto, Portugal
{rafpp,nps}@isep.ipp.pt
[2] LE2I UMR 6306 CNRS, University Bourgogne Franche-Comté, 21000 Dijon, France
christophe.cruz@u-bourgogne.fr

Abstract. One of the biggest challenges in Big Data is the exploitation of Value from large volumes of data that are constantly changing. To exploit value, one must focus on extracting knowledge from these Big Data sources. To extract knowledge and value from unstructured text we propose using a Hierarchical Multi-Label Classification process called Semantic HMC that uses ontologies to describe the predictive model including the label hierarchy and the classification rules. To not overload the user, this process automatically learns the ontology-described label hierarchy from a very large set of text documents. This paper aims to present a maintenance process of the ontology-described label hierarchy relations with regards to a stream of unstructured text documents in the context of Big Data that incrementally updates the label hierarchy.

Keywords: Maintenance · Multi-label classification · Hierarchy induction · Ontology · Machine learning

1 Introduction

The exponential growth of the amount of data available on the web requires new forms of processing to enable enhanced decision making, insight discovery and optimization. The term of Big Data is mainly used to describe datasets that cannot be processed using traditional tools.

To extract knowledge from Big Data sources we propose to use a Semantic HMC process [1, 2] that is capable of Hierarchically Multi-Classify a large Variety and Volume of unstructured data items. Hierarchical Multi-Label Classification (HMC) is the combination of Multi-Label classification and Hierarchical classification [13]. The Semantic HMC process is unsupervised such that no previous labelled examples or enrichment rules to relate the data items with the labels are required. The label hierarchy and the enrichment rules are automatically learned from the data through scalable Machine Learning techniques.

The automatic concept (label) hierarchy extraction from unstructured documents is not a trivial process and proper techniques for document analysis and representation are required. In the context of Big Data, this task is even more challenging due to Big Data characteristics. An increasing number of V-dimensions has been used to characterize

© Springer International Publishing Switzerland 2015
I. Ciuciu et al. (Eds.): OTM 2015 Workshops, LNCS 9416, pp. 492–501, 2015.
DOI: 10.1007/978-3-319-26138-6_53

Big Data further [3, 4]. Volume, Velocity, Variety are usually used to characterize the essence of Big Data [3, 5]. Volume concerns the large amount of data that is generated and stored through the years by social media, sensor data and other sources [3]. Velocity concerns the high speed of data production. Variety relates to the various types of data composing the Big Data. These types include semi-structured and unstructured data representing 90% of his content [5] such as audio, video, web page and text, as well as traditional structured data (e.g. XML, JSON or CSV).

Automatic concept hierarchy learning from text (i.e. taxonomy induction) has been extensively studied [6, 7]. In Big Data however, relearning the hierarchy for each new document is infeasible due to the Big Data characteristics. Most of the existing literature focuses in learning concept hierarchies from texts [6, 7]. Few works have been published in maintaining the hierarchy once it is created without relearning the whole hierarchy. This paper focuses in maintaining hierarchical relations of an automatically learned ontology-described concept hierarchy with regards to a stream of unstructured text documents in Big Data context. The process is implemented using technologies for Big Data that distributes the process by several machines in order to reach high performance and scalability.

The rest of the paper covers four sections. The second section presents the background knowledge and related work. The third section describes the hierarchy maintenance process from a stream of text documents. The fourth section describes the implementation in a scalable and distributed platform to process Big Data. Finally, the last section draws conclusions and suggests further research.

2   Background and Related Work

This section introduces some background and discusses the current related work about automatic concept hierarchy learning from text.

Two main different aspects of concept hierarchy extraction from text can be distinguished: (1) concept extraction and filtering (2) hierarchy creation. Several methods exist in literature for extracting concepts (i.e. terms) from a set of text documents, including linguistic [8–10] and statistical approaches [11, 12]. Many types of semantics can be captured using statistics-based methods [13] that offer better scaling performance than their alternatives [14]. Several statistic-based methods exist to create hierarchical relations between concepts, including [14, 15]:

- Hierarchical clustering that starts with one cluster and progressively merges the closest clusters.
- Subsumption methods that construct the concept broader-narrower relations based on the co-occurrence of concepts [16].

More advantages and drawbacks of each method are deeply studied by De Knijff et al. [14].

Most work in this area focus on the hierarchy creation and few works have been done on the hierarchy maintenance since it is created, even less in Big Data context. Liu et al. [17] automatically induce a hierarchy by combining phrases extracted from the collection using clustering with context knowledge derived from a knowledge base. Recent efforts have been made to organize text corpora using evolving multi-branch trees [18], known as topic trees. Cui et al. [19] present a visual topic analytics system, called RoseRiver, to help users better understand the hierarchical topic evolution at different levels of granularity.

Compared with existing approaches, maintaining an automatically induced hierarchy from Big Data requires simple and greatly scalable methods due to its high volume and velocity of data production. Due to the simplicity and its relation between the processing speed and ability to provide good concept hierarchical relations [14], the subsumption method is used to learn and maintain the relations between concepts. To the best of our knowledge, our approach is the first one to apply a subsumption method in order to maintain the concept hierarchy relations (Hierarchy Maintenance) with regards to a stream of unstructured text documents in Big Data.

3   Hierarchy Maintenance

This section describes in detail the hierarchy maintenance process that aims to incrementally update the label hierarchy using a stream of new documents. The label hierarchy is automatically learned based on a Description Logic ontology presented in Table 1. The *Item* class represents data items to be labeled/classified and is populated with data items (i.e. text document) in the assertional level (Abox). The *Term* class defines the extracted terms from data items and it is populated in the assertion level (Abox) with terms (e.g. words extracted from text documents, symbols representing subjects/objects in photos). The *Label* class defines the terms that are considered to classify the items i.e. the most relevant terms. The *broader* and *narrower* relations define the subsumption hierarchy between terms. The *hasTerm* relation links the asserted Items to the asserted Terms.

Table 1. Label hierarchy ontology

DL concepts	Description
$Item \sqsubseteq \top$	Data item to label (e.g. document)
$Term \sqsubseteq \top$	Extracted terms (e.g. word)
$Label \sqsubseteq Term$	Terms used to classify the items
$Term \sqsubseteq \exists broader.Term$	Broader relation between terms
$Term \sqsubseteq \exists narrower.Term$	Narrower relation between labels
$broader \equiv narrower^{-}$	Broader and narrower are inverse relations
$Item \equiv \exists hasTerm.Term$	Relation that links data items to the terms
$Item \sqcap Term = \emptyset$	Term is disjointed from Item

In previous work [2] the hierarchy relations (i.e. the hierarchy created using a traditional subsumption method) are induced from a collection of documents C using the co-occurrence of terms in documents. The terms in text documents can be either a unigram (i.e. a word, "CEO") or more complex n-grams (i.e. composed words, "chief executive officer"). This paper proposes to maintain the hierarchy relations by using a stream Stm of new documents. The new documents from Stm are included in the collection C originating a new collection C' impacting the term co-occurrence and consequently the hierarchy. In order to persist the co-occurrence values, a term co-occurrence frequency matrix is used to represent the co-occurrence of any pair of terms in a collection of documents [2].

Three steps comprise the maintenance process: (i) Co-occurrence matrix maintenance that calculates the impact of new documents in the co-occurrence matrix, (ii) Hierarchical relationship maintenance that calculates how the changes in the co-occurrence matrix impact the hierarchical relations, and (iii) Change detection that detects hierarchical changes and updates the hierarchy. These maintenance steps are described in the following subsections.

3.1   Co-occurrence Matrix Maintenance

The co-occurrence matrix used by the subsumption method is impacted with the inclusion of new text documents in the document collection. The set of documents C is a collection of n documents. The sub-set of $documents \subseteq C$ that contains a $term \in Term$ is represented by a set of vectors in the form: $vector_{term} < d_1, d_2, ..., d_n >$.

The co-occurrence frequency matrix cfm is used to represent the co-occurrence of any pair of terms $(term_i, term_j)$ in a collection C of documents, such that:

$$cfm_C(term_i, term_j) = \left|\left\{doc \in C: doc \in vector_{term_i} \wedge doc \in vector_{term_j}\right\}\right| \quad (1)$$

where $vector_{term_i}$ is the document vector for $term_i$ and $vector_{term_j}$ is the vector for term $term_j$. Let m denote the number of different terms in a collection of documents C, the term co-occurrence matrix for the collection C is a $m \times m$ symmetric matrix. The main diagonal of the co-occurrence matrix cfm_C $(term_i, term_i)$ denotes the occurrence of $term_i$ in all documents of C. Hence the main diagonal cfm_C $(term_i, term_i)$ is the maximum value for the line $term_i$ and the column $term_i$ of the co-occurrence table.

However, in document streaming context, the collection C will be constantly evolving. For each new text document doc' in the stream, the collection of documents C will evolve for a C' collection impacting the co-occurrence matrix. Assuming that no new terms are extracted from the new document, the set of terms $term_i$ in the new document doc' is defined as:

$$setTerms_{doc'} = \{term_i \in Term: term_i \in doc'\} \quad (2)$$

All vectors of documents $vector_{term}$ where $term \in setTerms_{doc'}$ are updated by adding the new document doc' such as: $vector_{term} < d_1, d_2, d_n, doc' >$. Hence for each pair of terms $(term_i, term_j) | term_i, term_j \in setTerms_{doc'}$ the co-occurrence matrix is impacted such as:

$$cfm_{C'}(term_i, term_j) = cfm_C(term_i, term_j) + 1 \qquad (3)$$

3.2 Hierarchical Relationship Maintenance

The hierarchical relations are maintained according to the evolved co-occurrence matrix without re-processing the entire hierarchy. A method based on [16] is used, which exploits the co-occurrence matrix to calculate the hierarchical relations between terms where term $term_x$ potentially subsumes term $term_y$ if (Fig. 1(A)):

$$(P_C(term_x | term_y) \geq st) \wedge (P_C(term_y | term_x) < st) \qquad (4)$$

where:

- $P_C(term_x | term_y)$ is the conditional proportion (number) of the documents from collection C common to $term_x$ and $term_y$, in respect to the number of documents in $term_y$ such that:

$$P_C(term_x | term_y) = \frac{term_x \cap term_y}{term_y} = \frac{cfm_C(term_x, term_y)}{cfm_C(term_y, term_y)} \qquad (5)$$

- $P_C(term_y | term_x)$ is the conditional proportion (number) of the documents from collection C common to $term_x$ and $term_y$, in respect to the number of documents in $term_x$ such that:

$$P_C(term_y | term_x) = \frac{term_x \cap term_y}{term_x} = \frac{cfm_C(term_x, term_y)}{cfm_C(term_x, term_x)} \qquad (6)$$

- $st \in [0,1]$ is the subsumption co-occurrence threshold.

Hence if $term_x$ appears in at least proportion st of the documents in which $term_y$ also appears, and $term_y$ appears in less than proportion st in which $term_x$ appears, then the hierarchical relationship between x and y is statistically relevant and $term_x$ potentially subsumes $term_y$, i.e. $term_y < term_x$. By applying this method to all terms, the result is a subsumption hierarchy of terms. The hierarchy relations can be induced with all statistically relevant hierarchical relationships (i.e. DAG) or with only some relationships (i.e. Tree).

Since the hierarchy is created from the initial collection of documents C it must be maintained according to the stream of new documents. Two types of changes in the co-occurrence matrix impact the conditional proportions used to calculate the hierarchal relations. That changes are (1) changes in the co-occurrence $cfm_C(term_i, term_j)$ where $term_i \neq term_j$ and (2) changes in the main diagonal $cfm_C(term_i, term_i)$.

Change in the Co-occurrence

A change in co-occurrences $cfm_C(term_i, term_j)$ where $term_i \neq term_j$, impact the numerator of the two conditional proportions described by equations (5) and (6), used by the subsumption method (4) to calculate the hierarchical relations. Hence, only the $P_C(term_i|term_j)$ and $P_C(term_j|term_i)$ proportions used to create the hierarchical relationships between $term_i$ and $term_j$ are impacted.

As an example, consider the set of terms $\{term_1, term_2, term_3, term_4, term_5\}$ with the induced hierarchy relation as depicted in Fig.1 (A). A co-occurrence change in the matrix $cfm_C(term_1, term_2)$ will impact the relationship between the terms $term_1$ and $term_2$ (Fig.1 (B)).

Change in the Main Diagonal

A change in the matrix main diagonal $cfm_C(term_i, term_i)$ for $cfm_{C'}(term_i, term_i)$ will impact the denominator of the two conditional proportions described by equations (5) and (6), used by the subsumption method (4) to calculate the hierarchical relations. Hence all proportions $P_C(term_i|term_n)$ and $P_C(term_n|term_i)$, where $term_n \in Term$ and $term_n \neq term_i$, are impacted. In other words, all the relationships between that term and all other terms from the collection C are impacted.

As an example, consider the set of terms $\{term_1, term_2, term_3, term_4, term_5\}$ with the induced hierarchy relation as depicted in Fig. 1(A). A main diagonal change in the matrix $cfm_C(term_2, term_2)$ impacts the hierarchical relationships with all other terms in the set (Fig. 1(C)). The broken line in Fig.1 (C) represents the impacted relation between $term_2$ and $term_3$ even it are not consider a hierarchical relation regarding the collection C.

3.3   Change Detection

Only the statistically relevant hierarchical relationships obeying to the subsumption method are induced as relations in the output hierarchy. After recalculating all the impacted proportions by C' (i.e. $P_{C'}(term_x|term_y)$ and $P_{C'}(term_y|term_x)$) the changes to the hierarchy relations regarding the previous collection C are detected. A change can be of two types: "Add", when a new hierarchy relation is induced and "Delete", when a hierarchy relation is no longer induced.

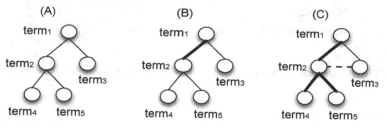

Fig. 1. Impact the hierarchical relations (example) where: (A) is the original, (B) impacted by a change in co-occurrence and (C) impacted by a change in main-diagonal.

An "*add*" change is detected when a relationship between two terms is not induced as a hierarchy relation in C but is induced in C'. On the other hand a "delete" change is detected when a relation is induced as hierarchy relation in C but is not induced in C'.

For example, consider the set of terms $\{term_1, term_2, term_3, term_4\}$ for the initial collection of documents C and that the subsumed terms of t_2 are calculated with a subsumption threshold $st = 65$. The proportions of $term_2$ and all other terms ($term_y$) in the collection C as well as the subsumption threshold are depicted in Fig. 2.

According to the subsumption method, one can observe in Fig. 2 that $term_1$ and $term_4$ are subsumed terms of $term_2$ as $(P_C(term_2|term_1) > st) \wedge (P_C(term_1|term_2) < st)$ and $(P_C(term_2|term_4) > st) \wedge (P_C(term_4|term_2) < st)$. However $term_3$ does not subsume $term_2$ because the subsumption condition with $st = 65$ is not granted $(P_C(term_2|term_4) > st) \wedge (P_C(term_4|term_2) > st)$. Hence the initial hierarchichal relations created for the $term_2$ are $term_1 \prec term_2$ and $term_4 \prec term_2$.

With the arrival of new documents with $term_1$ and $term_2$, the collection C will evolve to C'. Considering the impacted proportions as depicted in Fig. 3:

- A *delete* change is identified between $term_2$ and $term_1$ where the relation is no longer induced $(P_{C'}(term_2|term_1) < st) \wedge (P_{C'}(term_1|term_2) < st)$;
- An *add* change is detected between $term_2$ and $term_3$ where the hierarchical relationship is induced $(P_{C'}(term_2|term_3) > st) \wedge (P_{C'}(term_3|term_2) < st)$.

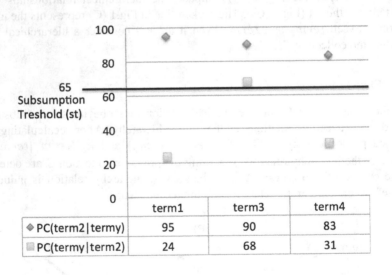

	term1	term3	term4
◆ PC(term2|termy)	95	90	83
▨ PC(termy|term2)	24	68	31

Fig. 2. Calculate the subsumed terms of $term_2$ in the collection C (example).

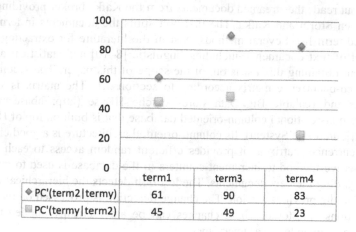

	term1	term3	term4
◆ PC'(term2|termy)	61	90	83
■ PC'(termy|term2)	45	49	23

Fig. 3. Calculate the subsumed terms of $term_2$ in the collection C'.

4   Implementation

In this section an implementation of the proposed hierarchy maintenance process is described. The proposed process is implemented in a scalable and distributed platform for Big Data. The hierarchical relations are maintained using documents streamed using a distributed and highly scalable broker Apache Kafka (http://kafka.apache.org).

The distributed real-time computation system Apache Storm (https://storm.apache.org) is used to process the text document streaming in order to maintain the hierarchy. The Storm architecture is based in: Tuples (Storm data item abstraction); Stream (unbound list of Tuples); Spout (source of a Stream); Bolts (Process the Streams of Tuples from Spouts to create new Streams) and Topologies (a directed graph of Spouts and Bolts). Four components comprise the maintenance topology (Fig. 4): a spout (in square) and three bolts (in ellipsis).

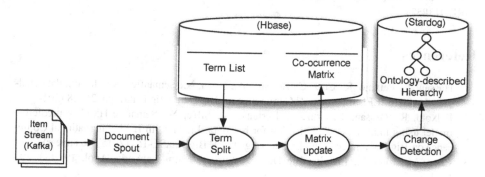

Fig. 4. Hierarchy Maintenance Topology

The spout reads the streamed documents from the Kafka broker providing an interface between Storm and Kafka. The first bolt splits the documents in terms using a pre-defined term list. Several methods exist in the literature for extracting the terms from a set of text documents, including linguistic [8–10] and statistical approaches [11, 12] but obtaining this list is out of the scope of this paper. The second bolt updates the co-occurrence matrix according to section 3.1. The matrix is stored in a distributed and scalable Big Data store Apache HBase (http://hbase.apache.org). HBase is a non-relational column-oriented database that is built on top of HDFS (Hadoop Distributed File System). Its column-oriented architecture is a good choice to fit the co-occurrence matrix as it provides efficient random access to each table cell. Also the native method to increment counters in the database is used to maintain the matrix regarding the new documents. The last bolt detects the hierarchical changes as described in the previous section. The change detection is processed on the fly where no proportions are stored. These changes can be automatically applied to the hierarchy or recommended to a supervisor.

5   Conclusions

To maintain the hierarchical relation automatically induced from text documents in Big Data context without relearn the whole hierarchy, this paper proposes a maintenance process from a stream of text documents. Three steps comprise the maintenance process (1) Co-occurrence matrix maintenance, (2) Hierarchical relationship maintenance and (3) Change detection.

The prototype was successfully implemented in a scalable and distributed platform to process Big Data. Our future research efforts will focus in studying the relevance and pertinence of using the proposed maintenance process in the Semantic HMC process to maintain the ontology-described concept hierarchy used to classify documents in Big Data context.

Acknowledgements. This project is funded by the company Actualis SARL, the French agency ANRT and through the Portuguese COMPETE Program under the project AAL4ALL (QREN13852).

References

1. Hassan, T., Peixoto, R., Cruz, C., Bertaux, A., Silva, N.: Semantic HMC for big data analysis. In: 2014 IEEE International Conference on Big Data (Big Data), pp. 26–28 (2014)
2. Peixoto, R., Hassan, T., Cruz, C., Bertaux, A., Silva, N.: Semantic HMC: a predictive model using multi-label classification for big data. In: The 9th IEEE International Conference on Big Data Science and Engineering (IEEE BigDataSE-15) (2015) (to appear)
3. Chen, M., Mao, S., Liu, Y.: Big Data: A Survey. Mob. Networks Appl. **19**, 171–209 (2014)
4. Hitzler, P., Janowicz, K.: Linked data, big data, and the 4th paradigm. Semant. Web. **4**, 233–235 (2013)

5. Syed, A., Gillela, K., Venugopal, C.: The Future Revolution on Big Data. Future **2**, 2446–2451 (2013)
6. Medelyan, O., Manion, S., Broekstra, J., Divoli, A., Huang, A.-L., Witten, I.H.: Constructing a focused taxonomy from a document collection. In: Cimiano, P., Corcho, O., Presutti, V., Hollink, L., Rudolph, S. (eds.) ESWC 2013. LNCS, vol. 7882, pp. 367–381. Springer, Heidelberg (2013)
7. Caraballo, S.A.: Automatic construction of a hypernym-labeled noun hierarchy from text. In: Proceedings of the 37th Annual Meeting of the Association for Computational Linguistics on Computational Linguistics, pp. 120–126. Association for Computational Linguistics, Stroudsburg (1999)
8. Hearst, M.A.: Automatic acquisition of hyponyms ftom large text corpora. In: Proc. 14th Conf. Comput. Linguist, vol. 2, pp. 23–28 (1992)
9. Toutanova, K., Manning, C.D.: Enriching the knowledge sources used in a maximum entropy part-of-speech tagger. In: Proc. Jt. SIGDAT Conf. Empir. Methods Nat. Lang. Process. Very Large Corpora, pp. 63–70 (2000)
10. Cimiano, P., Staab, S., Tane, J.: Automatic acquisition of taxonomies from text: FCA meets NLP. In: Proceedings of the International Workshop & Tutorial on Adaptive Text Extraction and Mining (2003)
11. Salton, G., Buckley, C.: Term-weighting approaches in automatic text retrieval. Inf. Process. Manag. **24**, 513–523 (1988)
12. Maedche, A., Volz, R.: The ontology extraction & maintenance framework text-to-onto. In: Proc. Work. Integr. Data, pp. 1–12 (2001)
13. Halevy, A., Norvig, P., Pereira, F.: The Unreasonable Effectiveness of Data. IEEE Intell. Syst. **24** (2009)
14. De Knijff, J., Frasincar, F., Hogenboom, F.: Domain taxonomy learning from text: The subsumption method versus hierarchical clustering. Data Knowl. Eng. **83**, 54–69 (2013)
15. Meijer, K., Frasincar, F., Hogenboom, F.: A Semantic Approach for Extracting Domain Taxonomies from Text. Decis. Support Syst. (2014)
16. Sanderson, M., Croft, B.: Deriving concept hierarchies from text. In: Proc. 22nd Annu. Int. ACM SIGIR Conf. Res. Dev. Inf. Retr. - SIGIR 1999, pp. 206–213 (1999)
17. Liu, X., Song, Y., Liu, S., Wang, H.: Automatic taxonomy construction from keywords. In: Proc. 18th ACM SIGKDD Int. Conf. Knowl. Discov. Data Min, pp. 1433–1441 (2012)
18. Wang, X., Liu, S., Song, Y., Guo, B.: Mining evolutionary multi-branch trees from text streams. In: Proc. 19th ACM SIGKDD Int. Conf. Knowl. Discov. Data Min. - KDD 2013, p. 722 (2013)
19. Cui, W., Liu, S., Member, S., Wu, Z., Wei, H.: How Hierarchical Topics Evolve in Large Text Corpora. IEEE Trans. Vis. Comput. Graph. **20**, 2281–2290 (2014)

A Conceptual Relations Reference Model to the Construction and Assessment of Lightweight Ontologies

Cristóvão Sousa[1,2(✉)] and António Soares[1,3]

[1] INESC TEC, Rua Dr. Roberto Frias, S/n, 4200 Porto, Portugal
[2] CIICESI - ESTGF, Polytechnic Institute of Porto, Rua Do Curral - Casa Do Curral-Margaride, 4610-156 Felgueiras, Portugal
[3] FEUP, University of Porto, Rua Dr. Roberto Frias, Sn, 4200-465 Porto, Portugal
cds@estgf.ipp.pt

Abstract. Lightweight ontologies are increasingly used by domain experts in a variety of activities. The development of these knowledge representation artefacts carries the challenge of the proper conceptualisation of the considered reality/situation. In particular, the elicitation of conceptual relations is widely acknowledged in the literature as being the most difficult part of the process. This paper proposes a technique to support domain experts in the elicitation of conceptual relations in the development of lightweight ontologies by providing the means to develop and ascertain the consistency of the produced conceptualisation results towards its reusability. Its innovation comes from the development of a reference model for the conceptual relations elicitation.

Keywords: Conceptual relations elicitation · Lightweight ontologies · Domain experts

1 Introduction

Although ontologies have a core role in the development of semantic web information systems [1] aiming at clarifying the structure of knowledge through a common vocabulary, enabling information sharing, its adoption in real world contexts of collaborative networks is still incipient. The common accepted justification is that *ontologies are expensive, complicated and difficult to build* [2]. To overcome this ontologies' stereotype it is argued that the paradigm associated to the development of this artefacts should be based upon the view that they *should be built according to pragmatic purposes*[3], where ontologies are typically *lightweight*[4] targeted at domain experts [2] and following a socio-semantic approaches [5]. In order to represent such pragmatic and lightweight representations of a specific domain, particular attention should be given to the conceptualisation phase, where the domain terms and the relationships among them are identified and understood by domain experts. The elicitation of the most adequate domain terms and the start up of the organisation of the concept

© Springer International Publishing Switzerland 2015
I. Ciuciu et al. (Eds.): OTM 2015 Workshops, LNCS 9416, pp. 502–511, 2015.
DOI: 10.1007/978-3-319-26138-6_54

system itself could constitute a "bottleneck" in the conceptualisation process, specially in what concerns to conceptual relations. According to literature, the most difficult problem in a conceptualisation process is the elicitation of conceptual relations [6, 7]. Indeed, conceptual relations may influence the organisation and, consequently, the interpretation of the conceptual structures, decreasing the probability of reusability and utility of the produced conceptual representations. For this reason, designing an artefact to assist the domain experts eliciting conceptual representations was needed, in order to streamline the process of creating lightweight ontologies. Thus, aiming at creating means that could ease a group of experts establish conceptual commitments, between the conceptual structures that they represent and the entities from their mental spaces or from reality, a Conceptual Relations Reference Model(CRRM) was developed and discussed in this paper. This artefact was built following a foundation ontological analysis with a twofold objective: i) to contribute, directly, to the conceptual relations elicitation, providing a common baseline for the creation of basic conceptual structures by means of the pre-defined templates; ii) to provide a set of metrics for conceptual representations (i.e., the conceptualisation result) evaluation; On the discussion of CRRM, it is presented a summary of the ontological analysis performed. Next, CRRM is presented and the way the reusability of the conceptual representations is calculated is also discussed. A short illustrative example is presented before closing the paper with its conclusion.

2 Conceptual Relations Elicitation

In order to accomplish the primary research goal, the authors seek to identify a set of domain-neutral conceptual relations. Thereunto we start on studying the main foundational upper-level ontologies, once those ontologies describe the very general concepts that are the same across all knowledge domains. "*Ontologies are often equated with taxonomic hierarchies of classes, classes definitions and the subsumption relations*" [8], however the aim is to identify other than only these ones. Hereupon, the approach was to follow through the main upper-level ontologies, namely: CyC[1], BFO[2], GFO[3], UFO [9], SUMO[4], COSMO[5], DOLCE[6], PROTON[7]. Summarising, and without going into the details (due to space constraints), the following ontological categories of formal relations where selected: constitution and containment dependence, existential dependence, generic dependence, historical dependence [10]. In this paper it will not be considered the Existential Dependence since it has to do with relations between entities and its examples and the intent, at this level, is to avoid mixing classes

---

[1] http://www.opencyc.org/
[2] http://www.ifomis.org/bfo
[3] http://www.onto-med.de/ontologies/gfo.html
[4] http://www.ontologyportal.org/
[5] http://micra.com/COSMO/
[6] http://www.loa.istc.cnr.it/DOLCE.html
[7] http://proton.semanticweb.org/

(concepts). But, in fact, the individuals which belongs to a specific category should be known in order to a new category/concept be added accurately. Constitution and Containment dependence was detailed as a Part-Whole conceptual relation as it is more common across literature. Following the same purpose, generic dependence was detailed into the Generic-Specific category. Historical dependence is related with temporal location relations. These kind of relations are treated differently (in terms of each taxonomy of categories used) in the available upper-lever ontologies. Historical dependence could have a space or time boundary considering physical or non-physical objects respectively, hence it was decided to detail it into two more specific conceptual relations, namely: Temporal Conceptual Relation and Spatial Conceptual Relation. Inspired mainly by GFO, it was decided to include Participation relation. Participation could be considered as an extension of historical dependence relation, however, in the context of collaborative networks, participation relation has an important role on offering an orthogonal view of an event or process. It can also offer a brief overview on the social interaction network around an event or process. Finally it was also considered the Cause-Effect Conceptual Relation. Casualty could easily be associated to space and time relations to describe events and consequently considered as not adding value for the current purpose. However, Cause-Effect Conceptual Relation is fundamental to add some dynamicity to conceptual representations on describing phenomenons and agents of change within some process or event or object state. The following categorisation is the end-result of this analysis.

- Constitution_and_Containment Dependence
  - Part_Whole Conceptual Relation
- Generic Dependence
  - Generic_Specific Conceptual Relation
- Time and Space Dependence
  - Spatial Conceptual Relation
  - Temporal Conceptual Relation
- Cause-Effect Conceptual Relation
- Participation Conceptual Relation

3 Supporting Domain Experts Eliciting Conceptual Relations

Conceptual relations are understood as the vehicle for building up the IT artefats that will provide support for the construction of explicit shared conceptual representations, e.g., lightweight ontologies. Hereupon, the CRRM provides a common baseline for conceptual representations construction. In practical term, CRRM is an ontology used to build and assess conceptual representations and includes the following information: 1) a taxonomy of conceptual relation types (or classes); 2) a taxonomy of classes of terms(e.g., Part, Whole, Generic, Specific, Cause, Effect, Local, ...); 3) a taxonomy of conceptual relation templates - one for each conceptual relation type. Each instance of a template encloses a conceptual structure in the basic form of *"concept - relation - concept"*. The ontology has 302 Axioms, 37 Classes and 27 Object properties.

In CRRM each conceptual relation is defined by: i) an intent; ii) a set o competency questions, and; iii) a linking phrase (derived from a linguistic marker) that designates and represents an instance of a conceptual relation. The intent is the goal or "usage scenario" of a certain type of relation, whereas the competency questions purpose is to define the scope of a conceptual relation. In this case it is possible to define more than one question. CRRM assists users along the conceptualisation process through templates. A template consists of a specific type of a conceptual relation and two distinct terms, allowing users to instantiate new conceptual structures. In practice CRRM is intended to be a baseline model which could be extended either by adding new linking phrases to designate conceptual relations or detailing the model adding more specific types of conceptual relations. Additionally, and besides the class taxonomy (and each class restrictions), CRRM also includes a set of Object Properties and SWRL rules. Object Properties are used to describe Conceptual Representations for its evaluation rather than its construction. Still in a perspective of evaluating a conceptual representation, there is a sub-set of Object Properties that allow, through inferred rules (using SWRL), to discover new knowledge used to determine if conceptual relations carry ambiguity or inconsistency. In this scenario it is assumed that the evaluated conceptual representations were created based on CRRM.Summarising, the procedure is as follows: 1) Conceptual representations are built by the domain experts and the conceptual structures are loaded into CRRM ontology and described using a set of *Object Properties*; 2) Through the reasoner engine, the SWRL rules are executed and extra knowledge is gathered; 3) Simultaneously the SWRL rules try to identify relationships that are ambiguous or inconsistent; 4) Additionally, SWRL rules also helps to identify the incompatible terms. Two terms are incompatible if they have ambiguous incoming and outgoing conceptual relations. At the end, the total number of terms, relations, linking phrases classified as Ambiguous Relations and the number of incompatible types of terms are the metrics used to determine the reusability degree of the conceptual representation. In CRRM ontology a relation is considered ambiguous if it violates at least one of the following conditions:

– if there is a CauseEffect relation among two terms (a cause and an effect respectively), then, no other relation between those terms may occur, except a temporal relation.[8]
– if there is a CauseEffect relation linking two terms (a cause and an effect respectively), then the Effect cannot be linked to other concepts connected to the Cause through the following conceptual relations: PartHood, GenericSpecific, CauseEffect, Participation or Temporal.

---

[8] **In SWRL**: $Cause\_Effect(?y), LinkingPhrase(?x), LinkingPhrase(?y), Term(?a), Term(?b), (Constituition\_and\_Containment$ or $Generic\_Dependence$ or $Participation$ or $Spatial)(?x), hasSource(?x,?a), hasSource(?y,?a), hasTarget(?x,?b), hasTarget(?y,?b) \rightarrow AmbiguousRelations(?y)$

- if there is a CauseEffect relation linking two terms (a cause and an effect respectively), then the cause always precede the effect.
- If there is term that is a specialization of another term, then the specific term cannot be linking by a CauseEffect relation to the generic term.
- if there is a Containment relation that does not meet the "one-to-one" cardinality between the part and the whole. It means that in a Containment relation the part can only be linked to a single whole, which calls for a nested relationship.

Furthermore, two term are considered incompatible when in the CRRM ontology:

- it is found that a term is both a part and a whole.
- it is found that a term is both te container and the content.
- it is found that a term is both a generic and a specific.
- it is found that a term is both a means and a end.

However, in order to determine the ambiguity of a relation or the incompatibility of terms, a set of facts must be inferred. In CRRM there are rules that define the conditions under which, from the stated facts, it is possible inferred:

- two terms related through an *isUsedBy Object Property*;
- two terms related through an *isPartOf Object Property* ;
- two terms related through an *isLocationOf Object Property*;
- two terms related through an *isTypeOf Object Property*;
- two terms related through an *isCauseOf Object Property*;
- two terms related through an *isContainedBy Object Property*;
- two terms are related through an *precedes Object Property*;

In addition to assisting the elicitation of conceptual relation and streamline the conceptualisation process, CRRM allows ascertain the degree of reusability of a conceptual representation. Reusability criterion measures the extent to which a common conceptual representation might be reused. A Conceptual Representation is prone to reusability if it is well-formed (computational ready) and its terms and conceptual relations are defined unambiguously, that is, there is a common understanding about the relations among terms. Considering a formalised conceptual representation, the reusability degree is expressed as a cumulative measure combining two components, wherein one provides a value (degree) for (i) Conceptual Relations ambiguity ($\deg_{CRa}$) and one for (ii) Concept Type incompatibility ($\deg_{CTi}$). Both ($\deg_{CRa}$) and ($\deg_{CTi}$) are determined with the support of the CRRM ontology, which implements a catalog of conceptual relations. At a glance, the process runs as follows: 1) The CRRM ontology is populated with the data from an existing conceptual representation (or Lightweight ontology) developed by the domain experts; 2) A set of (SWRL) rules is executed and a small set of indicators are gathered; 3) The indicators allow calculating $\deg_{CRa}$ and $\deg_{CTi}$ for a particular conceptual representation.

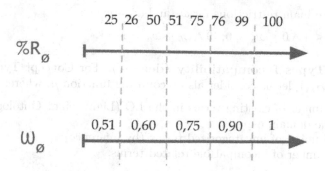

Fig. 1. Weight scale of uncategorized relations

Conceptual Relations Ambiguity ($\deg_{CRa}$). For Conceptual Relations ambiguity ($\deg_{CRa}$) let us consider a counting function μ, where:

- $\mu(R_t)$ = Number of existing relations in the LO (Lightweight Ontology) developed by the domain experts;
- $\mu(R_a)$ = Number of ambiguous relations inferred (according to the SWRL rules);
- $\mu(R^\theta)$ = Number of uncategorized relations;

The values of $\mu(R_a)$ and $\mu(R^\theta)$ are then normalized, by scaling between 0 and 1, obtaining:

- $N\mu(R_a)$, the normalized value of $\mu(R_a)$, calculated as follows: $\mu(R_a)/[\mu(R_t) - \mu(R_\theta)]$
- $N\mu(R^\theta)$, the normalized value of $\mu(R^\theta)$, calculated as follows: $\mu(R_\theta)/\mu(R_t)$

After normalizing these values, the conditions are met for calculating ($\deg_{CRa}$), which is obtained through the expression:

$$deg^{CRa} = \begin{cases} 1 & if \mu(R_\theta) = \mu(R_t) \\ N\mu(R_a) \times \omega_a + N\mu(R_\theta) \times \omega_\theta & if \mu(R_\theta) < \mu(R_t), where: \end{cases}$$

- ω_a and ω_θ, are weights reflecting the importance of R_a and R_θ respectively;

The Knowledge engineer might adjust the weight values, other wise it is used the default weight scale tables, however the proper identification of ambiguous relations, requires its classification through the CRRM ontology. Thereby, if $\mu(R_\theta)$ has a direct implication on $\mu(R_a)$, then the value of ω_θ should always be higher than ω_a. Figure 1, shows an indicative scale of how ω_θ can evolve according to the variation of R_θ percentage, having in mind that the higher the percentage of R_θ, the greater its weight (ω_θ) should be.

In short, the main restrictions for ω_θ and ω_a are:

- $0,51 \leq \omega_\theta \leq 1 \wedge 0 \leq \omega_a \leq 0,49 \wedge \omega_\theta + \omega_a = 1$

Conceptual Types Incompatibility (deg_{CTi}). For Concept Type incompatibility (deg_{CTi}), let us consider also a counting function μ, where:

- $\mu(T)$ = Number of existing terms in the LO (Lightweight Ontology) developed by the domain experts;
- $\mu(T_\theta)$ = Number of uncategorized terms (by inference);
- $\mu(T_i)$ = Number of incompatible related terms;

The values of $\mu(T_i)$ are then normalized, by scaling between 0 and 1, obtaining:

- $N\mu(T_i)$, the normalized value of $\mu(T_i)$, calculated as follows: $\mu(T_i)/[\mu(T) - \mu(T_\theta)]$

After normalization, the value for deg_{CTi} is equal to $N\mu(T_i)$, only if $\mu(T_\theta) < \mu(T)$. Otherwise, deg_{CTi} is impossible to calculate.

$deg_{CTi} = N\mu(T_i), if \mu(T_\theta) < \mu(T)$

Finally, the reusability degree results on the combination of deg_{CRa} and deg_{CTi}, by multiplying each other, in order to keep the proportionality of both. However, the two components might not have the same importance. Actually, deg_{CTi} is less relevant, because the classification of each term depends on the classification of the relation that binds to it. Moreover, even if there are no incompatible concepts, it is possible to calculate the reusability degree. The opposite however: despite the proportionally of the cumulative measure (degR), it should not be zero, even if deg_{CTi} is zero. The final expression for calculating the reusability degree is:

$$degR = \begin{cases} 1 - deg_{CRa} & if \mu(T_\theta) = \mu(T) \\ 1 - (deg_{CRa} \times (\omega_a + \omega_t \times deg_{CTi})) & if \mu(T_\theta) < \mu(T), where \end{cases}$$

- ω_a and ω_t, are weights reflecting the importance of deg_{CRa} and deg_{CTi} respectively;

Typically, domain experts might adjust the weight values for ω_a and ω_t as well, but there are some boundaries. deg_{CTi}, is a secondary importance factor, its calculation depends on deg_{CRa}. Actually, the reusability degree is always given by deg_{CRa} in the irst place. Afterwards, deg_{CRa} is obtained in order to fine-tune the reusability degree. Based on this, the value for ω_t obey to the following assumptions:

- $0 \leq \omega_t \leq 0,5 \wedge \omega_a + \omega_t = 1$
- $\omega_t = 0, if \mu(T_\theta) = \mu(T)$

Considering the assumptions listed before, Figure 2 presents an indicative scale of how ω_t can evolve according to the variation of of T_ω percentage.

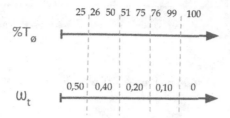

Fig. 2. Weight scale of uncategorized term types

4   Illustrative Example

In order to explain and demonstrate the reusability evaluation criteria, a simplification of the SEON[9] general concepts ontology was used and represented as shown in figure 3. A correspondence was made between the SEON general concepts ontology and CRRM, where all relations matched to some CRRM category were evidenced in the figure bellow with the CRRM prefix.

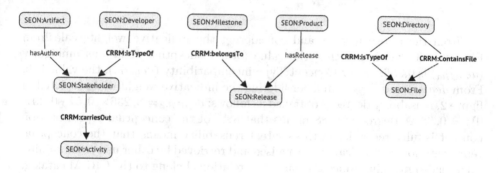

Fig. 3. SEON ontology example

Table 1. SEON ontology reusability metrics

$\mu(R_t)$	$\mu(R_\theta)$	$\mu(R_a)$	$\mu(T)$	$\mu(T_\theta)$	$\mu(T_i)$
7	2	1	9	2	0

The above ontology was populated into CRRM (see figure 4). The pellet reasoner was started up and the metrics gathered as summarized in table 1.

[9] SEON stands for Software Evolution ONtologies and representes an attempt to formally describe knowledge from domain of software evolution analysis and mining software repositories.

Fig. 4. SEON ontology populated in CRRM

From the above metrics and considering the indicative weight scale from Figure 1, it was found that the value form Conceptual Relations ambiguity (deg_{CRa}) is 0,236. As for Concept Type incompatibility (deg_{CTi}), the value is 0. From deg_{CRa} and deg_{CTi} and considering the indicative weight scale depicted in figure 2, reusability degree is obtained as follows: $deg_{CRa} = 0,236 \times (0,51 + 0,49 \times 0)) = 0,88$. A degree of $0,88$ means that 88% of the conceptual representation content is fully reusable. In this context reusability means that the conceptual representation content can be formalised and retrieved by other user, maintaining its intended meaning, since the employed relations belong to the CRRM catalog. The results indicate that 12% of the conceptual representation content is highly susceptible to misinterpretations when reused by others.

5   Conclusion

One of the most important key finding was that conceptual relations are recognised as an important enabler of the conceptualisation activities within a collaborative environment. In fact, the reusability of the conceptualisation results depends on the employed conceptual relations and the way they are interpreted by the domain experts. However, conceptual relations relevance is proportional to the difficulty of its proper elicitation. From the domain expert point-of-view, the elicitation of conceptual relations is not feasible without the adequate means to facilitate the identification, selection and application of conceptual relations in a awareness-driven process (i.e., the domain experts are aware of the context of use of a conceptual relations). In summary, the contributions of this paper are offered by means of CRRM, which provides the necessary support for domain experts to build reusable conceptual representations specifically in terms of: a) conceptual relations elicitation; b) a template-based construction of domain conceptual structures; c) assessment of the development conceptual representations.

Despite useful to build and assess conceptual representations, it might be necessary to add more specific relations to CRRM due to a couple of reasons: i) the specificities and the level of detail needed to describe a particular technical domain may require more specific conceptual relations, otherwise the concepts might remain underspecified; ii) it might be necessary to understand the restrictions of the associations between two or more concepts in order to fully axiomatize the conceptual representation. Let us consider two terms (A and B). At the moment, the domain experts can easily add (through CRRM) a "Part-Whole" conceptual relation between the two terms, but is not possible, in a pragmatic way, to detail the "Part-Whole" relation in order to define if term A is, for instance, a "proper part" of term B. Further research is planned to address this new demanding challenges. [1]

References

1. Horrocks, I.: Ontologies and the semantic web. Communications of the ACM **51**, 58–67 (2008)
2. Simperl, E.P.B., Tempich, C.: Ontology engineering: a reality check. In: Meersman, R., Tari, Z. (eds.) OTM 2006. LNCS, vol. 4275, pp. 836–854. Springer, Heidelberg (2006)
3. Bergman, M.: A new methodology for building lightweight, domain ontologies (2010). http://wiki.opensemanticframework.org/index.php/ightweight,_Domain_Ontologies_Development_Methodology
4. Davies, J.: Lightweight ontologies. In: Poli, R., Healy, M., Kameas, A. (eds.) Theory and Applications of Ontology: Computer Applications, pp. 197–229. Springer, Netherlands (2010). doi:10.1007/978-90-481-8847-5_9. http://dx.doi.org/10.1007/978-90-481-8847-5_9
5. Pereira, C., Sousa, C., Soares, A.L.: Supporting conceptualisation processes in collaborative networks: a case study on an R&D project. International Journal of Computer Integrated Manufacturing **26**(11), 1066–1086 (2013). http://doi.org/10.1080/0951192X.2012.684714
6. Auger, A., Barriére, C.: Probing semantic relations, Probing Semantic Relations: Exploration and Identification in Specialized Texts, vol. 23, p. 1 (2010)
7. Elsayed, A.: A framework for using semantic relations in conceptual structures. In: 2008 Eighth IEEE International Conference on Advanced Learning Technologies, pp. 1069–1070. Santander, Cantabria, Spain (2008)
8. Gruber, T.R.: A translation approach to portable ontology specifications. Knowledge Acquisition **5**(2), 199–220 (1993)
9. Guizzardi, G.: Ontological Foundations for Structural Conceptual Models, Ph.D. Thesis (CUM LAUDE), University of Twente, The Netherlands. Published as the book "Ontological Foundations for Structural Conceptual Models", Telematica Institute Fundamental Research Series No. 15, 05–74, ISBN 90-75176-81-3 ISSN 1388-1795; No. 015; CTIT Ph.D.-thesis, ISSN 1381-3617; No
10. Thomasson, A.L.: Fiction and Metaphysics. Cambridge University Press. ISBN-13: 9780521065214

Motivators and Deterrents for Data Description and Publication: Preliminary Results
(Short Paper)

Cristina Ribeiro[✉], João Rocha da Silva, João Aguiar Castro,
Ricardo Carvalho Amorim, and Paula Fortuna

INESC TEC—Faculdade de Engenharia, Universidade do Porto, Porto, Portugal
mcr@fe.up.pt

Abstract. In the recent trend of data-intensive science, data publication is essential and institutions have to promote it with the researchers. For the past decade, institutional repositories have been widely established for publications, and the motivations for deposit are well established. The situation is quite different for data, as we argue on the basis of a 5-year experience with research data management at the University of Porto. We address research data management from a disciplined yet flexible point of view, focusing on domain-specific metadata models embedded in intuitive tools, to make it easier for researchers to publish their datasets. We use preliminary data from a recent experiment in data publishing to identify motivators and deterrents for data publishing.

1 Introduction

Dataset description and publication raise many concerns. On the one hand, data are regarded as valuable assets to be explored but not disseminated. On the other hand, the publication of many datasets is hindered by issues of confidentiality and business contracts [3]. Based on a 5-year experience with research data management (RDM) at the University of Porto, working closely with researchers, we have identified requirements and designed tools to help with the associated tasks. Just as institutional repositories have been brought about by such powerful tools as DSpace, EPrints and Fedora, data repositories require tools that simultaneously engage researchers and are appealing to data curators. Such tools are being experimented, but the spectrum of requirements is so vast that no single tool can yet handle all [2]. We have proposed Dendro, an ontology-based staging platform for datasets in small research groups, and designed ontologies for the domains of the research groups that we have worked with [7,5].

The experience with researchers in RDM tasks provides us with a preliminary view on the motivators and deterrents in data publication. We started from the assumptions that (1) automated tools are essential in RDM and (2) metadata has to be fit to the domain of the data. This will allow data and metadata to be shared and to outlive the platforms where they are stored.

© Springer International Publishing Switzerland 2015
I. Ciuciu et al. (Eds.): OTM 2015 Workshops, LNCS 9416, pp. 512–516, 2015.
DOI: 10.1007/978-3-319-26138-6_55

2 Data Description and Publication

The main issue in RDM is that the incentives and penalties are either not clear enough for researchers or not in force yet. Take the example of mandates for data publication in H2020: the requirements and preferences for projects complying with data management rules are stated, but researchers are balancing the compliance with official mandates and the need to protect the data resulting from their projects.

The issues with RDM go along several lines, starting with the difficulties with the nature of data and their representation and storage. This has to be handled by researchers as part of any project setup. It is expected that data representation will evolve in the sense of more standard models and better storage facilities, but these are issues that go deep into the organisations and are therefore hard to influence.

A second issue, data description, has considerable work in many fronts. Basic descriptors are being used for datasets, in the tradition of library metadata, but many initiatives are in place for defining domain-specific metadata models, in areas such as life sciences, geospatial data, ecology and social sciences. More generic ontologies are also in use, namely for scientific experiments and project description.

A third issue, the engagement of researchers, is generally considered a major challenge. The problem is well known in institutional repositories, but data publication takes it to a new level. Here, the cooperation of researchers is no longer a convenience but rather an essential part. Several studies have obtained preliminary results on the influence of research culture on RDM [1]. It is widely recognised that researchers are essential stakeholders, but also that appropriate tools have to be provided [6].

A growing trend in RDM is the publication in so-called "data journals" [4]. Data papers resort to the traditional publication metaphors, and may prove to be important references for well-curated datasets. They will however not account for data in the long tail of science. For these, repository registries such as DataBib and re3data are already building access points to the more informally published data. DataCite, an organisation providing data identification and cross-referencing with publications, is promoting data citation.

3 Dendro and LabTablet, Ontologies in a Staging Platform

Tools are instrumental to set up a research data management workflow. To address researchers on the subject of publishing their data we need to provide or recommend an environment to store, link, visualize, describe, or identify datasets.

There is a clear advantage in capturing metadata at the earliest possible moment after data production. If data can be gathered and described early, not only more datasets will be preserved, but also their associated metadata will be of higher quality. In an environment where there are limited data management resources, researchers often have to manage data themselves, and data management tools play an important role.

Dendro targets the need for a flexible environment for data storage and description early in the research workflow. It fits in the category of staging platforms, designed to store data, describe them using domain-specific descriptors and later share them in a repository. Its goal is to make data management an integral part of the research workflow, reducing the delay from the moment of data creation to their description. Dendro uses a graph as an internal data model, where descriptors from existing ontologies or from purpose-built ones are linked to the produced descriptions, enabling external systems to easily retrieve metadata records [5]. The graph-based data model has an explicit semantics and is easy to transform into other representations. This simplicity will in turn help the generated metadata records survive the decommissioning of any Dendro instance.

Fig. 1. Project view in Dendro and in the LabTablet application.

A part of the description for a dataset may be collected automatically with common devices such as smartphones and tablets. It is encouraging for researchers to see that items such as location and temperature can be automatically filled in. LabTablet is an Android application for tablets and smartphones that uses the sensors on these generic devices and their API to serve as a comprehensive electronic laboratory notebook. Aside from these sources, the application can also be used as a traditional note taking application. The metadata records created on the LabTablet are represented using elements from established metadata schemas and sent to Dendro. Figure 1 shows the user interface of Dendro (on the left) an that of LabTablet (on the right), for the same metadata record.

4   Motivators and Deterrents for RDM

Dendro and the domain-specific ontologies allowed us to observe the researchers experience when describing datasets. A recent experiment involved 22 researchers from 11 domains in the task of selecting a dataset and assigning it metadata using generic (Dublin Core) and domain-specific descriptors.

The experiment involved the use of multiple ontologies and the observation of researchers using a recommendation system for Dendro. The preliminary results concern the ease of use of a system with a large number of descriptors. The controlled conditions of the experiment provided plenty of formal and informal feedback on aspects such as ease of use, sequence of operations, and interoperability. Based on the contacts with the researchers for an extended period, we enumerate on Table 1 a set of motivators and deterrents for RDM—at least for the first part of the workflow, which comprises the deposit and description of datasets.

Table 1. Motivators and deterrents for research data management

Motivators	Credit for the data collected, created or processed
	Increased citation for papers due to associated datasets
	Opportunities for new projects via contacts that arise from data publication
	Visibility of the institution, the research group and the individual researchers
	Reduced data loss within the research group
	Compliance with data management plans mandated by funding institutions
	Better communication of a senior researcher with the junior researchers collecting data
	Reduction of duplicate description efforts—"describe once, share many times"
	Having junior researchers contribute to early data description
	Faster research workflows through collaboration and standardised data management practices
	Improved knowledge of publication modalities (e.g. the possibility of publishing a metadata record and providing the data upon request)
Deterrents	Concerns over the ownership of the data (some researchers lack enough information about conditions for data disclosure)
	Confusion or lack of awareness about the intellectual property rights issues surrounding data sharing
	Loss of control over the data
	Additional time and effort required to perform data descriptions, diverting researchers from their main research activities
	Complexity of metadata standards
	Complexity of data management platforms
	Lack of knowledge of data management practices (e.g. embargoes, metadata requirements)
	Lack of awareness about the dangers of neglecting data
	Belief that their data management practices are good enough already

Besides this experiment, a lot of evidence concerning the behaviour of researchers with respect to their data has been collected. Although we have not observed a large number of groups, our observations have occurred over a long period (1 to 4.5 years, depending on the groups) and covered domains ranging from engineering to the social sciences. Moreover, we had contact with several researchers from each group, and we could gather feedback on usability of the tools, for example, because we had different people on each round.

5   Conclusions

The motivation of researchers is essential in data management. Our work involved the development of user-friendly applications to help researchers get their data ready for publication, namely Dendro as a data staging platform and LabTablet as a data and metadata collector. Our effort in description led to the development and test of domain-specific ontologies, to be plugged into these or other applications as metadata models. Ontologies can be preserved along with the metadata and the datasets to constitute self-explanatory datasets.

The experiments with researchers, while validating the tools, were also an opportunity to identify a set of factors that influence data publication initiatives. Our list is still open, and we expect to enrich it as we expand the data deposit process from an experimental stage to a university-wide endeavour.

Acknowledgements. Work supported by project NORTE-07-0124-FEDER000059, financed by the North Portugal Regional Operational Programme (ON.2–O Novo Norte), under the National Strategic Reference Framework (NSRF), through the European Regional Development Fund (ERDF), and by national funds, through the Portuguese funding agency, Fundação para a Ciência e a Tecnologia (FCT). J. Rocha da Silva supported by research grant SFRH/BD/77092/2011, provided by FCT.

References

1. Akers, K.G., Doty, J.: Disciplinary differences in faculty research data management practices and perspectives. International Journal of Digital Curation **8**(2), 5–26 (2013)
2. Amorim, R.C., Castro, J.A., Silva, J.R., Ribeiro, C.: A comparative study of platforms for research data management: interoperability, metadata capabilities and integration potential. In: Rocha, A., Correia, A.M., Costanzo, S., Reis, L.P. (eds.) New Contributions in Information Systems and Technologies. AISC, vol. 353, pp. 101–111. Springer, Heidelberg (2015)
3. Borgman, C.L.: The conundrum of sharing research data. Journal of the Association for Information Science and Technology **63**(6), 1059–1078 (2012)
4. Candela, L., Castelli, D., Manghi, P., Tani, A.: Data journals: A survey. Journal of the Association for Information Science and Technology **66**(9), 1747–1762 (2015)
5. Castro, J.A., Silva, J.R., Ribeiro, C.: Creating lightweight ontologies for dataset description: practical applications in a cross-domain research data management workflow. In: ACM/IEEE Joint Conference on Digital Libraries, pp. 313–316. ACM Press (2014)
6. Crystal, A., Greenberg, J.: Usability of a metadata creation application for resource authors. Library & Information Science Research **27**(2), 177–189 (2005)
7. Silva, J.R., Ribeiro, C., Lopes, J.C.: The Dendro research data management platform: applying ontologies to long-term preservation in a collaborative environment. In: Proceedings of the iPres 2014 Conference (2014)

MSC 2015 PC Co-Chairs' Message

Mobile and Social Computing for Collaborative Interactions (MSC) 2015

MSC 2015 PC Co-Chairs' Message

Mobile computing plays a crucial role in many social and collaborative activities as mobile devices are used more and more by people for working and entertainment in daily life. With this ever growing and pervasive use of tablets, smart phones and wireless technology, mobile computing is experiencing a new phase of innovation. The volume of data accessible from mobile devices is increasing ever more over the years, and new challenges in data management, situation-awareness, personalization, privacy, and security are emerging.

Social Computing considers relationships between the evolution of ICTs and the consequent changes in social behaviours. The emerging technologies are stimulated and stimulate social evolution, considering that they will be used by very heterogeneous people according to their social, cultural and technological features. Social computing addresses many challenges, such as increasing social interaction and collaboration, understanding social dynamics of people, socially constructing and sharing knowledge, helping people to find relevant information more quickly.

The second International Workshop on Mobile and Social Computing for collaborative interactions (MSC'15) was organized in conjunction with the OTM Federated Conferences to discuss such research topics. The workshop, held in Rhodes, Greece, 26-30 October 2015, provides a forum about artificial social systems, mobile computing, social computing, networking technologies, human-computer interaction, and collaborative environments.

This year, after a rigorous review process, five papers were accepted for inclusion in the workshop proceedings. Each of these submissions was rigorously peer reviewed by at least three experts. The papers were judged according to their originality, significance to theory and practice, readability, and relevance to workshop topics.

The topics of the accepted papers cover a wide range of interesting application areas such as social networking, collaborative applications and multimodal systems.

Papers on social networking propose a platform for measuring the individual features, such as authority and susceptibility, by using a semantic-based approach, as well as to discuss the role of social media in the co-creativity process by analysing the consumers' involvement in the different steps of the product development process.

Papers on collaborative applications propose a recommender system that provides personalized recommendations by using social collaborations in virtual learning environments to motivate students in their learning process, as well as an inventory of assistive technologies which target the disabled end-users, their facilitators and the professionals in the area of rehabilitation.

Finally, the paper on multimodal systems provides a discussion on the evolution from 2005 to 2015 of the approaches defined and used to face the main research questions, such as multimodal fusion and interpretation and context adaptation.

The success of the MSC'15 workshop would not have been possible without the contribution of the OTM 2015 organizers, PC members and authors of papers, all of whom we would like to sincerely thank.

September 2015

Fernando Ferri
Patrizia Grifoni
Arianna D'Ulizia
Maria Chiara Caschera

The mATHENA Inventory for Free Mobile Assistive Technology Applications

Georgios Kouroupetroglou[1,2(✉)], Spyridon Kousidis[1], Paraskevi Riga[1,2],
and Alexandros Pino[1]

[1] Department of Informatics and Telecommunications,
National and Kapodistrian University of Athens, Athens, Greece
{koupe,access}@di.uoa.gr
[2] Accessibility Unit for Students with Disabilities,
National and Kapodistrian University of Athens, Athens, Greece

Abstract. The entry of smartphones and tablets in the market yields new opportunities in the domain of Assistive Technology (AT) for persons with disabilities. The search process for mobile AT applications that fulfill specific user needs is not an easy task for the end-users, their facilitators as well as the professionals in the area of rehabilitation. Even, when they finally find what they are looking for, a number of questions are raised relative to the reliability, stability, compatibility and functionality of the AT applications. These questions can be answered safely only by a team of AT experts. In this work we present the methodological approach for the design and development of the mATHENA web-based inventory, which aims to make the search and selection of free mobile AT applications simple and sound. This methodology is based on the consistent and well-documented presentation of the information for each mobile AT application, after it is tested in an AT lab. mATHENA offers social interaction services for its diverse target groups. Moreover, we present the advantages of mATHENA compared with the functionalities of six other inventories for AT applications. Currently, mATHENA includes 420 free mobile AT applications, carefully selected among a total of 1,100.

Keywords: Assistive technology · Accessibility · Mobile-applications · Free of charge apps · Smartphones · Tablets · Online inventory · Persons with disabilities

1 Introduction

Computer-based Assistive Technology (AT) offers devices, tools, equipment and services that can be used to maintain, increase or improve the functional capabilities of persons with disabilities and the elderly. The last few decades, there is an increasing strong interest in the domain of AT. This interest comes out from the research institutes, the industry, the academia and various professional disciplines, such as rehabilitation sciences, computer engineers (mainly developers of human-computer interfaces, Web designers and Web content providers), ergonomists, therapists, teachers in inclusive and special education [1]. The main forces that boost this interest

© Springer International Publishing Switzerland 2015
I. Ciuciu et al. (Eds.): OTM 2015 Workshops, LNCS 9416, pp. 519–527, 2015.
DOI: 10.1007/978-3-319-26138-6_56

come from: i) the policy frameworks of the United Nations and the European Union, as well as the national legislation for the benefit of the disabled and their societal inclusion and participation, and ii) the increasing demographic figures of the aging population, given that the number of the disabled rises significantly for those above the 65 years old. In recent years, the field of AT has made substantial progress in consolidating theoretical approaches, scientific methods and technologies, as well as in exploring new application domains [2].

The recent developments in mobile technology, including the introduction of tablets and smartphones, and especially the mobile applications, yield new opportunities in the domain of AT, and had a new impact on the participation of the disabled and the elderly in the everyday life [3-6] but also on the behavior of the disabled and elderly as consumers [7]. Besides, the mobile AT applications can be used with a much broader scope. For example, under the framework of Universal Design for Learning (UDL), mobile AT apps have been found to engage all students, including those with disabilities, in collaborative learning, reasoning, and problem-solving activities [8-12].

Current statistics [13] show that Android and iOS users have the possibility to choose between 3 million mobile apps. Furthermore, the mobile app stores do not include a category for AT or a classification by disability. Thus, the search process for mobile AT applications that fulfill specific user needs is not an easy task by all the target groups: the end-users, their facilitators, as well as the professionals in the area of rehabilitation. Moreover, in many cases the users don't know the right keywords for searching in the app stores. Furthermore, the description of an AT app does not always include the proper keywords relative to the terminology used by the end users. Even when they finally find what they are looking for, a number of questions are raised relative to the reliability, stability, compatibility, functionality and usability of the AT applications [14-17]. These questions can be answered safely only by a team of AT experts following appropriate evaluation methodologies [18]. Also, the description of the AT apps is not consistent as the fields included to describe each app differ, as well as the amount of information provided in each field. Consequently, dedicated online databases or repositories have been recently developed for the elderly [19], the visually impaired [20], the communication impaired [4, 21] and for medical applications [22].

In this work we present the design and development of the mATHENA web-based inventory, which aims to make the search and selection of free mobile AT applications simple and sound. First, in section 2 we review the existing inventories of mobile AT apps. In section 3 we describe the methodological approach for the design and development of web-based inventories for mobile AT applications. Then in section 3 we present the results of the development of mATHENA and a comparison of its functionalities with the existing similar repositories.

2   Existing Inventories for Mobile AT Apps

Below we present a review of the most important existing inventories dedicated to mobile AT applications, along with their main characteristics.

Special Needs Apps [23]: currently lists 357 free of charge or commercial applications for iOS and Android. A description of each application is given. Users have the opportunity to download apps directly from the App Store or Google Play. Users can search for a specific application using three different ways: a) the general search field, using keywords, b) category-based search (Speech & Language, Scheduling, Education, Behavior, Life Skills, Social Skills, Games and Communications), and c) through sorting the entire app list by choosing: most popular, average rating, newest, price range. Furthermore, the inventory includes a rating system, a comments' field for members, screenshots and videos for each mobile AT application.

BridgingsApps [24] provides an inventory with 1,515 mobile AT apps (free or commercial). It includes nine main filters for searching: Keyword search, Skill levels, Mobile Devices, Embedded Skills, Independent Traits, Assistive Traits, Assistive/Independent, iTunes Categories, Android Market Categories. Moreover, there are more than 100 sub-filters for all the previous nine filters, which users can apply in order to fine-tune their search, a facility that is rather complicated for the inexperienced user. For each application there is a separate webpage with a description from AT reviewers, a rating system and a URL for downloading.

AppleVis [25] inventory includes more than 150 free of charge apps for iOS devices, specially designed for visual impaired people. The inventory provides an alphabetical list of applications. After selecting an application, the user is informed with a general description of the app and can search for similar apps using the filters or using the "More Like This" section. Moreover, there is a keyword search field and a field for user comments.

AppsforAAC [26] is a website that lists alphabetically about 300 commercial or free AAC applications in the domain of Augmentative and Alternative Communication (AAC) for Android and iOS users. There are three different ways to search the inventory choosing: device (iPad, iPhone, Android), type of app (Access, Education Support, Eye Pointing, Language Development, PECS, Photo Story, Phrase Bank, Set Phrases, Symbol Grid System, Text To Speech, Word Prediction) and price range. Each application has its own page with a description, a URL for downloading, a URL connecting with the developer's website, screenshots, a rating system and a field for user comments.

AssistIreland [27] provides a list of 70 iOS or Android, commercial or free, mobile applications for persons with disabilities and the elderly. Users can select apps according to five main classes of disabilities: Visual Impairment, Hearing Impairment, Alzheimer or Dementia, Autism and other related disorders, Mobility difficulties. Users can choose between sub-categories that classify the applications taking into account the purpose of use. Unfortunately, there is no extra page for each application, no download URL, no URL of the developer, no rating system and no field for user comments.

LowVisionBerau [28] lists 326 iOS mobile apps for the visual impaired. Search is facilitated through 22 application classes: Communication, Education, Entertainment, Food and Drink, Games, GPS/Navigation, Greeting Cards, Health, Magnification, Music/Radio, News, Pets, Photography, Productivity, Reading, Social Network, Sports, Travel, TV/Movies, Utilities, Voice Controlled. A team of experts is responsible for the selection and testing of each app. A small description, a download URL, system requirements and a rating field are included for each application.

Table 1 presents the main features of the different inventories discussed in this section showing the differences / similarities among them.

Table 1. Main features of existing inventories for mobile AT applications. a: SpecialNeedApps [23], b: BridgingApps [24], c: AppleVis [25], d: AppsforAAC [26], e: AssistIreland [27], f: LowVisionBureau [28]

	a	b	c	D	e	f
Number of apps	357	1,515	150	300	70	326
iOS	YES	YES	YES	YES	YES	YES
Android	YES	YES	NO	YES	YES	NO
Free	YES	YES	YES	YES	YES	YES
Commercial	YES	YES	NO	YES	YES	YES
Searching filters	3	9	3	3	5	1
User rating	YES	YES	NO	YES	NO	YES
User comments	YES	NO	NO	YES	NO	NO
Other				only AAC apps	only for the visual impaired	

3   Methodology

As we have described in the Introduction, it is crucial for an inventory of mobile AT applications: i) to be developed in a systematic way, ii) to include apps after a selection and evaluation process, preferable by experts in the field and c) provide a consistent description of all apps. Following these principles, we propose the following six-step methodology for the design and development of functional and reliable inventories of mobile AT applications:

a) Search and Locate Mobile AT Apps

Depending on the inventory scope, the exploration must cover either one or more mobile operating systems (iOS, Android, mobile MS-Windows). Moreover, the search must not include only the mobile app store(s) of the specific operating system(s), but has to include forums, websites, blogs, newsletters, databases, inventories, repositories and mailing lists in the domain of AT.

b) Download and Install the Apps

The identified mobile AT apps have to be installed on representative mobile devices (both smartphones and tablets) running one of the latest versions of mobile operating systems. The inventory has to include information on the specific models of the mobile devices and the version of the operating system that have been used for installation and testing. Mobile apps that cannot be installed or are failing to run are excluded from the next steps.

d) Test and Evaluate the Installed Mobile AT Apps

AT experts test and evaluate the installed mobile AT apps, in order to identify whether the application is in line with the scope and functionality referred by its manufacturer.

e) Create a Consistent Documentation for Each App

It is important to have a consistent description for each selected mobile AT app. The description must include the same fields for all apps and approximately the same amount of information. Optimally, the experts involved in the previous step must create the documentation. We propose the following fields to be included: the official app name, the name and URL of the manufacturer/developer, the app logo, the URL for downloading from the app store (iTunes App Store, Google Play), the required operating system and the minimum version, the latest app version, the disability/ies it addresses, a classification according to its application domain or scope, a description of its functionality and its main characteristics, the languages it supports, and the specific models of mobile devices used during the tests along with their version of their operating system.

f) Design the Facilities of the Inventory

It is crucial to select the appropriate search facilities and functionalities of the inventory. We propose the following five search and selection modes: a) by disability, b) by the operating system (Android, iOS, MS-Windows), c) by application category, d) using keywords, and e) in alphabetical order. A rating system along with a field for user comments are also suggested. It is preferable to present all the information for a specific app in a single webpage. Moreover, it is essential for the inventory to be accessible according to the Web Content Accessibility Guidelines (WCAG) 2.0 [29] at least for the level AA of conformance [30].

g) Update and Maintain the Inventory

Checking frequently for new mobile AT applications, as well updating the information of an existing app when a new version is released constitute an important part of the life cycle of the inventory.

4   Results

Following the above methodology, we have designed and developed the mATHENA Inventory of free mobile AT applications [31]. mATHENA is based on the approach followed in the ATHENA Inventory of Open Source AT software [32-33].

We decided to include only free of charge apps in mATHENA. Free Apps, are applications developed by an organization, company or freelancer developers and are available without any cost to users [34-37]. Many times, the purpose of a free app is the demonstration of the company's quality of app design, in order for the user to buy another commercial application from the same company in the future. The Organizations and freelancer developers who develop such applications don't have any financial profit, but just want to offer their services to the society in this way. Some Free Apps earn money from the advertisements in the pop-up windows that appear in frequent periods of time as the application runs. Free App Lite edition, is the application with less features than the commercial one. The user comes in contact with the interface and the basic function of the app, and he must pay for extra features if he needs them. Finally, a Free App Trial edition is the original commercial edition of the application but with a limitation in the usage period.

We explored and examined more than 200 different forums, websites, blogs, newsletters, application stores (iTunes App Store, Google Play), including the inventories mentioned in Section 2. We collected a total of 1,500 free applications (Table 2). Among them, thirty applications failed to download. Moreover, 15 apps failed to run smoothly (either because of software crashes, or because of failure of opening their interface on the device display). 190 applications, although they are referred as AT apps, were excluded after the evaluation as they were classified as non-AT apps. 75 applications that did not have their menu in English were also rejected. Finally, 420 mobile AT applications for iOS and Android devices were selected to be included in the mATHENA inventory (Table 2).

All the applications included in mATHENA have been tested by AT experts of the Speech and Accessibility Lab, University of Athens. Also, these experts are the authors of their documentation in mATHENA.

mATHENA is accessible according to the Web Content Accessibility Guidelines (WCAG) 2.0 [29] for the level AAA of conformance [30].

Table 3 presents the main fields of mATHENA, including details for each mobile AT application, as well as the inventory features, in comparison with the relative information for the six inventories presented in Section 2.

Table 2. Mobile AT applications located, tested, and selected by applying the proposed methodology

	Number	%
Total mobile AT apps located	1.100	100,0
Applications not free of charge	380	34,5
Applications failed to run	35	3,2
Non-AT apps	190	17,3
Applications not supporting the English language	75	6,8
Applications finally selected for mATHENA	420	38,2

Table 3. Overview of the information fields given for each product, and the most important website features for A: BridgingApps [24], B: SpecialNeedApps [23], C: AssistIreland [27], D: AppleVis [25], E: LowVisionBureau [28], F: AppsforAAC [26], G: mATHENA [31]

A	B	C	D	E	F	G	
				Details for each application			
•	•	•	•	•	•	•	Application Name
•	•	•	•	•	•	•	Description
•	•	•			•	•	Manufacturer
•	•	•			•	•	Application Logo
			•			•	Version
						•	Screenshots
						•	System Requirements for App
•	•		•	•		•	Download URL
•			•			•	Developer URL
			•			•	Add Comment
•						•	Languages
				Inventory features			
•	•		•	•		•	Search field
•	•	•	•	•	•	•	Filter Categories
		•				•	Filter Disability
					•	•	Only Free of charge Apps
•	•					•	Rating System
•	•		•		•	•	Alphabetical List of all Apps
•	•				•	•	Filter Operating System

5   Conclusions

We presented a methodological approach for the design and development of web-based inventories for mobile AT applications. This methodology is based on the consistent and well-documented presentation of the information for each mobile AT application, after it is tested in an AT lab. This methodology has been applied in the case of mATHENA, which targets the disabled end-users, their facilitators, as well as the professionals in the area of rehabilitation. Moreover, we presented the advantages of mATHENA compared with the functionalities of six other inventories for AT applications. Currently, mATHENA includes 420 free mobile AT applications, carefully selected after testing among a total of 1,100.

We plan to extend mATHENA by adding more languages, such as German and Spanish. Moreover, we plan to include apps related to new innovations in mobile technologies, both in hardware (e.g., smartwatch) and software that can benefit the disabled and elderly.

Acknowledgement. This research has been undertaken under the project UDLnet: Universal Design for Learning: A Framework for Addressing Learner Variability (540659-LLP-1-2013-1-GR-COMENIUS-CNW) [www.udlnet-project.eu] funded with support from the European Commission. This publication reflects the views only of the authors, and the Commission cannot be held responsible for any use, which may be made of the information contained therein.

References

1. Kouroupetroglou, G.: Assistive Technologies and Computer Access for Motor Disabilities. IGI Global, Hershey (2013)
2. Stephanidis, C.: The Universal Access Handbook. CRC Press, Florida (2009)
3. Scherer, M.J.: Living in the State of Stuck: How Technology Impacts the Lives of People with Disabilities. Brookline Books, Cambridge (2000)
4. McNaughton, D., Light, J.: The iPad and Mobile Technology Revolution: Benefits and Challenges for Individuals who require Augmentative and Alternative Communication. Augmentative and Alternative Communication **29**, 107–116 (2013)
5. Klasnja, P., Consolvo, S., McDonald, D.W., Landay, J.A., Pratt, W.: Using mobile & personal sensing technologies to support health behavior change in everyday life: lessons learned. In Proceedings of the American Medical Informatics Association (AMIA) Annual Symposium, pp. 338–342 (2009)
6. D'Ulizia, A., Ferri, F., Grifoni, P., Guzzo, T.: Smart Homes to support elderly people: Innovative Technologies and Social Impacts. In: Coronato, A., De Pietro, G. (eds.) Pervasive and Smart Technologies for Healthcare: Ubiquitous Methodologies and Tools, pp. 25–38. IGI Global, Hershey (2010)
7. Nikou, S.: Mobile technology and forgotten consumers: the young-elderly. International Journal of Consumer Studies **39**, 294–304 (2015)
8. Gavigan, K., Kurtts, S.: AT, UD, and Thee: Using Assistive Technology and Universal Design for Learning in 21st Century Media Centers. Library Media Connection **27**, 54–56 (2009)
9. Judge, S.: Using mobile media devices and apps to promote young children's learning. In: Proceedings of the Conference Embracing Inclusive Approaches for Children and Youth with Special Education Needs, pp. 142–145 (2014)
10. Bestwick, A., Campbell, J.: Mobile learning for all. Exceptional Parent **40**, 18–20 (2010)
11. Looi, C.K., Seow, P., Zhang, B., So, H.J., Chen, W.L., Wong, L.H.: Leveraging mobile technology for sustainable seamless learning: A research agenda. British Journal of Educational Technology **41**, 154–169 (2010)
12. Judge, S., Floyd, K., Jeffs, T.: Using Mobile Media Devices and Apps to Promote Young Children's Learning. In: Heider, K., Renck-Jalongo, M. (eds.) Children and Families in the Information Age. Springer, pp. 117–131 (2015)
13. Statista: Number of apps available in leading app stores as of May 2015. http://www.statista.com/statistics/276623/number-of-apps-available-in-leading-app-stores/
14. Hu, N., Pavlou, P.A., Zhang, J.: Can online reviews reveal a products true quality? empirical findings and analytical modeling of online word-of-mouth communication. In: Proc. 7th ACM Conf. on Electronic Commerce, pp. 324–330 (2006)
15. Khalid, H., Shihab, E., Nagappan, M., Hassan, A.E.: What Do Mobile App Users Complain About? IEEE Software **32**, 70–77 (2014)

16. Kaikkonen, A., Kekäläinen, A., Cankar, M., Kallio, T., Kankainen, A.: Usability testing of mobile applications: a comparison between laboratory and field testing. Journal of Usability Studies 1, 4–16 (2005)

17. Zhang, D., Adipat, B.: Challenges, methodologies, and issues in the usability testing of mobile applications. International Journal of Human-Computer Interaction 18, 293–308 (2005)

18. Billi, M., Burzagli, L., Catarci, T., Santuci, G., Bertini, E., Gabbanini, F., Palchetti, E.: A Unified Methodology for the Evaluation of Accessibility and Usability of Mobile Applications. Universal Access in the Information Society 9, 337–356 (2010)

19. Conde, M., Garcia-Peñalvo, F.J., Olivera, V.M.: Mobile apps repository for older people. In: Proceedings of the 2nd Int. Conf. on Technological Ecosystems for Enhancing Multiculturality, pp. 725–731 (2014)

20. Hakobyan, L., Lumsden, J., O'Sullivan, D., Bartlett, H.: Mobile assistive technologies for the visually impaired. Survey of Ophthalmology 58, 505–666 (2013)

21. Higginbotham, J.: The Future of the Android Operating System for Augmentative and Alternative Communication. Perspectives on Augmentative and Alternative Communication 20, 52–56 (2011)

22. Seabrook, H., Stromer, J., Shevkenek, C., Bharwani, A., de Grood, J., Ghali, W.: Medical applications: a database and characterization of apps in Apple iOS and Android platforms. BMC Research Notes 7, 573–581 (2014)

23. Friendship Circle, Special Needs Apps. http://www.friendshipcircle.org/apps/

24. BridgingApps. http://bridgingapps.org

25. AppleVis. http://www.applevis.com/

26. Apps for AAC. http://www.appsforaac.net/

27. Assist Ireland. http://www.assistireland.ie/

28. Low Vision Bureau, Podomatic. http://www.lowvisionbureau.com/

29. Web Content Accessibility Guidelines 2.0. http://www.w3.org/TR/WCAG20/

30. WCAG Conformance. http://www.w3.org/TR/UNDERSTANDING-WCAG20/conformance.html#uc-levels-head

31. mATHENA. http://access.uoa.gr/mATHENA/

32. Pino, A., Kouroupetroglou, G., Kacorri, H., Sarantidou, A., Spiliotopoulos, D.: An Open Source/Freeware Assistive Technology Software Inventory. Lecture Notes in Computer Science 6179, 178–185 (2010)

33. ATHENA. http://access.uoa.gr/ATHENA/

34. Pino, A.: Free Assistive Technology Software for Persons with Motor Disabilities. In: Kouroupetroglou, G. (ed.) Assistive Technologies and Computer Access for Motor Disabilities, pp. 110–152. IGI Global, Hershey (2013)

35. Richle, D.: The Economic Motivation of Open Source Software: Stakeholder Perspectives. IEEE Computer 40, 25–32 (2007)

36. Morelli, R., Tucker, A., Danner, N., de Lanerolle, T., Ellis, H., Izmirli, O., Krizanc, D., Parker, G.: Revitalizing Computing Education Through Free and Open Source Software for Humanity. Communications of the ACM 52, 67–75 (2009)

37. Chopra, S., Dexter, S.: Decoding Liberation: A Philosophical Investigation of Free Software. Routledge, New York (2007)

Improving Social Collaborations
in Virtual Learning Environments

Daniel González[✉], Regina Motz, and Libertad Tansini

Facultad de Ingeniería, Universidad de La República, Montevideo, Uruguay
danielgonzalezbernal@gmail.com, {rmotz,libertad}@fing.edu.uy

Abstract. This paper shows how to use social collaborations in virtual learning environments to motivate students in their learning process through recommendations of learning objects between peers. A hybrid recommender system is proposed and implemented in order to provide personalized recommendations for university students. An important contribution of this work is to show how to incorporate different recommendation approaches and techniques in order to produce useful recommendations in a real life scenario. Preliminary results indicate that information about groups of students as well as demographic information and previous evaluations of learning objects, processed with a combination of recommendation algorithms, show to be useful for the generation of personalized recommendations of learning objects.

Keywords: Learning objects · Hybrid recommender systems · Recommendation algorithms · Virtual learning environments

1 Introduction

Virtual learning environments are web-based tools which help students to improve their learning experience. In order to motivate students, different learning approaches have been proposed such as *blended learning*, which combines face-to-face methods with computer-mediated activities [1].

This work presents how to use social collaborations in virtual learning environments to motivate students in their learning process through recommendations of learning objects between peers. For that purpose, a hybrid recommender system is proposed and implemented in order to provide personalized recommendations for university students. An important contribution of this paper is to show how to incorporate different approaches and techniques in order to produce useful recommendations in a real life scenario. Specifically, the hybrid recommender system is used by university students of a technical career enrolled in an object-oriented programming course. In order to approve the course, all students must do a series of compulsory group tasks. A virtual learning environment called EVA[1] allows students to upload their group tasks as well as view and evaluate the recommended learning objects. When the course finishes, all the

---

[1] URL https://eva.fing.edu.uy

© Springer International Publishing Switzerland 2015
I. Ciuciu et al. (Eds.): OTM 2015 Workshops, LNCS 9416, pp. 528–535, 2015.
DOI: 10.1007/978-3-319-26138-6_57

learning objects are revised according to the evaluations through the course. The learning objects with acceptable evaluations are kept whereas the ones with unacceptable evaluations are candidates for being removed. Thus, a motivation for students is the fact that their evaluations of recommended learning objects can improve the resources for a particular course which helps their learning process.

The remaining part of this paper is organized as follows: In Section 2, the proposed hybrid recommender system is described. Section 3 presents the states and algorithms of the recommender system. Section 4 presents test cases and their preliminary results. Section 5 describes some conclusions and discusses improvements that could be made to the recommender system.

2   The Proposed Hybrid Recommender System

A hybrid recommender system combines two or more recommendation techniques in order to perform better than using any individual technique [2]. To combine the recommendation techniques, a hybridization method should be used [2]. As mentioned in the previous section, the proposed hybrid recommender system is used by university students enrolled in a programming course who must do a series of compulsory group tasks. The groups define the relationships between students. For simplicity, only one type of relationship between students is considered, that is the *membership* in a particular group of students. This information of the students and their relationships can be modeled as an undirected graph, where the vertices are the students and the edges are the relationships between them. For each student, an identifier, the identifier of the student group, his/her age, the courses that he/she is currently enrolled in, and the last access to the virtual environment platform are known.

A *course calendar* defines different periods and the learning objects suitable for them. A learning object can be suitable for one or more periods. Before the course starts, the correspondence between the periods and the learning objects is defined. For each learning object, an identifier, its type and its language are known. The learning objects available in the EVA are basically resources or activities. The students have the possibility to evaluate different quality attributes of the learning objects. Specifically, the quality attributes considered are: *intelligible*, which means the learning object is clear and easy to understand; *complete*, which means the learning object includes enough information to be understandable; and *agile to understand*, which means the learning object presents an agile explanation. For each evaluation, the identifier of the student who evaluates the learning object, the identifier of the learning object, the date of evaluation, and the ratings of the quality attributes are known. The average rating for each learning object is a calculated value based on the evaluations of the quality attributes. Weights, which are values between 0 and 1, set the importance for each quality attribute.

Regarding data privacy, a notice is published in the EVA expressing that the evaluations given by volunteer students will be processed automatically in a recommender system in order to improve the learning objects in the virtual learning environment for future editions of the course. It also expresses that no personal data will be published and that the given data is only used by the system for recommending learning objects in the context of this academic research.

3   States and Algorithms of the Hybrid Recommender System

The proposed hybrid recommender system uses a set of recommendation algorithms based on two different approaches: *crowdsourcing*, which uses the wisdom of the crowds [3]; and *friendsourcing*, which collects accurate information available only to a small, socially-connected group of people [4].

Let *current user* be the student who will receive the personalized recommendations. Considering the fact that the groups define the relationships between the students, four different states are defined: *S1*, in which there are no evaluations of learning objects in all the system; *S2*, in which there are no evaluations of learning objects made by any student of the same group as the current user but with evaluations made by students of other groups; *S3*, in which there are evaluations of learning objects made by any student of the group of the current user but with no evaluations made by students of other groups, and *S4*, in which there are evaluations of learning objects made by any student of all groups. For each state, a recommender algorithm is defined.

In *S1*, there are no evaluations of learning objects in all the system. Therefore, some recommendation mechanism is needed despite this problem known as the *cold-start problem*. Given the current date, the system recommends the most important learning objects which are suitable according to a predefined course calendar. Besides that, a criterion is used for giving importance to each learning object like the importance of the learning object in the web or teacher criterion based on knowledge and/or teaching experience. Taking into account that information, a recommendation algorithm called *RA1* is proposed. Let *c* be the course calendar, let *s* be the set of available learning objects, and let *i* be the importance for each learning object. These parameters are the inputs of algorithm. First of all, *RA1* gets the current date. With this date and the course calendar, the identifiers of the learning objects which are suitable for the selected period are obtained. Then, *RA1* orders them according to the importance criterion specified by the input. Finally, the recommended learning objects are returned. *RA1* is defined as shown in the following pseudocode:

```
RA1(CourseCalendar c, Set(LearningObject) s, Importance
i): Set(LearningObject){
  Date d = getCurrentDate();
  Set(LearningObject) cLO, result;
  cLO = getCurrentLO(c, s, d);
  result = orderByImportance(cLO, i);
  return result;
}
```

In *S2*, there are no evaluations of learning objects made by any student of the same group as the current user but with evaluations made by students of other groups. Therefore, the wisdom of the students of other groups contained in their evaluations of learning objects should be considered by using a collaborative filtering technique [3]. In traditional collaborative filtering, problems are broadcast to an unknown group of people in order to solve them [5]. In line with this approach, a *crowdsourcing recommendation algorithm* called *RA2* is proposed. Let *c* be the course calendar, let *s* be the set of available learning objects, let *u* be the current user, let *av* be the acceptance value for a learning object which indicates the minimum average ranking to be recommended by the algorithm, let *w* be the weights of the quality attributes, let *e* be the evaluations of learning objects, and let *i* be the importance for each learning object. These parameters are the inputs of the algorithm. Let *k* be a predefined variable used for limiting the maximum size of the best ranked learning objects for a particular group, and let *n* be a predefined variable used for limiting the maximum size of the set of recommended learning objects. First, *RA2* gets the current date. Considering this date and the course calendar, the set of learning objects which is suitable for the selected period is obtained. Then, *RA2* considers that set and the evaluations made by students of all groups except the group *g* of the current user *u* and obtains a map called *m* of the *k* best ranked learning objects and their average ratings, according to the acceptance value *av* and the weights of the quality attributes *w*. Then, *RA2* filters the map *m* removing the learning objects which the current user *u* previously evaluated. If the filtered map *m* is empty, *RA2* obtains the *n* most important current learning objects according to the importance criterion specified by the input, else *RA2* obtains the *n* best learning objects considering the average ranking in the map *m* and returns them. *RA2* is defined as shown in the following pseudocode:

```
RA2(CourseCalendar c, Set(LearningObject) s, User u,
float av, WeightsQA w, Evaluations e, Importance i):
Set(LearningObject){
  Date d = getCurrentDate();
  Set(LearningObject) cLO, result;
  cLO = getCurrentLO(c, s, d);
  Map(LearningObject, float avg_ranking) m;
  int g = myGroupID(u);
  m = getKBestRankedLO(g, cLO, av, w, e);
  m = filter(u, e, m);
  if(isEmpty(m))
    result = getNByImportance(cLO, i);
  else
    result = getNBestLO(m);
  return result;
}
```

In *S3*, there are evaluations of learning objects made by any student of the group of the current user but with no evaluations made by students of other groups. In this situation, the wisdom of the students who are close to the current user is considered. In previous research, a *friendsourcing recommendation algorithm* was defined [6]. This algorithm takes into account the similarity in the friendship relations, the similarity in the evaluations of items, and the similarity in the activity of rating items. The importance of each component of similarity is given by pondered values or weights. Therefore, an adaptation of the friendsourcing recommendation algorithm called *RA3* is proposed. Instead of considering the similarity in the friendship relations, we consider the similarity with the members of the group, taking into account the courses that the current user is enrolled in, the level of knowledge and demographic characteristics like age, gender and the distance from his/her house to the university. To determine the level of knowledge of a particular student, a multiple-choice questionnaire can be done in the virtual learning environment. Also, a short survey can be done to obtain demographic information of the students. Another difference to the original friendsourcing algorithm is the set of quality attributes considered. In this adaptation we only take into account the quality attributes previously described at the beginning of this section. Let c be the course calendar, let s be the set of available learning objects, let u be the current user, let av be the acceptance value for a learning object which indicates the minimum average ranking to be recommended by the algorithm, let w be the weights of the quality attributes, let e be the evaluations of learning objects, let i be the importance for each learning object, let α be the weight defined for the similarity of the current user u with the members of his/her group, let β be the weight defined for the similarity of evaluations of learning objects, and let γ be the weight defined for the similarity in the activity of rating learning objects. These parameters are the inputs of the algorithm. First of all, *RA3* obtains the current date. After that, the set of learning objects which are suitable for the selected period, according to the current date and the course calendar, is obtained. Finally, *RA3* returns the recommender learning objects according to the adapted friendsourcing algorithm. *RA3* is defined as shown in the following pseudocode:

```
RA3(CourseCalendar c, Set(LearningObject) s, User u,
float av, WeightsQA w, Evaluations e, Importance i):
Set(LearningObject){
    Date d = getCurrentDate();
    Set(LearningObject) cLO, result;
    cLO = getCurrentLO(c, s, d);
    result = friendSourcing(cLO, u, av, w, e, i, α, β, γ);
    return result;
}
```

In *S4*, there are evaluations of learning objects made by any student of all groups. Since there is wisdom of the crowds as well as wisdom of a small group of students we consider both by a combination of crowdsourcing and friendsourcing approaches and techniques, in order to improve the performance of the results given by the hybrid recommender system [2]. Therefore, a hybrid recommendation algorithm called *RA4* is proposed. Let c be the course calendar, let s be the set of available learning objects, let u be the current user, let av be the acceptance value for a learning object which indicates the minimum average ranking to be recommended by the algorithm, let w be the weights of the quality attributes, and let e be the evaluations of learning objects. These parameters are the inputs of the algorithm. First, *RA4* obtains a set of recommended learning objects using the *RA2* algorithm based on a crowdsourcing approach using collaborative filtering. Then, *RA4* obtains another set of recommended learning objects using the *RA3* algorithm based on a friendsourcing approach. Finally, *RA4* returns a combination of the previous sets of recommended learning objects. *RA4* is defined as shown in the following pseudocode:

```
RA4(CourseCalendar c, Set(LearningObject) s, User u,
float av, WeightsQA w, Evaluations e, Importance i):
Set(LearningObject){
    Set(LearningObject) s1, s2, result;
    s1 = RA2(c, s, u, av, w, e, i);
    s2 = RA3(c, s, u, av, w, e, i);
    result = combine(s1, s2);
    return result;
}
```

In order to combine the proposed recommendation algorithms, a switching hybrid-dization method is used [2]. The recommender system switches between recommendation algorithms depending on the current state. The decision of the current state is given by a *state machine*. To produce personalized recommendations for a current user, the system executes the recommendation algorithm of the current state. Figure 1 shows a state diagram of the proposed state machine. The initial state is *S1*, in which the cold start problem occurs, since there are no evaluations of learning objects in all the system. To mitigate this problem, *RA1* algorithm is executed until there are evaluations in the system. In *S2*, *S3*, and *S4* the hybrid recommender system executes a suitable recommendation algorithm: *RA2*, *RA3*, and *RA4* respectively.

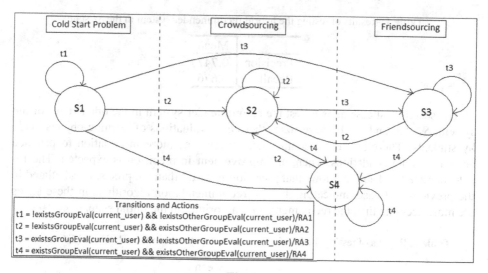

Fig. 1.

4   Test Cases and Preliminary Results

This section describes the test cases generated in order to test the efficiency of the hybrid recommender system. To create the proposed recommender system, a Java Project is developed which implements all the specified recommendation algorithms as well as its hybridization method. In order to test the hybrid recommender system in a real life scenario, the recommender system produces personalized recommendations of learning objects for students of the Computer Technologist career, which is a university career available in Montevideo, Uruguay. The students have the possibility to evaluate the recommended learning objects by ranking its quality attributes on a scale of 1 to 5; '1' means 'poor', whereas '5' means 'excellent'. The average ranking for a learning object is calculated as the weighted sum of the ranking of its quality attributes. The weights of the quality attributes have the same value, that is 1/3, and the acceptance value is 3. A total of 108 evaluations of recommended learning objects were made by students of the course. To evaluate the efficiency of the hybrid recommender system, two measures commonly used in the information retrieval are taken into account, which are *precision* and *recall* [7].

The first test case aims to test the recommender system in the initial state *S1*, which implies there are no evaluations of learning objects in all the system. In this state, the cold start problem occurs. Therefore, the expected precision and recall are at least 0.5, since the *RA1* recommendation algorithm aims to mitigate the cold start problem. The results depicted in Table 1, shows that the values of precision and recall are greater than the expected ones. This indicates that the teacher criterion used in the *RA1* recommendation algorithm is suitable for recommending learning objects in an initial state.

Table 1. Results of testing the hybrid recommender system in the *S1* state

	Mean
Precision	0.747
Recall	0.676

The second test case aims to test the recommender system in the other states of the system: *S2*, *S3*, and *S4*. In these states there are evaluations of learning objects made by students. Therefore, the recommender system has more information to produce accurate recommendations. Then, an improvement in precision is expected. The results depicted in Table 2, shows that precision is better than the precision calculated in the previous test case, indicating that the recommendation algorithms in these states are more accurate than the recommendation algorithm in the initial state.

Table 2. Results of testing the hybrid recommender system in the *S2*, *S3*, and *S4* states

	Mean
Precision	0.848
Recall	0.554

Preliminary results indicate that information about groups of students as well as demographic information and previous evaluations of learning objects, processed with a combination of recommendation algorithms, show to be useful for the generation of personalized recommendations of learning objects.

5   Conclusions and Future Work

A hybrid recommender system is proposed and implemented in order to provide personalized recommendations for university students. An important contribution of this work is to show how to incorporate different recommendation approaches like crowd-sourcing and friendsourcing, and recommendation techniques like collaborative filtering and demographic techniques, in order to produce useful recommendations of learning objects in a real life scenario. Regarding the results of the test cases, we may conclude that the information about groups of students as well as demographic information and previous evaluations, show to be useful for producing personalized recommendations of learning objects. Another conclusion is that a virtual learning environment like the EVA is a useful tool for students and also contains important information that can be used for recommending learning objects.

Extensions of the recommender system can be made. For instance, the recommender system can interact with learning object repositories when producing recommendations. Other future work includes generating larger test cases through the time to further analyze the performance of the hybrid recommender system. Another interesting line of future work is that the recommender system considers more than one course for recommending learning objects.

References

1. Guzzo, T., Grifoni, P., Ferri, F.: Social Aspects and Web 2.0 Challenges in Blended Learning. Blended Learning Environments for Adults: Evaluations and Frameworks, pp. 35–49 (2012)
2. Burke, R.: Hybrid Recommender Systems: Survey and Experiments. User Modeling and User-Adapted Interaction 12, 331–370 (2002)
3. Surowiecki, J.: The Wisdom of Crowds: Why the Many Are Smarter Than the Few and How Collective Wisdom Shapes Business, Economies, Societies and Nations. Doubleday (2004)
4. Bernstein, M., Tan, D., Smith, G., Czerwinski, M., Horvitz, E.: Personalization via Friend-sourcing. ACM Transactions on Computer-Human Interaction (2010)
5. Good, N., Schafer, J.B., Konstan, J.A., Borchers, A., Sarwar, B., Herlocker, J., Riedl, J.: Combining collaborative filtering with personal agents for better recommendations. In: Proceedings of the Sixteenth National Conference on Artificial Intelligence, pp. 439–446 (1999)
6. González, D., Motz, R., Tansini, L.: Recommendations given from socially-connected people. In: Demey, Y.T., Panetto, H. (eds.) OTM 2013 Workshops 2013. LNCS, vol. 8186, pp. 649–655. Springer, Heidelberg (2013)
7. Manning, C., Raghavan, P., Schütze, H.: Introduction to Information Retrieval. Cambridge University Press (2008)

A Platform for Measuring Susceptibility and Authority of Social Network Members

Gregorio D'Agostino[1,2] and Antonio De Nicola[1,3]([✉])

[1] ENEA-CR Casaccia, Rome, Italy
{gregorio.dagostino,antonio.denicola}@enea.it
[2] Boston University, Boston, MA, USA
[3] University of Rome Tor Vergata, Rome, Italy

Abstract. Social networks (SNs) offer the opportunity to define a new generation of services focused on users' needs and based on the SN topology and the temporal evolution of available information about their members. In this context we propose a platform for measuring some individual features of members, i.e. authority and susceptibility. The platform leverages on a semantics-based approach to represent members' interests and on a diffusion theory to model propagation of interests. Finally we present a case study concerning the American Physical Society (APS).

Keywords: Analytics for social networks · Semantic analysis · APS

1 Introduction

A *social network* (SN) consists of a community of "members" linked together with some kind of relationships (e.g., friendship, coauthorship). Depending on its context, it implicitly encompasses knowledge on personal activities, preferences and desires of members and their temporal evolution.

Making such a knowledge explicit requires multi-disciplinary competences from knowledge representation to natural language processing (NLP), to data analysis to social science to complexity science. Exploiting it could lead to a new generation of services tailored on personal needs of people by leveraging on available knowledge of all the members of the social network.

In this context we propose a software platform with three objectives. First it aims at gathering social network members data and organize them according to a predefined knowledge structure. Then it aims at estimating some individual features, i.e. people susceptibility to their neighbours and trends and people authority, by leveraging on an interest diffusion model. This means that we propose a method to measure the tendency of members to be influenced by their connections and their capability to influence others. Finally it aims at assessing the validity of the above mentioned diffusion model.

Our hypothesis is that the interests diffusion phenomenon results from the combined action of several factors: people connections, general trends, pre-existing interests and both the attitudes of people to be influenced by and to

© Springer International Publishing Switzerland 2015
I. Ciuciu et al. (Eds.): OTM 2015 Workshops, LNCS 9416, pp. 536–545, 2015.
DOI: 10.1007/978-3-319-26138-6_58

influence others. Furthermore, we assume that the temporal evolution of interests depends on the topics, since people can be susceptible to some specific information more than to others.

We tested the platform against the APS (American Physical Society) dataset (http://www.aps.org/) which provides a list of scientific papers in journals of physics. The analysis of APS publications is a representative application of our general framework as the dataset provides a rich amount of public available information on people belonging to a social network for a long time period.

The rest of the paper is organized as follows. Section 2 presents the related work in the field. How we organize social networks knowledge is described in Section 3. Section 4 briefly presents the interest propagation theory at the basis of the platform. Section 5 describes the software architecture together with the case study concerning the physics research community. Finally Section 6 provides conclusions.

2 Related Work

Social influence [6] is currently treated by different disciplines.

In [12], the authors propose a data mining approach to study the chain propagation of events (e.g. threads) and to identify leading influential members. Most of the efforts in the data mining community have been devoted to define progressive models. In such models, once a member becomes active (i.e. interested in a topic), it remains active. The most important propagation models are the Independent Cascade Model (ICM) [8], where diffusion events along every arc in the social network are mutually independent, and the Linear Threshold Model (LTM) [8], where members adapt their behaviour upon exposition to multiple independent sources.

Complexity Science includes the study of complex networks [2]. In particular, epidemics [11] studies the spread of viral processes in networks.

Merging the topological and semantic analysis of social networks represents a new research field which is providing promising results [10]. Along this line, our work uses a semantic conceptual representation of a *Domain of Interest* (DoI) in the social network context.

Finally, a social science approach is presented in [1] where an experiment on Facebook allows to estimate influential and susceptible members of social networks with respect to some social features, such as age and sex.

3 Social Networks Knowledge

In this Section we present how knowledge concerning social networks is organized in the proposed platform.

We refer to a DoI characterized by a set of products. It is worth mentioning that the term *product* here is employed in its broad sense, referring not only to goods, but also to cultural events and scientific products such as articles, books, etc. Conceptual images of products can be expressed in terms of a finite number of *concepts* belonging to a *semantic network* representing the DoI. Given the semantics structure, we further assume that there exists a set of elementary concepts, that we name *topics*, such that each product (or its abstraction) can be associated with a subset of topics. The identification of this set of basic topics plays a fundamental role and is a critical issue for the ontology engineering discipline [4]; the latter involves both automatic procedures (such as natural language processing) and human validation.

Then a *social network platform* can support the activities of a real *social network* which is composed by *social network members* connected together. SN members have *interest* in topics. Such interests vary with *time* (e.g., year) and can be estimated by means of a measure (i.e. degree of interest) which is inferred by *expressions of interest* of SN members as tweets, posts or published papers. Expressions of interest are events (e.g., publishing a post or a paper) demonstrating a positive attention by a member to a product. *Trends* depend on time, e.g., they can be determined every year by analyzing all the interests in topics of SN members.

The individual features characterize SN members with respect to the specific domain of interest. The susceptibility is the state of being easily affected, influenced, or harmed by something. *Susceptibility to neighbours* measures individual susceptibility from friends whereas *susceptibility to trends* measures susceptibility from the environment. *Authority* is the power to influence or command thought, opinion, or behavior.

Then we introduce a *semantic social network* consisting of a social network (SN), a semantic network [13], and a weighted interest graph connecting them.

A *Weighted Interest Graph* represents an abstraction of a community of people together with their interests with weight (i.e. degree of interest) assigned to the interests of people on topics. Such links may be viewed as either the probability to be interested or the degree of interest in a topic.

Semantic social networks are dynamic entities: they are born, grow, shrink and, finally, die (close). Appearance of new nodes may describe both inclusion of new members or emergence of novel topics. Similarly, disappearances of nodes may represent the cease of participation of people to the community or the obsolescence of topics. Moreover interests of members on topics may change their intensity during the time.

4   Interests Propagation

Here we briefly present the model of *interest propagation* [3] to describe the evolution of the interests in a *semantic social network*. It accounts for the structure of the social network and its temporal evolution without predicting it. It aims at estimating the probability for a person h_i to be interested in a topic c_k at a given time.

The evolution equations [3], resulting from the above assumptions, can be approximated for short time increments:

$$L_{h_i}(c_k, t + \Delta t) = [1 - x_i(c_k) - x_{is}(c_k)] \cdot L_{h_i}(c_k, t) + \frac{1}{|N_{h_i}|} \cdot \sum_{h_j \in N_{h_i}} x_{ij}(c_k) \cdot$$

$$L_{h_j}(c_k, t) + x_{is}(c_k) \cdot L_s(c_k, t) \tag{1}$$

The three terms at the right hand side model three different features: the personal tendency of a person to keep interest in a topic c_k, the influence of the neighbours, and that of the environment. In particular, $L_{h_i}(c_k, t + \Delta t)$ represents the probability of person h_i to be interested in the topic c_k at time $t + \Delta t$. $L_{h_i}(c_k, t)$ represents the probability of person h_i to be interested in the topic c_k at time t. $L_s(c_k, t)$ is the probability for the environment to provide some information on topic c_k at time t. $x_i(c_k)$ and $x_{ij}(c_k)$ are parameters (to be experimentally determined) characterizing the different individuals. We assume that, when all neighbours share the same interests (i.e. their profiles), the interest profile should not experience any variation, therefore:

$$x_i(c_k) = \frac{1}{|N_{h_i}|} \sum_{h_j \in N_{h_i}} x_{ij}(c_k) \tag{2}$$

and similarly, when the single member profile equals the trends source, no influence is expected.

$x_{ij}(c_k)$ is a positive number representing neighbours' susceptibility, i.e. the attitude of a member h_i to be influenced by each of her or his neighbours h_j with respect to the topic c_k. The $x_i(c_k)$ parameter measures the susceptibility of a member h_i to her or his neighbours' total solicitation with respect to the topic c_k. It is given by the average of x_{ij} over all j's (as in eq. 2). Finally, $x_{is}(c_k)$ represents the attitude of a member to be influenced by the general trends (i.e. *trends susceptibility*). Individual authority a_i is measured as following:

$$a_i \overset{def}{=} \sum_{h_j \in N_{h_i}} x_{ji}(c_k) \tag{3}$$

A complete description of the propagation model is available in [3].

5   Software Architecture

This Section presents the software architecture of the platform, devoted to manage knowledge concerning semantic social networks, together with a running example in the field of physics.

In particular, for the APS case study, we identified the members of the social network with the authors connected by the co-author relationships (representing the edges). Concerning the expressions of interest, we considered the publication of new scientific products (i.e. papers). In order to perform the analysis, we acquired the information about the topics defining the scope of the domain and the evolution dynamics of both the social relationships and the interests of the authors. The above information could be extracted from different sources, however the APS dataset provides both the information.

Results presented in this work refer to the dataset provided by the American Physical Society including paper up through 2013. The observation period has been limited to years from 1955 to 2005. In this temporal range, the number of considered papers is 357553.

The platform has the following three objectives. First it aims at gathering temporal knowledge about the domain of interest and social networks members, including their interests on topics. Then it aims at estimating individual features. Finally it aims at assessing the propagation theory.

The deployment and use of the platform is based on two phases, and the connected operations. The first phase concerns gathering and organizing knowledge whereas the last phase concerns assessment of the theory and estimation of the individual features.

5.1   Logical Software Architecture: Loading Phase

The logical software architecture is presented in Figure 1. During the loading phase, implicit knowledge is extracted from the social network data repository to make it explicit: the set of topics, the (dynamic) semantic social network at different time stamps and the trends are extracted and collected in the social network knowledge repository. The corresponding software modules are presented in the following.

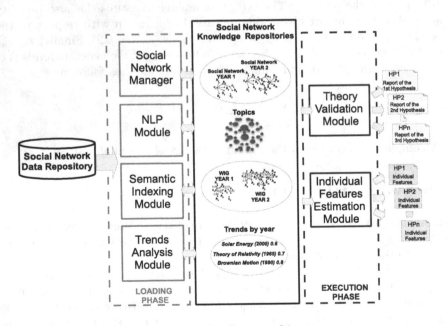

Fig. 1. Logical software architecture

Social Network Manager. The Social Network Manager extracts the social network by year as a directed graph $SoN = (H, F)$, where the set H of nodes $\{h_i\}$ represents the members of the social community $H = \{h_1, h_2, ..., h_{|H|}\}$ and the set F of links $f_{i,k}$ represents relationships between members as ordered pairs $F = \{f_{1,1}, f_{1,2}, ..., f_{|F|}\}$. For each year, the nodes are given by the authors that have written papers before that year and the edges are given by the co-authorships. According to this assumption, the social network evolves incrementally in time.

To identify SN members we considered the authors of the papers of the dataset. According to [15], we distinguish between an author and a person (i.e. referred as member in the following). The former is used to represent the available information on names (i.e. first name, surname, full name) and affiliation(s) obtained from the single entries of the APS dataset. The latter represents a real author entity, gathers information from one or more authors and it is collected in a proper set. The implemented protocol consists in checking for each author if it is compatible with the members already in the set. In case it is compatible, the corresponding information will enrich that of the compatible member, otherwise a new member will be created and added to the list. To fasten the process, the members considered for comparison are those with the same surname of the query author.

Disambiguation of authors is considered a relevant topic in social networks data analysis as demonstrated by [15], [5] and [14]. With respect to the existing protocols, we considered the case where a member uses both the first name and the hypocorism in signing papers. A hypocorism is a shorter or a diminutive form of a word or given name.

The implemented protocol is the following:

1. *Checking first name.* If the first name of the candidate author is the same of that of the already included person, the candidate author is compatible. Otherwise the next step of the protocol is applied.
2. *Checking hypocorism.* If the hypocorisms[1] of the first names of an author are compatible with the first name of a person, the author is compatible. Otherwise the next step of the protocol is applied.
3. *Checking first name initials.* If the first name initials are the same, the following two further checks are performed.
4. *Checking full names compatibility.* Please note that, even if the first name initials are the same, they still can be not compatible (e.g., H. Eugene is compatible with H. E. but it is not compatible with H. Edward). In case this check gives a positive response, a further step is performed.
5. *Checking affiliations* (e.g., the affiliation "Ohio University" is compatible with "Ohio University, USA" but it is not compatible with "ENEA, Italy").

If the checks pass, the author is compatible with the person. It should be noted that to check, for instance, that two affiliations or two first names are compatible, we computed the Levenshtein distance [9] between two strings.

---

[1] The list of hypocorisms was obtained from the following wikipedia page: http://en.wikipedia.org/wiki/Hypocorism

In our application the distance of the affiliations should be below the 40% and one character in case of first names.

The members of the social network identified with the above protocol are 257391. However, in order to study the evolution of authors' interests it is necessary to observe some change in their semantic profile during time; therefore only members that have published papers in, at least, two different years can be analysed. We named those members "treatable". Only 133058 members out of 257391 are treatable in the considered time period.

NLP Module. The NLP Module extracts topics from the data repository. It implements the following workflow.

1. *Replacing HTML tags* with characters (e.g., "Ë" with "Ë").
2. *Removing titles* containing words (e.g., editor in chief, poster) indicating that the titles do not refer to scientific papers.
3. *Removing not-English titles*, by means of the language-detection techniques available with Apache Lucene (https://lucene.apache.org/core) java library.
4. *Tokenizing titles*, to split titles in tokens by managing punctuation and function words (e.g., is, can, then).
5. *Stemming*, to reduce words to their lexemes. A lexeme is a unit of lexical meaning that exists regardless of the number of inflectional endings it may have or the number of words it may contain [7].
6. *Computing frequencies of lexemes and multi-words lexemes.*
7. *Identifying minimum annotation set of topics* corresponding to the single and multi word lexemes which permit to index all the papers of the APS dataset by means of at least one (single or multi word) lexeme.

We considered the whole APS dataset for this analysis and we identified 30967 topics.

Semantic Indexing Module. The Semantic Indexing Module allows to add a semantic profile to authors, to estimate the degree of interest in APS topics and, hence, to identify weighted interest graphs.

Within the observation period, we indexed papers and in turn we assigned a semantic profile to each member by means of the relative frequencies of "expressions of interest" (publications):

$$\xi_{h_i}(c_k, t) = \frac{\nu_{h_i}(c_k, t)}{\sum_{c_k} \nu_{h_i}(c_k, t)}, \tag{4}$$

where $\nu_{h_i}(c_k, t)$ represents how many papers, written before the considered year t, are indexed by the topic c_k. This function, by definition, spans the $[0, 1]$ range; the unitary value represents a total interest in the subject while a null value means no interest at all. These semantic profiles represent our estimates of the probabilities $L_{h_i}(c_k, t)$ evolving according to eq. (1); that is, one can estimate the likelihood of an author h_i to publish on a topic c_k through its share of interest $(L_{h_i}(c_k, t) \sim \xi_{h_i}(c_k, t))$.

Trends Analysis Module. The popularity of a topic ξ_s was estimated by its relative frequency over all published papers:

$$\xi_s(c_k, t) = \frac{\nu(c_k, t)}{\sum_{c_k} \nu(c_k, t)} \tag{5}$$

where $\nu(c_k, t)$ is the frequency of the topic c_k at time t. It can be regarded as the likelihood of a random person to be interested in the concept c_k at time t.

5.2   Logical Software Architecture: Execution Phase

During the execution phase, the platform validates the interest propagation theory (see eq. 1) and estimates individual features by means of the **Theory Validation Module** and the **Individual Features Estimation Module**.

To these purposes, we formulated three different hypotheses on susceptibility (x_{ij}) with increasing level of complexity that we tested against the APS dataset. The idea is to fit the free parameters (x_{ij}) by the maximum likelihood outcomes.

For the sake of simplicity (and to prevent possible overfitting), we assumed that x_i, x_{ij}, and x_{is} do not depend on the specific topic c_k. This means that a member influences her neighbours with the same intensity regardless of the subject.

In general, to estimate the susceptibility parameters, we constructed the mean square differences χ^2 between the predicted L's and the observed ones:

$$\chi^2 = \sum_{t, h_i, c_k} [L_{h_i}(c_k, t + \Delta t) - L_{h_i}(c_k, t) - \delta \xi_{h_i}(c_k. t)]^2; \tag{6}$$

where the symbol δ indicates the variation of a quantity from one year to the next ($\delta \xi(c_k, t) = \xi(c_k, t + \Delta t) - \xi(c_k, t)$).

One performs the optimization using the χ^2 as an object function, that is minimizing the deviation of prediction from observed values.

Since the L's represent likelihoods, they must be confined to the [0, 1] range. This implies that also the x_{ij} and x_{is} belong to the same interval. Therefore the feasible solutions of the optimization process must respect these constraints: $x_{is} \geq 0$, $x_{ij} \geq 0$, and $\sum_j x_{ij} + x_{is} \leq 1$.

The optimum values of the parameters are achieved analytically if the point at which the gradient of the χ^2 vanishes corresponds to a feasible solution ($\frac{\partial}{\partial \theta} \chi^2 = 0$). On the other side, when the analytical solution is unfeasible, we attribute to the parameters the closest value at boundary.

The first hypothesis (HP_1) states that all members have the same susceptibility to trends ($x_{is} = x_{s0}$) and are not influenced by neighbours ($x_{ij} = 0$). The second hypothesis (HP_2) states that all people have the same susceptibility to trends ($x_{is} = \bar{x}_s$) and to the neighbours ($x_{ij} = \bar{x}$). The third hypothesis (HP_3) states that people have both individual susceptibility to trends (x_{is}) and neighbours ($x_{i,j} = x_i$). Finally we introduced the $HP_{3\alpha}$ hypothesis where negative values of x_i and x_{is} are considered null.

Table 1. A Summary overview of the different hypotheses.

Hypothesis	Free Parameters	Estimated values	χ^2/dof
HP_1	$x_{ij} = 0$ $x_{is} = x_{s0}$	$x_{ij} = 0$ $x_{is} = x_{s0} = 0.086$	$3.26 * 10^{-7}$
HP_2	$x_{ij} = \bar{x}$ $x_{is} = \bar{x}_s$	$x_{ij} = \bar{x} = 0.059$ $x_{is} = \bar{x}_s = 0.051$	$3.23 * 10^{-7}$
HP_3	$x_{ij} = x_i$ x_{is}	$\bar{x} = 0.155$ $\bar{x}_s = 0.045$	$2.80 * 10^{-7}$
$HP_{3\alpha}$	$x_{ij} = x_i \geq 0$ $x_{is} \geq 0$	$\bar{x} = 0.156$ $\bar{x}_s = 0.067$	$2.96 * 10^{-7}$

Table 1 presents a summary of the testing hypotheses and the main results.

Table 1 shows that the fitness of the hypothesis improves with the complexity of the model behind the *interest propagation theory*. In fact, taking into account the degrees of freedom (dof) and the value of the χ^2/dof function (representing a good index for the method), HP_3 fits the dataset better than HP_2 and HP_1.

The hierarchical ranking of hypotheses supports the validity of the eq. 1.

According to the $HP_{3\alpha}$ hypothesis, the average susceptibility due to neighbours is 15.6%, whereas the contribution due to trends is 6.7% for a total average susceptibility of 22.3%. This means that about 77.7% of the subjects of papers are along the line of the previous works while some 22.3% do exhibit new topics due to the influence of collaborators and trends. The distribution profile of neighbours susceptibilities is presented in the Figure 2(a). This shows a very pronounced peak at null susceptibility (probably due to the quality of semantic analysis), while being smooth for other values. Similar considerations apply to trends susceptibilities.

The authority coefficients span the $[0, 352.27]$ range and are shown in Figure 2(b). Their mean value is $\bar{a} = 6.27$ and, as can be seen, there is a very long queue of few authors at high values.

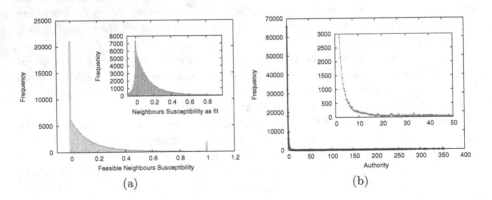

(a)   (b)

Fig. 2. (a) Histogram of neighbours' susceptibilities: feasible solutions and solutions as fit (in the inset). (b) Histogram of the authority coefficients.

6   Conclusions

In this paper we presented a software platform allowing to estimate some individual features characterizing social networks members. In particular the platform focuses on the susceptibility and the authority that quantify the tendency to influence and to be influenced by "friends" and the environment. The platform leverages on an interest propagation theory, on natural language processing techniques and on the semantic analysis of a domain of interest.

The platform was tested against the APS dataset. However, in principle, the model can be applied to big data from popular social networks such as Facebook and Twitter.

Acknowledgements. We kindly acknowledge Luis Amaral, Emiliano Casalicchio, Francesco Lo Presti, Walter Quattrociocchi, and Salvatore Tucci for stimulating discussions and the American Physical Society for providing us the dataset.

References

1. Aral, S., Walker, D.: Identifying influential and susceptible members of social networks. Science **337**(6092), 337–341 (2012)
2. Barabási, A.L., Albert, R.: Emergence of scaling in random networks. Science **286**(5439), 509–512 (1999)
3. D'Agostino, G., D'Antonio, F., De Nicola, A., Tucci, S.: Interests diffusion in social networks. Physica A: Stat. Mech. and its Appl. **436**, 443–461 (2015)
4. De Nicola, A., Missikoff, M., Navigli, R.: A software engineering approach to ontology building. Information Systems **34**(2), 258–275 (2009)
5. Deville, P., Wang, D., Sinatra, R., Song, C., Blondel, V.D., Barabási, A.L.: Career on the move: geography, stratification, and scientific impact. Sc. Rep. **4** (2014)
6. Guzzo, T., Ferri, F., Grifoni, P.: Social influence analysis. In: Encyclopedia of Social Network Analysis and Mining, pp. 1800–1807. Springer, NY (2014)
7. Hughes, H.: The cambridge encyclopedia of the english language. Reference Reviews **18**(3), 28–29 (2004)
8. Kempe, D., Kleinberg, J., Tardos, E.: Maximizing the spread of influence through a social network. In: Proc. of KDD 2003, pp. 137–146. ACM (2003)
9. Levenshtein, V.I.: Binary codes capable of correcting deletions, insertions, and reversals. Soviet physics doklady **10**, 707–710 (1966)
10. Mika, P.: Ontologies are us: A unified model of social networks and semantics. Web Semantics: Science, Services and Agents on the World Wide Web **5**(1), 5–15 (2007)
11. Pastor-Satorras, R., Vespignani, A.: Epidemic spreading in scale-free networks. Phys. Rev. Lett. **86**, 3200–3203 (2001)
12. Richardson, M., Domingos, P.: Mining knowledge-sharing sites for viral marketing. In: Proc. of 8th Int. Conf. on Know. Disc. and Data Min., pp. 61–70. ACM (2002)
13. Sowa, J.F.: Semantic networks. Encyclopedia of Cognitive Science (2006)
14. Stringer, M.J., Sales-Pardo, M., Amaral, L.A.N.: Effectiveness of journal ranking schemes as a tool for locating information. PLoS One **3**(2), e1683 (2008)
15. Wang, Peng, Zhao, Jianyu, Huang, Kai, Xu, Baowen: A unified semi-supervised framework for author disambiguation in academic social network. In: Decker, Hendrik, Lhotská, Lenka, Link, Sebastian, Spies, Marcus, Wagner, Roland R. (eds.) DEXA 2014, Part II. LNCS, vol. 8645, pp. 1–16. Springer, Heidelberg (2014)

Multimodal Systems: An Excursus of the Main Research Questions

Maria Chiara Caschera, Arianna D'Ulizia, Fernando Ferri[✉], and Patrizia Grifoni

Institute of Research on Population and Social Policies
(IRPPS) – National Research Council (CNR), 00185 Rome, Italy
{mc.caschera,arianna.dulizia,fernando.ferri,
patrizia.grifoni}@irpps.cnr.it

Abstract. Multimodal systems use integrated multiple interaction modalities (e.g. speech, sketch, handwriting, etc.) enabling users to benefit of a communication more similar to the human-human communication. To develop multimodal systems, several research questions have been addressed in the literature from the early 80s till the present day, such as multimodal fusion, recognition, dialogue interpretation and disambiguation, fission, context adaptation, etc. This paper investigates studies developed in the last decade, by analyzing the evolution of the approaches applied to face the main research questions related to multimodal fusion, interpretation, and context adaptation. As result, the paper provides a discussion on the reasons that led to shift attention from one methodology to another.

Keywords: Multimodal systems · Multimodal fusion · Interpretation · Context adaptation

1 Introduction

Multimodal systems represent a challenging issue for IT, since the use of integrated multiple interaction modalities (e.g. speech, sketch, handwriting, etc.) can provide value-added services by enabling users to benefit of approaches more and more similar with approaches used in human-human communication. Indeed, in multimodal interaction systems, different modalities are combined according to temporal and semantic constrains and according to different types of cooperation (e.g. complementarity, redundancy, etc.) [1,2]. In the literature, several multimodal systems have been developed from the early 80s till now [3,4,5,6,7,8,9,10]. The development of a multimodal system implies the resolution of several research issues, such as multimodal fusion, interpretation, disambiguation of interpretation, fission [11], adaptivity [12], etc.

This paper investigates multimodal systems developed in the last decade (from 2005 to 2015) by analyzing the evolution of the methodologies applied to face three of the main research issues that are multimodal fusion, interpretation, and context adaptation. For lack of space we have restricted the attention on these three research issues because they are faced during the input communication flow (from the user to

© Springer International Publishing Switzerland 2015
I. Ciuciu et al. (Eds.): OTM 2015 Workshops, LNCS 9416, pp. 546–558, 2015.
DOI: 10.1007/978-3-319-26138-6_59

the machine), as described also in the W3C multimodal interaction framework [13]. The output communication flow (from the machine to the user) will be addressed in a future work. To identify relevant works on multimodal systems we have utilized Google Scholar as reference database and we have gathered from it the literature limiting the search to the following works: published from 2005 to 2015, written in English, and containing at least one of the following keywords: multimodal system, multimodal interaction system, adaptive multimodal system, multimodal fusion, dialogue interpretation. Afterwards, we have selected the papers that provide a discussion on the following research questions:

- How to develop a synergistic fusion that combines, synchronizes and integrates input modalities?
- How to model and manage interpretation of the dialogue between users and multimodal interaction systems?
- How to utilize context information to adapt multimodal interaction?

The remainder of the paper is structured as follows. The first research question on fusion strategies is presented in Section 2. Section 3 answers the second research question on multimodal dialogue interpretation. Section 4 addresses the third research question on how multimodal systems utilize context information to adapt various aspects of multimodal interaction. Section 5 discusses some future perspectives emerged from the analysis and concludes the paper.

2   Multimodal Fusion

Several integration (or fusion) approaches have been developed in the literature, as surveyed in several papers [14,15]. A generally accepted classification of the fusion strategies considers the level at which the fusion takes place: *fusion at the recognition level*, *fusion at the decision level,* and *hybrid multi-level fusion.* These levels correspond to the main architectural levels of a multimodal system, as described in [14].

The *fusion at the recognition level* (named also *early fusion* or *recognition/feature-based fusion*) consists in merging the outcomes of each recognizer (i.e. the component devoted to recognize each specific unimodal input) by using integration mechanisms, such as, for example, statistical integration techniques, agent theory, hidden Markov models, artificial neural networks, etc. This kind of fusion has not been applied by any of the surveyed multimodal systems developed from 2005 to 2015 due to the necessity of a large amount of data for the training, and the high computational costs compared to the other two strategies. It was applied by several systems developed before 2005.

The *fusion at the decision level* (named also *late fusion* or *decision/conceptual-based fusion*) means merging the semantic information that is extracted from the specific decision managers (i.e. the components devoted to provide the most probable interpretation of the input). In fact, in this kind of fusion the outcomes of each recognizer are separately interpreted by the decision managers and the extracted semantic meanings are integrated by using specific dialogue-driven fusion procedures to yield the complete interpretation. Late fusion is mostly suitable for modalities that differ both in their nature and in the time scale. This implies that a tight synchrony among the various communicative modalities is essential to deliver the correct information at the right time. The main advantages of this kind of fusion rely on the use of standard and well-tested recognizers and interpreters for each modality, as well as the greater simplicity of the fusion algorithms. Decision-based fusion methods are further classified by Dumas et al. [16] according to the algorithmic solution adopted to fuse the input in: (i) *frame-based fusion*, a kind of fusion that uses data structures called frames or features for meaning representation of data coming from various sources or modalities; (ii) *unification-based fusion*, a fusion that is based on recursively merging attribute-value structures to obtain a logical whole meaning representation; (iii) *symbolic/statistical fusion*, a fusion that integrates unification-based approaches with statistical processing techniques. The surveyed multimodal systems (developed from 2005 to 2015) employ the following kinds of structures to fuse multimodal input at the decision level: *finite state automata* [17], *semantic frames* [18], *dialogue moves* [19], *feature value structure* (DTAC) [20], *behavioural matrix* [7], *multimodal generic dialogue node* [21], *XML Typed* [22], *communication acts* [23], *fusion agents* [24], and *interaction register* [25].

In the *hybrid multi-level fusion* the integration of input signals is distributed among the recognition and decision levels. In particular, the interdependence among modalities, which allows predicting subsequent symbols knowing previous symbols in the input data flow, is exploited to improve accuracy of the interpretation process. This implies that a joint multimodal language model, which relies on the symbols acquired during the acquisition phase and is governed by their semantic meanings extracted during the decision phase, is the basis of the hybrid multi-level fusion strategy. The following fusion methodologies have been applied in the surveyed literature: *multimodal grammars* [26,27,28,29,30], *scored hypothesis graphs* [31], and *transferable belief model* [32].

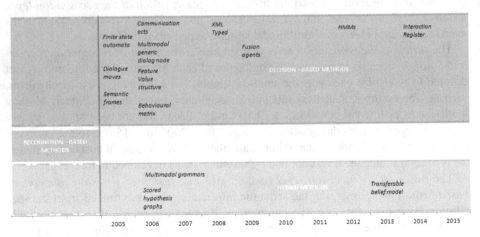

Fig. 1. Temporal evolution of fusion approaches

As depicted in Figure 1, from 2005 decision-based fusion results the most applied strategy due to its ability to extract meaning from loosely coupled modalities [10]. Specifically, decision-based fusion methods evolved from early approaches relying on a frame-based fusion, such as semantic frames [18], feature value structure (DTAC) [20], communication acts [23], dialogue moves [19], and multimodal generic dialogue node [21], to more recent methods relying on a unification-based fusion, such as fusion agents [24], to conclude with symbolic/statistical fusion, such as interaction register [25] and hidden Markov models (HMMs) [10]). This evolution toward symbolic/statistical approaches is justified by their ability to obtain more robust and reliable results [10]. Analogously, hybrid multi-level fusion is evolved from graph-based methods [31] to grammatical approaches [26,27,28,29,30] and approaches based on evidential reasoning [32].

3   Interpretation

The interpretation is an important process for correctly interacting with multimodal systems, consisting in capturing the meaning of the user's input. The interpretation process is strictly connected to different features, such as available interaction modalities, conversation focus, and context of interaction. Moreover, a correct interpretation can be reached by the system considering semantic, temporal and contextual constraints simultaneously. The literature provides different methods to interpret multimodal input and an overview of those approaches has been provided in [33]. As discussed in [33], the design of methods to interpret multimodal input implies the combination of more than two modes (spoken, gestural, facial expression, gaze, etc.) that can provide uncertain inputs and corrupted by noise. Note that some approaches sometimes aimed to consider the interpretation problem by dividing it in subproblems, such as ambiguity identification and resolution. Examples of resolution methods are mediation techniques [34] and probabilistic approaches [35]. A discussion on the main features of approaches to dialogue management has been addressed in [16], where these approaches have been divided into: finite-states and frame based approaches; information state-based and probabilistic approaches; plan-based approaches; and collaborative agent-based approaches.

In *finite-states and frame based approaches*, dialogue is represented by states transition networks where the nodes represent the system actions and the transitions are all the possible paths through the network. Frame-based approaches are more flexible than finite-states based approaches because the dialogue flow is more efficient and natural [36]. In [37] an example of a frame-based approach is presented and it uses interaction hierarchies.

In *information state-based and probabilistic approaches*, dialogue is modelled by information states (informational components, a set of dialogue moves, a set of update rules and an update strategy) that can be combined with probabilistic techniques such as Markov Decision Process and Bayesian Networks. Specifically, in the early surveyed period the following interpretation strategies have been applied: conversation discourse states [6], Partially Observable Markov Decision Processes [38,39], weighted finite-state automata with multimodal grammar [17], finite-state-based interpreter combined with an edit-based transducer [40]. Recently, a rule-based approach combined with Hidden Markov Models has been applied [41]. Moreover, in [42], the dialogue has been modelled using a hierarchical dialogue model.

Plan-based approaches model dialogue considering both that people communicate to achieve goals and that dialogue can change mental states in the listeners. An example of these approaches is provided in [43] where a greedy algorithm is used. More recently, probabilistic approaches [44], dialogue grammars [45], and ontology-based dialogue models [17] have been applied.

In *collaborative agent-based approaches*, dialogue is viewed as a collaborative process between intelligent agents. In the surveyed period, agent-based approaches have been mainly developed, such as BDI(belief–desire–intention) agents [46], agents tracking dialogue states and supporting dialogue [47], route construction agents [48], agents for verbal and non-verbal communication [49], and 3D Embodied Conversational Agents (ECA) [50]. Afterwards, behavioural control models [51,52] have been proposed to facilitate the conversational dynamics of embodied agents. Recently, an agent-based approach has been integrated with a service robot speech interface [53].

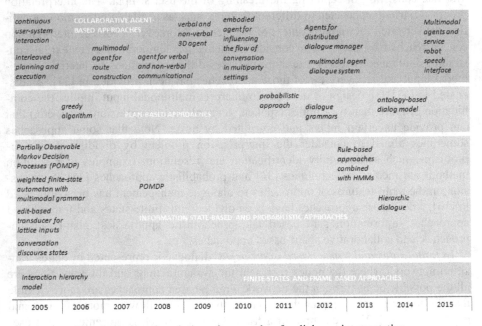

Fig. 2. Temporal evolution of approaches for dialogue interpretation

As depicted in Figure 2, from 2005 to 2015 the dialogue interpretation approaches have evolved from less flexible approaches, which model the system actions and the transitions (finite-state and frame-based), toward probabilistic approaches that model dialogue flow in a more efficient, natural and adaptive way. More recently, approaches able to capture people communicative goals and interaction behaviours (e.g. information state-based and probabilistic and plan-based) have emerged. Collaborative agent-based approaches are the most applied in the surveyed period (2005-2015). Specifically, collaborative agent-based approaches evolve from early approaches aiming to coordinate user-system interaction and to enable coherent user-system dialogue, to approaches able to support specific tasks and domain-specific customization and to simulate multimodal verbal and nonverbal behaviours.

4   Context Adaptation

Adaptive multimodal systems utilize context information to adapt various aspects of multimodal interaction. The context information can be used to adapt the language model in order to improve dialogue recognition accuracy and enhance the quality of semantic parsers [54,55,10,6,30,56]. Another use of context information is the adaption of the user interface [57,7,9,8]. Honold et al. [58] have categorized the kind of context information used in human computer interaction in eight models that are: application, task, environment, user, dialogue, information, presentation, and component models. In this review, we focus only on the models used in fusion and dialogue management that are: environment, user, dialogue, information, and presentation. In the remainder of this section, for each of these five models we describe the techniques used to adapt the interaction to the context.

Environment model-based approaches use the contextual information of the environment model to adapt the multimodal interaction. Environment model contains information that is not directly related to the user, but rather to the surrounding of the user sensed through a device/sensor. Important environment information include: location, time, and environmental conditions, such as temperature and lighting [58]. As depicted in Figure 3, the first surveyed environment model-based approaches rely on semantic models and adaptation rules [6,7]. Later, in 2011-2012 machine learning techniques have been mainly applied, such as case-based reasoning [9], HMMs [10], and heuristics algorithms [8]. More recently, adaptation rules and semantic models have been applied again in [3] to define the application's appearance (presentation) and behaviour dependent from different context.

Presentation model-based approaches use the contextual information of the presentation model to adapt the multimodal interaction. The presentation model holds information on the current presentation of the system, i.e. information about what is presented where and how. It is updated as soon as the fission module finished on deciding which information is to be presented in what kind of way [58]. As depicted in Figure 3, this kind of adaptation approach relies mainly on semantic models and adaptation rules [6,7,3].

User model-based approaches concern the dynamic knowledge of the user (such as user's preferences, user's current actions and working domain) and it influences the dialogue steps to be accomplished [58]. In the early surveyed period, dialogue systems tailored interaction by using semantic models [6] and multi-attribute decision theory [59]. Almost in the same period, for adaptive issues, automated clustering [60] and behavioural matrix [7] have been used. Later, in 2011, rule-based approaches

[61], automatic learning [44], and heuristics algorithms [8] have been used. Recently, semantic models and adaptation rules have been applied in [3].

Dialogue model-based approaches use the contextual information of the dialogue model to adapt the multimodal interaction. The dialogue model contains information on how adapting dialogue steps to the user model. In fact, it includes information about the tasks a user has to accomplish in cooperation with the system [58]. As for user model discussion, in the early surveyed period, systems tailored dialogue by using semantic models [6] and rule-based approaches [62]. Later, statistical approaches have been used [63] in order to achieve a more practical, effective, and theoretically well-founded approach to adaptivity, as well as semi-automatic rule-based methods [64]. A further approach recently used to model interaction dialogue is ontology, as proposed in [65].

Information model-based approaches use information on how representing communicable contents [58]. That information on how a user represents concepts in different contexts support a correct interpretation of the user's input avoiding incorrect and ambiguous interpretation. Issues concerning errors and ambiguities have been widely discussed both for modal interaction (e.g. sketch modality [66,67,68,69]) and for multimodal interaction [70,34,71,72]. Information model-based approaches are mainly based on rule-based techniques [73,74,54].

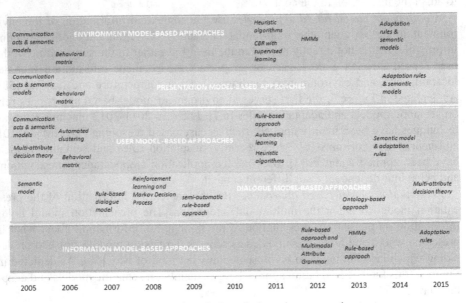

Fig. 3. Temporal evolution of adaptation approaches

From 2005 to 2015, the adaptation approaches for the different models (i.e. environment, presentation, user, dialogue and information) follow a similar trend, as Figure 3 shows. In fact, they evolved from approaches based on behavioural matrix, communication acts and semantic models to probabilistic approaches able to adapt dialogue flow in a more efficient and natural way and later to rule-based approaches, alone or combined with semantic models.

5   Conclusions and Future Research Directions

In this paper we have given an overview of three main research issues addressed in the multimodal interaction field: multimodal fusion, dialogue interpretation, and context adaptation. We have analysed how multimodal systems developed in the last decade have faced these research issues highlighting the evolution of the proposed approaches and the reasons that led to this evolution.

From the analysis of the evolution of methodologies applied to respond to the main research questions on multimodal fusion, dialogue management, and context adaptivity, two main directions of future research are emerged. First, the Web and the cloud can open up new perspectives in the research field of multimodality since they can provide the framework for structuring the complexity of multimodal human machine interaction, as well as all processes connected with multimodal fusion, dialogue interpretation, and context adaptivity, in a cloud perspective [75,76]. The Web can offer adequate computational resources to manage the complexity implied by the use of the five senses involved in human machine interaction and communication [77]. Analogously, cloud computing and Service Oriented Architectures (SOAs) - with their concepts of service, flexibility, scalability, adaptivity, evolvability, distribution, modularity, interoperability and computational power − allow managing multimodal interaction in a distributed, flexible, modular, interoperable and scalable manner. Second, multimodal corpora are emerging as a crucial tool for fine-tuning and improving information fusion and dialogue interpretation [78,79]. However, their development has traditionally been very time-consuming and expensive. Using the Web for collaboratively and incrementally creating multimodal corpora is another research direction that we envision in the next years.

References

1. Caschera, M.C., Ferri, F., Grifoni, P.: Multimodal interaction systems: information and time features. International Journal of Web and Grid Services 3(1), 82–99 (2007)
2. Caschera, M.C., Ferri, F., Grifoni, P.: Multimodality in mobile applications and services, encyclopedia of mobile computing and commerce. In: Taniar, D. (ed.) Monash University, Australia, pp. 675–681 (2007)
3. Nesselrath, R., Feld, M.: SiAM-dp: a platform for the model-based development of context-aware multimodal dialogue applications. In: Intelligent Environments 2014, pp. 162–169 (2014)
4. Caschera, M.C., D'Ulizia, A., Ferri, F., Grifoni, P.: An advanced multimodal platform for educational social networks. In: Meersman, R., Dillon, T., Herrero, P. (eds.) OTM 2010. LNCS, vol. 6428, pp. 339–348. Springer, Heidelberg (2010)

5. D'Andrea, A., D'Ulizia, A., Ferri, F., Grifoni, P.: A multimodal pervasive framework for ambient assisted living. In: Proceedings of the 2nd International Conference on PErvasive Technologies Related to Assistive Environments (PETRA 2009), June 9–13, Corfù, Greece. ACM, New York, pp. 1–8 (2009)

6. Chai, J.Y., Pan, S., Zhou, M.X.: Mind: a context-based multimodal interpretation framework in conversational systems. In: van Kuppevelt, J.C.J., et al. (eds.), Advances in Natural Multimodal Dialogue Systems, pp. 265–285 (2005)

7. Duarte, C., Carriço, L.: A conceptual framework for developing adaptive multimodal applications. In: Proceedings of the 11th International Conference on Intelligent User Interfaces, Sydney, Australia, January 29–February 01, 2006. ACM, New York, pp. 132–139 (2006)

8. Kong, J., Zhang, W.Y., Yu, N., Xia, X.J.: Design of Human-Centric Adaptive Multimodal Interfaces. International Journal of Human-Computer Studies 69(12), 854–869 (2011)

9. Hina, M.D., Ramdane-Cherif, A., Tadj, C., Levy, N.: A Multi-Agent Based Multimodal System Adaptive to the User's Interaction Context. INTECH Open Access Publisher (2011)

10. Dumas, B., Signer, B., Lalanne, D.: Fusion in multimodal interactive systems: an HMM-based algorithm for user-induced adaptation. In: Proceedings of the 4th ACM SIGCHI Symposium on Engineering Interactive Computing Systems, pp. 15–24. ACM (2012)

11. Grifoni, P.: Multimodal fission. Multimodal human computer interaction and pervasive services, pp. 103–120 (2009)

12. Caschera, M.C., D'Ulizia, A., Ferri, F., Grifoni, P.: Towards evolutionary multimodal interaction. In: Herrero, P., Panetto, H., Meersman, R., Dillon, T. (eds.) OTM-WS 2012. LNCS, vol. 7567, pp. 608–616. Springer, Heidelberg (2012)

13. Larson, J.A., Raman, T.V., Raggett, D., Bodell, M., Johnston, M., Kumar, S., Potter, S., Waters, K.: W3C multimodal interaction framework. W3C NOTE 6 (2003)

14. D'Ulizia, A.: Exploring Multimodal Input Fusion Strategies. Handbook of Research on Multimodal Human Computer Interaction and Pervasive Services: Evolutionary Techniques for Improving Accessibility, 34–57 (2009). IGI Publishing

15. Lalanne, D., Nigay, L., Robinson, P., Vanderdonckt, J., Ladry, J.F.: Fusion engines for multimodal input: a survey. In: Proceedings of the 2009 International Conference on Multimodal Interfaces, pp. 153–160. ACM (2009)

16. Dumas, B., Lalanne, D., Oviatt, S.: Multimodal interfaces: a survey of principles, models and frameworks. In: Lalanne, D., Kohlas, J. (eds.) Human Machine Interaction. LNCS, vol. 5440, pp. 3–26. Springer, Heidelberg (2009)

17. Johnston, M., Bangalore, S.: Finite-state multimodal integration and understanding. Nat. Lang. Eng. 11(2), 159–188 (2005)

18. Russ, G., Sallans, B., Hareter, H.: Semantic based information fusion in a multimodal interface. In: International Conference on Human-Computer Interaction (HCI2005), Las Vegas, June 20–23, pp 94–100 (2005)

19. Pérez, G., Amores, G., Manchón, P.: Two strategies for multimodal fusion. Proceedings of Multimodal Interaction for the Visualization and Exploration of Scientific Data, Trento, Italy, 26–32 (2005)

20. Portillo, P.M., García, G.P., Carredano, G.A.: Multimodal fusion: a new hybrid strategy for dialogue systems. In: ACM International Conference on Multimodal Interfaces, Banff, Canada, pp. 357–363 (2006)

21. Melichar, M., Cenek, P.: From vocal to multimodal dialogue management. In: Proceedings of the 8th International Conference on Multimodal interfaces, pp. 59–67. ACM (2006)

22. Dumas, B., Lalanne, D., Guinard, D., Koenig, R., Ingold, R.: Strengths and weaknesses of software architectures for the rapid creation of tangible and multimodal interfaces. In: Proc. of the 2nd Int. Conf. on Tangible and Embedded interaction (Bonn, Germany, 2008), pp. 47–54. ACM (2008)

23. Wasinger, R.: Multimodal Interaction with Mobile Devices: Fusing a Broad Spectrum of Modality Combinations. IOS Press (2006)

24. Mendonça, H., Lawson, J.Y.L., Vybornova, O., Macq, B., Vanderdonckt, J.: A fusion framework for multimodal interactive applications. In: ACM International Conference on Multimodal Interfaces (ICMI-MLMI), Cambridge, MA, pp. 161–168 (2009)

25. Griol, D., Garcia-Herrero, J., Molina, J.M.: A novel approach for data fusion and dialog management in user-adapted multimodal dialog systems. In: 17th International Conference on Information Fusion, pp. 1–7. IEEE (2014)

26. Sun, Y., Chen, F., Shi, Y.D., Chung, V.: A novel method for multi-sensory data fusion in multimodal human computer interaction. In: Proceedings of the 20th Conference of the Computer-Human Interaction Special Interest Group, Sydney, Australia, pp. 401–404 (2006)

27. D'Ulizia, A., Ferri, F., Grifoni, P.: A hybrid grammar-based approach to multimodal languages specification. In: Meersman, R., Tari, Z., Herrero, P. (eds.) OTM-WS 2007, Part I. LNCS, vol. 4805, pp. 367–376. Springer, Heidelberg (2007)

28. D'Ulizia, A., Ferri, F., Grifoni, P.: Toward the development of an integrative framework for multimodal dialogue processing. In: Meersman, R., Tari, Z., Herrero, P. (eds.) OTM-WS 2008. LNCS, vol. 5333, pp. 509–518. Springer, Heidelberg (2008)

29. D'Ulizia, A., Ferri, F.: Formalization of multimodal languages in pervasive computing paradigm. In: Damiani, E., Yetongnon, K., Chbeir, R., Dipanda, A. (eds.) SITIS 2006. LNCS, vol. 4879, pp. 126–136. Springer, Heidelberg (2009)

30. Ferri, F., D'Ulizia, A., Grifoni, P.: Multimodal Language Specification for Human Adaptive Mechatronics. Journal of Next Generation Information Technology 3(1), 47–57 (2012)

31. Wahlster, W.: Dialogue systems go multimodal: the SmartKom experience. In: SmartKom: foundations of multimodal dialogue systems, pp. 3–27. Springer, Berlin Heidelberg (2006)

32. Schüssel, F., Honold, F., Weber, M.: Using the transferable belief model for multimodal input fusion in companion systems. In: Schwenker, F., Scherer, S., Morency, L.-P. (eds.) MPRSS 2012. LNCS, vol. 7742, pp. 100–115. Springer, Heidelberg (2013)

33. Caschera, M.C.: Interpretation methods and ambiguity management in multimodal systems. In: Grifoni, P. (ed.) Handbook of Research on Multimodal Human Computer Interaction and Pervasive Services: Evolutionary Techniques for Improving Accessibility, pp. 87–102. IGI Global, USA (2009)

34. Mankoff, J., Hudson, S.E., Abowd, G.D.: Providing integrated toolkit-level support for ambiguity in recognition-based interfaces. In: Proceedings of ACM CHI 2000 Conference on Human Factors in Computing Systems, pp. 368–375 (2000)

35. Caschera, M.C., Ferri, F., Grifoni, P.: InteSe: An Integrated Model for Resolving Ambiguities in Multimodal Sentences. IEEE Transactions on Systems, Man, and Cybernetics: Systems 43(4), 911–931 (2013)

36. Bui, T.H.: Multimodal Dialogue Management - State of the Art. CTIT Technical Report series No. 06-01, University of Twente (UT), Enschede, The Netherlands (2006)

37. Bui, T.H., Zwiers, J., Nijholt, A., Poel, M.: Generic dialogue modeling for multi-application dialogue systems. In: Proceedings of the 2nd Joint Workshop on Multimodal Interaction and Related Machine Learning Algorithms, Edinburgh, UK (2005)

38. Williams, J.D., Poupart, P., Young, S.: Factored partially observable markov decision processes for dialogue management. In: Proceedings of 4th Workshop on Knowledge and Reasoning in Practical Dialog Systems, International Joint Conference on Artificial Intelligence (IJCAI), pp. 76–82, Edinburgh (2005)

39. Williams, J.D., Poupart, P., Young, S.: Partially observable markov decision processes with continuous observations for dialogue management. In: Dybkjær, L., Minker, W. (eds.) Recent Trends in Discourse and Dialogue, Springer Science + Business Media B.V., pp. 191–217 (2008)

40. Johnston, M., Bangalore, S.: Combining stochastic and grammar-based language processing with finite-state edit machines. In: Proceedings of IEEE Automatic Speech Recognition and Understanding Workshop (2005)

41. Caschera, M.C., D'Ulizia, A., Ferri, F., Grifoni, P.: Multimodal interaction in gaming. In: Demey, Y.T., Panetto, H. (eds.) OTM 2013 Workshops 2013. LNCS, vol. 8186, pp. 694–703. Springer, Heidelberg (2013)

42. Honold, F., Schüssel, F., Weber, M.: The Automated interplay of multimodal fission and fusion in adaptive HCI. In: Proceedings of the 2014 International Conference on Intelligent Environments, pp. 170–177. IEEE Computer Society, Washington (2014)

43. Chai, J.Y., Prasov Z., Qu, S.: Cognitive Principles in Robust Multimodal Interpretation 27, 55–83 (2006)

44. Muller, S., Schroter, C., Gross, H.M.: Adaptative input interpretation for dialogue management of an autonomous robot. In: 5th CompanionAble Workshop (2011)

45. Cutugno, F., Leano, V.A., Rinaldi, R., Mignini, G.: Multimodal framework for mobile interaction. In: Proceedings of the International Working Conference on Advanced Visual Interfaces, pp. 197–203. ACM (2012)

46. Nguyen, A., Wobcke, W.: An agent-based approach to dialogue management in personal assistants. In: Proceedings of the 10th International Conference on Intelligent User Interfaces, pp. 137–144. ACM Press, New York (2005)

47. Blaylock, N.: A collaborative problem-solving model of dialogue. In: SIGDIAL (2005)

48. Lieberman, H., Chu, A.: An interface for mutual disambiguation of recognition errors in a multimodal navigational assistant. Multimedia Syst. 12(4/5), 393–402 (2007)

49. Huang, H.-H., Cerekovic, A., Tarasenko, K., Levacic, V., Zoric, G., Pandzic, I.S., Nakano, Y., Nishida, T.: Integrating embodied conversational agent components with a generic framework. Multiagent and Grid Systems - Innovations in Intelligent Agent Technology 4(4), 371–386 (2008). IOS Press, Amsterdam

50. Niewiadomski, R., Bevacqua, E., Mancini, M., Pelachaud, C.: Greta: an interactive expressive ECA system. In: Proceedings of the 8th International Conference on Autonomous Agents and Multiagent Systems, Budapest, Hungary, vol. 2, pp. 1399–1400 (2009)

51. Bohus, D., Horvitz, E.: Facilitating multiparty dialog with gaze, gesture, and speech. In: ACM International Conference on Multimodal Interfaces, Beijing, China (2010)

52. Ondas, S., Juhar, J.: Design and development of the Slovak multimodal dialogue system with the BML realizer elckerlyc. In: Cognitive Infocommunications, pp. 427–432 (2012)

53. Ondáš, S., Juhár, J.: Event-Based Dialogue Manager for Multimodal Systems. Emergent Trends in Robotics and Intelligent Systems 316, 227–235 (2015)

54. D'Ulizia, A., Ferri, F., Grifoni, P.: Generating Multimodal Grammars for Multimodal Dialogue Processing. IEEE Transactions on Systems, Man and Cybernetics, Part A: Systems and Humans 40(6), 1130–1145 (2010)

55. D'Ulizia, A., Ferri, F., Grifoni, P.: A Learning Algorithm for Multimodal Grammar Inference. IEEE Transactions on Systems, Man, and Cybernetics - Part B: Cybernetics 41(6), 1495–1510 (2011)

56. Caschera, M.C., D'Ulizia, A.: Information extraction based on personalization and contextualization models for multimodal data. In: DEXA Workshops 2007, September 3–7, 2007, Regensburg, Germany, pp. 114–118. IEEE Computer Society (2007)

57. Motti, V.G., Vanderdonckt, J.: A computational framework for context-aware adaptation of user interfaces. In: IEEE Seventh International Conference on Research Challenges in Information Science (RCIS), pp. 1–12. IEEE (2013)

58. Honold, F., Schussel, F., Weber, M., Nothdurft, F., Bertrand, G., Minker, W.: Context models for adaptive dialogs and multimodal interaction. In: 9th International Conference on Intelligent Environments, pp. 57–64. IEEE (2013)

59. Foster, M.E., White, M.: Assessing the impact of adaptive generation in the COMIC multimodal dialogue system. In: Proceedings of the IJCAI 2005 Workshop on Knowledge and Reasoning in Practical Dialogue Systems, pp. 24–31 (2005)

60. Demberg, V., Moore, J.D.: Information presentation in spoken dialogue systems. In: Proceedings of EACL (2006)

61. David, L., Endler, M., Barbosa, S.D.J., Filho, J.V.: Middleware support for context-aware mobile applications with adaptive multimodal user interfaces. In: Proc. of U-Media 2011, Sao Paulo, Brazil, pp.106–111 (2011)

62. Dargie, W., Strunk, A., Winkler, M., Mrohs, B., Thakar, S., Enkelmann, W.: A model based approach for developing adaptive multimodal interactive systems. In: ICSOFT (PL/DPS/KE/MUSE), pp. 73–79 (2007)

63. Rieser V., Lemon, O.: Learning effective multimodal dialogue strategies from wizard-of-oz data: bootstrapping and evaluation. In: Proceedings of ACL, pp. 638–646 (2008)

64. Ertl, D.: Semi-automatic multimodal user interface generation: In Proceedings EICS 2009, pp. 321–324. ACM Press (2009)

65. Porta, D., Deru, M., Bergweiler, S., Herzog, G., Poller, P.: Building multimodal dialog user interfaces in the context of the internet of services. In: Wahlster, W., Grallert, H.J., Wess, S., Friedrich, H., Widenka, T. (eds.): Towards the Internet of Services: The THESEUS Research Program, Cognitive Technologies, pp 145–162. Springer (2014)

66. Avola, D., Caschera, M.C., Ferri, F., Grifoni, P.: Classifying and Resolving Ambiguities in Sketch-Based Interaction. International Journal of Virtual Technology and Multimedia 1(2), 104–139 (2010). Inderscience Publishers

67. Avola, D., Caschera, M.C., Grifoni, P.: Solving ambiguities for sketch-based interaction in mobile environments. In: Meersman, R., Tari, Z., Herrero, P. (eds.) OTM 2006 Workshops. LNCS, vol. 4277, pp. 904–915. Springer, Heidelberg (2006)

68. Avola, D., Caschera, M.C., Ferri, F., Grifoni, P.: Ambiguities in sketch-based interfaces. In: 40th Annual Hawaii International Conference on System Sciences (HICSS2007), p. 290. IEEE Computer Society (2007)

69. Caschera, M.C., Ferri, F., Grifoni, P.: The Management of ambiguities. Visual Languages for Interactive Computing: Definitions and Formalizations, 129–140 (2007). IGI Publishing

70. Caschera, M.C., Ferri, F., Grifoni, P.: From Modal to Multimodal Ambiguities: a Classification Approach. JNIT 4(5), 87–109 (2013)

71. Caschera, M.C., Ferri, F., Grifoni, P.: An Approach for Managing Ambiguities in Multimodal Interaction. In: Meersman, R., Tari, Z., Herrero, P. (eds.) OTM-WS 2007, Part I. LNCS, vol. 4805, pp. 387–397. Springer, Heidelberg (2007)

72. Caschera M.C., Ferri, F., Grifoni P.: Ambiguity detection in multimodal systems. In: Advanced Visual Interfaces, AVI 2008, pp. 331–334. ACM Press (2008)

558   M.C. Caschera et al.

73. Manca, M., Paternò, F., Santoro, C., Spano, L.D.: Generation of multi-device adaptive multimodal web applications. In: Daniel, F., Papadopoulos, G.A., Thiran, P. (eds.) Mobi-WIS 2013. LNCS, vol. 8093, pp. 218–232. Springer, Heidelberg (2013)
74. Caschera, M.C., D'Ulizia, A., Ferri, F., Grifoni, P.: Multiculturality and multimodal languages. In: Ghinea, G., Andres, F.,Gulliver, S. (eds.) Multiple Sensorial Media Advances and Applications: New Developments in MulSeMedia., pp. 99–114. IGI Global Publishing (2012)
75. Grifoni, P., Ferri, F., Caschera, M.C., D'Ulizia, A., Mazzei, M.: MIS: Multimodal Interaction Services in a cloud perspective. JNIT: Journal of Next Generation Information Technology 5(4), 1–10 (2014)
76. Jeong, H., Kim, M., Choi, E.: Build a Multi-modal Interaction in Cloud Computing, ASTL Volume 3, Information Science and Technology (Part 2), pp.36–38 (2012)
77. Caschera, M.C., D'Andrea, A., D'Ulizia, A., Ferri, F., Grifoni, P., Guzzo, T.: ME: multimodal environment based on web services architecture. In: Meersman, R., Herrero, P., Dillon, T. (eds.) OTM 2009 Workshops. LNCS, vol. 5872, pp. 504–512. Springer, Heidelberg (2009)
78. Caschera, M.C., D'ulizia, A., Ferri, F., Grifoni, P.: An italian multimodal corpus: the building process. In: Meersman, R., et al. (eds.) OTM 2014 Workshops. LNCS, vol. 8842, pp. 557–566. Springer, Heidelberg (2009)
79. Caschera, M.C., D'Ulizia, A., Ferri, F., Grifoni, P.: Methods for dynamic building of multimodal corpora. In: the Proceedings of the 6th Language & Technology Conference (LTC2013), December 7–9, 2013, Poznan, Poland, pp. 499–503 (2013)

Co-creativity Process by Social Media within the Product Development Process

Alessia D'Andrea, Fernando Ferri, Patrizia Grifoni$^{(\boxtimes)}$, and Tiziana Guzzo

Institute for Reaserch on Population and Social Policies (IRPPS), 00185 Rome, Italy
{alessia.dandrea,fernando.ferri,patrizia.grifoni,
tiziana.guzzo}@irpp.cnr.it

Abstract. Social media are computer-mediated communication tools frequently used for co-creating value because they promote communication, interaction and collaboration among all actors. This paper provides a description of the co-creativity process by Social Media within the product development process analysing the consumers' involvement in the different steps (product design and production, product improvement before market introduction; product sale and product innovation).

Keywords: Web 2.0 · Social media · Co-creativity · Business · Crowd-sourcing · Digital business eco-system · Product life cycle

1   Introduction

Social Media are defined in [1] as "groups of Internet-based applications that build on the ideological and technological foundations of Web 2.0 and that allow the creation and exchange of user-generated content". In the last years, with the wide use of mobile devices, Social Media are becoming more and more a pervasive phenomenon affecting the common people's daily life, changing the way they communicate, the social [2] and professional relationships [3], learning [4, 5] as well the way to co-create new products [6]. In fact, Social Media, in particular blog, micro-blogging, review sites, forum and Social Networks represent relevant data sources for the implementation of the co-creativity process that, according to Payne [7] indicates "an interactive process involving at least two willing resource integrating actors who are engaged in specific form(s) of mutually beneficial collaboration, resulting in value creation for those actors". The authors define the co-creativity process consisting of: "(i) active involvement between at least two actors; (ii) integration of resources that create mutually beneficial value; (iii) willingness to interact and (iv) a spectrum of potential form of collaboration". Based on these features, in the co-creativity process all members are equally important. Through interaction, each member gets an opportunity to influence the value creating process. During this direct interaction (in the Social Media environment), the value creating process is merging into one integrated dialogical process where all members are operating inside each other's processes/spheres and have the chance to be active, coordinate actions, learn and directly influence each other [8]. Social Media improved the

© Springer International Publishing Switzerland 2015
I. Ciuciu et al. (Eds.): OTM 2015 Workshops, LNCS 9416, pp. 559–569, 2015.
DOI: 10.1007/978-3-319-26138-6_60

opportunities of creating patterns of self organizing behavior that is a crucial issue for addressing participatory and knowledge sharing approaches of communities, devoted to stimulate co-creativity [9]. An ecosystem aggregating tools for co-creativity has been customised in the Sha.p.e.s. project (http://www.shapes-project.eu/) [10]. This is a common online toolbox of proven tools for supporting and promoting the Mediterranean creative excellence. On knowledge sharing and co-creativity process are also based the Knowing platform (http://www.knowing-project.eu/index.php?lang=en), funded by the STC programme MED that enhances the cooperation of key institutional and economic actors and promotes the "knowledge economy" by launching a transnational dialogue on policies, tools and strategies for co-creativity and innovation [9].

This important aspect of Social Media has important advantages in different domains. In the business domain, the concept of co-creativity involving the customer's knowledge and judgment to generate value is considered to be an upcoming trend for many companies. An increasing number of organizations is engaging customers in their product design and production activities via Social Media in order to evaluate and improve the efficiency of their strategies that are crucial for any company, as they explain how that company will earn revenue [11,12,13]. More specifically, they involve the set of activities, institutions and processes for communicating, creating, delivering and exchanging products/services with value both for companies and consumers [14]. Social Media allow companies performing better products/services development efforts as they can take into account consumers' needs [15].

Starting from these considerations this paper provides a description of the co-creativity process by Social Media within the product development process analysing the consumers' engagement in the different steps (product design and production, product improvement before market introduction; product sale and product innovation). Moreover the paper models the co-creativity process within the product development.

Co-creation is a very relevant approach for companies because ideas generate through this process will be closely mirror of consumer needs [16]. The paper is structured as follow. Section 2 provides a discussion on existing platforms for co-creativity in business domain. In Section 3 a description of co-creativity within the company's strategies is provided. In Section 4 a model of co-creativity process within the product development process is proposed and discussed. Section 5 concludes the paper.

2   Background

The co-creativity process allows identifying ideas and/or solutions that are perceived as novel, unique, useful and relevant for the design, development and innovation of a product. There is a body of theoretical knowledge that concerns the creative process in general [17, 18, 19, 20]. According to [21] the issue of co-creativity has been to the object of a very extensive psychological research, recently summarized with respect to the issue of group versus individual creativity, e.g., in [22, 23]. In these studies it is generally agreed that co-creativity is a multidimensional issue and its measurement requires expert assessments of many measures or criteria. Co-creativity can be defined as an action of collective creativity involving two or more people. According to [24] "an idea or product that deserves the label 'creative' arises from the synergy of many sources and not only from the mind of a single person". It is a different concept from collaboration, because its aim is to create something that is not known before. For companies, the co-creation process consists in developing ideas of new products or services with the active collaboration of customers. "Customers are no longer passive; they are informed and share information on products, services and their interactions with the company. Consequently, companies can no longer merely launch products on the market. On the contrary, they must work on their interactions with customers (customer experience) and involve customers in the design of this experience by making co-creation platforms available to them" [25].

Many platforms and tools have been developed mainly in business domain with the aim to provide co-creativity and knowledge sharing among consumers and companies. As an example the InnoCentive@Work (http://www.innocentive.com) is collaborative platform that allows companies engaging diverse innovation communities such as partners, employees, consumers etc. generating new ideas and solving problems. This platform enables companies to harness the power of crowds and give everyone a voice – consumers, employees, suppliers and partners mainly in the new products design and production. In the "InnoCentive Ideation Challenge" area a global brainstorm for producing a breakthrough idea is carried out. This could include ideas for a new product design, a new commercial application for a current product, creative solutions to technical problems or even a viral business idea for recruiting new consumers. The main advantages for companies in using this platform is that it allows them easily engaging and promoting collaboration with the right consumers and networks with less costs and risks than ever before.

Also SpigitEngage (http://www.mindjet.com/spigitengage) is a collaborative platform that allows companies performing the crowd participation and engagement for sustaining their business strategies. The aim of the platform is to promote innovation by involving the crowd. One of the more unusual features of Spigit Engage is the "Idea Market" that provides consumers a way to contribute new ideas for product innovation. Ideas can be evolved, teams can be built around them, and consumers can review and assess them. Each idea goes through a series of stages, where it is required to meet minimum requirements for the product innovation step.

Addressed to creative talents are the Edge Amsterdam and the Zooppa platforms. The Edge Amsterdam (http://www.edge-amsterdam.com/about-us) is a creative elite sourcing agency from Amsterdam created by companies for working with young creative talents for delivering fresh, new and unbiased concepts, designs and ideas. The platform through the "open call" section allows companies involving the crowd for generate creative ideas for both new products design and production and product innovation. This allows increasing the quality of the creative output and optimizing the product development process.

The Zooppa platform (https://zooppa.com/en-us) is a global Social network for creative talents. It is the world's largest source of user-generated contents. Zooppa allows companies involving consumers for new products design and production and product innovation. Community members are invited to create content in various formats producing viral videos and/or writing scripts/concepts for potential campaigns.

Table 1. Existing platforms in business domain

Platform	Product development process	Crowd involvement
InnoCentive@Work	- products design and production	In the "InnoCentive Ideation Challenge" area a global brainstorm for producing a breakthrough idea is carried out. This could include ideas for a new product line, a new commercial application for a current product, creative solutions to technical problems or even a viral marketing idea for recruiting new customers
SpigitEngage	- products innovation	In the "Idea Market" area consumers can contribute to the product innovation by providing new ideas.
Edge Amsterdam	- products design and production - product innovation	Through the "open call" companies can involve the crowd for generate creative ideas for both new products design and production and product innovation. This allows increasing the quality of the creative output and optimizing the product development process.
Zooppa	- products design and production - product innovation	Community members are invited to create content in various formats producing viral videos and/or writing scripts/concepts for potential campaigns.
DiCoDEv	- products design and production - product innovation	It provides real-time collaboration and facilitates synchronous and asynchronous communication of multiple users at different sites on the same project for the validation of a manufacturing product, from the early stages of the conceptual design until the latest stages of the production innovation.

A platform for problem solving is IdeaConnection (http://www.ideaconnection.com) that gives companies access to a worldwide network of experts; this allows companies solving technical problems, breaking development hurdles and finding technologies faster and more efficiently than their competitors. In [26] developed the DiCoDEv (Distributed Collaborative Design Evaluation) web-based platform for collaborative process and product design evaluation among distributed design expert groups or individuals, through a shared virtual environment. It provides real-time collaboration and facilitates synchronous and asynchronous communication of multiple users at different sites on the same project for the validation of a manufacturing product, from the early stages of the conceptual design until the latest stages of the production chain.

Table 1 synthesizes the platforms description according to their involvement in the product development process and the crowd involvement.

3   Co-creativity Within the Company's Strategies

The co-creativity process describes how customers can be involved as active actors in the design and development of products, services, and experiences [27]. Social Media enable the creation of more original ideas, allowing for more efficient selection of the best ideas and solutions, and, in some cases, permit these ideas to be implemented more easily".

The brand Converse, involved customers in creating their own videos advertisements for the product. Social Media include different form of co-creation, social communities became "ambassadors", "buzz agents", "smart mobs", and "participants" transforming the product experience. The integration of Social Media within the company's strategies has revolutionized relationships between companies and among companies and consumers. In [1] the authors define Social Media as "groups of Internet-based applications that build on the ideological and technological foundations of Web 2.0 and that allow the creation and exchange of user-generated content". This concept is successfully applied in the online travel community. In fact, backpackers, globetrotters, and other adventurers from all over the world join together at different online platforms to exchange information, experiences, and co-create new knowledge in building new travels. Consumers (travelers) are using these tools also to promote a sustainable tourism of their countries co-creating new and unique contents on uncontaminated places, not commercials and far from mass-tourism contributing to the improvement strategies of tourism companies [28]. Tourists and companies co-create value that can be of an economic nature, but can also be social (networking), emotional, cultural, educational, organisational or societal [29]. This process is facilitated by visualization systems for travel social network. In [30] the authors developed a multidimensional approach to visualize data and information about travel social network and their dynamics considering location, time and classes of interests.

This system is useful both consumers and Tour Operator for studying the trends of tourist market and offering innovative and targeted tourist services. In [31] the author explored internal and external uses of social media in a global corporation. Internally they were used for communication and knowledge transfer and to conduct internal idea crowdsourcing. Externally, they were used for communications related to the brand, to communicate with customers and to engage external stakeholders in creating a new idea via a crowdsourcing platform. In [32] the authors investigated contribution behavior to firm hosted commercial SNs, in which consumers interact to solve each other's service problems. Customers acquire a new role as they collaborate with companies producing a new shared knowledge. In this context, the concept of Digital business eco-system (DBE) is assuming a great relevance and it allows evolving traditional business models. In [33] the Digital business eco-system (DBE) is defined as "an economic community supported by a foundation of interacting organizations and individuals - the organisms of the business world. This economic community produces goods and services of value to customers, who are themselves members of the eco-system. The member organizations also include suppliers, lead producers, competitors, and other stakeholders. According to [34], DBEs represent the business model of the digital economy for two different reasons: i) the members contribute to the creation of the economic value of the company; ii) social environment and transactions are linked such that the social environment contributes to the value creation. The business potential of DBEs is mainly given in terms of added value they provide, resulting from new combinations of information, products and services and innovative integrations of resources, roles and relationships among business experts.

In [10] the authors provided a Web platform that combines, in an ecosystemic approach, online social media and services for the creation and management of distributed knowledge, and the creation of intelligent services for communities of creative enterprises. This platform allows knowledge creation, acquisition, storage and refinement in a dynamic way with the collective contribution of all members (crowd) in an ecosystemic approach.

Within the company's strategies the co-creation process is clearly expressed in the "crowd-sourcing" concept. Crowd-sourcing is defined in [35] as "an effort to leverage the expertise of a global pool of individuals and organisations, often across disciplines and sectors, generally enabled by the web, to as quickly and cost-effectively as possible develop and implement creative solutions to business innovation challenges". According to [36] crowd-sourcing is deeply changing the perspective of the company's strategies. It allows performing a revolution in knowledge management because they give power to a distributed network of consumers, which is able to produce knowledge that could not be produced by a restricted number of consumers within the network. By using the crowd's power, it is possible to grow services, tools and knowledge as well as to rapidly boost innovation by considering at wider number of ideas instead of someone. The crowd-sourcing paradigm stimulates the "co-creation process with consumer's stems from an active, creative and social collaboration between producers (retailers) and consumers (users) facilitated by the company" [37]. It is characterised by the direct involvement of people (consumers) in the product/service development. Many successful companies from Starbucks to LG, IBM, Mountain Dew to BMW show the potential of this business model that will continue to have a huge growth in the coming years. The brand Nike provided customer's online tools to design their own sneakers, other examples are Threadless (t-shirts) and customisable M&Ms. Social media is transforming the way we think of crowd-sourcing and will continue to do so as the benefits of using Social Media to crowd-source become more well-known.

Some strategies for crowd-sourcing have produced the development of the crowd-funding, where a group of people (in Social Networks) join and collect money to support particular initiatives/projects. Many social initiatives and projects are financed from money collections. According to [38] "charity help and money donations become an important and growing part of world economy ..... in era of globalization and expanding social networks it is a natural consequence that basking for money is moving from streets to virtual space where it is easier and cheaper to reach crowds of volunteers and build a community willing to donate".

4   Co-creativity Within the Product Development Process

The product development process includes different steps: product design and production, product improvement before market introduction; product sale and product innovation. These steps can imply different levels of co-creation then to different levels of customers and expert's involvement.

The first step includes the product design and production, in which tests, experiments, research activities, prototyping etc are carried out. In this step the company can involve customers or make a selective involvement of experts and lead users that have specific participation criteria [39].

Several companies like Google, Coca-Cola, MTV, Tata Group, Heineken, Audi, BMW realized that their users can offer new ideas, technologies, solutions and designs to businesses. An example of the consumer's involvement in the product design and production step is provided by Audi. This company involved consumers in its innovation and new product development process. It encouraged customers to visit its website and offer opinions or suggest new designs and ideas.

The collaboration among lead users can be enhanced by Social Media through informational gains and easier feedback from others. They in fact, can find information to solve an innovation problem. Moreover, prototypes can be shown through You-Tube videos improving the trial and error process during the build phase. Social media can be useful also to enterprises to find lead users with specific characteristics that otherwise required a lot of time. [40].

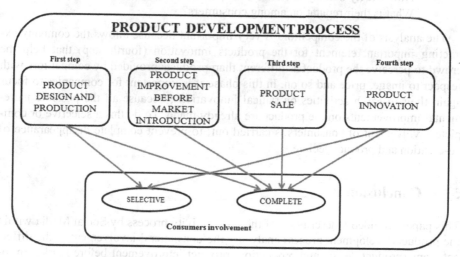

Fig. 1. Model of co-creativity process within the product development

The second step includes the product improvement before market introduction. In this step there is a complete customer's involvement in the co-creation process. Co-creation by knowledge and competences of early adopters create improvements in product functionalities [39]. Customers can communicate new ideas to the company through social media, blog, social networks, platforms and co-creation allows them to take an active and central role as participants in the product development. For companies social media are vital tools in the product life cycle, they use social media for new ideas and to test these ideas on an ideal audience. This could be consumers (the crowd of people), early adopters (kindred spirits), fellow specialists (experts) or other companies in another field (coalition of parties). According to the different audience, different kind of social media are chosen.

In the third step the product is accepted by the early majority of consumers so the sales grow. Social Media allow companies following their perceptions about and feelings toward the brand in real time in order to create interesting contents that can increase number of views and subsequently convert them in product sale. The ability to generate positive word-of-mouth (the passing of information from person to person) is another important element to increase sales [41]. During this phase there is a complete involvement of consumers in the continuous product improvements usually through online communities and crowd-sourcing.

When the sales growth and reach their highest point (maturity level), new competition appears and innovation pace decreases. In this phase very important is the analysis of competitors. In particular the company must analyse how they can cope with competitors on considering:

- How often do competitors improve or replace their products/services?
- What is their market share?
- How do they promote their products/services?
- How widely do they advertise their products/services?
- What is their reputation among consumers?

The analysis of the competitors is very important because allows the company extracting important element for the products innovation (fourth step) that help the crowd to perceive the product as different than products provided by competitors with respect to image, price and so on. In this phase it is important for companies to focus again their research activities on radical innovations, because all the possible incremental improvements on the product are already made. To do this a selective or complete involvement of consumers is carried out, to prevent complete disappearance of co-creation and product decline.

5   Conclusion

This paper provided a description of the co-creativity process by Social Media within the product development process analysing the consumers' involvement in the different steps (product design and production, product improvement before market introduction; product sale and product innovation). Co-creation process in the business domain allows involving people in the creation of meaning and value in the design and development of personalized products, services. Different companies like Converse, Nike, M&Ms etc. used this approach to improve their products; but in the last years this approach thanks to the social media use, is assuming a great relevance also in the tourism field, where tourists co-create new knowledge on new places increasing the company's strategies.

Co-creativity process is applied in the different phases of the product development process (product design and production, product improvement before market introduction; product sale and product innovation). These steps are connected to different levels of co-creation then to different levels of customers and expert's involvement for the development of the product innovation.

Despite the advantages of co-creativity some limitations and future perspectives have also been analysed. According to [42] limitations are related to:

- difficulties to monitor the quality of consumers suggestion;
- challenges in maintaining a relationship with crowd-sourced consumers throughout the duration of the company's strategies;
- vulnerability to faulty results caused by malevolent efforts given for example by a competitor;
- growing dependency on customers;
- cost to coordinate the co-creativity process;
- potential risk that customers can access to confidential information and proprietary skills.

For future research will be important to consider other types of crowd-sourcing within the company's strategies such as "crowd-funding" and "crowd-sourcing routine tasks" that are also increasingly used by companies in their strategies. Crowd-funding refers to "tapping into the crowd for raising capital for new project or businesses. This type of crowd-sourcing brings a new perspective in the world of investment" [43]. Crowd-sourcing routine tasks refer to "letting the crowd do simple tasks". This type of crowd-sourcing has a lot of potential since it is cheap for the company and it can deliver within a short timeframe" [44].

Therefore, future studies should propose measures that assess co-creativity based on intra-team social relations. These measures should adapt notions of social capital, measures of diversity, or measures of intra-team connectivity or intra-team conflict.

References

1. Kaplan, A.M., Haenlein, M.: Users of the world, unite! The challenges and opportunities of social media. Business Horizons 53(1), 59–68 (2010)
2. Guzzo, T., Ferri, F., Grifoni, P.: Social Network's Effects on Italian Teenager's Life. Journal of Next Generation Information Technology 4(3), 54 (2013)
3. Ferri, F., Grifoni, P., Guzzo, T.: New forms of social and professional digital relationships: the case of Facebook. Social network analysis and mining 2(2), 121–137 (2012)
4. D'Andrea, A., Ferri, F., Fortunati De Luca, L., Guzzo, T.: Mobile Devices to support advanced forms of e-Learning. In: Handbook of Research on Multimodal Human Computer Interaction and Pervasive Services: Evolutionary Techniques for Improving Accessibility, 389-407 (2009)
5. Guzzo, T., Grifoni, P., Ferri, F.: Social Aspects and Web 2.0 Challenges in Blended Learning. Blended Learning Environments for Adults: Evaluations and Frameworks, 35–49 (2012)

6. Guzzo, T., D'Andrea, A., Ferri, F., Grifoni, P.: Evolution of Marketing Strategies: From Internet Marketing to M-Marketing. In: Herrero, P., Panetto, H., Meersman, R., Dillon, T. (eds.) OTM-WS 2012. LNCS, vol. 7567, pp. 627–636. Springer, Heidelberg (2012)

7. Payne, A.F., Storbacka, K., Frow, P.: Managing the Co-Creation of Value. Journal of the Academy of Marketing Science 36(1), 83–96 (2008)

8. Grönroos, C.: Service Logic Revisited: Who Creates Value? And Who Co-Creates? European Business Review 20(4), 298–314 (2008)

9. Grifoni, P., Ferri, F., D'Andrea, A., Guzzo, T., Praticò, C.: SoN-KInG: a digital ecosystem for innovation in professional and business domains. Journal of Systems and Information Technology 16(1), 77–92 (2014)

10. Ferri, F., Grifoni, P., Caschera, M.C., D'Andrea, A., D'Ulizia, A., Guzzo, T.: An ecosystemic environment for knowledge and services sharing on creative enterprises. In: Proceedings of the International Conference on Management of computational and collective IntElligence in Digital EcoSystems (MEDES 2014), Buraydah, Saudi Arabia, September 15-17, 2014, pp. 27–33. ACM Publishing (2014)

11. D'Andrea, A., Ferri, F., Grifoni, P.: SNeM2S: a Social Network Model for Marketing Strategies. International journal of e-business development 2(3), 103–110 (2012)

12. Grifoni, P., Ferri, F., D'Andrea, A.: An integrated framework for on-line viral marketing campaign planning. International journal of business research 6(1), 22–30 (2013)

13. Ferri, F., D'Andrea, A., Grifoni, P.: IBF: An Integrated Business Framework for Virtual Communities. Journal of electronic commerce in organizations 10(4), 1–13 (2012). IGI Global

14. D'Andrea, A., Ferri, F., Grifoni, P.: The e-commerce business model implementation. Encyclopedia of Business Analytics and Optimization, pp. 2509–2520. IGI Publishing (2014)

15. D'Andrea, A., Ferri, F., Grifoni, P.: A business model framework for second life. In: E-Novation for Competitive Advantage in Collaborative Globalization: Technologies for Emerging E-Business Strategie, pp. 34–47. IGI Publishing (2011)

16. Hoyer, W.D., Chandy, R., Dorotic, M., Krafft, M., Singh, S.S.: Consumer cocreation in new product development. Journal of Service Research 13(3), 283–296 (2010)

17. Wierzbicki, A.P., Nakamori, Y.: Creative Space: Models of Creative Processes for the Knowledge Civilization Age. Springer Verlag, Heidelbert (2006)

18. Wierzbicki, A.P., Nakamori, Y.: Creative Environments. Springer, Heidelberg (2007)

19. Nonaka, I., Takeuchi, H.: The knowledge-creating company. Oxford University Press, Oxford (1995)

20. Bratteteig, T., Wagner, I.: Spaces for participatory creativity. CoDesign 8(2–3), 105–126 (2012)

21. Guilford, J. P.: Creativity: Yesterday, today, and tomorrow. Journal of Creative Behavior 1 (1967)

22. Bissola, R.: Organizing Collective Creativity. From People to Groups: a Multilevel Analysis. Cagliari, 10th WOA Conference (2009)

23. Kim, Y. K. M. K. T.: Analysis of team interaction and team creativity of student design teams based on personal creativity modes. In: ASME 2007 International Design Engineering Technical, Las Vegas (2007)

24. Csikszentmihályi: Creativity—Flow and the Psychology of Discovery and Invention. HarperCollins Publishers, New York (1996)

25. Prahalad, C., Ramaswamy, V.: Co-opting Customer Competence. Harvard Business Review (2000)

26. Pappas, M., Karabatsou, V., Mavrikios, D., Chryssolouris, G.: Development of a web-based collaboration platform for manufacturing product and process design evaluation using virtual reality techniques. International Journal of Computer Integrated Manufacturing **19**(8), 805–814 (2006)
27. Grönroos, C., Voima, P.: Critical service logic: making sense of value creation and co-creation. Journal of the Academy of Marketing Science **41**(2), 133–150 (2012)
28. Prahalad C.K., Ramaswamy, V.: The Future of Competition: Co-Creating Unique Value With Customers. Harvard Business School Press (2004)
29. Ferri, F., Grifoni, P., Guzzo, T.: Social Aspects of Mobile Technologies on Web Tourism Trend. In: Handbook of research on mobile business: technical, methodological and social perspectives, pp. 293-303 (2008)
30. Caschera, M.C., Ferri, F., Grifoni, P., Guzzo, T.: Multidimensional visualization system for travel social networks. In: 2009 Sixth International Conference on Information Technology: New Generations, 2009, ITNG 2009, pp. 1510–1516. IEEE (2009)
31. Vuori, M: Exploring uses of social media in a global corporation. Journal of Systems and Information Technology **14**(2) (2012)
32. Wiertz, C., De Ruyter, K.: Beyond the call of duty: Why customers contribute to firm hosted commercial online communities. Organization Studies **28**(3), 347–376 (2007)
33. Moore, J.F.: Predators and prey: the new ecology of competition. Harvard Business Review **71**(3), 75–83 (1993)
34. D'Andrea, A., Ferri, F., Grifoni, P., Guzzo, T.: Digital eco-systems: the next generation of business services. In: Proceedings of the International ACM Conference on Management of Emergent Digital EcoSystems (MEDES 2013), Neumünster Abbey, Luxembourg, October 28-31, 2013, pp. 40–44. ACM Publishing (2013)
35. Orcik, A., Tekic, Z., Anisic, Z.: Customer co-creation throughout the product life cycle. International Journal of Industrial Engineering and Management **4**(1), 43–49 (2013)
36. Piller, F.T., Vossen, A., Ihl, C.: From social media to social product development: the impact of social media on co-creation of innovation. Die Unternehmung **65**(1) (2012)
37. D'Andrea, A., Ferri, F., Grifoni, P.: Virtual communities in marketing processes: A marketing framework. Customer Centric Marketing Strategies: Tools for Building Organizational Performance, pp. 265-279, IGI Publishing (2012)
38. Wojciechowski, A.: Models of charity donations and project funding in social networks. In: Meersman, R., Herrero, P., Dillon, T. (eds.) OTM 2009 Workshops. LNCS, vol. 5872, pp. 454–463. Springer, Heidelberg (2009)
39. Howe, J.: The rise of crowdsourcing. Wired Inco-Production Journal of Marketing **67**(1), 14–28 (2006)
40. D'Andrea, A., Ferri, F., Grifoni, P.: CBM: An Integrated Crowd-sourcing Business Model. Journal of Contemporary Management **5**(2), 47–58 (2015)
41. Piller, F., Ihl, C.: Open Innovation with Customers Foundations, Competences (2009)
42. McDonald M.: Lost in the crowd: How crowd-sourcing can backfire on a business'. Robotic Blue (2007)
43. Belleflamme, P., Lambert, T., Schwienbacher, A.: Crowdfunding: tapping the right crowd. In: Proceedings of the International Conference of the French Finance Association (AFFI), July 30, 2011 (2010). http://papers.ssrn.com/sol3/papers.cfm?abstract_id=1836873
44. Heer, J., Bostock, M.: Crowdsourcing graphical per-ception: using mechanical turk to assess visualization design. In: Proceedings of the 28th international conference on Human factors in computing systems. doi:10.1145/1753326.1753357

Ontologies, DataBases, and Applications of Semantics (ODBASE) 2015 Posters

ODBASE 2015 PC Co-Chairs' Message

The International Conference on Ontologies, DataBases, and Applications of Semantics (ODBASE) provides a forum for exchanging ideas and research results on the use of ontologies and data semantics in novel applications. The 14th ODBASE conference is held in Rhodes, Greece, on 26-30 October 2015. As in previous years, ODBASE 2015 continues to draw a highly diverse body of researchers and practitioners. ODBASE is part of the OnTheMove (OTM 2015) federated event composed of three interrelated yet complementary scientific conferences. The other two co-located conferences are CoopIS'15 (Cooperative Information Systems) and C&TC'15 (Cloud and Trusted Computing'15). These three conferences together attempt to span a relevant range of the advanced research on, and cutting-edge development and application of, information handling and systems in the wider current context of ubiquitous distributed computing.

Of particular relevance to ODBASE 2015 are papers that bridge traditional boundaries between disciplines such as databases, conceptual modeling, ontology, social networks, artificial intelligence, information extraction, and knowledge management.

This year, we received 38 abstract submissions and invited a Program Committee (PC) of 66 dedicated colleagues. Each submitted full paper was reviewed by 4-5 PC members of different research areas. As a result, the final program consists of 8 regular papers (up to 18 pages), 6 short papers (up to 8 pages), and 1 poster (up to 4 pages). Their themes span a spectrum of studies on a number of modern challenges including querying and management of linked data and OWL documents, ontology engineering, semantic matching and mapping, social network analysis, web services discovery, and mobile data. We are also grateful for John Mylopoulos for giving us an insightful keynote speech on Data Semantics in the Days of Big Data.

We would like to thank all the members of the Program Committee for their hard work in reviewing the papers. We would also like to thank all the researchers who submitted their work to the conference.

We hope that you enjoy ODBASE 2015 and have a wonderful time in Rhodes, Greece!

September 2015

Yuan An
Min Song
Markus Strohmaier

Towards Flexible Similarity Analysis of XML Data

Jesús M. Almendros-Jiménez[1] and Alfredo Cuzzocrea[2]([✉])

[1] Informatics Department, University of Almería, Almería, Spain
jalmen@ual.es
[2] DIA Department, University of Trieste and ICAR-CNR, Trieste, Italy
alfredo.cuzzocrea@dia.units.it

Abstract. The problem of supporting *similarity analysis of XML data* is a major problem in the *data fusion* research area. Several approaches have been proposed in literature, but *lack of flexibility* represents a hard challenge to be faced-off, especially in modern *Cloud Computing* environments. Inspired by this motivation, we propose SemSynX, *a novel technique for supporting similarity analysis of XML data via semantic and syntactic heterogeneity/homogeneity detection.* SemSynX retrieves several *similarity scores* over input XML documents, thus enabling flexible management and "customization" of similarity tools over XML data. In particular, the proposed technique is highly *customizable*, and it permits the specification of *thresholds* for the requested *degree of similarity* for paths and values as well as for the *degree of relevance* for path and value matching. Also, *selection of paths* and *semantics-based comparison of label content* are supported. It thus makes possible to "adjust" the similarity analysis depending on the nature of the input XML documents.

1 Introduction

Semantic and syntactic heterogeneity can be found in data sources and detecting them is the major goal of the *data-fusion research initiative*. In this respect, *schema matching* and *duplicate detection* are two well-studied mechanisms. In addition to this, *data-conflict detection* and *data repairing/cleaning* strategies have been proposed in the data-fusion research area in order to deal with semantic heterogeneity, while syntactic heterogeneity has been typically addressed by *schema matching approaches*. Data heterogeneity has also been investigated via using *Ontologies*, whose main functionality is that of supporting semantics-based description of data sources. In this research area, *approximate data instance matching* aims at providing a measure of *data similarity*, which is later exploited to identify multiple instances of real-word (data) objects based on suitable *distance functions*. *XML data clustering* is also tightly connected to the data-instance matching problem, and the general goal here consists in classifying target XML documents in groups of similar content. Applications of XML similarity also include *data warehousing version control* and *change management*.

In order to be able of integrating data from multiple sources, a typical strategy consists in, first, identifying (data) objects to be integrated (usually, by

© Springer International Publishing Switzerland 2015
I. Ciuciu et al. (Eds.): OTM 2015 Workshops, LNCS 9416, pp. 573–576, 2015.
DOI: 10.1007/978-3-319-26138-6_61

means of unique keys), and, secondly, mixing attributes in the integrated data repository. Nevertheless, attributes of a certain object can have different names, even representing the same concept, or they can have the same names, even representing so-called *conflicting values*. In the first case, an *attribute name mapping* is required, while in the second one, a *conflict resolution strategy* is adopted. Strategies for conflict resolution range from the *most-frequent value* and the *most-trusted source* selection to more intuitive *date-based* selection. Also, values represented as strings can be compared via applying well-known *string comparison algorithms* (e.g., [4,6]).

In our research, we focus on *XML data* specially, for which several data fusion strategies have been proposed. XML data require specific mechanisms for data fusion since they are semi-structured data represented by *tagged trees* where leaf nodes have textual content. *Graph-based data*, e.g. *RDF data*, are also subject of recently-proposed targeted data fusion mechanisms, and they expose several "touching points" with the related XML data fusion research area. It is also significant to highlight that, in the semi-structured context (both XML and RDF data), conflicts of attribute values are more sophisticate since the same real-world (data) objects can be represented using different tree/graph structures. This makes the investigated problem harder.

Following the so-delineated research area, in this paper we introduce SemSynX, *a novel technique for supporting similarity analysis of XML data via detecting semantic and syntactic heterogeneity/homogeneity matches of objects* (i.e., elements, values, tags, attributes) *occurring in certain paths of the two* (*XML*) *trees* that model the input data sources. SemSynX retrieves a list of similarity/dissimilarity matches found in the target objects as well as a measure of similarity of the XML trees expressed by a *score*. A *local score* that takes into account path and value similarity is provided for each heterogeneity/homogeneity found. A *global score* that summarizes the number of equal matches as well as the local scores is also provided. Such a list of similarity/dissimilarity matches is suitable to support *automatic definition of schema mapping* and *conflicting strategies* of the target XML data. In addition to this, SemSynX is highly *customizable*, and it permits the specification of *thresholds* for the required *degree of similarity* for paths and values as well as for the *degree of relevance* for path and value matching, hence finally it makes possible to "adjust" the comparison of input XML trees depending on the nature of the trees themselves. Furthermore, in order to improve matching in some specialized scenarios, *selection of paths* to be matched between documents is supported, while assigning suitable *weights* to selected paths. *Semantics-based approach* has also been adopted in order to *compare label content*, thus introducing more precision during the matching of similar items characterized by a specific semantics.

2   Remarks

By analyzing active literature, we recognize that several studies on how to match string values exist, but there is a general lack of methods supporting the definition of *similarity functions* that work on "specific cases". Since SemSynX aims at offering a high degree of parametrization, our strategy is assigning a proper similarity function to each label. As an alternative to this, a *naive* strategy would assign similarity functions to types, indeed, but semantics of labels of the same type can vary one from another. As an example, labels of type `Integer` can represent the age of a person, the number of children as well as the population of a city, alternatively. Therefore, we would "lost" the specific semantics of the XML element. In order to avoid this, we would aim at semantically enriching meta-data of target documents (i.e., *DTD* or *XML Schemas*) with similarity functions. Unfortunately, neither DTD nor XML Schemas provide mechanisms for expressing semantics of element. As a consequence, our strategy embedded in `SemSynX` has been that of attaching a suitable *XML template* to each XML document, being this template capable of providing semantics to labels, and enabling a more fine-grained comparison of labels according to their semantics.

As far as we know, `SemSynX` is the first technique that fully-provides semantics-based similarity analysis of XML documents. All this confers highly *flexibility* to our proposed similarity analysis framework, with powerful benefits in the context of large-scale management of XML data over Clouds (e.g., [5]).

3   Extending SemSynX

In `SemSynX`, as highlighted above, a threshold can be set for path and value similarity. In more details, we admit the specification of a *percentage value* over which values should be considered equal or similar. The latter is a clear instance showing where the utility and the reliability of similarity thresholds are necessary and convenient in data similarity analysis tools, as highlighted in several studies. However, due to effectiveness and efficiency purposes, it is necessary to determine the bound over which a value is considered as equal or similar. This greatly depends on the *size* of strings of the target XML documents to be compared. Larger strings usually expose a "low" score when they are compared, and vice-versa.

Along this line, in `SemSynX` we introduce another percentage threshold value to distinguish equal from similar values. Obviously, this percentage has to be smaller than the previous percentage focusing on similarity of (data) objects. A threshold can also be specified for paths. The choice of these thresholds depends on the nature of XML documents to be compared. With highly-structured XML documents, path thresholds should be relaxed, while, when dealing with content-centered XML documents, value thresholds should be relaxed. As a particular case of the described, alternative application scenarios, when content-centered XML documents characterized by *small strings* are processed, then more strict thresholds should be specified for equality versus similarity. Indeed, taking "high" thresholds for equality and similarity causes that only very similar XML documents retrieve high (similarity) scores, while, with "low" thresholds for equality and similarity, higher (similarity) scores are found. By giving more relevance to paths, XML documents has to be similar in structure to get high (similarity) scores, whereas by giving more relevance to values, highly-different-in-structure XML documents can be matched.

4   Conclusions

In this paper, we have introduced SemSynX, a XML similarity analysis technique whose main benefits can be summarized by three main concepts: customization, flexibility and interoperability. The proposed technique retrieves the list of agreement/disagreement matches of two input XML documents, also determining suitable local and global similarity scores. SemSynX is fully customizable, thus enabling the specification of thresholds for path and value equality/similarity. Also, it makes possible to confer more relevance to paths versus values, and vice-versa, according to a proportional approach, as well as selection of paths and similarity functions. Some interesting extensions of SemSynX may include: *privacy-preservation* (e.g., [3]), *accuracy control* (e.g., [2]), and *adaptivity* (e.g., [1]).

References

1. Cannataro, M., Cuzzocrea, A., Mastroianni, C., Ortale, R., Pugliese, A.: Modeling adaptive hypermedia with an object-oriented approach and xml. In: Proceedings of the Second International Workshop on Web Dynamics, WebDyn 2002, May 7–11, 2002, Honolulu, HI, USA, pp. 35–44 (2002)
2. Cuzzocrea, A.: Accuracy control in compressed multidimensional data cubes for quality of answer-based OLAP tools. In: Proceedings of the 18th International Conference on Scientific and Statistical Database Management, SSDBM 2006, July 3–5, 2006, Vienna, Austria, pp. 301–310 (2006)
3. Cuzzocrea, A., Russo, V., Saccà, D.: A robust sampling-based framework for privacy preserving OLAP. In: Song, I.-Y., Eder, J., Nguyen, T.M. (eds.) DaWaK 2008. LNCS, vol. 5182, pp. 97–114. Springer, Heidelberg (2008)
4. Levenshtein, V.I.: Binary codes capable of correcting deletions, insertions and reversals. In: Soviet Physics Doklady, vol. 10, p. 707 (1966)
5. Lung, C.-H., Sanaullah, M., Cao, Y., Majumdar, S.: Design and performance evaluation of cloud-based XML publish/subscribe services. In: IEEE International Conference on Services Computing, SCC 2014, Anchorage, AK, USA, June 27 – July 2, 2014, pp. 583–589 (2014)
6. Winkler, W.E.: The state of record linkage and current research problems. In: Statistical Research Division, US Census Bureau (1999)

Author Index

Printed in the United States
By Bookmasters